THE NATIONAL INSTITUTE OF
ECONOMIC AND SOCIAL RESEARCH

Economic and Social Studies
XXIII

THE BRITISH ECONOMY

IN 1975

The National Institute of Economic and Social Research is an independent, non-profit-making body, founded in 1938. It has as its aim the promotion of realistic research, particularly in the field of economics. It conducts research by its own research staff and in co-operation with the universities and other academic bodies. The results of the work done under the Institute's auspices are published in several series, and a list of its publications up to the present time will be found at the end of this volume.

THE
BRITISH ECONOMY
IN 1975

BY

W. BECKERMAN
AND ASSOCIATES

CAMBRIDGE
AT THE UNIVERSITY PRESS
1965

THE NATIONAL INSTITUTE OF ECONOMIC
AND SOCIAL RESEARCH

1965

Bentley House, 200 Euston Road, London, N.W.1
American Branch: 32 East 57th Street, New York, N.Y. 10022

©

PUBLISHED BY
THE SYNDICS OF THE CAMBRIDGE UNIVERSITY PRESS

Printed in Great Britain by Metcalfe and Cooper Ltd., London, E.C.2

CONTENTS

CHAPTER II   *page* 44

DEMAND, EXPORTS AND GROWTH

BY W. BECKERMAN

CHAPTER III

THE FUTURE GROWTH OF
NATIONAL PRODUCT

BY W. BECKERMAN

TABLES

PART II. THE PATTERN OF OUTPUT AND EXPENDITURE

CHAPTER V *page* 146

BRITAIN'S VISIBLE TRADE

BY R. L. MAJOR

CHAPTER VI *page* 177

PRIVATE CONSUMPTION

BY D. A. ROWE

CHAPTER VII   *page* 201

THE PATTERN OF GROWTH OF OUTPUT,
EMPLOYMENT AND PRODUCTIVITY,
1960 TO 1975

BY W. BECKERMAN

TABLES

CHAPTER VIII   *page* 235

INVESTMENT REQUIREMENTS

BY W. BECKERMAN

CHAPTER IX   *page* 270

THE OVERALL PATTERN OF EXPENDITURE

BY W. BECKERMAN

TABLES

PART III. ENERGY, TRANSPORT, HOUSING AND SOCIAL SERVICES

CHAPTER XIII   *page* 404

HEALTH AND WELFARE

By D. C. PAIGE AND K. JONES

TABLES

CHAPTER XIV *page 458*

EDUCATION

By J. Vaizey and R. Knight

TABLES

APPENDICES

APPENDIX 14   *page* 595

TABLES

SYMBOLS USED IN THE TABLES

..   not available.

n.a. not applicable.

—   nil or less than half the unit stated.

PREFACE

This book has been compiled under my direction by a team at the National Institute. From the beginning the work was planned as that of a team and not as a collection of individual essays. The basic assumptions and the general pattern of expenditure and output were used as a common framework for the whole exercise so as to secure not only statistical consistency but also consistency in the general approach towards the social and economic problems and a reasonable balance in progress towards solutions.

Most of the work was done while I was working at the National Institute between the beginning of 1962 and early 1964, although a certain amount of revision went on during 1964 whilst I was the P.D. Leake Senior Research Fellow at Balliol College, Oxford. However we have not attempted to take account of many revisions to official statistics relating to the past that have appeared since the main work on this study was completed.

The central structure of the projections, contained in Parts I and II, was my work, with Mr D. A. Rowe contributing the analysis of private consumption in chapter 6 and Mr R. L. Major chapters 4 and 5 on the balance of payments. The special studies in Part III were the work of several authors: Energy, Mr G. F. Ray assisted by Mr R. E. Crum; Transport, Mr G. F. Ray and Mr C. T. Saunders assisted by Mr R. E. Crum; Housing, Miss D. C. Paige; Health and Welfare, Miss D. C. Paige and Mrs K. Jones; Education, Mr J. Vaizey and Mrs R. Knight.

I was assisted directly, at one stage or another, by Mr Z. Shardy, Mr E. A. Shirley, Mr A. D. Smith, Miss J. Sutherland and Mr W. Warren—almost all of whom, maddened by the attempt to cope with my own disorder and the files of their predecessors, have emigrated (Geneva, New Zealand, Paris) or become civil servants. Their main particular contributions are acknowledged in footnotes. Grateful mention must also be made of Miss M. Taylor and Mr L. Whitehead who did much of the computing for my own chapters; and for her care and patience I must thank my secretary, Miss B. Fuller, who typed most of the text.

I particularly want to acknowledge the help of those, who, when nearly everyone else had departed, saved the day by taking on the thankless task of tying up the innumerable loose ends. The responsibility was taken over by Mrs. Anne Jackson and the Director of the Institute, Mr C. T. Saunders, with the same patience that they have shown me from the outset. At all stages in this project Mr Saunders has been ready to examine and discuss its progress and to read early drafts, and anybody who has worked with him will share my deep appreciation not only of his technical expertise but also of his kindness and consideration. Mrs Jackson, too, has contributed in many ways throughout the project, both by dealing with all administrative headaches, and by giving us the benefit of her valuable judgement and experience on many matters of substance and presentation.

When the draft chapters were being prepared for the press Mr Blackaby kindly and ably edited two over-long chapters; Mrs Jones acted as final co-ordinator of chapters, resolving several conflicts which inevitably emerged at this stage between the (by now vested) interests of those responsible for thinking about particular sections of the economy and the master plan; and she and Miss Harington will be carrying the main load of proof correcting.

Very many people contributed to this study through conversation or advice or in other ways and they must forgive me if I fail to mention them all by name. At the National Institute, special mention must be made of Mr J. C. R. Dow, who first suggested that I should embark on this study and Mr R. Neild, who made valuable comments on earlier drafts of several chapters. I am indebted also to some of my colleagues at Oxford with whom I have discussed various points, particularly Mr Maurice Scott and Mr Paul Streeten.

It was the Treasury which made this study possible financially. The Treasury made a three-year grant in support of the project; and carried out the duty of following its progress by a series of meetings, at which the discussions in no way impinged on the independence of those engaged on the work and the interest displayed provided most welcome encouragement.

Finally, as in war, it is often some of the non-combatants at home who have to make the heaviest sacrifices. In this case it is my wife who had her home life disrupted and was obliged to live in temporary accommodation for the duration but who accepted it all uncomplainingly with her usual tolerance and understanding.

W. BECKERMAN

BALLIOL COLLEGF.

OXFORD

December 1964.

INTRODUCTION

By C. T. Saunders

This book is about the opportunities open to us for improving the efficiency of our economy and the welfare of our society. The discussion is centred on the economic opportunities—on the potential increase in our material resources and on how these resources might be used.

We are not attempting a forecast of what is most likely to happen; it is impossible to make meaningful forecasts for a period of ten years or so, except by assuming that past trends, in human behaviour, in policy, and in technical progress, simply continue. That would have been possible, but it is not what we set out to do. We have, on the contrary, assumed that productivity will grow faster than in the past and that British industry will become more competitive in international trade. We believe that we as a community have it in our power to realise these assumptions; we have tried to express them in numbers and to apply them in some detail.

We have, therefore, worked out a possible picture of the British economy in 1975, based on the assumption of a growth in the volume of national output per person employed of $3\frac{1}{2}$ per cent a year from 1963 onwards (implying an increase in total output of 3·8 per cent a year).

Purposes of the study

What purposes do we expect such a book to serve? First, there are some industries, or services, whose effectiveness several years hence depends upon decisions taken now, and for which a long-term policy of development and investment is necessary. The book contains (in Part III) special studies of five of these: transport and energy in the economic field; education and health services in the social field; and housing, in which both social and economic policies are concerned. For each, long-term policy is largely a matter for social decisions although, in some, private enterprise plays a large part. Our purpose is not to lay down ideal solutions. It is rather to explain the central issues which must be faced by the makers of policy, and to set out possible lines of development not only in general terms but, wherever it is relevant, in specific figures.

The quality of these activities touches the whole of society. To a certain extent, the faster growth of the economy itself depends upon them—although not in a measurable way. Moreover, they are sectors of our social infrastructure which absorb large resources in capital and (particularly the health and education services) call for large numbers of highly trained men and women. Yet their development in the post-war period—and long before—has had less

B

attention than it needed.   This is partly because our system of public finance, on which they largely depend, is ill-designed for promoting long-term development of a wide range of basic common services; it is partly because not much information has been available from which members of the public could inform themselves either on the costs of improvement or on the benefits that might flow from a higher quality of service; it is partly, too, because there has been no firm consensus of opinion about the criteria, economic and social, by which the quality of these services, and the need for improvement, should be judged.

It seems to us, therefore, that a considerable effort is needed before all these services are brought up to the standards which are appropriate for a country which is still among the richest in the world.   This inadequacy may be obvious enough even now.   But to study their potential development against the background of future economic growth throws a strong light both on the need for improvement and on the cost.

It is not suggested that a proper development of the public services must depend wholly on a faster growth rate for the economy as a whole, and must be slowed down proportionately for every percentage point by which the increase of gross national product falls short of the 'target' rate.   The kind of development of education and the health services and of transport facilities outlined here is not to be regarded as a luxury which can be afforded only out of some extra increment of gross national product.   It has by now become clear that adequate development of these public services cannot be achieved except by a social commitment to long-term programmes which should, at least up to a certain point, be regarded as a first charge on resources.

Our second purpose is to give some guidance about the probable pattern of changes in demand—for consumption, for investment, and for foreign trade— and about their consequences for output and inputs of capital and labour in different industries.   For the reasons already given, these cannot be used as unconditional forecasts.   There is no authority and no system of calculation which can tell industry X what the demand for its products *will* be ten years hence—or, for that matter, five years hence.   Nevertheless, the *pattern* of relative change in demand and output, although sensitive to the overall growth rate, is not wholly dependent upon it.   The reader who is unwilling to accept our general assumption about the overall growth rate may still gain useful indications of the relative prospects for a particular product or service.

One part of the study which is more nearly a forecast than most is the projection of the labour force (chapter 3); yet, although the size of the labour force for a decade or more hence is very largely determined by the present age structure of the population, possible variations in participation rates and in net migration introduce even into this calculation a considerable element of uncertainty and leave room for some influence of policy.   However, it seems certain (unless there is a very large change indeed in the amount of migration) that for about 10 years from the mid-1960s the size of the total labour force must remain approximately constant and that growth of output must come almost wholly from greater output per worker.

The third purpose of the book is to display in proportion the resources required for the development of the various sectors of the economy—to allow the reader to compare, at least in orders of magnitude, the suggested extra requirements for education against those for aid to developing countries, or for exports against consumption, or for private investment against the common services provided by the social infra-structure; and to compare each with the projected addition to our total resources. We do not suggest that the figures we have chosen represent, in any testable way, an optimal use or ideal allocation of resources. For a very long time to come, the major decisions must rest on value judgements rather than on scientific criteria of social benefits and social costs. Our object is simply that the necessary value judgements should be informed by a quantitative comparison of the results to be expected from alternative possible uses of resources. If the general proportions of our statistical framework are accepted, then a substantially greater use of resources for one purpose necessarily involves correspondingly less for another.

A fourth purpose is to see what kind of strains might be imposed on the balance of the economy—granted our overall growth assumption—by a set of reasonably ambitious programmes of development for its various parts. Three questions might be asked:

(a) The first is whether the projected investment requirements, including both directly productive investment in industry and trade and investment (largely public) in the social infra-structure, would in themselves impose a serious strain on the saving propensities of the economy. The answer is that they would not; total saving would be required, on our projections, to rise only from 18 per cent of gross national product in 1960 to 20 per cent in 1975[1]. There is no reason to expect more than a small increase in the proportion of saving to income, either for persons or for companies; the implication, however, is that the surplus of public authorities will need to rise to an extent which probably rules out any substantial reduction in the general level of tax rates.

(b) The second question is the feasibility of securing the necessary equilibrium in the balance of payments. This is, as already pointed out, the crux of the whole exercise. Faster growth—and perhaps even the maintenance of recent growth rates—requires a permanent shift in the relative competitiveness of the British economy. The projections indicate the scale of the changes required; they do little more.

(c) The third issue is the scale of the increase in consumption, in the standard of living—which is to be regarded as the major purpose of economic progress. Our projections show an increase of nearly two thirds

[1]See page 282 (table 9.10).

in the volume of private consumption between 1960 and 1975 (and about the same proportionate increase in public consumption, excluding defence, much of which may also be regarded as part of the standard of living)[1]. With the 13 per cent increase in population over the same period, this means a rise in total consumption of goods and services per head of nearly 50 per cent; it allows nothing for the increase in the standard of living, conceived more broadly, that should result from the improved quality of public services.   This increase of 50 per cent in consumption per head is about as large as the whole increase since the beginning of the century— for what the comparison is worth, since admittedly changes in the composition of consumption render any precise measurement over such long periods of doubtful significance[2].

Thus, lessons of rather differing kinds may be drawn from the projections in the different parts of the study.   The special studies of particular sectors are intended to emphasize the importance of long-term policy decisions and to give some guidance about possible lines of policy.   The study of consumption shows that as consumers we do in fact appear to behave in a fairly predictable way—although there are still problems to be solved in determining just what these laws of behaviour are (in particular, the pattern of consumers' expenditure on durable goods cannot yet be described as empirically determined).   So the projections for consumption may be regarded as predictions, although still conditional on the assumed rate of increase in real income.   The projections for investment in industry and trade are, as pointed out, rather arbitrary.   Past experience does not suggest clear regularities either in business behaviour or in technical relationships.   The result is, rather, to emphasize the need for flexibility in investment; this must mean accepting the risk of a certain amount of excess investment and over-capacity.   Finally, the projections for foreign trade (except for imports of industrial materials which are conditional on the rate of growth of output) are neither forecasts nor statements of policy.   They are statistical illustrations of what is meant by increasing competitiveness, which we regard as the fundamental condition for faster economic progress.

The growth rate assumption and the horizon for projection

The statistical structure is built on an average growth in output per worker of $3\frac{1}{2}$ per cent a year from 1963 to 1975, which implies—taking our labour force projections—a consequent growth in total output of 3·8 per cent a year[3].   This

---

[1]See table 9.1 (page 271).

[2]For estimates of consumption per head since 1900, see table 6.2 (page 180).   As pointed out in the accompanying text, the historical statistics reveal remarkably little increase in real consumption per head from 1900 until 1930.   From 1950 to 1960, the increase was nearly 25 per cent.

[3]For a summary of the projections in total labour force, productivity and gross national product, see tables 3.20 and 3.21 (page 102).

compares with a trend rate of growth in output per worker of about $2\frac{1}{2}$ per cent during most of the post-war period. The figure of $3\frac{1}{2}$ per cent is not the maximum conceivable growth of productivity. Faster rates of productivity growth—4 and 5 per cent—have been sustained in comparable conditions by comparable countries; more could doubtless be achieved by further exploitation of all the possibilities of technical progress. But $3\frac{1}{2}$ per cent does seem to represent a degree of improvement over past experience which is significant but not impracticable[1].

The other arbitrary element in the projections is the terminal date. The year 1975 is far enough ahead to give time for the necessary adaptations to be accomplished, yet not so far ahead that the projections are likely to be greatly upset by the appearance of new technical devices or by violent changes in external conditions. Our vision of the future will not be found to contain any great surprises and may seem prosaic. But perhaps a similarly conceived vision of 1965 constructed in the early 1950s would not be found surprising only because, disappointingly, so little has changed.

In fact, too much importance can be attributed to the time-span which such projections cover. In the pattern of the present study, there is little that would need to be altered if the projections were to be extrapolated a few years further ahead. It is true that we envisage some considerable investment expenditures for bringing up to date parts of our social equipment; and that such expenditure—even in 1975—may still be somewhat above the average for later periods. For example, it may well happen that the expansion of private car ownership and use will slow down at some stage in the 1970s; and that the capital-expensive task of providing for this expansion, as well as for catching up with past neglect, may become somewhat easier. It is inconceivable, however, that the immense process of reconstructing our towns to match contemporary ways of living will be complete by 1975, or by 1985[2].

It is true also that important technical developments will be apparent in 1975 which get no mention here. But our assumption is that such developments will not, in 10–20 years, greatly affect the pattern of output and expenditure between the broad categories used in our projections; at least we assume that the quantitative effect of such possible developments is not likely to exceed the margins of error already inherent in the projections for other reasons. This assumption may well be proved wrong in the event, and we are prepared to be convicted of lack of imagination.

In some sections of the study, notably in the special studies of education and the health service, the authors have looked beyond 1975; these are areas where a ten-year horizon is obviously too close for a long-term programme. In the

[1] For the considerations governing the choice of a growth rate in productivity see chapter 2.
[2] A separate study of the whole problem of urban redevelopment in Britain is being conducted at the National Institute of Economic and Social Research by Dr P. A. Stone.

study of housing, too, the general programme envisaged is one that looks well beyond 1975.

We considered, but rejected, the possibility of repeating the whole exercise for alternative growth rates and for different terminal dates. It would have been possible to perform the operation more or less mechanically but the effort—and the addition to the cost of this book—of a set of mechanically calculated alternatives seemed hardly to be justified[1].

The ways to faster growth

The study deals, then, with a possible future. It does not show how the economy can be steered into this new orbit. We have emphasized certain pre-conditions—in particular, greater competitiveness in international trade—which imply many changes in the attitudes of managements and workers towards wages, prices, productivity, investment and innovation, and the development of more effective forms of government policy for long-term economic progress. Our review in chapter 1 of the British post-war record, in comparison with that of other industrial countries, reveals no single cause for the relatively slow growth of the British economy in the post-war period; the slow rise of productivity does not seem to be the result simply of low investment, of the small increase in labour force, or of an unfortunate structure of markets and production. The obstacle to faster progress lies not in the amount of our resources but in how they have been used.

But to say all this is to state the problems and not to show how they might be solved. These are, indeed, the central problems for economic policy and for the direction of industry. Economists can contribute to their solution both by analysis of the actual operation of the competitive process, and of the effects of government policies, and by demonstrating the opportunities for more effective methods. Much of the work of the National Institute is in fact concentrated on this range of problems for government and industry, and will continue to be.

Notes on the book

The book is divided into three parts. Part I (chapters 1 to 3) is a general discussion of the factors underlying the growth rate in an open industrial economy and leads to the assumptions used about the projected growth rate of the British economy up to 1975; it includes, in chapter 3, the labour force projections. Part II (chapters 4–9) sets out a projected pattern of expenditure and output in considerable detail, between products and industries. Chapters 4 and 5 are concerned with foreign trade and the balance of payments, and

[1]In table 8.15 (page 268) we do in fact illustrate very roughly the effect of alternative rates of growth of gross national product on investment requirements.

chapter 6 with private consumption. In chapter 7, the projections of final demand are translated into demands for output by industry groups and estimates of relative productivity changes by industry are made to arrive at employment requirements by industry. Chapter 8 discusses investment requirements by industry, related to output. Chapter 9 brings together the pattern of expenditure and discusses the balance between savings and investment.

Part III (chapters 10 to 14) is a series of special studies of certain key sectors of the economy in which the government's long-term policies must play a large part—Energy (chapter 10), Inland Transport (chapter 11), Housing (chapter 12), Health and Welfare (chapter 13) and Education (chapter 14).

It would, of course, have been desirable to cover a wider range of such basic services. There are some of great importance which are not discussed in detail: for example, the improvement of ports and port facilities, and the development of water resources. Again, the whole problem of agricultural policy receives very little attention. But our resources did not allow a more comprehensive treatment.

There are several points about the statistical 'model' which we would ask the reader to bear in mind.

First, it will be recognized that the formulation of a set of internally consistent statistical projections is necessarily a circular process. It is never possible to deduce the whole structure logically from a single starting point. Thus, the production pattern by industry depends on the investment pattern, but investment is itself partly dependent upon the production pattern. A preliminary hypothesis about the investment pattern is introduced into the projections of production; the investment pattern is then modified; that in turn requires a modification of the production projections until consistency is arrived at by iteration. Thus, at several points the reader will find the conclusions of later chapters anticipated.

Second, statistical projections of this kind have now become fairly familiar. We have tried to emphasize that the answers at each point are of varying 'validity' depending upon the necessarily different methods used to arrive at them. One of the objects of the work is to suggest to what extent the economy is in fact subject to determinable regularities, at what points analysis of the past fails to reveal such regularities and at what points the pattern of events depends upon social decisions about policy. Thus, the discussion of how the projections are arrived at may be more significant than the resulting calculations. The result of research work, in our present state of knowledge, is often to suggest that no firm answer is possible.

Third, many readers may be shocked, or amused, at the *precision* of the statistical projections—a precision which admittedly goes far beyond our knowledge of the regularities of economic behaviour. The problem is simply one of presentation. There is really no useful compromise between, on the one hand, implausibly precise numbers and, on the other, vague verbal statements. It would be confusing and unwieldy to attach margins of uncertainty to every figure, especially when the figures are components of some more comprehensive aggregate. In any event, the nature of many of the projections is such that useful margins of error could not be established (though we have attempted to set rough limits on the possibilities at certain points[1]). In choosing an unconvincing accuracy, we have had in mind the convenience of the reader and not any unjustified conviction in our powers of precise deduction. Similarly, we have tried to avoid the use of the unqualified future tense; the word 'will', when it appears as something other than a statement of the obvious, should generally be taken as shorthand for 'will, on the specified assumptions'.

Fourth, the statistical structure of the work is based on the national accounts, as published in the annual series *National Income and Expenditure*—the Central Statistical Office 'National Income Blue Books'. These statistics are subject to continuous revision. Much of the basic statistical exercise was set up in 1962 when the latest version was *National Income and Expenditure 1961*. That Blue Book was also the basis for the input-output tables compiled at Cambridge (see below) on which we have drawn extensively. It has not been possible to revise the whole structure for more recent revisions of the national accounts[2].

In order to make full use of the elaborate work on the structure and inter-relationships of the British economy done by Richard Stone and his colleagues at the Department of Applied Economics at Cambridge[3], we have also adopted their classification of industrial output and of final expenditures, which differ in certain respects from those used in official statistics. We are extremely grateful to the Department for much help in the interpretation and use of their estimates.

Wilfred Beckerman asked me to introduce this book—the work of a team under his able and energetic direction. The bulk of the research was done in two years and the aim of completing a book for the printer within three years achieved. Study of the long-term prospects for our society cannot be contained within the compass of a single research project—it will continue at the National Institute and elsewhere. Perhaps the emphasis of research should now lie on the ways in which government policy on the one hand, and the practice of industrial management on the other, might be aimed more effectively at a progressive and well balanced economy and society.

---

[1]For example, table 7.6.

[2]Indeed in a few cases it was not worth while to carry through the input-output tables minor final revisions of some of our own expenditure estimates (*e.g.* in the special studies), so slight inconsistencies are implicit.

[3]*A Programme for Growth*, edited by R. Stone: 1, *A Computable Model of Economic Growth* (1962); 2, *A Social Accounting Matrix for 1960* (1962); 3, *Input-Output Relationships, 1954–1966* (1963); 4, *Capital, Output and Employment, 1948–1960* (1964), (London: Chapman and Hall for the Department of Applied Economics, University of Cambridge).

PART I

THE OVERALL RATE OF GROWTH

CHAPTER I

BRITAIN'S COMPARATIVE GROWTH RECORD

By W. Beckerman

1. THE RECORD IN SUMMARY

The starting point for any view of the possible future structure of the British economy must be a judgement about the overall growth rate that could and should be achieved. Such a judgement cannot be derived with any precision from historical comparison or from statistical analysis. Yet study of Britain's experience in the past, whether recent or more distant, in relation to that of other countries reasonably similar in level of economic attainment and in economic and social organization, can help to set the realistic limits within which a judgement must be reached.

Preoccupation with the desirability of faster economic growth in this country has been largely a response to the increasing awareness of our poor performance by comparison with other countries during the last decade or so. It is not a response to any failure to match earlier rates of growth; in fact, our average growth rate over the last ten years compares somewhat favourably with our longer-term historical growth rate[1]. It is simply that other countries in Europe appear to have done much better. As this is one of the few points on which there is fairly widespread agreement[2] we will confine ourselves here to a brief survey of the main indicators and qualifications.

The comparative statistics of Western growth rates are familiar, and need only be summarized (table 1.1). Over the whole period 1950–62, the trend rate of growth of total gross national product (GNP) of the British economy, at 2·6 per cent a year, was less than that of any other developed country in the Western world, except Ireland; it was much less than that of the other major industrial countries of Western Europe, although not very different from that of the United States. Per head of population or per employed person the

[1]Only in the 'golden age' in the third quarter of the nineteenth century have rates of growth of gross national product per head approached those recorded in the United Kingdom in the 1950s, as can be seen in Phyllis Deane and W. A. Cole, *British Economic Growth, 1688–1959* (Cambridge, 1962), table 73, p. 283 and table 74, p. 284. The fastest 8-year period of growth in GNP per man-year achieved by the UK in the last 100 years was from 1867 to 1875, when a rate of 2·7 per cent per annum was achieved, which was hardly greater than the rate in the 1950s. (See D. C. Paige, F. T. Blackaby and S. Freund, 'Economic Growth: The Last Hundred Years', *National Institute Economic Review*, July 1961, table 5, p. 34.)

[2]An exception to the general agreement that the British growth record in the 1950s has been 'poor' is the article by J. Knapp and K. Lomax, 'Britain's Growth Performance: the Enigma of the 1950s' (*Lloyds Bank Review*, October 1964).

comparison shows a somewhat reduced spread, but the British ranking is only slightly improved.

To set the stage for the discussion in chapter 2 where we select an appropriate future growth rate for Britain up to 1975 as a working basis for the whole of this study, we need to examine the comparative growth record more closely. In the rest of this chapter we shall discuss, first, whether the comparative statistical picture, as shown in table 1.1, can be accepted as a true account of the underlying differences between growth trends during the 1950s and early 1960s; how far it needs serious qualification because of the imperfections and incomparabilities of the statistical records and how much the superior growth record of some other countries owes to the choice of a particular period for examination. Then (page 19) we shall consider how far the differences in growth rates can be explained by measurable differences in the inputs of the basic factors of production, labour and capital; and how much is left to be explained by differences in the effectiveness with which additional labour and capital are used—in fact by their 'productivity'.

The question underlying this largely statistical examination of the past is, of course, the question of what changes could bring about a faster growth rate in Britain in future, or whether faster growth must be regarded as ruled out by certain immutable features of our economy differentiating it permanently from other apparently comparable economies. This is not a question to which a final answer can be given—except by time. But we can at least hope to see how much importance should be attached to some of the variables often believed to be significant in the growth equation.

Table 1.1. *Alternative indicators of growth rates, 1950–62: percentage annual average compound trend rates*

	GNP	GNP per head of population	GNP per head of employed labour force
Austria	6·0	5·8	4·9
Belgium	2·8	2·2	2·5
Canada	3·6	0·9	1·9
Denmark	3·8	2·9	3·2
France	4·4	3·5	4·2
Germany	7·2	6·2	5·1
Ireland	1·3	1·7	2·6
Italy	6·3	5·7	4·7
Netherlands	4·9	3·6	3·5
Norway	3·6	2·7	3·4
Sweden	3·7	3·1	3·2
United Kingdom	2·6	2·1	2·0
USA	3·0	1·3	2·0

Source: OECD, *Policies for Economic Growth* (Paris, 1962), *General Statistics*, and *Manpower Statistics, 1950–1962*; and appendix table 1.1.

Note: The 'trend' rates of growth in this and subsequent tables have been obtained by fitting least squares trend lines to the data for all the years.

2. QUALIFICATIONS OF THE RECORD

In making comparisons such as those in table 1.1, various qualifications and alternative approaches have to be considered. It may be claimed:

(a) that the methods and concepts used in the individual countries to measure the changes over time at constant prices (that is, in 'real' or 'volume' terms) may differ to a degree which invalidates the comparison;

(b) that measures, such as those shown above, of the 'trend' rates of growth over the whole period 1950 to 1962 may conceal genuine changes in 'trend' during the period, and that it is the latest trend with which we should be concerned;

(c) that the 'trends' in the 1950s may, in fact, simply reflect divergencies, due to the war, from some longer-run trend rates of growth. That is to say, those countries which, as a result of the war, had fallen greatly below their longer-run trend rates of growth grew more rapidly in the 1950s as part of the process of 'catching up'. This qualification is at the opposite extreme to the last one, since it amounts to saying that the period 1950 to 1962 is too short to identify a trend rather than too long;

(d) that the important comparison should be in terms of the growth of productive capacity, not output, of the different countries.

(a) *The international comparability of growth rates*

International comparisons of growth rates are occasionally regarded with scepticism on the grounds that different countries rely on different methods for estimating their growth rates, draw on basic data of varying reliability, or have different concepts of what they are trying to measure. A very strong attack on the international comparability of growth rates has been made recently by Professor Oskar Morgenstern who maintains that 'the computation, and hence the comparison, of international growth rates under these conditions is a most dubious undertaking'[1]. But Professor Morgenstern's criticism would carry greater weight if it were not for the fact that many of the errors in national income estimation to which he rightly draws attention are both systematic and relatively steady over time and also tend to be offsetting. This has been verified by the large-scale revisions that have been made to the past gross national product series for some countries and which left the average growth rate practically unaffected[2].

---

[1]'*Fortune*', October 1963, p. 180. For a fuller account see O. Morgenstern, *On the Accuracy of Economic Observation*, second edition (Princeton and Oxford, 1963).

[2]For example, in Germany the entire procedure for estimating year to year movements in net output by industry was revised in 1957 (see *Wirtschaft und Statistik*, November 1957, et. seq.), with the result that the measure of the growth rate for the period 1950 to 1955 was only changed from 9·4 to 9·1 per cent per annum, although other improvements in estimation procedures made at the same time resulted in the absolute level being raised by 7 or 8 per cent. Similar large-scale revisions made recently in Denmark changed the

There could be more substance in the contention that differences in treatment of quality changes could produce continuous disparities in measured growth rates, even where the 'true' growth rates were equal. If one country makes much less allowance for improvements in the quality of output than another, it will appear, *ceteris paribus*, to have a continuously slower growth rate. As Milton Gilbert has effectively argued, however, the criticism of failure to allow adequately for quality change is somewhat exaggerated since it is frequently based on a failure to recognize that not all changes in satisfactions are produced by genuine economic changes in quality[1]. In any case, there is no reason to believe that any country is more in error than others in its treatment of quality changes.

In practice, statistical allowance for 'quality change' is most effectively made when the greatest possible number of separate items are distinguished in the basic records of output or expenditure or prices. There is no reason to think that the basic records used for the British national accounts—although far from perfect—are less satisfactory than those of other Western European countries. It seems unlikely that the British growth rate has been under-estimated on this account more than theirs.

A detailed study has been made, at the Organisation for Economic Co-operation and Development, of the extent to which differences in methods and data deficiencies are likely significantly to affect the comparison of growth rates; it has been found that, among the more developed countries, no important incomparability could possibly result from these deficiencies[2]. The study also showed that no significant difference was made to the relative growth rates by

(i) adjusting the national estimates to ensure comparability in definitions; or

(ii) re-weighting the elements in national expenditure according to average European relative prices instead of national relative prices; or

(iii) re-calculating the European growth rates on concepts approximating as closely as possible to the concept of 'material product' used in Communist countries (which meant omitting government, banking, insurance and other services unconnected with the transport or distribution of goods). For the countries covered in these calculations the services

measure of the growth rate from 1950 to 1959 by only 0·1 per cent per annum as there were found to be offsetting errors in the estimates of net output of individual sectors. See J. McGibbon, 'The Statistical Comparability of Rates of Growth of Gross National Product' (*Productivity Measurement Review*, February 1964). The way this will arise is fairly obvious; for example, an underestimate of the rate of increase of inputs from manufacturing into services will tend to bias downwards the growth of manufacturing net output but bias upwards the rate of growth of net output of services. Similar insignificant corrections to estimates of growth rates have resulted in countries that have changed the base year for the calculation of the component indices.

[1] M. Gilbert, 'Quality Changes and Index Numbers' (*Economic Development and Cultural Change*, April 1961).

[2] See J. McGibbon, *op. cit.*

activities excluded from the gross national product amounted to about 25–30 per cent of total gross national product as defined in Western concepts. This check is of special interest since it amounts to omitting those elements of gross national product whose measurement is most arbitrary and therefore most likely to differ from country to country; or
    (iv) deleting completely one of the fastest growing items of final expenditures, namely consumer durables.

There remain, no doubt, many unknown and possibly undetectable differences in national procedures for estimating gross national product, so that it is always possible that some incomparability between the resulting implied growth rates exists. Yet such tests as can be made suggest that even if the absolute levels may be incomparable there is no reason to believe that the relative growth rates are equally suspect.

(b) *The time period*

How far are comparisons of growth rates affected if we use shorter periods to identify any possible changes in trend that may have occurred since 1950. The shorter the period selected, the less confident one can be that one is examining a 'trend' at all, rather than a cyclical movement; the identification of a 'trend' must depend on an economic interpretation rather than on statistical techniques. Nevertheless, the following table compares the average annual growth rates of gross national product per head of labour force over the whole period 1950 to 1962 with those prevailing in the two halves of the period; the trends are measured by fitting least squares regression lines to the data.

In the second half of the period, although the British growth rate did not

Table 1.2. *Annual average compound trend rates of growth of gross national product per head of employed labour force: alternative time periods*

	1950–56	1956–62	1950–62
Austria	5·7	4·2	4·9
Belgium	2·9	2·3	2·5
Canada	2·9	0·8	1·9
Denmark	1·9	3·4	3·2
France	4·3	4·0	4·2
Germany	5·9	4·4	5·1
Ireland	2·8	3·7	2·6
Italy	4·8	4·9	4·7
Netherlands	4·2	3·1	3·5
Norway	3·5	3·5	3·4
Sweden	3·6	2·1	3·2
United Kingdom[a]	2·1	1·9	2·0
USA	2·2	2·1	2·0

Source: As for table 1.1.

[a]Revised official data, published since this study was completed, suggest some acceleration in the UK growth rate between the two sub-periods shown.

improve, that of Germany was significantly reduced and there was possibly a slight fall in France. But the disparity remains substantial; Germany, Italy and France were still achieving rates of productivity increase over twice the British rate. As the figures shown in the table relate to fitted trend lines, and not to simple comparison of end years, no significant difference is made by adding or subtracting one year at either end of the time period[1].

(c) *The catching up hypothesis*

The view is sometimes taken that international differences in post-war rates of growth reflect deviations, caused by the war and its varying effects, from some longer-run trend[2]. This is very difficult to test, chiefly because of the uncertainty as to what is thought to be the longer-run trend.

To check this hypothesis, the best procedure seems to be to make alternative measurements of the pre-war trend in gross national product per man-year and hence arrive at alternative measures of the extent to which the various countries deviated from their trends in our base year, 1950. Four methods of selecting the pre-war trend in gross national product per man-year have been adopted, namely:

(i) the 'terminal year' method: this is a simple calculation of annual average rate of growth between the terminal years (i.e. beginning and end years) of the longest inter-war period for which data were available;

(ii) the 'least squares' method: this consisted of fitting a least squares trend line to the observations;

(iii) the 'equal capacity' method: this was similar to method (i), except that instead of selecting the first and last years for the whole inter-war period, years of roughly equal rates of capacity utilization, as far as could be judged (chiefly from employment data), were selected;

(iv) the 'upper capability' method: this involved selecting for each country a period when it appeared to be experiencing a fairly satisfactory upswing in growth. The acute depressions of the inter-war period are thus excluded from the measure of the long-term growth rates.

Clearly, methods (iii) and (iv) involve more judgement than the first two[3].

---

[1]This is partly, but not chiefly, because the fitting of a least squares line to a time series gives an average growth rate which is a weighted average of the growth rates between all pairs of successive years, the weights being much smaller for the growth rates nearer the beginning and end of the period than for those near the middle. This particular weighting pattern, which resembles the coefficients of a binomial expansion, has absolutely no economic significance.

[2]This view appears to be taken by J. Knapp and K. Lomax, 'Britain's Growth Performance: the Enigma of the 1950's', *op. cit.*

[3]The basic data used were obtained from A. Maddison, 'Economic Growth in Western Europe, 1870–1957', *Banca Nazionale del Lavoro Quarterly Review*, March 1959, and unpublished work-sheets prepared by D. C. Paige in connection with the article by D. C. Paige, F. T. Blackaby and S. Freund, 'Economic Growth: the Last Hundred Years', *op. cit.*

As will be seen in table 1.3, the economic disturbances of the inter-war period were so violent that alternative methods of measuring the trend lead to very different results, thereby illustrating the point made above that any concept of an underlying long-run trend is highly dubious. For example, the estimates of the French growth rate vary from 2·9 per cent per annum to 0·5 per cent per annum according to whether one selects method (i) or method (iii). Nevertheless, for what it is worth, we used these alternative trend rates to measure the percentage by which each country in 1950 deviated from the gross national product per man-year which it would have enjoyed in that year if the longer-run trend had been maintained up to that date. These indicators of deviation from trend were then correlated with the rates of growth of gross national product per man-year in the subsequent ten years 1950–60. The correlation coefficients were significant and of negative sign if all the ten countries shown in table 1.3 were included. However three extreme observations dominate the statistical results, namely Germany at one extreme and the United States and Canada at the other. Excluding these three countries, the correlation coefficients are completely insignificant, and with two out of the four methods (methods (ii) and (iii)) are of positive sign, which would indicate that the more a country had fallen below its trend line by 1950 the slower its subsequent growth rate would be[1]. So the tests tell us nothing relevant either to

Table 1.3. *Alternative measures of rate of growth of gross national product per man-year in the inter-war period*

	Method (i)	Method (ii)	Method (iii)	Method (iv)
Denmark	1·7	1·5	1·5	2·1
France	2·9	1·7	0·5	2·6
Germany	3·3	2·3	3·0	4·8
Italy	1·9	1·7	1·8	2·2
Netherlands	1·2	0·9	0·7	2·2
Norway	2·6	2·9	2·5	2·6
Sweden	1·9	2·0	2·6	3·4
United Kingdom	1·4	1·5	1·5	1·4
Canada	0·3	0·0	1·9	3·2
USA	1·4	0·7	1·3	1·0

Note: For description of alternative methods for measuring trend, see text page 16.

[1]The results are as follows:

		Correlation coefficient
Method	All ten countries	Excluding USA, Canada and Germany
(i)	− 0·74	− 0·20
(ii)	− 0·60	+ 0·05
(iii)	− 0·58	+ 0·28
(iv)	− 0·85	− 0·39

C

Britain, or to any other country that was not an extreme case of wartime destruction or economic progress.   For though it is true that the United States was, in 1950, well above, and Germany was well below, its respective trend line, the accelerated growth of, say, France or Norway or Italy cannot be explained by any earlier falling behind their longer-run trend rate of growth.

(d) *The growth of output and growth of capacity*

It may be argued that a comparison in terms of the growth of output as distinct from the growth of capacity is unfair to Britain since some Continental countries entered the 1950s with a considerable margin of spare capacity, so that much of their rapid growth of output could be achieved fairly easily simply by raising their rate of capacity utilization.   Furthermore it might be maintained that the reverse process has taken place in Britain: it may well be true that at the beginning of the 1950s our productive equipment was under heavier pressure than it has been since, so that our rate of growth of capacity has been faster than our rate of growth of output.

This seems a very plausible view, but there is no way of attaching unambiguous figures to it.   The notorious difficulties of finding a single and meaningful measure of long-term changes in the 'capacity' of an economy, taking into account both its capital equipment and the productive potential of the labour force, are too great.   'Capacity' depends too much on how equipment and labour are used and organized; it also depends on whether the pattern of potential supply matches the pattern of demand.

For Britain, one measure of production potential has been developed[1].   This is based on the trend rate of growth of productivity (gross national product per year per worker employed) during the years 1952–62.   The trend is derived by examining the growth of productivity between periods when the pressure of demand for labour (as expressed by unemployment) was equal—thus removing so far as possible the strong cyclical influence on the level of productivity. Allowance is also made for changes in hours of work and in the age-sex composition of the labour force.   When the trend rate of growth of the labour force is added to that of productivity, the result is a trend rate of growth of production potential per worker averaging 2·2 per cent a year over the period 1952–62. Moreover, it is shown that the growth of potential productivity has probably been accelerating during the post-war period and may now be put at about 2·7 per cent a year.   These calculations, when set against the fairly steady 2·0 per cent a year growth in actual output per worker (table 1.2) support the

[1]W. A. H. Godley and J. R. Shepherd, 'Long-term Growth and Short-term Policy', *National Institute Economic Review*, August 1964.

view that the capacity of the British economy may have been rising somewhat faster than its actual output, especially since the mid-1950s.

So far as we know, similar calculations have not been made for other countries. The higher growth rates of productivity in the early 1950s in Germany, Italy and Austria were no doubt the result of bringing back previously unused or unusable plant into operation as export markets were reopened and the balance of the economy was restored. But there is no reason to suppose that total capacity has failed to match the increase in total output since the mid-1950s[1].

Thus the broad picture of Britain's relatively slow growth in the last few years would probably be slightly modified, to Britain's advantage, if capacity rather than actual output trends were the criterion.

3. GROWTH OF OUTPUT AND INPUTS

We have seen that the British growth rate in the 1950s lagged behind that of most other European countries to an extent that cannot easily be explained away by alternative criteria or methods of measurement. This conclusion has been widely accepted for some time now and more serious attention has to be given to the question of how far our relatively slow growth record, in output or capacity, can be explained by a slow increase in the quantity and quality of inputs of the basic factors of production, capital and labour. It is this question which we shall examine in the rest of this chapter. It will be shown that differences in rates of growth of output can be explained only in part by differences in rates of change in the inputs of basic factors of production and that the most important reason lies in significant differences in rates of increase in productivity per unit of *total* factor input, that is of capital and labour together.

The problem has been posed here in terms of the relationships between output and factor inputs, not in terms of the extent to which the inputs have 'caused' the growth of output or any specific part of it. Statistical estimates can be made of the changes in output and in the quantity of factor inputs, and of the

---

[1] It could, perhaps, be maintained that capacity in Germany (and perhaps elsewhere), even in 1955, was still below trend because of high unemployment and the association between the increases in employment and in productivity. However, as pointed out on page 22 below, no such association exists over long periods; it is confined to cyclical upswings from a trend, and so would not apply to the 'trend' level of productivity in Germany in 1955. Furthermore, even should it apply, it would merely mean that output per head in Germany would have been higher in 1955 or 1956. It would not necessarily follow that the subsequent rise in output per head would be lower as long as there are other instances (such as France) of a tight labour market being accompanied by fast increases in output per head. In fact, there has been practically no slowing down of the rate of increase in industrial productivity in Germany after 1959 when the level of unemployment had become very low.

statistical relationships between them; it is much more difficult, if not impossible, to establish the *causal* relationships—to say how much more output is produced *as a result* of using an extra unit of capital or labour[1].   Some of the more important reasons are:

(a) neither capital nor labour is a homogeneous entity, and attempts to reduce a collection of disparate kinds of capital or labour to some common unit of equal quality invariably beg the whole question of what is the contribution to output of different types of capital and labour;

(b) even identical units of capital equipment and identical numbers of employees may produce different outputs of equally homogeneous products according to the particular economic and social situation in which they operate;

(c) attempts to measure the respective 'contributions' to output of capital and labour require that very strong assumptions be made concerning the form of the functional relationships involved, particularly assumptions about other things that change over time—such as technical progress, economies of scale and entrepreneurial dynamism—and there is, as yet, no firm evidence for such assumptions;

(d) finally, and most important, simple statistical correlations between outputs and factor inputs tell us nothing, by themselves, about the direction of causality.   For instance, they cannot confirm or contradict the view that a fast rate of growth of output will, after a time, induce a confident state of expectation about the long-run economic prospects which, in turn, will induce a high rate of investment and a more adaptable and mobile labour force.

Although we are unable to avoid completely certain theoretical questions concerning the interpretation of the statistical relationships, our primary object here is to see what statistical relationship does, in fact, exist between output and factor input changes in order to project the input requirements corresponding to our projected overall rate of growth of output[2].   However, from

---

[1] A succinct and not too technical critique of the theoretical basis for any unique causal relationship between capital and output remains Mr Kaldor's 'Increasing Returns and Technical Progress—A Comment on Professor Hicks's Article', *Oxford Economic Papers*, February 1961.   A much more detailed analysis may be found in the same author's 'Capital Accumulation and Economic Growth', chapter 10 of *The Theory of Capital*, edited by F. A. Lutz and D. C. Hague (London, 1961).   However, there is considerable disagreement about the conceptual issues involved and a variety of views have been brought together in *The Review of Economic Studies*, no. 80, June 1962.

[2] This is not to suggest that the question of the direction of the causal link between output and inputs of, say, capital, is irrelevant.   As Professor A. K. Cairncross has pointed out, the direction of causality cannot be dismissed as irrelevant on the grounds that 'if capital requirements must keep pace with the growth of income that is all we need to know for practical purposes; since the widespread view that a deliberate attempt to raise the rate of capital formation is a necessary condition for accelerating growth assumes the very causal relationship that is in dispute.' (*Factors in Economic Development*, London, 1962, p. 114.)

our analysis of the statistical relationships, certain hypotheses concerning the direction of causality in economic growth do emerge, and these are presented in the next chapter.

4. FACTOR INPUTS: LABOUR[1]

There are various possible mechanisms by which a change in labour inputs might influence the rate of growth of output, of which the following would appear to be the most likely[2]:

(a) without affecting productivity, different rates of increase in employment will be reflected in different rates of growth of output;

(b) different rates of increase in employment may affect the rate of growth of productivity;

(c) greater mobility of labour may raise the overall or sectoral rate of increase in productivity;

(d) the quality of the labour force may determine the rate of productivity increase.

As regards the first possibility, we have seen from table 1.1 above that the poor growth record of the United Kingdom is not improved if the comparison is made in terms of productivity rather than total output. However, the data in table 1.1 make no allowance for changes in hours worked or for changes in disguised unemployment. In his very comprehensive survey of the historical growth experience of the western world, Mr Maddison makes an attempt to allow for these changes; it appears that the gap between the British productivity growth rate and that of the major Continental countries is somewhat reduced, though the British growth rate still remains only about half that of the other countries, and the German productivity growth rate is still nearly three times

---

[1]For some of the methods of approach and statistical data in the rest of this chapter, acknowledgment is due to the very full study by the United Nations Economic Commission for Europe, *Economic Survey of Europe in 1961, Part 2: Some Factors in Economic Growth in Europe during the 1950s* (Geneva, 1964). We are grateful for the opportunity of seeing preliminary versions of sections of this report.

[2]The following discussion of the effect on productivity of changes in the employed labour force does not distinguish between the contribution made to the rise in the employed labour force by demographic changes, on the one hand, and by reduction in unemployment on the other hand. The precise composition of the increase in the labour force may, however, affect output per head. For example a re-absorption of unemployed, but skilled, labour would contribute more to output than the employment of school-leavers or unqualified immigrants. But in view of the vast increase in employment in Germany of agricultural labour from the East and unskilled labour from Italy, Spain and Greece, it is hardly likely that the British productivity growth rate has been relatively handicapped by this aspect of the composition of the increment in the labour force.

that of Britain[1].   Also Mr Maddison's method for adjusting for the reduction
in disguised unemployment may exaggerate the magnitude of this contribution
to the effectively employed labour force[2].   Hence, if the overall rate of increase
in the labour force is to explain a large part of inter-country differences in
growth rates it must have been by means of the second mechanism suggested
above, namely its effect on the rate of growth of productivity.

It is, of course, true that the employed labour force has grown much more
rapidly in the two countries with the fastest productivity increases (Germany
and Italy) than in Britain.   But the labour force has grown more slowly in
France than in Britain, although France has also achieved a much faster growth
of productivity, and it has not grown very rapidly in the Scandinavian countries
whose productivity performance has exceeded our own.   And in the United
States and Canada the labour force has grown very rapidly while productivity
has grown very slowly, though in these two countries one has to allow for a
marked fall in the level of capacity utilization over the last few years.   But if
we take enough countries to even out the special circumstances of individual
cases, there is no close correlation between inter-country rates of growth of
productivity and rates of growth of employment.   For example, the Economic
Commission for Europe, in its detailed comparison of international growth
experience in the 1950s finds that, among thirteen industrialized countries only
10 per cent of the variation in rates of productivity increase was 'explained'
statistically by variations in the rates of increase in the labour force[3].   Furthermore, Britain is shown to have achieved a rate of productivity increase even
lower than that which, given her rate of increase in the labour force, such
correlation as was found to exist would have implied.   Hence there does not
seem to be any prima facie evidence for the view that a high rate of increase
in the labour force is conducive to a high rate of increase in productivity, so
that the very slow growth of the labour force that we project for the future in
Britain (chapter 3) is not regarded as calling for any special restraint on the
productivity assumption that we should select.

---

[1]A. Maddison, in *Economic Growth in the West* (London, 1964), table II.7, p. 61, shows
the following figures for the annual average growth of output per man-hour, 1950–60,
after adjusting the data for the reductions in disguised unemployment (chiefly the fall in
agricultural 'employment' in France and Italy): France 3·1 per cent, Germany 5·2 per cent,
Italy 3·5 per cent, Netherlands 3·6 per cent, United Kingdom 1·9 per cent.   The abrupt
slowing down of the German growth rate as from 1953 does not detract from our main
comparison, which was in terms of the period 1956–62, a period in which there was a rapid
fall in average hours worked in Germany.

[2]This is because Maddison assumes that *all* the workers who left agriculture constituted
disguised unemployment.

[3]Economic Commission for Europe, *loc. cit.*, chapter II, p. 14, n. 20.   This inter-
country result confirms the results shown in the Appendix to chapter 7 where it can be
seen that, as among different industries in Britain (as in Germany), there is absolutely no
significant correlation at all between changes in productivity and changes in employment,
even between years at roughly equal stages in conjunctural fluctuations in activity.

The third possibility mentioned above, namely that immobility of labour has been partly responsible for our slow growth rate, is fairly deeply entrenched in current economic thinking.

One way by which mobility of labour can raise overall productivity is to accelerate the shift of labour out of low productivity industries into high productivity industries, thereby conferring a productivity bonus on the economy as a whole irrespective of how productivity in the individual sectors is changing, if at all. This might be described as the 'shift' effect, and it is possible to estimate its importance[1]. Estimates have been made by the Economic Commission for Europe which show that, at the level of industry detail used, the contribution to the overall increases in productivity made by inter-sectoral shifts in the labour force was practically negligible by comparison with the increases in productivity within the separate sectors and industries identified[2]. As can be seen in table 1.4 below the increase in overall productivity due to changes in the distribution of the labour force (the 'structural component') is very small in relation to the total increase in labour productivity, whatever the coverage of the indices. It is admitted that this kind of calculation does not tell us very much about mobility. A 'high productivity' industry is one in which value added per head is high. This simply means that wages plus profits, per person employed, are high; that may be the result of high efficiency, or it may be the result of monopoly, subsidies, etc. In a world of imperfect competition, there is no way of distinguishing the two. So the absence of any 'shift effect' in Britain or the United States in table 1.4 *may* be the result of lack of mobility, or it may be the result of the lack of any large differences between industries in wages plus profit per worker. The relatively large (though still not very important) 'shift effect' in Germany is the result not only of the large movement out of agriculture but also of the particularly large gap between added value per head in agriculture (with its disguised unemployment) and industry. (See Economic Commission for Europe, *loc. cit.*, chapter III, table 24, where added value per head is described as 'productivity' without qualification.) However, the main point is clear: the faster rates of growth achieved by some economies were almost entirely due to faster rates of productivity increase *within* individual sectors[3].

---

[1]This is done by comparing the actual overall increase in productivity that has taken place with the increase that would have occurred if the actual rates of productivity increase within each sector were applied to a constant distribution of the labour force between sectors. The difference between the two measures will reflect the additional productivity obtained through the shift in the labour force.

[2]Economic Commission for Europe, *ibid.*

[3]Whether the absence of any major contribution to growth by 'shift' in other countries is due to immobility of labour or the lack of large inter-industry differentials in net output per man is, of course, not shown by this calculation; but this is irrelevant to the hypothesis being tested. The same applies to the fact that 'net output per man' is not the same as labour productivity in the sense of efficiency.

Table 1.4. *Indices of the contribution of changes in distribution of labour force to overall growth of labour productivity, 1949–59*

	Total economy		'Productive' sectors of economy[a]		Manufacturing	
	Total labour productivity	'Structural component'[b]	Total labour productivity	'Structural component'[b]	Total labour productivity	'Structural component'[b]
Austria	142·8	104·5	147·8	106·5	142·5	101·0
Belgium	128·9	100·0	139·3	100·5	143·4	103·0
Canada	127·8	103·2	140·2	104·0	134·0	102·0
Denmark	125·6	100·9	139·9	101·0	125·4	100·8
France	152·4	102·6	164·3	103·8	158·9	104·0
Germany	154·2	105·5	173·0	107·1	157·0	99·5
Italy	160·0	103·5	183·0	104·0	194·0	102·0
Netherlands	138·7	99·5	150·9	100·0	156·7	103·5
Norway	137·2	105·1	142·8	106·4	137·1	102·0
United Kingdom	119·8	100·0	123·2	100·0	126·6	101·2
USA	126·4	99·0	133·2	100·1	141·6	101·0

Source: Economic Committee for Europe, *loc. cit.*, chapter III, tables 22, 25 and 26.

[a]Excluding dwellings and all services sectors except wholesale and retail trade.

[b]The index of the 'structural component' indicates how much labour productivity would have increased through the shift of labour among sub-industries. The method of calculation used by the ECE abstracts from the possibility that these shifts may affect the relative rate of productivity increase within sub-industries.

We have no comparative data from which to measure the actual movement of labour among industries in different countries. So far as Britain is concerned, the amount of movement is ceitainly not negligible (see chapter 7, page 232). Indeed, as table 1.5 shows, the rise in employment in manufacturing in Britain was much larger than in France—where a very large increase in manufacturing productivity was gained with hardly any net intake of labour.

We turn to the last aspect of the contribution of labour to the growth of productivity. This has to do with the 'quality' of labour. Attention has been drawn recently, especially since the publication of E. F. Denison's study of the growth of the American economy, to the impact on the growth of productivity of 'education'[1]. For example, in the United States over the period 1929 to 1957, Denison estimates that nearly half the growth of output per person employed was due to 'education'. Without in any way accepting the conceptual basis of Denison's estimates, it must be emphasized that such orders of magnitude may have been feasible when total output per head was growing at

[1]E. F. Denison, *The Sources of Economic Growth in the United States and the Alternatives Before Us* (Washington, 1962). The 'contribution' of education is here measured by weighting the increases in the proportions of people in the labour force attaining certain educational standards by the income differentials currently associated with such standards.

Table 1.5. *Indices of output, employment, output per man and output per man-hour in manufacturing, in 1960 (1950 = 100)*

	Employ-ment	Output	Productivity Per man	Per man-hour
Belgium	104	145	140	n.a.
France	106	188	177	178
Germany	164	260	159	173
Italy[a]	117	237	200	173
Netherlands	..	..	157[b]	146[c]
United Kingdom	**112**	**140**	**125**	**129**

Source: G. Bannock, 'Productivity in Manufacturing, Pre-war to 1960', *Productivity Measurement Review*, November 1962, tables 5, 7, 8 and 9, for all countries except Italy, which is taken from the ECE survey, *loc. cit.*, chapter III, tables A3, A5 and A8.

[a]1949 to 1959.
[b]Includes mining.
[c]1959, in which year the corresponding United Kingdom figure was 121.

only 1·6 per cent per annum. But in Europe we are faced with rates of growth of twice or three times this amount and, as shown later in this chapter, the 'residual' element in these growth rates alone (that is, the growth left unexplained by increases in inputs of labour and capital) is of the order of 3 to 4 per cent per annum. To ascribe to educational differences any significant part of this unexplained element in growth is plausible only if those differences have persisted over more than a generation—since present or recent differences in educational facilities or tradition, which are anyway not very pronounced[1], could affect only the new recruits to the labour force.

It is probable that growth in Britain has been impeded by the persistent shortage of people with certain specific qualifications or training—from advanced qualifications in engineering and other technologies to apprenticeships in manual skills. The reasons for this shortage lie in earlier failure—not yet removed in all cases—to appreciate that even a modest rate of economic growth leads to increasing demand for qualified people. Responsibility must be shared between the educational system, industrial managements, entry restrictions imposed by unions, and lack of foresight on the part of young people and those who advise them.

But these shortages are felt in greater or lesser degree in most of the industrial countries. It is difficult, for example, to ascribe any large part of the differences between the growth rates of Germany, France and Italy, on the one hand, and Britain and the United States on the other, to past or current developments in their respective educational systems.

[1]See the Cabinet Office, *Higher Education* (Robbins Report), Cmnd 2154 (London, 1963), table 17, p. 42.

In more general terms, the poor performance of the economy is sometimes attributed to the conservatism, restrictive practices or lack of effort of British workers, compared with other Europeans.   Such statements are hardly capable of proof or disproof.   But there are reasons for scepticism.   First, the statement is difficult to reconcile with the fact that gross national product per worker has until very recently been significantly higher than in most other European countries.   So if the statement is true, it has only recently become so.   Second, the fact that productivity, and changes in productivity, vary so much between different British enterprises strongly suggests that organization and management, rather than the innate attitudes of workers, are the important factor.   It does not seem sensible to assume that attitudes of British workers would render faster growth impossible, granted effective organization and techniques of production.

In conclusion, therefore, we find that different aspects of changes in the labour force so far as they are identifiable do not go very far towards explaining our slow advance in productivity.   However, the subject is complex; in the framework of this study, which is concerned more with the relationships to be applied to the future than with the analysis of the past for its own sake, we have not been able to formulate in a measurable fashion all the possible mechanisms by which a labour force that is changing, either in total or in composition, may influence the growth of productivity.   It is quite possible that a more detailed study would show that such changes have been more important than we have found them to be.   But, for purposes of our projections into the future, we have not found sufficient simple and clear evidence of the impact of the labour force on productivity growth to justify our making special allowance for it in arriving at the growth target which we adopt in chapter 2.   In short, such evidence to the contrary as may be found is hardly strong enough to offset the commonsense presumption, which is also verified by the experience of some countries (notably France), that a shortage of labour, by stimulating labour-saving investment may, indeed, be a stimulus rather than a handicap to the growth of labour productivity.

5.   FACTOR INPUTS: CAPITAL

The simplest and most commonly quoted relationship between capital and output is that which seems to exist between rates of growth of output or of labour productivity and the share of national product devoted to gross capital formation (referred to here, for brevity, as the investment ratio).   The poor growth performance of certain economies is frequently attributed to their low ranking in the 'investment league'.   As is shown in the following table, the ranking of countries by growth rates during the period 1956 to 1962 is correlated to some extent with their ranking in terms of the shares of investment (excluding

Table 1.6. *Trend rate of growth of gross national product (1956–62) and investment ratios (1955–61), including and excluding residential building*

	Gross national product rate of growth per annum[a]	Investment ratio (incl. residential building)[b]	*Percentages* Investment ratio (excl. residential building)[c]
Italy	6·7	21·3	15·7
Germany	5·9	23·3	18·0
Denmark	5·1	18·1	15·2
Austria	4·9	23·2	18·8
France	4·2	18·0	13·7
Netherlands	4·2	23·8	19·3
Sweden	4·1	21·1	15·9
Norway	3·9	29·3	25·1
USA	2·9	16·7	12·1
United Kingdom	**2·6**	**15·6**	**12·7**
Belgium	2·5	18·0	13·0
Canada	2·5	24·1	19·4
Ireland	2·0	14·0	12·0

Sources and notes:

[a]NIESR estimates based on OECD *General Statistics*. The rates of growth are based on trends and are annual average compound rates.

[b]Investment ratios: fixed domestic capital formation divided by GNP (current prices), both from OECD, *Statistics of National Accounts, 1950–1961.*

[c]Investment ratios: fixed domestic capital formation excluding residential building (current prices) both from OECD, *ibid.*

housing) in national product[1]. Similar results are found whatever precise period during the 1950s is adopted.

Of course, some relationship must be expected to hold between growth rates of output and investment ratios since common sense and economic theory generally attribute to capital an important role in determining levels of output,

[1]The correlation coefficients of growth of gross national product per head of labour force and investment ratios are 0·73 including residential construction and 0·68 excluding residential construction. In these and all subsequent correlations between investment ratios and growth, or between incremental capital-output ratios and growth, Canada and Norway have been excluded because of very exceptional factors responsible for the apparent low rates of return to capital formation in these two countries. In Canada, the boom up to the mid-1950s, which was largely due to the strength of world demand for primary products and to the booming American economy, led to very high investment. But with the ensuing relative stagnation of the American economy in the latter half of the 1950s, and the much weaker pressure of demand for Canadian primary product exports, considerable excess capacity emerged in Canada. In Norway the high investment ratio is caused by numerous factors including a relatively high price of capital goods, the determination to maintain fast growth in a country very poor in basic resources, the large overhead investments associated with widely separated urban centres with difficult internal communications, and a high share in total investment of very capital-intensive projects, particularly those associated with hydro-electric power production. For a discussion of Norwegian investment rate see G. A. Dean, 'Fixed Investment in Britain and Norway', *Journal of the Royal Statistical Society*, Series A, vol. 127, part 1, 1964.

other things being equal. That some such relationship does in fact exist, cannot be denied; but it is not a strong one.

Correlation analysis with the data in table 1.6 above, which makes no allowance for 'other things', particularly labour, shows that only 46 per cent of the variation in growth rates is associated with the variation in the investment ratios (excluding residential construction) even excluding two easily explained exceptional cases, Norway and Canada[1]. There are, of course, numerous conceptual and statistical reasons why the true association between the two variables might be higher or lower than that calculated, but before proceeding to these it is necessary to consider more carefully what such measures of statistical association mean in the context of the question being posed here.

A statistical relationship between growth rates and investment ratios would not necessarily mean that growth rates are *proportional* to investment ratios. Even with 100 per cent correlation between growth rates and investment ratios it would still be possible that, say, a 10 per cent increase in the investment ratio could be accompanied by a 30 per cent increase in the growth rate, and so on. The degree of proportionality will depend not on the amount of correlation between the two variables but on the form of the equation relating investment ratios to growth rates.

Now the data in table 1.6 above yield a relationship between investment ratios and growth rates which is rather like that in the simplified example of the last paragraph. That is, it shows that a given percentage increase in the investment ratio is associated with a *more than* proportionate increase in the growth rate. This is the same as saying that the higher the investment ratio and hence the faster the growth rate of output, the greater is the yield, or the return, on investment—that is the lower is the incremental capital-output ratio[2]. Hence we have to consider the possibility that inter-country differences in

[1]See footnote (1) to page 27.

[2]Where I = gross capital formation
  Y = gross national product, and $\dot{Y}$ = annual growth rate of GNP
  d = the increment sign
  and k and a are the parameters, the data in table 1.6 fit an equation of the form

$$\frac{I}{Y} = k + a\,\dot{Y} \text{ (with } k = 10 \cdot 13, \text{ and } a = 1 \cdot 22, r^2 = 0 \cdot 46) \tag{1}$$

From this it follows that:
$$\frac{I/Y}{\dot{Y}} = a + \frac{k}{\dot{Y}}$$

$$\text{or } \frac{I}{dY} = a + \frac{k}{\dot{Y}} \tag{2}$$

The left-hand side of the equation is what is known as the 'incremental' capital-output ratio (or ICOR for brevity) that is, the ratio of new gross capital formation to the accompanying increase in output. It would only indicate the 'rate of return on investment' as normally, and correctly, defined if other things were equal, notably the length of life of the assets being installed and the labour cost element in the total additional value added. For whole economies such as those we are considering, these conditions are approximately satisfied.

growth rates may be due at least as much to differences in their return to investment as to their investment ratios. A simple expression of the returns to investment is what is known as the 'incremental capital-output ratio', or ICOR for brevity. This is the relation between capital formation in any period and the increase in output during that period[1]. A high ICOR indicates—other things being equal, notably changes in co-operating factors—a low return to investment, and vice versa. The results obtained from the data in table 1.6 show that although the fast-growing countries have had higher investment ratios, these were not proportionately higher, so that they also had lower ICORs, or greater returns to investment.

How far the low British growth rate can be attributed respectively to the low investment ratio and the low return on investment (that is, the high ICOR) can be calculated on the basis of alternative assumptions. Such calculations have already been made by one analyst but the method employed is debatable[2]. The following table sets out the results obtained by an alternative method, from which it can be seen that differences in ICORs generally explain much more of

[1]Strictly speaking this definition of the ICOR cannot be applied to individual investment projects since the output resulting from the investment may not be obtained in the same time period. For large aggregates, however, one may ignore this point, though it is still preferable, in general, to follow the procedure we have adopted of lagging the period over which the increase in output is measured one year behind that taken for measuring the capital formation.

[2]A. Lamfalussy, *The United Kingdom and the Six* (London, 1963), top of page 74, calculates the respective contributions of the differences between the German and British ICORs and investment ratios simply by applying the British ICOR to the German investment ratio, comparing the resulting growth rate with the actual German growth rate and taking the difference as the contribution of the difference in investment ratios. Mr Lamfalussy overlooks the fact that the contribution of the difference in ICORs to the difference in growth rates is not independent of the difference in the investment ratios. For example, one could also apply the German ICOR to the British investment ratio and regard the difference between the resulting hypothetical growth rate and the actual British growth rate as being the contribution of the difference in the investment ratios. Theoretically, the most reasonable procedure (there is no unique method theoretically) would be to take the average of these two methods.

Algebraically, if A = investment ratio
B = reciprocal of ICOR
subscripts 1 and 2 indicate countries,
then A_1B_1 = growth rate of country 1
and A_2B_2 = growth rate of country 2
and the problem is to calculate the effects of $dA(= A_1 - A_2)$ and of $dB(= B_1 - B_2)$. Lamfalussy's method is to calculate the effect of dA as equal to $dA.B_2$ and the effect of dB as equal to $dB.A_1$. But one could equally take the effect of dA as $dA.B_1$ and of dB as $dB.A_2$. The average of these two methods, which is the method adopted above, would give the effect of dA equal to $dA\frac{(B + dB)}{2}$ and of dB as equal to $dB\frac{(A + dA)}{2}$, the sum of which also equals the total difference between A_1B_1 and A_2B_2. (When more than two variables are involved, of course, this method need not exhaust completely the difference between the two products concerned and a residual 'interaction' effect is left.) See technical note at the end of W. Beckerman and J. Sutherland, 'Married Women at Work in 1972', *National Institute Economic Review*, February 1963, p.60.

Table 1.7. *Influence of ICOR and investment ratio on difference between growth rates of Britain and other countries, 1956–62*

	ICOR	Difference of UK growth rate from that of country indicated	Of which due to difference in:		Percentage of difference in growth rate due to:	
			Investment ratio (excluding residential building)	ICOR	Investment ratio (excluding residential building)	ICOR
Austria	3·84	− 2·3	− 1·42	− 0·88	*61·7*	*38·3*
Belgium	5·20	0·1	− 0·06	0·16	*− 59·0*	*159·0*
Denmark	2·98	− 2·5	− 0·68	− 1·82	*27·0*	*73·0*
France	3·26	− 1·6	− 0·25	− 1·35	*15·9*	*84·1*
Germany	3·05	− 3·3	− 1·41	− 1·89	*42·7*	*57·3*
Ireland	6·00	0·6	0·13	0·47	*21·7*	*78·3*
Italy	2·34	− 4·1	− 0·95	− 3·15	*23·1*	*76·9*
Netherlands	4·60	− 1·6	− 1·39	− 0·21	*87·1*	*12·9*
Norway	6·44	− 1·3	− 2·23	0·93	*171·7*	*− 71·7*
Sweden	3·88	− 1·5	− 0·74	− 0·76	*49·3*	*50·7*
United Kingdom	**4·88**					
USA	4·17	− 0·3	0·13	− 0.43	*− 44·6*	*144·6*

Notes:
Col. 1: For investment ratios and trend rate of growth of GNP see table 1.6.
Cols. 2–6: For method see footnote 2, p. 29.

the difference between the growth rates of Britain and of other countries than the differences in investment ratios. For example, 57 per cent of the excess of the German growth rate over the British growth rate is explained by the lower German ICOR (that is, its higher return to gross capital formation). Table 1.7 implies that if we had had the same investment ratio as Germany our annual growth rate would have been higher by 1·4 per cent, but it would still have been 1·9 per cent lower than the German growth rate on account of the higher German rate of return on gross capital formation. The comparison between Britain and France or Italy is even more unfavourable to Britain since about three quarters of the excess of the French or Italian growth rate over the British growth rate is due to their lower ICORs. Only for Austria and the Netherlands does the higher investment ratio account for more than half of their faster growth as compared with Britain.

How far is it likely that our result, namely that fast-growing countries had generally lower ICORs, can be explained away by statistical or conceptual factors for which we have not yet made allowance? The most likely factor to bias our results is that we have used *gross* capital formation rather than *net* capital formation, and it is legitimate to argue that the relevant concept, in the context of an economy's addition to its productive capacity, should be *net* investment—that is gross investment minus some allowance for the wear and tear and scrapping of old equipment. For, with the same rate of depreciation in relation to gross national product, a country with a high rate of gross capital formation will tend to have a proportionately even higher rate of net capital formation[1]. The only relevant data available for several countries are estimates of 'depreciation', which is not the same as scrapping and is anyway calculated by very arbitrary methods in many countries. The Economic Commission for Europe's study referred to above includes estimates of net capital formation which, while admitted to be often inadequate, are probably the best available. Using these estimates to calculate the net ICORs, as in table 1.8 below, we find that although the spread between the ICORs for the various countries is on the whole somewhat narrowed, the net ICOR in Britain was still about 50 per cent higher than that of the other main Continental countries and that, in general, the faster-growing countries had the smaller net ICORs. It is true that the international comparability of the depreciation data we have used is weak, since they are largely based on national conventions concerning the length of life of assets, which differ considerably from country to country. But there is no reason to believe that these differences in conventions systematically bias the results in any way[2].

Table 1.8. *Growth rate of gross domestic product, net investment ratio and net incremental capital-output ratio in selected countries, 1949–59*

	Growth rate of GDP	Net investment ratio	Net ICOR
Austria	5·7	16·7	2·9
Belgium	3·1	7·4	2·4
Canada	4·3	15·3	3·6
Denmark	3·5	11·7	3·3
France	4·5	10·2	2·3
Germany	7·4	15·2	2·1
Italy	6·1	13·4	2·2
Netherlands	4·5	14·9	3·3
Norway	3·5	23·1	6·6
Sweden	3·4	11·2	3·3
United Kingdom	**2·5**	**8·0**	**3·2**
USA	3·5	10·0	2·9

Source: Cols. 1 and 2 from ECE, *loc. cit.*, chapter II, table 8, p. 22.   Col. 3 equals col. 2 divided by col. 1.

[1]For example, suppose there are two countries in each of which depreciation is the same at, say, 10 per cent of GNP. Then in the country with, say, 15 per cent of GNP devoted to gross capital formation, net capital formation will be only 5 per cent of GNP; whereas in the country with, say, 30 per cent of GNP devoted to gross capital formation, net capital formation will be 20 per cent of GNP. Hence if there were a strictly proportional relationship between the net investment ratio and the growth rate of output (say a *net* ICOR in both countries of 2·5) the former country would grow at 2 per cent per annum and the latter at 8 per cent per annum, but the gross ICOR would appear to be 7·5 in the former country and only 3·75 in the latter country.

[2]A most interesting part of the study by Mr Lamfalussy quoted above is the demonstration that the difference between the United Kingdom's return to investment and that of the other main Continental countries would persist even if widely different assumptions were made concerning depreciation rates (*op. cit.*, p. 80).

On the other hand, another weakness of the depreciation data would produce a bias in favour of the result we have found. This is that scrapping, or replacement, which is what we ideally wish to allow for, is not the same as 'depreciation' as conventionally measured, which includes an allowance for that part of any piece of equipment's useful economic life that is expected to have expired at the end of each accounting year. In a growing economy depreciation allowances will generally be greater than replacement[1]. The faster the growth of the economy and the capital stock the greater will be the excess of depreciation over replacement. Hence, in deducting depreciation to arrive at estimates of *net* capital formation, the excessive deduction will be greater in the faster-growing economies so that their *net* investment will have appeared lower than if only replacement had been deducted. This will tend to exaggerate their returns to net investment. Other features of the data, such as the tendency for the proportion of less productive investment (houses, roads, schools, etc.) in total investment to be lower in fast-growing economies, have been examined in detail in a recent study but have been found to have little effect on the conclusion that high rates of growth have been due as much to high returns on capital as to higher investment ratios[2].

Another statistical qualification is needed. The comparison of investment ratios as in table 1.8 above is at national prices, and the prices of investment goods relative to other prices within the economy differ from country to country. It is conceivable that an apparently low return to investment may, in fact, simply mean that the relative price of investment goods is high, so that in 'real' terms the amount of investment expenditure is not so great, compared to other countries, as it would appear. This is certainly so for Norway, though other incomparabilities also tend to exaggerate the Norwegian investment ratio. Fortunately, the international comparisons of relative price levels produced by Milton Gilbert and Associates[3] have made it possible to check how far investment ratios in different countries would need to be modified if they were re-calculated on the basis of some 'standard' relative prices of investment goods[4]. These adjustments tend to reduce the gap in investment ratios between Britain and the faster-growing countries. In fact, the British investment ratio at standard prices, as estimated by Maddison, is only 18 per cent below that of Germany, whereas at national prices it is about 30 per cent below the German ratio[5]. Hence, the relative rate of return on investment in Britain is even lower after

[1]See E. D. Domar, 'Depreciation, Replacement and Growth' (*Economic Journal*, March 1953).
[2]T. P. Hill, 'Growth and Investment according to International Comparisons' (*Economic Journal*, June 1964).
[3]*Comparative National Products and Price Levels: a Study of Western Europe and the United States* (Paris, Organisation for European Economic Co-operation, 1958).
[4]ECE, *loc. cit.*, chapter II, pp. 22 and 23; A. Lamfalussy, *op. cit.*, pp. 66–9, and A. Maddison, *Economic Growth in the West, op. cit.*, chapter III, table III.6.
[5]A. Maddison, *ibid.*

allowing for differences in the relative prices of investment goods, which tend to offset the unmeasurable bias in our results due to the discrepancy between depreciation and replacement.

6. THE JOINT CONTRIBUTION OF LABOUR AND CAPITAL

The most important element omitted from the above discussion of the investment ratio explanation of international differences in growth rates is the variation in the rates of increase in the labour force. For it is possible that the relatively low return on investment which we find in Britain has been caused by the slow growth of our labour force, since in countries with fast-rising employment the apparent return to capital, as measured by the ICORs shown above, is generally higher than in Britain[1]. And the returns to capital measured in this way include the contributions to output made by the increase in the labour force. Employment data may be used to assess the extent to which rising employment might have biased the ICORs towards the results we have found.

To do this we have calculated what is generally known as the ICOR(L). This is basically the same as the ICOR—it is the ratio between the amount of capital formation in any period and the increase in output over that period— the only difference being that the measure of the increase in output is adjusted to exclude that part of the increase that may be attributable to the rise in employment. The main conceptual question, therefore, is exactly how this adjustment should be made. For what is that part of the increase in output that is attributable to employment when capital is also changing? The simplest procedure, and one frequently adopted, is to regard it as being the base year output multiplied by the percentage increase in employment. This procedure corresponds exactly to a comparison between investment ratios and rates of growth of labour productivity instead of rates of growth of total output.

The defect of this method is that it exaggerates the effect of the rise in employment. For it implicitly assumes that output would rise in proportion to the rise in the labour force whatever was happening to capital formation (that is, even if there were no capital formation so that capital per head would be declining). Another way of interpreting this procedure is that all output in the base year is being credited to labour and none to the base year capital stock. The calculation of ICOR(L)s by this method would hence tend to exaggerate the contribution of any rise in employment and so bias the resulting ICOR(L)s against the countries where employment was rising rapidly by

---

[1]More generally, one would only expect a high correlation between investment ratios and growth rates of GNP if capital per head remained constant in all countries, so that a functional relationship between output, on the one hand, and the two factors capital and labour, on the other, is reduced to a relationship between output and either capital alone or labour alone.

D

requiring too great a deduction to be made from the output increase they achieved.

Hence we have supplemented the calculation of the simple ICOR(L)s with calculations of what we shall designate as the ICOR(L'). The increase in output in the ICOR calculation is adjusted to exclude the contribution of the increase in labour, measured by the increase in employment *multiplied by the share of wages in national income*, and the remaining change in output is then attributed to capital. Thus capital is credited with the contribution it makes by keeping capital per head constant as well as by raising capital per head[1]. The ICOR(L')s calculated by this method are shown, together with simple ICOR(L)s in table 1.9 below.

The assumption underlying this method, namely that the marginal product of labour is equal to its wage is, of course, a somewhat heroic one. The general assumption that factors of production are paid the value of their marginal products is central to the neoclassical theory of value and distribution. It has been effectively challenged on largely theoretical grounds with the emergence of the theory of imperfect competition. The more recent discussion of the production function in connection with the problems of economic growth, in which considerable emphasis has been placed on the role of technical progress and economies of scale, further weakened the operational value of the concept of the marginal product of labour. Finally, the difficulty of applying the static concepts of marginal productivity theory to a world of change and growth is manifested in the simple empirical fact that when employment rises output per head usually rises, which, in a static equilibrium model would mean that the marginal product of labour was greater than its average product so that if labour were to be paid the value of its marginal product this would more than exhaust the total national product[2].

[1]Symbolically, if I = gross capital formation, Y = national product, L = labour, and w = the proportion of national income going to labour; then the ICOR(L') = $\dfrac{I}{dY - dL\, w.\dfrac{Y}{L}}$

It should be noted that this form of the ICOR is a weighted harmonic mean of two simple familiar forms, namely (i) taking output unadjusted for any change in employment and (ii) adjusting output proportionately to the change in employment; the weights are w and $(1-w)$ respectively.

[2]It could, of course, be argued that the tendency for the average product of labour to rise with an increase in employment is due to an even faster rise in capital per head, thereby retaining consistency with the classical models in which the marginal product of labour will vary according to the amount of capital employed in the manner given by the law of variable proportions. But it is much more likely to be due to (a) the latent spare capacity and (b) the existence of overhead labour; so that a rise in the variable component of the labour supply will generally reduce real costs per unit of output. An alternative explanation would be along the lines of the important article by M. Frankel, 'The Production Function in Allocation and Growth: a Synthesis' (*American Economic Review*, December 1962), in which he shows how the 'realized' marginal products of capital or labour to the individual enterprise will be greater than their *ex ante* marginal products if many firms are increasing their inputs, since this will have a type of external economy effect though raising the ' development modifier' which he inserts in the production function of the individual firm.

Table 1.9. *Alternative measures of incremental capital-output ratios for selected countries*

	1956–62			1949–59
	Gross ICOR	Gross ICOR(L)	Gross ICOR(L')	Net ICOR(L')
Austria	3·84	5·52	4·27	3·48
Belgium	5·20	7·53	5·50	2·74
Canada[a]	7·76	30·12	16·65	7·28
Denmark	2·98	5·32	3·84	5·32
France	3·26	4·50	3·37	2·37
Germany	3·05	5·30	3·73	2·67
Ireland	6·00	3·78	3·88	..
Italy	2·34	4·35	2·81	2·79
Netherlands	4·60	7·68	5·57	4·14
Norway[a]	6·44	8·37	6·96	7·45
Sweden	3·88	6·39	4·54	3·86
United Kingdom	4·88	7·43	5·82	4·44
USA	4·17	7·95	5·37	5·00

Source: NIESR estimates.
[a]See footnote 1 to page 27.

However, at this stage we are still only concerned with what relationships can be found to exist between international differences in growth rates and factor inputs. If we do not accept that labour's contribution to changes in output can be equated with the change in employment multiplied by wages per employee (or by some other common value for the contribution to output of marginal increase in employment) we shall have to dismiss from the outset any possibility of being able to relate changes in output to changes in factor inputs. Experimenting with the ICOR(L) method will either show that there is some such relationship, or that the productivity of factor inputs has changed in a way which cannot be fully explained by changes in factor proportions and so must require an additional explanation. Also, there is no reason to believe that errors in the assumption that labour is paid the value of its marginal product would systematically bias the results of the international comparisons. In fact, we have found that our results would hardly be affected by assuming that the share of wages in national income is the same in all countries[1]. In the absence of any better procedure we have calculated the ICOR(L)s by the two methods described and the results are shown in table 1.9 above. In this table we also show the net ICOR(L')s, obtained by applying an adjusted contribution of rising employment to the net ICORs as given in table 1.8 above.

It can be seen from table 1.9 above that there is considerable variation between countries in the value of the ICOR(L')s, indicating that differences in

[1]On account of the slight inter-country variation in the share of wages in national income the correlation coefficients for ICOR(L)s on growth rates or ICOR(L')s on growth rates are almost equal.

rates of growth of output cannot be explained by differences in investment ratios even (a) after allowing for changes in labour input (on the basis of the marginal productivity equals wage assumption) and (b) after allowing for the difference between *gross* and *net* investment. Whatever the method used Britain always appears to have had a relatively high ICOR, that is, a relatively low rate of return (in terms of real product) on new capital formation.

With the aid of these ICOR(L')s, table 1.10 shows the respective contributions to the differences in growth rates between the United Kingdom and the main Continental countries of (i) the investment ratios and (ii) the ICOR(L')s. As with the similar calculations shown in table 1.7 above, it can be seen that the differences in the ICOR(L')s 'explain' a greater part of the disparities in growth rates than the differences in the investment ratios. However, the importance of the rate of return on investment (as measured by the ICOR(L')) is generally somewhat less when investment is measured net of depreciation than with gross investment.

The results shown so far relate to the total economy of the countries concerned. It might be argued that difference in aggregate ICOR(L)s may reflect differences in the pattern of investment; that is, countries with high aggregate ICOR(L)s may be those that allocated a higher proportion of capital formation to sectors where the technical conditions of production are such that the ICOR(L)s are high. The detailed study by the Economic Commission for Europe, however, contains an analysis of ICOR(L)s in individual industries and sectors, in which it is found that countries with relatively high aggregate ICOR(L)s had relatively high ICOR(L)s in nearly all individual sectors or industries[1]; and that though differences in the patterns of investment certainly contributed something to inter-country differences in rates of return on capital, the latter differences probably arise because returns on capital in given industries differed greatly from country to country. As regards the difference between the German and British growth rates, since the ICOR(L) s shown by the Economic Commission for Europe's study for individual sectors and manufacturing industries are generally higher in the United Kingdom than in Germany, we are able to dismiss the possibility that while the adverse effects on the British growth rate of differences in the pattern of employment changes or of investment taken separately may not be important their combined impact might be significant. In table 1.11 below we show our estimates of the ICORs and ICOR(L')s for manufacturing alone.

As has been noted already on page 28 above, the calculated relationship between growth rates of GNP and investment ratios imply that fast-growing countries obtained greater returns to capital. It is not simply that the low

---

[1]Similar results are shown by the ECE, *loc. cit.*, chapter II, table 17, p. 34, where ICOR(L)s for the period 1949 to 1959 are given.

[2]See in particular ECE, *loc. cit.*, chapter III, table 14, p. 18.

Table 1.10. *Influence of gross ICOR(L') and net ICOR(L') and investment ratio on difference between growth rates of the United Kingdom and other countries*

	Gross ICOR(L')					Net ICOR(L')				
	UK growth rate, 1956–62 minus that of country indicated[a]	of which due to:		% of difference in growth rate due to:		UK growth rate, 1949–59 minus that of country indicated[a]	of which due to:		% of difference in growth rate due to:	
		Investment ratio	ICOR(L')	Investment ratio	ICOR(L')		Investment ratio	ICOR(L')	Investment ratio	ICOR(L')
Austria	− 2·22	− 1·24	− 0·98	55·9	44·1	− 2·95	− 2·38	− 0·56	81·0	19·0
Belgium	− 0·18	− 0·05	− 0·13	27·8	72·2	− 0·91	0·19	− 1·10	− 20·9	120·9
Canada	1·02	− 0·78	1·80	− 76·5	176·5	− 0·71	− 1·57	0·86	221·1	− 121·1
Denmark	− 1·77	− 0·54	− 1·23	30·5	69·5	− 0·83	− 0·92	0·09	110·8	− 10·8
France	− 1·87	− 0·23	− 1·64	12·3	87·7	− 2·43	− 0·75	− 1·68	30·9	69·1
Germany	− 2·64	− 1·17	− 1·47	44·3	55·7	− 4·29	− 2·39	− 1·90	55·7	44·3
Ireland	− 0·91	0·15	− 1·06	− 16·5	116·5					
Italy	− 3·40	− 0·79	− 2·61	23·2	76·8	− 3·42	− 1·77	− 1·65	51·8	48·2
Netherlands	− 1·28	− 1·15	0·13	89·8	10·2	− 1·74	− 1·74	0·00	100·0	0·0
Norway	− 1·42	− 1·95	0·53	137·3	− 37·3	− 1·29	− 2·97	1·68	230·2	− 130·2
Sweden	− 1·32	− 0·63	− 0·69	47·7	52·3	− 1·03	− 0·84	− 0·19	81·6	18·4
USA	− 0·07	0·11	− 0·18	− 157·1	257·1	− 0·56	− 0·51	− 0·05	91·1	8·9

[a]The 'growth rate' here is the growth of output adjusted to exclude the contribution of the increase in labour force, valuing the marginal product of labour as equal to its wage. It is for this reason that the figures shown here are not the same as those in table 1.7. The growth rates here may be interpreted as the rate of growth of GNP ascribable to the increases in capital (and other unidentified factors), allowing for the contribution of labour.

British growth rate was associated with a low return on investment (as well as a low investment ratio); the association was general to all countries, though there were, of course, slight deviations in individual cases.   The same result is obtained from the ICOR(L)s in table 1.9 for, as can be clearly seen in the following diagram, they are inversely correlated with the growth rates of national product[1].   Again, the inverse association is fairly general.   The data shown in the diagram fit the following equation:

$$\text{ICOR(L)} = 10\cdot66 - 1\cdot36\,\dot{P} \tag{1}$$

(where $\dot{P}$ = annual rate of growth of GNP per employed person; the correlation coefficient for this equation is 0·829).

Fig. 1.1.   ICOR(L) and the growth of GNP: annual average percentage change, 1956-62

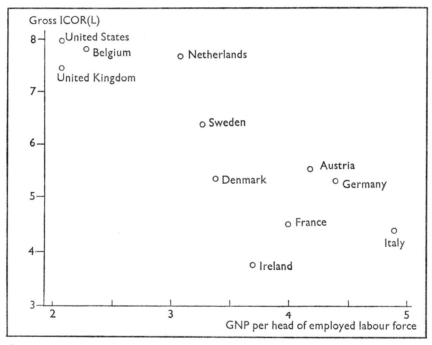

Source: Tables 1.9 and 1.2.

[1]It may be noted that the form of the inverse relationship between ICORs and growth rate expressed in the equation derived from the data shown in the diagram is not the same as that shown in footnote 2 to p. 28, where a linear relationship between investment ratios and growth rates entails a non-linear relationship between ICORs and growth rates. Conversely, the linear relationship between ICORs and growth rates shown below entails a non-linear relationship between investment ratios and growth rates of the form

$$\frac{I}{Y} = a\left(\frac{dY}{Y}\right) - b\left(\frac{dY}{Y}\right)^2$$

The above diagram can be interpreted in the following way. Faster rates of growth of output per man are associated statistically with higher returns to investment. Whether the latter result from greater economies of scale, faster technical progress, or a more dynamic management and hence better organization of production in conditions of fast-rising output, is a matter that will be discussed at greater length below. The point is that this relationship between fast growth and greater returns to investment is the same as that found by other methods of analysis of the relationship between growth of outputs and inputs, both on an inter-country basis and on an inter-industry basis, and is a result which is central to the whole theme of this part of the study.

Table 1.11. *Comparison of incremental capital-output ratios for manufacturing: United Kingdom and main Common Market countries*

	ICOR		ICOR(L′)	
	1955–60	1957–62	1955–60	1957–62
France	1·97	2·34	2·33	2·34
Germany	1·78	1·98	2·14	2·32
Italy	1·62	1·48	2·58	1·77
United Kingdom	3·93	4·84	4·11	4·84

Source: NIESR estimate.

Still at an international level, we may now consider an alternative method for assessing the joint effect on output of increases in both capital and labour. This method consists of assuming that the marginal product of capital, as well as of labour, is proportionate to its share in national income, so that the contribution to the output increase of changes in both factors equals the changes in the quantity of the factor inputs weighted by their respective shares in national product. The difference between the results obtained by this method and the ICOR(L) approach lies in the fact that the former may, and generally will, provide an explicit measure of a 'residual' increase in output, not resulting directly from the increases in either capital or labour.

This method is, in fact, an application of the well-known 'Cobb-Douglas production function'. As applied in the manner just described this function has shown remarkable powers of survival. Although it has been subjected to several powerful criticisms it is still used to measure the alleged contribution to growth made by capital and labour and hence to obtain a measure of the 'residual' which is generally ascribed to factors such as changes in technology, education, and any other fashionable elements in economic growth theory[1]. Whilst we sympathize with the various criticisms made of this function as an instrument for describing the real world, we use it in the following pages for three main reasons:

[1]See especially, E. F. Denison, *The Sources of Economic Growth in the United States and the Alternatives Before Us, op. cit.*

(i) it is instructive to demonstrate that, on the assumptions made by protagonists of this approach, the contribution of capital and labour to the explanation of differential growth rates would be negligible;

(ii) that, on the same assumptions, the 'residual' element in growth is not only highly correlated with the rate of growth of output (like the rates of return on capital) but is also so large in most countries that recent attempts to ascribe a large part of this 'residual' to education must be regarded with great scepticism[1]; and

(iii) we regard the procedure as being nothing more than a statistical device for obtaining a combined index of factor inputs and hence permitting the calculation of an index of 'total productivity'—that is, of total output per unit of total factor input[2].

In fact, it would be less misleading to conduct the whole discussion in terms of the productivity of the factors and to discard the whole concept of a 'residual'. For purposes of measuring this joint productivity, the two factor inputs have to be weighted together in some way or other, so the calculation of a 'residual' within the framework of a Cobb-Douglas production function is statistically the same operation as the calculation of the joint productivity of the factors labour and capital as long as the weights used are the same in both operations.

The Cobb-Douglas production function is generally written in the form:

$$Y = aL^w K^{1-w}$$

where Y and L represent output and labour as before

and K represents the stock of capital

and w and $(1-w)$ are respectively the shares of wages and non-wage incomes in national income.

As written above, the marginal products of labour and capital (the first differentials of output with respect to labour and capital) are simply the coefficients w and $(1 - w)$ respectively and, insofar as these are arbitrarily fixed at the outset as their respective shares in national income, it is assumed that the function is one where there are constant returns to scale[3].

The growth study by the Economic Commission for Europe, while stating some of the main reasons why the use of this function is very misleading anyway, proceeds to show empirically that inter-country differences in growth rates cannot be explained by the joint contribution of changes in capital and labour inputs, valuing the marginal products of these inputs by their respective shares

---

[1]See references on page 24 above to Denison's estimate of the contribution to growth of education.

[2]It is in this way that the procedure outlined has been used by W. B. Reddaway and A. D. Smith in 'Progress in British Manufacturing Industries in the Period 1948–54', *Economic Journal*, March 1960.

[3]More technically, it is assumed that the function is linear and homogeneous so that increasing both inputs in the proportion λ increases output in the same proportion.

in national income[1]. It is shown that a large unexplained 'residual' is left, which in most countries is greater than the combined contributions of capital and labour. Our own calculations lead to very similar results. The following table compares the two sets of results.

Table 1.12. *Contribution to growth of gross domestic product in selected countries of changes in (a) labour force and capital stock and (b) the 'residual'*

| | Annual average per cent of growth ascribed to: | | | |
| | Labour and capital | | 'Residual' | |
	ECE (1949–59)	NIESR (1950–60)	ECE (1949–59)	NIESR (1950–60)
Germany	2·9	3·75	4·5	4·05
Belgium	1·0	1·45	2·0	1·35
Canada	3·6	2·25	0·6	0·55
France	1·1	1·45	3·4	2·95
Norway	1·6	2·05	1·8	1·15
Sweden	0·9	0·75	2·5	2·15
Netherlands	2·2	2·85	2·6	2·25
United Kingdom	1·3	1·15	1·1	1·2
USA	..	1·9	..	1·2

Source: ECE, *loc. cit.*, chapter II, table 18, p. 36; and NIESR estimates. See appendix table 1.3.

The differences between the two sets of results are due to various factors— slightly different time periods and slightly different series for the basic data. But that such differences should lead to significantly different estimates, in some cases, of the contributions of the various factors is itself some reason for treating all such calculations with considerable suspicion. Nevertheless, both sets of results establish the importance of the statistical residual, that is, of the

---

[1]The ECE study, *loc. cit.*, chapter II, pp. 34–5, lists the following objections to the use of the Cobb-Douglas production function:

(a) Its dependence on highly dubious capital stock data.

(b) The assumption that the 'residual' trend found in practice—i.e. the part of the output increase left unexplained by capital and labour within the framework of the Cobb-Douglas function—is stable over time.

(c) The implausibility of the assumption that the function should be linear and homogeneous, i.e. should imply constant returns to scale.

Professor E. H. Phelps Brown, in 'The Meaning of the Fitted Cobb-Douglas Function', *Quarterly Journal of Economics*, November 1957, also shows that (a) for statistical reasons, chiefly the auto-correlation between the variables, 'The conclusion must be that the fitting of the Cobb-Douglas function to time series has not yielded, and cannot yield, the statistical realization of a production function. It can describe the relations between the historical rates of growth of labor, capital, and the product, but the coefficients that do this do not measure marginal productivity' (p. 551) and (b) if cross-section data relating to different industries are used, to avoid the serial correlation problem, the results 'do not necessarily throw any light on what will happen when we vary the proportion of labor to capital within one industry, with its given product and given technical requirements' (p. 556).

'unexplained' part of growth[1]. Secondly, there is again clear evidence that the residual is correlated with the growth rate. The two faster-growing countries, Germany and France, have high residuals and the two slow growers, the United Kingdom and the United States, have relatively small 'residuals'[2].

This result confirms the inverse correlation of ICOR(L)s with growth rates. Both mean that the faster the growth rate of the economy the less can be explained by the increases in labour and capital provided the combined marginal products of the latter are regarded as being equal to total product. Alternatively the faster the growth of output, the faster is the increase in the productivity of the factors labour and capital.

Hence, whilst qualitative statements to the effect that the poor British growth performance must be due to a slow-growing labour force or a small share of investment in national output are true as far as direction of effect is concerned, they are apt to be misleading as regards the quantitative importance of these factors. By obscuring the fact that a large part of our slow growth has been left unexplained by changes in factor inputs they tend to exaggerate the importance of policies designed to improve the supply or mobility of labour or to stimulate investment. We do not wish to give the impression that such issues are of no importance. Increased rates of investment and labour mobility will certainly contribute to growth of factor productivity. Nor do we imply that our attempts to measure the relative contribution of increased factor inputs are fully satisfactory: indeed we have indicated at the appropriate stages some of the

---

[1]Among the first studies to draw attention to the importance of the residual were R. M. Solow's 'Technical Change and the Aggregate Production Function', *Review of Economics and Statistics*, August 1957, and O. Aukrust's 'Investment and Economic Growth', *Productivity Measurement Review*, February 1959. A mystique of the 'residual' which was almost certainly not the original authors' intention has since developed, enshrined in the study by E. F. Denison (*op. cit.*). This study does not use the static marginal productivity theory of distribution as something to be tested and found inadequate as an explanation of the growth process but as a description of the real world of change, so that the resulting residual is not something which throws doubt on the theory, but something which has to be explained in terms of rather arbitrary valuations of the contribution of education, economies of scale, etc.

[2]It would be legitimate to ask why we (and the ECE) have made these calculations with fixed coefficients for labour and capital summing to unity, and why we have not left the coefficients free, in which case much higher estimates might have been obtained, implying greater contributions by the given increases in the stocks of capital and labour. For our own estimates we have, in fact, tried to fit production functions to the national data without any constraint on the coefficients of capital and labour. But the results were invariably absurd in that they showed negative coefficients for capital. The reason why this result is obtained from simple time series is that in years of falling off (or slower increase) in output, employment usually falls less than output, so that output per head falls. At the same time the capital stock increases at about the same rate as before so that capital per head rises faster. This must produce a negative correlation of output per head on capital per head, corresponding to a negative coefficient of capital in the framework of the Cobb-Douglas production function. In others words, if year to year changes are used the results are dominated by cyclical variations.

main qualifications to which they are subject. But we still find that much is left to explain.

Finally, it must be emphasized again that even had we found that, statistically, all the inter-country differences in rates of growth of output were associated with differences in rates of growth of inputs of labour or capital or both, it could still not be concluded that the higher rates of investment in some countries have been a major causal element in their faster growth rates. Such conclusions from the statistical relationships (even had they been better) are quite invalid in the absence of independent evidence of the direction of causality. Investment is not something autonomous and determined outside the economic system. In the following chapter we consider the question of why investment and growth rates have differed substantially between countries. In subsequent chapters we shall also consider how our results apply at the level of individual industries within Britain and what guidance they provide for projecting British investment requirements if a faster rate of growth of output is to be achieved. We shall also attempt to show that the inter-industry pattern of results is consistent with that obtained at the inter-country level once the necessary allowance is made for certain factors such as the stronger inter-industry differences in the technical conditions of production and the weaker inter-industry competition for markets.

CHAPTER II

DEMAND, EXPORTS AND GROWTH

By W. Beckerman

The outcome of the discussion in chapter 1 appears to be that international differences in growth rates can only in part be explained by different rates of increase in the employment of the basic factors of production, labour and capital, and that they are largely the result of different rates of increase in productivity per unit of factor input, whether the factor inputs are measured separately or are combined into some sort of weighted index. To arrive at a reasonable assumption about a feasible future growth rate for the British economy, therefore, will require not only an assumption as to the conditions under which there would be an increase in inputs of capital and labour but a view as to the reasons for the observed differences in rates of increase in the productivity of these factors of production.

Although this is, of course, *the* major problem in economic growth, the extreme complexity of the subject has, so far, made it difficult for economists to establish firmly the respective quantitative importance of different causes of increases in factor productivity. It is a simple matter to draw up long lists of probable contributory causes of growth, but the transition to an assessment of their relative quantitative importance is, so far, beyond our reach. The inherent methodological difficulty of separating cause from effect in economics is largely responsible for the little progress that has been made, particularly in view of the complex interrelationships between the variables[1]. This interrelationship applies with great force to the problem of economic growth, since almost anything that might be expected to contribute to growth might equally well be a cause of growth. For example, even had we found better simple statistical relationships between growth and rates of increase in the labour force there is abundant evidence showing that changes in the labour force are largely induced by changes in the demand for labour. The same applies to investment.

Furthermore, the main methodological handicap in economics is the limited opportunity for controlled experiments. To some extent international comparisons can provide the economist's substitute for the controlled experiment of other disciplines. But the economist still has to make the best of the conditions as found in the different countries. This means that whilst he may be able to say that, over the range of conditions that exist, certain generalizations

---

[1]The methodological difficulties are aggravated by our being limited to annual data for most of the relevant variables, though the mere provision of, say, quarterly data would not solve all problems. Also, one would probably require new kinds of data, for example, to measure differences in production techniques, in management, in organization, etc.

cannot be made, he may not be able to identify under what conditions the same generalizations could be made.   For example, the rate of investment does not seem to have played a decisive role in explaining differences among growth rates.   Yet it may well be that, under different conditions, the role of investment would be much greater.   In this chapter, we shall suggest that differences in competitive power in foreign trade have played a dominant role in explaining differences in growth rates among large countries with a high share of foreign trade in total output; yet it is not difficult to imagine conditions—such as much greater international co-ordination of economic planning and of balance of payments policies—in which this generalization would no longer be valid, and in which quite different factors, such as resource endowments, investment ratios, education, research, better management and so on, would predominate.

In view of these, and many other difficulties, it would be presumptuous in this study, which is directed at those aspects of the past that can help in assessing future possibilities, to attempt to provide a comprehensive explanation of inter-country differences in rates of growth of productivity.   But there are some reasons for believing that among the numerous factors which may explain these differences in productivity growth rates, one factor has been of particular importance, namely demand expectation.   Hence we concentrate on this factor in this chapter, although we do not maintain that many other factors, which we have not studied, are of no importance whatsoever, or that they could not be of prime importance in different circumstances, or that the rather qualitative, circumstantial, or quasi-theoretical reasons which we advance in support of the above view go further than being merely consistent with it.

1. THE GROWTH 'MODEL' IN OUTLINE

The essence of the view of the growth process expounded here is as follows[1]. Differences in growth rates among reasonably advanced countries are largely the result of differences in the expectations that may be held concerning future long-run demand prospects.   A high pressure of demand will not be enough to induce a fast increase in capacity unless it is accompanied by expectations of a fast increase in demand.   Confident expectations will stimulate a greater effort to expand productive capacity, both through a higher rate of investment and through improvements in productivity per unit of total input of capital and labour.   A faster rate of gross capital formation may have an automatically favourable effect on the productivity of net capital formation on account of

---

[1]Similar views have been presented elsewhere.   See, in particular, OECD, *Policies for Economic Growth, loc. cit.;* 'Policies for Faster Growth', *National Institute Economic Review,* February 1962; W. Beckerman, 'Projecting Europe's Growth', *Economic Journal,* December 1962; A. Lamfalussy, *The United Kingdom and the Six, op. cit.;* and same author, 'Contribution à une théorie de la croissance en économie ouverte', *Recherches Economiques de Louvain,* December 1963.

'embodied' technical progress[1]. If the increased capacity permits the confident demand expectations to be realized, so that output is able to expand rapidly, the productivity per unit of factor input is likely to rise on account of economies of scale both internal and external, as well as generally improved organization of production. In other words, the productive system, at least in most of industry, is believed to be very flexible, and the rate of growth that can be achieved is, within limits, partly a matter of the growth rate that the relevant bodies in society (particularly entrepreneurs) expect to be achieved.

For an economy in which foreign trade is a large proportion of output the most important determinant of confident expectations about the long-run rate of increase in demand is the buoyancy of exports[2]. Only in special circumstances can rapid increases in domestic demand be sustained for a long period in the absence of a rapid increase in exports. For large countries, whose exports are not heavily concentrated on a few products or a few markets, a favourable export position requires, above all, that exports be 'competitive'. Defined widely, 'competitiveness' may include all sorts of secondary characteristics such as packaging, punctuality of delivery, after-sales service, credit terms, and so on. But it must be basically a question of price and technological superiority.

The importance of competitiveness leads to the 'virtuous circle' element in the growth process. For insofar as fast growth is induced by rapidly expanding exports and, in turn, facilitates a fast rise in productivity, it will tend, other things being equal, to moderate the rise in costs per unit of output, thereby tending to perpetuate, or increase, the initial competitive advantage responsible for the rapid expansion of exports. This will maintain, or add to, the stimulus to invest by maintaining, or raising, profit margins on exports and hence the rate of profit on capital for the economy as a whole (corresponding to a rise in the share of profits in national income). Technological progress also enters into the virtuous circle process since faster growth and a higher rate of investment

[1]This depends on the assumption that a faster rate of gross capital formation is accompanied by a correspondingly faster rate of scrapping or retirement of old equipment, thereby leading to a sharper fall in the average length of life of the capital stock. 'Embodied' technical progress should have the same *proportionate* effect on the marginal product of the *gross* capital formation, whatever the level of the latter.

[2]The role of exports in growth has been of central importance in economic history, particularly in explaining differential national growth rates in the second half of the nineteenth century, and a substantial literature has been devoted to this topic. The mechanism suggested above is, in fact, very close to that which W. Arthur Lewis describes in 'International Competition in Manufactures', *American Economic Review*, May 1957; particularly the fact that, in the absence of rising exports, the rise in imports would result in deflationary pressures. The main difference is that in the circumstances Lewis is describing the deflation would be automatic, whereas today it would be under the control of the authorities. Also Lewis attributes considerable importance to the 'dynamism' (or lack of it) of British entrepreneurs at that time. See also H. J. Habakkuk and P. Deane, 'The Take-off in Britain', in *The Economics of Take-off into Sustained Growth*, ed. W. W. Rostow (London, 1963) for the view that acceleration of exports was responsible for British growth in the Industrial Revolution and for French growth in the 1860s.

may tend to accentuate any initial lead in 'new' products or technologically improved products (there is no hard and fast distinction), which confers a competitive advantage that cannot be represented by normal price comparisons[1]. And fast growth rates, accompanied by higher rates of investment, are likely to be associated with rapid rates of technological progress. Conversely, in a slow-growing economy with a poor export performance a vicious circle persists. Costs per unit of output will tend to rise relatively rapidly, even if money wages are rising more slowly than in fast-growing economies, and technical progress will be slower, thereby perpetuating, or aggravating, the competitive disadvantage. This will reduce the expected rate of increase in demand and lower the average rate of return on capital, thereby inhibiting investment as well as slowing down the subsequent rate of increase in productivity per unit of total factor input.

2. INVESTMENT AND EXPECTATIONS

The proposition that producers will expand capacity largely in the light of the expected increase in the demand for their products might appear such obvious commonsense that little need be said in support of it. Nevertheless, it is difficult to establish empirically the respective weight of demand expectations as compared with other possible influences, such as rates of interest, profit rates, changes in sales, investment allowances, depreciation provisions, and so on, chiefly because of the impossibility of obtaining any quantitative measure of expectations. The situation has been well summarized by J. C. R. Dow, in a recent survey of the information on the determinants of investment, as follows:

'In spite of much discussion among economists, there remains at best a rather general degree of agreement as to the determinants of investment, which leaves room for doubt as to precisely how important various possible influences in fact are. The results of empirical studies so far have not eradicated these uncertainties . . . The following rough picture would probably be fairly generally accepted as a starting point. First, the incentive to invest must depend primarily on the prospective evolution of final demand, and the degree to which productive capacity is at any time under- or over-employed in meeting demand'[2].

As Dow shows, most empirical studies then available led to the conclusion that past rates of increase of sales are the most important determinant of investment, even more important than past profits[3].

Another study confirms this view. This is G. J. Stigler's analysis of the determinants of investment in a large number of firms. He found that

---

[1]See T. Balogh, *Unequal Partners* (Oxford, 1963), vol. 1, pp. 36, 38 and 142.
[2]*The Management of the British Economy, 1945–60* (Cambridge, 1964), p. 286.
[3]The two most important studies at the time were J. R. Meyer and E. Kuh, *The Investment Decision: an Empirical Study* (Cambridge, Mass., 1957), especially p. 132; and R. Eisner, 'A Distributed Lag Investment Function', *Econometrica*, January 1960.

'All the possible regressions of relative increase in capital on relative increase of receipts [equals sales] and either current or preceding year profit rates have been calculated for the period 1948 to 1957 . . . In every case, the overridingly important influence on the rate of investment is the change in receipts: this is the only consistently significant regression coefficient, and even its magnitude is remarkably stable . . . The current profit rate plays a negligible role in the regression equations'[1].

Over the longer period, it is true that Stigler finds that profits were slightly more important than in the short-period annual changes, but still considerably less important than changes in receipts as 'In both periods [1938–47 and 1947–56] however, introduction of profit rates does not add appreciably to the 'explanation' of the variance of investment rates'[2].

In the absence of any direct evidence about management's expectations the past rate of change of receipts (sales) must be regarded as being the variable that is the most likely to be highly correlated with expectations. Expectations about the future are naturally dominated by experience of the past, so that when sales have risen fast it is very likely that expectations about the future will be optimistic. The empirical evidence, therefore, whilst not conclusive, does strongly confirm the commonsense view that demand expectations are the most important determinant of investment rates.

In Britain the role of long-run expectations in fixing the rate of growth of capacity is explicit in the plans made by some of the key industries. The various reports describing the expansion plans for coal, iron and steel and electricity leave no doubt that, whilst their earlier methods for projecting future demand may have been unsatisfactory in some cases, and whilst their expansion plans may have been curtailed by the authorities, the estimation of future demand played a central role in the formulation of the plans[3].

Though the projection techniques varied from one nationalized industry to

[1]G. J. Stigler, *Capital and Rates of Return in Manufacturing Industries* (Princeton, 1963), p. 76.

[2]Stigler, *ibid.*, p. 81.

[3]The National Coal Board's fifteen-year plan, presented in 1950 (*Plan for Coal*, London, 1950) was based on an estimate of coal demand for the period 1961 to 1965, which turned out to be too high, partly on account of the excessive estimate for export demand, which was acknowledged to be highly conjectural. Similar long-range demand estimates were key elements of subsequent revised plans for coal (*Investing in Coal*, London, 1956), including the *Revised Plan for Coal* (London, 1959), in which the earlier demand projections were revised downwards significantly. The electricity industry's plans for investment have also been made in the light of estimates of future demand though in the earlier post-war years it was recognized that the expansion plans would be insufficient either because of shortages of capacity in the supply industries (British Electricity Authority, *First Report and Statement of Accounts*, London, 1949, p. 30) or because of the government's limitation on the investment expenditure in the light of other economic considerations (*5th Report and Statement of Accounts, 1952–3*, p. 11). Future demand estimates, usually over a 5-year period, played a prominent part in all the steel industry's plans (notably Iron and Steel Board, *Development of the Iron and Steel Industry, 1953 to 1958*, London, 1955, and *Development in the Iron and Steel Industry: Special Report, 1957*).

another, the overall rate of growth of the economy was always one of the factors taken into consideration and assumptions as to this rate were generally discussed with the Treasury and the Ministry of Power[1]. The only public indication in the 1950s of official long-run growth expectations was Mr Butler's statement that this country should be able to double its standard of living in 25 years— that is 2·8 per cent per annum rate of growth of national product. This was the rate generally influencing the demand projections of the key industries[2]. Even the Iron and Steel Board in the latest comprehensive projections assumed a 3·2 per annum rise in gross national product, though this was an industry whose shortage of capacity was important in the 1955/6 import boom that contributed to the 1956 balance of payments crisis[3]. It is also well known that private industries, such as the chemical industry, the consumer durables industries (especially cars) and the petroleum industry have been very much influenced by long-range projections of demand for their products in determining their expansion plans, though the individual companies have naturally been under less obligation to publish their estimates.

In an economy that has been growing slowly, it is difficult to expect acceleration if future growth expectations are simply extrapolations of the past. Persuading the community that a 4 per cent growth rate will be achieved may not, alone, ensure that it is achieved, but persuading them that only 2·8 per cent will be achieved is a fairly safe way of ensuring that 2·8 per cent will not be exceeded. Capacity will not grow fast enough to sustain a prolonged acceleration of the growth rate, unless the acceleration is accompanied by changing expectations concerning the longer-run prospects.

The fact that demand expectations may be the most important determinant of investment does not mean that investment is not influenced at all by government policies or by rates of profit. The influence of governmental measures affecting investment will be limited by how far entrepreneurs wish to invest anyway. For example, there is little doubt that the exceptionally generous fiscal and other concessions to investment in Germany (at least up to 1958)

---

[1] See House of Commons *Report from the Select Committee on Nationalised Industries: the Electricity Supply Industry*, vol. 1 (London, 1963), pp. 31–3.

[2] The original statement, made in 1954, proposed a 20-year period, but this was subsequently modified to 25 years (see J. C. R. Dow, *op. cit.*, pp. 77–8). In addition to the Iron and Steel Board's 1957 report already referred to, see for example W. H. Glanville and R. J. Smeed, 'The Basic Requirements for the Roads of Great Britain' (*Proceedings of the Conference on the Highway Needs of Great Britain, 1957*), para. 24; also Dr G. H. Daniel (of the Ministry of Fuel and Power), in 'Britain's Energy Prospects', starts from the 'ambitious target for the expansion of economic activity . . . suggested by the Chancellor—doubling the standard of living in 25 years . . . this implies a growth rate of 3 per cent compound . . .' (*Institution of Production Engineers Journal*, February 1956, p. 79).

[3] Iron and Steel Board, *Development in the Iron and Steel Industry: Special Report, 1961* (London, 1961), p. 19. It is unfortunate that a more rapid expansion of capacity in this industry began to bear fruit at a time (1962 and first half of 1963) when, under the impact of demand restraint, steel demand fell much below capacity.

E

and in Austria after 1953 (except in 1956) helped to raise the rate of investment in these countries[1]. But this was chiefly because although the demand for investment was very high the capital markets in these countries were very imperfect. The various measures were required, therefore, to facilitate the finance of investment, even though the scope for self-financing (on account of high rates of profit and rapid growth) was substantial. The same desire to compensate for the inadequacy of the capital market in relation to the demand for investment prompted the French authorities to introduce special depreciation allowances and other tax concessions to investment. In both cases the measures were aimed at transforming investment opportunities into an effective demand for investment goods in spite of the inadequacies of the capital market. The authorities there took action to remove a brake on expansion that did not exist in Britain.

Furthermore, other countries, such as Norway and Switzerland, have maintained high rates of investment without any significant measures to facilitate or encourage investment. Finally, the poor private investment record in Britain in the early 1960s, in spite of very substantial tax concessions, suggests that, in the absence of buoyant long-run demand prospects (combined with some excess capacity at the time), any 'bargain' in investment provided by tax concessions is still thought by entrepreneurs, and rightly, to be an unjustified extravagance. On the other hand, it is important that, where the potential demand for investment *is* high, the authorities should have a policy designed to ensure that the demand can become effective. This will include not only fiscal concessions to investment but a policy with respect to the overall savings of the economy. Nor should we exclude policy aimed at achieving a pattern of investment nearer to the optimum pattern for longer-run growth than the free market mechanism is likely to be able to provide.

The influence of the rate of profit on capital must not be neglected. For the importance of the expected future rate of increase in demand is presumably related to the expected effect of higher demand on the profitability of new investment. In export markets, where prices are by and large determined by international costs, entrepreneurs will be unable to prevent profit margins falling when domestic costs rise faster than costs in other countries (in the absence of any change in exchange rates). Insofar as an important element in our poor export performance has been a fall in our competitiveness—that is a rise in our costs relative to world prices—a fall in profit margins on exports is inevitable. That such an adverse movement in relative costs has occurred is also supported by direct evidence of the rise in our wage costs per unit of output relative to

---

[1]In Germany, the measures included generous special and accelerated depreciation allowances, reduced rates of taxation on undistributed profits, and the extensive granting and guaranteeing of loans. It should be noted that most of these concessions were withdrawn after 1958, but that the high rate of investment persisted until the expansion of demand began to slow down in 1963.

our export prices[1]. As this will tend to reduce profit margins on exports it will tend to inhibit any desire by entrepreneurs to seek export markets and will also dampen the average propensity to invest.

The manner in which investment in Britain has been affected by 'stop-go' policies is too familiar to require much elaboration. The investment goods industries, particularly iron and steel, engineering, metal goods and construction have been affected directly and indirectly by the general climate of expansion or restraint, by symbols of this climate (such as changes in Bank Rate) and by specific measures such as changes in investment allowances, initial allowances, credit restrictions, restraint of public investment, and hire purchase restrictions on plant and machinery transactions.

Another way of looking at the developments during the period 1955 to 1958, when demand restraint was the rule rather than the exception (measures of restraint were operating for two out of the three years), is to compare the changes in output, capital-output ratios and net capital formation. As can be seen in the following table, in practically every manufacturing industry there was a sharp fall in output, adjusted for trend, between 1955 and 1958. At the same time the average capital-output ratio in each of the industries rose above trend, suggesting an emergence of excess capacity. This was accompanied in nearly every case by a sharp fall in net capital formation during the period. It is legitimate to conclude that the fall in capital formation was largely the effect of the exceptional rise in average capital-output ratios, which in turn was largely the effect of the adverse movements in output (although the preceding investment boom must, of course, have helped pave the way for the subsequent emergence of excess capacity).

Of course, the fact that cyclical fluctuations in investment have been associated with fluctuations in demand in Britain does not prove that this relationship is responsible for the relatively low average investment ratio in Britain. But it does confirm the view that investment cannot be treated as an autonomous element in the growth process, and is ultimately dependent on longer-run demand expectations, as the econometric results cited earlier suggest. One might also go further, as does Mr Maddison, and maintain that cyclical fluctuations, by increasing the risk element in investment, will tend to reduce the longer-run investment rate[2]. This view might appear to be supported by comparison of the growth experience of the post-war period with that of the

[1]As pointed out in the National Economic Development Council's report, *Export Trends* (London, 1963), para. 41, 'The fact that wage costs in the United Kingdom have risen about 3 per cent per annum faster than the average of other countries, whereas our export prices of manufactures have risen only about 1 per cent per annum faster, suggests that the profitability of exporting manufactures may have fallen relatively to what has happened in other countries.'
[2]This is a part of the thesis expounded by Angus Maddison, *Economic Growth in the West*, *op. cit.*, p. 50.

Table 2.1. *Changes in output, average capital-output ratios and net capital formation in manufacturing industry during period of general demand restraint*

	Per cent deviation of capital-output ratio from trend value		Per cent change in output adjusted for trend, 1955 to 1958	Change in net capital formation from peak to trough	
				Per cent change	Period
	1955	1958			
Food	0	+1	− 1·0	− 7·2	1955–7
Drink and tobacco	0	+3	− 0·6	− 19·3	1955–8
Mineral oil refining	−1	+5	− 11·7	− 66·9	1957–60
Other chemicals	−5	+8	− 8·3	− 15·7	1958–60
Iron and steel	−4	+6	− 13·6	b	
Non-ferrous metals	−11	+6	− 13·2	− 35·5	1956–8
Engineering	−4	+3	− 6·7	− 16·1	1955–9
Shipbuilding	a	a	− 1·3	b	
Motor vehicles	a	a	− 15·8	− 36·0	1956–9
Aircraft and railway rolling stock	−5	−2	− 10·9	− 27·2c	1956–8
Metal goods	−5	+8	− 12·1	− 22·8	1956–8
Textiles	−1	+7	− 9·6	− 95·9	1955–8
Leather and clothing	−1	+6	− 7·0	− 93·5	1955–8
Building materials	n.a.	n.a.	− 12·5	− 15·3	1955–8
Pottery and glass	−1	+7	− 8·7	− 47·9	1955–8
Timber and furniture	−5	+4	− 12·0	− 49·2	1955–8
Paper and printing	−7	+4	− 9·1	− 39·4	1957–9
Rubber and other manufacturing	−8	+4	− 11·0	− 5·9	1956–8

Source: Appendix tables 8.3, 8.7, 8.9.

Note: 'Net' capital formation here corresponds to the concept used in compiling the perpetual inventory series of capital stocks (see Appendix 8), namely gross capital formation minus estimated scrappings (instead of depreciation).

aThe changes in the actual capital-output ratios in shipbuilding and motor vehicles between 1955 and 1958 were 14 per cent and 20 per cent respectively.

bIn iron and steel and in shipbuilding net capital formation was rising during the period concerned, not falling.

cAircraft only.

pre-war period, where much lower average investment rates in the western countries in general were associated with a much sharper degree of cyclical fluctuation.

However, given the ceiling to output set by capacity, greater cyclical fluctuations also mean a lower average level of capacity utilization, so that it may be this, rather than instability as such, that caused the lower average investment rates. Furthermore, to return to the particular post-war experience of Britain, it can always be argued that it was the failure of investment in Britain to rise fast enough in recovery periods that was responsible for the inadequate increase in capacity and thereby, in turn, responsible for the ensuing balance of payments crises.

Another difficult question in connection with the nature of the causal process is the extent to which differences in the *pressure* of demand, as distinct from the longer-run expectations concerning the increase in demand, will influence investment and innovation in techniques or the organization of production. If demand is expected to rise by x per cent in a situation where there is plenty of spare capacity, the incentive to raise capacity by any means will be much less than if the same demand expectations are held in a situation of full capacity utilization. This implies that faster growth requires a fairly high level of capacity utilization.

Against this it can be, and has been, argued that (a) Britain has, on the whole, maintained a fairly high average pressure of demand during the 1950s without getting the fast growth and (b) that, indeed, it has been because of this that the delicate balance of payments situation has been an obstacle to faster growth[1]. The argument could be that fast growth requires considerable flexibility, which is prevented by a full utilization of capacity.

But in the absence of more information on the way entrepreneurs react to different levels of capacity utilization, one cannot readily accept the view that they would invest at the same rate if experience continued to teach them that demand was always managed in such a way that they were always left with a margin of unused capacity. Also, it is reasonable to maintain that fast growth permits a fuller utilization of capacity since the required flexibility will be achieved by the faster growth of newly installed capacity.

It is difficult to take a firm view on the relative importance of demand pressure as against demand expectation not only because of the lack of evidence but also because of the rather narrow range of demand pressure which is relevant for practical purposes. The relative importance of the two factors will clearly be very different at 20 per cent unused capacity and at 5 per cent, and in practice it is only the latter level that is relevant. Perhaps all that can be safely said is that, at roughly equal and high levels of capacity utilization, the more optimistic are demand expectations the more rapid will be the growth of capacity (in the widest sense of the term).

3. DEMAND EXPECTATIONS, THE FOREIGN BALANCE AND EXPORTS

(a) *The foreign balance*

Rather firmer conclusions can be drawn about the relationship between demand

---

[1]This is in line with the thesis set out in its most convincing form by F. W Paish in *Studies in an Inflationary Economy* (London, 1962). Some comments on the direct relationship between the pressure of demand in Britain and the foreign balance are presented on p. 60 below.

expectations and the foreign balance. In addition to the well-known experience of Britain, international comparisons seem to provide fairly safe guidance.

We shall not discuss in detail the relationship between exports and growth in other countries since this has already been done in the studies referred to above[1]. The main points that should be recapitulated are as follows. Apart from France, all the fast-growing countries, namely Germany, Italy, the Netherlands, Austria and Switzerland, had favourable foreign balances throughout most of the period from 1953 onwards, and rapid increases in exports. The slowest growing countries, namely Belgium, Canada, Denmark, the United Kingdom and the United States had the slowest increases in exports and precarious foreign balances (or the foreign balance was kept in equilibrium through a depressed level of home demand, as in Belgium).

The sluggish performance of United Kingdom exports which, as argued below, must be ascribed largely to falling competitiveness (in a wide sense of the term) has not meant that serious balance of payments deficits, when they occurred, were caused by a fall in exports. On the contrary, they were often accompanied by a reasonable rise in exports since such deficits, particularly in 1955, tended to occur at times of general world economic expansion. But in Britain, unlike the fast-growing countries, increases in export demand did not lead the overall demand expansion, which was triggered off mainly by the expansion in domestic demand. The immediate cause of the balance of payments deficits, therefore, was usually a sharp rise in marginal imports as the increase in home demand outran supply capacity in some critical industries (chiefly iron and steel in 1955 and 1959/60)[2]. In fact in 1955 exports rose by about 7 per cent in volume, but with imports rising by about 12 per cent the balance of trade deteriorated sharply. A similar pattern of events occurred in 1960. The direct impact of our export performance on the external balance—as distinct from the indirect impact on confidence and on the growth of capacity—has taken the form simply of a generally slow growth of exports leading either to a progressively more and more precarious trade balance or to more and more restraints on home demand designed to restrain imports[3]. By 1960, the United Kingdom had an exceptionally high trade deficit with a much lower level of

---

[1]See footnote 1 to page 45.
[2]See M. F. W. Hemming and G. F. Ray, 'Imports and Expansion', *National Institute Economic Review*, March 1959, p. 34.
[3]Detailed chronologies of demand restraints are given in *The Problem of Rising Prices*, by W. Fellner and others (Paris, OEEC, 1959), Appendix 2; J. C. R. Dow, *The Management of the British Economy, 1945–60, op. cit.;* and the 'Price Stability and the Policy of Deflation', by J. C. R. Dow and L. A. Dicks-Mireaux (*National Institute Economic Review*, May 1959); Dow also analyses the main demand restraints in the context of the contemporary state of the economy and the foreign balance. On this see also the annual *Economic Surveys*, especially that for 1956, Cmd 9728; P. B. Kenen, *British Monetary Policy and the Balance of Payments, 1951–1957* (Cambridge, Mass., 1960); and G. D. N. Worswick and P. H. Ady, *The British Economy in the nineteen-fifties* (Oxford, 1962).

'excess demand for labour' than in 1955 in spite of much better terms of trade, which suggests that the competitive position of exports, other things being equal, must have been getting progressively worse[1].

Apart from Britain, there are, among both the fast- and the slow-growing groups of countries listed above, exceptions to the relationship between the foreign balance (and/or exports) and growth rates. These can be used to prove the rule that the basic relationship is between demand expectations and growth rates. The growth of the French economy, in spite of the severe inflationary pressures and balance of payments crises which were experienced during the mid-1950s, illustrates the overriding importance of demand expectations even in the face of an adverse external balance. But this was because the French authorities were simply unable to cure the balance of payments problem by means of demand restraint. Their chief weapon for dealing with external imbalance was the extensive use of import restrictions, which merely added to the inflationary pressures. Hence, unlike entrepreneurs in most countries, French entrepreneurs became accustomed to a continuously fast-rising demand whatever the balance of payments or financial stability position. From being a relatively conservative-minded, backward and pessimistic body of entrepreneurs, a few years of sustained rapid demand expansion has converted French entrepreneurs into a relatively forward-looking and dynamic body. This is not to decry the contribution of French planning at critical growth points in the economy. The moral of the French story is that it is not even an exception to our general rule that demand expectations in most countries depend on the external balance: in any advanced country but France the same developments in this period would almost certainly have led to effective measures of demand restraint.

In the slow-growing group of countries, the United States is also an exception that underlines the overriding importance of demand. For here the demand restraints that were introduced in the mid-1950s were prompted solely by the fear of inflation; not by the foreign balance, which was still healthy. In all European countries *effective* demand restraints were introduced only in connection with the balance of payments—either directly to correct an imbalance, or, if aimed at checking inflation, because of the feared effects of inflation on the foreign balance[2]. The United States is the sole example, among developed countries, of effective demand restraints aimed at achieving price stability for its own sake. Hence in the United States, even the absence, at the time, of balance

---

[1] The NIESR index shows a negative excess demand for labour in 1960 and a very high positive excess demand for labour in 1955 (see *National Institute Economic Review*, Statistical Appendix, table 6). The terms of trade were 13 per cent better in 1960 than in 1955.

[2] See *The Problem of Rising Prices*, by Fellner and others, *op. cit.*, pp. 38 and 122.

of payments difficulties did not prevent long-run demand expectations being dampened. This is, of course, not simply the result of the greater importance that the United States authorities attached to price stability for its own sake, but also because of the much smaller importance of foreign trade in the United States economy.

Thus the experience of France and the United States, like that of the fast-growing surplus countries, leads to the view that (a) confident demand expectations are a necessary and possibly sufficient condition for rapid economic growth but that (b) a favourable external balance may be neither a necessary condition in countries where the authorities are expected to be unable (or unwilling) to restrain demand in the face of an adverse external balance, nor a sufficient condition in countries that are prepared to restrain demand or allow insufficient demand to persist uncorrected, even when the external balance is favourable.

A favourable foreign balance situation, however, probably does not have the same impact on demand expectations and on growth irrespective of the manner in which it is achieved. If it is achieved by demand restraint, of course, then it is self-defeating as far as its impact on expectations is concerned. But more relevant is the possibility of achieving it through import restrictions that permit a high pressure of demand to be maintained. For example, the quite rapid growth of the British economy from 1932 to 1937 was no doubt aided by the protectionist policy introduced in 1931–2. However, whilst some direct restraints on imports may be desirable as a short-run expedient for accelerating the growth rate these are hardly likely to be relevant for longer-run policy. Apart from the long-run inacceptability of beggar-my-neighbour commercial policies, a long-run policy of import substitution might involve a shift into diminishing-returns industries that would adversely affect the longer-run growth of productivity, at least in an advanced economy such as that of Britain.

Hence there appears to be no substitute for rapidly rising exports as a means of ensuring confidence in longer-run demand prospects[1]. The required degree of rapidity may not be simply a function of the marginal propensity to import. The international experience suggests that fast-rising exports provide a powerful stimulus to growth even when the rate is far in excess of that required to maintain a reasonably favourable foreign balance. The direction of causality is, again, difficult to establish rigorously and, indeed, it will be maintained below that it runs both ways, on account of the effects of faster growth on prices. But apart from this it can hardly be maintained that the rapid rise in exports of the fast-growing countries was simply the feedback of their rapidly rising imports (as may well have been the case for certain countries in the nineteenth century)

---

[1]Again, it should be recalled that this view is only thought to be valid as regards fairly advanced economies where foreign trade is a large item in total output. For relatively closed economies, such as the United States, it may not apply with so much force. Nor is it likely to apply in the same manner to developing countries where import controls can be accepted and reliance can be placed on indefinite long-term borrowing.

Table 2.2. *Changes in gross national product per head of employed labour force and the volume of exports, 1950–62: annual average compound trend rates*

	GNP per head of employed labour force	Volume of exports
Austria	4·9	12·6
Belgium	2·5	7·7
Canada	1·9	3·9
Denmark	3·2	7·3
France	4·2	7·7
Germany	5·1	14·8
Italy	4·7	17·9
Netherlands	3·5	9·5
Norway	3·4	6·0
Sweden	3·2	7·0
United Kingdom	2·0	2·3
USA	2·0	3·2

Source: Table 1.1 and OECD, *Manpower Statistics, 1950–1962.*

since we are faced now with a large number of countries, none of which could, by itself, sufficiently determine the purchasing power of overseas markets for its own products by changing its level of imports[1]. Nor could the rise in their imports have 'forced' the rise in exports since the countries with fast-growing exports generally had very comfortable external balances.

That buoyant exports, as much as, if not more than, an adequately favourable foreign balance, should stimulate growth is, of course, hardly surprising. In advanced, industrialized, and fairly open economies, many entrepreneurs will be affected directly, or indirectly, by the impact of export orders on their own demand prospects, particularly those engaged in manufacturing, where the mainspring of growth in such economies is to be found. Also, competitive exports permit a high rate of profit which is likely, by itself, to have some effect on investment, both for expansion and for modernization. Furthermore, competitive exports must greatly add to the confidence of entrepreneurs in their investment and production plans since it means, to take an extreme case, that they can dispose of any amount of output in export markets. In other words, they can regard exports as an outlet which will ensure that, even if they have overestimated home demand, they can maintain full capacity operation, thereby minimizing unit costs, by selling the surplus output abroad at a reasonable price.

Conversely, if total national export performance is inadequate, and the authorities react by deflating demand, so that the expectations of entrepreneurs (based on total demand) are frustrated, it is likely to make them slow down the

[1]See C. P. Kindleberger, 'Foreign Trade and Economic Growth: Lessons from Britain and France, 1850 to 1913', *Economic History Review*, December 1961.

rate at which they embark on new investments and changes in techniques. It is also likely to divert their energies from the task of improving organization and the efficiency of production into defensive action to try to maintain sales, to cope with accumulating stocks, to decide whether to reduce employment or hours worked and whether to curtail subcontracting and so on.

Thus, again, there can be no general answer to the question of what is the relative importance in growth of a favourable foreign balance and fast-rising exports, since so much will depend on the exact circumstances and the *absolute* position of each. Where there is a reasonably satisfactory foreign balance, the rate of increase of exports is probably predominant since this is likely to influence entrepreneurial behaviour directly. But where there is an unfavourable balance, this is likely to be the key factor in dampening demand expectations, if only indirectly, and different rates of export increase will have less effect on entrepreneurial expectations and behaviour since, as long as the aggregate is inadequate, domestic demand will be restrained.

(b) *Exports and competitiveness*

The next step in the thesis summarized in section 1 is the relationship between exports and competitiveness. The differences in export performance shown in the above table are closely related to differences in the changes in export prices, at least for manufactures, as is strikingly demonstrated in a recent National Economic Development Council report[1], where it can be seen that the countries with rapid increases in manufactured exports had the slowest increases in their prices of manufactured exports.

The differences in rates of increase of prices of manufactures were accounted for chiefly by different rates of increase in productivity, not in money wages. That is, the countries with the slowest increase in prices of manufactures were not, in general, those with the slowest increases in earnings. This again is clearly demonstrated in the National Economic Development Council report, where it can be seen, for example, that whereas German hourly earnings in manufacturing rose by 55 per cent from 1953/5 to 1959/61 as compared with only 43 per cent in Britain, the much faster rise in German manufacturing productivity meant that German wage costs per unit of output rose by only 11 per cent as against 22 per cent in Britain[2].

An alternative picture of the relationship between productivity, prices and exports is obtained by concentrating on changes in shares in world trade in manufacturing, as in the following table. It may be seen that the increase in the German share of world trade in manufactures is very high compared with her relative export price development. But the *ex post* changes in export prices are, of course, the prices at the margin of the equilibrium position (approximately) obtained *vis-à-vis* other countries' prices. That is, if British and

[1]National Economic Development Council, *Export Trends, loc. cit.*, table 11, p. 19.
[2]*Ibid.*, table 12, p. 20.

Table 2.3.   *Changes in shares in world trade in manufactures, productivity and export prices, 1953–61*

	Manu-facturing productivity	Export prices	Wholesale prices	Export shares		
	(Indexes 1961, 1953 = 100)			1953	1961	Change
				(Percentages of world trade in manufactures)		
Japan	197	91	91	*3·8*	*6·8*	*+ 3·0*
Italy	167	80	98	*3·3*	*5·7*	*+ 2·4*
France	165	99	91	*9·1*	*9·5*	*+ 0·4*
Germany	152	105	109	*13·4*	*20·4*	*+ 7·0*
Belgium	143	95	105	..	..	..
USA	124	121	111	*26·2*	*20·6*	*− 5·6*
United Kingdom	**122**	**114**	**116**	**20·9**	**15·7**	**− 5·2**

Source: Productivity and prices from B. Balassa, 'Trade Projections and Economic Model-Building' (in *The United States Balance of Payments*, Joint Economic Committee, 1963).   Export shares from *National Institute Economic Review*, no. 27, February 1964, Statistical Appendix, table 23.

American export prices (of manufactures) have risen by about 15 to 20 per cent, there is no need for German prices to remain stable in order for Germany to gain a very large increase in the share of the market.   Nevertheless, it is no doubt true that other factors have played some part in determining the export records even of large diversified economies.

One of the influences on British export performance has been the erosion of our protected position in most sterling area markets, and the fact that incomes, and total import demand, in our main sterling area markets have not been rising as fast as in continental Europe.   But it has now been firmly demonstrated in various studies that very little of the slow increase in British exports compared with the other main industrialized countries can be explained by the particular commodity or regional distribution of our exports.   The main factor has clearly been a general decline in our shares in individual markets for individual categories of product[1].   At a very detailed level of disaggregation of the commodity composition of trade, it appears that it is of some advantage to concentrate trade on certain technologically advanced 'newer' products, though the border-line between technological superiority and price competitiveness is difficult to define, so that the general importance of competitiveness is hardly diminished by this consideration[2].

[1]See R. L. Major, 'World Trade in Manufactures', *National Institute Economic Review*, July 1960; R. S. Gilbert and R. L. Major, 'Britain's Falling Share of Sterling Area Imports', *National Institute Economic Review*, March 1961; A. Lamfalussy, *The United Kingdom and the Six, op. cit.*, pp. 52–8; and National Economic Development Council, *Export Trends*, *loc. cit.*, para. 10.
[2]See 'Fast and Slow-Growing Products in World Trade', *National Institute Economic Review*, August 1963 and T. Barna, 'Export Growth Retarded by Technical Backwardness', *The Times*, 3 April 1963.

Some other partial explanations for our weak export performance are less easily acceptable.   For example, it is widely supposed that there was something 'inevitable' about the restoration of the German and Japanese shares to their pre-war levels.   But in the absence of an improvement in their competitiveness it is difficult to see what is 'inevitable' about such a restoration of a lost position.

One explanation of our poor export performance that must be taken seriously is that excessive pressure of home demand has directed potential exports into the home market.   We are not referring here to the view that excessive pressure of home demand has caused an unduly rapid rise in wages, since whether or not one subscribes to the view that increases in wages are largely demand induced, this doctrine would still be explaining our export performance in terms of competitiveness, and so in this respect would not be in conflict with the view advanced here.   We are referring here to the view that high pressure of demand at home 'sucks in' exportables, whereas low pressure gives producers an extra incentive to sell abroad.   However, there is no evidence that relative pressures of demand for labour explain the relative export performance of other countries. For example, the pressure of demand for labour has been at least as high, if not higher, throughout most of the 1950s in the Netherlands and Sweden, and in Germany since about 1959.   Conversely, a slack demand for labour in Belgium until the end of the 1950s did nothing to improve the export performance of that country.

Secondly, the doctrine that a lower pressure of demand must lead to an increase in exports, while superficially appealing, is not so obviously logical if we distinguish between the short-run and the long-run.   Roughly speaking the amount we will be prepared to sell to export markets, at any given price (that is our 'export supply schedule') will depend on the gap between domestic demand and our total potential supply at that price.   The converse applies to the overseas import schedule.   It follows that, if everything else remains unchanged, namely the domestic supply schedule and the foreign demand and supply schedules, a fall in our domestic demand schedule will increase our export supply, and hence the share of our exports in our total output and the share of our exports in world trade[1].

This implies two things.   First, a reduction in our demand schedule can only confidently be expected to improve our exports in the short run, since in the long run the 'other things' will not remain stable.   Secondly even if in the long run the other things did remain stable it can only give us a once-for-all increase in exports and export shares.   Given the rate of growth of world demand, in order for our exports to increase continuously at a faster rate than would otherwise have been the case (other things remaining equal) we should

---

[1]This type of model does not require the assumption of perfectly elastic demand for the products.   In the case examined above, total overseas demand would expand somewhat, as the general world trade prices would fall, and we should also gain a larger share of the -ncreased world trade.

require either (i) a continuous fall in the domestic demand schedule, or (ii) a continuous rise in the domestic supply schedule. Conversely, a failure of exports to increase rapidly could be explained by either (i) a continuous increase in domestic demand relative to supply or (ii) a slow growth of supply. Now it can hardly be maintained that the pressure of demand relative to capacity has shown any long-run increase over the last decade. Consequently the share of output that has been exported has remained fairly stable, as can be seen in table 5.12 of chapter 5. In terms of a quantitative description of events, therefore, though not in terms of a causal explanation, our slow export increase has been associated with an inadequate growth of our capacity and output[1].

In short, if we distinguish between once-for-all effects and continuous effects, a logical theory for ascribing our slow increase in exports to the pressure of home demand would have to be more complex than the usual straightforward theory encountered; and, at best, we could only expect variations in domestic demand relative to capacity to have a short-run impact[2]. Whether it has or not can be tested empirically. We present below three diagrams, in each of which we compare an indicator of the pressure of home demand against an indicator of our export performance. The three comparisons are:

(a) the pressure of demand for labour in the United Kingdom and our share in world trade in manufactures;

(b) home purchases of plant and machinery (as indicating domestic pressure of demand for these goods) and our shares in world trade in the same category of goods;

(c) home purchases of plant and machinery and the shares of total domestic production of those goods that were exported.

As our data were on a quarterly basis we experimented, in all cases, with various time lags between the indicator of the pressure of home demand and the effect on exports (which may be assumed to follow with some time lag), with the effect of combining the quarterly data into half-yearly data to reduce erratic variations, and with the effect of adjusting the data for trends. The diagrams show the results that gave the strongest correlation between the two variables. In spite of this, only in the second case could we find any correlation whatsoever, and that very low, even though, in the third case, the arithmetical identity of total output on the one hand, and home purchases plus exports on the other, should have biased the results in favour of a correlation[3]. Of course

[1]See also the National Economic Development Council's *Export Trends*, loc. cit., para. 24.
[2]An ingenious and perfectly logical model of the way in which a lower pressure of home demand could lead to a continuous rise in the share of exports in total output has been suggested by my colleague at the National Institute of Economic and Social Research, Mr Wynne Godley. A key assumption in this model is that the rate of growth of capacity will not be slowed down as a result of permanently operating at a somewhat lower level of capacity, which is somewhat doubtful. To test this model would require a longer period of excess capacity than we have endured so far.
[3]The correlation coefficient in the second case is 0·425.

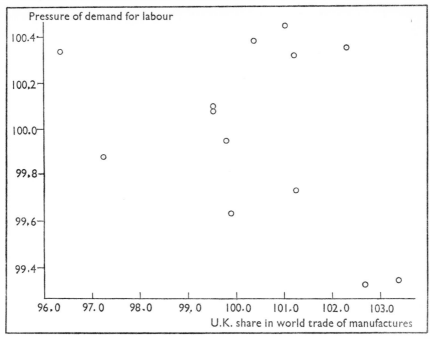

Fig. 2.1. Pressure of demand for labour in the United Kingdom and the UK share in world trade of manufactures
Half-yearly percentage relation to trend, seasonally adjusted, 1955 (2) to 1961 (2)

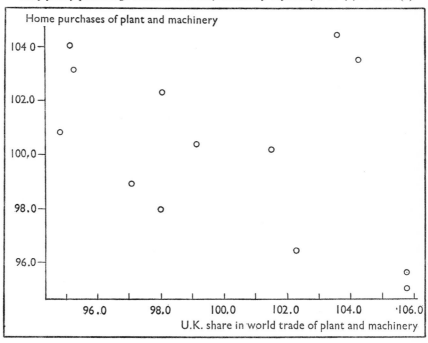

Fig. 2.2. Plant and machinery: home purchases and the UK share in world trade
Half-yearly percentage relation to trend, seasonally adjusted, 1955 (2) to 1961 (2)

Fig. 2.3. Plant and machinery: home purchases and the share of exports in total domestic production

Quarterly percentage relation to trend, seasonally adjusted, 1955 to 1961

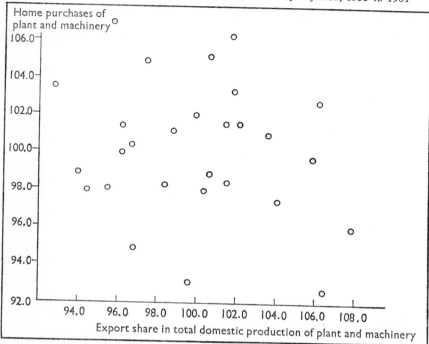

Export share in total domestic production of plant and machinery

Source: Appendix table 2.1.

it is possible that the time lags involved may be much greater than those we have been able to check. For example, it may require two, three or four years of slack demand for labour to have an impact on exports. But there has not been a sufficiently long period of slack demand for labour in Britain for such a relationship to be checked. And if, indeed, this is the sort of time lag that is believed to operate it is very difficult to maintain that the rate of growth of capacity would remain unaffected by such a prolonged period of slack demand, particularly in view of the way capital formation falls off after rather shorter periods of demand restraint. The short-term relation between exports and pressure of home demand is, no doubt, complex. For some firms, working near the desired limits of capacity, an increase in home demand will be associated with postponement of work on export orders; and in slack times a reduction of home demand will lead to more intensive efforts to sell abroad. For other firms, an expansion of home demand, by raising the rate of capacity utilization and reducing costs, and by providing a general stimulus to enterprise, will result in bigger exports; the discouraging effects of falling home demand will weaken export effort as well. It is presumably because these diverse reactions cancel out that the short-term correlation is so weak, and that restrictions on home demand have not, in British post-war experience, proved an effective instrument for raising total exports quickly.

Thus, whilst a full-scale study of export behaviour might be able to assess more precisely the respective influences on British export performance, there seems no powerful reason to believe that the slow growth of British exports has been exceptional in the sense of not being largely determined by competitiveness. Though, it should be emphasized once more, the concept of 'competitiveness' is not a simple one and will, for many products, include a technical quality element that cannot be readily translated into equivalent price comparisons.

It must also be emphasized that 'competitiveness', even widely defined, is probably much less important in determining the export performance of small countries. Countries whose exports are concentrated on a narrow range of products or on a limited number of markets will be much more dependent on the evolution of world trade in these products and on the growth rates in their main markets. For example, the rather slow growth of Danish exports until the late 1950s was largely the result of its particular commodity and country pattern of exports, whereas, at the other extreme, the rapid increase in Austrian exports was greatly aided by its dependence on the German market.

4. THE DIRECTION OF CAUSALITY

If export performance, among large countries, is largely determined by competitiveness, and if a good export performance, in turn, engenders greater confidence in future demand prospects, either directly or indirectly, we have at once the beginnings of a virtuous or vicious circle process. For it also appears that confidence in demand induces a higher rate of investment, and that, at the same time, high rates of investment are associated with greater rates of return in terms of output on new investment. This would lead to higher rates of growth of productivity of total factor input so that, other things being equal, prices would rise more slowly, and, in the manner indicated in section 1 above, the competitive advantage would be maintained or increased.

But all the evidence we have used in support of this virtuous-vicious circle hypothesis is, admittedly, rather circumstantial; it appears to be consistent with the hypothesis but in no way proves it. In this context, 'proof' (insofar as 'proof' is ever found in economics) requires, above all, substantiation of the *direction* of causality. For the same observed facts could be manifestations of a causal pattern that worked in the opposite direction to that suggested above. This possibility is particularly important given that we have, anyway, postulated a form of reverse causality in invoking the virtuous or vicious circle nature of the hypothesis advanced. In more concrete terms, it is possible that, for example, instead of the demand restraints associated with an inadequate increase in exports leading to a slowing down of investment, technical progress and productivity, it might have been the unresponsiveness of supply, resulting from quite different factors, that was responsible for the slow growth of exports and hence induced the demand restraints.

In more technical terms, there are two extreme causal hypotheses. The first is that supply is largely induced by demand prospects, which are initially autonomous, but which are then determined in turn by the related response of supply, thereby contributing a vicious or virtuous circle (according to whether the initial autonomous demand prospects were favourable or not). The alternative is that the growth of supply is mainly autonomous, in the sense of being relatively independent of demand, and it is then the permissible rate of growth of demand which is determined by whatever are the other factors governing supply—such as entrepreneurial ability, attitudes of workers to innovation, government policy to stimulate technical progress or to direct investment into the most productive channels or to raise the overall level of investment, the mobility of the labour market and so on.

As *ex post* supply is identically equal to demand (including stock changes), the unravelling of the relative importance of autonomous changes in supply or demand over the long run—that is excluding short-run conjunctural variations in the level of capacity utilization—is clearly a very difficult, if not impossible, task. Presumably neither of the two extreme possibilities mentioned above would attract much support, and most economists would agree that the truth lies somewhere in between, though there is scope for much disagreement as to how near it lies to one extreme rather than the other. We have indicated evidence for certain links in a causal chain running from demand to supply— notably the positive evidence concerning the determination of investment.

We have also indicated in this chapter, and in chapter 1, reasons why evidence purporting to substantiate the important independent role played by certain supply factors such as the attitudes of workers or the rate of growth of labour supply, is not necessarily conclusive. But another supply factor often believed to be responsible for the poor growth record of Britain is the quality of management. One of the most important recent studies of entrepreneurial behaviour has usually been interpreted as lending support to this view. This is the characteristically pioneering study by Professor Barna who has analysed the manner in which inter-firm differences in growth records are influenced by differences in managerial attitudes.

Of course, when one is examining relative performances at the level of, say, the individual firm, as in the investigations conducted by Professor Barna, the personality of the management will determine these performances almost entirely[1]. But in comparing individual performance in any capacity, such as the workers in any firm, individual abilities and personalities must necessarily

[1] T. Barna, *Investment and Growth Policies in British Industrial Firms* (Cambridge, 1962).

F

be the chief factor in explaining their performance. It is illogical to deduce from the Barna investigations that they establish the importance of innate psychological factors in explaining international differences in economic performance. For at the international level we are comparing the averages of whole frequency distributions of ability. More generally, at different levels of aggregation—the firm, the industry, the national economy, the world economy —different factors have to be taken as given, and as variables. An important variable at one level may be unimportant at another.

For example, if we suppose that Britain were to double her growth rate through doubling the dynamism and managerial ability of the whole managerial class, we might still find the same frequency distribution of ability and perform-ance within the managerial class. Hence, the existence of such a frequency distribution cannot prove anything about the average level of ability. Only if this evidence were to be supplemented by evidence that the processes of management selection in this country were such as to reduce the likelihood of management being drawn mainly from the most able people—which may well be the case in a society such as that of Britain—would the Barna results greatly strengthen the 'poor management' school of thought.

But the extent to which poor management is something innate, rather than induced by general economic circumstances, would still be an important element in the picture. We certainly do not exclude the influence on growth of 'dynamism'. Nor do we exclude—in fact we explicitly include—the possibility that the British growth rate and export record have been hampered by a deficiency in entrepreneurial dynamism. Such a deficiency certainly appears to exist[1]. But the experience of countries such as France or Italy suggests that 'dynamism' is largely induced by the expectations concerning long-run demand prospects. In other words there may be two different extreme views on the role of entrepreneurial dynamism in growth, both agreeing that it is an important role. One, which is often mistakenly supposed to emerge from Professor Barna's work, is that dynamism is something innate and hence autonomous in a given generation of management. The other is that it depends largely on economic conditions, particularly the past growth of demand. Very little evidence is available to discriminate between these alternative explanations. The example of France may be taken to illustrate strikingly the way in which a sustained dose of demand expansion can transform the attitude of entre-preneurs[2].

[1]See T. Barna, 'Some Contrasts in Export Performance: the Key Role of Management', *The Times*, 1 February 1961.
[2]A very relevant historical study is that by H. J. Habakkuk, *American and British Technology in the Nineteenth Century* (Cambridge, 1962). Whilst Professor Habakkuk provides a fascinating and comprehensive account of the historical, social and psycho-logical reason for the loss of the British comparative lead in technology, he also emphasizes the extent to which this was induced by poor growth prospects. For example '. . . But the abundance of entrepreneurial talent in the USA was the consequence rather than the

However, to cast doubt on the strength of the evidence in favour of autonomous supply factors by no means disposes of all or any supply-determined growth hypothesis. The question of how far growth is determined by supply rather than by demand is, of course, not merely of academic interest: it must greatly influence policies for growth and, for this study, the overall growth prospects which we need to assume in proceeding to the subsequent projections. It will be apparent from the above that we give considerable weight to demand expectations and, in particular, export demand.

5. THE CHANCE FOR FASTER GROWTH IN BRITAIN

Major importance has been ascribed to the extent to which the various groups in the economy (management and labour) could legitimately and reasonably have confident expectations about the future growth rate. This, in turn, we believe to depend very much on the external balance, and therefore on our competitiveness in foreign trade. Finally, whilst recognizing, indeed emphasizing, the vicious or virtuous circle nature of the growth-productivity-wage-costs-competitiveness process, we must underline the key role of an incomes policy in this process.

The manner in which Britain will move into a virtuous circle is hardly discussed here. The practical problems of introducing an incomes policy by itself are enormous, and the successful introduction of such a policy is, furthermore, not independent of the manner in which other parts of the equation are solved, such as the international liquidity problem or the measures taken to ensure that the business community and the nationalized industries can be relied upon to respond adequately to any 'breathing space' that may be engineered. But these are major problems in their own right, and an analysis of future growth, within the terms of reference which we have set for ourselves, does not give us any special insight into the most appropriate measures for solving these basic problems. Our position is that our study is relevant to the solution of problems that will arise within the context of a growth rate such as that we have projected.

Nevertheless, the temptation to say something, however gratuitous, about the likelihood of our hypothetical growth rate being achieved is irresistible. We will limit ourselves to two points. The first point, which emerges from the earlier discussion, is the importance in economic growth of the attitudes of the

cause of a high rate of growth; and it was the slow expansion of English industry which accounted for the performance of English entrepreneurs in the later nineteenth century not vice versa. Where market conditions were favourable to the expansion of capacity British business men were just as venturesome and dynamic as the American' (p. 213), and 'This was the first serious limitation on the comparative ability of British entrepreneurs: the slower rate of growth of the economy.' At the same time many of Habakkuk's comments on the unfavourable social and psychological factors at work at the end of the 19th century read depressingly relevant to conditions as they still exist today.

various groups of society to change and to expansion. Expectations are part of these attitudes, and in general expectations will tend to be based on the experience of the recent past. The viciousness of the vicious circle lies in the difficulty of changing expectations as a preliminary to speeding up growth. Once the faster growth has been achieved it is quite likely that the more confident expectations necessary for a continued rapid growth will be automatically aroused. Meanwhile, some change in attitude in this country, in a direction favourable to economic growth, has been discernible, both among employers (e.g., the interest in planning) and among labour (the attitude to trade union organization and to incomes policies). It might not be too optimistic, therefore, to believe that with appropriate direction from the authorities, this change in attitudes—which *can* be rapid (as in France)—might continue. If this is so, then the prospects for this country's economic growth seem very favourable. For many other aspects of the British character and British traditions are probably conducive to growth, such as the willingness to co-operate, to work as a team, and to make some sacrifice of narrow individual interest on behalf of the community. It is pre-eminently these characteristics which are required in, for example, the implementation of an incomes policy and the acceptance of effective economic planning. In these key fields, therefore, this country should be at least as well equipped as most of our Continental rivals.

In the past, of course, these and other favourable elements in British traditions have led to excessive complacency about traditions for their own sake, including many that have been an obstacle to economic growth. Perhaps this is part of the price to be paid for a stable society and possibly only an unstable society is capable of adaptation to new economic circumstances. But the growing frustration and *malaise* of British society in recent years demonstrate that, in the long run, even social contentment cannot survive a blatant failure fully to exploit our economic potential.

The second point to be made arises from the importance of international competitiveness as a condition of faster growth. 'Competitiveness' is relative. British competitiveness depends on what happens in other industrial countries as well as on what happens here. There are reasons for believing that our opportunities for becoming more competitive are more favourable now than they have been for several years. First, our Continental competitors have experienced since 1961 large increases in money incomes, far outstripping their increases in productivity. These increases in incomes can be associated with the equally recent achievement, especially in Germany and Italy, of levels of full employment and pressure of demand for labour more or less comparable to those maintained in Britain ever since the war. It remains to be seen whether other countries, now facing the problems of restraining the rise in money incomes so long familiar in Britain, will have better success in solving them. Whilst there has been recognition of the desirability of an incomes policy in France, there has been no such recognition in Germany or Italy. In none oı these countries does the prospect for any such progress look favourable. Secondly, the development of relative costs, although favourable to Britain, has not yet resulted in stemming the decline in our share of international trade[1]; and despite rising unit costs, Continental export prices have remained remarkably stable—their market shares have been held at the cost, it must be assumed, of falling profit margins on their exports. But this may lead to a reduced incentive to invest and hence to a move into a vicious circle. Such a tendency would be accentuated by reliance (as in Italy) on demand restraint to check inflationary pressures and balance of payments disequilibrium. Furthermore, the growing integration of the Common Market economies is likely to mean that failure in one or two large countries to contain the rise in money incomes (especially in France or Italy where trade union movements are divided along political or religious lines) will lead to 'imported' inflation in the others. We can do no more than suggest that some, at least, of the conditions for improving our competitiveness are more favourable than they were. We cannot be sure that full advantage will in fact be taken of these more favourable conditions.

6. A PRODUCTIVITY ASSUMPTION FOR BRITAIN

We now proceed to choose a growth rate for the British economy up to 1975 as a statistical basis for the rest of this book. Firstly, we propose to select a figure for the annual rate of growth in total output per man-year. The figure chosen should be generally regarded as technically feasible in the light of experience in this country and in comparable economies elsewhere. It is also based on the *assumption* that the conditions for faster growth in Britain, as described earlier in this chapter, are satisfied; this means, principally, that the incubus of a precarious balance of payments is removed by greater competitiveness, so that long-term expectations can be based on full use of the productive potential of our economic resources.

Secondly, the projected rate of growth of productivity will be applied to the expected growth of the labour force to yield a projection of gross national product up to 1975. This is done in the following chapter 3. The future growth of the labour force is more nearly a 'forecast' than the growth of productivity, since the former depends in great part on known demographic facts and social factors which are difficult to change. At the same time, we recognize that the future size of the labour force is not wholly independent of the growth of productivity and of the rate of economic progress.

The conditions suggested above for a future rate of growth of productivity leave us considerable room for choice. From the experience of other countries, as surveyed in chapter 1, rates anywhere in the range of about 3 to 5 per cent

[1]This declining share is explained in part, but only in a small part by a fall in Britain's share in the Common Market, where increasing tariff discrimination against us has offset some of our cost advantages.

per annum per employee might all be perfectly realistic. However, for present purposes we should exclude (a) small countries, whose growth rates are likely to be heavily dependent on the particular commodity structure of their exports and the extent to which their trade links have been chiefly with fast- or slow-growing large countries[1], and (b) countries, large or small, whose own growth rates during the 1950s are also generally considered to have been well below their potential (United States, Canada, Belgium).

We are left with three other European countries that are comparable with the United Kingdom in size and economic diversity, namely France, Germany and Italy. In chapter 1 it is maintained that 'exceptional' factors (for example, starting from lower levels of income, greater scope for increasing employment in industry, and so on) have not played a great role in explaining their faster rates of productivity increase. Nevertheless the contribution made by the exceptional factors cannot be completely excluded. Hence it is desirable to select a rate well below the rates of 4 to 5 per cent per employee achieved by these countries in the latter half of the 1950s; for example, a rate of productivity growth in the region of 3 to 4 per cent per annum.

Another possible guide to what might be a feasible rate is provided by British pre-war experience. Of course, earlier periods were so bedevilled by major fluctuations in economic activity that it is impossible to give any precise and useful meaning to the concept of a 'trend' rate of growth in such periods. Nor are there data of the kind needed to compare with any confidence rates of growth between years of equal utilization of productive capacity. In general, the environment of slumps and booms and the generally high level of unemployment which characterized the pre-war period certainly inhibited the longer-run growth of capacity, technical innovation and productivity. Hence an average rate of growth of productivity in the past (excluding historically exceptional periods such as the Industrial Revolution) will tend to be too low to be applicable to the general conditions of full employment and steady expansion that we are expecting to prevail. In order to offset this downward bias inherent in the inter-war period average growth rate, therefore, it is preferable to select that part of the period when output was expanding more or less uninterruptedly. Such a period would be 1932–7, when gross national product per employed person grew at over 3·5 per cent per annum[2]. It is true that this followed

[1]For example, Austria would hardly be comparable with the United Kingdom since as already mentioned the high Austrian growth rate during the 1950s certainly owes much to the very high proportion of her exports (more than 25 per cent) which go to Germany. The high Swiss growth rate should also not be used for selecting a rate for Britain, since the Swiss economy is hardly comparable in size and diversity with that of Britain (not to mention the special influences on the Swiss economy of having a labour force comprising over 25 per cent immigrant labour). In excluding small countries, therefore, this does not mean excluding only slow-growth countries, thereby imparting an upward bias to our selected 'comparable' growth rates.

[2]See D. C. Paige, F. T. Blackaby and S. Freund, 'Economic Growth: the Last Hundred Years', *op. cit.*

two to three years of unemployment and surplus capacity, but the expansion was well maintained, and in fact productivity was very little affected in the slump so that given the other factors dampening the longer-run growth of the inter-war period, it probably does not exaggerate the potential.

Finally, one can consider what growth rates have been regarded as feasible for other economies at a roughly similar level of development. Three sources of such estimates, which are shown in the following table, are as follows:

(a) The ministerial council of the OECD, at its meeting of the 16 and 17 November 1961, adopted a collective growth target for the decade 1960 to 1970 of an increase in gross national product of 50 per cent. A working party of the OECD has since published a first study of the possible pattern of growth rates among the largest countries. These projections do not commit the national governments at all, but neither can they be interpreted as representing the completely independent views of the OECD secretariat.

(b) The second source, a report by a special Common Market 'group of independent experts' (the Uri group) is even less the independent projection by the secretariat of an international organization and even more a set of quasi-official projections (except for Germany).

(c) The third source represents completely unofficial contributions to a volume of national projections (although the French projections have been based on official work carried out in connexion with the French plan).

It will be seen from the following table of projections that, with the exception of one of the projections for Italy, a growth rate substantially greater than 3.5 per cent per annum per man-year is expected for all three of the countries under consideration.

Whilst these various indicators still do not point to any precise figure as being the obvious one to draw for the projection in the study, they do suggest

Table 2.4. *Projected growth rates of gross national product per man-year for Germany, France and Italy, 1960–70*

	OECD[a]	European Economic Community[b]	ASEPELT[c] (1959–70)
Germany	3·8	3·55–3·85	6·0
France	4·2	4·35	4·4
Italy	4·1	4·3–4·9	3·3

[a]OECD, *Policies for Economic Growth, loc. cit.*, table 2, p. 28.

[b]Groupe de Travail pour les Problèmes de Structure et de Développement à Long Terme (Uri group), *Rapport sur les Perspectives de Développement Economique dans la CEE de 1960 à 1970* (Brussels, 1962). Data for Germany, p. 29; France, table 2.3, and p. 32; Italy, p. 37.

[c]*Europe's Future in Figures*, edited by R. C. Geary (Amsterdam, 1962). The figure for Germany is obtained by subtracting, from the total GNP projection shown on p. 340 the labour force projection in the chapter on Germany by Dr Krengel, p. 62; the French figure is from Professor Benard's chapter, on p. 85; the Italian figure is from Professor Cao-Pinna's chapter, pp. 142 and 145.

that an annual rate of growth of annual output per employee in the range of 3 to 4·5 per cent would be feasible. However, since we must select one figure for the statistical calculations, we have selected a rate of growth of labour productivity of 3·5 per cent per annum as being appropriate[1]. It is quite likely that very much higher rates of growth of output per employee could be achieved without necessarily reaching the boundary of technical progress and improvements in efficiency. But the precise measures needed to achieve such a rate are outside the scope of this study. For our purpose it is preferable to select a target that would be accepted by a sufficiently wide section of the interested bodies in the community.

In concluding this chapter two main points need to be stressed. Firstly, the hypothesis we have adopted for labour productivity is one which we regard as being technically feasible, given the general condition of export competitiveness. The important problems that must be solved in order to satisfy this general condition are not dealt with here.

Secondly, the 3·5 per cent per annum growth of labour productivity which we have adopted would, given our projection of the changes in the labour force and in working hours per year, imply certain variations over time in gross national product and in gross national product per man-hour. We examine these implications at the end of the next chapter, after analysing the probable course of the labour force; and only at that point do we specify the precise time path of the change in labour productivity per year that we finally adopt.

[1]The concept of the growth hypothesis adopted by the NEDC appears to be the same as that underlying the present study judging by Mr Selwyn Lloyd's budget statement of 9 April 1962 that 'What the Council must do is to set an ambitious but realistic target figure', House of Commons *Parliamentary Debates* (*Hansard*), vol. 657, no. 93, col. 569. Following the first meeting of the NEDC a statement was issued (press release, 9 May 1962) referring to the 4 per cent growth target adopted as being a 'reasonably ambitious figure'.

CHAPTER III

THE FUTURE GROWTH OF NATIONAL PRODUCT

By W. BECKERMAN

As explained in the Introduction to this study and in chapter 2, no attempt is made here to 'forecast' the rate of growth of British national product. Nor have we tried to show the implications of some exceptionally high rate of growth in order to isolate the main bottlenecks that a fast rate of growth might encounter. What we have done is to analyse the structure of demands and resources that might be expected to be associated with a rate of growth of productivity that would appear to most reasonable persons to be definitely feasible and, at the same time, more satisfactory than the rate achieved during the 1950s. In the preceding two chapters we presented our evidence and arguments for selecting such a rate of productivity growth. In this chapter we turn first to the projection of the labour force and then, given our productivity assumption of a 3·5 per cent annual average growth in productivity per man-year over the period 1963 to 1975, to the projection of total gross national product.

The projection of the employed labour force has been made in the light of the probable developments in firstly, the total population; secondly, the population of working age; and thirdly, the 'participation rates' or activity rates—that is, the proportion of people in each age group who are normally employed (or seeking employment).

1. TOTAL POPULATION[1]

The total population of the United Kingdom is projected to increase from 52·5 million in 1960 to 59·2 million in 1975. This increase of 6·7 million in fifteen years is, in absolute terms (though not in proportionate terms), greater than has ever occurred before, over a fifteen-year period, in the history of this country[2]. It will have a considerable impact on requirements in the field of social capital, such as housing, road transport, education and health, where

---

[1]Total population estimates include the armed forces serving overseas, and refer to population at mid-year.
[2]Proportionate rates of population increase over ten-year periods back to 1801 are given for England and Wales in A. M. Carr-Saunders, D. Caradog Jones and C. A. Moser, *A Survey of Social Conditions in England and Wales* (Oxford, 1958). See also, B. R. Mitchell and Phyllis Deane, *Abstract of British Historical Statistics* (Cambridge, 1962), table 1.1, p. 2. For England and Wales prior to 1801, and for the UK and Great Britain back to 1801 see Phyllis Deane and W. A. Cole, *British Economic Growth, 1688–1959, op. cit.*, table 75, p. 288.

Table 3.1. *Total births, deaths, net migration and population change in the United Kingdom: 5-year periods, 1950–75; mid-year estimates in thousands*

	1950–5	1955–60	1960–5	1965–70	1970–5	Total 1960–75
Births	3,978	4,344	4,849	5,295	5,558	15,702
Deaths	2,958	3,003	3,218	3,221	3,329	9,768
Total natural increase	1,020	1,341	1,631	2,074	2,229	5,934
Net migration[a]	−415	−23	458	175	100	733
Total population increase	605	1,318	2,089	2,249	2,329	6,667

Sources: For 1950–60, *Annual Abstracts of Statistics, 1952* and *1962*; for 1965–75, NIESR estimates.
[a] Births, deaths and consequently total natural increase figures are for *home* population, whereas population increase is for *total* population. Consequently net migration calculated as a residual differs slightly for the period 1955–60 from that implied in table 3.2 but would be approximately the same had we taken *home* population increase.

existing backlogs are already large. The costly social capital needs of an expanding population will not be offset by a corresponding increase in the population of working age, on account of the changing age structure of the population. Between 1960 and 1975, out of the population increase of 6·7 million, we expect the population of working age to rise by only 1·6 million; about half of this is due to the assumption about the exceedingly uncertain amount of net immigration.

The 0·8 per cent per annum (compound) rate of increase in population between 1960 and 1975 corresponds to an average annual absolute increase of 445,000 per annum. This, in turn, is the net result, on average, of 650,000 deaths per annum, 1,045,000 births per annum, giving a natural increase of 395,000 per annum, and net immigration of nearly 50,000 per annum.

The population projections adopted in this study follow closely the official projections prepared by the Government Actuary's Department[1]. The chief differences are:

(a) a higher birth rate has been projected[2]. This does not directly affect the labour force projection but does have a considerable influence on health, housing and education projections; and

(b) our more detailed breakdown of the projections by year and age group may not always correspond to the annual data implied by, but not shown in, the Government Actuary's projections (which are for five-yearly intervals).

In brief, the present study has not accepted the official projection of the natural rate of population increase, which is thought to be too low, but has

[1] *Monthly Digest of Statistics*, April 1963.
[2] The reasons for this have been set out in full elsewhere (D. C. Paige, 'Births and Maternity Beds in England and Wales in 1970', *National Institute Economic Review*, November 1962).

accepted the official projections of death rates and of rates of net migration.

The latter is a projection of net immigration of just over forty thousand per annum as from mid-1962 up to about 1975–6[1]. The acceptance of this projection in the present study does not signify conviction that it is, in fact, the most likely future course of net immigration, but rather the view that there is no strong case for adopting any other figure. The official projection appears to share this view since it is accompanied by the warning that '[migration] is a most difficult element in future population movements to estimate, particularly at the present time', and the same caution has invariably been shown by other official bodies that have, in the past, been faced with the need to take a view on likely migration trends[2].

The first obstacle to the prediction of future trends in migration is that our statistics on migration are notoriously incomplete, so that it is not possible to be certain what the gross flows of emigrants and immigrants have been in the recent past[3].

Reasonably good estimates can be made of *net* migration over the longer run on the basis of the decennial population censuses and there is little doubt that, until about 1931, there was a substantial net outflow from the United Kingdom[4]. Only in the 1930s was the net movement reversed, and during the war there was a substantial net inflow. The more traditional net outflow reappeared in 1946, but, as can be seen in the following table, this was short-lived[5].

[1]*Monthly Digest of Statistics*, April 1963.

[2]*Economic Trends*, September 1962, p. ii. The Royal Commission on Population stated in its *Report*, Cmd 7695 (London, 1949), in connection with projecting migration, that 'It is clear, however, that there is even less question here than elsewhere of choosing a single assumption as representing the "likely course of development" ' (para. 231). More bluntly, the Oversea Migration Board, in its *Sixth Report*, Cmnd 1243 (London, 1960), stated that 'Emigration is not a subject that lends itself to prediction' (para. 59).

[3]The Oversea Migration Board has felt obliged to complain about migration statistics in every annual report, particularly in its 1961 report, where it states that 'This is the seventh consecutive report in which we have found it necessary to urge the need for statistics of the considerable volume of immigration by long air routes' and 'Emigration policy . . . and immigration policy . . . are matters of considerable public interest and concern . . . yet full statistics of its volume and pattern are not available to Ministers and advisory bodies.' (*Seventh Report of the Oversea Migration Board*, Cmnd 1586, London, 1961, paras. 1 and 2). These reports include detailed descriptions of some of the inadequacies of available statistics.

[4]See Report of the Royal Commission on Population, *loc. cit.*, table VII, p. 15, for data back to 1871 for Great Britain, and Carr-Saunders, Caradog Jones and Moser, *A Survey of Social Conditions in England and Wales, op. cit.*, table 2.6, p. 16, for England and Wales. (This source is preferable to the table published in *The Registrar General's Statistical Review of England and Wales for the year 1960 part II: Tables, Population*, under table 5, p. 85, which includes wartime loss of life at sea in the emigration total.)

[5]The most reliable estimates of *net* migration in the more recent past are probably those based on comparisons of the 1951 and 1961 population censuses (after allowing for births and deaths). This shows a net gain for Great Britain of 87,000 over this ten-year period. However, there appears to have been a large change in the annual trend during this period from a net outward movement in the early years to a large net inward movement in the most recent years. The three available series are those of net migration prepared by the

Table 3.2.   *Summary table of estimated emigration, immigration and net migration, United Kingdom, 1953–62*

	Emigration	Immigration	Net migration
1953–5[a]	..	..	− 43,000
1956	220,000	203,000	− 17,000
1957	230,000	158,000	− 72,000
1958	142,000	187,000	+ 45,000
1959	130,000	174,000	+ 44,000
1960	124,000	206,000	+ 82,000
1961	124,000	294,000	+ 170,000
1962	127,000	263,000	+ 136,000

Source: Net migration and emigration from *Report of the Oversea Migration Board, loc. cit.*
[a]Annual average.

The second difficulty in projecting net migration is that this is a balancing item between what may be relatively large gross inward and outward flows, so that relatively small changes in either of these flows can produce proportionately large changes in the net movement.

Thirdly, the gross flows are, themselves, usually very small proportions of the total populations from which emigrants are going, so that relatively very small changes in the proportions of the population wishing to emigrate from any country can produce large changes in the absolute number of emigrants. For example, if the 0·25 per cent of the United Kingdom population presently emigrating were to cease doing so, and if 0·25 per cent more of the population of Pakistan were to emigrate to the United Kingdom, the net immigration into the United Kingdom would be raised from about 80,000 in 1960 to about 440,000 per annum, nearly four million more over a decade than provided for in the official projection.

Finally, the factors influencing emigration are varied and uncertain. 'Like the stock market it can be affected by the interplay of a variety of factors, some political, some economic, and sometimes by world events and sometimes by the inexplicable whims or hunches of individuals'[1]. There is a balance of

Registrar General (and published by the Oversea Migration Board) and the separate emigration and immigration series estimated by the Oversea Migration Board. Of these three series the immigration series is probably subject to the largest margin of error, being based on data on entrants into national insurance from overseas. They also relate to Great Britain only. These data relate entirely to persons over school-leaving age, exclude non-working dependants and do not take account of withdrawals from British national insurance by citizens of overseas territories. In table 3.2 above it has seemed preferable to estimate immigration by adding the Registrar General's net migration estimates to the Oversea Migration Board's emigration estimates.
[1]*Sixth Report of the Oversea Migration Board* (*loc. cit.*, 1960), para. 54. See also Julius Isaac, *British Post-War Migration* (Cambridge, 1954), p. 235, for summary of determinants of British migration.

evidence that the forces of the 'push' (from countries of origin of emigrants) rather than of 'pull' (into the countries of destination) have been historically more important, but it is not possible to distinguish relative strengths of 'push' and 'pull' from different sensitivities to each force[1].

Nevertheless, in spite of the gaps in our statistical information and the obvious analytical difficulties of projecting migration, it is necessary to consider briefly the extent to which the official forecast—admitted to be very tentative—could be proved wrong. The main factor that should be considered in this study is the possible effect of the faster overall growth rate which is assumed here (see section 5 of this chapter) to be achieved in Britain over the next decade. This is likely, other things being equal, to reinforce two tendencies, which the Royal Commission on Population already foresaw in its 1949 report, namely a decline in the volume of spontaneous emigration from Britain and difficulty in recruiting 'an adequate supply of native labour for industries that are comparatively unattractive'[2]. As the Royal Commission observed, the beginning of this process had already been evident before the war. Given that gross emigration seems to have been declining since the peak in the mid-1950s, in spite of the relatively slow growth rate of the economy, a faster growth rate of the economy might be expected at least to perpetuate the rate of decline of emigration. At the same time, the shortage of labour in the less desirable occupations could become progressively more acute.

The problem of the capacity of the labour market to absorb a much higher net immigration would only be serious if net immigration represented a particularly abnormal and unfavourable age or occupational structure—an exceptionally high proportion of dependants or of highly specialized skills the demand for which could not be expanded adequately by general measures of economic policy. But, in fact, the reverse is the case[3]. Furthermore, there is a widespread belief (to which this study does not subscribe) that faster economic growth, even in terms of output per employee, in certain Continental countries has been greatly facilitated by a faster growth in the labour force (conferring benefits from greater mobility of the labour force, less labour hoarding and so on). Protagonists of this view, therefore, should welcome encouragement of greater net immigration[4].

---

[1]Some of the evidence is quoted in Brinley Thomas, *Migration and Economic Growth* (Cambridge, 1954), p. 83, though Thomas, in this study, develops a complex explanation of the interdependence of the two forces.

[2]*Report* of the Royal Commission on Population, *loc. cit.*, paras. 325 and 326.

[3]There are numerous sources concerning the occupational qualifications of immigrants. For coloured immigrants in general, see J. A. G. Griffith and others, *Coloured Immigrants in Britain* (Oxford, 1960); and for West Indian immigrants, in particular, see Ruth Glass, *Newcomers* (London, 1960).

[4]The fact that there has been no advocacy of an increase in immigration suggests that the belief referred to is, perhaps, not so firmly held after all. For if the main obstacle to a faster British growth rate were the slow rise in the labour force, the policies required to rectify the situation would be obvious and relatively simple from an economic point of

How far could an increased 'pull' in this country in the direction of more net immigration be checked by lack of spontaneous supply of immigrants from overseas? No such check is easy to see. In 1961, the net immigration into Britain from the West Indies, India and Pakistan amounted to about 115,000[1]. This is a negligible fraction of the population in the countries of origin (about 540 million in 1960). Even for the West Indies, where emigration to Britain in 1960/1 averaged about 55,000 per annum out of a total population of just over 3 million, the percentage of the population involved is only about 1·7 per cent per annum, which still leaves the West Indies population rising at an annual average rate of well over 2 per cent per annum[2].

Lack of available immigrants or of suitable employment opportunities in Britain is unlikely to check immigration on this scale. The chief obstacle would almost certainly be social. The Royal Commission on Population recognized this problem in stating that 'Immigration on a large scale into a fully established society like ours could only be welcomed without reserve if the immigrants were of good human stock [sic] and were not prevented by their religion and race from intermarrying with the host population and becoming merged with it'[3]. At what level of immigration such difficulties become important obviously depends on national attitudes and traditions. The passing of the Commonwealth Immigrants Act in 1961 very soon after coloured immigration showed a sharp increase, suggests that net immigration much

---

view, if not from a social point of view. One exception to this schizophrenic attitude to the role of a growing labour force in facilitating economic growth is H. Wincott, 'Do the British Really Want to Grow' (*The Financial Times*, 7 January 1964) who does make the perfectly valid point that if we believe in the contribution of a rising labour force to growth *and* we really want growth then we should open our country to immigrants as has been done by Germany and Australia.

[1]Economist Intelligence Unit, *Studies on Immigration from the Commonwealth, 2. The Immigrant Communities* (London, 1962), p. 4. A similar estimate is quoted in R. B. Davison, *West Indian Migrants* (Oxford, 1962), table 1, p. 4.

[2]Population from United Nations *Demographic Yearbook, 1960*, pp. 106 and 120. Emigration to destinations other than the United Kingdom is relatively negligible, judging from comparisons of West Indian immigrants to UK with total passports issued to West Indians, and from sample surveys among persons leaving the West Indies, according to R. B. Davison (*op. cit.*, pp. 3–14). The same study also identifies the extent to which emigration fails to prevent the population from rapidly rising (page 40, tables 22 and 23). The estimate of the percentages of the West Indian population emigrating does not allow for the fact that emigrants tend to comprise a relatively high proportion of people of working age. A very detailed analysis of emigration from Jamaica (G. W. Roberts and D. O. Mills, *Study of External Migration Affecting Jamaica, 1953–55*, Jamaica, 1958) showed the disproportionate effect of migration on the growth of the Jamaican labour force (pp. 114, 116 and 129). Thus, even though increased emigration might fail to check the rise in population in the West Indies it might significantly reduce the working population, leading eventually to a smaller incentive to leave.

[3]*Report* of Royal Commission on Population, *loc. cit.*, para. 329. The term 'human stock' is not interpreted here as excluding Martians but as a euphemism for certain cherished species of humans.

larger than the official projection would rapidly encounter powerful social objection[1].

To summarize, therefore, the projection of net migration is generally recognized as a hazardous operation and the official projection represents, if anything, a rather bold revision of earlier official projections in the light of latest trends. There would seem to be ample scope, however, for much greater net movement from the purely economic point of view both in this country and in the countries from which immigrants come. However, social difficulties here seem likely to prevent a volume of net immigration much larger than the official projection. In view of this and of the uncertainties of projection in this field, the official projection has been adopted in this study.

2. POPULATION OF WORKING AGE[2]

If there were no change in the school-leaving age, the population of working age would increase by 1·6 million between 1960 and 1975, that is, at an annual average rate of 0·34 per cent (compound). Furthermore the gap between the rates of increase in total population and in the population of working age will be much wider towards the end of the 1960s than in the next few years. This is because the entry into the working age groups of the post-war baby boom is concentrated into the years 1961 and 1962. Between 1961 and 1964 the population of working age will rise by about 1 per cent per annum, whereas towards the end of the 1960s the rate will be only about 0·2 per cent per annum when the total population will be rising by about 0·9 per cent per annum.

The fall during the 1960s in the proportion of the total population of working age continues a trend that has already been operating for some time. In the 1950s, out of a total population increase of nearly two million, the population of working age rose by only 130,000. By 1975 the proportion of the total population that will be of working age will have fallen, before allowing for a rise in the school-leaving age, to only 58 per cent from 64·3 per cent in 1950 and from a peak in this century of 66·6 per cent in 1931[3]. The decline in the

---

[1]At the time the Act was passed the official estimate of the number of immigrants from Commonwealth countries other than those predominantly white, that had arrived since the end of the second world war, was over 400,000, representing roughly 1 per cent of the total population of the United Kingdom. (Reply by Mr R. A. Butler to parliamentary question, House of Commons *Parliamentary Debates (Hansard)*, vol. 649, no. 13, col. 81, 16 November 1961). An earlier official estimate which provides more detailed breakdown by country of origin was given in November 1959 by Mr Renton (House of Commons *Parliamentary Debates (Hansard)*, vol. 613, no. 20, col. 1129, 17 November 1959).

[2]Population of working age is defined here as comprising males from 15 to 64 and females from 15 to 59. As is shown in the next section, however, it is assumed that the school-leaving age will in fact be raised to 16 years in 1967 and allowance has been made for this in projecting the total labour force.

[3]For data prior to 1950, see Carr-Saunders, Caradog Jones and Moser, *op. cit.*, table 1.3, p. 4.

working age proportion of total population is accounted for by roughly equal increases in the proportions of old and of very young people. Between 1960 and 1975 the proportion of the population over working age will rise from 14·6 to 16·0 per cent whilst the proportion aged 0 to 14 years will rise from 23·3 to 26·0 per cent[1].

The unfavourable movement in the age structure of the population should not, however, persist after 1980, when the rising birth rate of the post-war period and the low birth rate of the pre-war period will begin simultaneously to have a favourable effect on the age structure. At present the reverse is the case. The low birth rate of the inter-war period means that the proportion of older people to people in the 20 to 60 age bracket is rising, at the same time as the rising birth rate of recent years is increasing the relative size of the population aged 0 to 14.

3. THE ACTIVE LABOUR FORCE

The next step in projecting the active labour force—that is, the number of people working or seeking work—is to apply to each age/sex group of the population a 'participation' rate, which is the percentage of the total population of any given age/sex group that works or seeks work. For this purpose it is preferable to divide the population of working age into three categories, each raising quite different considerations. These are (a) young people in the age group 15 to 19, and, to a lesser extent, 20 to 24, for whom the major consideration is educational—that is, what proportion may be still at school or at some other educational institution, (b) other males, for whom no special consideration arises, and (c) other females, whose participation rates are largely determined by marriage rates and the ages at which they have children.

(a) Effect of education on labour force

The projection of the participation rate for the age groups between 15 and 24 raises many vital issues of education policy, and the proposals concerning the policies that should be adopted have an important quantitative effect on the labour force projection. Educational estimates are discussed in detail in chapter 14, where a case is argued for larger numbers in higher and further education in 1975 than we have allowed for in our projection of the labour force.

The labour force projections made here have been based on the assumptions that:

(i) the school-leaving age would be raised to 16 by 1970, and
(ii) closely following the Robbins report, the total numbers in full-time

---

[1]The raising of the school-leaving age to 16 removes a further 254,000 from the 1970 labour force and 221,000 from the 1975 labour force, corresponding to about 0·4 per cent of the total population.

Table 3.3. *Education and labour force for population aged 15 to 24
in Great Britain*[a]*: thousands*

1960	15–19	20–4	15–24
Population	3,448	3,297	6,745
In full-time education[b]	719	74	793
In labour force	2,604	2,714	5,318
Not seeking work	143	547	690
1975			
Population	4,008	3,707	7,715
In full-time education[b]	1,747	255	2,002
In labour force	2,250	2,767	5,017
Not seeking work	38	792	830

[a]The numbers in full-time education, in the labour force and those not seeking work, exceed the population because students who hold insurance cards are included both in education and in the labour force.

[b]These figures differ from those in chapter 14 because overseas students are excluded here.

higher education and full-time non-advanced further education should be 540,000 by 1975.

As explained in chapter 14 on education, subsequent analysis suggested that this higher education target needed to be substantially raised in order to allow for (a) the higher figure for the number of qualified school-leavers, and (b) the unlikelihood of reaching the teacher-pupil ratio objectives without exceeding the Robbins report provisions for teacher-training. However, these revisions to the education targets could not, in the time left, be incorporated in the form of revised labour force projections. Furthermore, there is some doubt whether it would be feasible by 1975 to reach the higher education objectives in chapter 14. But insofar as it did prove possible to do so, the actual increase in the labour force would be even smaller than that projected in this chapter.

(b) *Total male labour force*

Apart from the age groups affected chiefly by the education assumptions, male participation rates for specific age groups have been very stable in the past, and the projections in this study for males aged 25 years and above are practically the same as the official projections[1]. Combining the latter with our own educational projections produces the set of male participation rates shown in table 3.4.

Given these participation rates the male labour force is projected to rise, between 1960 and 1975, by 717,000 in the United Kingdom and by 745,000 in

[1]*Ministry of Labour Gazette*, October 1963, *loc. cit.* Apart from a few very small differences, the only deviations from the official projections are in the 60+ and 70+ age groups in 1975.

G

Table 3.4.   *Male participation rates in Great Britain:*
percentage in each age group

Age	1952	1960	1970	1975
15+	79·0	76·0	60·1	56·7
20+	98·0	99·0	93·7	90·7
25+	98·5	99·5	99·5	99·6
30+	97·5	99·5	99·5	99·6
35+	99·5	99·5	99·5	99·6
40+	98·0	99·5	99·5	99·5
45+	97·5	97·5	98·5	98·3
50+	96·0	95·5	95·5	95·5
55+	93·5	95·0	94·5	94·4
60+	87·0	88·5	89·9	90·0
65+	48·0	45·0	40·8	36·4
70+	19·5	17·5	15·4	12·9

Source: 1952 and 1960, *Economic Trends*, September 1962; 1970 and 1975, appendix
tables 3.4 and 3.15.
Note: Our projection of participation rates in the 15–24 age groups differs from official
projections on account of the different estimates for education mentioned above. In
particular, we assumed that the school-leaving age would be raised to 16 by 1970 and
that there would be a considerable increase in higher and futher education (see pages 80
and 81 above).

Table 3.5.   *Relative contribution to changes in male labour*
force in the United Kingdom, 1960–75: thousands

	Age groups	
	25+	15+
Labour force		
1960	13,567	16,631
1975	14,376	17,348
Change	809	717
of which:		
Northern Ireland	−30	−28
Great Britain	839	745
Great Britain change due to:		
rise in population	1,300	1,731
change in participation rates	−134	−649
change in age structure	−326	−335
'residual interaction'	−1	−2
Percentage of change in Great Britain		
due to rise in population	*155*	*232*
change in participation rates	*−16*	*−87*
change in age structure	*−39*	*−45*
'residual interaction'	—	—

Note: For method used to calculate components of total change, see W. Beckerman and
J. Sutherland, 'Married Women at Work in 1972', *National Institute Economic Review*,
op. cit., Appendix.

Great Britain. The latter is the net outcome of an increase of 1,731,000 due to the rise in the male population aged 15 and over which is offset to the extent of 335,000 on account of changing age structure and to the extent of about 649,000 on account of lower participation rates (chiefly in the 15–24 group).

(c) The female labour force

Females now (1962) comprise 33·8 per cent of the total active labour force, and 35·6 per cent of the total number of employees in the United Kingdom[1]. Since the proportion of part-time workers among females is much greater than among males, these percentages exaggerate the contribution of females to the active labour force. Nevertheless, without an increase in the employment of women, at least of married women, over the next decade or so the total labour force would decline under the twin impact of changes in age structure and increasing education. The rise in employment of married women is by far the most important factor in determining the projection of the labour force into the future. Hence it is necessary to calculate the respective effects of demographic and other factors on the changes in the employment of women in order to identify which ones dominate the situation.

(i) *Changes in the female labour force 1950–60.* The rapid increase in the

Table 3.6. *Role of females in United Kingdom labour force, 1950 and 1960*

		1950	1960	Increase 1950–1960	
		'000s		'000s	%
1.	Total working population	23,526	25,010	1,484	6·3
2.	Males	16,069	16,631	562	3·5
3.	Females	7,457	8,379	922	12·4
4.	*of which:* married	(2,966)[a]	4,236	(1,270)	(42·8)
5.	Total employees	21,054	22,702	1,648	7·8
6.	Males	13,939	14,675	736	5·3
7.	Females	7,115	8,027	912	12·8
8.	*of which:* married	2,893	4,147	1,254	43·3
		Percentages			
9.	3 as % of 1	*31·7*	*33·5*		
10.	4 as % of 1	*12·6*	*16·9*		
11.	7 as % of 5	*33·8*	*35·4*		
12.	8 as % of 5	*13·7*	*18·3*		

Source: Annual Abstract of Statistics, 1960, 1961 and *1962* except for data on married women in total working population in 1960, which are from *Economic Trends,* September 1962 for the year 1960.

[a]The 1950 estimate of married women in the total working population has been obtained by applying the 1952 ratio of married women in the total working population to the 1950 figure of working population.

[1]*Annual Abstract of Statistics, 1963.*

proportion of females in the total labour force is fairly recent[1].   It corresponds to a rise in the female participation rate from 43 pei cent in 1950 to 48·2 per cent in 1960[2].   The rise in the overall female participation rate is also relatively recent; in the longer run it has been very stable[3].   But this long-run stability of the female participation rate has concealed large but offsetting changes in marital status, age structure and the participation rates for given age groups or marital status groups.   During the first half of this century the increase in the proportion of married women or of older women (both having particularly low participation rates) has tended to reduce the aggregate female participation rate.   But if allowance is made for these two changes, the 'adjusted' female participation rate in the United Kingdom, as in most other countries, has risen significantly over the longer run[4].   During the last decade too, the rise in the aggregate female participation rate in Britain has been the resultant of opposing forces—a rise in the participation rate for given age and marital status groups much more than offsetting the changes in the marital status and age structure of the total female population of working age.

The proportion of married women in the total female population aged 15 to 64 rose during the 1950s, on account of a rapid rise in the proportion of married women in the younger age groups.   This trend is expected to continue into the 1960s, thereby tending to reduce—if other things were to remain equal—the overall female participation rate.

[1]Cf. C. D. Long, *The Labor Force under Changing Income and Employment* (Princeton, 1958), Appendix table A.9, p. 302.   Long's data relate to 1911 and 1951, and to Great Britain, not the United Kingdom.

[2]The percentages here indicate the female members of the labour force as a percentage of the total female population aged 15 to 64.

[3]C. D. Long's data (*op. cit.*, p. 304), which, as noted above, are on a different conceptual basis, show, in fact a slight fall in the crude female participation rate from 1911 to 1931 followed by a very slight rise to a level in 1951 that was still below the 1911 figure.   Similar results are shown in United Nations, *Demographic Aspects of Manpower, Report I*, Population Studies 33 (New York, 1962), table 5.3.   Calculations by C. E. V. Leser in 'The Supply of Women for Gainful Work in Britain' (*Population Studies*, November 1955), show a slight long-term upward trend in the crude female participation rate, but this is on the basis of female employees as a proportion of the total female population *of all ages*.   Leser's estimate, therefore, reflects the declining proportion of females below working age in the total female population over the period he covers (1881 to 1951).

[4]For example, on an 'adjusted' basis, Long (*op. cit.*) obtains a rise in the female participation rate from 32·2 per cent in 1911 to 41·6 per cent in 1951 (p. 304); the United Nations, *Demographic Aspects of Manpower, loc. cit.*, shows a rise over the same period from 33·2 to 39·0 per cent for England and Wales; and Leser ('The Supply of Women for Gainful Work in Britain', *op. cit.*) shows absolute amounts that imply a rise, on his concepts, from 27·2 per cent in 1911 to 32·5 per cent in 1951.   For other countries, the main exceptions to the long-run rise in female participation rates are France and Switzerland.   Declines in other countries are noted by Leser ('Trends in Women's Work Participation', *Population Studies*, November 1958) and C. Vimont, *La Population Active: Evolution Passée et Prévisions* (Paris, 1960) but both these sources are on an unadjusted basis.   In spite of the almost universal inter-temporal rise in female participation rates, there is no close cross-country correlation between these rates and relative levels of income per head (see A. Collver and E. Langlois, 'The Female Labor Force in Metropolitan Areas: an International Comparison', *Economic Development and Cultural Change*, July 1962).

Table 3.7. *Married women as percentage of total female population in each age group in the United Kingdom*

Age group	1952ª	1960	1970	1975
15+	4·1	6·0	8·4	8·0
20+	48·1	56·3	63·1	64·1
25+	77·2	83·3	86·1	87·3
30+	84·1	88·6	90·1	90·9
35+	83·3	86·7	89·8	90·1
40+	81·5	86·2	89·3	89·6
45+	77·5	81·9	87·0	88·6
50+	74·3	77·1	82·5	84·6
55+	66·9	69·6	74·1	77·3
60+	56·8	60·7	64·4	67·3
65+	34·3	33·5	35·8	35·9
15–64	66·8	69·9	72·7	73·8

Source: Appendix table 3.10.

ªThe ratios shown here relate to Great Britain only; in Northern Ireland they are estimated to be somewhat lower for all age groups.

The downward influence on the aggregate participation rate of the changed age structure during the past decade has been due to a slight fall in the proportion of women aged 15 to 64 in the total female population, and within this group, a change in the age structure in favour of the age groups that have the lowest participation rates (for given marital status). Both these trends are expected to continue in the 1960s. The effects of these changes on the female labour force both in the recent past and in the future are shown in tables 3.10 and 3.13 below.

Table 3.8. *Age composition of female population in the United Kingdom*

	1952	1960	1975
Percentage of female population aged 15 to 64			
15–19	9·4	10·1	11·2
20–4	9·9	9·7	10·5
25–9	10·5	9·4	11·7
30–4	10·7	9·9	10·0
35–9	10·7	11·0	9·4
40–4	11·2	9·8	9·1
45–9	10·8	10·9	9·3
50–4	9·9	10·7	10·3
55–9	8·9	9·9	8·9
60–4	7·9	8·8	9·6
Percentage of total female populationª			
0–15	21·4	22·0	25·0
15–64	65·8	64·1	59·4
65+	12·8	13·9	15·6

Source: Appendix table 3.10.
ªPercentages do not add to 100 on account of rounding.

Table 3.9.   *Female participation rates by age groups, Great Britain:*
percentage in each age group

| | 1952 | | 1960 | |
	Single women	Married women	Single women	Married women
15–19	78½	55½	77	45
20–4	92½	42	99½	39½
25–9	91	29	99	32
30–4	89	26½	98½	31½
35–9	77	29½	86	36½
40–4	80½	31	96	39½
45–9	73	31	81	41½
50–4	65½	27	74	37
55–9	54½	21	58½	29½
60–4	26	9½	30½	16
65+	6	6	6	6

Source: *Ministry of Labour Gazette*, October 1963, *loc. cit.*

The effects of changing marital status and age structure on the overall female participation rate have been much more than offset by a sharp rise in the participation rates for individual age and marital status groups, except for the age group 15 to 19.

There is no theoretically unique measure of the separate effects of each of the three changes described above on the overall female labour force, because the changes were simultaneous so that the effect of any one change was partly determined by the others.   However, a reasonable approximation to an estimate of their respective contributions can be made, the results of which are summarized in the following table[1].

Table 3.10.   *Relative contribution to changes in female labour*
force in the United Kingdom[a], 1952–61: thousands

UK female labour force, 1952	7,608
UK female labour force, 1961	8,508
Change	+ 900
Of which:	
Northern Ireland	+ 5
Great Britain	+ 895
Great Britain change due to:	
rise in female population 15–64	+ 275
change in participation rates	+ 1,189
change in age structure	− 171
change in marital status	− 410
'residual interaction'	+ 12

[a]In this and other related tables we have shown 1961 estimates consistent with latest published estimates (at December 1963), without revising certain calculations based on earlier estimates since the amount of revision involved would be negligible.

[1]See note to table 3.5.

If participation rates for given age and marital status groups had remained constant, the increase in the female labour force in Great Britain due to the rise in population (275,000) would have been more than cancelled out by adverse changes in the age and marital status, so that the female labour force would actually have declined by 306,000. In fact it rose by 895,000, reflecting the addition of 1,189,000 due to the rise in participation rates for given age and marital status groups. Thus these participation rates are numerically by far the most important elements in the changes currently taking place in the female labour force, and, for purposes of projection it is necessary to analyse them in some detail.

The factors responsible for changes in participation rates may, of course, be as numerous as the considerations that determine the decision by females to seek employment, and it is unlikely that the separate and independent influence of each can be measured[1]. Nevertheless, some factors seem to predominate, particularly the number of children per married female and the age of the children. It will be seen in table 3.9 above that the rise in participation rates has been least for the younger groups of married women, and highest for the groups aged 35 to 45. This pattern corresponds to the trend towards earlier marriage with a corresponding tendency to have children at an earlier age. As a result fewer married women tend to be employed in the age groups 20 to 24 and 25 to 29, when they have very young children to look after; but their return to work, when these children have passed the age requiring their constant attention, is also at a younger age than hitherto, so that participation rates have been rising sharply in the 35 to 50 age groups. The role of children in influencing participation rates is also apparent in the longer-run trends in Britain and elsewhere that have been mentioned above; the almost universal character of the upward trend in the 'adjusted' participation rate in the first half of this century is due largely to the general decline in the birth rate and hence in average family size[2].

That participation rates are considerably influenced by the number and age of children has also been established, in Britain, by means of direct surveys. For example, a sample survey in 1949 showed that, among all mothers born between 1910 and 1919, those that had children under five years of age

---

[1] C. D. Long, *The Labor Force under Changing Income and Employment, op. cit.*, pp. 8–9, provides an apparently exhaustive list of factors which seem to have had an influence on female participation rates on the basis of a very extensive analysis of a mass of data. Following Long's study, however, relationships have been found between female participation rates and yet further variables in numerous other studies, of which the most quantitative has been R. N. Rosett's 'Working Wives: an Econometric Study', in *Studies in Household Economic Behaviour*, by T. F. Dernberg, R. N. Rosett and H. W. Watts (New Haven, Conn., 1958).

[2] According to Long (*op. cit.*, p. 10), the lower birth rate since 1890 combined with the longer life span of women in the United States, Great Britain and Canada 'could have been the source of the entire rise in female participation in these nations, areas and groups'.

represented 45·8 per cent of the total; but, of working mothers those with children under five years of age represented only 21·9 per cent. As the children become older, however, this disparity disappears rapidly[1].

Another survey has shown how the participation rate of mothers increases rapidly as the age of the child rises through the 0–4 years age group[2]. For the United States much more precise data are available. A detailed analysis of the relationships between number and age of children and participation rates has been made by Richard Rosett, who measures the effect on female participation rates of a large number of variables, one of the most important of which is found to be the age of the youngest child if he is under six years of age[3]. Rosett's estimates show that the existence of a child under six years of age has a much greater impact on the female willingness to enter employment than any of the other variables he considers, such as husband's earnings, personal or mortgage debt, education, number of years married and so on. The age of a child (under six years of age) was also more important than any other variable except the mother's educational status and the length of time she had been married. National data for the United States show that the participation rate for mothers of children under five years old (which varies from about 7 to 9 per cent according to the age of the mother) is about one quarter to one third

[1]In the same survey it was found that among mothers born during the same period (1910–19), those having children in the age group 5–9 were 25·8 per cent of the total, whereas mothers of children of this age were an even higher percentage of working mothers: 27·1 per cent (R. K. Kelsall and Sheila Mitchell, 'Married Women and Employment in England and Wales', *Population Studies*, July 1959, table 5, p. 23). See also Viola Klein, *Employing Married Women*, pp. 12–13 and *Working Wives*, pp. 39–42 (London, 1961 and 1959 respectively). A more qualitative description of the influence of family duties on participation rates in the United Kingdom is given in Barbara Thompson and Angela Finlayson, 'Married Women who Work in Early Motherhood' (*British Journal of Sociology*, June 1963).

[2]J. W. B. Douglas and J. M. Blomfield, *Children Under Five* (London, 1958), chapter 16, table 69, p. 118. This survey shows the actual participation rates of the (surveyed) mothers to be as follows:

Age of child	% working full-time	% working part-time
1 year	2·0	1·6
2 years	3·4	3·4
3 years	4·6	5·6
4 years	5·2	8·3

[3]R. N. Rosett, *op. cit.*, especially equation (5.1), p. 75. Rosett's analysis is the only one known to the present writer which attempts to isolate quantitatively the effects of the individual variables examined, and to give precise measurements within the framework of a comprehensive theoretical model, of the 'elasticities' of female participation with respect to each variable. However, as he points out himself, to derive his estimates from the type of cross-section data used required making, on scanty evidence, the assumption that there was no upward trend in participation rates for given age groups. Also there are certainly other variables affecting participation rates, such as those elucidated in the studies by V. Klein and the Department of Scientific and Industrial Research (see below), some of which are related to the number and age of children so that even Rosett's elasticities for the age of children effect are not 'pure' elasticities.

that of mothers with children over five years of age (in both cases over a range for mothers from 20 to 40)[1].

Nevertheless, important as it clearly is, the number and age of children is only one of the many factors influencing female participation rates. The effect on the participation rates of younger mothers of an increase in the number of their children during recent years appears to have been offset by other influences, as can be seen from the sharp rise in participation rates for mothers of all age groups, including groups where there has been no 'adverse' change in the number or age of their children. In fact, since another very important influence on married women's participation rate is the desire to improve the family's financial situation, the existence of more children creates, to some extent, a greater financial incentive to go to work[2].

(ii) *The projection of female participation rates in the labour force.* One method of projection is simply to examine the trends in each group's participation rate over the past and to make judgements about the future trend. However, it is necessary to be quite clear what such a trend really represents. A series showing the participation rates of females of a given age group over the years must relate, each year, to a different group 'cohort' of women. But whether a given woman is in employment at the age, say, of fifty, depends largely on whether the same woman was in employment when she was aged, say forty-five[3]. Consequently, a judgement about the participation rate in 1970 for women who will be aged 50 to 54 in that year has a precise implication concerning the net rate at which the *same* cohort of women (who were aged 40–4 in 1960) will withdraw from employment in the next ten years. As the number of such women in employment in 1960 is known it is natural to project their employment in 1970 on the basis of their present employment and the rate at which women who are employed at age 40 to 44 continue to be employed ten years later. This approach is the method of 'cohort' analysis familiar in demography.

For this method we require 'cohort participation profiles' which show, for a given cohort of females, at specified dates, the proportion of the same cohort in employment as they advance through life to successively higher age groups[4].

[1] US Bureau of Labor Statistics, 'Tables of Working Life for Women, 1950', Bulletin 1204 (Washington, 1957).
[2] Viola Klein, *Working Wives, op. cit.,* table 6, p. 25 and Department of Scientific and Industrial Research, *Woman, Wife and Worker* (London, 1960), pp. 9–12; Thompson and Finlayson, *op. cit.,* table 6, p. 157; and 'Why do Housewives go out to Work?—A Survey', *New Society,* 28 March 1963, p. 27 (review article).
[3] It is probably also true to say that whether a woman enters the labour force after her children have passed the infant stage is largely determined by whether she was employed before she began to have children.
[4] In fact, the cohorts we show are not pure cohorts in the sense of relating to an identical group of women throughout their lives, on account of (a) changes in their marital status and (b) the fact that the *net* changes are composed of partially offsetting gross flows in and out of the labour force.

As can be seen from table 3.12 in the Appendix to this chapter, on the basis of data for Britain from 1952 to 1961 the shape of the cohort participation profiles can be established within fairly narrow limits at least over the range necessary for the present projections. The results obtained are also fairly consistent with such studies on cohort participation profiles as are available for the female labour force in the United States[1].

The method of cohort analysis used here for the projection of female participation rates has already been described elsewhere[2], and is illustrated briefly with the aid of the following key table.

This table shows the participation rate for married women born during the periods indicated in the stub of the table at the ages indicated along the top of the table. The figures in brackets are projections for 1967, 1972 and 1977, the remaining figures being the rates recorded during the period 1952 to 1962, adjusted for trend (see footnote 2 on this page). Reading any column from bottom to top corresponds to the trend *over time* in the participation rate *for a given age group*. Reading horizontally, from left to right, corresponds to a 'cohort participation profile'. To project the participation rate for the age group, say 30 to 34, on the basis of the time trends in the rate for this group, one would observe that the rate for 30- to 34-year-olds has risen from 27·8 per cent in 1952 (the year in which the generation born 1918 were aged 30 to 34) to 29·0 per cent in 1957 and to 32·8 per cent in 1962. On the basis of this one would be inclined to project a further rise. The official projection for this group is, in fact, 37 per cent in 1972 and 34·5 per cent in 1967[3]. But such figures would imply a pattern of horizontal reading—that is, a cohort profile— that bears little resemblance to such cohort profiles as can be established.

[1]Diagrams corresponding to cohort participation profiles for the USA, for women born in 1876–85 and the subsequent four decades, are given in *Womanpower*, a statement by the National Manpower Council (New York, 1957), figure 3, p. 128.

[2]W. Beckerman and J. Sutherland, 'Married Women at Work in 1972', *op. cit.* The projections in the present study incorporate certain revisions to the Beckerman and Sutherland projections, notably:

(i) To establish the cohort profiles for the past years, the female participation rates in each year have been adjusted according to the level of unemployment in each year. This is in order to reduce the impact of conjunctural variations in the *demand* for labour.

(ii) Curvilinear trends have then been fitted to the resulting adjusted female participation rates to obtain estimates of the 'trend values' of the cohort profiles.

(iii) Over the range of the cohort profiles where the participation rates are rising the slope of the profiles has been measured, for purposes of their projection into the future, from the point of view of the rate of change in the proportion of non-active females on the grounds that a measure of the rise in participation rates is basically a proposition about the behaviour of non-active females; namely a measure of how fast they are returning to the labour force. Strictly speaking, of course, there is a flow in and out of the labour force, and it is when the *net* movement is inwards that it is predominantly non-active females who are changing their status.

(iv) The 'swing' method, explained in the text below, has been adopted.

[3]*Ministry of Labour Gazette*, October 1963, *loc. cit.* (after interpolation from 1973 to 1972 and 1968 to 1967).

Table 3.11. *Cohort profiles of participation rates of married women in Great Britain*

Year of birth	Age last birthday										
	15–19	20–4	25–9	30–4	35–9	40–4	45–9	50–4	55–9	60–4	65+
1948–52	(50·0)	(40·0)	(29·7)								
1943–47	50·0	(40·0)	(29·7)	(29·3)							
1938–42		37·3	(29·7)	(29·3)	(42·7)						
1933–37		42·1	32·2	(31·7)	(43·0)	(45·2)					
1928–32		43·1	31·6	32·8	(42·4)	(45·7)	(55·0)				
1923–27			31·0	29·0	37·5	(42·2)	(51·0)	(55·7)			
1918–22				27·8	34·8	41·0	(48·8)	(52·9)	(51·2)		
1913–17					29·6	37·6	44·6	(48·2)	(46·6)	(28·4)	
1908–12						31·2	37·5	40·6	(39·3)	(23·9)	(12·4)
1903–07							31·2	33·6	32·6	(19·9)	(10·3)
1898–1902								27·4	26·4	16·5	(8·5)
1893–97									21·0	12·5	7·0
1888–92										9·5	4·5

Source: Appendix tables 3.12 for back years and 3.11 and 3.16 for projections.

Taking the average of the generations born 1928–32 and 1923–7 it can be seen that their participation rates fell off as they moved from age 25–9 to 30–4. Thus, the participation rate in 1967 for the 30- to 34-year-olds (born 1933–7) should be slightly less than the participation rate for the same generation of women in 1962 (when they were aged 25–9) which was 32·2 per cent. The same procedure can be adopted for all the other rates that require projection.

The reliability of this method can be evaluated to some extent by the speed with which the shapes (slopes) of the cohort profiles appear to be changing. The complete set of figures used, which have already been published, show that, in fact, the change in slope between any two cohorts at five-year intervals has been very small during the 1950s[1]. Nevertheless it must be emphasized that the gap between two cohort profiles at any given age represents the joint effect of (a) a difference in participation rates at the beginning of the profiles (when they enter the labour force) and (b) the cumulation, up to the given age, of changes in the slope of the profiles. Thus the fact that the cohort profiles do change shape over time must be recognized. This means that, instead of taking the average slope from the last two cohorts, as was done in the original article by Beckerman and Sutherland, it has been considered more appropriate to follow the swing in the cohort shapes between the successive cohorts.

The complete set of participation rates which we have projected, on the basis of the method outlined above, are compared, in table 3.12 below, with the official projections for 1973. It will be seen that, among married women, our figures are below the official figures for the age groups 25 to 49, which is partly because our method makes more allowance for the tendency towards earlier age of marriage and childbirth. Conversely, our projected participation rates are significantly higher than the official projections in the older age groups. Overall, our participation rate for married women is somewhat higher than the official projection and implies a married female labour force only 44,000 higher than that contained in the official projection[2]. The alternative projections of the female married labour force are thus broadly in agreement, with the principal difference, small but definite, to be found in the age structures. For single women, too, we project higher participation rates except in the 15 to 24 age groups (on account of our educational assumptions).

It is now possible to bring together the results, for females, of the projections made above of the population, age structure, marital status and participation rates. The respective contributions of the various items are shown in table 3.13 below. It will be seen that the female labour force in Great Britain will rise by about 693,000 between 1960 and 1975, almost all of which may be attributed to the change in participation rates, since the increase attributable to the rise

[1] W. Beckerman and J. Sutherland, *op. cit.*, upper section of table 1, p. 57.
[2] About 14,000 of this difference is due to our projection having a higher proportion of married women in the total female population.

Table 3.12. *Female participation rates, Great Britain*

Married	1960	1973 NIESR	1973 Official	1975 NIESR
15–19	45·0	50·0	40·0	50·5
20–4	39·5	40·0	36·0	40·0
25–9	32·0	29·5	32·0	29·5
30–4	31·5	29·5	37·5	29·5
35–9	36·5	43·0	43·5	42·5
40–4	39·5	45·5	50·0	45·0
45–9	41·5	52·0	54·0	53·5
50–4	37·0	53·5	50·0	54·5
55–9	29·5	47·5	42·0	49·0
60–4	16·0	22·5	23·0	26·5
65–9	6·0	11·0	6·0	11·5
Total	32·0	37·5	34·2	37·7
Single				
15–19	77·0	57·5	66·3	56·0
20–4	99·5	92·0	93·8	91·0
25–9	99·0	99·0	99·0	99·0
30–4	98·5	99·5	99·0	99·5
35–9	86·0	98·5	95·0	98·5
40–4	96·0	97·5	92·5	98·0
45–9	81·0	91·0	85·0	93·0
50–4	74·0	81·0	75·0	83·0
55–9	58·5	66·5	60·0	68·0
60–4	30·5	37·5	30·0	38·0
65–9	6·0	6·5	5·0	7·0
Total	53·0	45·5	46·2	44·8

Source: 1960 and 1973, official projections from *Ministry of Labour Gazette*, October 1963, *loc. cit.* and population estimates of the Government Actuary's Department (*Annual Abstract of Statistics, 1962*); NIESR projections from appendix tables 3.11, 3.12, and 3.16.

Table 3.13. *Relative contributions to changes in female labour force in the United Kingdom, 1960–75: thousands*

UK female labour force, 1960[a]	8,315
UK female labour force, 1975	9,002
Change	687
of which:	
Northern Ireland	− 6
Great Britain	693
Great Britain change due to:	
rise in population	538
change in participation rates	778
change in age structure	−277
change in marital structure	−346
residual interaction	—

[a]The actual figure for the female labour force in the United Kingdom in 1960 was 8,379,000. The figure given above is our 'trend' figure.

in female population of working age (538,000) will be more or less cancelled out by changes in age structure and marital status.

The age and marital status composition of the female labour force in the United Kingdom in 1975 is shown in table 3.14. The total increase since 1960 of 687,000 is the net result of a fall of nearly 620,000 in the number of active single women (due to more education and a higher marriage rate) and a rise of about 1,307,000 in married female workers. The percentage of married women in the total female labour force will have risen from 40·7 per cent in 1950 and 51·7 per cent in 1960 to 61·9 per cent in 1975.

The increase of 1,307,000 in the number of married women in the labour force between 1960 and 1975 will, in fact, be almost equal to the entire rise in the labour force (male and female) over this period. The complete structure of the labour force in the terminal years is as follows:

Table 3.14. *Total labour force in the United Kingdom, 1952–75: thousands*

	1952	1955	1960	1965	1970	1975
Males						
15–19	1,297	1,304	1,373	1,693	1,166	1,198
20–4	1,675	1,661	1,691	1,767	2,056	1,774
25–59	11,654	11,781	11,837	11,881	11,945	12,328
60–4	945	999	1,068	1,261	1,342	1,358
65+	683	728	662	672	726	690
Total males	16,254	16,473	16,631	17,274	17,235	17,348
Females						
(i) Married						
15–19	37	38	48	75	78	81
20–4	344	355	377	427	530	480
25–59	2,756	3,167	3,616	3,992	4,265	4,518
60–4	74	86	146	186	243	300
65+	23	53	76	111	148	191
Total, married	3,234	3,699	4,263	4,791	5,264	5,570
(ii) Single						
15–19	1,204	1,252	1,264	1,481	1,006	1,030
20–4	826	777	720	675	724	606
25–59	1,064	1,973	1,741	1,590	1,460	1,379
60–4	152	181	178	205	215	209
65+	128	131	149	171	181	208
Total, single	4,374	4,314	4,052	4,122	3,586	3,432
Total	23,862	24,486	24,946	26,187	26,085	26,350
of which: females	7,608	8,013	8,315	8,913	8,850	9,002

Source: 1952 and 1955, Ministry of Labour. Projections, appendix tables 3.13, 3.14 and 3.17. 1952 and 1955 figures are 'actual'. Trend figures, given for 1960, differ negligibly from 'actual' for males; 'actual' 1960 labour force was 25,010,000 and female force 8,379,000. Our projected time path assumed the school-leaving age would be raised in 1967 whereas the latest officially announced date is early 1970s. This does not, of course, affect our 1975 projection.

(d) *The total labour force projections*

Taking males and females together, the United Kingdom labour force will rise by 1,404,000 over the period from 1960 to 1975. For Great Britain, the combined downward impact due to the changing marital structure and the change in the age structure (accounting together for a loss of 958,000) is offset only to the extent of about one third by the positive effect of the rise in participation rates and the favourable change in the sex ratio (accounting together for a gain of 325,000). The negative effect of the movement of male participation rates cancels out most of the gain due to the improvement in female participation rates. The net result of all this is that the rise in the total labour force is rather less than the rise in the total population of working age (1,797,000).

Our projection of the total United Kingdom labour force in 1973 (we do not possess an official figure for 1975) is lower (by about 270,000) than the official projection, our slightly higher figure for married women being more than offset by our lower figures for single women and men, both of which are principally due to our educational assumptions.

The increase in the British labour force of about 1·4 million between 1960 and 1975 will not be evenly spread over the years. Most of the increase will occur in the first half of the 1960s, as can be seen in table 3.14[1]. The increase in the employment of married women will also be of great importance in determining the time path of the change in the labour force, since it will be *relatively* steady throughout the period. In fact, in the absence of the projected rise in participation rates for married females, the labour force would fall,

Table 3.15. *Relative contributions to changes in total labour force, 1960–75: United Kingdom and Great Britain; thousands*

UK labour force, 1960	24,946[a]
UK labour force, 1975	26,350
Change	1,404
of which:	
Northern Ireland	− 34
Great Britain	1,438
Great Britain change due to:	
change in participation rates	129
change in age structure	−612
change in marital structure	−346
interactions	− 2
rise in population	2,269
of which:	
change in aggregate male/female ratio	196

Source: Appendix table 3.17 and NIESR estimates.
[a]Trend figure, actual figure is 25,010,000.

[1]For detailed year by year evolution of the labour force see appendix table 3.17.

Table 3.16. *1973 labour force estimates: official and NIESR; thousands*

	NIESR	Official	Difference[a]
United Kingdom			
Males	17,387	17,610	−223
Females	8,938	8,986	− 48
of which:			
Married	5,482	5,443	+ 39
Single	3,456	3,543	− 87
Total	26,325	26,596	−271
Great Britain			
Males	16,994	17,211	−217
Females	8,755	8,784	− 29
of which:			
Married	5,413	5,369	+ 44
Single	3,342	3,415	− 73
Total	25,749	25,995	−246

Source: NIESR, appendix table 3.17; official, *Ministry of Labour Gazette*, October 1963, *loc. cit.*
[a]Where the NIESR estimate is higher than the official estimate the difference is recorded with a plus sign, and vice versa.

from 1966 to 1970, by 262,000; and even excluding the years 1967 and 1968, which are dominated by our educational assumptions, the labour force over the following four years would fall rather than rise without the projected rise in married female employees.

The major role of the increase in married women employees in the labour force has many implications, quite apart from those affecting the purely statistical measurement of the labour force. In the first place, the utilization of this particular source of increasing labour supply will call for continued adaptation, by employers, of their conventional attitudes to the employment of married women. Secondly, there are implications for the staffing of certain social services where more married women employees may be the only way of filling serious gaps (see chapter 13 on health, page 445). This is, of course, only part of the special problem of the occupational and regional distribution of this particular component of the increase in the labour force. It may well be that the extra married women employees can be suitably integrated into the labour force only in selected occupations and areas. Hence, as the labour force *excluding married women* will be declining in the early part of the 1970s, the global contribution that will be made by increasing numbers of active married women should not obscure the generally adverse trend in the labour force that will be taking place[1]. Finally, the economic and social problems of employing

[1]Between 1970 and 1975, out of an increase of 265,000 in the total labour force, the married women account for a rise of 306,000. That is, excluding married women the labour force would fall by 41,000 (see appendix table 3.17).

more married women, especially those with fairly young children, are numerous and complicated—the absence, so far, of any official policies in this vital field will have to be rectified[1].

4. WORKING HOURS AND HOLIDAYS

The last step required to translate the projections of the active labour force into an aggregate labour input projection is to make an allowance for probable changes in (a) weekly hours worked and (b) paid holidays. As regards the former, if we ignore short-period fluctuations which reflect changes in the pressure of demand for labour, there has been no trend change in average *actual* hours worked over the period 1950 to 1960. The index of average weekly hours actually worked, with 1950 = 100, rose to 102·4 in 1955 when the pressure of demand was at a peak and fell, after a slight fluctuation, to 100·7 in 1960[2]. Since 1960, however, there does seem to have been some longer-term reduction in actual hours worked. Average hours actually worked remained very stable over the whole period 1950 to 1960 although the share of part-time female employees in the total labour force rose from about 3·5 per cent in 1950 to about 4·3 per cent in 1960[3]. Such small changes in the share of part-time employees in the total labour force can obviously have a negligible effect on average hours worked over a ten-year period. For the next ten years, even the projected large rise in the employment of married women (about 20 per cent of whom are part-time) cannot reduce average hours worked by more than about one per cent over the whole decade, as can be seen in table 3.18. But there is likely to be an extra reduction of at least three per cent in the length of the working week.

Holidays with pay also show no trend over the last ten years. But it is necessary to allow for the possible effect of emulation here of conditions overseas[4]. It is very likely that the fairly large gap between the amount of paid holidays in Britain and in the member countries of the European Economic Community will be largely eliminated by 1975, even though at the time of writing it appears that this would be caused not by the deliberate implementation of any treaty but merely the force of spontaneous emulation adding to the

[1] See F. Le Gros Clark, *Women, Work and Age* (London, 1962); and 'Study Needed on Married Women in Industry', *The Times*, 28 January 1963, p. 10.
[2] Ministry of Labour, *Statistics on Incomes, Prices, Employment and Production*, no. 1, April 1962, table D.1, p. 68.
[3] This estimate has been based on the assumption that the proportions of married and single female employees who worked part-time in manufacturing were the same in 1950 as in 1961 (as shown in *Ministry of Labour Gazette*, December 1962).
[4] If Britain were, after all, to enter the Common Market by 1975, then of course statutory obligations to harmonize working conditions would enter the picture. For Article 120 of the Rome Treaty lays down that 'Member States shall endeavour to maintain the existing equivalence of paid holiday schemes': see *Treaty establishing the European Economic Community, Rome 1957* (English translation published in London by H.M. Stationery Office, 1962) Article 120, p. 45.

H

natural desire for more leisure and the general trend over time towards greater leisure.

Accurate brief comparisons of paid holidays in Britain and other countries are not possible; the institutional arrangements governing the length of paid holidays are often complex and vary between countries—for example, the degree to which statutory minima are supplemented by collective agreement, the extent to which holidays vary with length of service, the extent to which public holidays are normally paid and other factors. Nevertheless one beneficial outcome of the negotiations for British entry into the Common Market was a fairly detailed comparison of holidays here and in the Common Market countries. The following table attempts to summarize paid holiday provisions on a reasonably comparable basis.

It will be assumed here that even if Britain has entered the Common Market by 1975 the number of public holidays in the United Kingdom will not be influenced by overseas conventions (we assume that 'entry into Europe' would not involve the recognition of more saints' days or celebrations of British military victories). Hence harmonization of holidays would have to be concentrated on the annual holidays. If the length of British annual holidays were to be raised, by 1975, to that *now* prevailing, *on the average*, in the European Common Market (15½ days) this would involve an increase of 3½ days in British holidays. Furthermore, the present average in the Common Market is also likely to rise by 1975 since any further standardization—whether by enforcement or mere emulation—will tend to take the form of standardization upwards[1]. Thus it

Table 3.17. *Approximate total paid holidays in the United Kingdom and the European Economic Community*[a]

	Number of days holiday		
	Total	Public holidays	Annual holidays
Belgium	22–7	10–15	12
France	20–4	1–5	19
Germany	24–31	10–13	(14–18)[b]
Italy	30–3	17	(13–16)[b]
Luxembourg	28	10	18
Netherlands	20–2	7	(13–15)[b]
United Kingdom	**17–18**	**5–6**	**12**

Source: Ministry of Labour Gazette, February 1962, p. 59.

[a]Including a number of public holidays for which payment is normally made. The basis of calculation has been to add the latter to the number of days paid annual holidays *generally* granted to workers with about 10–15 years service.

[b]The figures are particularly uncertain because of the considerable extent to which collective agreements supplement statutory minima.

[1]In fact the agreement at the end of 1962 to give the Renault workers a fourth week of paid holidays suggests that the upward movement may proceed fastest in the country where these are already the longest.

H2

is likely that pressures in Britain would lead to one further week's paid holiday by 1975, which would still leave the British total, at $22\frac{1}{2}$–$23\frac{1}{2}$ days, below the present Common Market average of $25\frac{1}{2}$ days. This corresponds to a reduction of one forty-ninth of the existing working year (allowing for public holidays)— that is a reduction of about 2 per cent. Given the above views on the likely reduction in the working week and the influence of part-time female employees on hours worked per week this would imply a total decline of about 6 per cent in the length of the working year. For estimating labour input it is immaterial how this 6 per cent is allocated between longer holidays and shorter hours per week.

A reduction in hours per year obtained by longer holidays is not a very large proportionate change in the total working year, but it will mean both a significant change in established holiday conventions and a very large (nearly 50 per cent) proportionate change in the potential length of stay at holiday resorts. The stability of the length of paid annual holidays in Britain during the 1950s has been remarkable, as has also the uniformity between occupations and industries. Out of over three hundred categories of employees in 1961 for whom paid holiday data are available only about ten had over two weeks holiday and nearly all these were special cases which had the same length of holiday ten years earlier[1]. It is difficult to foresee the distribution over time of the possible 6 per cent fall in working hours. Consequently the purely arbitrary assumption is made here that the total fall in working hours per year due to longer holidays will be spread evenly over fifteen years as from 1960.

Given the negligible rate of increase in the active labour force projected for the later 1960s, even such a slight fall in working hours per year is important since it implies a fall in total hours worked per year during the last few years of this decade. Consequently the somewhat arbitrary nature of the assumption made concerning yearly hours must be stressed. Fortunately, the slight change in average hours worked that we project here is not expected to have a significant impact on the rate of increase of productivity per man-year, though it then implies that productivity per man-hour will rise faster than the 3·5 per cent per annum rate of increase in productivity per man-year projected. The historical evidence suggests that, in the longer run, changes in hours worked are compensated for by changes in the organization of production apart from long-run trends in productivity, so as to leave productivity per man-year roughly constant: though short-run fluctuations in hours worked are more

[1]See Ministry of Labour, *Time Rates of Wages and Hours of Work, 1 April 1961*, Appendix III, and *Time Rates of Wages and Hours of Labour, 1st October 1951*, Appendix III (London, 1961 and 1952). This stability of conventional holidays during the last ten years would appear to justify the Ministry of Labour's statement that 'At the present time (April 1962) there is no indication that this period [2 weeks] is likely to be increased to 3 weeks in the near future' (*Statistics on Incomes, Prices, Employment and Production*, April 1962, D.10, p. 77).

often accompanied by short-run variations in productivity per man-year[1].

The following table summarizes the changes in labour input. It shows the difference between simple measures of labour input (row 8) in which no account is taken of changes in the male/female composition of the labour force or of our projected changes in holidays and/or the length of the working week, and indicators in which account is taken of one or both of these factors (row 7 and row 9). It will be seen that the latter indicator implies that the total input declines as from 1965.

Table 3.18. *Projection of labour input, 1960–75*

	1960	1965	1970	1975
Hours worked per week (million)				
1. Males	765·5	794·6	792·8	798·0
2. Married females: full-time	139·8	157·1	172·7	182·7
3. part-time	18·8	21·1	23·2	24·5
4. Single females: full-time	157·8	160·6	139·7	133·7
5. part-time	4·3	4·3	3·8	3·6
6. Total hours worked per week	1,086·1	1,137·7	1,132·1	1,142·5
7. Index of yearly hours worked adjusted for male/female mix	100·0	104·8	104·2	105·2
8. Index of labour force unadjusted for male/female mix	100·0	105·0	104·6	105·6
9. Index of yearly hours worked adjusted for male/female mix and for increased holidays and/or shorter working week	100·0	103·4	100·1	98·9

Source: Appendix table 3.19.

5. THE DEVELOPMENT OF GROSS NATIONAL PRODUCT, 1960 TO 1975

Given the projected year by year evolution of the labour force and the adopted 'norm' for the average annual increase in national product per head of labour force, the projection of total gross national product is a matter of simple arithmetic once the base year from which the 'norm' is to apply is selected. In this study we have taken 1963 as the base year; that is, output per head of labour force is projected to rise by 3·5 per cent per annum, on the average, from 1963 to 1975. This gives an increase in output per head over the whole

[1]See, in particular, E. F. Denison, 'Measurement of Labor Input: Some Questions of Definition and the Adequacy of Data', in National Bureau of Economic Research, *Output, Input and Productivity Measurement* (Princeton, 1961), especially pages 352–4. The main historical evidence is that given by H. M. Vernon, *The Shorter Working Week* (London, 1934) and P. Sargant Florence, *Economics of Fatigue and Unrest* (London, 1924). Both these authors find that reductions in hours from about 70 to 55 per week raised productivity per man-hour thereby leaving productivity per man more or less unchanged or even raising it; but below eight hours per day 'Reduction of hours . . . does not increase hourly output sufficiently to increase the daily total . . .' (Sargant Florence, p. 348).

period 1963 to 1975 of 51·1 per cent. (The reader who thinks that this degree of precision violates the spirit of the exercise should wait for the denouement in the final paragraph of this chapter.)

Our projection of the 'trend' levels of the labour force gives a rise of 2·1 per cent over the whole period 1963 to 1975. But in 1963 the actual labour force appeared to be about one per cent below the 'trend' value (as adopted in section 3 above)[1]. Hence, assuming that this deviation from 'trend' is eventually absorbed, the labour force would increase by about 3 per cent between 1963 and 1975. Combining this with the projected 51 per cent increase in output per head of labour force yields an increase in gross national product of 56 per cent between 1963 and 1975. This corresponds to an average annual compound rate over the period 1963 to 1975 of 3·8 per cent, and, over the whole period 1960 to 1975, of 3·5 per cent. As can be seen in the following table, if the 'excess supply' of labour in 1963 is absorbed by 1966, the annual rate of increase of gross national product should be about 4·5 per cent per annum over the three years 1963–6, when the labour force will still be rising fast. After that, there would be some fluctuations in the 'trend' rate of increase in the labour force, and hence in gross national product, on account chiefly of changes in the school-leaving age, and then, in the early 1970s, gross national product should rise at about the same rate, 3·5 per cent per annum, as gross national product per head of labour force.

But it would be highly artificial to project such fluctuations in the time path of gross national product solely on account of variations in the rate of change of the labour force. Hence our final projection assumes that, apart from some extra boost arising from the fast rate of increase of the labour force between

Table 3.19. *Projection of rates of increase in labour force and gross national product assuming steady rate of growth of productivity*

Annual average per cent compound rates of change

	Labour force	GNP per head of labour force	Total GNP
1960–3	0·7	1·7	2·4
1963–6	1·0		4·5
1966–9	− 0·3		3·2
1969–72	0·3	3·5	3·8
1972–5	0·0		3·5
1960–75	0·4	3·1	3·5
1963–75	0·3	3·5	3·8

[1] The 'trend' values of the labour force referred to here are those corresponding to the 'trend' values of the participation rates for each age, sex and marital status group. Short-run fluctuations in the demand for labour appear to have a significant effect on participation rates in any given year, particularly for women. Our 'trend' value of the UK active labour force in 1963 is 25,807,000 as compared with an actual figure in that year of 25,579,000.

1963 and 1966, the rate of growth of gross national product will be steady from 1966 to 1975.   This implies both that (a) the course of the labour force may be steadier than that shown in the above table—as would happen if, for example, the school-leaving age were raised in 1970 instead of 1966/7 and that (b) variations in the rate of increase in the labour force are more or less offset by variations in the rate of increase in productivity.   The final projections, on this basis, are shown in table 3.20 below.   It will be seen that we have assumed that the rate of productivity increase between 1963 and 1966 will be somewhat less than the longer-run rate, partly because of the greater opportunities for expanding output by increasing employment, and partly because the various basic changes in attitudes, planning, and arrangements for incomes policies, on which we believe that the growth rate will largely depend, cannot be introduced overnight and should have a gradually increasing effect.

Table 3.20.   *Final projected time path of gross national product*

| | Annual average per cent compound rate of growth | | |
	Labour force	GNP per head of labour force	GNP
1960–3 (actual)	0·7	1·7	2·4
1963–6	1·0	3·2	4·2
1966–75	0·0	3·6	3·6
1960–75	0·4	3·1	3·5
1963–75	0·3	3·5	3·8

Table 3.21.   *Indices of gross national product, labour force, gross national product per head of labour force and gross national product per man-hour in 1975*

| | Index in 1975 | |
	1960 = 100	1963 = 100
Gross national product	166	156
Labour force	105·6	103
GNP per head of labour force	157	151·5
GNP per man-hour	170	161

For the whole period 1960 to 1975 the above projections imply a rise of about 66 per cent for gross national product (3·5 per cent per annum compound) and of about 57 per cent for gross national product per head of the labour force[1]. Because of the likely decline in hours worked per year, productivity per man-hour would have to rise by about 70 per cent from 1960 to 1975, or at about

[1]Assuming, at the time of writing, that GNP in 1963 was about 2¾ per cent greater than in 1962.

3·6 per cent per annum.   As from about 1966, the implied rate of growth of productivity per man-hour would be even higher than this, at about 4·1 per cent per annum[1].

In money terms, at constant 1960 prices, our projection of gross national product in 1975 is £39,800 million.   In order to emphasize once again the interpretation that should be attached to this sort of exercise, this figure will be rounded off to £40,000 million—which may be an easier figure to remember than to achieve.

[1]Assuming that the school-leaving age is raised to 16 in 1966, the man-hours worked per year will fall by about 0·45 per cent per annum between 1966 and 1975 (see appendix table 3.19).

PART II

THE PATTERN OF OUTPUT AND EXPENDITURE

CHAPTER IV

CAPITAL AND INVISIBLE TRANSACTIONS IN BRITAIN'S BALANCE OF PAYMENTS

By R. L. Major

In this chapter and the next we consider the prospects for the balance of payments in 1975 on our underlying assumptions about economic conditions in Britain and on what seem to us to be reasonable hypotheses about the course of world trade and payments. Chapter 4 discusses first how big a surplus Britain will need to earn on current account if the overseas capital position is to be strengthened and a worthy contribution made to the development of poorer countries. The outlook for invisible transactions is then examined, and an estimate is thus obtained of the kind of balance which might be required on visible trade. After allowance has been made, in the earlier part of chapter 5, for likely developments in the classes of trade which are less dependent on competitiveness (mainly imports of food, fuel and materials), this balance is converted into projections for the exports of British manufacturing industry as a whole and for the imports which compete with output in the domestic market. Finally the totals are distributed industry by industry in the light of the varying rates of growth in demand to be expected here and abroad and of relative competitiveness over the past ten or twelve years.

1. THE SURPLUS NEEDED: POLICY ASSUMPTIONS

It may, however, be useful first to clear away some misconceptions about past estimates of our current surplus requirements in relation to future needs. It is sometimes suggested that the annual current surplus required year in and year out was officially put at £350 million in 1953, that in 1959 the target was raised to £450 million (approximately the surplus then thought to have been achieved in the previous year), and that therefore the difference between £450 million and the surplus of £121 million actually recorded for 1963 is the measure of the improvement that is necessary. But there are several fallacies in this.

The statement in the *Economic Survey for 1953* that 'the annual surplus on current account needed to provide for commitments, and for some increase in the gold reserves, might amount to something like £300–£350 million' was made in the context of likely capital calls 'over the next few years', notably Indian drawings on sterling balances and the need to repay the large debt then owed to the European Payments Union[1]. Similarly the figure of £450 million

---

[1] *Economic Survey for 1953*, Cmd 8800, p. 43.

mentioned to the Radcliffe Committee was stated to be illustrative only and to mean that 'in present circumstances the United Kingdom should conduct its internal policies in such a way that the resources available to attain a current surplus of this order would be available if required'[1]. It related specifically to the early 1960s and allowed for the repayment in the period of nearly £300 million of borrowed dollars. Comparison with these former estimates is, moreover, largely invalidated by subsequent changes in the figures.   In each case the estimate of the current surplus for what at the time was the latest year (1952 in one case and 1958 in the other) has since been written down by well over £100 million.   The figures for other years have been brought down in much the same way.   The corresponding changes elsewhere in the accounts have affected mainly long-term capital and the 'balancing item'.   Thus the calls upon the current surplus as officially estimated have been scaled down in much the same way as the surplus itself, so that the starting point for forecasts of the future has changed.

But even if a common basis of comparison existed, and the former estimates were accepted as valid in their own contexts, the requirements of the mid-1970s are unlikely to be the same as those of the 1950s.   The claims envisaged both in 1953 and 1959 were to a considerable extent non-recurring ones which have already been met.   On the other hand there are others, such as private investment and official aid, which assume greater importance as trade expands and the needs of the developing countries become more apparent.

The framework adopted here—of determining, at the end of the analysis, the surplus required of exports over imports of manufactured goods—is a framework chosen as one convenient and logical way of setting out the issues. It does not, of course, mean that all the other items in the balance of payments are fixed, and that it is only trade in manufactures which can be varied, or which is amenable to policy.   Policies can be, and indeed no doubt will be, brought to bear on other sectors of the accounts as well: and so some assumptions have to be made about them before projections can be made.   The following paragraphs set out the main policy assumptions, and also those about trends in the world economy in general.

Perhaps the main policy assumption which has to be made, before a target is fixed for the surplus required on current account, is about the size of aid to developing countries[2].   Currently, the British government's official contribution is about £150 million a year (net of repayments of principal).   To this can be added about £100 million of commercial investment in developing

---

[1]Committee on the Working of the Monetary System, *Minutes of Evidence* (London, 1960), pp. 938–9.

[2]Part of this aid is in the form of loans, and part in the form of grants: so it is divided between the capital and current accounts in the balance of payments.   However, there is not much difference between loans and grants in their impact on the British economy, and any forecast of the division of aid between the two forms is bound to be arbitrary.   So both forms of aid are considered together here.

countries. Together, the two make up about 1 per cent of national income—roughly in line with current United Nations targets. For the projection, we have assumed that aid to developing countries will rise by 1975 to £450 million—made up of some £350 million of official aid, and £100 million of commercial investment. As this is a rate of increase of over 5 per cent per annum, it probably implies that a slightly higher proportion of national income than at present will by then be going into aid. We have not allowed, however, for any revolutionary change in the scale of provision.

If in fact aid were to become very much more important than it is now in the hierarchy of objectives of economic policy, then the figures could be very much larger. For 1 or 1¼ per cent of national income does not in any sense represent a limit to what Britain could 'afford', in terms of real resources. Particularly if the government of the day were able both to tie the additional aid given to the supply of British goods, and also to ensure that the resources required were withdrawn from home consumption, and not from commercial exports, then both the aid and the export figures in our statistical projection might be much larger, and the figure for total domestic use of resources correspondingly smaller.

Another policy assumption which lies behind the figure of the current surplus required in 1975 concerns Britain's reserves and liabilities; we assume that it will still be a concern of policy to try to improve the ratio of reserves and other short-term assets to liabilities. It is conceivable that during the next decade the international monetary system might be radically reorganized—for instance, in such a way that Britain's sterling liabilities became liabilities of an international organization instead, and that Britain accepted a funded debt to that organization. If this were to happen, Britain would presumably have a contractual obligation to repay the debt; so this possible reorganization of the international monetary system would not necessarily make any difference to the size of the required surplus on current account. It could merely mean that what had previously been a general policy objective, without any specific figure attached to it, would become a fixed obligation to repay certain sums on certain dates.

Thirdly, we assume that in 1975 there will be no more restrictions on the movement of long-term capital in and out of the country than there are at present: indeed, there may be fewer. As a consequence, both the inflow and outflow of private capital is assumed to continue to rise between now and then.

Given these various policy assumptions then, the current balance of payments surplus required in 1975 might be of the order of £550 million: table 4.1 illustrates how this total is made up. The figures are meant to indicate rough orders of magnitude only.

We have assumed, fairly arbitrarily, that £100 million of official aid is in the form of grants and so included in the current account: but whether the proportion given in grant form is greater or less than this does not matter much

Table 4.1. *The composition of the current surplus required in 1975:* £ *million*

Official loans to developing countries (net of repayments)	250
Private net long-term capital outflow to developing countries	100
Other net official long-term capital outflow	50
Other net private capital outflow	150
Improvement of balance between reserves and net short-term liabilities	50
Less Balancing item	− 50
Surplus required on current account	550

(unless the interest charges were to be so high that the object of the aid was defeated). For if a larger part of aid is in the form of loans, then the current surplus on invisible account will be correspondingly greater, and vice versa. We also assume that the balancing item—the 'errors and omissions' item—continues to be positive, as in the past: and that it is roughly as big as the annual improvement required in the balance between reserves and net short-term liabilities.

Turning to the invisible account, perhaps the main policy assumption (apart from the figure for aid in the form of grants) is about the scale of overseas military expenditure. This has risen rapidly in the last decade. If there were a general move towards world disarmament, or if forces under the control of the United Nations assumed much wider responsibilities, then the figure might fall. This sort of assumption, however, can hardly be written into a statistical projection of this kind; we have assumed that the figure does rise much more slowly in the future than in the past—but we have not postulated any radical change in defence policy.

There are two other main points about the general economic setting of the projections. One is about the terms of trade. We assume some further deterioration in the terms of trade of the developing countries. It is, however, quite possible that prices of primary products might keep pace with the prices of manufactures, or even outstrip them—either through new market forces or through organized commodity schemes. If that were to happen and the benefits were to extend fairly generally to developing countries, then it would be logical to regard the target for aid and the related current surplus objective as less pressing. Nevertheless circumstances could arise in which a large increase in the prices of primary products could not be accommodated in this way. The projected improvement in the volume of net exports and invisible earnings would then be inadequate. But, since on this assumption the primary producing countries would be much more prosperous, the outlook for British exports would then be brighter.

The second point is about the price assumptions in the projections. The balance of payments has to balance—obviously—at current prices. It does not have to balance in any given year at the prices of some other year, and in fact would only do so if the terms of trade, in the widest sense, themselves remained constant.   If the terms of trade improve, this makes it easier (prima facie at any rate) to achieve a given surplus; if they worsen the converse applies. Partly for this reason, and partly because of the difficulty of distinguishing in any detail the effects of price changes in the past, the discussion here is in terms of current prices.   Price changes are for the most part mentioned only when there is reason to think that their net effect is likely to be significantly different in the future from what it has been in the past.

2. NET CLAIMS ON THE CURRENT SURPLUS

(a) *Short-term capital and reserves*

The need to improve the balance between reserves and short-term liabilities was discussed in the Treasury's note to the Radcliffe Committee which has already been quoted[1].   The relevant paragraphs read as follows:

'Ever since the war, a great weakness in the external position of the United Kingdom has been the existence of short-term liabilities too greatly in excess of the reserves of gold and convertible currencies.   This makes sterling vulnerable to confidence movements, because of the possibility that the reserves may approach or even fall below a comfortable working level.   From a domestic point of view, an exchange crisis may compel more drastic action than would be desirable if there were more freedom of manoeuvre.   It is therefore an important objective to reduce the excess of short liabilities over reserves.   This means that surpluses on current account should exceed net long-term investment.

In considering the potential stability of the whole system, however, it is necessary to consider not only the arithmetical difference between total reserves and liabilities, but the ratio between them, and the composition of the liabilities themselves.   The ability to withstand a drain will depend to a considerable extent on the absolute size of the reserves at the beginning of the drain.   These reserves are needed to finance any temporary deficit in the United Kingdom balance of payments on current and long-term capital account combined, as well as to meet withdrawals of sterling balances.   It follows from this that a reduction in any of the sterling holdings is inadequate compensation for an equal fall in the reserves. Experience has shown, moreover, that there is a significant difference between the attitude of the various holders, which corresponds roughly to the difference between the sterling area countries (RSA) and the rest of the world.   In the crises through which sterling has passed, a major factor has normally been the liquidation of the balances held by non-sterling area countries.   The sterling area on the whole has shown much more cohesion.

---

[1] *Minutes of Evidence, loc. cit.*, pp. 937–8.

Thus a reduction in the sterling holdings of the RSA improves the position less, in relation to what may happen in a subsequent crisis, than an equal reduction in the holdings of the non-sterling world.

In order to increase the stability of the system, it is therefore desirable not only that the current surplus should be enough to match net long-term investment, but that in addition the balance of liquid assets and liabilities should be improved. This means that we should aim at a current surplus which makes provision for moderate reductions in the sterling holdings so that these reductions are not met out of the reserves. Indeed the reserves need to be increased. While it might not be feasible to cover a very substantial fall in sterling holdings over a short period out of the current surplus, the aim in such circumstances should be to improve somewhat the present *ratio* of reserves to liabilities, even if the absolute level of the reserves declines. A further requirement, in view of the instability of the holdings of non-sterling countries, is that any increase in these particular holdings should be matched by a corresponding increase in the reserves.'

On this view, the extent of the arithmetical improvement required depends on the relationship—not greatly changed as yet—between the various assets and liabilities involved. A modest annual net gain should be sufficient if much of it could be added to the reserves (especially now that international co-operation has been improved and will probably be developed still further). But to avoid dangerous losses of reserves it would be necessary to budget for something bigger if large falls in sterling balances or other forms of short-term capital outflow, particularly to the non-sterling area, were to be expected. In practice it is clearly impossible to predict short-term capital movements over a given twelve months still ten years distant. It is, however, possible to form some view, if no more than a very tentative one, as to whether in the mid-1970s any markedly adverse trend is probable. This in fact is all that matters. Temporary fluctuations can within reason be afforded in 1975 as in any other year.

In previous forecasts of the balance of payments over a period of years it has commonly been assumed that substantial net drawings on sterling balances would occur in the fairly near future—whenever this might be[1]. In fact, however, this has not happened. Other countries' holdings of sterling were almost exactly the same at 31 December 1962 as they had been twelve or fifteen years previously in money terms (though in terms of their purchasing power over imports they had of course been appreciably reduced). The proportion held within the sterling area was also much the same as it had been at the end of 1950 although there had been intermediate fluctuations both in the total and in the area distribution (see table 4.2).

Holdings of sterling by particular groups of countries have shown some important changes. The balances of Ceylon, India and Pakistan fell by about

[1]See, for example, *Economic Survey for 1953*, pp. 43–4.

Table 4.2. *Overseas sterling holdings*[a]: *£ million at end of year*

	1950	1952	1954	1956	1958	1960	1962
Ceylon, India and Pakistan	787	648	652	541	228	198	138
Jordan, Libya and Persian Gulf	19	35	100	211	310	368	413
Brunei, Burma, Hong Kong and Malaysia	279	423	420	490	507	678	749
Australia, New Zealand and South Africa	640	429	485	371	383	285	452
Other sterling area countries:							
African	426	593	755	720	652	529	427
Other	346	354	410	397	439	420	496
All sterling area countries	2,497	2,482	2,822	2,730	2,519	2,478	2,675
Non-sterling area countries	986	737	881	692	834	1,405[b]	826
All countries	3,483	3,219	3,703	3,422	3,353	3,883	3,501

Source: **Bank of England Quarterly Bulletin,** December 1963, pp. 276–7.

[a]These comprise British government and government-guaranteed stocks (if held by or for the account of banks and other official bodies overseas), as well as other net assets, in sterling or other sterling area currencies, of overseas holders, official or private, with banks in the United Kingdom, or with the Crown Agents for Oversea Governments and Administrations. A fuller description is given in the source. The series does not extend beyond 1962.

[b]Includes a temporary holding of £131 million by the Ford Motor Company of the United States.

£650 million between 1950 and 1962. Data published by the International Monetary Fund suggest that Egyptian balances probably fell over the same period by some £250 million. If so, there must have been a net rise of some £900 million in other countries' balances. The Persian Gulf territories account for a large part of this. Their balances combined with those of Libya and Jordan increased from £19 million in 1950 to £413 million in 1962. There were also big rises in the balances of Far Eastern members of the sterling area, principally Malaysia and Hong Kong. The holdings of the former African colonies increased for a time but have since declined. The rest have fluctuated.

There is still no sign of any permanent downward tendency. Indeed, from the new series of the United Kingdom's net external liabilities in sterling, it seems probable that the balances have risen since the end of 1962. Nor, except in the Persian Gulf area and perhaps Hong Kong, are there holdings now which are far in excess of reserve requirements on the old Indian or Egyptian pattern. As Kuwait's spending capacity and aid to other Arab countries increase, it is unlikely that balances there will go on rising as they did in the last decade, but there are now indications that Abu Dhabi may become the Kuwait of the next decade. Libya's income also will probably be very large in relation to its needs.

The most reasonable hypothesis for the period around 1975 seems to be that the total of other countries' holdings of sterling will be neither rising nor falling.

It seems unlikely also that any change will be occurring in the area distribution such as would substantially affect Britain's own reserve requirements, though, if anything, non-sterling area countries' balances may be rising with the growth of trade, and the rest falling because of development programmes in some of the sterling area countries. It is, of course, quite possible that for political or other reasons the Persian Gulf states might abandon sterling as their reserve currency or further diversify their holdings. If so, the effect on Britain could be quite serious. This sort of thing is, however, quite unpredictable and can hardly be taken into account in the context of 1975 or any other particular year.

British transactions with the International Monetary Fund—the payment of an additional subscription in sterling in 1959 and purchases and resales of non-sterling area currencies in various years—have produced some big changes in the Fund's holdings of sterling. Again, however, there is no reason to expect any transactions of this kind in 1975.

On other short-term capital items apart from the reserves there has on balance been a small net outflow of capital (see table 4.3). This seems likely to continue. At times in the last few years there have been substantial inflows of funds to local authorities, but now that their facilities with the Public Works Loan Board have been improved there is no particular reason to expect that they will be borrowing from abroad in 1975. At the same time the expansion of trade and particularly of exports will probably mean a progressive increase in the net amount of normal commercial credit extended to borrowers overseas, though there will probably be less sterling credit made available to other countries through the International Bank for Reconstruction and Development and the International Monetary Fund[1].

On the whole it seems reasonable to expect some small net outflow of short-term capital, but a surplus of £50 million a year should be sufficient to cover this and perhaps allow United Kingdom reserves to rise in line with those of the world as a whole[2].

A case could clearly be made for a much bigger addition to the reserves in view of the size of Britain's liabilities compared with those of other countries.

[1]Other countries borrowed about £20 million of sterling a year through the IBRD between 1957 and 1960. This virtually exhausted the funds available. Drawings of sterling through the IMF were at a similar rate over the ten years 1953–62, but they are likely to be small in future now that sterling can be used for repayments as well as borrowing. Indeed in 1963 there was a small net repayment of sterling.

[2]The United Kingdom accounts for about 6 per cent of the gold held by official institutions outside the Sino-Soviet bloc. Over the past decade these institutions have received just about half the gold produced in the non-Communist world. If output continues to increase at about the same rate (5 per cent per annum) as in the past ten years or so, its value in 1975 should be about £850 million, of which on past experience official institutions might be expected to receive some £425 million. On this basis an addition of £25 million to United Kingdom reserves, which are held predominantly in the form of gold, would be needed to maintain their share of the total.

Table 4.3. *Short-term capital account: £ million, annual rates*

	1952 -63	1952 -57	1958 -63	1958	1959	1960	1961	1962	1963
Changes[a] in:									
Other countries' sterling holdings[b]	+ 5	−51	+60	+ 80	+154	+376	−337	− 45	+131
IMF sterling holdings[c]	+39	+27	+51	—	+103	+127	+386	−308	—
Miscellaneous short-term assets and liabilities[b]	−13	− 9	−16	+ 2	+ 29	−136	− 38	+ 78	− 31
Reserves	−10	+ 4	−23	−284	+119	−177	− 31	+183	+ 53
Total short-term capital, etc.[b]	+22	−29	+72	−202	+405	+190	− 20	− 92	+153

Source: Central Statistical Office, *United Kingdom Balance of Payments, 1964* and *Economic Trends*.

[a] A plus sign denotes a rise in liabilities or fall in assets, a minus sign the reverse.
[b] The coverage is not the same for 1963 as for earlier years.
[c] Includes only changes due to the additional sterling subscription paid in 1959 and to purchases and resales by the United Kingdom of the currencies of other countries. Other changes in IMF sterling holdings are included in 'miscellaneous short-term assets and liabilities'.

But the machinery for dealing with temporary balance of payments difficulties of individual countries has been strengthened considerably in recent years and will probably be improved still further. Thus, even without this, sterling should be assured of international support in case of sudden need to a much greater extent than in the past. The need to rely on national reserves is correspondingly reduced, and it does not seem necessary to budget for any larger annual increment in the reserves if at the same time net short-term liabilities are declining even to a modest extent.

(b) *Private long-term capital*

There is in general no exchange control on the movement of private long-term (or short-term) capital from Britain to other parts of the sterling area. (The only exception is that since July 1957 United Kingdom residents have not been free to buy non-sterling securities from other sterling area residents.) Outflows to the non-sterling area are, however, controlled. Portfolio investment is in general not permitted, though there are certain exceptions, notably in favour of other countries in the European Free Trade Association. Direct investment may be allowed on terms which have varied from time to time. But since May 1962 direct investment not approved on its own merits can be financed by the sale of non-sterling securities to non-residents of the sterling area. (This has the effect of increasing the cost to the investor, since within the sterling area such securities command a premium, which at times has been large, over their normal market price.) As from April 1964, the same arrangements apply to purchases of property from the non-sterling area, in which there was formerly a separate market (also involving the payment of a premium by purchasers).

There has been a good deal of fluctuation in total movements of private long-term capital, due only in part to known abnormalities such as heavy buying in some years, particularly 1956 and 1957, of United States and Canadian securities, the sales of the Trinidad Oil Company in 1956, and the minority holdings in the Ford Motor Company in 1961 (see table 4.4) and the acquisition by Shell in 1964 of a share in Montecatini's petrochemical interests. No clear trend emerges despite the change from a net outflow of about £150 million in 1953 and 1954 to a small net inflow from 1961 to 1963. In the early 1950s the outflow was stimulated by the high level of commodity prices in the Korean boom and by the relatively low level of domestic interest rates. High interest rates in 1961 and the early part of 1962, combined with the more restrictive policies then in force, helped to produce the opposite effect. In the intervening period the outflow showed some tendency to rise, after the initial check which accompanied the sharp rise in interest rates in 1954 and 1955. But 1956 and 1957 were both abnormal years, at least for oil investment, because of the Suez crisis and the purchase of new concessions in Venezuela.

Interpretation is difficult except in general terms because of the absence of detail in the official statistics, and particularly because of the blanket of secrecy that covers the operations of the oil companies. As from 1958 the Board of Trade has published an analysis of direct investment other than by oil and

Table 4.4.   *Total private long-term investment*[a]: *£ million*

Year	Outward	Inward	Net	Yield on long-term government securities Per cent
1952	127	13	114	*4·25*
1953	173	28	145	*3·95*
1954	238	75	163	*3·55*
1955	182	122	60	*4·24*
1956	258	139	119[b]	*5·13*
1957	298	126	172	*5·46*
1958	307	165	142	*5·54*
1959	311	176	135	*5·23*
1960	314	228	86	*5·77*
1961	321	416[c]	−95	*6·27*
1962	253	250	3	*5·89*
1963	309	259	50	*5·29*

Source: Central Statistical Office, *United Kingdom Balance of Payments, 1964, Economic Trends* and *Monthly Digest of Statistics.*

[a]Net of disinvestment.
[b]Includes the sale for £63 million of the Trinidad Oil Company, with interests inside as well as outside the United Kingdom.
[c]Includes the sale to the Ford Motor Company of the United States of holdings in the United Kingdom firm, to the value of £131 million.

insurance companies. We, therefore, discuss this investment first. For private long-term capital flows of other types only aggregate figures have been given, except for portfolio investment from 1960 onwards. The aggregates include direct investment by oil and insurance companies, as well as all identified portfolio investment in securities excluded from the sterling holdings series (see footnote (a) to table 4.2), miscellaneous investment of various kinds, for example in building societies or real estate, and a few special items such as compensation from Egypt for sequestrated British assets.

(i) *Direct investment* (*other than by oil and insurance companies*). What does clearly emerge, from the Board of Trade's analysis of direct investment other than by oil and insurance companies, is that these particular flows, both inward and outward, have been increasing fast. Of the total estimated book value of £3,600 million, net of depreciation, for British investment overseas at

Table 4.5.   *Direct private long-term investment*[a]: *£ million*

	Overseas sterling area	North America	Western Europe	Other countries	Total	Capital acquisitions and unremitted profits of subsidiaries	Changes in branch indebtedness and inter-company accounts
United Kingdom investment overseas							
1958	79	38	14	13	144	115	29
1959	106	52	20	18	196	145	51
1960	155	45	26	21	247	165	82
1961	128	37	39	22	226	156	70
1962	116	18	52	19	205	159	46
1963	128				223	170	53
1958–63 annual average	119				207	152	55
Overseas investment in United Kingdom							
1958	10	72	6	−1	87	65	22
1959	8	120	18	—	146	131	15
1960	14	104	16	1	135	102	33
1961	10	202	24	—	236	207	29
1962	2	102	24	2	130	107	23
1963	9				150	125	25
1958–63 annual average	9				147	123	24

Source: Board of Trade Journal and Central Statistical Office, *United Kingdom Balance of Payments, 1964.*

[a]All figures are net of disinvestment. They exclude transactions of oil companies and, except in 1963, of insurance companies.

the end of 1962, over £1,000 million can be accounted for by investment in the previous five years.   For foreign assets in this country, which are predominantly American, investment during this period constituted a much higher proportion still: all but half of a total book value at the end of 1962 of £1,500 million. Within the last six years also the rate of investment has risen rapidly, particularly on the inward side.   Both for United Kingdom and for foreign investment, increases in holdings on inter-company accounts reached a peak in 1960 from which they have since declined (see table 4.5), but their inclusion here is rather questionable.   In general items which are more clearly long-term are continuing to rise, but probably more slowly than before, though establishment of the European Economic Community and European Free Trade Association seems to have provided a great stimulus to the flow of capital to and from the Continent.

There may be particular years of balance of payments difficulty in which the Government takes steps to restrict direct investment overseas, particularly in the non-sterling world; but it is a reasonable policy assumption (though not, of course, a certain one) that such intervention would be short-lived, and that the long-term trend is for a continued increase in both the inward and the outward flows.   Lower interest rates in this country would in themselves tend to stimulate the normal net outflow.   On the other hand relatively faster expansion here should have the opposite effect.   In 1975 outward investment might perhaps be put at £375 million, and inward at £250 million.   Each of these figures represents an annual rate of increase of about 4 per cent on the 1958–63 average.

(ii) *Other private long-term capital.* On other private long-term capital (including portfolio investment and oil companies' investment) there has been a change from a net outflow of about £85 million in both 1958 and 1959 to a net inflow averaging just over £50 million a year in the next four years.

Overseas investment by British oil companies fell away at the beginning of the present decade, though it is known to have risen again since, and to have been particularly high in the first half of 1964.   Investment in this country by foreign oil companies has apparently fluctuated, but has tended to increase. In 1963 the two flows were approximately in balance, but this seems to have been quite exceptional[1].   The book value at the end of 1962 of the net assets abroad of British oil companies is estimated at £1,100 million, compared with only £700 million for the net assets in Britain of Continental and American companies[2].

Oil investment generally has been less buoyant in the 'free world' in the last few years, partly because of the declining rates of profit.   But a further rapid rise is generally expected in the future.   For example, one authority has predicted an increase of about 75 per cent at constant prices between 1960 and

[1]See *Economic Trends*, June 1962, p. xv and March 1964, p. iv.
[2]See *Bank of England Quarterly Bulletin*, March 1964, pp. 27 and 30.

1975 on admittedly conservative assumptions about the growth of demand[1]. Net investment by the United Kingdom thus seems likely to be much higher than it has recently been, particularly if the British companies continue to increase their share of world trade (see page 140).

On portfolio transactions there was a net inflow into this country between 1960 and 1963 which averaged £70 million a year, although it was as high as £119 million in 1961 and fell to £15 million in 1963. Issues for other countries on the London market (net of redemptions) accounted for an average net outflow of £11 million, but there were net sales of other portfolio holdings overseas by British investors, to the amount of £18 million a year on average. On balance, therefore, there was a small reduction in United Kingdom holdings overseas, and this was accompanied by a substantial net flow of overseas investors' funds into this country, mainly into British company securities and government stocks (in which investment up to 1959 is believed to have been very small). Including also small net additions to overseas holdings of securities and mortgages offered by local authorities in this country, portfolio investment, net of disinvestment, in this country averaged £63 million a year from 1960 to 1963 and ranged from £115 million in 1961 to £31 million in 1963.

It is difficult to predict what is likely to happen to portfolio investment in 1975. Much will depend on the conditions prevailing at the time, and particularly perhaps the degree of freedom accorded by the authorities in this country for United Kingdom residents to buy securities from residents of the non-sterling area. With the present restrictions, British securities held by non-residents are normally dealt in at a small discount, while non-sterling securities held by residents command a premium which at times during the last few years has been in the region of 15 per cent. This, however, does not necessarily mean that there would be substantial net transfers from non-resident to resident ownership on a free market. Demand for non-sterling securities has been artificially increased now that the proceeds of sales to non-residents of the sterling area can be used to finance direct investment in the non-sterling area which would not otherwise be allowed. Conversely, investors from the non-sterling area might be encouraged to put more of their money into this country if they could count on being able subsequently to repatriate their funds at the official rate.

On the whole it seems at the best improbable that the balance on portfolio transactions will remain as favourable as it has been in recent years. Relatively faster growth in this country should encourage the inflow of funds. On the other hand lower interest rates would tend to reduce it. It is likely, for example, that the relatively high rates ruling in 1961 and the early part of 1962 played an important part in stimulating the inflow of funds in this period. Also there

[1]See A. S. Ashton, 'Oil, Finance and the Future', *Esso Magazine*, Summer 1962, p. 3. Estimates by the Chase Manhattan Bank (*Future Growth of the World Petroleum Industry*, New York, 1961) point in much the same way.

have been substantial sales of South African securities in recent years and these can hardly continue for another decade[1]. Either British investors will take a more favourable view of the outlook in South Africa or their stock of holdings will become progressively exhausted. Much the same applies to investments in Southern Rhodesia and in African countries which have recently attained independence. Finally, if the balance of payments evolves satisfactorily between now and 1975, as we are assuming, any changes in exchange control regulations are likely on balance to be in the direction of greater freedom and to work to the detriment of the long-term capital account even if they increase net invisible earnings.

Altogether a net outflow of £125 million might be a reasonable allowance for the various types of private long-term capital not covered by the Board of Trade's inquiry into direct investment. Net investment by the oil companies is likely to be the main element.

(c) *Official long-term capital*

There is wide agreement that a further big increase is needed in the flow of aid to underdeveloped countries. A resolution was passed at the United Nations' Conference on Trade and Development at Geneva that industrial countries should aim at making available to the less developed countries financial resources equal to about 1 per cent of national incomes. The United Kingdom (which supported the resolution) is probably achieving the target already—thanks to the inclusion of private investment. This, however, falls into rather a different category from official aid. The British government's contribution, running at some £150 million a year, is roughly 0·7 per cent of national income, and slightly below the recent average for all the governments which are members of the Development Assistance Committee of OECD. A reasonable assumption might be that in the absence of any major changes in policy (page 109) the United Kingdom will move towards the figure of 1 per cent of national income which is sometimes suggested as a reasonable target. In the face of a price rise of perhaps 1 per cent per annum and an underlying annual rate of growth in gross national product of $3\frac{1}{2}$ per cent from 1960, this could mean increasing the net outflow to about £350 million[2].

Official aid is at present divided evenly between grants and loans. But as the number of colonies becomes fewer and fewer, the grant element—on present

---

[1]According to the Bank of England's estimates of transactions in overseas securities in which there are dealings on the London Stock Exchange or which have a registrar or buying agent in this country, United Kingdom residents' net sales of South African company securities alone amounted to £85 million in the five years from 1959 to 1963, despite restrictions imposed by the South African authorities (see *Bank of England Quarterly Bulletin* for June 1961, p. 31, June 1963, p. 119 and June 1964, p. 119).

[2]The Brookings Institution assumes a faster rate of increase—to £245 million by 1968. See Walter S. Salant and associates, *The United States Balance of Payments in 1968* (Washington, 1963), p. 187.

policies—is unlikely to rise much. On this assumption, loans, net of repayments, might be put at £250 million, but the distinction between grants and loans may not in any case have much real significance for the balance of payments in 1975.

Repayments on loans to developed countries are likely to be negligible in 1975, and it may be assumed that there will be no new lending in either direction between these countries and Britain. Loans to Britain should also have been repaid, apart from those from the United States and Canada, on which nearly £50 million will be due in 1975.

(d) *Total long-term capital*

On this basis and with some small miscellaneous items the net outflow of long-term capital in 1975 would be £550 million—£300 million official and £250 million private funds. These are very high figures by the standards of past years (see table 4.6). But private investment was actually running at about £300 million a year in the first half of 1961 and again in the first half of 1964, if the Ford and Montecatini deals are excluded. This was in spite of substantial sales of South African securities. The intervening decline, culminating in a net inflow of £50 million in 1963, seems to have been due to temporary factors—first the big inward portfolio investment and the restraints on direct investment overseas, and later a dip in oil investment. In the case of official capital an important reason for expecting a rise in net lending is that repayments to Britain for aid given to other governments of Western Europe during and immediately after the war will have been completed by 1975. The main cause is, however, the assumption of a deliberate policy of increasing aid to the underdeveloped countries.

(e) *Balancing item*

There is a tendency for the change in known monetary assets and liabilities such as the reserves to be more favourable than the balance on identified current and capital transactions. Part at least of the difference, which is officially known as the 'balancing item', is believed to represent unidentified net current earnings. The item fluctuates a great deal and in individual years has at times been a minus quantity. But it seemed until recently that the underlying positive element had risen to something like £100 million a year and might well increase further as the volume of transactions grew[1].

In the last two or three years some additional receipts on current account have been identified. The latest periods have been the most affected, with the result that, for the present at any rate, the balancing item has become smaller on average and its rising trend seems to have disappeared. Indeed for 1963

[1]See Treasury, *United Kingdom Balance of Payments, 1959 to 1961*, Cmnd 1671 (London, 1962), p. 8.

Table 4.6. *Long-term capital account: £ million, annual rates*

	1952–7	1958–63	1958	1959	1960	1961	1962	1963
Private direct investment[ab]								
Outward	..	−207	−144	−196	−247	−226	−205	−223
Inward	..	+147	+87	+146	+135	+236	+130	+150
Balance	..	− 60	− 57	− 50	−112	+ 10	− 75	− 73
Portfolio investment[a]								
Outward	..	..	..	..	+ 28	+ 4	+ 12	− 16
Inward	..	..	..	..	+ 43	+115	+ 64	+ 31
Balance	..	+ 6	− 85	− 85	+ 71	+119	+ 76	+ 15
Other private long-term capital (net)	..				− 45	− 34	− 4	+ 8
Total private long-term capital (net)	−129	− 54	−142	−135	− 86	+ 95	− 3	− 50
IMF subscription	—	− 39	—	−232	—	—	—	—
Loans to HMG from other governments								
Borrowings	+ 19	+ 9	—	+ 37	—	+ 18	—	—
Repayments	− 50	− 81	− 60	−183	− 72	− 82	− 44	− 45
Loans from HMG to other governments[a]								
Western Europe	+ 23	+ 35	+ 23	+ 63	+ 28	+ 97	—	—
Other	− 5	− 40	− 7	− 35	− 48	− 49	− 47	− 52
Other official long-term capital (net)	− 14	− 12	− 6	− 6	− 10	− 29	− 13	− 8
Total official long-term capital (net)	− 27	−127	− 50	−356	−102	− 45	−104	−105
Total long-term capital (net)	−156	−181	−192	−491	−188	+ 50	−107	−155

Source: Central Statistical Office, *United Kingdom Balance of Payments, 1964* and *Economic Trends.*

[a]Figures are net of disinvestment and repayments.
[b]Excluding oil and excluding insurance except in 1963.

there was a change to a negative entry of about £100 million. But it is probably best to assume that this was no more than a temporary fluctuation, due to unidentified movements of short-term capital, such as has occurred on previous occasions, and to make some allowance for a positive item in 1975[1].

(f) Implied current surplus

If the balancing item is put at £50 million, which is equal to the postulated improvement in the short-term capital position, a net outflow of long-term capital of £550 million (at current prices) in 1975 implies a current surplus

[1]*Economic Trends*, March 1964, p. vi and *National Institute Economic Review*, March 1964, pp. 12–14.

Table 4.7. *Summary balance of payments: £ million, annual rates*

	1952–7	1958–63	1958	1959	1960	1961	1962	1963
Private long-term capital	−129	− 54	−142	−135	− 86	+ 95	− 3	− 50
Official long-term capital	− 27	−127	− 50	−356	−102	− 45	−104	−105
Short-term capital (excluding reserves)	− 33	+ 95	+ 82	+286	+367	+ 11	−275	+100
Reserves (increase, −)	+ 4	− 23	−284	+119	−177	− 31	+183	+ 53
Identified capital balance	−185	−108	−394	− 86	+ 2	+ 30	−199	− 2
Balancing item		+ 67	+ 30	+ 49	− 67	+256	− 29	+ 84	−111
Identified current balance	+118	+ 78	+345	+153	−258	− 1	+115	+113

Source: Central Statistical Office, *United Kingdom Balance of Payments, 1964* and *Economic Trends.*

the same size. This is about £200 million above the biggest surplus so far achieved (in 1958), and it compares with an average of less than £100 million for the last twelve years (see table 4.7). But a higher capital outflow tends in itself to improve the current balance by increasing both exports and invisible earnings, in particular investment income. Moreover the deficit on visible trade has over a long period tended to decline (see page 148). The main trouble has been the big reduction in the surplus on invisibles. This has been largely due to factors which should have relatively much less force in future.

3. PROSPECTS FOR INVISIBLES[1]

In 1952 the invisible surplus was nearly £450 million; from 1960 to 1963 it averaged less than £150 million a year. One element in the decline has been a big worsening in the balance on shipping transactions. But this has been outweighed by rising surpluses on other items, particularly miscellaneous services and property income (see table 4.8). The main trouble has been the rising deficit on government account. With interest on government loans excluded, this has increased to something like £400 million from little more than £50 million in 1952. On other invisibles the surplus fell from about £500 million to £300 million between 1952 and 1955. Since then, however, it has risen again, with some fluctuations, to £550 million or thereabouts in 1962 and 1963.

[1]Throughout this chapter account has been taken, both in the estimates for past periods and in the projections, of the revisions of previously published figures which were made by the Central Statistical Office in *United Kingdom Balance of Payments, 1964, loc. cit.* It was, however, impracticable to carry the changes into the chapters concerned more specifically with national accounts and industrial output, where their effect would in any case have been unimportant in relation to the magnitudes involved. The main result is that the figures used in this chapter are more favourable for shipping and less favourable for travel and miscellaneous services than those used elsewhere. The differences cancel out on balance.

Table 4.8. *Invisibles: £ million, net annual rates*

	1952–7	1958–63	1958	1959	1960	1961	1962	1963
Government	−116	−305	−224	−233	−286	−335	−363	−387
Shipping	+ 31	− 4	+ 43	+ 16	− 32	− 28	− 12	− 11
Civil aviation	− 1	+ 18	+ 8	+ 18	+ 18	+ 20	+ 20	+ 23
Travel	− 9	− 23	− 18	− 20	− 15	− 19	− 20	− 45
Other services	+155	+214	+193	+201	+203	+235	+232	+219
Property income	+230	+292	+297	+270	+234	+244	+329	+377
Private transfers	− 3	+ 2	+ 5	+ 3	+ 6	+ 9	+ 1	− 14
Total	+287	+194	+304	+255	+128	+126	+187	+162

Source: Central Statistical Office, *United Kingdom Balance of Payments, 1964.*

(a) *Government*

There appear to be four main reasons for the big rise in net government expenditure overseas. The first is the cessation of defence aid from the United States government, the second is the cessation of direct contributions from the government of West Germany to the foreign exchange costs of the British troops there, the third is the big rises in pay and allowances for government employees, and particularly troops, serving overseas (or at home) and the fourth is the increase in the level of aid and other contributions to international causes.

Government receipts have fallen sharply during the past decade. At first this was due to the decline in defence aid, which came to an end during 1958, but the trend still seems to be slightly downward. The main element is military receipts, which include expenditure by United States and Canadian forces, contributions by other governments to the costs of common defence projects, and, probably, the proceeds of disposals of supplies to newly independent and other Commonwealth countries assuming increasing responsibilities for their own defence. Some of these are likely to diminish, for example the receipts from the United States. The United States Air Force is gradually relinquishing its bases in this country and it is now the policy of the United States government to achieve substantial reductions in procurement and other expenditure, especially in the more developed countries. On the other hand there should be higher receipts on other items, including co-operative undertakings in NATO. Altogether, therefore, receipts may recover a little to around the 1958–60 level of £50 million.

British military expenditure overseas has risen very sharply, particularly—on the net basis of estimation which is used—in West Germany. In the early 1950s the great bulk of the gross expenditure there, which has risen fairly steadily, was covered by contributions from the West German government. Subsequently these contributions followed an erratic but generally downward course until they ceased entirely in 1960[1]. Expenditure is now believed to b

[1]Press statements, etc. suggest that net expenditure in West Germany was about £4 million in 1958, £29 million in 1959, £45 million in 1960, £63 million in 1961 and perhaps £75 million in 1962 and £80 million in 1963.

Table 4.9. *Government overseas payments and receipts: £ million, annual rates*

	1952 –57	1958 –63	1958	1959	1960	1961	1962	1963	1975
Payments									
Military	151	212	180	167	206	225	243	251	275
Bilateral aid grants }	50	63	51	52	58	73	74	69	85
Other grants }		13	5	6	12	12	15	26	40
Subscriptions, etc. to international organizations	10	19	11	13	18	21	21	29	55
Other transfers	6	10	8	9	10	10	11	12	20
Other administrative and diplomatic, etc.	21	33	26	29	31	37	36	42	75
Total	238	350	281	276	335	378	400	429	550
Receipts									
Defence aid and other US grants (net)	64	—	3	—	—	—	—	—	—
US and Canadian forces' expenditure	23	18	25	18	21	16	17	12 }	}40
Other military } 36 {		22	27	22	24	20	13	25 }	
Other		5	2	3	4	7	7	5	10
Total	122	45	57	43	49	43	37	42	50
Net	−116	−305	−224	−233	−286	−335	−363	−387	−500
of which:									
Services	−117	−201	−152	−153	−188	−219	−242	−251	−300
Transfers	+ 1	−104	− 72	− 80	− 98	−116	−121	−136	−200

Source: Central Statistical Office, *United Kingdom Balance of Payments, 1964* and *Economic Trends;* and NIESR estimates.

running at about £85 million a year.   Other expenditure in the non-sterling area (about £25 million a year, including contributions to NATO infra-structure and other common defence projects) has remained below its previous level since the Suez operations and the abandonment of the former bases in Egypt. But, despite the ending of the emergencies in Malaya, Kenya and Cyprus, expenditure in the overseas sterling area more than doubled between 1950 and 1960 and still continues to rise.   Works expenditure on overseas bases—most of it presumably a charge to the balance of payments—increased particularly fast, notably in the area of Aden and the Persian Gulf[1].   Conversion of pay and allowances, which is probably the largest single element in the total, must also have risen sharply in recent years.   The size of the forces was halved between 1952 and 1963, but pay, etc. of service personnel rose by about 40 per cent.

Future expenditure largely depends on international developments and on military and political decisions.   According to the 1962 White Paper on defence, British garrisons overseas, other than those in Germany, were to be reduced

[1]See *Tenth Report from the Estimates Committee . . . Session 1962–63: Military Expenditure Overseas* (London, 1963), appendices I-IV.

progressively[1]. Previous pronouncements on the same lines have proved incorrect, but the movement towards independence of former colonial territories such as Kenya, Aden and Singapore seems almost bound to have this effect in course of time whether or not it is considered desirable on strategic or financial grounds. There should, in any case, be substantial savings in works expenditure with the completion of the new building programme caused by the post-Suez redeployment and by the need for additional married quarters following the ending of national service. Rates of pay, however, will probably go on rising, if more slowly, and, as on the receipts side, there may be higher contributions to joint allied undertakings, particularly in NATO. On balance total military expenditure overseas might be put at £275 million, that is about 12 per cent above the 1962–3 level.

Higher rates of salary and allowances must also have been one of the main causes of the big rise in transfers to persons (i.e. pension payments) and miscellaneous administrative and diplomatic expenditure. The latter doubled between 1955 and 1963, and continues to rise despite the government's proclaimed intention of cutting it. Even so the recent rate of increase can hardly continue, and given greater stability of prices and incomes, further rises by 1975 of 70 per cent for pension payments and 80 per cent for the rest should be an adequate allowance.

The assumptions already made about aid to the less developed countries imply that the grant element, consisting mainly of bilateral grants to other countries, will amount to £100 million in 1975. Other grants to overseas governments and payments to international organizations have increased from £16 million in 1959 to £43 million last year. The rise will probably continue but much more slowly, as the recent figures will have been inflated by grants to India and Malaysia for special military purposes and contributions to the cost of operations in the Congo by the United Nations.

(b) *Transport*

(i) *Shipping*. The balance of payments for shipping has worsened substantially over the past decade though it improved for a period around 1958 and to a minor extent between 1960 and 1962 (see table 4.10). On both these occasions the balance of visible trade was more favourable than usual, and tramp freight rates were falling, while liner freights remained high. (High rates are to Britain's advantage in the case of liners but probably not in the case of tramps, for which payments are believed normally to exceed receipts.)

Much the biggest worsening has been on charter hire. Though earnings from foreign chartering of British ships have risen steadily, and latterly quite fast, they remain quite small. But payments for foreign shipping chartered in

[1]See Ministry of Defence, *Statement on Defence, 1962: The Next Five Years*, Cmnd 1639 (London, 1962), pp. 4–12.

Table 4.10. *Shipping*[a]: £ million, annual rates

	1952	1958–63	1958	1959	1960	1961	1962	1963	1975
Freight on imports Total	−343	−408	−378	−391	−440	−417	−403	−417	−650
Less Paid to UK shipping	+218	+245	+235	+244	+256	+250	+243	+243	+360
Paid to foreign shipping	−125	−163	−143	−147	−184	−167	−160	−174	−290
Freight on exports earned by UK shipping	+145	+145	+150	+148	+148	+148	+135	+139	+190
Freight on cross-trades earned by UK shipping	+305	+341	+338	+328	+337	+341	+348	+355	+450
Balance on freight	+325	+323	+345	+329	+301	+322	+323	+320	+350
UK payments of passage money Total	− 31	− 36	− 34	− 34	− 31	− 34	− 39	− 41	− 60
Less Made to UK shipping	+ 26	+ 29	+ 28	+ 27	+ 25	+ 27	+ 33	+ 33	+ 50
Made to foreign shipping	− 5	− 7	− 6	− 7	− 6	− 7	− 6	− 8	− 10
Receipts of foreign passage money by UK shipping	+ 43	+ 51	+ 54	+ 52	+ 53	+ 48	+ 50	+ 51	+ 60
Balance on passage money	+ 38	+ 45	+ 48	+ 45	+ 47	+ 41	+ 44	+ 43	+ 50
Charter payments	− 54	−167	−137	−149	−172	−180	−180	−182	−300
Charter receipts	+ 17	+ 26	+ 23	+ 24	+ 24	+ 28	+ 32	+ 26	+ 50
Balance on charter hire	− 37	−141	−114	−125	−148	−152	−148	−156	−250
Disbursements abroad by UK shipping	−241	−306	−300	−299	−304	−313	−313	−307	−400
Disbursements in UK by foreign shipping	+ 49	+ 75	+ 64	+ 66	+ 72	+ 74	+ 82	+ 89	+150
Balance on disbursements	−192	−231	−236	−233	−232	−239	−231	−218	−250
Balance on shipping account *of which:*	+134	− 4	+ 43	+ 16	− 32	− 28	− 12	− 11	−100
UK shipping's net receipts from overseas trade	+459	+365	+391	+375	+367	+349	+348	+358	+460
Less receipts from UK	−244	−274	−263	−271	−281	−277	−276	−276	−410
Foreign shipping	+215	+ 91	+128	+104	+ 86	+ 72	+ 72	+ 82	+ 50
	− 81	− 95	− 85	− 88	−118	−100	− 84	− 93	−150

Source: Central Statistical Office, *United Kingdom Balance of Payments, 1964* and *Economic Trends*, and Chamber of Shipping of the United Kingdom, *Annual Report, 1962–63*, p. 228, and *1963–64*, p. 200.

[a] Foreign shipping on United Kingdom charter and United Kingdom shipping on foreign charter are included in United Kingdom and foreign shipping respectively.

this country more than trebled from 1952 to 1961. The main reason for this is understood to be that during the Suez crisis oil companies chartered tankers at very high rates for a number of years ahead. These charters are now running out and current rates for new fixtures are much lower. It is difficult to judge what the position may be in 1975. But from what is known of the companies' building programmes and assumed about the future level of their trade, a reasonable guess might be that in 1975 they will have over twice as much tonnage on charter as in 1963. This would mean that trade and chartering would rise at similar rates. The tankers chartered are predominantly foreign; of the world tonnage not owned by oil companies probably not more than 8 per cent was British at the end of 1963[1]. In view of the speed with which tankers can now be built, a reasonable balance can be expected in future between supply and demand. Hence rates are likely to move in line with operating costs, in which there is a downward trend because of falling building and fuel costs, improving port facilities and the use of bigger and faster ships[2]. The rates effective in 1975 might consequently be as much as 20 per cent lower than in 1963. Chartering of foreign dry cargo ships is likely to increase more slowly but is probably much less important. Thus, total overseas payments for chartering might be put at £325 million in 1975 compared with £182 million in 1963. Receipts, which have recently averaged between £25 million and £30 million, might reach £50 million.

Even with the use of all the foreign shipping chartered by the British industry its share of trade seems to have declined steadily. Tramp rates fell by about a fifth between 1952 and 1963 and liner rates rose by about a third. Yet the share of payments for freight on imports going to foreign shipping rose from 36 to 42 per cent and the amount involved by about 40 per cent. In the meanwhile British shipping's earnings on cross-trades went up by only a sixth while seaborne world trade more than doubled, and 4 per cent less was received from the carriage of United Kingdom exports, although their volume was 40 per cent higher.

Except in the United States, the industries of other major shipping countries for which figures are available all seem to have been increasing their earnings on ocean-going traffic (including receipts from their own residents) much faster than the British shipping industry (table 4.11). Moreover Britain's share of the world's ocean-going merchant fleet (in terms of gross tonnage) fell by one seventh between 1958 and 1963, from 17·7 to 15·2 per cent[3]. But these may be rather unfair comparisons. The emergence of new countries to independence, the increasing use of flags of convenience, and the rapid building

[1]See S. G. Sturmey, *British Shipping and World Competition* (London, 1962), p. 165, and Lloyd's Register of Shipping, *Statistical Tables, 1964.*

[2]See W. L. Newton, 'The long-term development of the tanker freight market', *Journal of the Institute of Petroleum*, September 1964, pp. 214–16.

[3]See Lloyd's Register of Shipping, *Statistical Tables, 1959* and *1964.*

Table 4.11. *International shipping earnings*[a]

	Value of earnings in 1958 US $m.	1952	1958	1959	1960	1961	1962	1963	1975
			Indices (1958 = 100)						
Gross earnings									
Denmark[b]	224	77	100	105	103	102	107		
West Germany[bc]	549	29[d]	100	101	109	113	120		
Italy[e]	450	61	100	95	116	124	130		
Japan	436	43	100	112	133	151	165		
Netherlands[f]	418	89	100	99	107	106			
Norway[b]	754	81	100	110	109	114	118		
United Kingdom	2,318	91	100	99	102	102	102	102	140
United States	1,015	123	100	96	101	97	100		
Freight earnings on cross-trades									
Italy	169	56	100	89	109	120	120		
Japan	70	35	100	90	81	73	71	75	
United Kingdom	946	90	100	97	100	101	103	105	133
United States	130	135	100	108	105	124	140		
Freight earnings on exports ÷ volume of exports									
Italy	38	46	100	93	80	75	71		
Japan	107	74	100	105	108	103	100	92	
United Kingdom	420	114	100	96	91	89	79	77	67
United States	429	142	100	86	89	89	84		
			Percentages						
Share of earnings in total freight on imports									
Denmark	17	*19*	*17*	*17*	*18*	*16*	*17*		
West Germany	157	*19*	*26*	*25*	*21*	*20*	*21*		
Italy	122	*45*	*44*	*37*	*36*	*35*	*36*		
Japan	259	*40*	*58*	*56*	*55*	*48*	*52*	*56*	
Norway	28	*59*	*57*	*57*	*51*	*55*	*53*		
United Kingdom	658	*64*	*62*	*63*	*58*	*60*	*60*	*58*	*55*
United States	336	*48*	*31*	*31*	*28*	*27*	*28*		
Share of earnings in total passenger payments									
Italy	45	*66*	*85*	*88*	*86*	*88*	*90*		
United Kingdom	78	*84*	*82*	*79*	*81*	*79*	*85*	*80*	*83*
United States	88	*34*	*35*	*32*	*28*	*21*	*19*		

Source: International Monetary Fund, *Balance of Payments Yearbook*, Chamber of Shipping of the United Kingdom, *Annual Report, 1962–63*, p. 228, and *1963–64*, p. 170, US Department of Commerce, *Balance of Payments: Statistical Supplement to the Survey of Current Business* (revised edition, 1963), pp. 136–9, and Industrial Bank of Japan, *Japanese Industries, 1964* (Tokyo, 1964), p. 200.

[a]Earnings by ocean-going ships including earnings from residents.
[b]Excludes passenger earnings from residents.
[c]Excludes earnings from charter hire.
[d]Includes a NIESR estimate of passenger earnings from non-residents.
[e]Includes aviation earnings except for exports and passenger fares from non-residents.
[f]Excludes tanker earnings.

K

of a Russian fleet, were bound to have adverse effects on the established shipping nations. The British industry, because of its former pre-eminence on the world's shipping routes, is particularly vulnerable to such competition. British shipping has also been handicapped by the relatively slow growth of sterling area trade and of United Kingdom exports in particular, and by the orientation of United Kingdom trade towards continental Europe and away from the more distant countries of the sterling area such as Australia.

The tendency for domestic shipping industries to receive a diminishing share of freight payments on imports seems to be common to most countries. Those few for which the relevant figures are available also show, like the United Kingdom, a considerably worsening ratio of freight earnings on exports to export volumes (that is if allowance is made for the period of recovery of the former Axis powers from their wartime losses). It is perhaps on cross-trades that the British industry's performance looks weakest in relation to that of other countries, but even here it has recently compared surprisingly well with Japan's, and the big loss of share to the United States since 1960 may be due to some extent to the expansion of the Canadian grain trade with the Communist countries.

In the case of trade in manufactures we have assumed that British industry will improve its share of trade by 1975 (see chapter 5). In the case of shipping some further loss of ground can hardly be avoided as more and more countries begin to develop national fleets. But consistency requires the assumption that British shipping will at any rate be more competitive than it has been in the past. At the same time freight rates are likely to improve. Liner rates will probably go on rising, perhaps more slowly, as they depend largely on costs. Tramp rates may be higher also, since it is unlikely that they will continue to be depressed, as they were at times in the early 1960s, by the existence of a substantial tonnage of laid-up shipping.

In chapter 5 we show the volume of both imports and exports as rising by about 60 per cent between 1963 and 1975, with the freight content of imports declining very slightly. Even if their share of the trade rises more slowly than in the past, payments to foreign shipowners for the carriage of imports might on this basis be expected to increase by about two thirds. Higher export earnings might, however, compensate for about half the worsening, and earnings on cross-trades should also improve substantially even if the expansion of world trade is rather slower than it has been in the past.

As a reflection of their growing share in British trade, foreign ships' disbursements in this country have been increasing at a faster rate than disbursements abroad by British ships. This tendency has become more marked in the last few years, when, presumably because of falling oil prices, British ships' fuel costs have declined. But their total foreign disbursements greatly exceed those of foreign ships in this country. Thus the balance has improved only marginally and may tend to worsen again as it did between 1952 and 1958 if oil prices become more stable.

On the assumption that the surplus on passage money will continue to rise a little, these forecasts imply that the deficit on shipping will rise to £100 million by 1975. The surplus of British shipping's foreign receipts over foreign payments, recently down to little more than a third of the 1952 figure of £215 million, would fall to £50 million. The industry's total net earnings from external trading, including receipts from British importers and passengers, would recover to their level of 1952. But at the same time net payments to foreign shipping, which in recent years have fluctuated around an average of rather less than £100 million, would rise to £150 million. In other words, the shipping industry as a whole will gain from a faster rise in British trade, but this will mean a faster deterioration in the balance of payments on shipping unless the British industry's competitiveness improves a good deal more than we have assumed.

(ii) *Civil aviation.* Debits and credits were close to balance throughout the years 1952–58, both rising during this period by some 70 per cent. From 1958 to 1961 on a rather different basis of estimation debits rose by 70 per cent but credits rose by 80 per cent. This meant that by 1963 there was a net surplus of £23 million, with credits nearly a quarter higher than debits. In the absence of any detailed analysis of the figures for the years before 1962 it is difficult to predict their future pattern. But a surplus of £50 million in 1975 seems likely to be somewhere near the mark.

(c) *Travel*

Net expenditure on travel was negligible ten years ago. After a gradual rise in the mid-1950s it fluctuated between £15 and £20 million from 1957 to 1962, but then jumped to £45 million in 1963. Between 1952 and 1963 the annual rates of increase were about $10\frac{1}{4}$ per cent for debits and $8\frac{1}{2}$ per cent for credits. They are not a good guide for the future, however, because they will have been affected by the easing of currency restrictions. In particular debits will have been stimulated by the easing of this country's regulations[1]. Similar moves by other countries, especially those in Western Europe, probably had a smaller impact, largely because the geographical distribution of payments and receipts is quite different. There is normally a substantial deficit with Western European countries (see table 4.12) partly balanced by a surplus with other areas and particularly the United States. Because of balance of payments difficulties the official American attitude towards foreign travel has been rather more restrictive in the last few years, and this has probably had some adverse effect on United Kingdom earnings.

Apart from the effects of changes in official policies and regulations, the

[1]The most important over the last ten years occurred late in 1954 when the annual allowance for holiday travel outside the sterling area was raised from £50 to £100, in the middle of 1957 when it became available for travel in the dollar area, and late in 1959 when restrictions were effectively removed.

THE BRITISH ECONOMY IN 1975

Table 4.12. *Travel*

£ *million, annual rates*

	1952–7	1958–63	1958	1959	1960	1961	1962	1963
Debits								
Overseas sterling area	42	47	40	39	44	49	55	58
Western Europe	⎫	130	101	112	127	135	139	166
North America	⎬ 70	11	8	9	10	11	12	13
Other countries	⎭	5	3	4	5	5	6	7
Total	113	193	152	164	186	200	212	244
Credits								
Overseas sterling area	42	61	50	50	60	67	71	68
Western Europe	⎫	39	27	32	37	41	46	53
North America	⎬ 62	55	49	52	59	55	56	58
Other countries	⎭	15	8	10	15	18	19	20
Total	104	170	134	144	171	181	192	199
Balance	−9	−23	−18	−20	−15	−19	−20	−45

Source: Central Statistical Office, *United Kingdom Balance of Payments, 1964* and *Economic Trends.*

underlying trend of the travel balance seems to have been quite favourable. This, however, must be due partly to the fact that the British economy has been expanding more slowly than that of the Continental countries. A fast rise in incomes is clearly associated with an even faster rise in travel expenditure (see figure 4.1). Moreover, United Kingdom travel earnings rose more slowly between 1954 and 1963 than those of any of the major Continental countries except Switzerland. This is partly because Europeans, whose expenditure has risen particularly fast, provide a smaller proportion of total travel earnings for the United Kingdom than for the Continental countries. Even so, this expenditure has been rising more slowly in this country than in continental Europe. On the other hand Britain's share of American tourists' expenditure in Europe and the Mediterranean area has remained fairly steady over the past ten years at around 16–17 per cent (compared with 23 per cent in 1937).

It is mainly the rising income from the United States which has enabled Western Europe as a whole to improve its balance on travel account so markedly. The number of American visitors to Western Europe and the Mediterranean is nearly three times as big as it was ten years ago. It is also nearly three times as large as the number of Europeans travelling to the United States. For Britain the ratio was as high as four to one (539 thousand coming from the United States against 138 thousand going there in 1963). The number coming to Europe by sea has risen by less than a quarter in ten years, but arrivals by air have increased five-fold and now account for well over three quarters of the total, thanks partly to declining average rates of fare[1]. The

[1]*Survey of Current Business*, June 1963, pp. 27–32.

Fig. 4.1. National incomes and travel expenditure and receipts, 1954-63: annual percentage increase at current prices

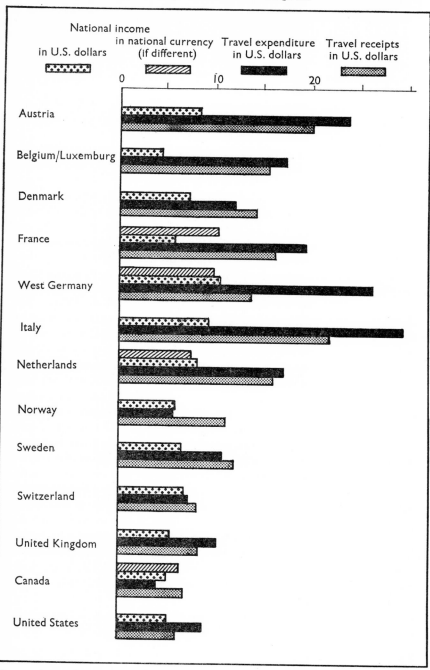

Source: Appendix table 4.1.

recent big reductions in transatlantic air fares have further accelerated these trends. According to the Brookings Institution, United States travel expenditure in Western Europe is likely to rise by about 75 per cent at constant prices between 1961 and 1968 and Western European travel expenditure in the United States to be approximately doubled[1]. This would mean a rise of over 70 per cent in the United States deficit.

On balance higher traffic across the Atlantic should benefit Britain. For most British tourists a trip to North America is probably an alternative to a Continental holiday; it may be more costly, but no great increase in net expenditure is likely to result. There will be some corresponding diversion of Europeans who would otherwise come to this country, but this should be far outweighed by the potential increase in visitors from North America. Stabilization of the deficit at something like the current level thus seems a reasonable aspiration for 1975. As payments were nearly 25 per cent higher than receipts in 1963 this means that over the next ten or twenty years the rise in receipts will need to be substantially greater. This is probably conditional on a much greater effort to improve roads and, perhaps even more important, to increase accommodation. Big rises must be expected in the numbers of travellers, particularly with a channel tunnel. The British Travel Association expects twice as many visitors as in 1963 to be coming here even by 1970.

The increase in available tourist accommodation since 1958 has varied greatly between the various Continental countries according to OECD statistics[2]. For Italy it is over 50 per cent; for most of the others much less. Nowhere, however, is it anything like so small as the 8 per cent recorded for the United Kingdom[3]. Moreover the pressure on accommodation in 1958 was probably much greater already here than it was, for example, in Italy and France—the only Continental countries whose gross receipts from travel are as large as our own. The number of available beds in relation to the number of travellers who arrive from overseas is much higher here, but the average length of stay is also very much greater. (This, however, is mainly because those who come from other parts of the Commonwealth often do so for long periods—the average was two months in 1963—and for the most part do not occupy what is normally classed as tourist accommodation.) Furthermore, in this country tourists from overseas (rather more than 2 million in 1963) are only a small fraction (about 6 or 7 per cent) of the total holidaymakers. In France the $6\frac{1}{2}$ million incoming travellers in 1963 probably accounted for more than a fifth of the total and the $10\frac{1}{2}$ million Italians taking holidays in their own country only just about equalled the number of visitors. (Figures exclude excursionists for both France and Italy.)

[1] W. S. Salant and Associates, *The United States Balance of Payments in 1968* (Washington, 1963), p. 57.
[2] *Tourism in OECD Member Countries.*
[3] This is on the assumption that the sharp fall recorded for France since 1961 is due to some change in classification.

(d) *Other services*

This item includes payments and receipts in respect of education, films, royalties, fees and banking facilities (excluding interest earnings); on the debit side it includes sales of gold for industrial use, and on the credit side net earnings from insurance (up to 1963) and merchanting, private receipts from the expenditure of foreign government agencies in the United Kingdom, and the personal expenditure of United States and Canadian service personnel[1].

From 1952–3 to 1962–3 credits rose rather faster than debits—probably at about $5\frac{1}{2}$ per cent against $4\frac{1}{2}$ per cent per annum. But in the second half of the period the position was the other way round. The annual rate of increase was 5 per cent for debits and probably not more than $4\frac{1}{2}$ per cent for credits[2]. Moreover in both cases there has been a marked slowing down in the most recent years although the general easing of exchange controls both here and in other countries, and particularly the restoration of convertibility for the major European currencies at the end of 1958, will have helped to increase the turnover of financial transactions. But at the same time credits will have been adversely affected by declines in the profitability of insurance business in the United States, where British companies have been reporting underwriting losses in the last few years, and in the expenditure of the United States and Canadian forces. These private receipts from the forces probably rose quite fast to a peak of £50 million in 1957, from which they have since declined (at least up to 1961— the last year for which the figures have been published), though more slowly than the corresponding government receipts.

For the future, world trade is expected to grow less rapidly (see chapter 5), and there is little scope for further liberalization of commercial transactions generally. These factors point towards a rather slower increase in both debits and credits. At the same time the decline in the forces' expenditure will probably continue. Changes in strategy and the United States government's desire to save foreign exchange might even mean a faster fall. On the other hand the deterioration on insurance in North America can hardly continue indefinitely. On balance it might be reasonable to allow for an annual rate of increase of $3\frac{1}{2}$ per cent in both debits and credits (excluding insurance) from 1962–3 to 1975. This would mean a rise in the net surplus from about £225 million to £350 million (see table 4.13).

(e) *Property income*

As in the case of the investment itself, not much information is available about earnings on British investment overseas or on foreign investment in Britain except, from 1958 onwards, for direct investment other than by oil and insurance

[1]See Central Statistical Office, *United Kingdom Balance of Payments, 1964, loc. cit.*, p. 30.

[2]This is on the assumption that the insurance companies' earnings excluded from the official figures for 1963 only were about £20 million.

Table 4.13. *Other services: £ million, annual rates*

	1952–7	1958–63	1958	1959	1960	1961	1962	1963	1975[a]
Debits	197	256	222	239	263	264	271	275	425
Credits	352	470	415	440	466	499	503	494[b]	775
Net surplus	155	214	193	201	203	235	232	219	350

Source: Central Statistical Office, *United Kingdom Balance of Payments, 1964* and *Economic Trends.*

[a]Estimate.
[b]Excludes earnings from overseas branches, subsidiaries and associates of United Kingdom insurance companies.

companies.   Earnings on portfolio investment are, however, separately covered in official statistics, again from 1958 onwards, and some information about other types of property income, of which oil earnings are the most important, can be derived from miscellaneous sources.

(i) *Direct investment, excluding oil and insurance.*   Earnings on British investment overseas (net of depreciation and taxes paid abroad) probably rose by about a half between 1958 and 1963.   Foreign earnings in this country similarly calculated rose by two thirds.   Even so the credits are so much larger than the debits that the net surplus increased by a third (see table 4.14).   But 1958 was almost certainly a year in which both debits and credits were unusually low, because of the rather depressed level of economic activity both here and in other industrial countries and the adverse effects on the profitability of investment in primary production as well as manufacturing.

Figures of the book value of investments (net of depreciation) are available only as at the end of 1962.   But changes in book values over short periods are likely to correspond fairly closely with net investment (or disinvestment). Since details of the latter are available from 1958 onwards, it is possible to estimate end-year book values from 1957 to 1963 without much risk of serious error.   It appears that over this period the value of the British investments overseas rose from about £2,575 million to £3,825 million (or by just under half), while the value of foreign investment in this country increased by some 120 per cent (from about £750 million to £1,650 million).   Our estimates of the future growth of investment imply, on the assumption that it takes place at an even rate, that by mid-1975 outward investment will be worth about £7,300 million and inward investment nearly £4,000 million.

To calculate yields it seems best to compare earnings in a given year, which will be accruing throughout the period, with the mean of the values of the investment at the end of the year in question and at the end of the previous year. On this basis it appears that in 1962 and 1963 British investment overseas was earning just under 8 per cent per annum and foreign investment in Britain about 10½ per cent.   The figures for British investment do not change much if

Table 4.14. *Earnings on direct investment*[a]: £ *million*

	Earnings						Percentage share in 1962 in total:	
	1958	1959	1960	1961	1962	1963	earnings on invest-ments	value of invest-ments[b]
United Kingdom investment overseas[c]								
United States	18	21	18	18	20		7·3	9·5
Canada	21	22	19	19	20		7·3	18·7
Western Europe	15	25	23	29	31		11·3	10·1
Latin America	11	12	14	11	12		4·4	4·9
Australia	24	30	34	27	36		13·1	14·5
India	16	18	20	22	24		8·7	7·1
Malaya	11	16	20	21	20		7·3	3·5
Rhodesia and Nyasaland	8	10	12	12	11		4·0	3·0
South Africa	21	22	28	27	35		12·7	7·5
Other countries	50	62	70	65	66		24·0	21·3
All countries	195	238	258	251	275	312[d]	100·0	100·0
Overseas investment in United Kingdom[c]								
United States	72	103	105	98	103		76·9	72·1
Canada	6	10	11	11	8		6·0	9·5
Western Europe	14	19	17	14	18		13·4	15·6
Other countries	3	4	4	5	5		3·7	2·9
All countries	95	136	137	128	134	158	100·0	100·0
Net United Kingdom earnings	100	102	121	123	141	154[d]		

Source: Board of Trade Journal, 19 April 1963, pp. 877–83, and 7 August 1964, pp. 286–95; Central Statistical Office, *United Kingdom Balance of Payments, 1964*, and *Economic Trends.*

[a]Excludes oil and insurance companies.
[b]Excludes banks as well as oil and insurance companies.
[c]Except for 1958 the area distribution of earnings is partly estimated.
[d]Includes earnings from overseas branches, subsidiaries and associates of United Kingdom insurance companies (probably some £20 million).

they are carried back over a longer period. They come out higher in 1959 and 1960 but lower in 1958 and 1961. But foreign earnings seem to have been a good deal higher in the earlier years, and perhaps as much as 15½ per cent over the two years 1959–60 when company profits in this country were rising particularly fast.

On the whole it seems reasonable to assume that yields on foreign investment in this country will remain close to recent levels. Faster growth would in itself tend to increase them, but we are assuming that it will be accompanied by greater stability in prices. Yields on British investment overseas might if any-thing improve a little. They have recently been held down by the low level of profitability of investment in Canada (which is very evident also in the case of investment by the United States).   British investment in Canada, which was officially encouraged during the 1950s, accounted for only 7 per cent of identified United Kingdom earnings in 1962 although it represented nearly 19 per cent of known book values at the end of the year.   It has, however, fallen away recently, and the economic outlook in Canada seems in any case to have improved.   On the other hand slower growth in Western Europe would have adverse effects, and investment there has recently risen very fast, in EFTA as well as in the Common Market.

Prices of primary products are another important factor.   (Agriculture and mining provide about a quarter of the total United Kingdom earnings and manufacturing rather less than half, with distributive trade as the next biggest element.)   Here we are in effect assuming that for commodities other than petroleum prices in 1975 will be above the level to which they fell in 1962. This, however, would probably mean that they would be fairly close to the average for the period 1958–63, which was itself some 5 per cent above the 1962 level.   On this assessment credits in 1975 might be put at £600 million, or just under double the 1963 figure, and debits at £400 million, which represents a rise of about 150 per cent.   The yields implied are about $8\frac{1}{4}$ per cent for British investment overseas and 10 per cent for foreign investment in the United Kingdom.

(ii) *Oil*.   The growth in consumption of oil outside the Communist bloc shows little sign of slackening.   Indeed it was $7\frac{1}{2}$ per cent in 1963 compared with annual rates of 7 per cent over the whole period from 1958 and rather under $6\frac{1}{2}$ per cent in the previous five years.   The rise is fastest in Western Europe (about 14 per cent per annum) and slowest in the United States (about 3 per cent per annum).   Supplies of Russian oil to the 'free world' are now increasing much more slowly than they were a few years ago—by some 9 per cent in 1962 and 1963, compared with about 50 per cent in 1958 and 1959.   Consequently 'free world' output has accelerated rather more than 'free world' consumption. It is now rising at about $6\frac{3}{4}$ per cent per annum, compared with $5\frac{1}{2}$ per cent per annum from 1953 to 1958.   Output is still increasing much faster in the Middle East than in the big producing areas of the Western Hemisphere (see table 4.15), but the fastest rate of growth is now in North Africa.

The patterns of supply and demand have both been changing favourably for the British companies.   BP and Shell control nearly half Middle Eastern output as against about a fifth for the non-Communist world as a whole.   Similarly Western Europe accounts for little more than a quarter of 'free world' consumption but for about a third of combined Shell and BP sales, which have risen at an annual rate of over 8 per cent in volume since 1955.   Though Shell have important interests in North America and BP's stake there has also been growing, the American companies are the main sufferers from the relatively slow growth of demand and hence of output in the United States and Canada.

Table 4.15. *Oil consumption and output by areas*[a]: *percentages*

	Annual rate of increase		Share of total		
	1953 to 1958	1958 to 1963	1953	1958	1963
Consumption					
USA and Canada	4·1	3·3	67	60	51
Western Europe	12·8	14·1	15	19	26
Other countries	9·4	9·5	18	21	23
Total	6·4	7·0	100	100	100
Output					
USA and Canada	1·5	3·0	56	46	38
Other Western Hemisphere	8·0	5·7	19	21	20
Middle East	12·0	9·8	20	27	31
Other countries	9·0	21·8	4	5	10
Total	5·5	6·8	100	100	100

Source: British Petroleum Company, *Statistical Review of the World Oil Industry, 1963.*
[a]Sino-Soviet bloc excluded throughout.

Most authorities seem to expect the annual rate of increase in 'free world' demand to slow down to about 5 per cent over the decade of the 1960s with a continuing decline thereafter and a particularly marked deceleration in Western Europe. One forecast (which the author admits to be cautious) allows only $3\frac{1}{2}$ per cent per annum from 1960 to 1975, falling to less than 3 per cent by the end of the period[1]. But forecasts of oil consumption have tended consistently to underestimate the rate of increase, particularly in Western Europe. The 1960 report of OEEC's Energy Advisory Commission is a case in point. On the basis of forecasts of total energy requirements which were prepared separately by the OEEC Secretariat, by member governments and by four major oil companies, but were in broad agreement, the Commission predicted that Western Europe's consumption of oil would approximately double between 1955 and 1965[2]. But their highest figure for 1965 was attained as early as 1962, and consumption is already within their range of forecasts for 1975.

It may be reasonable to suppose that demand for energy in Western Europe will not maintain its recent rapid rate of growth and that natural gas will increase its share of the total. Even so, consumption of oil should continue

[1]A. S. Ashton, 'Oil, Finance and the Future', *op. cit.*, p. 2. See also P. H. Frankel and W. L. Newton, 'The State of the Oil Industry', *National Institute Economic Review,* September 1960, p. 16; Shell Transport and Trading Company, 'The Way Ahead', *Shell Review,* 1961; Chase Manhattan Bank, *Future Growth of the World Petroleum Industry, loc. cit.*; 'Peering into the Seventies', *Petroleum Press Service,* July 1962, p. 243; 'Energy Patterns in a Changing World', *Petroleum Press Service,* November 1962, p. 406; and 'Forty Years On', *Petroleum Press Service,* December 1963, p. 447.
[2]See *Towards a New Energy Pattern in Europe* (Paris, 1960), p. 59.

to rise fast. Energy policy in the Common Market is still undecided, particularly as regards the degree of protection for national coal industries. It seems probable, however, that there will be a fairly liberal attitude towards oil imports, except from Russia.

Russian and Saharan oil may continue to increase their share of the market to the detriment of the British companies. But Shell and BP both have a stake in Saharan oil, and the EEC Commission has recommended on strategic grounds that exports from Russia to the Common Market, which have recently accounted for nearly half of total Russian oil exports to the non-Communist world, should not be allowed to exceed 10 per cent of EEC's oil imports (compared with about $7\frac{1}{2}$ per cent for the Six as a group in 1963). Moreover of the main producing areas in the 'free world' the Middle East still offers the greatest scope for increasing output. Not only is the oil there relatively easy, and consequently cheap, to extract, but the ratio of reserves to output is exceptionally high. In 1963 the Middle East accounted for 70 per cent of 'free world' reserves compared with 31 per cent of production, whereas the corresponding figures for the Western Hemisphere were 20 per cent and 58 per cent.

Altogether it seems that the trade of the British companies should continue to increase faster than 'free world' consumption up to 1975. A reasonable assumption might be that the volume of their sales will rise at about $6\frac{1}{2}$ per cent per annum from 1962 (probably a better base year than 1963 with its abnormally severe weather). This implies that sales in 1975 will be about two and a quarter times the 1962 level and this is about the rate of increase assumed in chapter 10 for consumption in the United Kingdom. Thus the volume of trade of foreign companies operating here might be expected to show a similar rate of growth. Separate figures of the oil component of interest, profits and dividends are not published. It is, however, known that net earnings have risen considerably in the last few years, and some idea of their previous level can be obtained from the scale of various revisions in the estimates and from information supplied to the Radcliffe Committee about interest earnings[1]. It seems probable that by 1962 the net annual contribution of oil was in the region of £200 million. An increase of 125 per cent would bring this to about £450 million in 1975.

Profits in the oil industry have, however, been lagging far behind the growth of trade. Despite stringent economies in the last few years, the combined net profits of Shell and BP were only about 20 per cent higher in 1963 than in 1956, although the volume of their sales expanded in this period by about 75 per cent. While the market has weakened considerably both for crude oil and for products, royalties and taxes due to Middle East governments are now based on fictitious prices only slightly lower, since August 1960, than those previously fixed. Even so there is continual pressure from the Organization of

---

[1]Committee on the Working of the Monetary System, *Principal Memoranda of Evidence* (London, 1960), vol. 1, part II, p. 120.

Petroleum Exporting Countries for more favourable terms and the companies have already offered concessions. The scope for further squeezing of the companies' profit margins is not unlimited and they will probably not fall so fast as in the last few years. But some further worsening in their terms of trade must be expected through a combination of higher output costs and lower selling prices. The allowance for this can only be arbitrary, but might perhaps be put at £100 million for 1975. On this basis, the forecast of net earnings becomes £350 million.

(iii) *Other*. Net earnings on portfolio investment rose gradually from 1958 to 1962 largely because of increasing rates of dividend from South African companies. But they fell back in 1963; following the net investment in this country in the previous year. There seems to be no reason to expect much net change in yields as between the United Kingdom and other countries between now and 1975. United Kingdom interest rates should be relatively lower, but rates of dividend may move the other way. Moreover, it has been assumed that portfolio investment inward and outward will be in balance, and this may be a reasonable estimate for the intervening period also. Thus net earnings may remain close to the recent average of £75 million.

Net interest payments on overseas sterling holdings averaged £75 million in 1952–5. In 1956, when rates were much higher, they rose to £114 million. Figures for later years are not available. In 1975 the total level of the balances (other than those of the International Monetary Fund, which earn no interest) may be much the same as it was ten years or so ago. A rise in the proportion held by countries outside the sterling area would now tend to reduce interest payments, as the balances of the overseas sterling area contain a much higher proportion of long-term securities. But the disparity was probably a good deal smaller in the early 1950s, when Egypt had large holdings of securities. Also even if interest rates fall below recent levels they are still likely to be somewhat higher in 1975 than they were then. In 1952–5 the average discount rate on Treasury bills was only $2\frac{3}{4}$ per cent, nearly 1 per cent less than in 1963, and short-term and long-term government bonds yielded little more than 3 per cent and 4 per cent respectively as against $4\frac{3}{4}$ per cent and $5\frac{1}{2}$ per cent in 1963. £100 million seems a reasonable allowance for net payments in 1975.

Interest payments on the North American loans will fall from £46 million in 1958 and £38 million in 1963 to about £30 million in 1975 if the instalments due in the intervening years are all paid. On the other hand there should be a considerable rise in interest receipts, which were probably in the region of £25 million a year in 1963[1]. On the assumption that net lending to underdeveloped countries increases at an even rate to the £250 million estimated for 1975 and that other loans will by then have been paid off, the amount by then outstanding will be over £2,000 million. Not long ago the rates of interest

[1] Interest received on aid loans amounted to £16 million compared with only £1 million in 1952 (see *Bank of England Quarterly Bulletin*, December 1964, p. 284).

being fixed on these loans averaged something like $6\frac{1}{2}$ per cent. If this remained typical, receipts by 1975 could thus be something over £125 million. There has, however, been a considerable easing of conditions recently (in part because market rates have fallen and perhaps in part also because of pressure from OECD's Development Assistance Committee, whose members seem on average to have been charging about $3\frac{1}{2}$ per cent for loans recently granted)[1]. Indeed the government has indicated that in suitable cases interest will in future be waived altogether for the first seven years after a loan has been made[2].

On the assumption that net lending rises at an even rate to the level of £250 million assumed for 1975, well over half the amount outstanding would by then be on loans less than seven years old. Such concessions on their terms could thus make a big difference to interest receipts in 1975. £50 million may in the circumstances be an adequate allowance for them.

Miscellaneous net receipts, for example from interest on trade credits, were probably somewhere in the region of £50 million in 1963. This figure should tend to rise a little as turnover increases, particularly if the recent net inflow of miscellaneous capital is reversed.

(iv) *Total property income.* On this assessment net earnings of property income in 1975 should be around £600 million (£350 million from oil, £200 million from other direct investments and £50 million from all other items). In the past the surplus has fluctuated. It was, for example, just over £250 million in 1954 but under £175 million in 1955, and it slumped again from £300 million in 1958 to £238 million in 1960 before its latest recovery (see table 4.16). Apart from the varying rates of payment on sterling balances, the varying fortunes of the oil industry have been mainly responsible. The upward trend in the British companies' earnings was interrupted after 1954 first by a retrospective increase in rates of payment to the governments of producing countries, then by the Suez crisis in 1956–7, and finally by the sharp decline in product prices in 1959–60[3]. On each occasion, however, the advance has been resumed. We are in effect assuming that a similar process will operate in the future. The recent rate of rise in the surplus is unlikely to be maintained over the full period, since checks may be expected to recur. They should, however, be less severe than in the past in view of the big contraction in the oil companies' margins of profit which has already taken place.

(f) *Private transfers*

This item covers transfers of assets by migrants to or from the United Kingdom and unofficial grants and gifts of all kinds. It was virtually in balance over the whole period 1952–63, ranging from a deficit of £20 million in 1957 to a

---

[1]See OECD, *The Flow of Financial Resources to Less-developed Countries, 1956–63* (Paris, 1964), p. 36.

[2]See Treasury, *Aid to Developing Countries*, Cmnd 2147 (London, 1963), p. 14.

[3]See also R. S. Gilbert, 'The Fall in Britain's Invisible Earnings', *National Institute Economic Review*, November 1960, pp. 50–1.

Table 4.16. *Property income: £ million, annual rates*

Direct investment (excluding oil and insurance)	1958–63	1958	1959	1960	1961	1962	1963
Debits	131	95	136	137	128	134	158
Credits	255	195	238	258	251	275	312[a]
Net	+124	+100	+102	+121	+123	+141	+154[a]
Portfolio investment							
Debits	56	55	49	56	53	53	70
Credits	131	115	121	133	133	142	141
Net	+ 75	+ 60	+ 72	+ 77	+ 80	+ 89	+ 71
Other (net)	+ 93	+137	+ 96	+ 36	+ 41	+ 99	+152
Balance	+292	+297	+270	+234	+244	+329	+377[a]

Source: Central Statistical Office, *United Kingdom Balance of Payments, 1964* and *Economic Trends.*

[a]Includes earnings from overseas branches, subsidiaries and associates of United Kingdom insurance companies (probably some £20 million).

surplus of £11 million in 1953. The fluctuations tend to follow the patterns of net migration, and the fairly small net immigration expected over the next ten years or so seems likely to leave the figures close to balance.

Table 4.17. *Invisible balance: £ million*

	1952	1963	1975[a]
Defence aid	+120	—	—
Other government	−174	−387	−500
Transport	+134	+ 12	− 50
Travel	− 3	− 45	− 50
Other services	+122	+219[b]	+350
Property income	+252	+377[b]	+600
Private transfers	− 2	− 14	—
Balance	+449	+162	+350
of which:			
Property income	+252	+377[b]	+600
Transfers	+ 75	−150	−200
Services	+122	− 65[b]	− 50

Source: Foregoing tables and forecasts.

[a]Estimate.

[b]Earnings from overseas branches, subsidiaries and associates of United Kingdom insurance companies are included in property income for 1963. For other periods they are in other services. The amount involved for 1963 is probably about £20 million.

(g) *Invisible balance*

These tentative forecasts for 1975 combine to produce a surplus on all invisible transactions in the current account of £350 million. This is more than twice the 1963 figure, but only about £25 million up on 1952, even if the £120 million of defence aid received in that year is excluded (see table 4.17). For reasons just discussed the surplus on property income rises faster than in the past. Transfer payments increase rather more slowly, because a higher proportion of official aid to other countries is assumed to be provided in the form of loans. The deterioration in the balance on services is halted at about the present point, mainly because overseas military expenditure is taken to be now about at its peak. The worsening on transport continues, but so also does the improvement on miscellaneous services.

4. IMPLICATIONS OF THE FORECASTS

Our figures of £550 million for the required current surplus in 1975 and £350 million for the surplus on invisibles are, of course, subject to wide margins of error. This applies with relatively much greater force to some of the individual items than to the final outcome, in the sense that in most cases errors should be mutually cancelling rather than complementary. There is some tendency for individual pairs of debits and credits to move in parallel and there are similar links in other cases, for example, between property income and investment. Even so, the fact that we arrive at a figure of £200 million for the required surplus on visible trade implies merely that a satisfactory balance of payments, including a worthy contribution to the development of poorer countries, is unlikely to be achieved in the mid-1970s without at least a modest surplus of exports over imports.

Whether the balance of payments will in fact be satisfactory in these terms depends, more than on any other single factor, on the competitiveness of British manufacturing industry at home and overseas. To this extent it is logical as well as convenient to treat visible trade, and ultimately net trade in manufactures, as in effect a balancing item. This is done in the next chapter. It does not, however, follow that the blame for any ultimate shortfall must necessarily lie in this quarter. There is scope also in other sectors of the balance of payments for bigger improvements than we have allowed. It has been assumed in this chapter, for instance, that the deficit on shipping will continue to increase; also that this country will remain one of the few in Western Europe with a deficit on travel account, despite its advantages in terms of geography, language and common antecedents in competing for the custom of tourists from the United States and indeed from many other parts of the world. In the latter case at least it is not clear that there are inherent reasons why the adverse tendency should persist. It may be, for example, that government assistance in improving tourist accommodation on a scale commensurate with that available in most Continental countries would greatly improve the travel balance. Other possibilities include much greater reliance on transport aircraft rather than garrisons to meet military commitments overseas, on the lines apparently contemplated by the United States. Moreover other recommendations for economies in military expenditure have been made by the Estimates Committee[1].

It is sometimes questioned also whether the return on private overseas investment justifies the outlay which it constitutes. This problem is too big to be considered in detail here, involving as it does such issues as benefit to underdeveloped countries, effects on exports, the continuance of the sterling area system, and the choice between foreign and domestic investment. But to the limited extent that it can be inferred from these forecasts the answer is a favourable one. If our figures are anywhere near the mark, the total cost in 1975 of direct British investment overseas, including investment in oil but ignoring foreign investment in this country, should be almost covered by the increase compared with 1963 in income from the investment. Failing a really marked improvement in competitiveness, of which there is so far less sign, rising property income emerges as the main ground for hope of a more favourable trend in the balance of payments over the next ten or fifteen years.

[1] *Ninth Report from the Estimates Committee . . . Session 1963–64: Military Expenditure Overseas* (London, 1964), pp. vi–lxxi.

L

CHAPTER V

BRITAIN'S VISIBLE TRADE

By R. L. Major

In this chapter an attempt is made to analyse the likely pattern of Britain's visible trade given the overall rate of growth assumed in this study. In other parts of the study the difficulties involved in trying to predict the future, even in a highly conditional sense, have been emphasized. In the field of foreign trade these difficulties are, of course, greatly magnified. Whilst imports can be related without too much uncertainty to developments within the economy, exports depend largely on developments in other economies for which no counterpart studies are available. Furthermore, imports and exports of many commodities are relatively small balancing items between the major aggregates of domestic demand and supply. For these and other reasons the very special character of this chapter and the limited objectives to which it has been addressed must be clearly understood.

In the first place it is essential to form some idea, however rough, of the extent to which faster growth may encounter a bottleneck on the side of the balance of payments. This means that some estimate is needed of the increase in net imports of food, fuels and materials that would accompany the faster growth assumed. This then indicates what increase is necessary in net exports of manufactures if the surplus on visible trade that was postulated at the end of chapter 4 is to be achieved. The first object of this chapter is to identify this increase in order to see what conditions need to be satisfied, in terms of the likely evolution of world trade and our shares in this trade, for this target to be reached.

Secondly, net exports (or imports) are an important determinant of total output for many industries. Hence it has been necessary to form some view of the way in which net exports by industry or commodity are likely to develop within the framework of the constraints on total imports and exports set by the preceding considerations. At the same time, this breakdown of imports and exports into the groups required for purposes of projecting output by industry provides the most satisfactory method of assessing the feasibility of the overall target for net exports. This is because the growth of British imports and exports depends partly on their commodity structure in relation to the likely changes in the commodity pattern of demand at home and abroad.

However, as has been stated in chapter 2, competitiveness is undoubtedly the main determinant of our export performance and an increase in our competitiveness is the major assumption of the whole exercise. If it is not realized, the export projections contained in this chapter will probably not be realized and

L2

so the overall growth target, too, will probably not be reached. On the other hand, all the estimates in this chapter could be invalidated by other factors, such as a different evolution of the terms of trade from that which we have assumed, or unforeseen changes in the degree of protection accorded to domestic industries in this country or others. The various possible permutations and combinations need not be enumerated here in full, but it is important to note that, because of interdependence between many of the items, errors in some of the assumptions do not necessarily destroy the possibilities of achieving an overall balance similar to that projected. For example, if commodity prices are higher than we assume and this country's terms of trade are consequently less favourable, then although the required increase in the volume of our exports would be greater, the purchasing power of primary producers would also be greater, other things being equal. On the other hand, if our terms of trade improved even more than projected, it is possible that this might be matched by a greater increase in aid.

1. GENERAL TRENDS IN BRITISH OVERSEAS TRADE

Traditionally Britain has had a deficit on merchandise trade. This appears to be true not only of the balance recorded in the trade accounts, where the valuation of imports includes the cost of insurance and freight, but also under the system of estimation now used for balance of payments purposes, in which payments for freight and insurance to non-residents of the United Kingdom are treated as invisible transactions and payments to residents are not recorded at all.

On a trade account basis the deficit has risen fairly steadily. Before the 1914–18 war it was in the region of £125–£150 million a year. Between the wars it was very much bigger, with a peak of £426 million in 1926 (the year of the general strike) and an annual average of about £360 million for the last four years of peace. Since the last war the deficits have been larger still. They averaged about £625 million from 1948 to 1963—rather more than £650 million a year in the first half of the period, rather less than £600 million in the second.

The worsening shown in the trade accounts was, however, due to the inclusion of higher absolute amounts for freight and insurance (these are estimated at about 11 per cent of c.i.f. values in recent periods)[1] which resulted from the higher level of trade. The balance of payments accounts present a different and far more encouraging picture. Fully comparable figures are not available for periods before the last war, but in the 1930s this deficit probably never fell much below £200 million[2]. But since the war the position had, until recently,

[1]See Central Statistical Office, *United Kingdom Balance of Payments, 1964*, p. 5.
[2]The c.i.f. value of imports was seldom more than £1,200 million in the 1920s and fell to more like £750 million in the early 1930s. It is clear that even the exclusion from these figures of the cost of freight and insurance would still have left a substantial excess of imports over exports. Throughout this chapter 'imports' means retained imports, i.e. re-exports have been deducted.

become much more favourable.   Over the whole period from 1956 to 1963 the deficit averaged well under £100 million a year on a far bigger turnover of trade, and in two of these years there were surpluses of the order of £50 million. The sterling value of exports was about nine times as high by 1963 as it had been just before the war; the value of imports was only about five or six times as high.

These favourable post-war developments were not on the whole attributable to changes in the terms of trade.   Despite the big improvement since the early 1950s, these may still have been marginally less favourable in 1963 than they had been in 1938.   In volume terms imports and exports had risen in roughly equal proportions in the past fifteen years.   But compared with 1938 exports had apparently risen about three times as much as imports[1].

The improvement partly reflected a general tendency for world trade in manufactures to rise faster than trade in primary products.   For Britain manufactures constitute a much bigger proportion of exports than of imports (see table 5.1); this, therefore, was a highly advantageous development.   But it was also true up to 1963 that British exports had risen faster than imports since 1935–8 for manufactures as well as for trade in total.   For non-manufactures exports were also increasing the faster in the early 1960s, because of the stabilizing effect on the other side of big food imports.   But in the case of manufactures, imports began to rise much faster than exports in the mid-1950s.   By the early 1960s the surplus on trade in manufactures was already tending to fall, while under the prevailing conditions of slow economic growth the deficit on non-manufactures was rising very little.

The initial phase of faster growth, since the summer of 1963, has, not surprisingly, brought with it a sharp worsening in the balance of trade, due in the main to a rapid rise in imports of manufactures and non-manufactures alike. The deterioration should, however, be no more than a temporary one.   There seems to be no inherent reason why the country should not be able, not merely to reverse it, but also to achieve the modest improvement which is here postulated in the previous merchandise balance.   There has already been one period of twelve months, the financial year 1962/3, when the deficit in balance of payments terms was no more than £20 million.   To move from this to a surplus of £200 million in 1975 requires a net swing of about 1½ per cent on the total turnover of trade which we envisage in that year.   It seems inevitable, however, that faster growth will continue to involve a rising deficit on non-manufactures. Thus it is on trade in manufactures that the improvement must be achieved.

For a country which lives by exporting manufactures, the prospect of retaliation, if nothing else, must rule out restriction of manufactured imports as a long-term policy, whatever its possible merits as a means of overcoming

---

[1]See London and Cambridge Economic Service, *Key Statistics of the British Economy, 1900–1962* (London, 1963).

Table 5.1. Composition and growth of United Kingdom trade: annual averages

	£ million					Indices (1935–8 = 100)			
	1935–8	1948–51	1952–5	1956–9	1960–2	1948–51	1952–5	1956–9	1960–2
Retained imports									
Food, beverages and tobacco	386	1,027	1,297	1,465	1,502	266	336	380	389
Basic materials	217	896	1,023	963	916	412	471	443	422
Mineral fuels and lubricants	41	203	345	442	497	494	839	1,074	1,206
Total for above groups	644	2,126	2,665	2,870	2,915	330	414	445	452
Manufactured goods	175	490	721	907	1,389	279	411	517	793
Total[a]	824	2,635	3,403	3,792	4,323	320	413	460	524
United Kingdom exports									
Food, beverages and tobacco	34	120	159	193	206	349	462	562	599
Basic materials	28	73	98	119	135	265	353	431	488
Mineral fuels and lubricants	42	67	142	142	134	159	337	337	319
Total for above groups	104	260	399	454	475	250	383	436	456
Manufactured goods	348	1,723	2,200	2,719	3,100	496	633	782	891
Total[a]	465	2,031	2,687	3,258	3,676	437	578	701	790
Balance of trade									
Food, beverages and tobacco	− 352	− 907	− 1,138	− 1,272	− 1,296				
Basic materials	− 189	− 822	− 925	− 843	− 781				
Mineral fuels and lubricants	+ 1	− 136	− 204	− 301	− 363				
Total for above groups	− 540	− 1,865	− 2,267	− 2,416	− 2,440				
Manufactured goods	+ 172	+ 1,233	+ 1,479	+ 1,812	+ 1,711				
Total[a]	− 359	− 604	− 716	− 534	− 647				

Sources: Annual Abstract of Statistics and *Accounts relating to Trade and Navigation of the United Kingdom.*
[a]Includes miscellaneous.

temporary difficulties. Thus the improvement can only come as a result of increased competitiveness.

In the rest of this chapter we first discuss the prospects for the volume of trade in non-manufactures and imports of semi-manufactures of which domestic requirements are supplied mainly from overseas. These are all categories in which trade depends mainly on the strength of demand, at home or overseas, and on policy decisions, with competitiveness playing no more than a minor part. When the figures have been adjusted to a balance of payments basis and allowance has been made for possible price changes, this leads to a target balance for the competitive trade of British manufacturers which is then distributed over the imports and exports of the main groups of industry in the light of past performance and of the level of demand to be expected at home and overseas. Finally the general implications of the forecasts are briefly discussed.

For United Kingdom trade the classification adopted follows where possible that used up to the beginning of 1963 in *Trade and Navigation Accounts*. The published figures for 1963 and 1964 not being strictly comparable in all cases, the analysis of the past generally ends with 1962.

2. TRADE IN FOOD, FUELS, MATERIALS

(a) *Food, drink and tobacco*

The volume of exports in class A in *Trade and Navigation Accounts* increased by over one fifth between 1954–6 and 1960–2 and the volume of imports by about one sixth.

Exports of food changed very little in total. While there was a fairly slow but steady rise on other items, exports of refined sugar fell rapidly until the recent flurry in prices. At 1960 prices they seem to have been worth only about £12 million by 1962—less than half the 1954 figure. There is a rather similar story on tobacco products, of which exports, also worth around £25 million at 1960 prices in the mid-1950s, had fallen by a third by 1962. Exports of beverages—predominantly whisky— have, however, risen fast. In 1962 they were worth about £85 million at 1960 prices—over double the 1954 figure.

Western Europe is an important market for food exports, and the prospects of increasing sales there in the face of present agricultural policies in the Common Market do not seem good. On the other hand the scope for further falls on sugar and tobacco is now limited, whereas there seem to be good prospects for exports of whisky in view of its growing popularity in Western Europe. Exports of whisky to the United States are rising steadily and still accounted in 1963 for over half the total of £85 million at current prices, but exports to Sweden, Denmark and the Common Market increased by a quarter to £13 million. Altogether the exports of the group might rise by about 50 per cent in volume between 1960 and 1975. This forecast assumes that there will be little change in food exports, but a doubling on drink and tobacco together.

Forecasts of consumers' expenditure in this country are given in chapter 6. They imply increases between 1960 and 1975 of just over 30 per cent for food, non-alcoholic beverages and beer, 35 per cent for tobacco and about 65 per cent for wines and spirits. Part of this increase in expenditure is likely to take the form of payment for improved services in the form of packing and so on. In an elaborate series of forecasts by the Institute for Research in Agricultural Economics of Oxford University of the likely pattern in 1975 of demand for agricultural products in this country, it is suggested that this element might account for about 6 per cent of the 22 per cent rise in expenditure at retail level which they envisage (on the basis of a substantially smaller rise in population than we have assumed)[1]. Our own expenditure forecasts, therefore, probably imply a rise of about 25 per cent in consumption of food at farm/ import level. Of this, population changes would account for nearly half— rather less than the increase envisaged in the total population, because there would be a bigger proportion of young children, who eat less food than adults[2]. We should expect the fastest increase on fruit and vegetables, followed by the meat and dairy products groups. Only a small rise is likely on cereal foods (see tables 5.2 and 6.15).

Home production has recently been supplying a steadily rising proportion of consumption of most of the main foods—bacon is a notable exception[3]. Agreements have, however, recently been concluded with overseas suppliers of cereals[4] providing for a balance between home production and imports 'broadly based upon the present supplies to the United Kingdom market' and for an opportunity for domestic producers and overseas suppliers to share 'in a fair and reasonable way' in its future growth. There are also broadly similar arrangements with bacon exporters, and attempts are understood to have been made, so far unsuccessfully, to extend them to meat. On sugar too the tonnage covered by the Commonwealth Sugar Agreement is being raised as consumption in this country increases. Our forecasts of imports of these commodities generally assume, therefore, that apart from stock changes they will increase in similar proportions to consumption. We have, however, allowed for a considerably higher proportion of poultry in the total of meat consumed and

---

[1] *United Kingdom: Projected Level of Demand, Supply and Imports of Farm Products in 1965 and 1975* (Washington, 1962), p. 82.

[2] Institute for Research in Agricultural Economics, *op. cit.*, p. 6.

[3] See also K. Jones, A. Maizels and J. Whittaker, 'The Demand for Food in the Industrial Countries, 1948–1960', *National Institute Economic Review*, May 1962, p. 46 and A. Maizels, 'Trade and Development Problems of the Under-developed Countries: the Background to the United Nations' Conference', *National Institute Economic Review*, May 1964, p. 37.

[4] Foreign Office, *Cereals: Exchange of Letters and Notes . . .*, Cmnd 2339, 2383 and 2404 (London, 1964).

Table 5.2.   *Imports and consumption of food*

	Consumption				Imports	Value of imports in 1960[b] (£ m.)
	1954–6 to 1957–9	1957–9 to 1960–2	1954–6 to 1960–2	1960 to 1975[a]	1954–6 to 1960–2	
Butter	8·6	2·2	5·3	1·5	4·7	122
Cheese	2·1	2·4	2·3	1·4	0·5	32
Beef and veal	1·8	0·4	1·1	1·6	− 1·3	71
Mutton and lamb	0·4	3·3	1·8	1·5	0·8	72
Bacon and ham	0·5	2·7	1·6	1·1	4·5	101
Canned meat	4·1	− 0·5	1·8	1·3	0·9	63
Wheat	− 1·5[c]	− 0·3[c]	− 0·9[c]	0·4[c]	− 1·0	105
Sugar	1·7	1·1	1·4	1·2	− 0·4	76
Dried fruit	− 1·4	− 0·2	− 0·8	1·5	0·1	17
Other fruit	1·5	2·1	1·7	3·0	2·7	83
Maize	14·3[d]	14·5[d]	14·4[d]	3·2	15·9	65
Tea	0·8	0·1	0·4	0·1	0·9	108
Coffee beans	8·5	10·2	9·5	4·0	9·4	13

Sources: H.M. Customs and Excise, *Annual Statement of the Trade of the United Kingdom; Trade and Navigation Accounts; Board of Trade Journal; Monthly Digest of Statistics.*

[a]NIESR estimates.
[b]The items listed cover over two thirds of the value of imports of food and feeding-stuffs.
[c]All grain products consumed as food (of which flour accounts for over 90 per cent).
[d]Disposals (estimated from home production, imports and known stock changes).

expect the great bulk of the additional poultry supplies to be produced in this country[1].

Imports of shell eggs have also been dwindling and are likely to be negligible by 1975[1]. It is assumed also that there will be no substantial importation of liquid milk. On the other hand imported lard is accounting for a rising proportion of usage of cooking oils and fats, and the biggest increases in consumption are expected to be of products of which imports account for a particularly high proportion of total consumption, notably tropical fruit and tomatoes. On balance the import content of food consumption will probably remain about stable, but our forecasts of consumption imply bigger increases in imports of wines, spirits and tobacco. Also the rising livestock population is likely to mean substantially higher imports of feeding-stuffs. This applies particularly to maize (although changes in price relationships, which may not continue, are partly responsible for the very rapid increase in imports of maize over the last ten years or so). Altogether, therefore, the rise in the volume of imports covered by the group may be around 30 per cent.

[1]See Institute for Research in Agricultural Economics, *op. cit.* p. 83.

(b) *Fuels*[1]

Between 1954–6 and 1960–2 the volume of imports of fuels rose by about one half; the volume of exports changed very little. The contrast is partly due to the big fall in coal exports in the middle 1950s. Petroleum exports rose by about one third and imports by about two thirds.

Coal exports have recently been recovering, particularly to Western Europe. In 1963 the volume of exports was up by nearly two thirds on 1962. There are possibilities of further big increases. The outlook is very uncertain, particularly with future energy policy in the Common Market still undecided, but a further rise of about 50 per cent to over twice the 1960 level has been allowed for. It is assumed that coal imports will remain negligible.

Consumption of oil in Britain and total sales by British companies are both likely to rise at about $6\frac{1}{2}$ per cent per annum, and refining in this country will probably increase at a similar rate. How far the companies operating here will choose to supply their overseas markets with oil refined in Britain is difficult to predict. But the most reasonable assumption seems to be that a similar relationship will apply and that both imports and exports in 1975 will be about 130 per cent higher than in 1960.

Imports of natural gas may well have reached substantial proportions by 1975. The value is difficult to predict but might be put at £75 million.

(c) *Basic materials*

Manufacturing industries' consumption of imported materials, including semi-manufactures, of those items of which imports are the main source of supply has not merely failed to keep pace with the rise in output, but has actually been falling slightly. Adjusted for identified stock changes the decline in imports, excluding precious metals, was only about 1 per cent between 1957–9 and 1960–2, compared with 5 per cent in the previous three-year period. But the rise in total output of manufacturing industry was 5 per cent in the first period and 12 per cent in the second. Thus the disparity between imports and output was tending to increase.

There are a number of reasons for the favourable relationship between output and consumption of imported materials. One cause is the decline in production of textiles, which have a particularly high import content. In addition, however, there is an improving trend in most individual industries (see table 5.3). This has been found to apply over long periods both in Britain and in other countries[2].

[1]A full discussion of energy prospects is given in chapter 10.
[2]See M. F. W. Hemming and G. F. Ray, 'Imports and Expansion', *op. cit.*, p. 33; J. A. Rowlatt and F. T. Blackaby, 'The Demand for Industrial Materials, 1950–57', *National Institute Economic Review*, September 1959, pp. 24–5; A. Maizels, 'Trade and Development Problems of the Under-developed Countries', *op. cit.*, p. 38; and M. FG. Scott, *A Study of United Kingdom Imports* (Cambridge, 1963), pp. 125 and 133.

Table 5.3.   *Output of selected manufacturing industries and their consumption of imports of materials, etc. of mainly imported type*

Indices
(1957–9 = 100)

	Value of imports 1960	Estimated net output[a]		Estimated import consumption[b]		Estimated net output	
						Estimated import consumption	
	(£ m.)	1954–6	1960–2	1954–6	1960–2	1954–6	1960–2
Chemicals n.e.s.	120	87	124	111	98	78	127
Iron and steel (melting, rolling and casting)	115	101	108	91	104	111	104
Non-ferrous metals	222	98	112	106	93	92	120
Textiles	250	107	101	108	92	99	110
Leather goods, clothing, footwear	24	98	111	115	86	85	129
Paper, printing, publishing	99	93	119	93	106	100	112
Other manufacturing	42	91	114	116	95	78	120
Total for above industries	872[c]	97	113	105	96	92	118

Source: NIESR estimates.

[a]The 'net' output indices shown here are, as usual, largely based on the application of gross output indicators to components of the industries which are combined together by net output weights. Hence they are likely to depart from true measures of net output in the direction of gross output indices (see also chapter 7, table 7.8 for further details).

[b]Estimated consumption of imports of materials, including semi-manufactures, of which imports are the main source of supply to the United Kingdom.

[c]Other imports of basic materials, etc., supplied mainly from overseas amounted to about £225 million. The main element was timber to the value of about £140 million, used partly by the construction industry.

In the present case the most striking fall in import content occurred in the chemical industry, where between 1954–6 and 1960–2 net output appears to have risen by a good 40 per cent, while the volume of related net imports, adjusted for stock changes, probably fell by about 12 per cent. This is presumably the result of changes in the pattern of output within the industry and particularly the swing away from the processing of oilseeds and vegetable oils, of which the imports very largely consist, towards the production of synthetic resins and plastics. There has been a similar switch to synthetics in the rubber industry (an important element in 'other manufacturing') and in textiles; also in leather goods, clothing and footwear a switch towards clothing, which has a very small direct consumption of imports, as well as a substantial rise in output of hides from slaughtering in Britain. On non-ferrous metals the improvement may be associated with the substitution of aluminium for copper.

In paper, printing and publishing, imports of materials, adjusted for identified stock change, seem to have moved fairly closely in line with output from 1954 to 1959. Since then, however, usage of mainly imported materials appears to have fallen marginally, while production has continued to increase. Probably as a result of tariff reductions, imports of wood pulp from the countries in the European Free Trade Association are tending to be replaced by semi-manufactured forms of paper which compete with the output of the British industry. In other words there seems to be a tendency, which is likely to continue until the tariff changes are complete and have had their full impact, for an increasing part of the manufacturing process to be carried out overseas.

There seems to be no industry group where imports of materials have risen consistently faster than output. In iron and steel, however, the import content rose fairly sharply up to 1957–9 before declining again. This was probably in part because output was rising considerably faster in the earlier period. As domestic production of iron ore is relatively inelastic, imports tend to fluctuate more than output. Thus the recent improvement in the ratio is likely to be reversed again. Moreover relative price movements, and the fact that new centres of production are tending to be sited near the coast, probably imply greater reliance on imported iron ore than on domestic scrap becoming available.

But while iron and steel will probably remain an exception, the general tendency towards a more favourable industry by industry ratio of output to imports of materials should continue. It should indeed be encouraged to the extent that higher investment leads to the use of more efficient machinery[1]. But the industries which we expect to grow considerably faster than before (see table 7.6) include several, notably textiles and timber, furniture, etc., which are relatively high consumers of imports. With the pattern of production which we envisage, a continuation of past trends in individual import/output ratios would mean that total consumption of mainly imported materials would rise between 1960 and 1975 by something like 20 per cent, instead of falling as in the past. Our import forecasts allow for an increase of this order in consumption, heavily concentrated on iron ore, timber and papermaking materials; also for identified changes in stocks and the relatively small exports of the commodities concerned (mainly of wool originating in this country). In 1960 there was an abnormally big rise (worth about £60 million) in identified stocks of these commodities. On the other hand exports are rising quite fast and should be substantially higher by 1975.

(d) Adjustments to balance of payments basis

On the items so far considered, that is trade in food, drink, fuels and mainly imported materials, etc., the forecasts produce a deficit in 1975 at 1960 prices of £3,625 million (see table 5.4). This is after allowance for miscellaneous items, principally parcel post. The deficit is not, however, directly comparable with the required surplus of £200 million on all visibles in the balance of payments. It makes no allowance either for changes in the terms of trade or

[1] See M. FG. Scott, *A Study of United Kingdom Imports, op. cit.*, pp. 127–8.

Table 5.4. *The balance of trade in 1960 and the projected balance in 1975: £ million*

	Retained imports			Exports			Balance		
	1960	1975		1960	1975		1960	1975	
		1960 prices	Current prices[a]		1960 prices	Current prices[a]		1960 prices	Current prices[a]
Food, beverages and tobacco	1,510	1,950	1,910	197	300	290	− 1,314	− 1,650	− 1,620
Mineral fuels and lubricants	478	1,175	1,105	133	300	295	− 345	− 875	− 810
Mainly imported materials, etc.									
Basic materials	825	925	875	36	50	50	− 789	− 875	− 825
Semi-manufactures	275	325	365	—	—	—	− 275	− 325	− 365
Total	1,100	1,250	1,240	36	50	50	− 1,064	− 1,200	− 1,190
Miscellaneous[b]	25	55	60	110	155	175	+ 85	+ 100	+ 115
Total of above items	3,113	4,430	4,315	475	805	810	− 2,638	− 3,625	− 3,505
Other competitive trade of British industry									
Processed materials	169	320	300	90	170	170	− 79	− 150	− 130
Manufactures	1,117	2,700	3,050	2,990	5,200	6,085	+ 1,873	+ 2,500	+ 3,035
Total	1,286	3,020	3,350	3,080	5,370	6,255	+ 1,794	+ 2,350[c]	+ 2,905[c]
Total as in trade accounts	4,399	7,450	7,665	3,555	6,175	7,065	− 845	− 1,275	− 600
Adjustment for freight and insurance on imports							+ 483		+ 825
Other adjustments (net)							− 24		+ 25
Total adjustments							+ 459		+ 800
Visible balance of payments							− 386		+ 200[c]

Source: Annual Statement of the Trade of the United Kingdom and NIESR estimates.

[a] For simplicity the food, fuel and materials groups have all been revalued at 1962 prices, though it is perhaps more likely that fuel prices will be lower and the rest rather higher.
[b] Including works of art.
[c] Target figures.

for differences between the trade account figures so far used in this section and the balance of payments figures.

So far as the terms of trade are concerned, we have allowed for a further improvement, but a much slower one than has been taking place over most of the last ten or fifteen years—about 11 per cent from 1960 to 1975 (or 8 per cent from 1964 to 1975), compared with 20 per cent in the ten years from 1952 to 1962. The value of the improvement from 1960 to 1975 is £675 million. This is based on the assumption that prices of manufactures will rise at 1 per cent per annum between 1962 and 1975, while prices of non-manufactures will remain at the 1962 level. This applies to both imports and exports. Fuel prices are likely to fall, and indeed trade in fuels is unlikely to expand at the rate here envisaged if this does not happen. The assumption, therefore, leaves room for some increase over the 1962 level in prices of food and materials, as in fact has so far occurred.

The rises in primary product prices since 1962 have been due to a large extent to failures of a number of food crops and, more recently, to shortages of base metals, which are partly due to re-stocking in consuming countries and are unlikely to persist for long. Factors tending to depress prices will probably prove more lasting, though this depends to some extent on the future level of imports by the Sino-Soviet countries.

Demand from the industrial countries is limited by development of synthetics, by protection of domestic industries, and in some cases by taxation policy. At the same time the underdeveloped countries are unable to take much advantage of the improved productivity resulting from the use of more advanced techniques to switch resources to other types of economic activity[1]. It has been estimated that world industrial output needs to rise at about 6 per cent a year for prices of metals and agricultural products other than food to be maintained[2].

On the other hand there is increasing international support for measures to improve the export earnings of underdeveloped countries and some stabilizing of their export prices, through such means as commodity agreements, seems a probable development. Furthermore the government is attempting to restrict low price food imports into this country in order to limit the cost of support for home agriculture. There may, moreover, be some rise in freight rates, which would affect c.i.f. import prices.

World export prices for manufactures have been rising at about 1 per cent per annum in recent years and British export prices a good deal faster. From 1955 to 1964 world prices rose by 10 per cent and British prices by 19 per cent. Our assumption implies that as from 1962 British prices will now conform with the general trend as one aspect of improved competitiveness.

[1]See A. Maizels, 'Trade and Development Problems of the Under-developed Countries', *op. cit.*, pp. 46–7; and United Nations, *Towards a New Trade Policy for Development*, Prebisch report (New York, 1964), pp. 14–17.
[2]See *National Institute Economic Review*, February 1962, p. 36.

The freight and insurance content of the c.i.f. value of imports has lately been running at about one ninth but tending to decline a little. The relationship depends upon the source and commodity composition of imports as well as upon the relationship between freight rates and f.o.b. prices. But it does not seem likely that this would change much up to 1975 on the assumptions made here. The commodity distribution is probably the most important factor, and the import groups which are expected to show the biggest rises—manufactures and fuel—are respectively cheap and expensive to ship in relation to their value. Other differences between the trade account and balance of payments figures vary from year to year but on the whole come near to cancelling out. If anything the tendency in recent years has been for more to be added to imports than to exports[1].

Altogether the net effect of the balance of payments adjustments might be an improvement of some £800 million in 1975 (compared with £459 million in 1960). This would make the required surplus in 1975 on the competitive trade of manufacturing industry on a trade account basis £2,350 million at 1960 prices. A relatively small amount of trade in processed materials is included[2]; in 1960 this showed a deficit of some £75 million, which, with imports tending to rise faster than exports, will perhaps double by 1975. This would leave a surplus of £2,500 million to be achieved on the manufacturing component as normally defined. The effects on this figure of different assumptions about the terms of trade are discussed on page 172.

3. COMPETITIVE TRADE OF MANUFACTURING INDUSTRY

(a) *Recent trends in world trade in manufactures*

World trade in manufactures[3] has risen very fast over the past decade. Between 1954 and 1963 its volume almost doubled. Total trade of the 'free world' increased in the same period by only 80 per cent and the rise in the volume of manufacturing output was under 60 per cent.

The chief rise has been in trade among industrial countries. Between 1954 and 1963 the eleven biggest exporters of manufactures increased the value of their exports to industrial countries (including trade with one another) by almost 170 per cent. Their exports to all primary producers, apart from the Soviet and Chinese blocs, rose over the same period by only 50 per cent, and for Latin America the figure is under 10 per cent.

[1]See Central Statistical Office, *United Kingdom Balance of Payments, 1964, loc. cit.,* p. 5.
[2]A little trade included under 'Manufacturing' in table 5.11 is, however, excluded here because the items are classed as 'food, drink and tobacco'.
[3]Throughout this section 'world trade in manufactures' means, unless otherwise indicated, exports in sections 5–8 of the Standard International Trade Classification of the following eleven countries: Belgium/Luxembourg, Canada, France, West Germany, Italy, Japan, Netherlands, Sweden, Switzerland, United Kingdom and United States (excluding 'special category' exports of military supplies, etc.).

The increases recorded for the main commodity groups vary in the same sort of way. At one extreme, world exports of machinery and electrical equipment rose by over 140 per cent in value. At the other, exports of textile manufactures rose by little more than a third. Exports of metals and chemicals occupied an intermediate position. In the case of chemicals falls in prices partly offset a particularly steep rise in the volume of trade.

(b) *Britain's share*

Britain's share of the eleven countries' exports of manufactures has fallen by nearly a third in ten years—from 20 per cent of the total in 1954 to well under 14 per cent in 1964. If Britain had maintained its 1954 share of the total (excluding the other ten countries' exports to it) the value of its manufactured exports in 1964 would have been well over £5,000 million (compared with an actual value of little more than £3,500 million). An analysis of world trade in eight classes of manufactures with ten different areas, that is in a total of eighty area/commodity groups, suggests that changes in the composition of trade may have been marginally favourable to Britain at least up to 1963 (see table 5.5). Different classifications would naturally produce rather different results, but it is unlikely that they would substantially affect the broad conclusion that the fall in Britain's share has not been due to any significant extent to adverse movements in trade patterns.

Of the eighty groups adopted here Britain's share improved in twenty-five between 1954 and 1963, with all the eight commodity classes represented at least twice. But this is because the countries of the overseas sterling area (apart from Iceland and the Irish Republic, which are members of OECD) are treated as a single bloc, whereas the non-sterling area countries are divided into much smaller groups. In trade with the overseas sterling area the share fell heavily for each of the eight classes. But there were gains in two or more commodity classes with each of the subdivisions of the non-sterling world except the European Economic Community. With the Sino-Soviet bloc and to a lesser extent Latin America its share improved. It was, moreover, just about maintained in other primary producing countries and in the United States, though only because these areas' imports included a rising proportion of goods in which Britain's share of trade, at least in 1954, was relatively high—particularly exports of cars to the United States.

Outside the sterling area shifts of this kind in the pattern of trade, by area as well as by commodity, were generally favourable to Britain, which also gained a little from commodity changes within the sterling area. Altogether movements of this kind fully compensated for the disadvantage of a relatively slow growth in the overseas sterling area's total imports of manufactures. But Britain's share of trade is still so much higher with the overseas sterling area than with the rest of the world (nearly 38 per cent against 12 per cent in 1963) that differences in the rates of growth of their respective imports could clearly

Table 5.5. *The United Kingdom's loss of share in world exports of manufactures, 1954–63[a]: £ million*

	Value of UK exports			Effects of changes in:			
	1954	1963	Changes, 1954–63	Size of markets[b]	Composition of markets[c]	Size and composition of markets	UK shares of markets
Exports of:							
Chemicals	206	368	+ 162	+ 242	− 9	+ 233	− 71
Textiles	321	254	− 67	+ 117	− 18	+ 99	− 166
Iron and steel	136	205	+ 69	+ 151	− 35	+ 116	− 47
Other metals and metal goods	157	228	+ 71	+ 125	− 2	+ 123	− 52
Non-electrical machinery	407	859	+ 452	+ 629	+ 8	+ 637	− 185
Electrical equipment	176	318	+ 142	+ 278	+ 14	+ 292	− 150
Transport equipment	406	630	+ 224	+ 460	+ 58	+ 518	− 294
Other manufactures	313	506	+ 193	+ 404	− 11	+ 393	− 200
All manufactures	2,122	3,368	+ 1,246	+ 2,399	+ 12	+ 2,411	− 1,165
Exports of manufactures to:							
United States	106	254	+ 148	+ 154	+ 69	+ 223	− 75
Canada	109	147	+ 38	+ 89	− 10	+ 79	− 41
EEC	242	646	+ 404	+ 630	+ 28	+ 658	− 254
EFTA	215	382	+ 167	+ 301	+ 2	+ 303	− 136
Other OECD members in Europe	108	206	+ 98	+ 148	− 6	+ 142	− 44
Japan	9	37	+ 28	+ 30	—	+ 30	− 2
Sino-Soviet countries	16	119	+ 103	+ 47	+ 6	+ 53	+ 50
Latin America	106	131	+ 25	+ 15	− 3	+ 12	+ 13
Other non-sterling area primary producers	181	297	+ 116	+ 114	+ 16	+ 130	− 14
Non-sterling area[d]	1,092	2,219	+ 1,127	+ 1,325	+ 305	+ 1,630	− 503
Overseas sterling area[d]	1,030	1,149	+ 119	+ 747	+ 34	+ 781	− 662
All countries	2,122	3,368	+ 1,246	+ 2,399	+ 12	+ 2,411	− 1,165

Source: Board of Trade.

[a]Exports to the United Kingdom are excluded.

[b]This column shows for each commodity group and area how the value of the United Kingdom's exports of manufactures would have risen by 1963 if their 1954 share had been maintained in total world exports of that group of commodities or to that area.

[c]This column shows how the rise would have differed from that given in the previous column if the 1954 share had been maintained in exports of each commodity group to each area.

[d]Iceland and the Irish Republic are included with the non-sterling area.

have important effects in future. We have therefore considered the sterling and non-sterling areas separately both in analysing the past performance of the individual British industries concerned and in assessing their future prospects.

(c) *Share of imports in demand for manufactures in industrial countries*

Not surprisingly, the loss of share in overseas trade has been paralleled in the domestic market. But as one aspect of the faster growth of trade than of output, there has been a general tendency for a rising share in demand for manufactures in the main industrial countries to be supplied by imports. This has applied both to consumer and to capital goods (see table 5.6). The share of imports in consumption varies so much between the bigger countries and the smaller ones, which naturally tend to specialize more, that international comparisons are difficult. On the whole the upward tendency has perhaps been rather more pronounced in Britain than elsewhere, but the disparity has not been particularly marked, even in the case of clothing and footwear, of which imports have risen particularly fast.

The implication seems to be that under the most favourable assumptions imports of manufactures into this country are likely to go on rising quite rapidly, particularly under conditions of accelerated economic growth. But given an improvement in competitiveness and the existing degree of protection for domestic industries, the rate at which imports have been outstripping output must be expected to decline.

(d) *Outlook for world trade in manufactures*

The much faster growth in exports than in production of manufactures by the industrial countries is unprecedented since the beginning of the century. The disparity has clearly been associated with the reduction or elimination of trade restrictions[1]. It is unlikely to continue on its recent scale, and trade must be expected to slow down even if recent rates of growth in income per head are maintained in the large industrial countries and increased elsewhere. One of the most uncertain elements is the future purchasing power of the underdeveloped countries. But on fairly optimistic assumptions about the growth of their export earnings and receipts of aid and private capital, it has been estimated that the volume of world trade in manufactures might about double between 1959 and 1970–5[2]. Allowing for growth during the first half of the 1970s, this would represent an approximate doubling of volume from 1960 to 1975 also, that is an annual rate of increase of about $4\frac{3}{4}$ per cent (compared with about $7\frac{1}{2}$ per cent from 1954 to 1962).

Past disparities in rates of increase for the different commodity groups are likely to be somewhat reduced—a projection up to the middle of the next century would give as big a value for machinery and transport equipment as for manufactures in total. Chemicals similarly may now increase their share only slowly. On reasonable assumptions about relative growth rates the same tendency should apply to exports to the different areas[3]. In particular, imports

[1] A. Maizels, *Industrial Growth and World Trade* (Cambridge, 1963), pp. 384–5.
[2] A. Maizels, *op. cit.*, p. 403.
[3] A. Maizels, *op. cit.*, pp. 391–2 and 402–3.

M

Table 5.6. *Imports and total demand for manufactures in industrial countries*

	Percentages[a]							Value of imports in 1960 ($ billion)
	1956	1957	1958	1959	1960	1961	1962	
Share of imports in fixed capital formation in machinery and equipment[b]								
Belgium/Luxembourg	51·7	54·8	54·7	52·4	57·2	··	··	0·56
Canada	53·7	48·3	51·4	54·3	53·4	64·4	61·2	1·50
France	12·3	12·8	11·0	13·5	16·8	17·1	19·0	0·85
West Germany	5·1	7·2	8·7	9·4	10·0	11·2	11·5	0·85
Italy	14·9	15·9	14·9	24·8	19·7	22·1	25·8	0·59
Netherlands	50·0	55·3	59·8	57·4	60·3	70·5	69·5	0·81
Sweden	51·9	57·9	56·6	55·3	58·9	53·6	57·6	0·59
United Kingdom	**9·7**	**9·9**	**10·8**	**11·5**	**14·4**	**14·5**	**16·7**	**0·86**
United States	1·7	1·7	2·6	3·1	3·1	3·8	3·9	0·86
Share of imports in consumers' expenditure on household equipment and personal effects Total[c]								
Belgium/Luxembourg	34·5	35·2	38·9	38·7	39·7	··		0·63
Canada	39·5	40·3	38·4	39·5	40·7	42·2		1·30
France	5·5	5·0	5·3	5·5	7·5	9·2		0·48
Italy	11·7	11·7	11·2	12·4	15·8	17·0		0·40
Netherlands	49·6	51·3	46·7	51·9	53·8	59·8		0·84
Sweden	36·2	37·2	36·4	33·3	37·7	36·3		0·55
United Kingdom	**11·8**	**12·5**	**12·7**	**14·1**	**17·8**	**18·4**		**1·49**
United States	4·6	4·5	4·5	5·5	5·8	5·6		3·02
Clothing[d]								
Belgium/Luxembourg	5·2	5·9	6·1	6·4	7·3	8·4	8·6	0·06
Canada	3·2	3·4	3·5	4·3	4·4	3·9	4·0	0·09
France	0·3	0·3	0·2	0·3	0·5	0·7	0·9	0·02
West Germany	1·0	1·4	2·0	2·7	3·1	3·7	4·3	0·16
Italy	6·9	8·1	7·7	7·7	11·2	15·4	18·3	0·01
Netherlands	8·3	7·6	6·8	7·4	8·1	8·8	10·4	0·08
Sweden	5·3	5·8	5·5	6·4	7·7	8·1	8·6	0·07
United Kingdom	**1·6**	**1·7**	**2·0**	**2·6**	**3·5**	**3·8**	**4·1**	**0·16**
United States	0·7	0·7	0·8	1·2	1·4	1·3	1·6	0·43

Sources: OECD trade statistics, *National Accounts, 1955–1962* (supplement to the *General Statistics Bulletin*, 1964), United Nations, *Yearbook of National Accounts Statistics*.

[a] There are some minor inconsistencies due to changes in classification and in exchange rates.

[b] Imports of machinery and transport equipment, apart from passenger cars, etc. and their components (section 7, less groups 732.1, 732.6, 732.8 and 732.9 of the revised Standard International Trade Classification), as a percentage of gross domestic fixed asset formation in plant and machinery (item 3.c in the OECD tables of national product and expenditure).

[c] Imports of manufactures, apart from chemicals, machinery and transport equipment and metals (sections 6 and 8, less divisions 67 and 68 and groups 667 and 897, of the revised Standard International Trade Classification), as a percentage of consumers' expenditure on clothing and other personal effects and furniture, furnishings and household equipment (as in Standard Table VII of the UN *Yearbook of National Accounts Statistics*).

[d] Imports of clothing, etc. (divisions 84 and 85 of the revised Standard International Trade Classification), as a percentage of consumers' expenditure on clothing (item 1.b in the OECD tables of national product and expenditure).

into the semi-industrial countries will probably account in future for a bigger share of the rise in trade and imports into the industrial countries for a smaller share[1]. In the semi-industrial countries locally produced goods have been replacing imports of textiles and other consumer goods and there is less scope for similar substitution in the case of the capital equipment, other metal products and chemicals of which their imports now mainly consist. On the other hand the industrial countries' imports have been the most affected by relaxation of restrictions. This might account for as much as half of the increase in their mutual trade in manufactures between 1950 and 1959[2].

(e) Targets for United Kingdom imports and exports of manufactures

It is estimated that the combined volume of imports of manufactures of the large industrial countries other than the United States might rise annually from 1959 to the early 1970s at about 9 per cent with a rise of $5\frac{1}{2}$ per cent per annum in national incomes, or $8\frac{1}{2}$ per cent with a rise in national incomes of about 5 per cent[3]. A gradual slowing down is, however, implied. Thus for Britain, with an annual growth rate assumed to be $3\frac{1}{2}$ per cent, a comparable rate of increase in imports of manufactures over the whole period from 1959 to 1975 would probably be somewhere in the region of $6\frac{1}{2}$ per cent. This is equivalent to rather less than 5 per cent per annum from 1960, as there was a rise of 34 per cent in that year, when imports of manufactures were inflated by a number of abnormal items[4]. It implies that the volume of manufactured imports would rather more than double from 1960 to 1975—from just under £1,400 million to about £2,850 million at 1960 prices.

This country's imports of manufactures include some semi-manufactures which serve primarily as materials for British industry. On the view which we have already taken of industry's requirements, these might amount in 1975 to about £325 million at 1960 prices, compared with £275 million in 1960. A total of £2,850 million for all manufactures would on this basis leave £2,525 million, compared with just over £1,100 million, for the items competing in the home market with British manufactures. If at the same time the manufactured exports of British industry rose after 1962 at the $4\frac{3}{4}$ per cent rate assumed for the growth of world trade in manufactures, their value in 1975 at 1960 prices would be about £5,725 million (compared with about £3,000 million in 1960). Thus the surplus on this trade would be £3,200 million, or £700 million more than is assumed to be required. If the difference is distributed between imports and exports roughly in proportion to their total values in 1960, imports are raised to £2,700 million and exports lowered to £5,200 million.

[1] A. Maizels, Industrial Growth and World Trade, op. cit., p. 392.
[2] A. Maizels, op. cit., pp. 385 and 390.
[3] A. Maizels, op. cit., p. 386.
[4] National Institute Economic Review, January 1961, pp. 9 and 34–6.

Table 5.7. *Volume of trade and output in manufactures: percentage annual rate of change*

	World exports	UK exports	UK imports	UK output[a]
1955	+12	+9	+26	+7
1956	+ 9	+6	—	−1
1957	+ 9	+3	+ 5	+2
1958	− 2	−4	+ 1	−2
1959	+ 9	+4	+15	+6
1960	+14	+6	+34	+9
1961	+ 4	+3	− 3	—
1962	+ 6	+1	+ 4	—
1963	+ 9	+5	+ 9	+4
1964	+12	+5	+21	+7
1954–64	+ 8	+3½	+10½	+3½
1960–75	+ 4¾	+3¾	+ 5¼	+4¼
1964–75	+ 3¾	+4	+ 4	+4¾

Source: National Economic Development Council, *Export Trends, loc. cit.; Economic Trends* and NIESR estimates.

[a]Excludes food, drink and tobacco.

It should hardly be necessary to emphasize that the calculations by which we arrive at the projections for 1975 of £2,700 million for retained imports and £5,200 million for exports, both at 1960 prices, are extremely arbitrary and hypothetical. For what they are worth however, they are intended to serve two main purposes. The first is to make it easier to judge whether an overall surplus of £2,500 million is a reasonable aspiration for British industry as a whole. The second is to make it easier to distribute between the various sectors of industry. Their individual balances between exports and competing imports will depend to some extent, though perhaps not a great deal, upon the level of trade at which the overall balance is struck.

It is clear that the achievement of the surplus that we are postulating on total trade in manufactures will be a formidable task. Because of the serious fall during 1964 in Britain's share in sales of manufactures both at home and in overseas markets, our figures imply that a big improvement in competitiveness will now be required.

If our export target is to be achieved, the annual rate of increase in the volume of British exports of manufactures will need to be about ½ per cent more than it has been over the past ten years (table 5.7). Moreover, unless our assumptions about the future growth of world trade are too pessimistic, as recent trends suggest that they may be, British exports will need to rise substantially faster in volume terms than those of competing countries. British export prices for manufactures have so far risen faster since 1962 than the prices of world exports of manufactures generally. Thus our assumption that they will rise equally from 1962 to 1975 means some relative decline in British prices from now on. But we are implying also that in 1975 this country will account for 14 per cent, by value at 1960 prices, of world exports of manufactures.

Recently, its share has been only about 13½ per cent at current prices, and this is equivalent to no more than about 13 per cent at 1960 prices.

We are at the same time assuming that demand for manufactures will be increasing a good deal faster in this country than in the world at large. This means that the share of British output of manufactures that goes to export markets will continue to decline a little. It also means that British imports of manufactures will continue to rise faster than world trade generally. We are, however, implying that this disparity will be a good deal smaller than it has been in the past and that the share of imports in the British market for manufactures will fall a little after its very rapid rise in recent years. An upward trend in the share of imports in the total home market for manufactures seems, moreover, to have been fairly universal in recent years. Thus it may be even harder for Britain to reverse it than to improve its share of markets overseas.

(f) Past performance of individual United Kingdom industries in world markets

Analysis of the recent performance in world export markets of the various sectors of British manufacturing industry reveals a number of general tendencies, but there are also some important differences (see table 5.8).

Nearly all groups have fared much worse in the overseas sterling area than in the rest of the world. One very striking example is the iron and steel industry. Its share improved between 1954 and 1962 in trade with the non-sterling area, but with the sterling area it was cut almost in half, partly owing to a spectacular rise towards the end of the period in exports to India and Pakistan from the United States. Non-ferrous metals and paper and printing also lost heavily in the overseas sterling area, while gaining ground in non-sterling area trade. The exceptions were three groups which suffered severe losses all round—shipbuilding, aircraft and railway locomotives and rolling stock.

In total trade most industries lost fairly steadily. The railway vehicle industry fared worst of all, with a loss of over half its share between 1954–6 and 1960–2, mainly in the latter part of the period. The aircraft industry, which had gained ground at first, also fared very much worse in the last few years. This change followed the advent in 1960 of the Boeing 707, which gave the United States a much higher share of the market. On the other hand the decline in the position of the shipbuilding industry was concentrated in the earlier years. Apart from these three the leather and clothing industry did particularly badly.

Only in the case of non-ferrous metals—always an erratic group—was Britain's share of trade higher in 1960–2 than in 1954–6, and even here it declined in the last few years. But the paper and printing trade virtually maintained its share. The motor industry too lost very little ground. Of the other three big groups, chemicals also did relatively well, but engineering and textiles both

Table 5.8. *United Kingdom industry in world trade in manufactures: percentages*

| | United Kingdom share in world exports[a] | | | | | | | Annual rate of rise in volume of exports | | |
| | Overseas sterling area[b] | | Other | | All areas | | | United Kingdom | | World |
	1954	1962	1954	1962	1954-6[c]	1957-9[c]	1960-2[c]	1954-5 to 1960-1	1960 to 1975	1960 to 1975
Chemicals n.e.s.	53·2	38·1	9·6	9·6	15·3	14·3	13·4	9·4	4·7	5·1
Iron and steel	58·4	30·9	8·0	8·6	13·3	12·8	11·1	5·1	2·0	2·5
Non-ferrous metals	46·3	26·2	9·1	14·7	12·6	15·2	12·9	6·9	3·6	2·0
Engineering and electrical goods	64·5	42·3	14·2	11·6	22·4	18·8	16·4	1·8	4·7	6·6
Shipbuilding and marine engineering	57·1	24·2	17·3	7·1	21·3	13·2	12·9	2·4	-1·1	2·0
Motors and cycles	61·5	52·6	21·0	20·3	26·1	25·5	25·0	5·7	4·9	5·2
Aircraft	64·9	43·1	34·6	23·7	44·5	46·3	30·6	12·5	4·2	5·4
Railway locomotives and rolling stock	56·4	34·9	12·6	6·5	28·4	25·5	13·2	-17·7	0·7	2·8
Metal goods n.e.s.	64·2	44·3	11·8	11·5	20·2	18·7	16·2	1·3	2·7	3·4
Textiles	51·0	26·9	20·2	14·5	25·9	22·5	18·0	-2·2	0·9	3·0
Leather, clothing, footwear	66·5	27·6	13·6	9·4	20·3	16·0	11·4	—	5·4	7·1
Paper, printing, publishing	47·2	36·6	2·8	3·9	6·9	6·9	6·8	0·4	4·2	2·6
Other manufacturing	57·5	41·8	12·2	11·3	18·9	16·7	15·2	7·6	1·8	2·6
Total products of above industries	58·2	39·1	13·4	12·0	19·9	18·1	15·9	3·1	3·8	4·7
Total manufactures	57·8	39·0	12·4	11·6	19·3	17·6	15·6	3·1	3·8	4·7

Source: United Nations, OECD and national trade statistics, Board of Trade and NIESR estimates.

[a] In the analysis by industry Swiss exports are excluded. The items covered for each industry group are listed below, numbered according to the Standard International Trade Classification (revised) and with the value of United Kingdom exports in 1960 shown in brackets. The separate area figures are partly estimated. Canadian exports of aircraft engines (711.4) are included in 'engineering and electrical goods'.

Chemicals n.e.s. (£326 million)	081.3, 231, 263.2, 274.1,4 and 5 (less 52)
Iron and steel (£203 million)	67 (less 671.5 and 677)
Non-ferrous metals (£100 million)	671.5 and 68 (less 681)
Engineering and electrical goods (£832 million)	71 (less 711.4 and 712.5), 72, 812, 861, 862, 864 and 951
Shipbuilding and marine engineering (£52 million)	735
Motors and cycles (£555 million)	712.5, 732 and 733
Aircraft (£20 million)	711.4 and 734
Railway locomotives and rolling stock (£166 million)	731
Metal goods n.e.s. (£135 million)	667, 677, 681, 69, 821 and 897
Textiles (£344 million)	26 (less 261, 262.1, 263.1 and 263.2) and 65
Leather, clothing, footwear (£71 million)	61, 83, 84 and 85
Paper, printing and publishing (£75 million)	25, 64 and 892
Other manufacturing (£108 million)	62 and 89 (less 892, 896 and 897)

[b] Excluding Iceland and the Irish Republic.

[c] The unweighted average of the percentages for each of the three years.

fared worse than manufacturing industry as a whole (textiles particularly in the overseas sterling area).

(g) *Future prospects for exports of individual British industries*

Mention has already been made of the relative rates of increase in trade in the main groups of manufactures—fastest for machinery and transport equipment and, in volume, for chemicals, slower for metals and miscellaneous manufactures, slowest of all for textiles—and of the likelihood that recent divergences will be somewhat reduced in future. Within these broad groups there have also been important differences, particularly in the transport section.

Between 1954 and 1962 the value of exports of aircraft and aircraft engines increased by something like 230 per cent, and exports of road vehicles more than doubled. Exports of ships on the other hand increased by less than half and exports of railway vehicles actually declined a little. Similarly in the miscellaneous group, clothing and leather exports rose very sharply (by some 165 per cent), but world exports of the paper and printing industry by little more than 50 per cent.

Trade in clothing is still expanding very fast, particularly with the overseas sterling area. On the other hand world exports of aircraft and of railway vehicles seem to have reached respectively a temporary peak and a temporary low point round about 1960, which was also a year of very high exports of base metals, particularly iron and steel. Our projections of the growth of world trade between 1960 and 1975 allow for these various tendencies. They also assume that exports to the overseas sterling area will not in future lag so far behind the rest. This follows from the view taken about the trade of the semi-industrial countries, which include Australia, India, New Zealand, Pakistan and South Africa.

On our hypotheses about the total value and composition of world trade in manufactures in 1975, British exports of manufactures in that year would exceed their target by over £600 million, or 12 per cent, if the 1962 share were maintained industry by industry both inside and outside the sterling area. They would, however, fall short of it by nearly £1,000 million, or more than 18 per cent, if these shares continued to change (and in the aggregate to decline) at the same rate as from 1954 to 1962. That is to say, to achieve the collective target they will need to make good about 60 per cent of the gap between the figure which represents a projection of past trends in their shares and the figure which represents maintenance of 1962 shares. Our individual targets are based on the assumption that this sort of relationship will apply industry by industry, subject to modification in a few cases. For example, we have taken a higher figure for the aircraft industry than this method would produce, as it is probably not sensible to assume that the phase of supremacy for the Boeing and the Caravelle denotes an underlying decline in the British industry's competitiveness. And for non-ferrous metals we have allowed for a slightly slower rise in share.

Table 5.9. *Japanese industries' shares in world trade in 1962 and changes in British industries' shares from 1954 to 1962[a]: percentages*

Japanese share		Annual rate of change in United Kingdom share	
Shipbuilding and marine engineering	21.5	Railway locomotives and rolling stock	− 9·2
Textiles	16·4	Leather, clothing, footwear	− 9·0
Leather, clothing, footwear	15·8	Shipbuilding and marine engineering	− 8·7
Railway locomotives and rolling stock	14·7	Textiles	− 6·2
Pottery and glass	12·8	Engineering and electrical goods	− 4·5
Iron and steel	9·9	Pottery and glass	− 4·4
Metal goods n.e.s.	8·8	Iron and steel	− 3·9
Engineering and electrical goods	5·2	Metal goods n.e.s.	− 3·0
Chemicals n.e.s.	3·8	Chemicals n.e.s.	− 2·0
Motors and cycles	2·6	Motors and cycles	− 1·5
Paper, printing, publishing	1·9	Paper, printing and publishing	+ 0·4
Non-ferrous metals	1·8	Non-ferrous metals	+ 2·7

Source: United Nations, OECD, and national trade statistics.

[a]Of the industries specified in table 5.8 the aircraft industry is omitted as a special case, and the 'other manufacturing' group because of its mixed composition. For all manufactures the Japanese share was 7·5 per cent and rate of fall of the United Kingdom share 3·5 per cent.

On this basis we arrive at figures of the volume of exports in 1975 which range from 220 per cent of the 1960 level for clothing to under 85 per cent for shipbuilding. Of the biggest groups textiles are given only a 15 per cent increase, but chemicals, motor vehicles and engineering goods apart from transport equipment are all shown as doubling.

It should perhaps be emphasized again at this point that the whole operation is highly conjectural. It does, however, seem reasonable to suppose that if an improvement in competitiveness is to be achieved most of it is likely to come where present deficiencies seem most marked. A further consideration is that past losses of share appear to be connected very closely with Japanese competition. They have consistently been biggest where Japan has gained a substantial part of the market, as has happened with shipbuilding, textiles and clothing, and railway rolling stock, and least where Japanese exports play the smallest part, on non-ferrous metals and paper and printing (actual gains) and on motor vehicles and chemicals (see table 5.9). Japanese exports are now becoming increasingly diversified, and the process is likely to continue. Their competition is now seriously felt in heavy engineering, for example, and the same thing is likely to happen before long in the motor vehicles industry[1].

(h) *Prospects for competing imports of manufactures*

As might be expected, the industries which have shown themselves most competitive overseas have, on the whole, been the most successful also in

[1]L. A. Dicks-Mireaux and others, 'Prospects for the British Car Industry', *National Institute Economic Review, op. cit.,* p. 33.

maintaining their share of the domestic market. This is true, for example, of the paper and printing and chemical industries, in which the share of imports in United Kingdom consumption does not seem to have changed very much between 1954 and 1960 (see table 5.10). Similarly the shipbuilding, aircraft and textile and clothing industries fared badly in both respects. In the non-ferrous metal and motor vehicle industries on the other hand, imports increased particularly fast in relation to consumption despite their good export records. For both, however, 1960 was an abnormal year. Stock accumulations and the liberalization of car imports were probably largely responsible.

It is impossible to distinguish at all clearly how far foreign gains in the United Kingdom market have been due to liberalization and how far to declining competitiveness in British industry. Accordingly a combination of two methods has been used to distribute, group by group, the total allocated for competing imports of manufactures in 1975. The first method assumes that this distribution will depend on the relative competitiveness of the British industries concerned, measured by their performance in world markets. That is to say, it assumes that for a given industry imports as a proportion of United Kingdom consumption will rise between 1960 and 1975 more or less than the average according as the industry concerned has been taken to be less or more successful than the average in maintaining (or exceptionally, increasing) its share of world exports over the same period. Under the second method separate calculations have been made, much as in the case of exports, of the value which imports would reach in 1975 industry by industry if their share of consumption remained as in 1960, and of the value which they would reach if it continued to change at the 1954–60 rate. The former values have been scaled up or down to the extent necessary to produce the required total, in proportion to the difference between the two sets of figures.

The first method is open to the objection that competitiveness may not be the same at home as it is abroad. For example, high tariffs may enable an industry to maintain its position domestically even though its underlying competitiveness is deteriorating. Similarly, future tariff reductions might mean a loss of share to foreign imports even though competitiveness was maintained, or the effects of past liberalization may not have fully worked themselves out. Also competition may come from different sources. Overseas, account has been taken only of the exports of other big industrial countries. But in the case of clothing, for instance, the biggest rise in imports has been from the underdeveloped countries[1]. The second method, on the other hand, gives too much weight to what may be temporary consequences of liberalization, or even more ephemeral developments such as British Overseas Airways Corporation's purchase of Boeings. It was not applied at all to non-ferrous metals, where it would have produced an obviously absurd result.

In practice the results of the two methods were in most cases not very

[1]*National Institute Economic Review*, November 1963, p.13.

different, at any rate in absolute amounts. But the second produced substantially lower figures than the first for engineering products and chemicals, and higher ones for paper and printing and motor vehicles. The first two groups both contain some highly protected items, whereas the competition in the home market in paper goods is to a large extent with the EFTA countries and car imports in 1960 were, as already mentioned, abnormally high. In general the mean of the two results was used, but downward adjustments were made for aircraft and cars, and an upward adjustment on clothing in view of the big further rise in imports which has already taken place since 1960.

Table 5.10.   *Imports and home consumption: percentages*

	Annual rate of rise in volume of retained imports		Share of imports in consumption		
	1954–6 to 1960–2	1960 to 1975[a]	1954	1960	1975[a]
Chemicals n.e.s.	11·2	8·1	9·5	11·2	11·6
Iron and steel	−6·0	4·0	2·2	4·1	4·7
Non-ferrous metals	20·7	1·6	4·4	10·7	8·8
Engineering and electrical goods	14·0	6·8	4·6	7·7	10·2
Shipbuilding and marine engineering	32·8	8·9	1·6	3·6	8·5
Motors and cycles	15·7	6·9	1·5	4·0	5·3
Aircraft	12·7	5·1	5·4	11·3	12·7
Metal goods n.e.s.	16·5	5·7	1·3	3·0	3·8
Textiles	8·6	4·5	5·1	8·8	11·6
Leather, clothing and footwear	18·2	7·3	3·4	6·8	11·9
Building materials	9·4	3·5	1·2	2·1	3·3
Pottery and glass	10·9	5·2	4·7	7·1	9·0
Timber, furniture, etc.	6·8	4·3	9·2	11·1	12·1
Paper, printing, publishing	8·6	4·3	6·4	7·2	6·6
Other manufactures	14·3	6·3	3·2	4·4	5·0
Total for above industries	10·8	5·9			
Total manufactures	9·7	5·3			

Source: NIESR estimates.
[a]Estimates.   Share figures at 1960 prices.

4.   IMPLICATIONS

(a) *Balances of individual industries on competitive trade*

The projections imply annual rates of growth in exports between 1960 and 1975 of about 5 per cent for leather goods and clothing, motor vehicles, other engineering products (apart from vehicles) and chemicals, 4 per cent for the products of the aircraft, paper and printing and non-ferrous metal industries, 3 per cent for miscellaneous metal goods, 2 per cent for iron and steel and other miscellaneous manufactures, and 1 per cent for textiles apart from clothing. Exports of ships and railway vehicles are both taken as falling by about 1 per cent per annum.   In comparison with the past this would mean big improvements for machinery and leather goods and clothing (because of increased competitiveness and strong demand, notably in the overseas sterling area). Textiles too would do a good deal better, as is in fact happening now that man-made textiles account for a much higher proportion of the total. Chemicals, however, would suffer from slower growth in world demand, and metals would rise relatively little because of their high level in 1960.

On the import side the implication is that for most manufacturing industries competing imports would rise at about half the rate that applied from 1954–6 to 1960–2. The reduction would be greater where the rate was particularly high, as it was for ships, leather goods and clothing, and miscellaneous metal goods, but smaller for chemicals, for which demand in Britain is expected to increase particularly fast. Metals are again a special case because of year to year fluctuations. If they are excepted the annual rate of rise from 1960 to 1975 would range from 9 per cent for ships to $3\frac{1}{2}$ per cent for building materials.

Engineering goods (apart from transport equipment) and road vehicles would greatly improve their balances of trade, which are already very favourable. For all other manufacturing industries combined there would, however, be a worsening. Metals and metal goods and aircraft would all substantially increase their surpluses, but there would be big deteriorations on chemicals (where imports are already higher absolutely than in any group but engineering, and have been rising faster than exports), on textiles, and on three groups in which competing imports are already higher than exports—clothing and leather goods, wood products and paper and printer matter (Appendix table 5.2).

Altogether the surplus on the competitive trade of manufacturing industry would amount to about £2,400 million, compared with rather more than £1,800 million in 1960 and around £1,900–£2,000 million in other recent years for which we have estimates (Appendix 5.2). In other classes of industry the corresponding balances would not change much, except that the deficit on agricultural trade and food, drink and tobacco products would rise from about £500 million to £600 million[1].

(b) *Competitive trade in relation to output in individual industries*

Our projections make no great change in the orientation of British industries' production. In most cases they imply that a lower proportion of output will go into exports in 1975 than in 1960 and that the balance of trade in relation to output will also be less favourable, though the deterioration will be slower than in the past (Appendix 5.3). The industries in which we expect these

---

[1]The import figures on which these balances are calculated exclude products for which United Kingdom demand is supplied mainly from abroad (such as crude petroleum, most basic materials and many types of food). On the other hand they include freight and insurance costs.

relationships to be better in 1975 than in 1960 are mainly the ones in which they had already been improving before 1960. The only ones where we expect a deterioration between 1954 and 1960 to be followed by a significant improvement between 1960 and 1975 are coal mining, drink and tobacco, railway locomotives and rolling stock and, for net exports only, non-ferrous metals. The relatively favourable outlook for coal and whisky exports has already been discussed, as has the erratic course of trade in non-ferrous metals. In railway vehicles we are allowing for a sharp fall in United Kingdom demand.

(c) *Total overseas trade*

Altogether, with mainly imported food, fuels, and materials etc., included, we envisage that the volume of retained imports will increase at an annual rate of 3·6 per cent per annum from 1960 to 1975, and the volume of exports at 3·7 per cent (see table 5.11). Imports in 1960 were, however, inflated by a number of special factors. The underlying rate of rise would be more like 3·8 or 3·9 per cent. Moreover even on the figures as they stand the faster growth of exports than of imports would be due to the faster growth of trade in manufactures than in non-manufactures. Class by class exports would be increasing the more slowly, except in the food and materials groups, where they are in any case small.

Because on a trade account basis imports in 1960 exceeded exports by £850 million, or nearly a quarter, the 'trade gap' measured at constant prices would increase substantially in trade account terms and would be somewhat higher even in the balance of payments. The big improvement comes on the terms of trade, from which our assumptions imply a gain of £675 million on a trade account basis to 1975. Without it we should have had to raise the annual percentage rate of increase in the volume of exports of manufactures from 3·8 to 4·3, and to reduce that for imports of manufactures from 5·3 to 4·8 (assuming the same method of calculation—see page 163). However over half of the assumed gain from more favourable terms of trade had already accrued by 1962 as a result of the improvement since 1960 (and the subsequent worsening has been largely due to factors which are clearly temporary). The price rise assumed for manufactures between 1962 and 1975 adds almost £425 million to imports as well as £750 million to exports—a net gain of only £325 million.

The hypothesis of a further improvement in the terms of trade, like many of the other assumptions made, is clearly a highly debatable one, but the amounts involved are so large that it seemed necessary to take what appeared to be the most reasonable view rather than follow the easy way of assuming no change. Our hypotheses imply more favourable terms of trade than those of the 1930s. They are, however, fairly similar to those adopted by the Brookings Institution in its recent forecasts of the American balance of payments in 1968. These were that raw material prices would be stable as between 1961 and 1968, while for manufactures Western Europe's export prices would rise by 1 or 1½ per cent per annum and those of the United States by about ½ per cent per annum[1].

If the implied deterioration in the terms of trade of the underdeveloped countries does not occur, their need of international assistance will be to that extent diminished. But the scope for saving by reducing aid from Britain below the level envisaged in chapter 4 would be relatively small even if such a reduction could be justified. The main effect on Britain would be that the considerable improvement in competitiveness that will in any case be required would need to be even bigger.

(d) Competitiveness and current policies

Competitiveness has many aspects and may be affected by official policies in a number of different fields. Some of them, where the issues involved are mainly domestic, are discussed in other chapters of this book. This applies not only to education, energy and transport, where the influence of policy decisions is likely to be fairly long-term and indirect, but also to prices and incomes, where success or failure can have a more immediate impact. Here, however, internal and external considerations are closely linked. Not only can achievement in export markets be influenced to an important extent by the domestic price structure, but the domestic price structure can itself be influenced by trade policies.

There is an increasing readiness to accept reductions in the degree of protection enjoyed by manufacturing industry in Britain. Such changes have indeed already been taking place in EFTA and through the 'Dillon round' of tariff negotiations, and may be carried further by the 'Kennedy round'. The hope is that tariff cuts will cheapen costs to the consumer, both directly by lowering the prices of imports and indirectly through the influence of competition on the selling prices of British industry, and that they will stimulate exports both by promoting greater efficiency and by increasing the relative attractiveness of overseas markets.

In the case of agriculture, on the other hand, policy appears to be moving in the opposite direction, namely by making imports more expensive and so restricting competition from them. This is a little surprising. It is true that greater competition from imports would be unlikely to have much effect on agricultural exports. But food has an important impact on the cost of living (accounting for well over a quarter of total consumers' expenditure), and the disparities between the prices paid to home and overseas producers are in some cases very large—compared for example with the general level of protection of manufacturing industry.

[1]See Walter S. Salant and Associates, *The United States Balance of Payments in 1968*, *op. cit.*, pp. 59, 83, 86 and 226.

Table 5.11. *Projected growth of trade by commodity group: £ million*

	1960	1975 At 1960 prices	1975 At current prices	Annual percentage rate of increase, 1960–75 At 1960 prices	Annual percentage rate of increase, 1960–75 At current prices
Retained imports					
Food, beverages and tobacco	1,510	1,950	1,910	*1·7*	*1·6*
Basic materials	994	1,245	1,175	*1·5*	*1·1*
Mineral fuels and lubricants	478	1,175	1,105	*6·2*	*5·7*
Manufactured goods[a]	1,399	3,050	3,440	*5·3*	*6·2*
Miscellaneous	18	30	35	*3·5*	*4·5*
Total	4,399	7,450	7,665	*3·6*	*3·7*
Exports					
Food, beverages and tobacco	197	300	290	*2·9*	*2·6*
Basic materials	126	220	220	*3·8*	*3·8*
Mineral fuels and lubricants	133	300	295	*5·6*	*5·4*
Manufactured goods[a]	3,000	5,225	6,115	*3·8*	*4·8*
Miscellaneous	99	130	145	*1·8*	*2·5*
Total	3,555	6,175	7,065	*3·7*	*4·7*
Balance of trade	−845	−1,275	−600	n.a.	n.a.

Sources: Table 5.4, *Annual Statement of the Trade of the United Kingdom* and NIESR estimates.

[a]Includes works of art.

The value of subsidies under price guarantees for domestically produced cereals, eggs and livestock has recently been running at close on £200 million a year. There are in addition direct payments of various kinds which cost the exchequer about £100 million a year and must relate to quite a large extent to the same products. Their total cost in subsidies must, therefore, be something like a third of their value at 1962 import prices of around £800 million (and also equivalent to nearly half the yield from purchase tax). Moreover against the import saving must be set probably the major part of imports of feeding-stuffs, fertilizers, store cattle and so on totalling around £300 million.

The position on sugar is slightly different in that the consumer, broadly speaking, pays a price based on the total cost of all sugar, both home-produced and imported. Also, when credit is taken for the value of the by-products obtained in the processing of the beet, home output for the last few years has probably been costing much the same as imports at the prices negotiated under the Commonwealth Sugar Agreement, or even a little less. But these have usually been well above the price at which sugar was available in the free market. There is probably a good case for aid to sugar producers in the West Indies and the colonies. But it is difficult to see why it should be given indefinitely under arrangements which have obliged the British consumer to subsidize producers in Australia and, for a time, in South Africa also.

The latest policy of controlling subsidies by enforcing minimum import prices for cereals and perhaps for meat, if necessary by levies, similarly deprives the consumer of the benefit of cheap supplies and at the same time maximizes the foreign exchange cost of the share of the market which is allocated to imports. The same sort of effect is achieved by quota arrangements for butter and bacon. There would be more merit in such schemes if a substantial part of the benefit from them could be expected to accrue to the underdeveloped countries. But in 1963 these countries supplied only 25 per cent of British imports in the meat group, 3 per cent in the dairy produce and eggs group and 6 per cent in the cereals group.

Clearly there is a case for saving expenditure on imports at some cost in terms of domestic price inflation. It seems doubtful, however, whether the balance has been struck at the right point in all cases, and the latest policies in some respects combine the worst of both worlds. Moreover direct savings on food imports will have relatively less value as time goes on, since consumption of food is one of the least expansive elements in the economy, whereas competitiveness in the field of manufactured goods will be increasingly important. The total turnover of trade in manufactures was £5,000 million in 1963 and on our figures its value will nearly double by 1975.

There is evidence that, in Britain at least, export prices of manufactures are linked fairly closely to costs of production (of which wages and salaries account for about half, materials and fuels for about 30 per cent and services for about 20 per cent)[1]. There is a clear association also between changes in the relative export prices of the chief manufacturing countries and their success or failure in export markets. Of the ten biggest exporters of manufactures in most recent years the two countries (Italy and Japan) which recorded the biggest falls in the prices of their exports between 1953 and 1963 also achieved the biggest increases in their value. The three which recorded the biggest price rises (Switzerland, the United States and the United Kingdom) occupied three of the last four places in order of value rise (see table 5.12).

Comparisons between recorded export prices of different countries may be somewhat misleading for various reasons[2]. All the same, these results can hardly result from mere coincidence. On the other hand it is clear too that other factors must have played important parts. The order of the Common Market countries apart from Italy is exactly reversed between one list and the other, and for most countries relative performance measured by changes in export values did not change much between the first half of the period and the second although there were some big divergences in the movements of export prices. Canada, for example, seems to have gained very little from the decline in the exchange value of the Canadian dollar after 1959. West Germany's

[1]See R. R. Neild, *Pricing and Employment in the Trade Cycle* (Cambridge, 1963), pp. 9 and 50.
[2]See Walter S. Salant and Associates, *op. cit.*, p. 74.

Table 5.12. *World exports of manufactures: percentage changes from 1953 to 1963 in prices and values*[a]

	Prices				Values		
	1953–8	1958–63	1953–63		1953–8	1958–63	1953–63
Italy	−14	−6	−19	Japan	+141	+ 96	+373
Japan	− 7	−5	−12	Italy	+ 95	+124	+336
Belgium/				West Germany	+112	+ 66	+253
Luxembourg	− 2	−4	− 6	Netherlands	+ 59	+ 67	+165
Canada	+ 5	−6	− 1	France	+ 46	+ 62	+136
France	+ 2	−2	—	Belgium/			
Netherlands	+ 1	+3	+ 4	Luxembourg	+ 41	+ 56	+121
West Germany	—	+7	+ 7	Switzerland	+ 26	+ 55	+ 96
Switzerland	− 1	+9	+ 8	United States[b]	+ 36	+ 28	+ 75
United Kingdom	**+10**	**+7**	**+18**	**United Kingdom**	**+ 29**	**+ 27**	**+ 64**
United States	+12	+6	+19	Canada	+ 22	+ 27	+ 55
Total[c]	+ 5	+2	+ 7	Total[c]	+ 53	+ 51	+131

Source: United Nations, *Monthly Bulletin of Statistics; Board of Trade Journal.*

[a]In terms of US dollars.
[b]Excludes special category exports of military supplies, etc.
[c]In addition to countries listed includes Sweden, for which separate price figures are not available for 1963.

smaller gains in the later period might, it is true, be attributed to the revaluation of the German mark in 1961. On the other hand Switzerland shows the opposite pattern in terms of export values, although in each period Swiss export prices moved in much the same way as German.

The conclusion appears to be that the United Kingdom can hardly hope to achieve the required improvement in export earnings if British export prices continue to rise appreciably faster than those of most competing countries. But even an improving price relationship would not guarantee success. Other factors too must make their contribution.

CHAPTER VI

PRIVATE CONSUMPTION

By D. A. Rowe

The purpose of the present chapter is to provide a detailed projection of consumers' expenditure for 1975, allocating the figure of total expenditure arrived at in chapter 9 between thirty or so separate commodities or commodity groups. From these figures the industrial output needed to meet these demands may be calculated and, ultimately, the requirements in terms of the basic factor resources.

The projection of consumer demand must, inevitably, rely mainly on the extrapolation of past patterns of consumer behaviour. But we shall also take account of special factors, such as policy decisions affecting transport and fuel, which are likely to influence significantly the consumption of particular items.

The evidence regarding consumer behaviour to be chiefly drawn on consists of annual estimates of expenditure covering the period 1900 to 1960. It is debatable, perhaps, how far into the past it is reasonable to pursue the search for insight into the future. In other sectors of the economy it may be hardly worth looking beyond the last decade or, at most, the post-war period. There is reason to believe, however, that movements in consumer demand can best be viewed in a longer perspective. Aggregate demand is the outcome of innumerable separate decisions, and while very many of the transient influences affecting individual choices cancel out for the community as a whole, there are also long-term shifts in tastes and social structure which are unlikely to emerge clearly from an examination of a short period only.

It is not possible in the present state of our knowledge to identify more than a few of the factors responsible for long-term shifts in demand. We can only assume them to be, in aggregate, gradual in operation and very largely independent of short-term changes in income and prices. Analysing past behaviour in this way, it is possible to take a middle course between, on the one hand, simply extrapolating the past trend of sales and, on the other hand, introducing a multitude of special factors whose effect can only be assessed in broad, qualitative terms.

The projections are made on the assumption that real expenditure per head increases at an average rate of $2\frac{1}{2}$ per cent a year between 1960 and 1975. This is a rather higher rate of growth than has been achieved in any comparable period of this century. Conceivably, this fact in itself will tend to invalidate projections based too closely on past experience. Processes of technical development and social change are intimately related to the rate of growth in the standard of living; where new products are being continually

N

introduced, price effects and innovation effects are hard to disentangle. It is to be hoped, nevertheless, that the income and price responses derived from the analysis of the past will reflect persistent underlying relationships; the evidence of family budget inquiries may be drawn on to confirm and to improve the precision of these estimates.

In the present context, where there is a fixed total expenditure to be distributed, the essential interrelation of all demands cannot be overlooked. It is not enough simply to sum a series of independent estimates for individual commodities considered in isolation; more than average increases in one category can only be achieved at the cost of some retrenchment elsewhere.

The procedure adopted for making the projections has been accomplished in two stages. The first stage is a projection of eight main commodity groups based on an econometric analysis of the time series covering the whole period 1900 to 1960. The aim of this analysis was to assess the relative importance of the main determinants of demand: income, prices and changing taste; and it has been formulated in such a way as to pay special attention to the interrelation of demands. For items within the main groups, in the second stage of the projection, less systematic methods have been employed. The more narrowly commodities are defined, the more important are special factors in determining demand. For many items it has been necessary to rely to a large extent on the extrapolation of recent trends; in certain cases it has been possible to incorporate information from cross-section analysis as well.

A particularly difficult problem arises in dealing with price changes. To the individual consumer prices present themselves, in almost every case, as extraneously determined; he allocates his expenditures in terms of a given set of prices. It is evident, nevertheless, that price changes in the past were determined in part by movements of demand. The introduction of a new commodity, for example, has often been associated with rapid technological advance, making for cost saving and a falling price, while competing goods, for which the demand has declined, have been subject to price increases—the recent history of coal prices and railway fares provides examples of this process. To incorporate a completely determinate system of price formation in the present projections would require an extremely detailed and complex formulation. It seems best for the present purpose, therefore, to make only the simplest assumptions as to relative price movements. It would not be reasonable, clearly, to suppose that all prices would change in the same proportion, since this would imply very special and peculiar assumptions regarding supply conditions and autonomous shifts of demand in the future. In the event, the solution adopted must be an uneasy but expedient compromise. For the eight main commodity groups it is assumed that relative prices remain unchanged at the 1960 levels. Within these groups, where price substitution is more marked, it will be assumed that there are continuing shifts in relative prices in line with recent experience.

N2

In the following section the changing pattern of consumption since the beginning of the century will be briefly sketched. In section 2 the model of consumer demand is presented. Projections for the main commodity groups, derived from the model, are given in section 3, and in section 4 they are further subdivided between thirty-one individual items of consumption. In a final section the estimates for all items are brought together and some conclusions on the general reliability and significance of the figures are drawn.

1. CONSUMERS' EXPENDITURE, 1900 TO 1960

The changing pattern of consumption between 1900 and 1960 is summarized in tables 6.1 and 6.2. In order to simplify the picture, figures for seven years only are shown, illustrating the principal changes in each decade.

There are many problems, conceptual and statistical, likely to impair the comparability of expenditure figures over so long a period[1]. Apart from purely statistical difficulties due to the lack of accurate and comprehensive data, quality changes and the introduction of new products and the disappearance of old ones do much to invalidate comparisons over sixty years. But only broad groups of commodities, representing fairly distinct and stable categories of wants, are dealt with here[2]; the more striking shifts in taste mostly take place within the groups. Had the comparison been limited to the post-war years, the results would have been unduly dominated by the effects of the war and the subsequent period of readjustment.

While total consumption, at constant prices, increased at an average annual rate of 1·2 per cent over the period 1900 to 1960 as a whole, the population had also been rising by a little over 0·5 per cent a year, so that total consumption per head rose at an average rate of only 0·7 per cent[3]. The rate of growth was far from uniform throughout the period. This was primarily due, of course, to the disturbing effects of two wars. As a consequence, the greater part of the increase was concentrated in the 1930s and the last decade of the period.

So far as their pattern of growth over the period is concerned, the eight commodity groups fall into three distinct classes. Communications, transport and entertainment have all grown extremely rapidly; drink and tobacco has

[1]Those interested in details should consult the original sources: *Consumers' Expenditure in the United Kingdom, 1900–1919*, by A. R. Prest and A. A. Adams (Cambridge, 1954); *The Measurement of Consumers' Expenditure and Behaviour in the United Kingdom, 1920–1938*, by Richard Stone and others (Cambridge, 1954); Central Statistical Office, *National Income and Expenditure, 1957* and *1962*, together with *National Income Statistics: Sources and Methods* (London, 1956).

[2]The composition of the eight main commodity groups is shown in table 6.15. The estimates discussed in the present and two following sections, however, exclude expenditure on 'housing maintenance' and the 'net tourist balance'.

[3]The actual magnitude of the increase depends on the base-year prices chosen; the nearer the base year is to the end of the period, the smaller is the apparent increase. This is a familiar feature of base-weighted aggregates. The choice of 1938 as the base year represents a convenient compromise between the more extreme positions.

Table 6.1. *Consumers' expenditure at current prices, 1900–60*

	1900	1910	1920	1930	1938	1950	1960
							£ per head
Food	12·89	13·99	39·23	27·80	27·39	56·67	93·68
Clothing	3·71	3·96	18·18	9·11	9·22	21·29	31·06
Household expenses	9·37	9·84	23·80	21·67	24·64	36·64	66·43
Communications	0·12	0·18	0·39	0·48	0·63	1·24	2·65
Transport	1·99	2·25	5·67	5·80	6·61	11·10	29·25
Drink and tobacco	5·20	4·45	13·03	9·61	9·90	30·55	39·86
Entertainment	1·00	1·11	3·22	3·03	3·16	7·13	11·06
Other	5·19	5·77	12·09	9·83	12·28	17·59	36·22
Total	39·47	41·55	115·61	87·33	93·83	182·21	310·21
							Percentages
Food	32·7	33·7	33·9	31·8	29·2	31·1	30·2
Clothing	9·4	9·5	15·7	10·4	9·8	11·7	10·0
Household expenses	23·7	23·7	20·6	24·8	26·3	20·1	21·4
Communications	0·3	0·4	0·3	0·5	0·7	0·7	0·8
Transport	5·0	5·4	4·9	6·7	7·0	6·1	9·4
Drink and tobacco	13·2	10·7	11·3	11·0	10·5	16·8	12·9
Entertainment	2·5	2·7	2·8	3·5	3·4	3·9	3·6
Other	13·2	13·9	10·5	11·3	13·1	9·6	11·7
Total	100·0	100·0	100·0	100·0	100·0	100·0	100·0

Table 6.2. *Consumers' expenditure at constant (1938) prices, 1900–60*

	1900	1910	1920	1930	1938	1950	1960
							£ per head
Food	21·34	21·18	21·12	25·83	27·39	31·47	33·94
Clothing	8·30	7·86	8·76	8·74	9·22	9·60	11·50
Household expenses	18·16	18·19	19·59	22·37	24·64	23·06	28·23
Communications	0·24	0·29	0·32	0·46	0·63	0·90	1·16
Transport	2·28	2·47	3·86	5·14	6·61	7·19	12·96
Drink and tobacco	16·67	12·54	12·28	9·51	9·90	9·51	11·19
Entertainment	1·26	1·51	2·70	3·01	3·16	4·47	4·81
Other	10·07	9·86	8·55	9·85	12·28	9·17	14·37
Total	78·32	73·90	77·18	84·91	93·83	95·37	118·16
							Percentages
Food	27·2	28·7	27·4	30·4	29·2	33·0	28·7
Clothing	10·6	10·6	11·3	10·3	9·8	10·1	9·7
Household expenses	23·2	24·6	25·4	26·4	26·3	24·2	23·9
Communications	0·3	0·4	0·4	0·5	0·7	0·9	1·0
Transport	2·9	3·3	5·0	6·1	7·0	7·5	11·0
Drink and tobacco	21·3	17·0	15·9	11·2	10·5	10·0	9·5
Entertainment	1·6	2·0	3·5	3·5	3·4	4·7	4·1
Other	12·9	13·4	11·1	11·6	13·1	9·6	12·1
Total	100·0	100·0	100·0	100·0	100·0	100·0	100·0

shown a noticeable decrease; while the four remaining groups, which between them account for the largest part of expenditure, have on the whole risen only slightly more or less than the average.

(a) *Food*

Expenditure on food accounts for more than 30 per cent of total expenditure in most years and consumption has tended to rise slightly faster than total consumption over the period as a whole. This may appear surprising in view of the considerable amount of evidence from cross-section studies that the income-elasticity of demand for food is in the region of a half. In part it is accounted for by the increased consumption of better quality food with the rising standard of living; it also reflects the fact that in the course of time a growing proportion of manufacturing and retail services, processing and packaging, have been incorporated in food consumption. Prices have also been a contributory factor; apart from the war periods, food prices tended to fall more and rise less than other prices.

(b) *Clothing*

Over the period as a whole consumption of clothing has risen less than total consumption. Again, this would seem to conflict with the findings of cross-section analysis, which have usually shown that demand for clothing is income-elastic. It would appear that there were quite substantial forces at work to offset the ordinary income effect. It does not look as if adverse price movements have contributed to this result to any great extent. It will be important in making projections to be able to assess the strength of this element of trend.

(c) *Household expenses*

This is a large and apparently heterogeneous group, but the various commodities represent quite closely interrelated demands. It includes expenditure on rent which has been subject in a large measure to statutory control over much of the period. It also includes domestic service, which has declined steeply during the period as alternative and more congenial forms of employment have been offered to young women. This decline has stimulated, and to some extent been promoted by, the greater use of domestic appliances. Expenditure on household durable goods, especially electrical equipment, has constituted a rapidly growing proportion of the total. It is also possible that the limited amount of new housing and the increasing inadequacy of the ageing stock of houses has been a cause of greater expenditure on furnishings, fuel and cleaning materials than would have otherwise been the case. In spite of the divergent trends of these components there is good reason for taking them together as a single group.

(d) *Communications*

Though relatively small, this group is sufficiently different from other items to be worth treating separately. It has been one of the most rapidly growing groups in the period since 1920. It has grown, moreover, at a steady rate, unimpeded by the second world war. This expansion has been mainly due to the growth of the telephone service, which was negligible at the beginning of the century and now accounts for half of the total.

(e) *Transport*

Expenditure on transport, at constant prices, has risen more than any other group during this period. Both expenditure on public transport and purchases of motor cars and motor cycles, together with their running costs, are included here. The rapidly growing importance of the petrol engine is the principal feature of the changing pattern of expenditure on transport. The motor bus has ousted the tram and begun to replace the train, while the growth of private motoring has diverted a continually increasing part of the total traffic away from the public services. This process was severely disrupted during the second war when production of new motor vehicles for civilian use was drastically curtailed and the supply of petrol for private purposes restricted. In the first world war road transport was altogether less important and war conditions seem to have encouraged a greater mobility of the population and an increased demand for transport services. Allowing for the effect of the war periods, the demand for transport appears to have risen at an accelerating rate over the period as a whole.

(f) *Drink and tobacco*

Both components of this group have exhibited strong trend movements, but they have been in opposite directions. The declining consumption of alcoholic drink has in part reflected a change in social habits but it has also been induced to some extent by a continually rising price as duty rates were repeatedly increased. Tobacco consumption has risen in spite of an equally marked increase in price. It is probable that these trends are not unrelated and something is to be gained from treating the two commodities together.

(g) *Entertainment*

This is the only group that has increased more rapidly during each of the war periods than at other times. The rise was particularly marked during the first war when the cinema was enjoying its first wave of popularity. Apart from the wartime interludes, the rate of growth was very even until the last decade of the period. In these final years the rapid spread of television had begun to make its impact on cinema-going.

(h) *Other goods and services*

This large and miscellaneous group of goods and services is the one that was most severely affected by war restrictions; they are, in effect, the 'inessential' components of consumption.   Apart from the war periods, the trend has been upwards, but for the most part this has only been just sufficient to make good the wartime losses.

2. A MODEL OF CONSUMER DEMAND

The model of consumer demand which has been applied to the analysis of the eight main groups of expenditure over the period 1900 to 1960 is a version of the linear expenditure system[1].   This system postulates a linear relationship between expenditure on each commodity, total expenditure and the prices of all commodities.   The simplicity of a formulation where expenditures are directly determined by total expenditure and prices will be evident, but it is too general for practical purposes.   By imposing certain theoretically desirable conditions the degrees of freedom in the system (the number of parameters to be estimated) can be considerably reduced.   These conditions are:

(i) that the sum of the expenditures on the individual commodities is always equal to total expenditure;

(ii) that there is no 'money illusion'.   If all prices and total expenditure were raised in the same proportion, the quantities purchased would remain unchanged;

(iii) that the substitution effects are symmetric between all pairs of commodities[2].

As a consequence of these restrictions, in a system with n commodities the number of independent parameters is reduced from a possible maximum of $n(n + 2)$ to no more than $2n - 1$.   It is also apparent from the mathematical form of the equations that these parameters may be given a particular meaning. Expenditure on each commodity can be said to consist of two parts: a committed part, the cost of purchasing a fixed quantity, c, at the current price, and a discretionary part which is a proportion, b, of the money left over after all committed expenditures have been made[3].   While this interpretation is certainly not put forward as a complete resolution of the complexities of consumer behaviour, it is sufficiently plausible to lend colour to a useful working hypothesis.

The benefits to be gained from using so relatively simple a formulation are also offset by certain limitations.   The present system can accommodate neither

[1]See 'Linear Expenditure Systems and Demand Analysis: an Application to the Pattern of British Demand', by Richard Stone (*Economic Journal*, September 1954).   Two alternative formulations of demand models with a similar aim are: 'Commodity Group Expenditure Functions for the United Kingdom, 1948–1957', by C. E. V. Leser (*Econometrica*, January 1961), and 'A Method for Estimating Price and Income Elasticities from Time Series and its Application to Consumers' Expenditures in the Netherlands, 1949–1959', by W. H. Somermeijer, J. G. M. Hilhorst and J. W. W. A. Wit (Netherlands Central Bureau of Statistics, *Statistical Studies*, no. 13, 1962).

[2]This is the Slutsky condition for consistent choice.

[3]Since the b's must sum to unity if condition (i) is to be fulfilled, the number of independent parameters is only $2n - 1$.   See Appendix 6 for a mathematical statement of the model.

inferior nor complementary goods.   Further, unless negative c's are admitted, all demand curves are necessarily price-inelastic.   While these limitations might be serious if the analysis were concerned with a very detailed classification of individual goods, in many applications their effect may be minimized by a judicious grouping of commodities.   In the present instance only eight broad classes of commodities are distinguished and they are so chosen as to be unlikely to conflict with the basic assumptions of the model.

The model is also open to certain extensions which, at the cost of added complexity, make for greater realism.   For instance, in the formulation adopted here the fixed parameters of the basic equations have been replaced by straight-line trends.   In this way, while all the other useful properties of the system are retained, allowance is made for a gradual adjustment of behaviour patterns through time.   The committed quantities are now no longer fixed but are assumed to be subject to a process of gradual change.   They are still 'committed', however, in the sense of being determined independently of current income and prices.   At the same time the distribution of discretionary spending between commodities is also changing.   This formulation, it may be noted, is more complex than the usual residual trends which are often introduced as a means of allowing for changes in taste.   There is a danger, nevertheless, in the rigidity of the assumed trends.   This defect might be overcome by substituting specific variables for the simple trends; for example, some function of past purchases would be a plausible alternative and would introduce a genuine dynamic element into the formulation.

In theory, the number of commodities in the system is unlimited.   In practice, however, the limitations of the basic model are likely to become increasingly apparent as it is applied to a more detailed list of commodities.   The computing difficulties also constitute a limiting factor.   All the parameters must be determined simultaneously by an iterative procedure, and even with no more than eight commodity groups the amount of computation involved is formidable.

There is a further property of the system, however, which offers a way round this difficulty.   The equations for any subgroup of items may be rewritten in terms of expenditure on the group and the prices of the group alone, the form of these equations being similar to that of the total system.   This subsystem may then be treated in exactly the same way as the total system, but quite independently of all other items[1].

In the present instance it has not been possible to carry out an analysis of more than the eight aggregate groups discussed in the preceding section. Eventually it may be possible to undertake a further analysis of subgroups as well, but in its absence some alternative procedure must be used to make estimates for items within the groups.   The independence of subgroups suggests one method of doing this.   It can be shown that, subject to certain

[1]See Appendix 6.

additional restrictions and assuming that there are no relative price changes within the group, the proportionate change in expenditure on each item is a weighted average of the proportionate changes in total and committed expenditure on the group as a whole[1]. The weights are determined by the expenditure elasticities of the items and may be derived extraneously from cross-section data. For the present application, where the parameters of the main groups are assumed to be changing through time, this method for subgroups involves the further assumption that within groups the relative values of the parameters are fixed. In this way, while remaining within the framework of the model, it is possible to extend its scope by making use of information from cross-section analysis.

At best, this method is only a makeshift, and in many cases the fairly stringent assumptions required will not be appropriate. Marked shifts in tastes may take place within the groups as well as between groups. In these cases a more flexible, but more arbitrary, procedure must be adopted, relying to a large extent on the extrapolation of past trends. The dangers of such a method are manifestly great where the period of the projection is relatively so long, but the predetermined totals for the groups do something to reduce the degree of arbitrariness involved. A method of simple extrapolation also carries the implication that all determinants of demand will vary in the future in very much the same way as they have done in the past. But this is not necessarily a disadvantage. It is to be expected that the relative shift in some prices will continue into the future; an assumption of fixed price ratios for all commodities would imply a radical change in supply conditions that no expectations about the future would warrant.

3. PROJECTIONS FOR THE MAIN EXPENDITURE GROUPS

The model of consumer demand described in the preceding section has been applied to annual data covering the period 1900 to 1960 for the eight main expenditure groups[2]. The broad pattern of consumption during this period has been briefly described in section 1 above. All expenditures were converted to values per head and the years 1914–19 and 1940–7, which were clearly abnormal, were omitted from the calculations. The estimating procedure was an iterative one and was directed to determining the set of parameters which minimized the sum of squares of the discrepancies between actual and calculated expenditures at current prices. In this way greatest weight is given to observations for which expenditure is largest. Not only do the larger groups gain at the expense of the smaller ones, but the later years of the period are also given more weight than the earlier. Though this is not in all cases clearly the

---

[1]See Appendix 6.
[2]For a more detailed account of this application of the model see 'Demand Analysis and Projections for Britain: 1900–1970', by Richard Stone, Alan Brown and D. A. Rowe, in *Europe's Future Consumption*, edited by J. Sandee (Amsterdam, 1964), p. 200.

Table 6.3.   *Demand parameters for the main expenditure groups*

	c	Δc	b	Δb
Food	33·73	0·33	0·0805	− 0·0039
Clothing	9·26	0 04	0·1569	0·0021
Household expenses	24·59	0·15	0·2263	0·0021
Communications	1·13	0·03	0·0023	− 0·0004
Transport	8·97	0·17	0·2342	0·0016
Drink and tobacco	10·20	0·06	0·0956	− 0·0019
Entertainment	5·05	0·08	− 0·0143	− 0·0008
Other	9·99	0·06	0·2186	0·0012

best procedure, it has an advantage from the point of view of making projections. The underlying trends are unlikely to be as simple as the linear forms specified and it is desirable to give greatest emphasis to recent experience when assessing the probable effect of these trends in the future.

In spite of this limitation, however, good agreement between actual and calculated values was found over the whole of the period[1]. Not only were the broad trend movements of the series well represented, but a considerable part of the short-term variation was accounted for as well; the post-war movements were particularly well explained. The goodness of fit obtained in the past, under quite widely varying conditions, is some indication of the reliability to be expected with regard to the projections.

The estimated values of the parameters are shown in table 6.3.

In this table the parameters c and b relate to 1960, the final year of the observed period. They represent, respectively, the committed quantities (£ per head at 1938 prices) and the proportions of discretionary or supernumerary expenditure allotted to each group in that year. The increments Δc and Δb, are the annual changes in these parameters. Thus the values of c and b for any future year may be obtained and, for given levels of total expenditure and prices, expenditure on each commodity group can be calculated. One of the dangers involved in the assumption of linear trends is already manifest in this table: in 1960, as throughout the post-war years, the parameter b for entertainment has a theoretically unacceptable negative value.[2]

The usual demand elasticities may also be calculated, but, since the equations are linear in expenditure and prices, they are not constants[3]. They vary not only with the level of expenditure and prices but also with the annual shifts in the parameters. Estimated values for three years of the period are shown in table 6.4. The changes shown are fairly large but need not be rejected on this ground alone. There is support from budget inquiries, for example, for the declining expenditure elasticity for food and the 1960 value agrees well with

[1] R. Stone, A. Brown and D. A. Rowe, 'Demand Analysis and Projections for Britain: 1900–1970', *op. cit.*, figure 1, pp. 214–15.

[2] It implies a positive elasticity of substitution with respect to ow price.

[3] The Engel curves in this system are linear in form, while the ord ary demand curves, relating quantity and own price, are hyperbolic.

Table 6.4. *Estimated demand elasticities for main expenditure groups*

	Expenditure elasticity			Own-price elasticity		
	1900	1938	1960	1900	1938	1960
Food	0·96	0·55	0·26	− 0·57	− 0·22	− 0·11
Clothing	0·35	1·09	1·57	− 0·17	− 0·22	− 0·32
Household expenses	0·42	0·73	1·05	− 0·25	− 0·25	− 0·33
Communications	5·19	1·54	0·27	− 2·02	− 0·19	− 0·04
Transport	4·10	2·47	2·48	− 1·53	− 0·43	− 0·47
Drink and tobacco	1·54	1·23	0·74	− 0·69	− 0·26	− 0·18
Entertainment	1·38	0·09	− 0·40	− 0·56	− 0·02	0·06
Other	1·06	1·68	2·02	− 0·50	− 0·35	− 0·41

estimates from recent cross-section data. It will be recalled that throughout this period the proportion of total expenditure spent on food has remained nearly constant. Marketing costs have often been invoked to reconcile this fact with the low elasticities invariably obtained from cross-section analysis. From the present analysis, however, the explanation seems to lie rather in the continued increase in the relative importance of the committed expenditure on food. For clothing and household expenses, it may be noted, changing tastes have resulted in a rising expenditure elasticity through the period. This is supported by the generally observed tendency for these goods to be increasingly associated with prestige expenditure.

In 1975 it is calculated that total private consumption will be £27,260 million at 1960 prices[1]. With an estimated population of 59,206 million in 1975, an increase of 12·7 per cent on 1960, this represents an expenditure of £460 per head. The corresponding figure for 1960 is £317·7, so that an annual rate of increase in consumption per head of 2½ per cent is implied. It will be assumed that the relative prices of the eight main groups in 1975 remain unchanged at the 1960 level. As no money illusion is incorporated in the model, it is only relative prices that matter here.

The concept of consumers' expenditure employed in the analysis excludes occupiers' maintenance expenditure on houses and makes no adjustment for consumers' expenditure abroad or expenditure by foreign tourists in the United Kingdom. The value of these items in 1975 has been estimated separately[2]. Excluding these items, the total figure to be allocated between the eight main groups is £450·8. The details of the calculation are shown in table 6.5.

The parameters c and b in this table are derived directly from those in table 6.3 by the addition of fifteen annual increments. The prices (1938 = 1·000) are given in the first column. Committed expenditure is the value of the committed quantities, c, at these prices. The difference between total expenditure and total committed expenditure is then allocated in accordance with the b's to obtain supernumerary expenditure on each group.

[1]See chapter 9, page 271 below.
[2]See pages 192 and 197 below.

Table 6.5. *Projected expenditures on eight main groups in 1975*

				Expenditure (£ per head at 1960 prices)		
	p	*c*	*b*	Com-mitted	Super-numerary	Total
Food	2·760	38·71	0·0220	106·8	3·2	110·0
Clothing	2·702	9·91	0·1884	26·8	27·0	53·8
Household expenses	2·353	26·90	0·2577	63·3	37·0	100·3
Communications	2·262	1·52	− 0·0037	3·4	− 0·5	2·9
Transport	2·256	11·45	0·2582	25·8	37·0	62·8
Drink and tobacco	3·562	11·07	0·0671	39·5	9·6	49·1
Entertainment	2·300	6·18	− 0·0263	14·2	− 3·8	10·4
Other	2·520	10·95	0·2366	27·6	33·9	61·5
Total	—	116·69	1·0000	307·4	143·4	450·8

The extrapolation of the linear trends has now produced a negative value of *b* for communications as well as for entertainment. Although these negative values raise difficulties for theoretical interpretation, in the context of the analysis the estimated parameters probably provide the most satisfactory basis for projection; in both cases there are offsetting increases in committed expenditure. Nevertheless there are clearly limits beyond which projections on this basis cannot be usefully made. Already in 1975 almost the whole of expenditure on food is committed expenditure, with the implication that food consumption is becoming increasingly insensitive to changes in income and prices. Moreover, as this committed expenditure is increasing at a slower rate than expenditure on all commodities, the proportion spent on food falls. This is shown more clearly in table 6.6.

It can be seen from this table that the reduction in the proportion spent on food is mostly taken up by the increased share going to transport. The other groups whose shares also increase are clothing and the residual group of miscellaneous goods and services. The increase in expenditure on transport, which is expected to more than double in these fifteen years, is perhaps the most striking feature of this table.

Both communications and entertainment, which have been among the most rapidly expanding groups in the past, show no such movement for the projected period; indeed, expenditure on entertainment actually falls. So far as communications are concerned, the past rate of growth has been fostered both by the relative fall in price and by the fact that wartime restrictions, while restraining expansion of other competing groups, have had little adverse effect on these services. Neither factor is operative for the projection. The decline of the cinema is manifest in the marked slowing down in the growth of expenditure on entertainment in the 1950s, and it is probably not surprising that this should turn into an actual fall in succeeding years. It is likely, however, that the effect of the linear trend is to overstate this fall.

Table 6.6. *Expenditure on main groups in 1960 and 1975*

| | Expenditure per head at 1960 prices | | | | Percentage change, 1960–75 |
| | 1960 | | 1975 | | |
	£	Per cent	£	Per cent	
Food	93·7	30·2	110·0	24·4	17·4
Clothing	31·1	10·0	53·8	11·9	73·2
Household expenses	66·4	21·4	100·3	22·3	50·9
Communications	2·6	0·8	2·9	0·7	9·8
Transport	29·2	9·4	62·8	13·9	114·9
Drink and tobacco	39·9	12·9	49·1	10·9	23·1
Entertainment	11·1	3·6	10·4	2·2	− 5·7
Other	36·2	11·7	61·5	13·7	69·9
Total	310·2	100·0	450·8	100·0	45·3

In general, it is to be expected that the changes in the pattern of consumption to emerge from the projection should diverge to a certain extent from the experience of the past. In part this is due to the assumption of a higher average rate of growth for total expenditure than has obtained for any comparable period in the past. At a slower rate of growth changes in committed expenditure play a more dominant part and tend to maintain a stable pattern of expenditure. In earlier periods, moreover, shifts in relative prices, though rarely very large, have also influenced the pattern of expenditure. To make an adequate projection of price movements, allowing for the interaction of demand and supply in both commodity and factor markets, would be extremely difficult, and the assumption of fixed relative prices at the level of aggregation used so far is the only feasible alternative in the present instance. This assumption will be partially relaxed in dealing with subgroups.

4. PROJECTIONS FOR THE SUBGROUPS OF EXPENDITURE

In the present section the eight main expenditure groups are discussed in turn and the methods used to make projections for the component items of each group are described.

(a) Food

Six items of food expenditure are separately distinguished for the present purpose. In the past changes in the pattern of expenditure on these items have not suggested the presence of any special factors affecting tastes other than the normal development associated with a rising standard of living. The demand shifts, moreover, have hardly been such as to influence greatly relative prices, which have been largely determined by supply conditions in a world market. In these circumstances it seems reasonable, as a preliminary step at least, to

Table 6.7.   *Expenditure elasticities for food items, 1960*

	Expenditure (pence per week)	Expenditure elasticity
Bread	21·98	− 0·09
Flour	3·05	− 0·21
Cakes and biscuits	21·24	0·18
Other cereals	8·20	0·28
Bread and cereals	54·47	0·06
Carcase meat	50·27	0·27
Other meat and products	50·80	0·29
Fish	15·68	0·37
Meat, bacon, fish	116·75	0·29
Liquid milk	33·44	0·22
Other milk and cream	3·47	0·45
Cheese	7·85	0·23
Eggs	18·46	0·26
Dairy products	63·22	0·25
Fresh fruit	19·11	0·64
Other fruit	8·95	0·56
Potatoes	12·12	0·07
Fresh green vegetables	8·01	0·66
Other vegetables	10·87	0·26
Fruit and vegetables	59·06	0·44
Fats	22·65	0·11
Sugar and preserves	12·67	0·03
Miscellaneous foods	8·81	0·35
Other food	44·13	0·13
Beverages	18·10	0·19
All food	355·73	0·25

make projections for the separate food items by the systematic method for sub-groups discussed in section 2[1].   The expenditure elasticities, derived from family budget data for 1960[2], which have been used for this purpose, are set out in table 6.7.

The figures of expenditure given in this table are averages per household over the whole year of the inquiry: they have been used as weights to calculate elasticities corresponding to the subgroups of the present analysis.   The very close agreement between the expenditure elasticity for all food obtained here and that derived from the time series analysis will be noted.

With this additional information a preliminary projection of the six food subgroups can be made.   As was noted above, committed expenditure forms a large part of the projected total expenditure on food, and in consequence consumption tends to be relatively insensitive to variations in income and prices.

[1] See pages 184-5 above, and Appendix 6.
[2] Ministry of Agriculture, Fisheries and Food, *Domestic Food Consumption and Expenditure, 1960*, pp. 160–2.

Table 6.8. *Expenditure on food items in 1960 and 1975*

| | Expenditure per head at 1960 prices | | | | Percentage change, |
| | 1960 | | 1975 | | |
	£	Per cent	£	Per cent	1960–75
Bread and cereals	12·30	13·1	12·18	11·1	− 1·0
Meat, bacon, fish	28·48	30·4	34·31	31·2	20·5
Dairy products	14·66	15·7	17·59	16·0	20·0
Fruit and vegetables	15·34	16·4	18·73	17·0	22·1
Other food	16·96	18·1	20·11	18·3	18·6
Beverages	5·94	6·3	7·08	6·4	19·2
Total	93·68	100·0	110·00	100·0	17·4

A similar rigidity in the pattern of expenditure is also apparent in regard to the subgroups. This result is largely inherent in the assumptions on which the projection is made, since no relative changes in committed expenditures are permitted for the individual items in the group. Indeed, it seemed likely that the shift away from cereal products to more expensive foodstuffs was understated by the method and a further adjustment in this direction was made, the small discrepancy being redistributed proportionately among the other food items to obtain the figures shown in table 6.8.

Expenditure on fruit and vegetables shows the largest proportionate increase over the 15-year period, most of the gain being at the expense of bread and cereals and, to a lesser extent, the residual group of fats, sugar and miscellaneous foods. The other two groups to have increased noticeably more than the average are meat, bacon and fish, and dairy products, the main sources of protein in the diet. The share of beverages is almost unchanged.

(b) *Clothing*

For the present purpose only two subgroups have been distinguished here: footwear and other clothing. Any further subdivision between different types of apparel, though of considerable interest in many ways, has little significance in terms of industrial requirements and will not be attempted here in view of the approximate nature of the methods used.

While 'taste' factors have probably played an important part in determining total expenditure on clothing, there is little reason to think that they have affected footwear very differently from other clothing. The same method as for food may be used to allocate the projected total between the two component items. The expenditure elasticities from cross-section data[1] are found to be 0·94 for footwear and 1·30 for other clothing. The combined figure for all clothing is 1·24, which agrees reasonably well with the estimate from the time series analysis.

[1]Ministry of Labour, *Family Expenditure Survey: Report for 1960 and 1961* (London, 1962).

Table 6.9. *Expenditure on clothing items in 1960 and 1975*

	Expenditure per head at 1960 prices				Percentage change,
	1960		1975		1960–75
	£	Per cent	£	Per cent	
Footwear	5·50	*17·7*	8·65	*16·1*	*57·3*
Other clothing	25·56	*82·3*	45·14	*83·9*	*76·6*
Total	31·06	*100·0*	53·79	*100·0*	*73·2*

The estimates for 1975 obtained on this basis are shown in table 6.9. The effect of the higher elasticity for other clothing is to produce a proportionate increase for this item which is a third as large again as that for footwear. As the standard of living rises, the demand for all types of clothing is increasingly influenced by fashion, apart from genuine improvements in quality. It is probable that footwear offers less scope for this sort of sophistication than does other clothing.

(c) *Household expenses*

This large mixed group is one of the most difficult to allocate. Certainly the assumptions adopted for food and clothing are not appropriate here. There are many special factors to be taken into account in projecting the future pattern of expenditure. A great deal of reliance, therefore, has to be placed on a broad assessment of recent trends.

Expenditure on housing (rents, rates and water charges) depends primarily on the stock of houses and this magnitude is determined as much by political as by economic forces. It is estimated that the number of private houses will increase by 17 per cent between 1960 and 1975[1]. There will also be some improvement in the quality of the stock as the poorest houses are replaced by additions of higher quality. This improvement in quality alone probably accounts for an increase of a little over one per cent a year in expenditure on housing. Together these two factors imply an increase of 38 per cent in the total expenditure on housing, or an increase of 22·5 per cent in expenditure per head.

A somewhat larger increase is expected in expenditure on maintenance, including repairs and improvements. While the volume of improvements and major repairs will probably increase less rapidly than in the past, it seems likely that this will be offset by a more than proportionate expansion in minor repairs and maintenance work undertaken by occupiers.

Even in 1975 the standard of housing may still leave much to be desired. There will be a continuing demand for greater comfort and convenience in the home. In recent years it has been expressed in a widespread substitution of electricity for coal and a growing interest in central heating. Future developments in fuel consumption, however, depend to a great extent on policy

[1]See chapter 12 below for the details of this calculation.

Table 6.10.   *Expenditure on household items in 1960 and 1975*

| | Expenditure per head at 1960 prices | | | | Percentage change, 1960–75 |
| | 1960 | | 1975 | | |
	£	Per cent	£	Per cent	
Rents, rates, etc.	24·48	*34·2*	29·98	*27·8*	*22·5*
Housing maintenance	5·12	*7·2*	7·60	*7·1*	*48·4*
Coal	5·41	*7·6*	2·63	*2·4*	*− 51·4*
Electricity	4·49	*6·3*	15·20	*14·1*	*238·5*
Gas	2·59	*3·6*	3·38	*3·1*	*30·5*
Other fuels	1·75	*2·4*	2·33	*2·2*	*33·1*
Household durables	22·55	*31·5*	41·79	*38·7*	*85·3*
Matches, soap, etc.	3·52	*4·9*	4·31	*4·0*	*22·4*
Domestic service	1·64	*2·3*	0·65	*0·6*	*− 60·4*
Total	71·55	*100·0*	107·87	*100·0*	*50·8*

decisions in the nationalized industries.   In chapter 10 estimates of domestic consumption have been arrived at in the context of a wide review of the whole pattern of energy resources and requirements[1].   Those estimates are simply adopted here.

Total consumers' expenditure on fuel and light is expected to almost double between 1960 and 1975.   While coal consumption will fall by nearly a half, consumption of electricity is expected to increase fourfold.   Much more moderate increases of only 50 per cent are expected for gas and other fuels. Increases in terms of expenditure per head are shown in table 6.10.

The volume of private domestic service was much reduced by the war and has continued to decline fairly rapidly ever since.   It has been assumed that between 1960 and 1975 it will continue to decline at the same rate, 6 per cent a year, as in the preceding decade.

The remaining part of household expenses, after deduction of these specific items, comprises expenditure on all kinds of household goods, durable and non-durable.   The non-durable items, matches, soap and cleaning materials, are less than one tenth of the combined figure and may, with little loss of precision, be assumed to increase proportionately with expenditure on housing. The remainder is allotted to durable goods.   They include, in addition to the major durables such as furniture and electrical appliances, all sorts of furnishings, household textiles, hardware and pottery.   It has not been possible to subdivide the group further or provide any precise cross-check on this residual figure.   Nevertheless it is not implausible.   Expenditure per head is expected to almost double between 1960 and 1975, implying a gross expenditure elasticity of 1·7.   In view of the mixed nature of the group, this is a reasonable figure[2].

[1]See pp. 295–6 below.
[2]For a discussion of future trends in sales of individual durables see 'The Demand for Domestic Appliances', by L. Needleman in *National Institute Economic Review*, November 1960.

o

Table 6.11. *Expenditure on communication services in 1960 and 1975*

| | Expenditure per head at 1960 prices | | | | Percentage change, 1960–75 |
| | 1960 | | 1975 | | |
	£	Per cent	£	Per cent	
Postal service	1·37	51·7	1·44	49·5	5·1
Telephone and telegraph service	1·28	48·3	1·47	50·5	14·8
Total	2·65	100·0	2·91	100·0	9·8

(d) *Communications*

The only subdivision that is made here is between the postal services and the telephone and telegraph services. The projection for the group as a whole implies only a modest rate of increase, rather lower than in recent years. The margin of uncertainty must necessarily be large for so small a group as this, but, accepting the figure, it seems reasonable to attribute most of the increase to the telephone service. Accordingly, it has been assumed that expenditure per head on the postal services in 1975 is only 5 per cent higher than in 1960. The results for the group are shown in table 6.11.

(e) *Transport*

The future pattern of expenditure on transport is governed to a very large extent by a single factor: the private ownership of motor cars. It is possible that even within the period of the projection attitudes on this question may change radically and policy be directed to restrict rather than facilitate the use of the private car. For the present purpose, however, it will be assumed that the widespread urge to car ownership, clearly manifest in the last decade, will continue unhampered.

In a comprehensive review of the determinants of car sales made in 1961[1], it was estimated that between 1960 and 1970 registrations of new cars in Great Britain would probably expand at an average annual rate of between 7·2 and 8·6 per cent. This estimate was based on a projection of the car stock and assumed that real disposable income per head would rise at an average rate of $2\frac{1}{2}$ per cent a year. In addition, allowance was made for a residual trend factor to increase purchases by 3 per cent a year up to 1965 and $1\frac{1}{2}$ per cent a year thereafter. The alternative rates of growth reflect different assumptions about the rate of stock replacement.

This projection was only intended to establish an equilibrium position and not to provide short-term forecasts of sales. In 1961 and 1962 actual registrations were well below the trend; 1963 showed a marked recovery and the current level in the first quarter of 1964 is some way above the projected trend. But there is no indication of a systematic departure from the trend and there

[1]See 'Prospects for the British Car Industry', by L. A. Dicks-Mireaux, C. St. J. O'Herlihy, R. L. Major, F. T. Blackaby and C. Freeman in *National Institute Economic Review*, September 1961.

Table 6.12. *Expenditure on transport items in 1960 and 1975*

	Expenditure per head at 1960 prices				Percentage change, 1960–75
	1960		1975		
	£	Per cent	£	Per cent	
Motor vehicles	10·28	35·2	27·89	44·4	171·3
Running costs	8·28	28·3	23·65	37·6	185·6
Railway travel	2·76	9·4	2·53	4·0	− 8·3
Other travel	7·93	27·1	8·78	14·0	10·7
Total	29·25	100·0	62·85	100·0	114·9

seems no reason yet for any substantial revision of the projection. The assumptions on which it is based are sufficiently close to those of the present study for it to be adopted in essence here. However, we are concerned with expenditure and not simply the number of vehicles. The present trend is towards smaller cars and it is unlikely that this will be reversed. On the other hand, the probable effect of price changes must not be overlooked. There is clearly a tendency for car prices to fall relatively to other prices, and a recent reduction in purchase tax produced a significant upward shift in the level of sales. It seems reasonable, therefore, to assume an average rate of increase midway between the two alternatives, say 7¾ per cent a year, for expenditure between 1960 and 1975. This figure has been applied to all expenditure on motor vehicles as defined for the present purpose, that is, including expenditure on motor cycles and the dealers' margin on second-hand purchases.

Estimates of consumers' expenditure on other items of transport are made in chapter 11 below[1]. The results are shown in table 6.12. They are derived from an assessment of the total demand for travel and take into account the possibilities for some modification of the recent trend away from public transport towards private transport. Nevertheless, total expenditure on the use of cars, as shown by the estimate of running costs, is expected to grow by 8 per cent a year. Of the category 'other travel', about three quarters now consists of expenditure on bus fares. A reversal of the recent decline is projected. Of the rest, the largest amount is for expenditure on sea travel, which is expected to continue growing fast. Relatively small amounts are included, too, for expenditure on taxis and hire cars, which should rise, and on air travel, which should rise fast (although most of air travel expenditure is taken to be on business account).

(f) Drink and tobacco

Total expenditure on drink and tobacco has been subdivided between beer, other alcoholic drink and tobacco. For this purpose we have made use of the systematic method of dealing with subgroups outlined in section 2[2]. This requires knowledge of the expenditure elasticities for each of the items. It is

[1]See page 340 below.
[2]See pages 184-5 above, and Appendix 6.

Table 6.13. *Expenditure on drink and tobacco in 1960 and 1975*

| | Expenditure per head at 1960 prices | | | | Percentage change, 1960–75 |
| | 1960 | | 1975 | | |
	£	Per cent	£	Per cent	
Beer	10·72	26·9	12·48	25·4	16·4
Other alcoholic drink	7·44	18·7	10·39	21·2	39·7
Tobacco	21·70	54·4	26·19	53·4	20·7
Total	39·86	100·0	49·06	100·0	23·1

notorious that most family expenditure inquiries show serious deficiencies in respect of expenditure on these commodities. The understatement of spending on drink often amounts to as much as a half of the true figure. Although this bias may be independent of the level of income, the discrepancy is so large as to throw considerable doubt on estimates of the elasticities from this source. It seems better, therefore, to rely on figures from time series analysis.

For the post-war period 1950–6, expenditure elasticities of 0·52, 2·18 and 0·83 were found for beer, other drink, and tobacco, respectively[1]. The average for the group as a whole is 1·00. This is a higher figure than that obtained from the present analysis, but the margins of error are fairly large, particularly for other drink, and the two estimates are not significantly different. On this basis the estimated expenditures on the three items are as shown in table 6.13.

No very marked shift in the pattern of expenditure on these items is foreseen. The demand for wines and spirits, which is highly income-elastic, is expected to increase the most. Although the method employed for the projection makes no allowance for the secular shift in tastes which has favoured smoking at the expense of drinking, this is not so unreasonable as it might appear. Recent changes in social habits have probably arrested, if not wholly reversed, the long-term decline in the consumption of alcoholic drink. At the same time the warnings of the dangers of cigarette smoking have produced, along with some shift to other forms of tobacco consumption, a temporary fall in total sales, and may be expected in the longer run to weaken the force of the upward trend.

(g) *Other goods and services* (*including entertainment*)

As was indicated in discussing the analysis of the main expenditure groups, it seems probable that the results for entertainment are unduly dominated by the recent decline of the cinema. This was apparent in the reversal of sign for the elasticities in the later years of the period. As a consequence, the extrapolation of the linear trends for the parameters probably produces an increasing understatement of expenditure on entertainment. It seems more reasonable, therefore, to combine this group with the residual group of miscellaneous goods and services before attempting to allocate the projected figure between items.

[1] See 'Dynamic Demand Functions: Some Econometric Results', by Richard Stone and D. A. Rowe (*Economic Journal*, June 1958), p. 256.

Table 6.14. *Expenditure on other goods and services in 1960 and 1975*

| | Expenditure per head at 1960 prices | | | | Percentage change, |
| | 1960 | | 1975 | | |
	£	Per cent	£	Per cent	1960–75
Books, newspapers, etc.	4·66	*9·6*	4·26	*5·8*	*− 8·6*
Cinemas	1·28	*2·6*	0·26	*0·4*	*− 79·7*
Other entertainments	3·65	*7·5*	7·54	*10·3*	*106·6*
Chemists' goods	4·66	*9·6*	7·60	*10·3*	*63·1*
Other goods	9·96	*20·4*	14·66	*19·9*	*47·2*
Other services	23·07	*47·3*	37·63	*51·1*	*63·1*
Net tourist balance	1·47	*3·0*	1·64	*2·2*	*11·6*
Total	48·75	*100·0*	73·59	*100·0*	*51·0*

Expenditure on books, newspapers and magazines, at constant prices, has increased very little in the post-war period, with the result that expenditure per head has been decreasing slowly. This movement probably reflects some broad shift in tastes and may be expected to continue in the future. Accordingly, a figure for 1975 has been calculated on this assumption.

In 1963 admissions to cinemas were little more than a quarter of what they had been ten years earlier. Expenditure at constant prices has been falling at an average rate of ten per cent a year. There seems no reason to expect a reversal of this trend and it has been extended to 1975 at the same rate.

The remaining items included in this group are: other entertainments, chemists' goods, other miscellaneous goods, and other services. Expenditure per head on the group as a whole is estimated to increase by a little under two thirds between 1960 and 1975. The evidence of cross-section analysis suggests that expenditure elasticities are not very different for these items[1]. It seems not unreasonable, therefore, to assume a similar distribution in 1975 as obtained in 1960. Recent experience, however, suggests a somewhat faster rate of expansion for expenditure on other entertainments, while expenditure on miscellaneous goods may rise rather less than that on other items. With these adjustments, the projections are as shown in table 6.14.

A final item to be included here is the net balance of tourist expenditures. This is the difference between consumers' expenditure abroad and expenditure by foreign tourists and others in the United Kingdom. In the post-war period it has risen quite rapidly as the popularity of holidays abroad has outstripped the tourist attraction of this country. In part, however, this movement has reflected the progressive relaxation of travel allowances both here and abroad. For the future, developments more favourable to this country may be expected, and only a relatively small increase in the net balance is projected.

[1]See, for example, *The Analysis of Family Budgets* by S. J. Prais and H. S. Houthakker (Cambridge, 1955), p. 107.

5. SUMMARY AND CONCLUSIONS

The projections for all items of consumers' expenditure are brought together in table 6.15; the figures for 1950 and 1960 are also included for comparison. The changes in the pattern of expenditure have been discussed in some detail in the preceding sections and no further comment is called for here.

It will be apparent from the account of the methods used that the projections for individual commodities and commodity groups are strictly neither forecasts nor targets. While the figure of total expenditure is in the nature of a target to be reached if the specified growth rate is to be achieved, it is not implied that the estimates for individual items represent either desirable norms or standards by which to judge the success or failure of particular industries.

The figures are clearly not simple forecasts either. They are an attempt to discern a possible future pattern of expenditure, subject to particular prior assumptions. It is one of the implications of the formulation of consumer behaviour adopted here that the pattern of expenditure varies with the rate of growth of expenditure. With the assumption of a different rate of increase in total expenditure the projected pattern of expenditure would also be altered[1]. Specific assumptions have also been made with regard to relative price movements. While the rather simple assumptions made probably provide a reasonable first approximation, the absence of a detailed price forecast almost certainly produces some distortion in the results[2].

The formulation of the demand model is of equal importance with the assumptions in determining the outcome. In the present state of knowledge any model is at best a working hypothesis. The one employed here possesses certain advantages of simplicity and theoretical coherence. There are equally some obvious limitations. No explicit demographic factors are introduced, for instance, though changes in the composition of households might be expected to play a significant part in the long-run development of spending patterns. In fact, a whole range of long-term influences, definitional, distributional and behavioural, have had to be subsumed in the linear trends of the parameters. The importance attaching to these trends is a measure of our ignorance concerning the true determinants of demand.

It will hardly need emphasizing that the seemingly precise figures presented in table 6.15 are really no more than indications of the central region of a wide range of probabilities. Any assessment of the margin of error would vary from item to item and, at this stage, would be largely a matter of subjective judgement. While a projection over a period as long as fifteen years clearly offers scope for a considerable accumulation of errors, there is evidence from the past of a notable stability in the pattern of expenditure and this may be

[1]See, for example, the results for alternative rates of growth shown in the paper referred to in footnote 2 on page 185 above.
[2]Some calculations of the effect of alternative price assumptions are presented in Appendix 6.

Table 6.15. *Consumers' expenditure in 1950, 1960 and 1975*[a]

Expenditure at 1960 prices

	1950		1960		1975		Annual rate of change (per cent)	
	£m	Per cent	£m	Per cent	£m	Per cent	1950–60	1960–75
Bread and cereals	733	5·5	631	3·8	700	2·6	− 1·5	0·7
Meat, bacon and fish	1,234	9·3	1,461	8·8	1,972	7·2	1·7	2·0
Dairy products	687	5·2	752	4·5	1,011	3·7	0·9	2·0
Fruit and vegetables	626	4·7	787	4·7	1,077	4·0	2·3	2·1
Other foods	641	4·8	869	5·2	1,156	4·2	3·1	1·9
Beverages	224	1·7	304	1·8	407	1·5	3·1	2·0
Food[b]	4,145	31·2	4,804	28·8	6,323	23·2	1·5	1·8
Footwear	261	2·0	289	1·7	512	1·9	1·0	3·9
Other clothing[c]	1,057	8·0	1,350	8·1	2,676	9·8	2·5	4·7
Clothing	1,318	9·9	1,639	9·8	3,188	11·7	2·2	4·5
Rents, rates, etc.	1,090	8·2	1,286	7·7	1,775	6·5	1·7	2·2
Housing maintenance	234	1·8	269	1·6	450	1·7	1·4	3·5
Coal	289	2·2	284	1·7	156	0·6	− 0·2	− 3·9
Electricity	102	0·8	236	1·4	900	3·3	8·7	9·3
Gas	145	1·1	136	0·8	200	0·7	− 0·6	2·6
Other fuels	59	0·4	92	0·6	138	0·5	4·5	2·7
Household durables	766	5·8	1,185	7·1	2,474	9·1	4·5	5·0
Matches, soap, etc.	175	1·3	185	1·1	255	0·9	0·6	2·2
Domestic service	153	1·2	86	0·5	38	0·1	− 5·6	− 5·3
Household expenses	3,013	22·7	3,759	22·5	6,386	23·4	2·2	3·6
Postal service	54	0·4	72	0·4	85	0·3	2·9	1·1
Telephone and telegraph	48	0·4	67	0·4	87	0·3	3·4	1·8
Communications	102	0·8	139	0·8	172	0·6	3·1	1·4
Motor vehicles	83	0·6	540	3·2	1,650	6·1	20·6	7·7
Running costs	145	1·1	435	2·6	1,400	5·1	11·6	8·1
Railway travel	146	1·1	145	0·9	150	0·6	− 0·1	0·2
Other travel	424	3·2	417	2·5	520	1·9	− 0·2	1·5
Transport	798	6·0	1,537	9·2	3,720	13·6	6·8	6·1
Beer	510	3·8	563	3·4	739	2·7	1·0	1·8
Wines, spirits, cider	246	1·9	391	2·3	615	2·3	4·7	3·1
Tobacco	914	6·9	1,140	6·8	1,551	5·7	2·2	2·1
Drink and tobacco	1,670	12·6	2,094	12·5	2,905	10·7	2·3	2·2
Books, newspapers, etc.	242	1·8	245	1·5	252	0·9	0·1	0·2
Cinemas	178	1·3	67	0·4	15	0·1	− 9·3	− 9·5
Other entertainments	126	0·9	192	1·2	446	1·6	4·3	5·8
Sport and travel goods[d]	47	0·4	77	0·5	132	0·5	5·1	3·7
Entertainment	593	4·5	581	3·5	845	3·1	− 0·2	2·5
Chemists' goods	166	1·3	245	1·5	405	1·5	4·0	3·4
Other goods	255	1·9	446	2·7	781	2·9	5·7	3·8
Other services	1,144	8·6	1,369	8·2	2,438	8·9	1·8	3·9
Net tourist balance	61	0·5	77	0·5	97	0·4	2·4	1·6
Other	1,626	12·3	2,137	12·8	3,721	13·7	2·8	3·8
Total	13,265	100·0	16,690	100·0	27,260	100·0	2·3	3·3

See next page for footnotes.

expected to continue into the future. The procedures employed attempt to exploit this inherent stability and to limit the elements of pure guesswork in the projection. Though many will find cause to disagree with the figures and some, perhaps, will have the means to improve on them, much more detailed analysis is needed before any real precision can be attained. No more than a preliminary review of the problem, with some suggestions for approaching a solution, is offered here.

Notes to table 6.15, page 199.

[a]The classification of items used here follows that of the official statistics in *National Income and Expenditure, 1963*. The few exceptions are indicated in the following notes.

[b]Includes 85 per cent of 'income in kind not included elsewhere', which was distributed proportionately between component food items. In this table, following the official practice, food supplies to caterers are valued at wholesale prices. In the preceding tables of this chapter, however, caterers' supplies are valued at retail prices and expenditure on 'other services' is reduced by a compensating amount. The amount involved is approximately 3 per cent of total expenditure on food.

[c]Includes 15 per cent of 'income in kind not included elsewhere'.

[d]This item is not separately distinguished in the official figures. For the present purpose it has been roughly estimated by taking 10 per cent of expenditure on the residual group of other goods, including chemists' goods.

CHAPTER VII

THE PATTERN OF GROWTH OF OUTPUT, EMPLOYMENT AND PRODUCTIVITY, 1960 TO 1975

By W. Beckerman

Some chapters of this study have been concerned with establishing a reasonable assumption for the future overall growth rate of the economy and others with providing some guidance as to the manner in which the final output should be allocated among different end-uses, private and public consumption, the foreign surplus and so on. We have here to consider what such a pattern of final demand would imply for the output of individual industries, and from this we shall also go on to project the likely pattern of labour productivity and employment in the individual industries.

It will become increasingly clear, as we describe the techniques used, that no method has been found of estimating with much precision the changes in output by individual industry that correspond to the overall projection of the growth of gross national product and the pattern of final demand. How serious this limitation on the results is depends on the particular needs of the user. For an industrialist it would obviously be valuable to have a fairly precise estimate of future market trends whatever the industry in which he is engaged. But for the economic planner, there are probably very few problems of which the solution requires a precise figure of the growth rate of every branch of industry over the next ten or fifteen years. Apart from the flexibility of the relationships between outputs and inputs in most industries, to which we shall return in more detail in the next chapter, it would be naïve to believe that economic policy can proceed by laying down a detailed blue-print for ten years or more hence, deciding how this should be achieved, and then abandoning further responsibility for continuous adjustment and modification in the light of changing circumstances as well as for the errors in the initial projections.

Apart from errors made in the prediction of some of the factors influencing the demand for individual industries, there are numerous other factors which cannot be, or are not, predicted at all, so that economic policy must combine long-range strategy with considerable tactical flexibility. It would be foolish to think that, if the demand for the output of industry X grows by only 3 per cent per annum instead of 4 per cent as predicted, overall strategy will be seriously jeopardized and the authorities obliged, idly and hopelessly, to watch the imbalances in the economy multiply and accumulate.

Given, therefore, that it is impossible to make accurate projections of output by industry, that precision in this field is hardly necessary anyway, and that the presentation of apparently 'precise' results can be very misleading to some readers, we have not, in fact, made a precise estimate for the future output of each industry.   In the main table of projections (table 7.6) we show only a range within which the output of each industry is likely to fall in the projection year 1975.   It is purely for the sake of simplicity of presentation and of computation that the subsequent related tables referring to output, employment and productivity projections are based on the mid-points of the ranges, and so appear to indicate a precise output projection for each industry.

Although precise figures for each industry's 1975 output may be unnecessary and subject to large margins of error, a purpose is served by making the rough estimates of the kind presented here.   In the first place it is important to see whether, on the whole, some industries are likely to be required to grow exceptionally fast or exceptionally slowly.   Such cases might call for special investigation even allowing for the margins of error in the estimates.   But 'planning' or any form of attempt to influence the long-run growth of the economy must comprise a continuous exchange of, and mutual testing of, information and estimates between those engaged in more or less back-room statistical analysis and those that possess much more specialized knowledge than that which has been used in our very general approach.

Secondly, major changes in the pattern of output have implications for the desirable changes in the pattern of employment and the degree of inter-industry labour mobility that will be required.

Thirdly, the description in chapter 9 below of the overall balance in the economy requires some rough estimate of relative price changes, at least between major sectors of final demand, and a projection of output, employment, and hence labour productivity in individual industries is an obvious method of arriving at a view about the likely pattern of change in relative prices.

1.   SUMMARY OF PROCEDURE

It would be out of place in this study to present a full-scale exposition of the way that the pattern of outputs by industry is determined jointly by (i) the pattern of final demand by industry—that is, the sales to final demand by individual industries and (ii) the pattern of inter-industry relationships—the relationships between each industry's total outputs and its purchases of intermediate products (goods and services) from other industries.   There are many standard texts on this subject[1].   But it will be apparent that final sales of, say, cars to private consumers will not only have a direct impact on the output of the motor industry but will also have an indirect impact on the output of industries supplying raw materials to the motor industry, such as steel, rubber, textiles and the like.   Conversely, the total output of the steel industry will be determined not only by how much steel is sold direct to final buyers (e.g. for

[1]See, for example, Burgess Cameron, *The Determination of Production* (Cambridge, 1954), and Richard Stone, *Input-Output and National Accounts* (Paris, OEEC, 1961).

capital formation, or exports) but how much is sold as inputs into the car industry and other steel-consuming industries. The magnitude of these secondary, or indirect, effects will depend on the technical production relationships such as those between the output of cars and inputs, into the car industry, of steel, rubber and so on. To project the complete pattern of industrial output, therefore, it is not enough to know the total final demand for cars, steel, textiles or other products. It is also necessary to know the pattern of transactions between industries in intermediate products.

The most convenient and comprehensive description of the pattern of inter-industry transactions is an 'input-output' table. From such a table a matrix of 'technical coefficients' (or 'input-output coefficients') can be derived expressing inputs into each industry in relation to the total outputs of each industry. The major problem in using such a matrix for projection is that these technical coefficients are likely to change over time. For example, there may be substitution of other fuels in place of coal in the production of steel or gas, or of synthetic fibres in place of natural fibres in the production of clothing, or of aluminium for steel in the production of cars. The problem of the stability of input-output coefficients has been given considerable attention in the literature[1] and the most comprehensive attempt to predict the future changes in these coefficients in the United Kingdom has been that published as part of the Cambridge Department of Applied Economics long-term growth project under Professor J. R. N. Stone (hereafter referred to as the 'DAE Growth Project')[2]. In this study we have relied very heavily on the Cambridge work for the input-output matrix in the base year 1960 though for our projections we have been obliged to adopt some crude rule-of-thumb procedures for extrapolating to 1975 the effect on industries' outputs of changes in the technical coefficients. Before explaining our method for doing this, however, it is necessary to summarize briefly the entire procedure we have followed in this chapter.

In the first place, on the basis of the various projections of final demand by *function* given in other chapters, we have estimated final demand in terms of the various commodities identified in the DAE Growth Project's social accounting matrix (hereafter referred to as 'SAM')[3]. The distinction between the 'functional' and 'commodity' classification of final demand is as follows. A functional classification of final demand indicates a classification in terms of the functions that are being served: that is, private consumers' expenditures would be classified by functions under food, clothing, household durables, operation of transport equipment and so on. Almost every single function in

[1] A comprehensive bibliography on this topic is provided in *A Programme for Growth, 3: Input-Output Relationships, 1954–1966* (London, 1963), pp. 54–7.
[2] A series of volumes under the general title *A Programme for Growth* is being published for the Cambridge University Department of Applied Economics by Chapman and Hall.
[3] For definition of industry classification used in SAM in terms of the 1958 Standard Industrial Classification see *A Programme for Growth, 4: Capital, Output and Employment, 1948–1960* (London, 1964), pp. 50–1.

such a classification would represent expenditures on different 'commodities'. For example, expenditure on the operation of transport equipment would include purchases of petrol, insurance, licence fees, maintenance and other items, each of which represents a different 'commodity'. Equally, public expenditure on the function 'education' would include payments of teachers' salaries, purchases of stationery, heating and lighting of school premises, and so on, all of which are different 'commodities'.

Hence, the first step has been to translate the functional classification of each category of final demand in 1975 into a commodity classification. This has been done, in some cases, as part of the detailed projection of the category concerned. For example, the projection of educational expenditures included an explicit projection of the number of teachers required. In other cases it has simply been assumed that the commodity content of each function would be proportionately the same in 1975 as in 1960 (as given by 'SAM'). In yet other cases, a mixture of the two approaches has been used. This applies chiefly to the initial projection of capital formation: a provisional projection of total fixed capital formation has first been broken down in terms of the likely share, in this total, of different types of physical asset (buildings and works, plant and machinery, and different types of vehicle) and the 1960 relationship between commodities and these distinct types of asset has been applied to the 1975 projections for each type of asset. Finally, for foreign trade, as is explained in chapter 5 above, the projection has been made directly in terms of the SAM commodity classification.

The second step has been to make a provisional projection of total output by commodity, using methods described below to allow for likely changes in the technical coefficients of production. These provisional output projections have then been used to modify some of the final demand projections, chiefly the foreign trade projections, since many imports have been projected in the light of the projected changes in output of the consuming industries (which have been assumed to be proportionate to changes in the outputs of the corresponding commodities). The revised final demand projections have then been used to obtain revised, and final, projections of output by commodity. Output of the corresponding industries (namely those of which the commodities identified are the principal products) has then been assumed to change in the same proportion as the commodity outputs. Henceforth, therefore, the terms 'industry' and 'commodity' will be used interchangeably. Final *pro rata* adjustments to each industry's projected net output have been made to ensure consistency with the projection of total gross national product.

Clearly, a more satisfactory procedure would be to adjust, at each stage, all the components of the initial final demand projection (for example, by allowing for the effect on consumers' expenditure of the projected changes in output and hence in productivity and prices, or by re-calculating the pattern of capital formation by type of asset). Only in some cases, however, have we proceeded to a second round of re-calculations of the final demand pattern—notably for capital formation by industry, and imports of raw materials (both linked to the first-round output projections). We have not tried to make second-round adjustments to the pattern of consumers' demand, nor to proceed at all to third-round adjustments, partly through lack of time, partly because we are not convinced that they add substantially to the reliability of the results, and partly because a full-scale computable model of the economy, designed precisely to be able to handle manipulations on this scale, is being developed elsewhere[1].

The various sources of possible error in the procedure outlined above include, as a minimum, the following:

(a) Uncertainty as to the pattern of final demand by function. This applies chiefly to net exports, certain items of government consumption, and, perhaps to a lesser extent, the size and pattern of capital formation by type of asset. For example, the predictions made of exports of particular commodities must be subject to a large margin of error since so much depends on factors external to the British economy. Again, if by 1975 defence expenditures were to reflect the cessation of aircraft construction together with an almost total reliance on nuclear submarines, the relative output requirements for the aircraft industry and the ship-building industry would be greatly affected (though this might make very little difference to the metal goods or similar industries supplying inputs to shipbuilding or aircraft).

(b) Given final demand by function, the cross-classification of each function with its commodity content may change over time and there are no satisfactory estimates of such changes in the past for more than a handful of functions (chiefly consumers' expenditure on food).

(c) Very little is known about changes in the technical coefficients of production in Britain, and it is clear from the past that such changes can be very important (see next section), so that even if the final sales of each commodity were accurately projected, total output of each commodity would still be subject to a large margin of error in industries where inter-mediate sales to other industries are an important proportion of total sales[2].

(d) As the projected increases in *commodity* output have been used to project outputs of the corresponding *industries* major changes in the proportion of any commodity produced by the corresponding industry could be a source of error, though at the level of detail used here this is unlikely to be important[3].

---

[1] *A Programme for Growth, 1: A Computable Model of Economic Growth* (London, 1962).
[2] A concise survey of work in other countries on the stability of input-output coefficients is given in K. J. Arrow and M. Hoffenberg, *A Time Series Analysis of Inter industry Demands* (Amsterdam, 1959), pp. 15–24.
[3] Comparison of the 1954 and 1960 'make matrices' in *Input-Output Relationships, 1954–1966* (vol. 3 of *A Programme for Growth, op. cit.*) shows relatively small changes in the commodity/industry output ratios.

2. THE PROJECTION OF OUTPUT BY INDUSTRY

(a) *Changes in final sales by industry*

The crucial steps in the procedure outlined above are (i) the final demand projections for each industry and (ii) the transition from the final demand projections to the projections of total output by industry. The manner in which total final demand by function has been converted into final demand for the outputs of different commodities as classified in SAM has already been explained. The relationship between this classification and gross national product is summarized in table 7.1.

Tables 7.2 and 7.3 show the increases in final demand for each of the 31 industries used in SAM and the respective contribution to these increases made by the various categories of final expenditure shown above. As the most uncertain elements in the final demand projections for each industry are net exports followed by defence and capital formation, table 7.3 enables the incidence of this uncertainty in individual industries to be assessed.

Although private consumption by and large dominates the changes in final sales for each commodity there are several commodities where net exports or fixed capital formation are more important. Where it is the change in net exports that is very important the projection of output is particularly

Table 7.1. *Relationship between final expenditures on SAM classification and GNP, 1960 and 1975*

	£ *million, 1960 prices*	
Category of final expenditures	1960	1975
Change in stocks	591	600
Gross fixed capital formation	4,103	7,980
Net exports of 'competitive' goods and services[a][b]	2,286	3,200
Public consumption:		
(i) Civil	2,578	4,188
(ii) Military	1,611	2,222
Private consumption[b]	16,823	27,735
Total	27,992	45,925
less 'complementary' imports	− 2,939	− 4,275
less indirect taxes on imports	− 1,443	− 2,400
plus net property income from abroad	179	750
equals: GNP at market prices	23,789	40,000

[a]'Competitive' imports are 'imports of goods which are also produced in this country and of which half the total supply or less comes from abroad' (*A Programme for Growth, 2: A Social Accounting Matrix for 1960*, London, 1962, p. 3). All British exports are regarded as 'competitive'.

[b]Foreign tourist expenditures in the UK (£215 million in 1960 and £475 million in 1975) are included here in private consumption and hence are excluded from net exports. Hence in *National Income and Expenditure, 1961* the figure of net exports of goods and services (national accounts definitions) of − £259 million, is composed of £(2,286 + 215 − £2,939 + 179) million.

Table: SAM industry group by category of expenditure, 1960 and 1975 (£m.)

No.	SAM industry group	Change in stocks 1960	Change in stocks 1975	Gross fixed capital formation 1960	Gross fixed capital formation 1975	Net exports 1960	Net exports 1975	Public civil consumption 1960	Public civil consumption 1975	Defence 1960	Defence 1975	Private consumption 1960	Private consumption 1975	Total 1960	Total 1975	Index, 1975 total (1960=100)	SAM number
1	Agriculture, forestry and fishing	18	21	16	30	−231	−275	20	32	2	4	1,532	2,119	1,339	1,897	141·7	1
2	Coal mining	−14	−13			34	75	9	15			212	328	259	439	169·5	2
3	Mining and quarrying	−2	8									15	21	19	34	178·9	3
4	Food processing	26	24			−310	−410	23	38			1,966	2,505	1,705	2,157	126·4	4
5	Drink and tobacco	27	25			103	205					553	760	683	990	144·9	5
6	Coke ovens, etc.											21	35	59	87	147·5	6
7	Mineral oil refining	2	6			11	−80	17	28	4	8	136	302	176	357	202·8	7
8	Chemicals n.e.s.	2	2			−34		13	29	59	104	253	415	548	687	125·4	8
9	Iron and steel (excluding tinplates and tubes)	59	56			−139	−55	72	117	25	44	−17	−44	83	35	42·2	9
10	Iron and steel (tinplates and tubes)	57	54			43	25							100	122	122·0	10
11	Non-ferrous metals	8	7			30	85					−27	−66	25	43	172·0	11
12	Engineering and electrical goods	22	24	1,282	2,936	631	1,065	20	51	180	319	240	500	2,464	4,974	201·9	12
13	Shipbuilding and marine engineering	111	103	178	369	56	15			93	164			326	547	167·8	13
14	Motors and cycles	−1	−1	255	683	564	1,120			31	54	394	1,012	1,301	2,922	224·6	14
15	Aircraft	57	53	89	156	80	135			209	369			337	666	197·6	15
16	Railway locomotives and rolling stock	6	2	33	64	15	15							106	81	76·4	16
17	Metal goods n.e.s.	2	2		75	105	115	4	5	27	48	98	233	301	508	164·8	17
18	Textiles	34	32			200	105	9	19	1	1	202	470	442	623	141·0	18
19	Leather, clothing and footwear	30	28			92	115	7	14			935	1,851	967	1,845	190·8	19
20	Building materials	22	20				−40	11	27					40	45	112·5	20
21	Pottery and glass	14	13			15	5	6	9	1	1	53	129	95	168	176·8	21
22	Timber, furniture, etc.	4	4	29	53	−31	25	13	24	2	4	125	305	148	328	221·6	22
23	Paper, printing, publishing	23	27			−44	−85	16	39			239	315	259	338	130·5	23
24	Other manufacturing	28	29			−24	−45	32	65			130	273	236	377	159·7	24
25	Construction	20	19	1,845	2,931	54	20	105	237	95	168			2,307	3,716	161·1	25
26	Gas			10	6	10	10	13	25	3	5	252	370	170	237	139·4	26
27	Electricity			64	142	8	10	35	75	6	10	236	191	347	551	158·8	27
28	Water			9	16	6	5	8	17	1	1	60	70	86	114	132·6	28
29	Transport and communications			90	177	577	640	36	79	5	9	942	1,702	1,645	2,598	157·9	29
30	Distributive trades			29	58	16	25	37	87	18	32	2,928	5,161	3,015	5,340	177·1	30
31	Services n.e.s.			55	111	96	240	260	393			1,441	2,660	1,870	3,436	183·7	31
	less subsidies											−118	−137	−118	−137		
	Customs duties	1	1					8	17			988	1,448	997	1,466		
	Excise duties											400	592	400	592		
	Purchase taxes			77	173							450	1,044	527	1,217		
	Rates							26	50	10	18	377	438	413	506		
	Other											74	164	74	164		
	Distribution of property income											524	608	524	608		
	Persons							1,620	2,433	718	718	204	274	2,542	3,425		
	Depreciation on buildings							132	203	1	1	296	343	429	547		
	Complementary imports[a]	27	50					26	60	120	140	573	1,025	746	1,275		
	TOTAL	591	600	4,103	7,980	2,286 / +215 = 2,501	3,200 / +475 = 3,675	2,578	4,188	1,611	2,222	16,823 / −215 = 16,608	27,735 / −475 = 27,260	27,992	45,925	164·1	

[a] Excluding complementary imports used by industries.

	1960 £m.	1975 £m.
Total final demand by SAM category of expenditure as above (i)	27,992	45,925
less SAM complementary imports(ii)	−2,939	−4,275
less indirect taxes on imports	−1,443	−2,400
plus net property income from abroad	179	750
equals GNP at market prices (*National Income and Expenditure, 1961*)	23,789	40,000

(i) This total corresponds to the total of the categories 'consumers' expenditure', 'public authorities' current expenditure on goods and services', 'gross fixed capital formation at home', 'value of physical increase in stocks and work in progress' (table 11 of *National Income and Expenditure, 1961*), and of SAM category 'net exports'.

(ii) *National Income and Expenditure* net exports of goods and services (excluding indirect taxes on imports) = SAM net exports less SAM complementary imports (excluding the import content of re-exports from both SAM net exports and SAM complementary imports).

Table 7.3. *Increase in final sales, 1960–75*

SAM industry group	Total change in final sales (£m. at 1960 prices)	Percentage of change accounted for by						Index of final demand, 1975 (1960 = 100)
		Change in stocks	Gross fixed capital formation	Net exports	Public civil consumption	Defence	Private consumption	
1 Agriculture, forestry and fishing	558	0·5		−7·9	2·3		105·0	141·7
2 Coal mining	180	0·6	7·8	22·8	3·3	1·1	64·4	169·5
3 Mining and quarrying	15	40·0		20·0			40·0	178·9
4 Food processing	452	−0·4		−22·1	3·3		119·2	126·4
5 Drink and tobacco	307	−0·7		33·2			67·4	144·9
6 Coke ovens, etc.	28			−3·6	39·3	14·3	50·0	147·5
7 Mineral oil refining	181			−25·4	8·8	24·9	91·7	202·8
8 Chemicals n.e.s.	139	−2·2		−60·4	32·4	13·7	116·5	125·4
9 Iron and steel (excluding tinplates and tubes)	−48	6·2		37·5			56·2	42·2
10 Iron and steel (tinplates and tubes)	22	−4·5		104·5				122·0
11 Non-ferrous metals	18	11·1		305·6			−216·7	172·0
12 Engineering and electrical goods	2,510	−0·3	65·9	17·3	1·2	5·5	10·4	201·9
13 Shipbuilding and marine engineering	221		86·4	−18·6		32·1		167·8
14 Motors and cycles	1,621	0·2	26·4	34·3		1·4	38·1	224·6
15 Aircraft	329		34·7	16·7		48·6		197·6
16 Railway locomotives and rolling stock	−25		100·0					76·4
17 Metal goods n.e.s.	207	−1·0	20·3	4·8	0·5	10·1	65·2	168·8
18 Textiles	181	−1·1		−52·5	5·5		148·1	141·0
19 Leather, clothing and footwear	878	−0·2		−4·9	0·8		104·3	190·8
20 Building materials	5	−20·0		−200·0	320·0			112·5
21 Pottery and glass	73			−8·2	4·1		104·0	176·8
22 Timber, furniture, etc.	180	2·2	13·3	−22·8	6·1	1·1	100·0	221·6
23 Paper, printing, publishing	79	1·3		−26·6	29·1		96·2	130·5
24 Other manufacturing	141	−0·7		−24·1	23·4		101·4	159·7
25 Construction	1,409		77·1		9·4	5·2	8·4	161·1
26 Gas	67		−6·0	3·0	17·9	3·0	82·1	139·4
27 Electricity	204		38·2	−0·5	19·6	2·0	40·7	158·8
28 Water	28		25·0	7·1	32·1		35·7	132·6
29 Transport and communications	953		9·1	6·6	4·5		79·7	157·9
30 Distributive trades	2,325		1·2	0·4	2·2	0·2	96·0	177·1
31 Services n.e.s.	1,566		3·6	9·2	8·5	0·9	77·8	183·7
less subsidies	−19						100·0	116·1
Customs duties	469				1·9	8·6	98·1	147·0
Excise duties	192						100·0	148·0
Purchase taxes	690		13·9				86·1	230·9
Rates	93				25·8		65·6	122·5
Other	90						100·0	221·6
Distribution of property income	84						100·0	116·0
Persons	883				92·1		7·9	134·7
Depreciation of land and buildings	118				119·8		80·2	254·7

vulnerable[1]. As can be seen in table 7.3, this applies most to iron and steel, non-ferrous metals, and building materials, but the absolute amounts here are comparatively small. For other industries, where the absolute amounts involved are much larger, changes in net exports are an important part of the total projected change in final sales for the drink and tobacco industry, the motor vehicles and cycle industry, and the aircraft industry. There are also some important industries where declines in net exports are expected to have a large dampening impact on the evolution of total final sales, notably the food processing industry, the chemical industry, the shipbuilding industry, and the textile industry.

For about six industries the projection of domestic fixed capital formation is the most important element in the final demand projections, notably engineering, shipbuilding, railway locomotives and construction, and these are all industries for which sales to final demand account for about two thirds of total output, so that the possible error in the capital formation projections by asset would seriously distort the output projections for these industries (table 7.5).

(b) *Methods used to project changes in total sales (output) by industry*

Given the composition of sales by each industry to final demand, total gross output by industry can be computed (using the techniques of matrix inversion) provided one knows the matrix of inter-industry transactions. Such a matrix is available for 1954[2] and has been adapted as part of the DAE Growth Project to fit the SAM classification[3]. The authors of this adaptation have also estimated a corresponding matrix for 1960 and a provisional projection of the 1966 matrix.

It is quite clear from comparison of the DAE Growth Project's 1954 and 1960 matrices that very important changes have taken place between 1954 and 1960 in the pattern of inter-industry transactions. For example, if the 1960 pattern of final demand by commodity is applied to the 1954 input-output table and the resulting output figures are compared with the actual outputs of each commodity in 1960, the differences between the two sets of results—shown in table 7.4 below—should indicate the impact on the output of individual industries of all the changes, between 1954 and 1960, in the estimated matrices of inter-industry transactions. It will be seen for example that the net effect of changes in technical coefficients on the output of the chemical industry has been to raise its output (given the pattern of final demand) by 15·4 per cent

[1]It should be noted that 'net exports' here comprise total exports minus 'competitive' imports only, these being imports of goods of which domestic production supplies over half of total domestic consumption.
[2]From Board of Trade and Central Statistical Office, *Input-Output Tables for the United Kingdom, 1954* (London, 1961).
[3]*A Programme for Growth, 3: Input-Output Relationships, 1954–1966, op. cit.*

P

Table 7.4. *Percentage effect on output of commodities in 1960 of changes in input-output coefficients between 1954 and 1960*

SAM industry group

1.	Agriculture, forestry and fishing	− 15·5
2.	Coal mining	− 24·9
3.	Mining and quarrying n.e.s.	− 1·3
4.	Food processing	+ 3·2
5.	Drink and tobacco	− 22·4
6.	Coke ovens, etc.	− 23·7
7.	Mineral oil refining	+ 5·3
8.	Chemicals n.e.s.	+ 15·4
9.	Iron and steel (excluding tinplates and tubes)	+ 2·6
10.	Iron and steel (tinplates and tubes)	+ 16·7
11.	Non-ferrous metals	+ 7·8
12.	Engineering and electrical goods	− 0·1
13.	Shipbuilding	− 22·9
14.	Motors and cycles	− 6·6
15.	Aircraft	+ 25·3
16.	Railway locomotives and rolling stock	− 13·4
17.	Metal goods n.e.s.	+ 15·2
18.	Textiles	+ 24·0
19.	Leather, clothing and footwear	− 13·8
20.	Building materials	− 1·1
21.	Pottery and glass	− 8·4
22.	Timber, furniture, etc.	+ 22·8
23.	Paper, printing and publishing	+ 31·4
24.	Other manufacturing	+ 20·2
25.	Construction	+ 3·1
26.	Gas	− 0·3
27.	Electricity	+ 21·8
28.	Water	− 25·7
29.	Transport and communications	+ 5·2
30.	Distribution	− 1·0
31.	Services n.e.s.	+ 22·3

over the six-year period 1954 to 1960[1]. This change is readily understandable in view of the substitution of chemical products (such as plastics) for other raw material inputs. However, some of the other changes seem more difficult to

[1] The changes in technical coefficients referred to here comprise all changes in the input-output matrix, not only those directly affecting the chemical industry (though these will be the most important). It should be emphasized that the DAE's input-output matrix for 1960 is based not on direct information about inputs (since the latest comprehensive statistics of inputs by industry derive from the 1954 Census of Production) but on indirect estimates.

P2

interpret[1], and examination of the DAE matrix for 1966 shows that the estimated changes in technical coefficients between 1954 and 1960 are, in many cases, not expected to continue at the same rate[2].

In view of this uncertainty about the likely changes in technical coefficients, we have projected each industry's ouput by a variety of methods; the final projections, shown in table 7.6 below have been based on our comparison of the results of the different methods, allowing for our evaluation of their reliability as applied to each industry. The methods used, for industries other than those (the energy and transport industries) for which special projections have been made in chapters 10 and 11 below, are as follows:

Method 1.   This comprised simply the application of the 1975 final demand pattern by industry to the DAE input-output matrix for 1960.

Method 2.   This is the same as method 1, except that the DAE's 1966 input-output table has been used.

Method 3.   (i) Each industry's total sales have been separated into intermediate sales and sales to final demand.   For many industries, as can be seen in table 7.5 below, final sales comprise 70 per cent or more of total output, these being industries producing either capital goods or certain consumer goods such as food, drink and tobacco;

(ii) to the final sales component of total output we have applied the index of total final sales, as already calculated (see last column of table 7.3 above), to obtain final sales in 1975;

(iii) intermediate sales in 1975 have been estimated with the aid of a crude measure of substitution in favour or against the industry concerned[3];

(iv) the sum of the resulting projection of final and of intermediate sales in 1975 equals total 1975 output.

[1]For example, the upward effect of changing coefficients on the output of the textile industry, on the paper, printing and publishing industry, and on the aircraft industry. In fact, the DAE Growth Project team apparently shares our doubts as to the continuity of some of the estimated changes in technical coefficients between 1954 and 1960 since, in extrapolating to 1966 they depart substantially from the estimates of the 1966 coefficients that would be obtained by adhering rigidly to the method of extrapolating the changes in the '*r* and *s* multipliers' that are implied by their 1954 and 1960 matrices.   They also emphasize the need to make such forecasts of changes in technical coefficients in close co-operation with experts from the industries concerned, and work along these lines is apparently leading to large revisions to the coefficients used in this study.

[2]One test made was as follows.   A provisional breakdown of 1975 final demand by industry was applied to the SAM 1966 matrix.   We then extrapolated the effect, to 1975, of further changes in coefficients on the outputs of each industry, taking for this the average of such effects as given by the difference between the DAE's 1954 and 1960 matrices, and 1960 and 1966 matrices.   This produced some very curious results, for example, that output of the textile industry would rise twice as fast as output of the chemical industry, even though we had inserted a rise in final demand for chemicals twice as fast as the rise in final demand for textiles.

[3]This involved multiplying 1960 intermediate sales by the provisional projected increase in total manufacturing output adjusted by the ratio between the rise in total output of the

Table 7.5.   *Sales to final demand as percentage of total sales, by commodity in 1960*

SAM industry group

Drink and tobacco	98·0
Leather, clothing and footwear	92·0
Water	87·8
Agriculture, forestry and fishing	85·7
Distribution	84·0
Motors and cycles	77·3
Construction	75·8
Food processing	72·9
Shipbuilding	72·0
Engineering and electrical goods	63·4
Aircraft	55·1
Transport and communications	54·3
Railway locomotives and rolling stock	52·2
Services n.e.s.	46·2
Gas	45·6
Electricity	44·7
Pottery and glass	43·0
Other manufacturing	36·1
Mineral oil refining	34·3
Coal mining	32·1
Iron and steel (tinplates and tubes)	30·9
Chemicals n.e.s.	27·5
Timber, furniture, etc.	26·4
Coke ovens, etc.	25·2
Metal goods n.e.s.	21·2
Textiles	21·1
Paper, printing and publishing	17·8
Mining and quarrying n.e.s.	12·7
Building materials	9·2
Iron and steel (excluding tinplates and tubes)	4·7
Non-ferrous metals	3·5

Source: Cambridge University DAE Growth Project, *A Programme for Growth, 2: A Social Accounting Matrix for 1960, op. cit.,* 3rd fold-out, table 1.

industry concerned and total manufacturing output over the period 1954 to 1960.   The inclusion in the ratio, however, of the change in final sales of the commodity concerned over the period 1954–60, obviously distorts the measure.   The possible distortion in the measure of this ratio will be bigger the greater the share of final sales in total output. But the larger the share of final sales in total output the larger the proportion of total output that is projected directly from the separate final sales projection and the smaller the share of total output to which the possibly erroneous ratio is applied.   While this means that the effect of the error on the projection of total output is probably not too great, the fact remains that the error in the projection of intermediate sales can be very large.   Hence it seemed desirable to attempt an alternative method of projecting intermediate sales, which is described in method 4.

Method 4. This method follows method **3**, steps (i) and (ii) to obtain the projection of 1975 final sales, but a slightly different method has been used to project intermediate sales[1].

For certain industries a variant of method 4 has been adopted for the projection of intermediate sales. These industries are those where the method 4 results seemed inherently very implausible and where, at the same time, sufficient reliance could not be placed on the results of the other three methods. This variant consisted of identifying separately the intermediate sales of each given commodity to the main purchasing industries, and then projecting each separately in proportion to provisional output projections for the purchasing industries (based on methods 1 to 4), but without assuming any change in the relevant technical coefficients[2]. The projection of intermediate sales by this method was then added to the projection of final sales, as with methods 3 and 4, to obtain the projection of total output.

In evaluating the results obtained by the various methods the following properties had to be borne in mind:

(i) Method 1 implies no changes in technical coefficients at all from 1960.

(ii) Method 2 is based on the technical coefficients as extrapolated to 1966 in the DAE study. Whatever reservations may be held concerning the order of magnitude of the changes in coefficients shown in this study, the difference between the method 1 and method 2 results has been taken as providing some guidance as to the direction of change (as far as it affects the output of individual industries).

(iii) Methods 3 and 4 employ a crude measure of the effect of technical change in the past which is extrapolated *pro rata* into the future (except for a few industries where the projection is based solely on the projection of final sales, and where, therefore, no allowance for technical change is made); and of the two methods, method 4 was considered to be less reliable, if more logical, on account of data deficiencies.

[1]This follows method 3 (step (iii)) except that the ratio by which the projected increase in manufacturing output has been adjusted is the ratio over the period 1954 to 1960 of the increase in the intermediate sales only of the industry concerned to the increase in total manufacturing output. This method is certainly more logical than method 3, but the estimates of intermediate sales in 1960 are probably subject, in some cases, to significant margins of error, which become very important when attempts are made to express intermediate sales in 1954 and in 1960 at constant prices. As applied in the manner just described, these estimates of changes in intermediate sales from 1954 to 1960 led to startling and obviously absurd results in some cases. For example, intermediate sales by the aircraft industry, at constant prices, would appear to have risen, from 1954 to 1960, over five times as fast as total manufacturing output. Extrapolation of this relationship to 1975 would lead to an estimate of intermediate sales in 1975 over ten times as large as final sales by this industry, implying a tenfold increase in the total output of the industry.

[2]The industries for which this adjustment seemed appropriate and the percentages of their total intermediate sales to other industries covered by the individual sales identified were as follows: metal goods, n.e.s. (63 per cent), non-ferrous metals (82 per cent), iron and steel (tinplate and tubes) (77 per cent), textiles (80 per cent), paper and printing (85 per cent).

Table 7.6. *Comparison of projected changes in net output by industry, 1960–75, with changes 1950–60: indices or annual average compound rates of change*

	Index 1975 (1960 = 100)	Projected rate of change 1960–75	1950–60 rate of change
A. Industries growing significantly faster than in past			
Coal mining	95–115	0·3	− 1·1
Engineering and electrical goods	180–210	4·6	3·8
Shipbuilding and marine engineering	140–160	2·7	0·6
Metal goods n.e.s.	150–200	3·7	2·4
Textiles	130–150	2·2	− 0·4
Leather, clothing and footwear	150–170	3·1	1·3
Building materials	130–150	2·2	1·7
Pottery and glass	150–170	3·1	2·0
Timber, furniture, etc.	160–180	3·5	1·8
Other manufacturing	200–250	5·5	4·6
Water	120–140	1·9	0·8
Transport and communications	145–165	2·9	1·6
B. Industries growing at about the same rate as in past			
Agriculture, forestry and fishing	130–140	1·9	2·0
Mining and quarrying (excluding coal)	145–165	2·9	2·7
Drink and tobacco	135–155	2·4	2·2
Chemicals n.e.s.	260–320	7·3	6·4
Iron and steel (excluding tinplates and tubes)	130–160	2·6⎫	2·5
Iron and steel (tinplates and tubes)	165–185	3·7⎭	
Non-ferrous metals	150–170	3·1	3·1
Paper, printing and publishing	200–220	5·0	4·5
Construction	150–160	2·9	2·7
Electricity	280–340	7·8	8·4
Distributive trades	145–165	2·9	2·9
Services n.e.s.	150–170	3·2	2·8
C. Industries growing significantly slower than in past			
Food processing	130–140	1·9	2·5
Coke ovens	105–115	0·6	1·8
Mineral oil refining	210–250	5·7	11·3
Motors and cycles	200–240	5·3	7·2
Aircraft	165–195	3·9⎫	5·4
Railway rolling stock	70–80	− 1·9⎭	
Gas	60–80	− 2·3	− 0·8[a]
Total manufacturing		4·2	3·6
Total gross domestic product		3·5	2·5

[a]In the interests of comparability with the past the output index shown here is the currently used index which is largely based on gas made at gas-works. If account were also taken of value added to natural gas, refinery gas or other gas bought for processing and distribution, the results would be very different. The 1975 index would probably be in the region of 100 to 150, representing an average annual compound rate of increase of 1·5 per cent (see table 7.10 below). This is largely because of the rapid increase expected in sales of imported or natural gas.

(c) *The main results*

The results shown in table 7.6 are presented firstly in terms of ranges. Where the various methods produced widely different results, a larger range has been shown, in order to emphasize the greater margin of error to which the projections for these industries are presumably subject. The ranges shown are not mechanically derived from the averages of the different methods, since it was preferable to interpret the different sets of results more flexibly[1]. Also, it should be recalled that the projections for the various industries entering into fuel and transport were derived from the special chapters on these two sectors. Finally, as explained above, the projected increases in gross output by industry have also been applied to base-year net output by industry to obtain projected net output by industry, small proportionate adjustments then being required to preserve consistency with the overall gross national product projection.

Out of 31 industries, 13 are projected to grow at about the same rate as in the past, 11 significantly faster than in the past and 7 significantly slower than in the past. Table 7.7 below compares the ranking of the industries by rate of growth between 1950 and 1960 and projected rate of growth and indicates how their projected growth rates compare with those of the past. From this one can see that in general the rankings do not change much. On the whole the fast-growing industries in the past are expected to remain the fast-growing industries and vice versa. But the differences between the rates of growth of fast- and slow-growing industries are expected to diminish, so that the dispersion of growth rates around the average will be narrower. At the bottom of the ranking, the six industries with the slowest growth rates in the past (including negative growth) all show appreciable increases over the past rates, and in two or three cases substantially improve their ranking.

To explain fully the differences between the past and the projected growth rates it would be necessary to identify separately the differences between the past and the future with respect to (a) final sales and (b) intermediate sales for each industry as classified in SAM. Unfortunately reliable data of this kind do not exist for most industries. However, certain aspects of the changes can be identified as follows:

(i) The general narrowing of the dispersion of growth rates may be caused by excessive caution in extrapolating into the future the apparent effect of changes in technical coefficients in the past. If more reliance had been placed on the various measures of these substitution effects (for example, as given by comparing the DAE 1954 and 1960 input-output tables), the dispersion of growth rates would have been about as great as in the past, notwithstanding the considerations mentioned below, though the ranking of industries would have been very different.

(ii) Some of the fast-growing industries will slow down because they tend to be industries that were producing 'new' products (in the wide sense

---

[1]For example, where the results of methods 1 and 2 indicated substitution against some particular industry but method 3 gave a higher projection than method 1, the method 3 result was interpreted as being near the upper end of the probable range (i.e. the measure of substitution employed in method 3 was interpreted as being too high).

Table 7.7. *Ranking of industries by percentage annual average compound growth rate of net output, 1950–60 and 1960–75*

SAM number	Industry	1950–60 Growth rate	Rank	1960–75 Growth rate	Rank	Relation of projection to past growth rate[a] F	E	S
7	Mineral oil refining	11·3	1	5·7	3			X
27	Electricity	8·4	2	7·8	1		X	
14	Motors and cycles	7·2	3	5·3	5			X
8	Chemicals n.e.s.	6·4	4	7·3	2		X	
15	Aircraft ⎫	5·4	5	3·9	8 ⎫			X
16	Railway rolling stock ⎭			− 1·9	29 ⎭			
24	Other manufacturing	4·6	6	5·5	4		X	
23	Paper, printing and publishing	4·5	7	5·0	6		X	
12	Engineering and electrical goods	3·8	8	4·6	7	X		
4–24	*Total manufacturing*	*3·5*	n.a.	*4·2*				
11	Non-ferrous metals	3·1	9	3·1	12/13/14		X	
30	Distributive trades	2·9	10	2·9	15/18		X	
25	Construction	2·7	11/12	2·9	15–18		X	
3	Mining and quarrying (excluding coal)	2·7	11/12	2·9	15–18		X	
4	Food processing	2·5	13/14	1·9	24–26			X
9	Iron and steel (excluding tinplates and tubes ⎫	2·5	13/14	2·6	20 ⎫		X	
10	Iron and steel (tinplates and tubes ⎭			3·7	9/10 ⎭			
17	Metal goods n.e.s.	2·4	15	3·7	9/10	X		
5	Drink and tobacco	2·2	16	2·4	21		X	
1	Agriculture, forestry and fishing	2·0	17/18	1·9	24/26		X	
21	Pottery and glass	2·0	17/18	3·1	12/13/14	X		
6	Coke ovens	1·8	19/20	0·6	27			X
22	Timber, furniture, etc.	1·8	19/20	3·5	11	X		
20	Building materials	1·7	21	2·2	22/23	X		
29	Transport and communications	1·6	22	2·9	15/18	X		
19	Leather, clothing and footwear	1·3	23	3·1	12/13/14	X		
28	Water	0·8	24	1·9	24/26	X		
13	Shipbuilding and marine engineering	0·6	25	2·7	19	X		
18	Textiles	− 0·4	26	2·2	22/23	X		
26	Gas	− 0·8[b]	27	− 2·3	30			
2	Coal mining	− 1·1	28	0·3	28	X		
	Total gross domestic product	2·5		3·5				

[a]F = significantly faster, E = roughly equal, S = significantly slower.
[b]See footnote (a) to table 7.6.

of the term). This applies to *oil products*, which started the decade as a relatively unimportant part of total fuel consumption, so that after a period of rapid substitution for other forms of fuel the proportionate increase in oil consumption would inevitably slacken off, and has, in fact, already shown signs of doing so[1]. *Aircraft* and *motors and cycles* are industries producing durable goods, the purchases of which are determined by the rate of change in the stock (and by scrapping rates). For motor cars, the rate of increase in the stock in this country has been, also inevitably, slowing down after rising rapidly from an initially very low level, though much will depend here on the uncertain prospects in export markets. For aircraft, of course, although similar dynamic relationships between stocks and purchases apply, the determinants of the stock, and of scrapping rates, are more volatile, especially for military aircraft.

(iii) Among the slow-growing industries, higher growth rates are projected simply because the overall growth rate for gross national product is projected to be substantially higher than in the past; some industries should henceforth experience moderate growth rates that will represent a big improvement over the negligible or negative growth rates in 1950–60, when the overall growth rate was low[2]. The improved growth rate projected for one of these industries, however, namely *shipbuilding*, reflects our much more optimistic projection of final demand specifically for ships. This is largely based on our projection of only a moderate fall in net exports, whereas in the 1950s net exports of ships fell rapidly. Over the last half of the 1950s, Britain relied increasingly on ships built abroad for British registry and there was a fall in the number of ships built here for export. During the last two or three years, however, there has been a great improvement in the export order situation and in the domestic order situation, though the latter may be short-lived insofar as it has been stimulated only temporarily by the government's £75 million shipbuilding credit scheme. Nevertheless, while there are some grounds for taking a slightly more optimistic view of the prospects for this industry, much will clearly depend on how far the British shipbuilding industry, with its multitude of shipyards constructing a unique variety of tailor-made size and type of ship, and facing special problems of labour relations and job demarcation, can become sufficiently competitive to reverse the adverse trends of the 1950s. The prospects of another of the industries in this category, namely the *textile* industry, must depend heavily on wider issues of commercial policy, particularly as this affects cotton textiles. Now that the first phase of the government's reorganization scheme has been completed, with the aid of public financial assistance, it remains to be seen how far this will be followed by a continuation of the recent favourable productivity performance and how far, if this is not continued, the authorities are prepared to reduce restrictions on imports of manufactured cotton

---

[1] This may, however, represent partly a once-for-all effect of the excise duty on oil imposed in April 1961.

[2] The six industries showing the greatest proportionate acceleration in growth rates all grew at less than 2 per cent per annum from 1950 to 1960.

cloth (particularly from Hong Kong and other Asian sources).   If general world pressures in favour of easing obstacles to world trade in such goods were to prevail then, failing further rapid productivity increases, the prospects for this industry might be no more favourable than in the past, and our projections would be proved to have been over-optimistic.

(iv) Apart from the industries falling in the categories described above, the projected acceleration of growth rates for many other industries is roughly in line with the projected overall acceleration of the growth of GNP. This applies, for example, to *engineering and electrical goods, building materials, metal goods n.e.s., pottery and glass*, and so on.

(v) This leaves, for explanation, two categories of industries, namely (a) those that, without having experienced exceptional growth rates in the past (i.e. category (ii) industries) do not seem to share in the general acceleration of growth, and (b) those whose future acceleration seems to be more than can be explained by their relatively very slow (or negative) growth rate in the past.

The first group includes *non-ferrous metals, construction, iron and steel, drink and tobacco, food processing, distribution* and *agriculture, forestry and fishing.* Some of these, such as *drink and tobacco, food processing* and *agriculture*, reflect the declining income-elasticities of demand for the products concerned as incomes rise. This applies also, to some extent to *distribution* where the composition of total private consumption seems to be shifting away from distributed goods and in favour of services and other goods. But, in addition, the ratio of value added to final demand goods in distribution appears to have declined from 1954 to 1960 and we have assumed that this decline will continue at the same rate. Others, notably *iron and steel*, and *non-ferrous metals*, are industries for which output is difficult to project by the general methods used above since such a large proportion of their output consists of intermediate products where unpredictable changes in technical coefficients are very important. The final demand increases for these products are slower than in the past (largely because of small or negative changes in net exports combined with large increases in sales of scrap by consumers), but as can be seen in table 7.5 above, this can only explain a small part of the output projection. In fact, methods 3 and 4 indicated rather higher output projections than those we have finally adopted, and the downward adjustment has been made in the light of the apparent substitution against these industries as indicated by comparing the results obtained from methods 1 and 2[1]. It is quite possible,

---

[1]Substitution against steel, as has been recognized for some time, has taken many forms in different industries. In building, reinforced concrete has been replacing structural steel; in motor cars, smaller cars and the use of lighter sheets have effected economies; and in other industries technical progress has often been at the expense of steel or has taken the form of more economical kinds of steel.

therefore, that the latter comparison exaggerates the amount of this substitution and that methods 3 and 4, however crude, gave a fairer picture of the true substitution, entailing a higher output projection for iron and steel and non-ferrous metals.

For the last industry in this group, namely the *construction* industry, final demand is 75 per cent of total output, and the bulk of this final demand is, of course, gross capital formation in housing, public works and industrial and commercial construction. The reliability of the output projection hangs on the projection of this final demand. The housing, health, education and road-building elements of construction have been estimated in the special chapters devoted to these topics so that, given the objectives selected in these chapters, the estimates are comparatively well founded. Capital formation in manu-facturing is estimated by more general methods, but this is only about 13 per cent of the total. Hence, the projection of total construction output is regarded as being among the more reliable of the industry projections. And while the projected growth rate is about the same as in the past few years, it should not be overlooked that this was by no means negligible. For example, total construction of dwellings and other non-industrial construction rose by 160 per cent over the decade 1951 to 1961, and a large part of this consisted of social overheads (houses, roads, etc.) which are not necessarily closely related to the rate of increase of total GNP.

On the other hand, the projections of the quasi-social expenditures (houses, schools, hospitals, roads), not being determined completely by economic calculations, could be substantially amended if it were found that the resources involved would bear the extra strain. For road-building, in particular, as is apparent from chapter 11, a much higher figure could be adopted without approaching satiation of social needs, particularly if urban renewal on a large scale is attempted. In terms of total output, but not productivity, the con-struction industry should be able to meet the longer-term demands, as here projected, without any improvement over its past growth record. The main query, however, is whether this very labour-intensive industry can raise its rate of productivity increase; its past productivity record is not striking. The productivity and employment implications of the projections are discussed in the second half of this chapter.

Industries that appear to show a sharp acceleration of growth rates are the *timber and furniture*, and the *leather, clothing and footwear* industries. In the former, final demand is only about one quarter of total output, and our estimate of the 'substitution' effect indicates a sharply rising 'timber intensity' of production. It would require a special study of the timber industry to identify the reliability of this estimate, but it is possibly related to the increasing timber content of construction, including the growing use of laminated beams and of timber framing and chipboard. This is particularly true of houses built for local authorities according to standardized systems of construction, and matches one of the areas, mentioned above, where steel is losing ground[1].

A final qualification to these projections must be emphasized. In general we assumed that net output for each industry will rise in the same proportion as gross output, and it is the latter that is actually projected by the various methods used since they are all, in one form or another, estimates of the future changes in total sales. This has two main implications.

Firstly, in comparing the projection with the past rates of growth we have used, as measures of the latter, changes which are conceptually changes in net output, and it is not possible to say how far these comparisons are invalidated by errors in the assumption that net output in the future will rise at the same rate as gross output. For a selection of industries we compare, in table 7.8, the evolution of net and gross output, and it will be seen that although the movements have been very similar, given the methods used (which automatically reduce the scope for discrepancy between the two series) there is enough divergence in a few industries to justify the conclusion that the projections are more reliable as projections of gross output than of net output.

Table 7.8. *Comparison of rates of growth of net and gross output for selected industries*

	Period	Net output	Gross output
Agriculture	1953–62	2·5	2·9
Coal mining	1950–60	− 1·1	− 0·9
Coke ovens, etc.	,,	1·8	1·8
Mineral oil refining	,,	11·3	13·0
Iron and steel	,,	2·5	2·8
			(3·1 unweighted)
Construction	1955–63	4·8	5·5
Gas	1950–60	− 0·8	− 1·4
Electricity	,,	8·4	8·1
Motor vehicles and cycles	,,	7·2	9·1
Other mining	,,	2·7	1·8

Note: Gross output has been calculated by applying indices of physical output (e.g. tons of different kinds of steel, or numbers of different sizes and types of vehicles) to the gross output weights measured by their sales value, given in the 1958 Census of Production. To a large extent, the net indices are obtained by applying the same indicators to base-year net output weights on the assumption that, for each item for which a separate indicator is used, the net/gross output ratio remains constant. Thus, by contrast with a net output index obtained by means of a complete double deflation of outputs and inputs, the net output indices can only differ from the gross output indices shown above by virtue of the difference in the base-year weighting pattern.

[1]Apparently such 'system-built' houses use twice as much timber as conventional houses. Also research, largely under the auspices of the Timber Research and Development Association, reducing the dangers to timber from insects, dry rot and fire has added to the growing popularity of timber in construction. But the rising use of timber also applies to large constructions where timber roofs have greater insulation value and lower maintenance costs.

The other main implication of the net/gross assumption is that it implies an internal inconsistency in the results since we have assumed, in making the projections, that there would be substitution for or against certain products in the production of other products. It is quite possible, of course, for such substitution to take place without affecting the ratio of total intermediate inputs to total output of any industry[1], but such an outcome would be highly coincidental. Nevertheless, it seems preferable to allow for such substitutions whenever the evidence for it exists even though this almost certainly means that, for some purchasing industries, there is an unidentified implied deviation between the evolution of gross and net output[2].

3. THE PROJECTION OF PRODUCTIVITY AND EMPLOYMENT BY INDUSTRY

(a) *Methods used*

Given the projection of output by industry obtained in the manner indicated above, the next step has been to project the corresponding pattern of productivity. This requires some estimate of the relationship between changes in output and changes in productivity in individual industries. The ideal method for obtaining such estimates would be within the framework of a comprehensive 'production function' showing the relationship between net output on the one hand and individual factor inputs, particularly capital and labour, on the other hand. A common simple form of such a production function, namely the Cobb-Douglas function, expresses the relationship in such a way that output would be functionally related to capital and labour in each industry according to coefficients separately estimated for each industry. But, as is shown in detail in the next chapter, our experiments with variants of such production functions for individual industries failed to provide any firm basis for proceeding along these lines. The only close correlation found was between changes in output per head and changes in total output.

A close correlation between rates of change of output and productivity has been found to hold for different time periods and in many different countries. In all cases the values of the parameters in the equations linking output per head to output are very similar. The data we have used to establish these relationships are of the following nature. For individual industries we have calculated the trend rates of change over a period of years in both output and output per head. We have then correlated the results across industries; that is,

---

[1]For example, the above-mentioned substitution of timber for steel in construction might leave the net/gross output ratio in the construction industry unchanged.

[2]This is confirmed by the fact that the sum of the projected gross outputs for industries 1 to 31 rises by 74 per cent, whereas the sum of projected final sales rises by only 69 per cent over the 1960 level.

for each industry we have one pair of observations, namely the average rate of change in output and in output per head over the period of years concerned, and the pairs of observations for a number of industries constitute our two series of changes in outputs and output per head.   Table 7.9 shows the results for British manufacturing industries for the whole period 1950 to 1960, as well as for other periods (for which non-manufacturing industries have been added).   Some of the industries are clearly rather special cases on account of exceptional conditions of production (such as coke being essentially a by-product).

Table 7.9.   *Regressions of proportionate changes in output per head on proportionate changes in output*

		Number of industries	c	e	R^2
	United Kingdom				
1.	Fast growth period (1952–5)	29	− 0·02	0·72	0·70
2.	„ „ „ (1958–60)	29	1·22	0·57	0·74
3.	Slow growth period (1950–2)	28	− 0·58	0·79	0·97
4.	„ „ „ (1955–8)	29	0·44	0·49	0·49
5.	'Peak to peak' period (1955–60)	29	0·77	0·56	0·70
6.	'Trough to trough' period (1952–8)	29	0·45	0·63	0·67
7.	1950–60[a] (i) including mineral oil refining	14	0·07	0·78	0·65
8.	1950–60[a] (ii) excluding mineral oil refining	13	0·02	0·81	0·61
9.	Average 1953/4/5 to average 1959/60	20	0·99	0·50	0·72
10.	1924 to 1950 (i) including mineral oil	28	0·47	0·56	0·74
11.	1924 to 1950 (ii) excluding mineral oil	27	0·39	0·62	0·69
	USA				
12.	1899 to 1953	18	− 0·29	0·51	0·84
	New Zealand				
13.	1950–60	12	− 0·18	0·62	0·81
	Australia				
14.	1948/9 to 1954/5	13	− 0·56	0·56	0·64
	Germany				
15.	Fast growth period (1950–5)	24	0·78	0·33	0·71
16.	Slow growth period (1955–8)	24	− 0·92	0·39	0·44
17.	Fast growth period (1958–60)	24	3·48	0·48	0·29

Sources of basic series:

United States from J. W. Kendrick, *Productivity Trends in the United States* (Princeton, 1961), pp. 468–75.

New Zealand from A. D. Brownlie, 'Some Aspects of the Measurement of Aggregate Productivity with Special Reference to New Zealand Manufacturing' (*Productivity Measurement Review*, February 1963), p. 5.

Australia from E. J. Thomson, 'Productivity Change in Australian Manufacturing Industry, 1948–49 to 1954–55' (*Productivity Measurement Review*, February 1962), p. 26.

Germany from Deutsches Institut für Wirtschaftsforschung, *Produktionsvolumen und Produktionsfaktoren der Industrie im Gebiet der Bundesrepublik Deutschland: Statistische Kennziffern 1950 bis 1958* (Berlin, 1960) and . . . *Statistische Kennziffern 1959 bis 1960/61* (Berlin, 1962).

[a]Trend values of output and output per head in terminal years, manufacturing industries.

Excluding such cases, the equation for the period 1950 to 1960 is
$$P = 0.07 + 0.78\ Y$$
where P = rate of change of output per head (*i.e.* labour productivity)
Y = rate of change of total output[1].

Exactly the same sort of relationship is found from data drawn from various periods and various countries. The coefficients shown in table 7.9 correspond to an equation of the form $P = c + eY$ (where P and Y are as defined above, and c and e are the parameters of the equation in each case).

In only three cases (two of them relating to Germany) does the proportion of the variation in productivity that is associated with variation in output fall below 60 per cent. Also, the regression coefficient, e, varies only slightly about an average value of approximately 0.6 to 0.7. There is more variation in the constant term in the equation, c, which is sometimes negative, but which is generally positive. The close similarity between the results for the various countries and time periods is illustrated on the following diagram in which are shown the lines corresponding to the equations fitted to the data for each country.

How far does this type of cross-section cum time series equation indicate the manner in which any *individual* industry's productivity would change in relation to a change in its output[2]? In terms of figure 7.1 below, for example, we wish to know how a line connecting various observations (that is for different time periods) for any one industry would differ, if at all, from the cross-section line. Assuming linearity in all cases, the differences could be of two kinds. Either the constant term in the equation for a given industry could be systematically and significantly different from that obtained from the cross-section line or the slope could be different; or there might be some combination of the two.

The constant term of the equation can be interpreted as indicating the rate of change in productivity that, over any reasonable period of time, could be expected to prevail in the absence of any increase in output. Alternatively, differences in the constant terms for the equations of various industries would indicate differences in the rate of productivity increase they tend to achieve for equal rates of increase in output. If then there are systematic and significant differences in the constant terms of the equations for individual industries one would expect to find that some industries have tended systematically to have larger increases in productivity than others irrespective of the rate of change in their outputs.

This may be investigated by analysing the productivity and output performance of selected industries in various periods of time and in different countries. For several individual industries, therefore, we have examined the relationship

[1] The correlation coefficient being 0.807, this indicates that 65 per cent of the variation in output per head is associated with the variation in output.
[2] Other aspects of this relationship between output and productivity are discussed in chapter 2.

Fig. 7.1. Regression equations of changes in output per head and output: percentage average annual compound rates of change

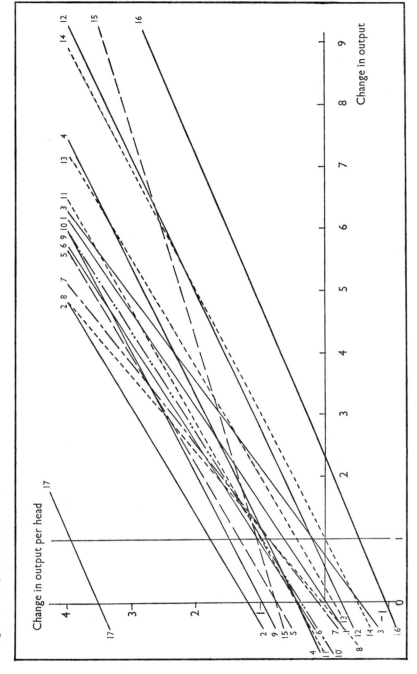

Source: Table 7.9.

between productivity and output in the different circumstances of three countries (the United Kingdom, Germany and the United States) and for varying periods within each country. The selection of industries was determined by the need to obtain reasonable comparability among the three countries and different time periods and hence does not cover all the industries with which we are concerned here; nor are the classifications identical. The analysis of these data did, in fact, suggest that certain industries achieved systematically different productivity performances for given rates of output increase, and that some classification of industries along the following lines was possible:

Group 1. *Industries where relative productivity increases were generally high for a given rate of increase in output:* vehicles; chemicals; tobacco.

Group 2. *Industries where relative productivity increases were generally low for a given rate of increase in output:* food; clothing; stone, clay and glass; primary metals; metal goods n.e.s.

Group 3. *Industries where relative productivity increases were about average for given rates of increase in output:* electrical engineering; mechanical engineering; paper and printing; leather.

But an alternative check (on the extent to which the productivity/output relationship for individual industries differed from the average) suggested that no such systematic differences could be established. For the industries used in the projections, the 1950–60 period has been divided into four sub-periods, two of fast growth of output (1952–55 and 1958–60) and two of slow growth (1950–52 and 1955–58). In each sub-period the rate of growth of output and employment has been calculated. The results for the two slow growth periods have been averaged as well as the results for the two fast growth periods. Thus there are two observations for each industry; one representing the rate of growth of output and productivity in periods of slow growth and one in periods of fast growth. Both points for each industry have been plotted on the following scatter diagram and joined by straight lines. The slopes of these lines indicate roughly how the ratio of the productivity increase to the output increase changes *in the individual industries concerned* when they move from slow to fast growth.

As can be seen in the diagram the slopes of the lines for the individual industries are remarkably similar to each other and to the cross-section line for the whole period 1950–60. Also, most of the lines pass very close to the origin—that is, their constant terms are very similar—suggesting that differences in industries' productivity performance for given rates of increase of output are hardly significant. And in cases where the constant terms, for some industries, do differ from the average constant term, the differences do not confirm the classification referred to above. For example, one of the industries

Q

Fig. 7.2. Relations between output change and productivity change: comparison between fast growth and slow growth periods, percentage average annual rates of change

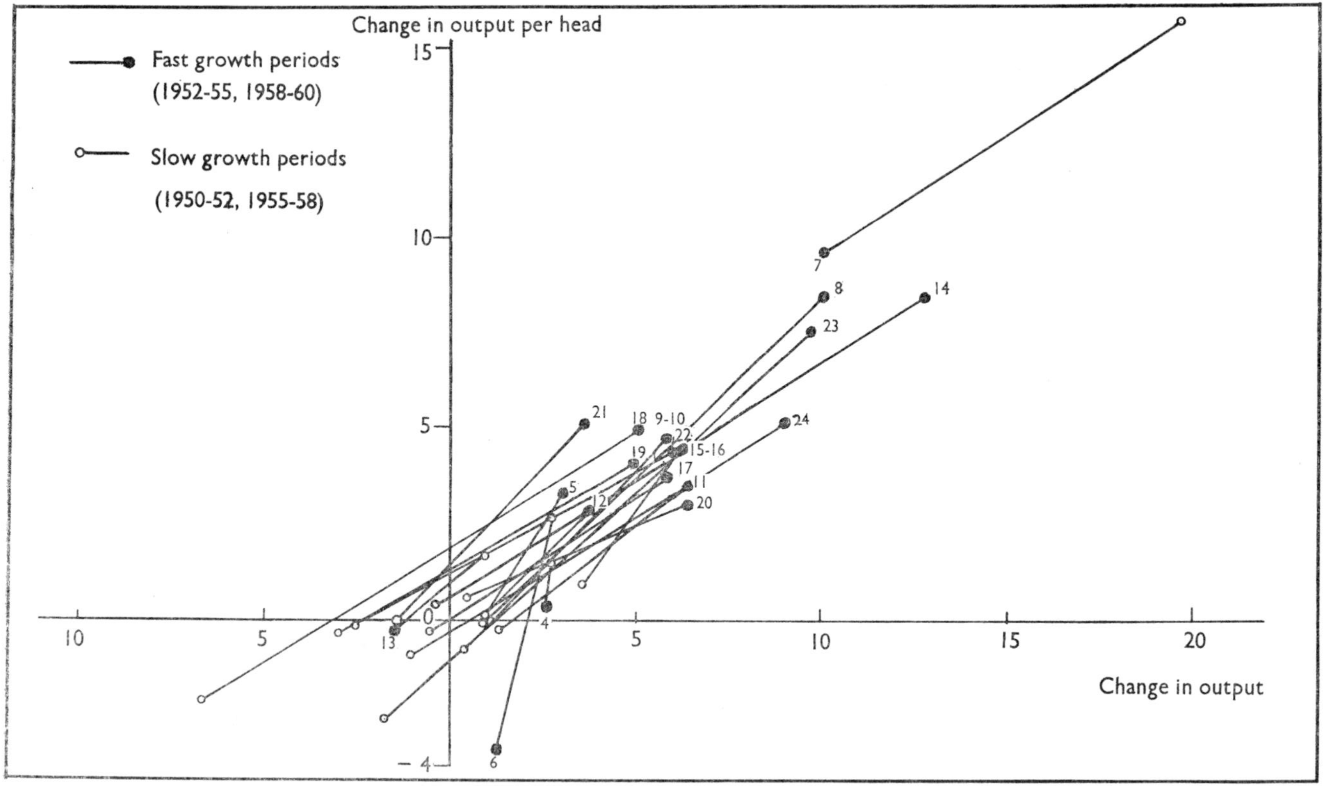

Source: Appendix tables 8.10, 8.11.

Note: Numbers attached to lines refer to SAM industries.

whose constant term appears relatively high is the textile industry (probably accounted for by the exceptional amount of rationalization during the 1950s), though this is not in group 1 above. Conversely, the chemical industry, which is in group 1, does not show an above-average constant in figure 7.2. But this may be partly because the chemical industry in the SAM classification excludes mineral oil refining, and the latter, which is shown separately in figure 7.2, does appear to have an above-average constant term. Although many of the other industries cannot be matched exactly in terms of coverage and definition, some other contradictions seem to be implied. For example, in figure 7.2, where we have followed the SAM classification, the drink and tobacco industry (number 5) seems to show a negative constant term, though tobacco is in group 1 in the above classification.

On the whole, allowing for a few apparently freak results (e.g. industries 4 and 6), figure 7.2 strongly suggests that, with two or three exceptions, there is no firm basis for discriminating among most British industries with respect to the relationship between their changes in labour productivity and changes in their output, and that this relationship is, for most industries, remarkably similar. The main exceptions appear to be a high constant term for mineral oil refining and, possibly, though to a smaller extent, textiles; and possibly a low constant for iron and steel and non-ferrous metals.

In view of these results the procedure adopted has been as follows. For most industries we have applied the elasticity of productivity with respect to output given by the regression equation obtained from the cross-section data for all industries combined over the two periods 1955 to 1960 and 1952 to 1958 (which were periods of which the terminal years were at roughly equal stages in the cyclical variations in output during the 1950s). The equations for these periods are

$$P = 0{\cdot}773 + 0{\cdot}562\,Y \text{ (1955 to 1960; } r^2 = 0{\cdot}699)$$
$$\text{and } P = 0{\cdot}448 + 0{\cdot}628\,Y \text{ (1952 to 1958; } r^2 = 0{\cdot}673)$$

The average of these two results is

$$P = 0{\cdot}610 + 0{\cdot}595\,Y$$

(where P and Y, as before, indicate changes in productivity and output and relate to annual average rates of change).

Because of the approximate nature of the whole exercise, we have rounded off the elasticity from $0{\cdot}595$ to $0{\cdot}6$. But to obtain the constant term in the equation we have calculated what the constant term has to be, given this elasticity and given also the projected increases in total employment and output. These implied a constant term of unity, which may be justified on the grounds that the constant term, being an indicator of technical progress, is related to the rate of growth of output.

The manner in which the resulting equation ($P = 1{\cdot}0 + 0{\cdot}6\,Y$) has then been used is as follows. The projected output increases for each industry have been inserted into the above equation to obtain the increases in output per head.

For example, as output in the food processing industry is projected to rise by 1·8 per cent per annum, we suggest that output per head in that industry should rise by 1·0 + 0·6 (1·8) per cent per annum, that is 2·08 per cent per annum. This means that employment in this industry would fall by (1·8 − 2·08) per cent per annum, that is by 0·28 per cent per annum.

For certain special industries this estimating equation has not been used at all. This applies chiefly to the energy and transport industries where the more specialized knowledge of the authors of the chapters on their industries was drawn upon, and to industries such as the services, the construction industry and agriculture where the past relationships between changes in output and productivity indicate special problems. On account of the departure from the estimating equation in many cases, the sum of the initial set of employment projections for all the industries was found to be well above the overall employment projection of chapter 3. Consequently a *pro rata* downward adjustment was made to the projected level of employment in all industries (similar to that made to net output to preserve consistency with gross national product) which implied a corresponding upward adjustment to the initial productivity estimates.

A major problem encountered in projecting employment by industry arises for public administration and defence. This, together with some other services (such as ownership of dwellings, and domestic service) is not included in the 31 basic SAM industries so that in the tables below, a 'new' industry called 'public administration, defence and other services' has been added[1].

It is on the possible manpower requirement of this industry and of the 'services n.e.s.' industry that the feasibility of the output targets in the rest of the economy may be heavily dependent. Output of these two industries combined is likely to rise by about 45 per cent between 1960 and 1975, and in 1960 they accounted for 6.8 million out of a total employment of 24·7 million. They include activities where productivity, as conventionally measured, can show very little increase; if productivity in these industries did not improve compared with the past, they would need, by 1975, to employ about 2·5 million more people. Given that total employment is only expected to rise by about 1·7 million, this would imply a fall of 0·8 million employment in the rest of the economy, with correspondingly very high rates of increase in productivity.

In fact, over the period 1948 to 1960, the average rate of increase in output of the 'services n.e.s.' industry was shared about equally between increasing productivity and increasing employment; so that for this industry we have felt justified in assuming that, as in most other industries, faster output growth can lead to faster productivity growth. For the 'public administration, defence and other services' industry, we have also assumed that employment in certain component parts of this industry (education and health) will rise in accordance with the special projections for these activities contained in the chapters thereon, but

---

[1]The detailed breakdown of the projections of final expenditures in table 7.2 shows, ' below the line ', the elements required to project the output of this 'new' industry.

for all other such services we have assumed that productivity will rise faster than in the past. For the remainder of this industry (namely, public administration, defence and other services) we have assumed that productivity will rise by 1 per cent per annum, as compared with about 0·4 per cent per annum during the period 1950 to 1960[1].

(b) *The results*

Table 7.10 below compares the final projection of output and employment by industry and the reconciliation of the industry totals with total gross national product.

In tables 7.11 and 7.12 we compare the projected changes in employment and productivity with the changes in the period 1950 to 1960. Given the methods used, the difference between the past and the projected pattern of productivity change is inevitably very similar to the change in the pattern of output. That is, a much narrower dispersion of productivity changes is projected than occurred from 1950 to 1960. However, although ten industries are projected to have a slower rate of growth of output than in the past, in only four (mineral oil refining, motors and cycles, electricity and agriculture) is the rate of increase of productivity projected to be slower than in the past. This is the counterpart of the higher overall rate of productivity increase underlying the basic gross national product projection which, in turn, has been incorporated in the individual industry projections through the use of the equation specified on page 227 above (and the subsequent *pro rata* adjustments to maintain consistency with the total labour force projection).

It will be recalled that the overall gross national product objective adopted in chapter 3 was based on an overall increase in productivity per head of labour force of 3·1 per cent per annum for the whole period 1960 to 1975 (see chapter 3, table 3.19), or about 50 per cent higher than the rate achieved during the 1950s. But because of the projected pattern of output (and the particularly rapid proportionate acceleration for several industries) and the large absorption of labour in the service industries, future rates of productivity growth will have to be more than twice as fast as in the past in six manufacturing industries and more than 50 per cent higher than in the past in another four. Among all industries, nineteen will have to achieve rates of productivity growth of over 3 per cent per annum, whereas in the past only seven managed to do so. Only three industries are projected to raise productivity by less than 2 per cent per annum (distributive trades, water and public services), whereas in the past sixteen industries had failed to surpass this limit. Clearly the improvement

[1]Output, employment and productivity for public administration, defence and other services are projected to rise by 0·8 per cent, −0·2 per cent and 1·0 per cent per annum respectively, by comparison with −1·1 per cent, −1·5 per cent and 0·4 per cent during the period 1950 to 1960.

Table 7.10. *Net output and employment by industry, 1960 and 1975*

	SAM industry group	1960 Output[a] (£m.)	1960 Employment ('000s)	1975 Output (£m.)	1975 Employment ('000s)
1	Agriculture, forestry and fishing	914	1,062	1,220	746
2	Coal mining	562	692	588	375
3	Mining and quarrying	108	72	167	58
4	Food processing	546	634	728	615
5	Drink and tobacco	305	215	438	204
6	Coke ovens, etc.	34	19	37	15
7	Mineral oil refining	56	40	129	50
8	Chemicals n.e.s.	720	474	2,083	606
9	Iron and steel (excluding tinplates and tubes)	521	419	770	404
10	Iron and steel (tinplates and tubes)	110	67	190	68
11	Non-ferrous metals	178	133	283	122
12	Engineering and electrical goods	1,819	2,078	3,589	2,327
13	Shipbuilding and marine engineering	181	278	268	268
14	Motors and cycles	487	488	1,062	555
15	Aircraft	281	294	502	306
16	Railway locomotives and rolling stock	65	145	49	104
17	Metal goods n.e.s.	493	557	855	570
18	Textiles	625	906	871	810
19	Leather, clothing and footwear	379	677	602	673
20	Building materials	190	198	265	185
21	Pottery and glass	121	145	192	144
22	Timber, furniture, etc.	209	315	352	318
23	Paper, printing, publishing	602	613	1,258	677
24	Other manufacturing	247	306	554	348
25	Construction	1,285	1,607	1,984	1,574
26	Gas	146	128	183	199
27	Electricity	403	212	1,243	298
28	Water	62	37	82	37
29	Transport and communications	1,915	1,691	2,958	1,656
30	Distributive trades	2,811	3,355	4,341	4,107
31	Services n.e.s.	2,917	3,107	4,702	3,426
32	Public administration, defence and other services	3,393	3,727	4,455	4,505
	Total[b]	22,684	24,691	37,000	26,350
	less stock appreciation	− 133		− 150	
	residual error	303		—	
	GDP at factor cost	22,248		36,850	
	less indirect taxes on imports	− 1,444		− 2,400	
	plus taxes on expenditure	3,389		} 4,800	
	less subsidies	− 498			
	GDP at market prices	23,695		39,250	
	plus net property income from abroad	236		750	
	GNP at market prices	23,931		40,000	

[a]All figures in this table correspond to those in *National Income and Expenditure, 1963*, in the interests of more accurate breakdown of net output by industries.

[b]For the total of manufacturing, namely the sum of industries 4–24, 1975 net output and employment are projected as £15,077 million and 9,362,000 respectively, implying annual average growth rates of output, employment and productivity of 4·2 per cent, 0·3 per cent and 3·9 per cent, respectively.

Table 7.11.   *Comparison of past and projected rates of change of productivity in individual industries*

	SAM industry group	Annual average percentage rate of growth of change of productivity		Ratio, 1960–75 to 1950–60
		1960–75	1950–60	
	Manufacturing industries			
13	Shipbuilding and marine engineering	2·9	1·0	2·9
4	Food processing	2·1	0·8	2·6
12	Engineering and electrical goods	3·9	1·5	2·6
11	Non-ferrous metals	3·7	1·5	2·5
18	Textiles	2·9	1·4	2·1
17	Metal goods n.e.s.	3·5	1·7	2·1
20	Building materials	2·7	1·4	1·9
22	Timber, furniture, etc.	3·5	2·0	1·8
23	Paper, printing and publishing	4·3	2·6	1·7
24	Other manufacturing	4·6	2·8	1·6
5	Drink and tobacco	2·7	1·8	1·5
19	Leather, clothing and footwear	3·1	2·1	1·5
9/10	Iron and steel	3·0	2·3	1·3
21	Pottery and glass	3·1	2·5	1·2
8	Chemicals n.e.s.	5·6	4·9	1·1
15/16	Aircraft and railway rolling stock	3·6	3·2	1·1
14	Motors and cycles	4·4	5·6	0·8
7	Mineral oil refining	4·2	8·1	0·5
6	Coke ovens, etc.	2·2	− 1·1	n.a.
4–24	Total manufacturing	3·9	2·4	1·6
	Other industries			
26	Gas[a]	3·2	0·4	8·0
30	Distributive grades	1·5	0·7	2·1
31	Services n.e.s.	2·5	1·5	1·7
25	Construction	3·1	1·9	1·6
29	Transport and communication	3·1	2·2	1·4
3	Mining and quarrying n.e.s.	4·3	3·8	1·1
1	Agriculture, forestry and fishing	4·2	4·5	0·9
27	Electricity	5·5	6·9	0·8
2	Coal mining	4·3	− 0·4	n.a.
28	Water	1·9	− 0·4	n.a.
32	Public administration, defence and other services	0·5	0·6	0·8
	Total gross domestic product per person employed (factor cost)	3·1	1·8	1·7

[a]This estimate attempts to take account of the value added to natural or other gas bought for processing and distribution.   The present index of production omits this.

over the past will need to be not only substantial but widespread over the whole of industry if the pattern and level of demand projected is to be met.

Substantial improvements over past productivity performances are required in several key industries.   In *engineering*, for example, on which the achievement of the export target largely depends, productivity will need to grow between twice and three times as fast as in the past. The *construction* industry, as indicated above, need not expand output much faster than in the past, but because of the prospective developments in the labour force it will need to raise its rate of productivity increase from about 1·9 per cent per annum (1950 to 1960) to over 3 per cent per annum. The growth of productivity in the *distributive trades* is also of great importance on account of the large numbers employed in this industry. Its output is not projected to grow any faster than in the past, but during the period 1950 to 1960 it was adding to its employment at a rate of 2·2 per cent per annum and raising productivity by only 0·7 per cent per annum. We have projected a productivity growth rate twice as fast as this, in order to keep its employment growth rate down to 1·4 per cent per annum. Failure to achieve any improvement on past productivity performance in this industry would mean (assuming its output growth to be unaffected) that it would absorb half a million more employees than we have allowed for, thereby calling for an even greater improvement over past productivity performance in industries on which our exports and rate of investment largely depend.

The projected changes in employment by industry are shown in table 7.12 below. Again, the projected narrowing of the dispersion in rates of growth of output, combined with the methods used to estimate the corresponding changes in productivity and employment, has meant some narrowing of the dispersion in rates of change of employment. In one sense this would appear to facilitate the achievement of the projected output pattern, since the main conclusion emerging from table 7.12 is that inter-industry labour mobility will not have to be so great in the future as in the past. Whereas in the past six industries increased employment by more than 2 per cent per annum, only one, electricity, is projected to require this in the future.

However, this is the result not only of the narrower dispersion in rates of change in employment but also of the generally higher productivity growth projected and the lower rate of increase in the labour force.

Thus, whereas in the past only ten industries experienced declines in employ-ment, for the period 1960 to 1975 sixteen industries are projected to experience declines, or no increase, in employment. In the sense of the extent to which industries will release manpower, therefore, labour mobility will have to be greater than in the past. While the labour force is expanding it is relatively easy for the most rapidly growing industries to add to their labour force. But when, as we have projected for the years following 1967, the total labour force will be more or less stationary, so that the fastest-growing industries must rely on labour released from other industries (which will also, on the whole, be expanding faster than in the past and therefore less likely to release labour) the difficulties of achieving the required redistribution of the labour force will be greater.

Certain issues related to these manpower projections are obvious candidates for further analysis. First, the labour mobility problem in aggregate could be

Table 7.12. *Comparison of past and projected rates of change of employment in individual industries : percentage annual average rate of change*

SAM industry group		1960–75	1950–60
15	Aircraft	0·3	4·5
7	Mineral oil refining	1·5	3·2
6	Coke ovens, etc.	−1·6	2·9
12	Engineering and electrical goods	0·7	2·3
30	Distributive trades	1·4	2·2
15/16	Aircraft and railway rolling stock	−0·5	2·2
23	Paper, printing and publishing	0·7	1·9
24	Other manufacturing	0·9	1·8
11	Non-ferrous metals	−0·6	1·8
4	Food processing	−0·2	1·7
14	Motors and cycles	0·9	1·6
8	Chemicals n.e.s.	1·7	1·5
27	Electricity	2·3	1·5
28	Water	—	1·2
25	Construction	−0·2	0·8
17	Metal goods n.e.s.	0·2	0·7
5	Drink and tobacco	−0·3	0·4
20	Building materials	−0·5	0·3
9/10	Iron and steel	−0·2	0·2
22	Timber, furniture, etc.	—	−0·2
13	Shipbuilding and marine engineering	−0·2	−0·4
21	Pottery and glass	—	−0·5
29	Transport and communications	−0·2	−0·6
2	Coal mining	−4·0	−0·7
19	Leather, clothing, footwear	—	−0·8
3	Mining and quarrying n.e.s.	−1·4	−1·1
26	Gas	−1·7	−1·2
18	Textiles	−0·7	−1·8
1	Agriculture, forestry and fishing	−2·3	−2·5
4–24	*Total manufacturing*	*0·3*	*1·1*
	Total economy	*0·4*	*0·7*

translated into calculations of the type and sex of the labour required in the different industries. For example, it has been shown in chapter 3 that the economy will have to rely extensively on a further increase in the employment of married women if the total labour force is not to decline as from about 1967; but the pattern of employment change projected in table 7.12, given the different male/female ratio of the labour force in each industry will not necessarily correspond to the projected overall change in the male/female mix of the total labour force. Another aspect of the same problem that could be investigated is the composition of the labour force by skill and qualification—a problem which is gaining increasing recognition. Finally, the projected pattern of employment is also likely to have important consequences for the regional distribution of manpower.

In suggesting these follow-up investigations, however, we have not overlooked the margin of error attached to the projections of output and employment by industry.   Firm and detailed conclusions about the male/female balance of the labour force, the skill qualifications required and the regional impact can be drawn only if projection methods can be improved and specific industries studied in a less general manner.

CHAPTER VIII

INVESTMENT REQUIREMENTS

By W. Beckerman

This chapter is concerned with the problems encountered and the methods used to project capital formation in 1975. The probable sources of savings to match the investment requirements are discussed in chapter 9.

Physical capital has traditionally played a predominant role in the study of economic growth, though changing fashions have sometimes shifted the emphasis on to other factors of production, land, labour, and more recently education. But no great economic sophistication is required to observe that, on the whole, large differences in output per head, whether over time, or between countries or industries, are related to differences in capital per head. Simple comparisons of this nature are convincing evidence of the role of capital whether they refer to the difference between the United States and Europe, between the advanced countries of Europe and, say, Greece or Portugal, between Britain today and Britain fifty years ago, or between, say, the electricity industry and the textile industry.

That the clear and simple conviction of the connection between capital and output conveyed by such comparisons cannot be translated into an equally simple pure theory of capital is largely because of the inherent complexities of the concept of capital, some of which have been referred to in chapter 1 above. Most of these complexities, such as the difficulty of reducing to homogeneous units capital of different vintages employed in different uses with different techniques of production used in combination with different amounts and qualities of other factors of production, not only complicate the theory but also make it difficult to verify empirically the precise relationship at any period of time between capital and output. There is still a long way to go before the broad simple comparisons of the type mentioned above can yield precise measures of exactly how much more capital is required today in industry X if output is to be raised by a given amount.

Nevertheless, in any long-range projection of the economy some attempt must be made to evaluate the rough order of magnitude of the investment requirements associated with the growth hypothesis adopted. In this study, in particular, where we have given a special emphasis to objectives in the fields of health, housing, education, transport and foreign trade, it is essential to stand back and try to obtain an overall view of the extent to which the objectives adopted might impose an intolerable level of investment either in the sense of an excessive sacrifice of present consumption for the sake of future standards of living or in the sense of implying a strain on internal financial stability.

As with the output projections discussed in the last chapter, however, we do not believe that great precision in projecting investment requirements ten years hence is either necessary or feasible. It is not necessary because, within limits, a tendency towards excess capacity or a shortage of capacity in most industries can be corrected as it emerges. It is not feasible because, in addition to the uncertainty as to the 1975 output projections by industry, there is simply no foolproof method of knowing what will be the latest techniques of production in 1975 and it is largely these techniques that will determine the investment requirements per unit of additional output in 1975. Much of this chapter comprises a description of the attempts made to find precise relationships between investment requirements and the output projections, although the conclusions are, on the whole, very agnostic. In making these attempts we have concentrated on manufacturing investment, although this accounts for only about one quarter of total gross domestic capital formation. We have done this for two reasons. Firstly, if any precise relationships between capital and output can be expected to exist at all it is in manufacturing above all (rather than, say, in distribution or transport) that they should be identifiable. Secondly, most of the other large items of capital formation have been projected in the specialized chapters concerned, namely housing, education, energy and transport.

In the first section of this chapter we present our estimates of capital stocks in individual manufacturing industries and discuss their reliability and the trends in the average capital-output ratios that they show for the period 1950 to 1960. It is found that these trends are generally rising, in some cases rapidly. But as we have assumed here a higher growth rate for the period 1960–75 than that achieved during the 1950s, simple extrapolation of these rising trends into the future would be inconsistent with the evidence, presented in chapter 1, of the inverse correlation between growth rates and incremental capital-output ratio (ICORs) at the level of total gross national product. Hence we have also examined to what extent this negative correlation between growth rates and capital requirements per unit of additional output also applies at the level of individual industries. The results suggest that it does. In the end, therefore, the methods used to project investment requirements per unit of additional output in individual industries make some allowance for changes in their growth rates as well as for the different technical conditions of production in each industry as represented by their average capital-output ratios.

1. THE USE OF CAPITAL STOCK DATA

Industries are expected to differ with respect to their investment requirements per unit of additional output because they differ with respect to the capital-intensity of their techniques of production, whether capital-intensity is defined in terms of capital per unit of output (the capital-output ratio) or capital per employee. Hence it is desirable to allow for these differences in techniques of production among industries in projecting how much new capital is required to produce a given increase in output.

(a) *Reliability of capital stock data*

If this approach is to be adopted it is necessary, first, to have some confidence in the conceptual relevance of the concept of capital that is selected and in the reliability of the estimates of the capital stock in individual industries. One of the main conceptual issues is whether to measure capital stocks on a gross basis, rather than net of depreciation. The main consideration determining the choice between the gross and the net (of depreciation) concept is whether the productive ability of the capital stock is believed to be a function of the capital consumption which should be spread over the life of the assets. This will include wear and tear and obsolescence. We have taken the view that, for the analysis of the productive capacity of the capital stock, while it is necessary to allow for scrappings and retirements, it is unrealistic to assume that productive capacity is reduced proportionately to the capital consumption allowances that should, from the accountant's point of view, be spread over the life of the assets in one way or another.

Hence we have preferred to adopt the concept of the gross capital stock before deducting depreciation. Estimates have been made of the gross capital stock at constant prices for the twenty-four manufacturing industries identified in 'SAM' by means of a cumulation, over the estimated length of life of the assets, of past gross capital formation, minus only the estimated scrappings and retirements during this period (which also depend on the estimated lengths of lives of the assets)[1]. The results are shown in table 8.1.

One way of checking the reliability of the capital stock data is to use a well-known theoretical relationship between capital per head and output per head.

This theoretical relationship is the proposition that, under conditions of perfect competition and homogeneity of capital and labour, if all industries were in long-run equilibrium they would all have the same rate of return on capital. If P = profits, r = rate of return on capital, E = employment, w = wages per employee, W = wage bill, K = capital stock, and O = value of net output in a given year, then for each industry,

$$O = W + P$$
$$= wE + rK$$

so that $\dfrac{O}{E} \equiv w + \dfrac{rK}{E}$ ....(1)

[1]These estimates were prepared by A. D. Smith. The main data used are shown in appendix tables 8.1 to 8.5. In brief, the method adopted is that known as the 'perpetual inventory method', and which has been used, notably, by R. W. Goldsmith in 'The Growth of Reproducible Wealth of the United States of America from 1805 to 1950' in International Association for Research in Income and Wealth, *Income and Wealth, Series II* (Cambridge, 1952); and P. Redfern, 'Net Investment in Fixed Assets in the United Kindom, 1938–1953', *Journal of the Royal Statistical Society*, Series A, part 2, 1955. See also notes to table 8.1.

Table 8.1. *Capital and output per employee and average capital-output ratios for British manufacturing industries, 1950 and 1960[a] : £ at 1960 prices*

SAM number	1950			1960		
	Capital per employee	Output per employee	Capital-output ratio	Capital per employee	Output per employee	Capital-output ratio
7	2,033	400	5·08	9,470	1,400	6·77
8	2,363	980	2·41	4,337	1,520	2·85
9 and 10	2,326	1,000	2·33	3,966	1,321	3·00
5	2,825	1,221	2·31	3,448	1,463	2·36
18	2,407	599	4·02	3,249	684	4·75
11	2,575	1,062	2·43	3,074	1,246	2·47
20	1,733	796	2·18	2,442	959	2·54
4	1,852	801	2·16	2,343	874	2·37
23	2,017	773	1·98	2,340	988	1·88
14	1,388	703	2·31	2,100	1,115	2·68
24	1,305	652	2·01	1,729	815	2·12
12	1,295	755	1·72	1,557	885	1·76
15 and 16	1,305	601	1·72	1,535	793	1·94
17	939	751	1·25	1,318	898	1·47
13	844	604	1·27	1,310	645	1·52
21	834	658	1·40	1,276	839	2·03
22	782	580	1·35	1,113	710	1·57
19	635	478	1·33	724	577	1·25
Total manufacturing	1,590	730	2·18	2,196	922	2·38

Source: Appendix tables 8.4, 8.11 and 8.12.

Note: The capital stock data have been prepared at the National Institute of Economic and Social Research by A. D. Smith and are based largely on estimates by Mr C. Feinstein of the gross capital stock in 1955, broken down by industry largely in accordance with Professor T. Barna's 1955 estimated distribution (see footnote 2 to page 239 below), and extrapolated backwards and forwards to each year of the decade 1950 to 1960 in the light of Feinstein's estimated capital formation series for these years (and for earlier years) in order, given estimates of the length of life of the different types of assets, to deduct annual scrapping during the period 1950 to 1960. See appendix tables 8.1 to 8.4.

[a]Industries ranked in order of capital per employee in 1960.

Thus if w is the same for all industries, the values of $\dfrac{O}{E}$ and $\dfrac{K}{E}$ for all industries in long-run competitive equilibrium would fall along a regression line of the form shown by equation (1) above[1]. Deviations from the regression line could

[1]An alternative algebraic derivation and interpretation of the same result is that of the economy as a whole operated in accordance with a linear homogeneous production function, so that

$$O = \frac{\delta O}{\delta E} \cdot E + \frac{\delta O}{\delta K} \cdot K$$

then,

$$\frac{O}{E} = \frac{\delta O}{\delta K} \cdot \frac{K}{E} + \frac{\delta O}{\delta E}$$

Hence if the observation of $\dfrac{O}{E}$ and $\dfrac{K}{E}$ fit a straight line of the form $\dfrac{O}{E} = w + r\dfrac{K}{E}$ the mean that industries are not paying the same wages per employee or that they are not in long-run competitive equilibrium and are earning excess or sub-normal profits (which could be accounted for, in some cases, by their not operating at a normal full level of capacity utilization).

Cross-section comparisons of output per head and capital per head have, in fact, been used by some writers as a means of measuring the relationship between capital and output for the economy as a whole (or that part of it covered by the comparisons)[1]. But it is now generally recognized that such cross-section comparisons are not measures of any technical production relationship at all because although the single observations for each industry represents the particular position which that industry happens to occupy on the curve relating changes in its capital stock to changes in its output, the intercept of such points, which is what the fitted cross-section regression line constitutes, must, for the reasons given in the last paragraph, have a slope equal to the rate of return on capital. And the rate of return on capital (that is, the rate of profit) for the economy as a whole is in no sense a technical production-output relationship[2]. It will depend on many factors such as the general degree of competition in the economy and what is conventionally accepted as a 'normal' rate of profit. For example, if the conventionally accepted normal

constant w must be interpreted as the real wage $\left(\dfrac{\delta O}{\delta E}\right)$ and the slope of the line, r, must be interpreted as the rate of return on capital, $\left(\dfrac{\delta O}{\delta K}\right)$. If the point on an industry's capital-output curve at which the slope of the curve was tangential to the slope represented by the cross-section regression line were above the regression line then that industry would be earning above 'normal' profits and the process of perfect competition would, through the price mechanism, force down the price of that industry's output to the point where its curve is tangential to the cross-section line.

[1]Notably by M. Bronfenbrenner and P. H. Douglas, 'Cross-Section Studies in the Cobb-Douglas Function', *Journal of Political Economy*, December 1939; J. Williams, 'Professor Douglas' Production Function', *Economic Record*, June 1945; and G. W. G. Browne, 'The Production Function for South African Manufacturing Industry', *South African Journal of Economics*, December 1943.

[2]See, in particular T. Barna, 'The Replacement Cost of Fixed Assets in British Manufacturing Industry in 1955', *Journal of the Royal Statistical Society*, Series A, part 1, 1957. Early criticisms of the interpretation of the inter-industry cross-section results were made by H. Mendershausen, 'On the Significance of Douglas' Production Function', *Econometrica*, April 1938, and more recently by E. H. Phelps Brown, 'The Meaning of the Fitted Cobb-Douglas Production Function', *op. cit.*, in 1957. Considerable constructive clarification of the interpretation of the cross-section studies has been provided by T. Barna, *ibid.*, and in simple diagrammatic form, in 'Du Capital Envisagé comme une Variable Economique', *Cahiers du Séminaire d'Econométrie*, no. 5 (Paris, 1959). Following T. Barna, but in English, R. M. Solow has summarized the cross-section regression lines as being '. . . simply not a production function. The points should lie on or near a straight line whose vertical intercept should be the real wage and whose slope should be the real return on capital. The line will be the envelope of the production functions of the several industries'. (See Solow's 'Comment', page 65, on Stigler's 'Economic Problems in Measuring Changes in Productivity', in the National Bureau of Economic Research, *Output, Input and Productivity Measurement* (Princeton, 1961.)

Fig. 8.1. Relationship between output per employee and capital per employee (1960 prices)

(a) Output and capital per head, 1950

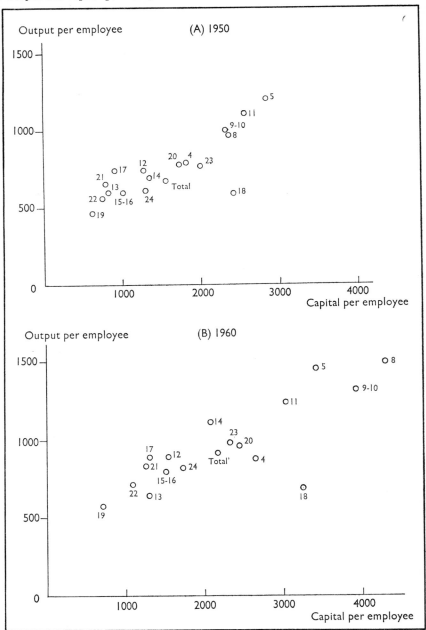

(b) Output and capital per head, 1960

(c) Change in output and capital per head, 1950 to 1960

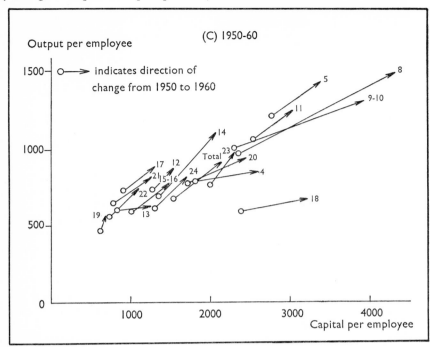

Source: Table 8.1.

Note: Numbers refer to SAM industry numbers.

rate of profit were to fall for some reason or other (e.g. increased planning of the economy or expectation of a generally faster rate of growth, both of which could decrease the 'risk' element) then the slope of the cross-section regression line would simply become flatter, as the competitive process would reduce the prices of all industries' outputs. Clearly this does not require any change in the technical relationships between physical quantities of output and capital in the individual industries.

Nevertheless, whilst cross-section analysis of the type discussed cannot be used to estimate how much more capital stock is required to produce the projected level of output, the theoretical requirements which the data should satisfy provide us with some check on whether the orders of magnitude of the 'perpetual inventory' estimates of the capital stocks in the individual industries are reasonable, since we can see how well they fit the equation (1) above.

In figure 8.1 (a) and 8.1 (b) we show the relationship between output per head and capital stock per head in the various industries with which we are concerned, in 1950 and 1960, on the basis of the perpetual inventory data shown in table 8.1 above. It will be seen that the fit in both cases is good considering the inevitable errors in the capital stock estimates, and that, at any point of time, industries are not likely to be in long-run competitive equilibrium (or be operating at normal levels of capacity utilization)[1].

Hence we may conclude that, considering the theoretical assumptions required to produce a perfect statistical fit for the equation specified are most unlikely to be satisfied, the perpetual inventory data are probably reasonably accurate guides to inter-industry differences in average capital-output ratios.

(b) *Average capital-output ratios in British manufacturing industries, 1950 to 1960*

Having selected a series of capital stock estimates, the next step, if capital-output ratios are to be used as a guide to investment requirements, is to check how stable they are. Table 8.2 shows the indexes of the average capital-output ratios, as measured by the perpetual inventory method, over the period 1950 to 1960. With the exception of three industries (motor vehicles, leather and clothing, and paper and printing) those ratios have all risen between 1950 and 1960, in some cases substantially. But the value of these ratios in any one year will reflect, among other things, short-term changes in the degree of capacity utilization.

For this reason a more satisfactory way of assessing the stability of the capital-output ratios, is to examine the evolution of these ratios each year throughout the period. These are shown in the following diagrams. In these diagrams the fluctuations in the ratios corresponding to short-period conjunctural fluctuations in output relative to capacity are clearly apparent. At the same time it is clear from figure 8.2 that the excess of the 1960 capital-output ratios over the 1950 ratios cannot be ascribed to the special circumstances of those two years but reflect fairly constant upward trends in these ratios throughout the 1950s.

On the other hand, it would be inconsistent with other results in this study simply to extrapolate these capital-output ratio trends over the next fifteen years. For we are assuming that output will grow significantly faster over the period 1960 to 1975 than over the period 1950 to 1960. And in chapter 1 we have shown that, at the level of total gross national product, *incremental* capital-output ratios (ICORs) are inversely correlated with growth

[1]The fit for the 1950 data here ($r = 0.828$) is slightly, though statistically not significantly, better than for the 1960 data ($r = 0.823$) (in both cases excluding mineral oil and textiles), even though for purposes of figure 8.1 (c), where the movements over time for each industry are shown at constant prices, the 1960 data in figures 8.1 (a) and 8.1 (b) are at constant (1960) prices, and on theoretical grounds the 1950 data at 1960 prices should show more deviations from the regression line than at 1950 prices, since the equilibrating mechanism involves changes in net output prices. Estimates of capital stocks for the same industries were prepared by Mr Z. Shardy on the basis of accounting data published by the Board of Trade in *Company Assets, Income and Finance in 1960* (London, 1962). These data showed a weaker correlation in the form of the equation (1) above, largely no doubt because of the historical cost basis of the data.

R2

Table 8.2. *Indexes of average capital-output ratios in British manufacturing industries, 1950–60*

	Index 1960 (1950 = 100)
Coke	183·3
Shipbuilding	145·0
Mineral oil refining	133·3
Iron and steel	128·8
Pottery and glass	119·7
Other chemicals	118·3
Textiles	118·2
Metal goods n.e.s.	117·6
Building materials	116·5
Timber and furniture	116·3
Food processing	116·0
Aircraft and railway rolling stock	112·8
Other manufacturing	105·5
Engineering	102·3
Drink and tobacco	102·2
Non-ferrous metals	101·6
Motor vehicles	94·9
Leather and clothing	94·0
Paper and printing	90·8

Source: Appendix table 8.9.

rates of output. Hence, one should expect that ICORs in the future will be lower than in the 1950s. This would mean that capital-output ratios in the future would rise less rapidly (if at all) than in the past. On the evidence in chapter 1 of comparative ICORs in different countries, we feel justified in regarding part at least of the rise in the capital-output ratio *not* as an expression of basic technical changes but rather as evidence that investment has not been yielding its full return in terms of output. In a later section of this chapter, therefore, we examine how far any inverse relationship between ICORs and rates of growth of output can be established at the level of individual industries, and we find that the same relationship does exist. Furthermore, we find that at the industry level, as at the total level of gross national product discussed in chapter 1, 'progress' or the 'residual' is positively correlated with rates of growth of output. Consequently our final projections of capital formation by industry make some allowance for the effect of changes in their growth rates on the ICORs.

But before proceeding to the analysis of the ICORs it must be conceded that the exploitation of capital stock data for purposes of projecting investment requirements has a strong theoretical appeal. This is because ideally what is required is the identification of the 'production function' for individual industries—that is, a more complete specification of the relationship between inputs and outputs than is provided by partial measures such as ICORs, or average capital-output ratios. Hence we have experimented with production functions with the aid of our capital stock data.

Fig. 8.2. Index numbers of capital-output ratios, 1950 = 100

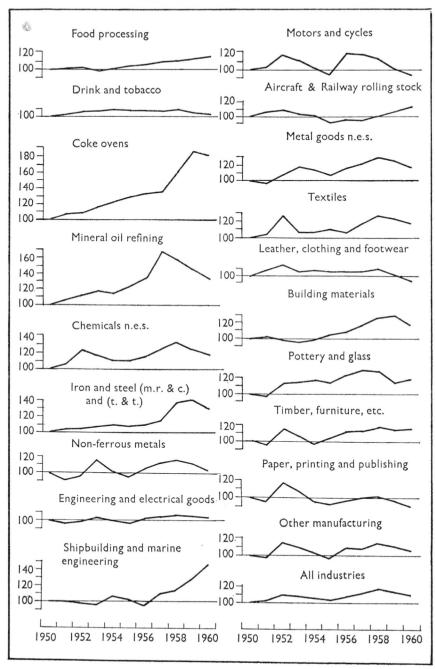

Fig. 8.2 (*continued*)

Source: Appendix table 8.9.

Note: The relationship between the SAM industry groups in this chart and the Standard Industrial Classification (the 'index of production' industries) is shown below.

SAM group	SIC order	Minimum list headings
Food processing	III	211 to 229
Drink and tobacco	III	231 to 240
Coke ovens	IV	261
Mineral oil refining	IV	262 and 263
Chemicals n.e.s.	IV	271 to 277
Iron and steel	V	311 to 313
Non-ferrous metals	V	321 and 322
Engineering and electrical goods	VI	331 to 369
Shipbuilding and marine engineering	VII	370
Motors and cycles	VIII	381 and 382
Aircraft and railway rolling stock	VIII	383 to 385
Metal goods n.e.s.	IX	391 to 399
Textiles	X	411 to 429
Leather, clothing and footwear	XI, XII	431 to 450
Building materials	XIII	461, 464 and 469
Pottery and glass	XIII	462 and 463
Timber, furniture, etc.	XIV	471 to 479
Paper, printing and publishing	XV	481 to 489
Other manufacturing	XVI	491 to 499

(c) *Production functions*

First, for each of two industries, the food, drink and tobacco industry and the textile industry, four forms of production function were used, and each form was tried on the basis of (i) actual value of the variables in each year and (ii) the values obtained from a three-year moving average of the variables. The various forms of equation fitted were:

(i) a simple 'Cobb-Douglas' production function, $O = AK^{\alpha}E^{\beta}\epsilon^{rt}$, with $\alpha + \beta = 1$ (indicating constant returns to scale) where O, K and E are as defined above; and t = time, so that r = the 'residual' trend rate of growth of output that is not explained by changes in K or E;

(ii) the same as (i) but without any restriction on the sum of α and β;

(iii) a function obtained by expressing, initially, the changes in capital stock as a lagged adjustment between the actual capital stock in any year and the 'optimum' capital stock[1] but without any trend term;

(iv) the same as (iii) but with the trend term re-introduced.

The results obtained with the eight experimental calculations for the two industries indicated are shown in table 8.3. The coefficients of capital and labour, α and β, do not only vary greatly according to the precise form of equation adopted but often have quite unacceptable values, in some cases being negative and large[2]. Also, the 'residual' trend, which, in similar contexts, is often widely used as an indicator of the contribution of factors such as education, economies of scale and so on, also varies enormously, being negative in two cases. Finally, although the textile industry has had a generally lower rate of capacity utilization than the food, drink and tobacco industry throughout

---

[1]This formulation of the function, due to L. A. Koyck, is attained as follows:

Denoting K^* as the 'optimum' or 'desired' level of capital stock in a given year corresponding to the actual level of output and employment in the same year, the equation shown above can be rewritten as

$$\text{Log } O = \log A + \alpha \log K^* + \beta \log L \qquad (1)$$

and with K_{-1} indicating actual capital stock in the preceding year,

$$\log K - \log K_{-1} = \lambda (\log K^* - \log K_{-1})$$

where λ represents the coefficient by which, in a year, the actual capital stock is adjusted towards the desired stock, so that

$$\log K = \log K^* + (1 - \lambda) \log K_{-1} \qquad (2)$$

From (1) and (2) we have

$$\log K = -\frac{\lambda}{\alpha} \log A + \frac{\lambda}{\alpha} \log O - \frac{\lambda\beta}{\alpha} \log L + (1 - \lambda) \log K_{-1} \qquad (3)$$

Writing $b_0 = -\frac{\lambda}{\alpha} \log A$; $b_1 = \frac{\lambda}{\alpha}$; $b_2 = -\frac{\lambda\beta}{\alpha}$ and $b_3 = 1 - \lambda$

our data can be fitted to the equation

$$\log K = b_0 + b_1 \log O + b_2 \log L + b_3 \log K_{-1}$$

and the calculated values of the coefficients correspond to the basic coefficients of capital and labour respectively, as follows:

$$\alpha = \frac{1 - b_3}{b_1}, \text{ and } \beta = \frac{-b_2}{b_1}$$

[2]The multiple correlation coefficients obtained in all cases were very high, but this is no indicator of the 'reliability' of the results given the small number of degrees of freedom and the high serial correlation.

Table 8.3. *Results of experimental production function calculations for the food,
drink and tobacco industry and the textile industry, 1950–60*

Type of equation	Series	Capital coefficient	Labour coefficient	'Residual' trend
Food, drink and tobacco				
(i)	A	0·93	0·07	— ·004
	B	— 0·78	0·22	— ·003
(ii)	A	— 0·36	0·01	·016
	B	— 0·95	0·05	·025
(iii)	A	0·91	— 0·29	
	B	1·80	— 1·96	
(iv)	A	— 27·70	1·38	·013
	B	— 2·41	· 0·01	·021
Textiles				
(i)	A	— 1·01	2·01	·020
	B	— 0·52	1·52	·013
(ii)	A	— 3·06	2·13	·032
	B	— 3·04	2·29	·033
(iii)	A	4·05	— 2·95	
	B	1·06	— 0·02	
(iv)	A	— 4·21	2·65	·005
	B	9·08	5·44	·004

Note: Series A relate to the actual values of the variables in each year and series B to the values obtained from a three-year moving average.

the period and a slight downward trend in output, it appears from this sort of calculation to have had a greater positive 'residual'. Equally unacceptable results were obtained applying functions of type (i) and (ii) to various other industries. For example, in three industries, drink and tobacco, coke, and mineral oil refining, the 'residual' was negative. The currently popular tendency to ascribe 'residuals' obtained by such calculations to changes in knowledge, would imply, for these industries, a continuous loss of memory.

Inter-industry comparison of the 'residuals' tends, in fact, to support the view advanced in chapter 1 to the effect that faster growth is accompanied by lower capital requirements per unit of additional output, since these residuals are highly correlated with rates of growth of output. It also appears that the residual is only very slightly correlated with the rate of increase in the capital stock, suggesting that it is economies of scale in one form or another, rather than the 'embodied' technical progress, which are important in obtaining the productivity increases. Using the data shown in the most careful available inter-industry comparisons of changes in inputs and output in British industry, namely those published by Reddaway and Smith, and where $x_1 =$ the 'residual' (corresponding to what the authors call 'progress'), $x_2 =$ the index of net output and $x_3 =$ the index of the capital stock, the following correlation results are obtained[1]:

$$R^2_{1.23} = 0·78; \ r_{12} = 0·85; \ r_{13} = 0·13$$

[1]W. B. Reddaway and A. D. Smith, 'Progress in British Manufacturing Industries in the Period 1948–54', *op. cit.* The data for x_1, x_2 and x_3 here correspond to those shown in table I, col. (5) and table II, cols. (1) and (3) respectively.

One obvious possible explanation for the unsatisfactory results of the production function experiments is that the methods used do not contain adequate correction for short-run variations in the degree of capacity utilization. In particular, the usual course of events when, say, output falls in one year, is that employment will fall less rapidly, if at all, so that output per head will fall. At the same time, the capital stock will generally continue to rise, at least over a period as short as a year, so that capital per head will rise. Hence the statistical results obtained from time series based on annual data will tend to show an inverse correlation of capital per head on output per head. The above experiments attempt to overcome this difficulty to some extent in the equations based on three-year moving averages of the data and those using the lagged investment demand function. But it has to be recognized that these may be quite inadequate to avoid the problem of varying capacity utilization.

(d) *Influence on estimated capital coefficients of choice of capital stock indicator*

One possible substitute for an index of the capital stock which should make some allowance for changes in capacity utilization is an index of fuel inputs into each industry. This has been used recently in an attempt to derive production functions for individual industries by Hilhorst, who points out that 'As a machine cannot work without being powered by energy, more machines will be utilized as more energy is used in the productive process'[1]. However there are also numerous limitations on fuel input as an indicator of the capital stock. Some additions to the capital stock (such as office or storage space) may require no corresponding increase in fuel, some of the fuel input may be required for heating so that temperature variations can affect the input and there may be big changes in the fuel utilization rates of existing machinery unrelated to changes in their level of operation, not to mention increased fuel efficiency of new machinery. Hence if, in the event of no change in the degree of utilization of capacity, fuel input is an unreliable indicator of changes in the capital stock, it will also be an unreliable indicator of changes in the 'utilized' capital stock. Comparisons of the evolution of the time series of capital stock with indices of fuel input into various industries strongly suggest that the latter must be very poor indicators in some cases[2].

In one industry, the iron and steel industry, we have been able to compare alternative indicators of the capital stock and calculate the values of the

[1] J. G. M. Hilhorst, 'Measurement of Production Functions in Manufacturing Industry', Netherlands Central Bureau of Statistics, *Statistical Studies*, no. 13, 1962. It should be noted that fuel had been used as an indicator of capital stock much earlier by M. Frankel, *British and American Manufacturing Productivity* (Urbana, Illinois, 1957).

[2] For example, our perpetual inventory index of the capital stock in the chemicals industry (excluding mineral oil refining) shows an increase of 123 per cent in the capital stock of this industry between 1950 and 1959, whereas the fuel input index increases by only 36 per cent over the same period. Even allowing for substantial errors in the former, a large part of the discrepancy must be accounted for by the latter.

equations used above on the basis of the alternative series. The three capital stock indicators used were an index of fuel input, the perpetual inventory series already mentioned, and a special series compiled by the staff of the Iron and Steel Board in which allowance has been made for known scrappings, unlike the hypothetical scrappings used in the perpetual inventory series[1]. Furthermore, the latter two indices have been adjusted according to estimates of the degree of capacity utilization kindly provided by the staff of the Iron and Steel Board[2].

The results obtained with the alternative capital stock figures are shown in table 8.4. It can be seen that (i) the results are generally much more acceptable than those of table 8.3, (ii) the results obtained with the fuel input series do not differ greatly from our perpetual inventory series, except as regards the labour coefficient when constant returns to scale are not assumed, but that (iii) the Iron and Steel Board series lead to much lower capital coefficients. In view of the methods used to construct the three series, the benefit of the doubt must be in favour of the Iron and Steel Board series, though it is not possible to say exactly where, between the two sets of results, the 'best' estimate would lie, nor even that the alternative sets of results define the limits to the range of reasonable estimates.

Table 8.4. *Alternative estimates of production functions for the iron and steel industry*

Nature of data and equation	Capital coefficient	Labour coefficient	'Residual' trend
A. Cobb-Douglas production function with constant returns to scale			
A.1. Perpetual inventory capital stock series	0·766	0·234	− 0·006
A.2. Grieve Smith and Miles (Iron and Steel Board) capital stock series	0·464	0·536	0·002
A.3. Fuel input as indicator of utilized capital stock	0·704	0·296	0·008
B. Cobb-Douglas production function with variable returns to scale			
B.1. Corresponding to A.1	0·647	0·804	− 0·004
B.2. Corresponding to A.2	0·441	1·321	0·002
B.3. Corresponding to A.3	0·656	0·468	0·008

These results for the iron and steel industry show that the estimated labour and capital coefficients are too sensitive to the precise capital stock series

[1] The Iron and Steel Board estimates are given by J. Grieve Smith and T. P. Miles in *Productivity in the Iron and Steel Industry*, Iron and Steel Institute Special Report 75 (London, 1962), p. 24.
[2] The basis of this index of capacity utilization is simply the ratio of actual output to estimated capacity output. The interpretation of the index depends, therefore, on the nature of the Iron and Steel Board's estimate of capacity utilization. It is here that a fundamental problem in measuring degrees of capacity utilization arises, for there is no simple concept of what is capacity to start with.

selected for any confidence to be attached to measures of these coefficients. This result has been obtained even though two of the capital stock series, ours, and the Grieve Smith and Miles series, show almost identical trend changes in capital stock over the whole period 1950 to 1960—the main differences being the greater degree of annual variation in the latter.

(e) *Combination of cross-section and time series capital stock data*

As the poor results obtained from time series data may be partly the result of conjunctural variations in output, rather than accurate reflections of the flexibility of the relationships, it might appear reasonable to combine time series with cross-section data in a manner designed to eliminate the main defect of time series. This would involve taking, for each industry, the values of the changes over time in capital per head and output per head, between comparable years in terms of conjunctural variations in output or between averages of early and late years during the 1950s, and compensating for the loss of observations by combining the pairs of observations remaining for each industry into a cross-section analysis of the form

$$d \log \left(\frac{O}{E}\right) = a + b.d \log \left(\frac{K}{E}\right)$$

This amounts to examining the relationship, *across industries*, between proportionate changes in capital per head and proportionate changes in output per head. However, attractive as this procedure may appear at first sight, there is no sound theoretical reason why any such cross-section relationship should exist[1].

It is true that at the extremes changes in output per head appear to be correlated with changes in capital per head (table 8.5). For example, output per head rose most (excluding mineral oil refining) between 1950 and 1960 in 'other chemicals' and motor vehicles (55·3 per cent and 58·3 per cent respectively) and these were the industries where capital per head rose most, by 83·5 per cent and 51·3 per cent respectively as compared with a rise of 38·1 per cent for the total of manufacturing industry.

But apart from these extreme cases, changes in output per head in individual industries during the 1950s show very little systematic correlation with changes in capital per head. In fact, much the most interesting result to emerge from this type of analysis is that if proportionate changes in output per head are correlated with both (a) proportionate changes in capital per head and (b) proportionate changes in output, the latter variable explains most of the

[1]The ratios of the proportionate changes in capital per head to proportionate changes in output per head would only be the same for all industries if, in terms of the logarithm of the variables, the observations of capital per head and output per head fell along a straight line that passed through the origin of a scatter diagram having these two variables along the two axes. But it follows from the equation discussed on page 237 above that they should not do so.

Table 8.5. *Indexes of capital per employee and output per employee in British manufacturing industries, 1960 (1950 = 100)*

	Capital per employee	Output per employee
Mineral oil refining	466	342
Other chemicals	184	155
Coke	175	96
Iron and steel	170	132
Shipbuilding	155	107
Pottery and glass	153	128
Motor vehicles	151	158
Aircraft and railway rolling stock	148	132
Timber and furniture	142	123
Building materials	141	121
Metal goods n.e.s.	140	120
Total manufacturing	*138*	*127*
Textiles	136	115
Other manufacturing	133	125
Food processing	127	109
Drink and tobacco	122	120
Engineering	120	117
Non-ferrous metals	119	118
Paper and printing	116	128
Leather and clothing	114	121

Source: Appendix tables 8.8 and 8.10.

Table 8.6. *Results of correlations between proportionate changes in (a) output per head, (b) output and (c) capital per head, in British manufacturing industries*

Nature of correlation	R^2	$r^2_{12 \cdot 3}$	$r^2_{13 \cdot 2}$
1. Average 1953/5 to average 1959/60	0·75	0·70	0·17
2. Peak to peak (1955 to 1960)			
(a) Capital per head lagged one year	0·78	0·74	0·05
(b) Capital per head unlagged	0·77	0·77	—
3. Trough to trough (1952 to 1958)			
(a) Capital per head lagged one year	0·70	0·65	—
(b) Capital per head unlagged	0·70	0·67	—

Notes: $r^2_{12 \cdot 3}$ indicates the proportion of the variation in output per head explained by the variation in output after allowing for the variation in capital per head.

$r^2_{13 \cdot 2}$ indicates the proportion of the variation in output per head 'explained' by the variation in capital per head after allowing for the variation in output.

R^2 is the multiple correlation coefficient, indicating the proportion of the variation in output per head explained by the combined variation in capital per head and in output.

variations in output per head and the changes in capital per head play no significant role at all. This can be seen in table 8.6.

In conclusion, therefore, we find that whilst it is theoretically logical to allow for inter-industry differences in average capital-output ratios in projecting investment requirements, the use of capital stock data by themselves does not seem to provide a firm basis for the projections since it has not been found possible to establish firm relationships between capital stocks and output. Furthermore, other evidence suggests that variations in growth rates are accompanied by variations in capital requirements per unit of output. This means that one of the illusory advantages of working in terms of average capital-output ratios rather than ICORS is, in fact, a disadvantage. This illusory advantage is their greater relative stability[1]. But if ICORs are inversely correlated with rates of growth of output, any such correlation will be easier to identify in the more sensitive ICORs than in the corresponding evolution of the average capital-output ratios.

2. INCREMENTAL CAPITAL-OUTPUT RATIOS IN BRITISH MANUFACTURING INDUSTRIES, 1950 TO 1960

(a) *Gross fixed capital formation by manufacturing industry, 1950 to 1960*

Gross fixed capital formation in British manufacturing industries has risen from a total of £659 million in 1950 to £995 million in 1960 (both at 1960 prices), or by 50 per cent. Over the same ten-year period, net output of manufacturing at 1960 prices rose from £5,833 million to £8,132 million. Between 1950 and 1959 the cumulative total of capital formation was £7,763 million and in 1960 manufacturing net output was £2,043 million higher than in 1951. In other words, if all the increase in net output could be ascribed to the capital formation over the period, it required about £3·85 of new capital to produce an extra £1 per annum of net output.

During this period, however, some capital equipment was retired from active use, so that manufacturing net capital formation, defined as gross capital formation minus estimated retirements (which is not the same as the accounting provision for depreciation) was only about £6,475 million[2]. On this basis it required only about £3·2 of net new capital formation to produce an extra £1 of net output per annum.

The classification of the industries followed in this study, following that used in the DAE study, has been adopted in the interests of product homogeneity and not in the light of the relative size of the different industries. For this, and other reasons, the total capital formation in manufacturing is distributed

[1]It would be an illusion to believe that this enables capital formation requirements to be projected more accurately than on the basis of more unstable ICORs, since a given proportionate error in the projection of the average capital-output ratio would imply a much greater error in the projection of the implied capital formation than the same proportionate error in the projections of the ICOR.

[2]The estimates of 'net' capital formation used throughout this section refer to those, already mentioned above, on which the 'perpetual inventory' estimates of capital stocks were based. As stated in the text they are net of hypothetical retirements only, not of depreciation allowances.

Table 8.7. *Gross and net capital formation in British manufacturing industries, 1950 and 1960: £ million at 1960 prices*

	Gross fixed capital formation		Net fixed capital formation[a]	
	1950	1960	1950	1960
Food processing	58	85	51	68
Drink and tobacco	20	29	17	19
Mineral oil refining	48	16	9	15
Coke	9	16	48	16
Other chemicals	76	138	71	118
Iron and steel	73	169	65	150
Non-ferrous metals	14	22	13	20
Engineering	84	165	75	141
Shipbuilding	8	14	7	12
Motor vehicles	29	64	27	61
Aircraft and railway rolling stock	19	23	18	20
Metal goods n.e.s.	27	44	25	36
Textiles	79	65	67	23
Leather and clothing	16	15	11	1
Building materials	21	30	19	21
Pottery and glass	8	12	7	5
Timber and furniture	16	20	15	16
Paper and printing	36	68	29	54
Other manufacturing	18	39	17	30
Total manufacturing	659	1,034	589	825

Source: Appendix tables 8.2 and 8.3.

[a]See footnote (2) to previous page.

far from evenly among the constituent industries. Some industries, such as 'other chemicals' and iron and steel have invested about ten times as much as industries such as glass and china or leather and clothing (table 8.7).

Corresponding to the differences in investment between industries there has been, of course, a large range in the absolute amounts by which outputs of the different industries increased. But the amount of new investment required to produce an extra £1 per annum of net output (i.e. the ICOR) has not been the same for each industry since (i) as explained at the outset of this chapter, different techniques of production imply different ICORs, and (ii) there have been conjunctural variations in output and in the degree of capacity utilization, which have not been exactly synchronized in time and which have varied in severity.

(b) *Alternative measures of the ICORs*

To assess the amount of new investment required to produce an extra £1 of net output per annum in each industry we have examined alternative measures of the ICORs in order to see whether any one measure appeared to be more stable, for each industry, than any other. In the first place, we have the choice between gross ICORs and net ICORs—that is, before or after allowing for retirements in estimating the cumulative capital formation over the period selected. Secondly, we can simply relate the cumulative capital formation over the period selected to the total increment of net output, or we can adjust the latter to allow for the contribution of the change in employment in each industry to the change in net output. The latter measure corresponds to the ICOR(L') already defined and used in chapter 1[1]. Combining the two sets of alternatives gives us four methods of measuring the ICOR.

Furthermore, we can select alternative time periods over which the ICORs can be measured. Clearly, it is desirable to minimize, as far as possible, the effect of conjunctural variation in output and capacity utilization. For this purpose it seemed preferable to calculate the ICORs and ICOR(L')s between pairs of years that corresponded roughly to each other in their conjunctural phase. That is, we have measured the ICORs from 'peak to peak' years and 'trough to trough' years, and for some industries estimates have been made for two 'peak to peak' periods. The results are shown in table 8.8.

In this table, the ICOR(L')s are, of course, always greater than the ICORs (except for the textile industry in some cases on account of a fall in employment), since the ICOR(L') excludes the contribution to output made by the change in employment. It can be seen that according to the time period selected the ICORs for any given industry vary substantially—even as between two 'peak to peak' estimates. For the average of all the manufacturing industries, the ICOR(L')s vary less than the ICORs, which should be expected since, insofar as the terminal years used for the measurements are unlikely to represent precisely equal stages in the cyclical movements of output and capacity utilization, the ICORs will be affected more by conjunctural fluctuations in employment.

However, the relative stability of the ICOR(L')s at the level of total manufacturing does not apply to individual industries. A crude measure of the stability of the ICOR and ICOR(L')s is the ratio of the spread between the upper and lower estimates to the average of the estimates for each industry separately. On this basis it is found that, for the average of all industries, the spread is about one half of the average—that is, on the average the upper and lower estimates of the ICORs or ICOR(L')s are about 25 per cent above and below the average ICOR or ICOR(L') for each industry. In fact, this indicator of the stability of the ICORs shows that the ICOR(L')s are rather less stable, according to the time period selected, than the ICORs. This is because

[1] The ICOR(L')s used in this chapter correspond to those used in chapter 1, in that the contribution of the increase in employment in each industry has been based on the share of wages in net output in each industry as well as the increase in employment, a procedure which implicitly assumes that the marginal product of labour in each industry is equal to its wage. For algebraic definition, see chapter 1, page 34, footnote (1).

Table 8.8. *Incremental capital-output ratios for British manufacturing industries between selected years during period 1950 to 1960*

		Gross ICOR Peak to peak	Gross ICOR Trough to trough	Gross ICOR(L') Peak to peak	Gross ICOR(L') Trough to trough	Net ICOR Peak to peak	Net ICOR Trough to trough	Net ICOR(L') Peak to peak	Net ICOR(L') Trough to trough
Food processing		7·2	5·8	24·0	10·0	5·8	3·8	19·4	6·7
Drink and tobacco		2·6	3·8	3·1	4·2	1·9	2·8	2·3	3·1
Mineral oil		14·8	22·2	17·3	27·1	7·2	7·2	8·4	8·8
Other chemicals		3·8	4·2	4·2	4·6	3·4	3·9	3·8	4·3
Iron and steel		9·6	22·7	12·3	22·7	7·9	18·8	10·1	18·8
Non-ferrous metals	(a)	4·5	3·9	10·6	5·7	4·3	3·5	10·0	5·2
	(b)	4·7		5·0		4·2		4·4	
Engineering	(a)	2·2	3·1	4·1	6·0	2·0	2·7	3·7	5·2
	(b)	3·0		4·6		2·6		3·9	
Shipbuilding		1·7	3·0	2·3	3·5	1·6	2·6	2·1	3·1
Motor vehicles		1·9	2·7	2·4	3·1	1·8	2·5	2·2	2·8
Metal goods	(a)	3·1	3·3	3·5	4·1	2·8	2·9	3·1	3·5
	(b)	3·7		8·7		3·0		7·1	
Textiles		−14·6	13·7	10·9	8·1	−7·3	9·3	5·4	5·5
Leather and clothing	(a)	4·1	3·4	2·8	2·5	1·8	1·2	1·3	0·9
	(b)	1·6		1·3		0·2		0·2	
Building materials		7·7	14·5	7·7	12·3	6·1	12·3	6·1	10·4
Pottery and glass	(a)	9·5	4·7	7·6	3·8	7·6	4·7	6·1	3·8
	(b)	3·4		2·4		2·5		1·8	
Timber, etc.		13·5	2·9	11·6	2·8	10·3	2·4	8·8	2·3
Paper and printing	(a)	2·5	1·5	3·1	1·9	1·9	1·2	2·5	1·5
	(b)	3·2		4·4		2·3		3·3	
Rubber and other	(a)	2·4	2·1	3·0	3·0	2·2	2·0	2·7	2·7
	(b)	3·7		5·0		3·2		4·3	
Average		4·15	6·9	6·7	7·4	3·3	4·9	5·1	5·2

Source: Appendix tables 8.2, 8.5 and 8.12.

Notes: (i) For definition of 'net' see footnote (2) to page 252.

(ii) For significance of 'peak to peak', 'trough to trough', ICOR, and ICOR(L') see text preceding table.

(a) and (b) are alternative 'peak to peak' periods.

although the average of the ratio indicated is 0·5 for the gross ICORs, the gross ICOR(L')s and the net ICORs, it is 0·7 for the net ICOR(L')s.

However, although the ICORs (and ICOR(L')s) are clearly unstable for given industries, it is still possible to say that some industries have significantly higher ICORs than others. For in general, a change from one time period to another for purposes of measurement (e.g. from 'peak to peak' to 'trough to trough') affects the measures of the ICORs of most industries in the same direction, so that the ranking of industries by size of ICORs is not completely dependent on the precise time period or concept adopted (though this generalization cannot be carried very far). For example, the iron and steel industry has a relatively high ICOR in every column of table 8.8, and the

Table 8.9. *Regressions of ICORs on average capital-output ratios and rates of growth of output in manufacturing industry*

Type of data	R^2	Coefficients of partial determination	
		$r_{12 \cdot 3}$	$r_{13 \cdot 2}$
1. 1950 to 1960 (a) ICORs before allowing for scrapping	0·449	0·393	− 0·669
(trend values of output) (b) ICORs after allowing for scrapping	0·467	0·609	− 0·625
2. 'Peak to (a) ICORs adjusted for labour	0·383	0·454	− 0·588
peak' years (b) ICORs unadjusted for labour	0·560	0·534	− 0·734
3. 'Trough to (a) ICORs adjusted for labour	0·667	0·754	− 0·772
trough' years (b) ICORs unadjusted for labour	0·661	0·729	− 0·780

Note: $r_{12 \cdot 3}$ is the coefficient of partial determination of the ICORs on average capital-output ratios after allowing for variations in rates of growth of output, $r_{13 \cdot 2}$ is the corresponding coefficient of partial determination of the ICORs on rates of growth of output after allowing for variations in the average capital-output ratios. The actual equation obtained, in the same order as the results above, and with $x = \dfrac{dK}{dO}$, y=average capital ratio over the period concerned $\dfrac{K}{O}$ and z = average annual trend rate of change of output over the same period $\dfrac{dO}{O}$, are as follows:

$$x = 4 \cdot 096 + 1 \cdot 742 \, (\pm 1 \cdot 129)y - 0 \cdot 986 \, (\pm 0 \cdot 304) \, z$$
$$x = 0 \cdot 710 + 2 \cdot 633 \, (\pm 0 \cdot 952)y - 0 \cdot 739 \, (\pm 0 \cdot 256) \, z$$
$$x = 4 \cdot 488 + 4 \cdot 193 \, (\pm 2 \cdot 377) \, y - 2 \cdot 051 \, (\pm 0 \cdot 815) \, z$$
$$x = 4 \cdot 317 + 2 \cdot 513 \, (\pm 1 \cdot 150)y - 1 \cdot 475 \, (\pm 0 \cdot 394) \, z$$
$$x = 3 \cdot 283 + 7 \cdot 531 \, (\pm 1 \cdot 894)y - 1 \cdot 788 \, (\pm 0 \cdot 425) \, z$$
$$x = - 2 \cdot 986 + 7 \cdot 369 \, (\pm 1 \cdot 996)y - 1 \cdot 937 \, (\pm 0 \cdot 448) \, z$$

motor vehicle industry a relatively low ICOR in every column. Thus there is some support for the theoretical expectation that, on the whole, industries would differ with respect to their ICORs according to whether they were capital-intensive industries or not.

Since this inter-industry variation in capital intensity has been the justification, in the first place, for the analysis of capital stock data and of the possibility of using average capital-output ratios, the obvious next step is to see how far the ICORs are, in fact, correlated with the average capital-output ratios in the different industries. At the same time, there is some evidence, if far from conclusive, that ICORs are affected by the rates of growth of output. Hence we have carried out a multiple correlation of the ICORs of the different manufacturing industries on both (a) average capital-output ratios and (b) rates of growth of output. The results are shown in table 8.9.

This table confirms both that (a) ICORs are, as should be expected, positively correlated with average capital-output ratios in industrial industries, but that (b) differences in the rates of growth of output explain even more of the inter-industry variation in the ICORs than the differences in the average capital-output ratios. And, as with the other related results, the correlation of the ICORs on the rates of growth of output is negative in sign.

(c) *Conclusion concerning the relationship between rates of growth of output and incremental capital-output ratio (ICORs)*

We may summarize the various results obtained as follows:

(i) at the level of total gross national product, international comparisons (chapter 1) show that faster rates of growth are associated with lower ICORs;

(ii) corresponding to this it is also found that, in the context of conventional 'production-function' estimates, in which capital stocks are introduced as a variable, the 'residual' in growth (i.e. the growth unexplained by change in inputs of capital and labour) is also greater the faster is the rate of growth of total gross national product;

(iii) at the level of the individual manufacturing industry in the United Kingdom over the period 1950 to 1960, it is difficult to establish reliable 'production functions' and hence it is difficult to use average capital-output ratios as a means of projecting capital formation requirements;

(iv) nevertheless, average capital-output ratios do partially explain inter-industry differences in ICORs;

(v) however, where allowance is made for average capital-output ratios (i.e. for differences in techniques of production), inter-industry variations in ICORs are negatively correlated with their rates of growth of output. This result is completely consistent with (i) above when allowance is made for the fact, that, as between whole countries, differences in techniques of production will be much less important, particularly between large countries combining fairly similar economic structures with highly diversified patterns of output.   It is for this reason that the inter-country differences in ICORs discussed in chapter 1 are more closely correlated with differences in rates of growth of output than are the inter-industry differences in ICORs.

This confirmation, at different levels, of the fact that faster growth of output is associated with lower investment requirements per unit of additional output is, of course, of crucial importance in assessing how much sacrifice of present consumption is necessary in the interests of faster growth.   Unfortunately, while the various results justify confidence in the direction of the relationship between ICORs and rates of growth of output, only those at the level of total GNP were highly significant statistically.   The results at the level of the individual manufacturing industry, while statistically significant, were not so to a degree that would justify categorical answers to the question of how much greater, if at all, would be the investment burden associated with faster growth. In the concluding section of this chapter we present some tentative answers to this question, but the margin of error attached to them is considerable.

Finally, it must be acknowledged that we have not felt competent to consider possible alternative theoretical interpretations of the results.   As stated at the

S

outset our primary objective has been the identification of measurable relationships that can be used for purposes of projecting the items and aggregates as conventionally defined and measured in the national accounts. There is no doubt, however, that, even given this modest objective, 'measurement without theory' can be hazardous. But any theoretical objections to our interpretation of the results must be left to those better equipped for this kind of activity.

3. METHODS FINALLY ADOPTED AND RESULTS FOR MANUFACTURING CAPITAL FORMATION IN 1975

To obtain an approximate breakdown of manufacturing investment in 1975, we have preferred, in view of the results above, to make allowance both for average capital-output ratios for each industry and for rates of growth of output, by using an equation of the type referred to in table 8.9. The introduction of the average capital-output ratios does, at least, add to the explanation of inter-industry variations in the ICORs, so that it is desirable to use them, particularly when, as the analysis of the ICORs in isolation has shown, the ICORs themselves are not sufficiently stable to provide a firm basis for projection. At the same time, the results shown in table 8.9 confirm those of chapter 1 in suggesting that ICORs are inversely correlated with growth rates, so that an equation having this propensity will probably produce results in the right direction, even if the exact figures obtained for 1975 may be subject to a substantial margin of error.

However, we have preferred not to rely exclusively on this one method of calculating the ICORs for each industry and have supplemented it with alternative methods. The various methods used were as follows:

Method 1. The average capital-output ratios in 1975 were assumed to be the same as in 1960. Corresponding estimates have then been made of capital stocks in 1974 and 1975 and of retirements in order to obtain the gross capital formation figures.

Method 2. An equation of the type shown in table 8.9 has been estimated excluding shipbuilding and mineral oil refining. The resulting equation was:

$$\text{ICOR} = 1\cdot70 + 2\cdot26\frac{K}{O} - 0\cdot71\frac{dO}{O}(\text{R}^2 = 0\cdot6107)$$

Method 3. The average of the peak to peak and trough to trough ICORs (gross) from table 8.8 have been applied to the 1975 increments of output in each industry.

Method 4. An equation has been calculated from inter-country comparisons of manufacturing ICOR(L)s. In the neighbourhood of the growth rate for total manufacturing projected here this is linear of the form:—

ICOR(L) = 3·8 − 0·3 × rate of growth of output per employee.

Each of these methods yields a different investment projection not only for each industry but also for total manufacturing (method 4, of course, gives only a figure for total manufacturing). The various results are as follows:

Total manufacturing GCF in 1975 (£ m., 1960 prices)

Method 1	2,470
Method 2	2,190
Method 3	2,420
Method 4	1,660
Average	2,185

As only methods 2 and 4 allow for the downward effect on ICORs of the assumed acceleration of growth rates, the final total manufacturing gross capital formation in 1975 was rounded off to £2,000 million. Given this total, the other methods have been used mainly as alternative indications of the percentage distribution by industry of the total gross capital formation[1].

The figure of about £2,000 million finally selected corresponds to an ICOR(L) in 1975 of 3·3[2]. As can be seen from table 1.11, although this represents a substantial improvement over the past it would still be well above the ICOR(L)s achieved by the three other large European countries, and so should not underestimate future requirements.

An important point is the degree to which our estimate would vary according to the different hypotheses as to the overall growth rate. The evidence of inter-country comparisons of ICORs, as also indeed of the inter-industry comparisons shown in table 8.8, is that whilst ICORs fall rapidly as growth rates rise up to about 3 per cent per annum, they decline much less rapidly as yet higher growth rates are achieved. Hence, whilst raising the overall growth rate of the economy from about 2·5 per cent in the past to about 3·5 per cent in the future may imply a much lower ICOR and hence not much increase in the share of investment in gross national product, further increases in the growth rate would not be much offset by a lower ICOR. In the following table we show rough illustrative calculations of the impact on manufacturing investment of alternative growth rates of gross national product over the range 2·5 per cent to 5·0 per cent per annum, in 1975.

It can be seen from table 8.10 that raising the growth rate of gross national product from 2·5 per cent per annum (approximately the 1950–60 rate) to 3·5 per cent per annum (the projected rate for the whole period 1960 to 1975) raises the share of manufacturing investment in gross national product by only about 13 per cent, as over this range the ICOR(L)s tend to fall sharply with

[1]For this purpose, the constant term in the equation in method 2 was adjusted downward so that the total GCF produced by this method would approximately equal the total selected. This adjustment will not, of course, affect each industry's GCF in the same proportion.

[2]This figure was slightly modified in the light of final revision to the output projection for certain industries and of other considerations, so that the final figure for manufacturing GCF was £2,015 million.

Table 8.10. *Influence of variations in growth rate hypothesis on manufacturing investment requirements in 1975*

1. GNP growth rate (per cent per annum, 1960–75)	2·5	3·0	3·5	4·0	4·5	5·0
2. Manufacturing growth rate (per cent per annum 1960–75)[a]	3·0	3·6	4·2	4·8	5·4	6·0
3. Manufacturing output per head growth rate (per cent per annum 1960–75)[b]	2·9	3·4	3·9	4·4	4·9	5·4
4. GNP in 1975 (£'000 million)	34·6	37·4	40·0	43·0	46·5	50·0
5. Manufacturing net output in 1975 (£'000 million)	12·6	13·7	15·0	16·3	17·8	19·4
6. 1975 increment of manufacturing net output (£ million)	380	495	630	780	960	1,160
7. Contribution of increase in manufacturing employment (£ million)	8	16	27	39	53	70
8. Row 6 adjusted for row 7	372	479	603	741	907	1,090
9. ICOR(L) for manufacturing	4·17	3·70	3·34	3·16	2·98	2·80
10. Manufacturing investment requirements in 1975 (£ million)	1,551	1,772	2,015	2,342	2,703	3,052
11. Row 10 as per cent GNP	4·48	4·74	5·04	5·45	5·81	6·10

[a] Assuming ratio of growth rates of manufacturing to GNP (1·2 : 1) is same for alternative growth rates as forecast (chapter 7) for the growth rate assumed in this study.

[b] A rough allowance has been made for higher intakes into manufacturing employment accompanying higher growth rates of manufacturing output.

faster rates of growth of output. And given the small share of manufacturing investment in gross national product this implies only about an extra 0·5 per cent of gross national product to be directed to manufacturing investment. Of course, if there were no improvement in the ICOR(L) by comparison with, say, the period from 1957 to 1962 the manufacturing investment requirements for the 2·5 per cent and the 3·5 per cent growth rates would be £1,800 million and £2,920 million respectively, representing 5·2 per cent and 7·3 per cent of gross national product respectively. Hence our relatively modest projection of manufacturing investment requirements depend heavily on the observed relationship between ICORs and growth rates of output. However, as this correlation is found both in international comparisons and in cross-industry comparisons (when allowance is made for different average capital-output ratios in individual industries) it seems to be fairly firmly based.

Our final figure of about £2,000 million for total manufacturing investment was first distributed among industries according to the average per cent distribution of the total as given by the four methods indicated. Various other adjustments have then been made to allow for special circumstances affecting the ICORs of individual industries in the recent past. Also, as some industries deviated considerably from the regression equations in the past the strict application of the equations produced apparently very dubious results. This applied particularly to the food processing industry, and the drink and tobacco industry, where the equations implied very sharp declines in capital formation in the future; at the other extreme, the regression equation for the 'other

Table 8.11. *Projections of capital formation by manufacturing industry in 1975 : £ million at 1960 prices*

SAM industry group	GCF in 1960	GCF in 1975	Col. (2) as per cent of 1960	Per cent distribution, col. (2)	Actual change 1960–75 (£m.)	Per cent composition of total change
	(1)	(2)	(3)	(4)	(5)	(6)
4 Food processing	85	78	*91·8*	*3·9*	− 7	*− 0·7*
5 Drink and tobacco	29	31	*106·9*	*1·5*	+ 2	*0·2*
6 Coke ovens, etc.	16	31	*193·8ᵃ*	*1·5*	+ 15	*1·5*
7 Mineral oil refining	16	105	*656·3*	*5·2*	+ 89	*9·1*
8 Chemicals n.e.s.	138	444	*321·7*	*22·0*	+306	*31·2*
9 Iron and steel (excluding tinplates and tubes)	169	208	*123·1ᵃ*	*10·3*	+ 39	*4·0*
10 Iron and steel (tinplates and tubes)						
11 Non-ferrous metals	22	37	*168·2*	*1·8*	+ 15	*1·5*
12 Engineering and electrical goods	165	334	*202·4*	*16·6*	+169	*17·2*
13 Shipbuilding and marine engineering	14	31	*221·4ᵃ*	*1·5*	+ 17	*1·7*
14 Motors and cycles	64	115	*179·7*	*5·7*	+ 51	*5·2*
15 Aircraft	19	52	*273·7*	*2·6*	+ 33	*3·4*
16 Railway locomotives and rolling stock	4	10	*250·0*	*0·5*	+ 6	*0·6*
17 Metal goods n.e.s.	44	78	*177·3*	*3·9*	+ 34	*3·5*
18 Textiles	65	105	*161·5*	*5·2*	+ 40	*4·1*
19 Leather, clothing and footwear	15	47	*313·3ᵃ*	*2·3*	+ 32	*3·3*
20 Building materials	30	37	*123·3*	*1·8*	+ 7	*0·7*
21 Pottery and glass	12	21	*175·0ᵃ*	*1·0*	+ 9	*0·9*
22 Timber, furniture, etc.	20	37	*185·0ᵃ*	*1·8*	+ 17	*1·7*
23 Paper, printing, publishing	68	141	*207·4*	*7·0*	+ 73	*7·4*
24 Other manufacturing	39	73	*187·2*	*3·6*	+ 34	*3·5*
Total manufacturing	1,034	2,015	*194·9*	*99·7ᵇ*	981	*100·0*

ᵃIf the average per cent composition of gross capital formation in 1958–60 were used as a base, the indexes in 1975 for coke ovens; shipbuilding and marine engineering; timber, furniture, etc.; pottery and glass; iron and steel; and leather, clothing and footwear would be 107·6; 173·2; 232·7; 210·0; 143·2 and 364·3 respectively.
ᵇDetail does not add to total on account of rounding.

chemicals' industry and the non-ferrous metals industry seemed to indicate unreasonably fast increases in investment. This emphasizes once more the uncertainty attached to these projections, an uncertainty that increases the greater the degree of detail in which the projections are made.

The final results are shown in table 8.11. For several industries the changes in annual capital formation between 1960 and 1975 differ considerably from the average. This reflects three factors: (a) 1960 may have been far from 'normal' with respect to capital formation in a given industry, (b) deviations from the average rate of growth of output and (c) deviations from the average ICOR.

For example, the fastest projected increase in capital formation is for mineral oil refining. Although the estimate for this industry is derived from chapter 10 and not from our equations, it does reflect both a high ICOR, a relatively fast increase in output, and, in addition, the fact that capital formation in this industry in 1960 was rather below the average of the three years 1958 to 1960. The latter factor was particularly important in the railway rolling stock industry, though the ICOR for this industry is also inflated by the projected fall in its output.

Two industries in which annual capital formation would appear to require little or no increase between 1960 and 1975 are food processing and drink and tobacco. In these industries 1960 capital formation was rather higher than in the preceding two years but not to an exceptional extent, since 1960 as a whole was a year of relatively high activity and investment. It is possible, of course, that the projections for these two industries are greatly in error, but these are industries which were found to require even less capital formation in 1975 according to the regression equations than in the estimates finally adopted.

This illustrates a general feature of our results and of the projection which is of some importance. Differences between the values of the ICORs calculated for industries from the regression equations and those they actually experienced in the past are to some extent indicators of over- or under-investment in the individual industries. That is to say, when an industry such as the chemical industry shows an ICOR in the past which is more than can be accounted for by its particular average capital-output ratio and the rate of growth of its output, this is some evidence that it has been over-investing relative to its contribution to the increase in output. In using these regression equations to obtain the projections, therefore, industries whose investment appears to rise very little compared with the past are generally those where, according to the equations, past investment has been excessive. In table 8.12 we compare the ICORs calculated from the best-fit regression equation for the past with the actual ICORs and with those implied by our projections, for all industries (other than those for which direct estimates have been made in the special chapters concerned). We have projected substantial improvements (i.e. reductions) in the ICORs for the shipbuilding, chemicals n.e.s., building materials and mineral oil refining (though for this industry the estimates of the 1950–60 ICORs are more or less meaningless). But no improvement has been projected in the ICOR for the motor vehicle industry, in spite of its appearing, from table 8.12, to have had an excessive ICOR in the 1950s. This is because the measure used in table 8.12 is probably 'unfair to the motor car industry' by virtue of the linearity of the equation used to calculate the theoretical ICORs for the past[1].

---

[1]As the equations in table 8.9 are of the form $ICOR = a + b\,(K/O) - c\,(dO/O)$, very fast rates of increase in output would imply negative ICORs. A more realistic form of the equation, therefore, would be curvilinear as with the international ICOR equation, so that after a point faster growth rates do not imply much reduction in ICORs.

Table 8.12. *Actual and theoretical ICORs, 1950 to 1960, and projected*
1975 ICORs, for manufacturing industries

	Actual 1950–60 ICOR (1)	Theoretical 1950–60 ICOR (2)	Ratio col. (1) to col. (2) (3)	Projected 1975 ICOR (4)
Mineral oil refining	67·80	3·3	20·55	14·58
Motor vehicles	2·18	0·4	5·45	2·17
Shipbuilding	11·50	6·5	1·77	4·77
Other chemicals	4·00	2·4	1·67	3·11
Building materials	8·21	6·5	1·26	6·73
Iron and steel	7·47	6·3	1·19	8·22
Aircraft and railway rolling stock	2·16	2·0	1·08	3·54
Pottery and glass	4·26	4·5	0·95	3·75
Food processing	5·48	6·0	0·91	6·09
Other manufacturing	2·86	3·2	0·89	2·53
Metal goods n.e.s.	3·32	4·1	0·81	2·62
Timber and furniture, etc.	3·85	4·9	0·79	3·19
Non-ferrous metals	3·95	5·3	0·75	4·46
Engineering and electrical goods	2·52	3·4	0·74	2·15
Paper and printing	2·75	4·0	0·69	2·38
Leather and clothing	3·01	5·1	0·59	2·67
Textiles	− 27·09	12·1	− 2·24	5·90

Note: The actual and 'theoretical' ICORs have been calculated from the *trend* rates of
growth of output, 1950 to 1960, and the corresponding equation in table 8.9.

In fact, this industry had the lowest ICOR of any. Another industry for which
the projected ICOR is no lower than in the past, in spite of the latter being
greater than the theoretically calculated ICOR for the 1950s, is iron and steel.
This is because the ICOR shown for 1975 is already well below that given by
the average of the four projection methods used.

For the industries whose past ICORs were apparently better (i.e.lower)
than their values as calculated from the regression equation, not much further
improvement is projected. However, on the whole, all industries are projected
to show lower ICORs than in the past. This is the result of using methods
which make allowance for the downward effect on the ICORs of the faster
overall growth rates projected, though the importance of this adjustment will,
of course, vary from industry to industry.

In examining the projected investment requirements for individual industries,
it should not be overlooked that they differ considerably as regards the absolute
amounts involved. As can be seen from table 8.11, the absolute amounts
involved are very small for many industries so that errors in the projection
may not be of much significance for the economy as a whole. Between 1960
and 1975 total capital formation in manufacturing is expected to increase by
about £900 million, but about 30 per cent of this arises in the 'other chemicals'

industry, and a further 17 per cent in engineering.   It is in these two industries, therefore, accounting for nearly 50 per cent of the total increase in capital formation, that the margins of error are most significant.   And it must be recognized that, according to the method adopted, very different estimates are obtained for future investment requirements in these two industries.

In concluding this section on manufacturing capital formation, therefore, it must be acknowledged that the difficulty is not of finding a method which can produce a satisfying proliferation of figures but of finding too many methods, each of which gives very different figures.   The fairly popular method of simply applying ICORs as measured by data about the past has been shown above to lead to very different results according to the precise time period or concept used. Also, this method as generally used is not subjected to statistical checks on the extent to which the ICORs are 'explained' by the sort of variables likely to be relevant.   We have proceeded therefore to check how far they are, indeed, explained by two theoretically plausible determinants, namely average capital-output ratios and rates of growth of output.   This test itself produces further alternative methods, namely the regression equations employed therein, and these equations too lead to different results.   Only for total manufacturing investment do alternative methods lead to a relatively narrow range of results, while for individual industries some methods give results which are twice as high as those obtained by others.   And this conclusion, already sufficiently agnostic, is made more so when it is borne in mind how much margin of error is attached to the output projections to which the alternative methods for projecting investment have to be applied.

4. TOTAL GROSS CAPITAL FORMATION, 1960 AND 1975

Manufacturing capital formation accounts for only about one quarter of total capital formation.   The remaining items have been estimated by a variety of methods, the important ones being described below.   The results are sum-marized in table 8.13.   Total gross fixed domestic capital formation, as shown in table 8.13, at £7,980 (1960 prices) million in 1975 would represent about 20 per cent of gross national product.   This total may be compared with that which would be obtained by applying the inter-country equation for this coverage of capital formation shown in chapter 1 (page 38); according to that equation, the ICOR(L) = 10·66 — 1·36 (rate of growth of gross national product per employed person), which would imply, for Britain, with a projected rate of growth of gross national product per employed person of 3·5 per cent per annum in the year 1975, an ICOR(L) of 5·9[1].   As we have assumed no increase in employment in 1975 the entire increase of about £1,400 million would be

---

[1]Substituting 3·5 per cent for the rate of growth of GNP per employed person in the equation.

Table 8.13. *Gross domestic fixed capital formation by industry of use,
1960 and 1975 : £ million at 1960 prices*

	1959–61 average	1960	1975	Increase 1960-75 Per cent	Absolute
Housing	742	753	1,200	59·4	447
Energy[a]	498	484	1,005	107·6	521
Other mining	15	11	20	81·8	9
Water	42	43	100	132·6	57
Health (including National Assistance)	52	51	200	292·2	149
Education and child care	155	147	290	97·3	143
Transport[b]	412	439	710	61·7	271
Roads and public lighting	92	83	550	562·7	467
Manufacturing[c]	1,009	1,016	1,910	88·0	894
Total, above items	3,017	3,027	5,985	97·7	2,958
Agriculture	156	140	200	42·9	60
Construction	72	63	150	138·1	87
Distribution[d]	604	615	1,130	83·7	515
Communications	100	96	235	144·8	139
Public services (excluding roads and lighting)	101	107	180	68·2	73
Legal fees, etc.	54	55	100	81·8	45
Total, all items	4,104	4,103	7,980	94·5	3,877

Note: As in other tables in this chapter, in the interests of consistency with SAM, the 1960 data shown here are from *National Income and Expenditure, 1961*. Hence, for certain items the 1960 figures may differ from those shown in the special chapters concerned.

[a]Excluding mining other than coal, and water, but including mineral oil refining.
[b]Railways, road passenger transport, shipping, harbours and air transport.
[c]Excluding mineral oil refining, which is included here in energy.
[d]Wholesale trade, retail trade and 'other transport and services'.

ascribed to capital, so that the total fixed domestic investment requirement would be £8,260 or 20·7 per cent of gross national product[1]. This is remarkably close to the estimates shown in table 8.13, which we have obtained as the sum of independent estimates of fifteen components of total fixed capital formation. Thus again, although we have emphasized the large margin of error attached to the estimates of capital formation in individual manufacturing industries and have been sceptical of the feasibility of projecting these very accurately, the overall results suggest that much more confidence can be placed on the projection of total investment requirements.

The increase in investment requirements for many 'industries' is much more rapid than the projected increase in gross national product. This applies chiefly to certain social or quasi-social investments such as roads, health and communications. The detailed justification for the projections of investment

[1]The figure of £8,260 is the product of the ICOR(L) of 5·9 and the increase in output of £1,400 million.

in health services and in roads is given in the special chapters on health and transport. In the case of *communications* the projection has been based largely on official plans for this sector. Among the more 'productive' forms of investment, the most rapid increases are projected for energy and construction. For *energy* this is largely the counterpart of the continued rapid increase in fuel demand and output that, as is explained in chapter 10, is expected to take place. The *construction* industry is one for which firm projections of investment requirements are difficult to make, partly because of the apparently relatively short life of the capital assets used therein. However, in addition to rough estimates based on incremental capital-output ratios we have added an arbitrary amount to allow for the results obtained in chapter 7, which makes it clear that the future growth of output in this industry must depend on productivity rising very much faster than in the past.

One item which does not rise very much faster than gross national product but which is very important in absolute amounts is investment in distribution. This too is a very difficult item to project with much confidence; so much of it will depend not on the growth of the volume of distribution but on changes in the organization of distributive outlets. As explained in Appendix 8, an attempt has been made to estimate distribution investment separately, but the estimates must be treated with considerable reserve.

On the whole the 'productive' investments are expected to rise rather less rapidly than the 'non-productive' investments. It is impossible to draw any sharp dividing line, of course; even health and education clearly contribute to the productive capacity of the economy, not to mention roads and communications. The criterion that may be used here is whether or not the investments have been estimated as a function of the output projection rather than in the light of relatively independent judgements as to social or quasi-economic needs[1]. On this basis the investments may be classified as in the following table 8.14.

It can be seen that, as defined here, 'non-productive' investments are projected to rise about 15 per cent faster than 'productive' investments. This has two main implications.

Firstly, the overall projection shows a rise in the share of investment in gross national product (at constant prices) partly because of the large increases projected in social or quasi-social investments, and this in turn is largely because of existing serious backlogs in certain types of social or quasi-social

---

[1] In applying this criterion we have included communications investment under 'non-productive' largely because the methods underlying the official projections for the telephone service, while responsive to rising incomes and similar demand factors, are of a different character from an 'output-oriented' projection (see *The Inland Telephone Service in an Expanding Economy*, Cmnd 2211, London, 1963, paragraph 4). The projection of investments in transport including shipping is partly based on output projections but also allows for improvements that are only quasi-economic in character.

Table 8.14. *'Productive' and 'non-productive' capital formation, 1960 and 1975 : £ million at 1960 prices*

	1960	1975	Per cent increase	Absolute increase
Housing	753	1,200	59	447
Education and child care	147	290	97	143
Health[a]	51	200	292	149
Transport	439	710	62	271
Roads	83	550	563	467
Communications	96	235	145	139
Total 'non-productive'	1,569	3,185	103	1,616
Total 'productive'	2,534	4,795	89	2,261
Grand total	4,103	7,980	94	3,877

[a]Including National Assistance.

capital. Roads are an extreme example of such a backlog, and health (particularly hospitals) is another important case. But such investments also provide a form of social consumption. Hence, in weighing up the loss of private consumption caused by the projected rise in investment, it should not be overlooked that the sharp rise in social investments is a means of either raising social consumption in a measurable form (i.e. as allowed for in national accounts conventions) or of improving these aspects of standards of living which are not conventionally measured in the national accounts statistics.

Secondly, the importance of non-productive investments affects significantly the way in which different rates of growth of gross national product are associated with different shares of investment in total output (the 'investment ratios')[1]. Insofar as they have been estimated largely independently of the output projections, the projected levels of investment would not necessarily be greater had a higher rate of growth of output been assumed. Hence, even if ICORs for productive investment were assumed to remain constant (instead of being inversely correlated with growth rates), so that productive investment requirements rose proportionately to the growth rate of gross national product, yet total investment requirements would not do so. In the following table we show illustrative calculations of the way investment requirements would vary with the growth rate of gross national product, assuming (a) that non-productive investment is invariant and (b) that the ICOR for productive investment remains constant, instead of declining as the growth rate rises. The differences made by these simplifying assumptions to the total investment ratio are in opposite directions, of course, as the growth rate increases—though there is no reason why they should cancel each other out exactly. It will be seen

[1]This point is very carefully analysed in 'Growth and Investment according to International Comparisons', T. P. Hill, *op. cit.*

Table 8.15. *Influence of alternative rates of growth of GNP on share of total fixed capital formation in GNP*

1. GNP growth rate (% p.a. 1960–75)	2·5	3·0	3·5	4·0	4·5
2. GNP in 1975 (£'000 million)[a]	34·6	37·4	40·0	43·0	46·5
3. 1975 increment of GNP (£ million)	865	1,120	1,400	1,720	2,080
4. Assumed ICOR of 'productive investment'[b]	3·42	3·42	3·42	3·42	3·42
5. 'Productive' investment (£ million)[c]	2,960	3,830	4,795	5,880	7,115
6. 'Non-productive' investment (£ million)[c]	3,185	3,185	3,185	3,185	3,185
7. Total fixed capital formation (rows 5 and 6)	6,145	7,015	7,980	9,065	10,300
8. Total fixed capital formation as percentage GNP (row 7 as % row 2)	17·8	18·8	20·0	21·1	22·2
9. ICOR from inter-country equation	7·3	6·6	5·9	5·2	4·5
10. Total fixed capital formation as percentage GNP from inter-country equation (row 9 × row 1)	18·3	19·8	20·7	20·8	20·3

[a]See table 8.10, row 4.
[b]This is the ratio of productive investment as actually projected with assumed 3·5 per cent rate of growth of GNP *in* 1975, to total GNP increment in that year (£1,400 million).
[c]See table 8.14.

from row (8) that if the gross national product growth rate is raised by one third from 3·0 per cent per annum to 4·0 per cent per annum, the share of total fixed capital formation in gross national product would rise by about 10 to 15 per cent (from about 18·8 to about 21·1 per cent). These results are also compared with the investment ratios that would be obtained by strict application of an equation relating ICORs to growth rates from cross-country data[1].

In addition to total fixed domestic capital formation, of course, allowance must also be made for the change in stocks and for net investment overseas. The estimate of net investment overseas has been derived in chapter 4, where an objective for this figure of £150 million has been selected *at 1960 prices*. The estimate of the change in stocks suggests a figure in the region of nearly £600 million in 1975.

[1]The best fit for such an equation gave ICOR $= 11·2 - 1·5 P$ (where $P =$ annual rate of growth of output per head). To obtain the same figure for investment in 1975 as that selected here, we have adjusted the constant term in the equation to 11·0. It will be observed that, according to this equation, the investment ratio actually declines after a point. This is because a linear equation for the ICORs yields a curvilinear equation for the investment ratios of the form $dK = (a - bP') P'$, where $dK =$ capital formation, $P' =$ rate of growth of GNP, and a and b are the parameters of the ICOR equation. This investment ratio equation has a maximum value where $P = 3·7$ per cent per annum. Thus, if the ICOR equation alone were used to project investment, we would seem to have selected just about the GNP growth rate that implies the highest investment ratio—a higher or lower growth rate of GNP yielding a lower investment ratio !

Thus, at 1960 prices, total investment is projected to change as follows:—

Table 8.16.   *Total investment, 1960 and 1975 : £ million at 1960 prices*

	£ million		Per cent GNP[b]	
	1960	1975	1960	1975
Housing	753	1,200	*3·2*	*3·0*
Other gross fixed domestic capital formation	3,350	6,780	*14·1*	*17·0*
Change in stocks	591	600	*2·5*	*1·5*
Net investment overseas[a]	−259	150	*− 1·1*	*0·4*
Total	4,435	8,730	*18·6*[c]	*21·8*[c]

[a]The figure here is the national accounts concept of net investment overseas and so includes current transfers (net) overseas.
[b]GNP in 1960 = £23,789 million.
  GNP in 1975 = £40,000 million.
[c]Detail does not add to total on account of rounding.

It can be seen that total investment as a share of gross national product is projected to rise from about 18·6 per cent in 1960 to about 21·8 per cent in 1975. This increase is expected to occur in spite of a decline in the share of housing and of the change in stocks[1]. The overall rise in the total investment ratio, therefore, is accounted for by the rise in fixed investment (excluding housing) and the objective of an external surplus of £150 million (at 1960 prices; it would be about £750 million at 1975 prices) by comparison with a deficit of about £250 million in 1960. This swing in the net investment overseas is thus responsible for a rise of nearly 3 percentage points in the overall investment ratio.

The implications of these projections for the overall balance of the economy are examined more fully in chapter 9, where the investment ratio is also discussed at current 1975 relative prices.

[1]The latter change however does not reflect the *trend* rate of change in stocks, but is heavily dependent on the actual change in stocks in 1960 which is being compared here with a 'trend' value from the change in stocks in the projection year.
A more satisfactory comparison is between the projected change of stocks of £600 million with what the trend change in 1960 would have been assuming the same stock/output ratio. This would have been about £250 million (2·5 per cent increase in total stocks of about £10,000 million) which would imply a rise in the share of the change in stocks in total GNP of from 1·09 to 1·5 per cent of GNP.

CHAPTER IX

THE OVERALL PATTERN OF EXPENDITURE— 1960 TO 1975

By W. BECKERMAN

In this brief chapter we present in summary form the projected changes in the pattern of national expenditure and discuss the balance of investment and savings. The detailed pattern of final expenditures is shown in table 7.2, and here we are concerned only with the major aggregates. In order to extract from this pattern some idea of the magnitude of the investment 'burden' and hence of the likely changes in the sources of savings we also show here the pattern of expenditure at 1975 *relative* prices, as well as at 1960 prices.

The main results are shown in table 9.1 below. The derivation of the capital formation estimates is described in full in chapter 8 ('Investment Requirements'). The foreign balance objective is explained in chapter 5. The projection of public civil consumption is composed partly of special projections of the health and education components (chapters 13 and 14) and partly of a fairly rough projection of the remainder (see page 272 below). The latter is explained in Appendix 9. Total private consumption has been obtained as a residual.

1. NATIONAL EXPENDITURE BY MAJOR CATEGORY

In terms of the major aggregates shown in table 9.1 no drastic changes in the composition of final expenditures are projected. At constant relative prices, there is a rise in the share of fixed investment, and the foreign balance, which is shown to swing from a deficit in 1960 to a small surplus (at 1960 prices) in 1975. The combined rise of 4.2 percentage points in the share of these items is matched by slight falls in the shares of private consumption, military expenditures and the changes in stocks.

Table 9.1 shows the composition of national expenditure by major category in 1960 and 1975, and table 9.2 compares these shares with the shares in past years. Although there are sharp changes in the volatile items such as changes in stocks or net exports, the shares of the other major categories of gross national product, although projected relatively independently of their past trend, appear to follow them fairly closely. The projected rise between 1960 and 1975 in the share of fixed capital formation is a continuation—albeit at a much slower rate—of the rising trend from 1950 to 1960. The projected slight decline in the shares of public civil and military consumption (at constant prices) is also in line with the 1950 to 1960 trend in their shares. The share of private

Table 9.1 *National expenditure by major category, 1960 and 1975 : £ million at constant 1960 prices*

Category of final expenditure	1960	% GNP	1975	% GNP
Change in stocks	591	*2·5*	600	*1·5*
Gross fixed domestic capital formation	4,103	*17·2*	7,980	*19·9*
Public consumption				
(i) Civil	2,578	*10·8*	4,188	*10·5*
(ii) Military	1,611	*6·8*	2,222	*5·6*
Private consumption	16,608	*69·8*	27,260	*68·1*
Net exports of goods and services	− 259	*− 1·1*	150	*0·4*
less Indirect taxes on imports	− 1,443	*− 6·0*	− 2,400	*− 6·0*
GNP at market prices	23,789	*100·0*	40,000	*100·0*

Table 9.2. *Percentage composition of national expenditure by major category, 1950–75 (at constant 1960 prices)*

Category of expenditure	1950	Average 1954–6	Average 1959–61	1960	1975
Change in stocks	− 1·6	1·0	1·5	2·5	1·5
Gross fixed domestic capital formation	13·3	14·8	17·2	17·2	19·9
Public consumption					
(i) Civil	11·1	10·5	10·9	10·8	10·5
(ii) Military	7·6	9·5	6·8	6·8	5·6
Private consumption	70·0	68·3	69·7	69·8	68·1
Net exports of goods and services	5·3	1·5	− 0·1	− 1·1	0·4
less Indirect taxes on imports	− 5·7	− 5·6	− 6·0	− 6·0	− 6·0
GNP at market prices	100·0	100·0	100·0	100·0	100·0

consumption, however, is projected to fall rather more rapidly than between 1950 and 1960.

As is explained more fully in chapter 8, the rise in the share of gross fixed capital formation is mainly because of the fast rise projected in energy investment and in certain quasi-productive investments, chiefly transport, roads and health, though investment in manufacturing and in distribution also rises faster than gross national product.   The rise in the share of net exports is in accordance with the projected trends in the balance in private capital movements and invisibles plus the objective selected for overseas aid.   But, as chapter 5 shows, given what appears to be a reasonable assumption about the future trends in (i) the terms of trade, of manufactures *vis à vis* primary products, (ii) the volume of world trade in manufactures and (iii) British competitiveness, the net foreign surplus projected here should be quite feasible.

Of the items that decline as a proportion of gross national product the first, namely the change in stocks, is purely the difference between a 'trend' projection for 1975 and what the actual change in stocks happened to be in 1960.   As this is a very volatile item such comparisons do not have to signify any basic structural change.   The very slight decline in the share of public civil consumption is the net outcome of two offsetting factors. On the one hand education expenditures are expected nearly to double (at 1960 prices). But both health and miscellaneous civil consumption are projected to rise by only about one half. The health expenditures are explained in chapter 13. Much of the miscellaneous civil expenditure (police and justice, finance and tax collection etc.) may be regarded as a form of overheads. In the past they have risen at roughly the same rate as gross national product, but it is unlikely that they would accelerate in proportion to the projected acceleration in the growth of total gross national product. Hence we have, rather arbitrarily, assumed that they would rise at about the average of the rate of growth of total gross national product in the past and in the future[1].

The decline in the share of military expenditures is necessarily an arbitrary assumption. After the ending of the post-Korean armaments boom, defence expenditure in absolute amounts actually declined continuously (at constant prices) from a peak in 1953 to a level, in 1959, about 25 per cent below the 1953 peak. As gross national product was rising, the share of defence expenditures fell sharply. In the last three years, however, there has been a rapid rise in defence expenditures. For the period 1960 to 1975 we have assumed that defence expenditures will rise at roughly the average of the rate given by two hypotheses, namely that (i) the absolute level will remain constant—which implies that the downward trend of the 1950s, after 1953, will not continue, and (ii) the share of defence in total gross national product will remain constant. If this projection proved an overestimate in the sense that the international political situation and the evolution of strategy and techniques were such as to lead to a much lower defence effort, the error in our assumption would not be too serious; it would tend to facilitate the solution of other problems such as the amount of resources that could be devoted to investment or exports. On the other hand, if the error were in the reverse direction, the burden on the engineering, shipbuilding and aircraft industries would jeopardize the achievement of other elements in the projection.

The projected decline in the share of private consumption is, as explained above, simply the counterpart of the other items, since private consumption is obtained as a residual after deducting from the projected total gross national product the independent direct projections of the other components. This statistical procedure implies, of course, a particular view as to the process by which overall equilibrium is achieved. This is, in a nutshell, that the authorities will take such fiscal and other action as may be necessary, given their estimates of the likely claims on resources from the other components of final expenditures, to ensure that personal disposable incomes are such that (given

---

[1]This appears to be broadly in line, after excluding the health, education and defence components, with the rates of growth assumed in *Public Expenditure in 1963–64 and 1967–68*, Cmnd 2235 (London, 1963), Annex B. See also Appendix 9 on projection of total public consumption.

an assumed savings ratio) private consumption will be just about right to achieve full employment equilibrium. The other way of looking at this is that the authorities will aim roughly at that budget surplus which, together with other expected savings, will yield total savings roughly equal to expected total investment without undesirable equilibrating movements in the level of income.

2. CHANGES IN RELATIVE PRICES

What this would mean for the public authorities' current surplus in 1975, however, will depend not on the balance of investments and *ex ante* savings in 1975 *at 1960 prices*, but on what this balance will look like *at 1975 prices*. It will be recognized that any projection of the pattern of relative prices over a period of fifteen years would have to be treated with considerable caution, even if it were the fruit of a special analysis of the determination of past trends. For this study, we have not in fact been able to make elaborate calculations for projecting relative price changes; the estimates of these changes made here must therefore be interpreted as highly impressionistic.

The method used to project relative price changes has been as follows. It has been assumed that earnings per employee would remain constant in all industries, so that wage costs per unit of output would vary according to the different rates of increase of productivity as projected in chapter 7. Non-wage factor incomes (i.e. profits) per unit of output have been assumed to remain constant. Thus estimates can be made of the pattern of change in total factor incomes per unit of output in each industry. These are applied to the 1960 table of inter-industry transactions to yield estimates of the changes in final prices of each industry's outputs[1]. The possible errors in this procedure are numerous, so that it cannot be claimed to provide much more than a rough guide to the direction of relative price changes[2]. No change has been assumed in indirect tax rates. Because of the approximate nature of the exercise, it is preferable to show the projections of relative price change quite explicitly before discussing their effects on the pattern of expenditures, so as to indicate the most likely weaknesses and errors.

[1]The inter-industry transactions matrix for 1960 is that given in the Cambridge University Department of Applied Economics, *A Programme for Growth, 3: Input-Output Relationships, 1954–1966, op. cit.* Where A = the familiar matrix of input-output coefficients, P = the vector of final prices and F = the vector of factor costs per unit of output, $P = (I - A)^{-1} F$.

[2]Clearly the assumption of constant profit margins per unit of output is dubious, particularly in view of the results shown by W. E. G. Salter in *Productivity and Technical Change* (Cambridge, 1960), p. 117. Also, since the final projections made in chapter 7 we have not adhered to the 1960 input-output matrix, the latter is only an approximate guide to the indirect effects on final prices of any given industry of changes in the prices of its inputs from other industries. Finally, as capital formation by industry has been projected in chapter 8, one obvious check would be to estimate the change in output prices required to maintain the same rate of profit on capital as in the recent past (see chapter 8, page 239 for exposition of the relationship here).

T

Table 9.3 compares the projected rates of change in the relative prices of the major categories with the past changes. On the whole the direction of change is very much the same as from 1950 to 1960. But the orders of magnitude are significantly different for some items. The relative price of capital goods is expected to fall rather faster than in the past, reflecting mainly the projected improved productivity performance in these industries. The most debatable projection is that of the relative price of military expenditures, which is projected to rise very much more slowly than in the past. The concept of the 'price' of military equipment is very difficult to define because of the impossibility of converting units of present day equipment into corresponding units of obsolete equipment. A military aircraft produced today may be ten times as expensive as one produced ten years ago, but how much of this is a genuine price increase and how much represents a higher quality aircraft which is conceptually the equivalent of several older aircraft cannot be established by conventional methods. It is quite possible that the 'price' increase shown for the period 1950 to 1960 really incorporates a substantial amount of quality improvement[1].

This would mean that the past slow rise in the *volume* of military expenditures which has influenced our projections of this item, is an underestimate. This would, in turn, imply that to be consistent with the past it would be necessary either to adjust upwards our projection of the volume of defence expenditure or to project a faster rise in the price than that obtained by the method outlined above, which makes no special allowance for the peculiar character of rapid technical change in military hardware leading to rapidly rising costs of items defined simply as, say, 'aircraft' or 'ships'. In fact, the methods we have used have been such that the relative rise in the 'price' of military expenditures is accounted for entirely by the relative rise in the 'price' of the personnel element contained therein[2].

A projected relative rise in personnel costs is the main reason also for the relative price rise projected for public civil consumption. It has been assumed that incomes in this sector will have to rise *pari passu* with gross national product per head of the labour force, and as a relatively low productivity increase for this sector has been projected, its relative price must inevitably rise sharply.

The relative price changes projected above have a considerable impact on the pattern of national expenditures. The three most important differences between

---

[1]Much of the rise in the 'price' of military equipment must represent the fact that the services are getting a lot more equipment in terms of base-year units of quality. On the other hand, there is no doubt a considerable increase in the research expenditures accompanying the development of techniques which are rarely spread over long runs, as would be the case, for example, with new drugs. This is presumably the explanation for the rapid rise between 1950 and 1960 in the within-industry transactions in the aircraft industry.

[2]No productivity increase has been assumed for the personnel component of defence, whereas their incomes, as with public civil administration, have been assumed to rise.

Table 9.3. *Annual average rates of change in relative prices of major categories of national expenditure, 1960–75 and 1950–60*

Category of final expenditure	Price indexes relative to GNP price index		Annual average % compound rates of change		Composition of 1975 GNP (£m.)	
	1960 (1950= 100)	1975 (1960= 100)	1950–60	1960–75	1960 prices	1975 relative prices
Change in stocks	96·0	91·1	− 0·4	− 0·6	600	547
Gross fixed domestic capital formation	97·4	88·6	− 0·3	− 0·8	7,980	7,066
Public consumption						
(i) Civil	111·6	121·4	1·1	1·3	4,188	5,086
(ii) Military	112·9	112·7	1·2	0·8	2,222	2,504
Private consumption[a]	92·6	97·4	− 0·8	− 0·2	27,260	26,551
Net exports of goods and services	n.a.	n.a.	n.a.	n.a.	150	637[b]
less Indirect taxes on imports	81·9	99·6	− 2·0	—	− 2,400	− 2,390
GNP at market prices	100·0	100·0	0·0	0·0	40,000	40,000

Note: 'n.a.' indicates 'not applicable'.   The implied price index of the balancing item net exports is of little significance.   Clearly a small increase, say, in the price of total exports, with import prices remaining constant, can lead to a proportionately very large rise in net exports (*cet. par.*), so that the implied price index of net exports will be virtually meaningless.

[a]The slower fall in the relative price of consumer goods is largely because of the reduction of purchase tax rates over the period 1950 to 1960, whereas we have assumed these to remain constant up to 1975.

[b]See note to table 9.4 below.

the pattern of expenditures in 1975 at 1960 and at 1975 prices would be:

(i) the share, in gross national product, of fixed capital formation would be only 17·6 per cent at 1975 prices, as compared with 19·9 per cent at 1960 prices, but

(ii) the share of public civil consumption in 1975 would be 12·7 per cent of gross national product in 1975 prices as compared with 10·5 per cent at 1960 prices, and

(iii) the share of net exports would be 1·6 per cent at 1975 prices as compared with 0·4 per cent at 1960 prices.

Thus whereas, on the one hand the required savings to match the total investment is a slightly lower proportion of gross national product at 1975 prices than at 1960 prices (20·6 per cent as against 21·8 per cent at 1960 prices; combining gross fixed capital formation, net exports and changes in stocks), on the other hand, the higher share of gross national product absorbed by public expenditure at current prices will not facilitate the achievement of a larger public surplus in the event of a shortfall of autonomous private savings.

It will be seen from table 9.4 that the pattern of change at current prices is on the whole in line with the direction of change during the past, though there are differences in the orders of magnitude.   Thus, for example, there is a slightly

Table 9.4. *Per cent composition of national expenditure by major category, 1950-75 (at current prices)*

Percentage of GNP

Category of expenditure	1950	Average 1954–6	Average 1959–61	1960	1975
Change in stocks	− 1·7	1·1	1·5	2·5	1·4
Gross fixed domestic capital formation	13·6	15·5	17·2	17·2	17·6
Public consumption					
(i) Civil	9·9	9·3	10·8	10·8	12·7
(ii) Military	6·7	8·7	6·8	6·8	6·3
Private consumption	75·7	71·1	69·6	69·8	66·4
Net exports of goods and services	2·7	0·5	0·1	− 1·1	1·6
less Indirect taxes on imports	− 7·0	− 6·2	− 6·0	− 6·0	− 6·0
GNP at market prices	100·0	100·0	100·0	100·0	100·0

Source: National Income and Expenditure, 1961 and *1962.*

Note: The share of net exports shown here, applied to the total GNP figures in table 9.1 would imply net exports, at 1975 prices, of £637 million (as in table 9.3) instead of £750 million as indicated in chapter 5. This is because the £750 million is at 1975 absolute prices. The above table, however, is at 1975 relative prices, and has been obtained by applying to the relative price changes an increase in the overall GNP price corresponding to (i) the estimated change in the net export relative price and (ii) the assumed absolute rise in the price of our exports of 1 per cent per annum and the assumed stability in the import prices of complementary imports. The resulting pattern of expenditures at 1975 absolute prices has then been reconverted into the price pattern relative to the constant price GNP projection (£40,000 million).

faster rise projected in the share of public civil consumption, and a much slower fall in the share of private consumption. The share of military expenditures is projected to decline only slightly, by comparison with a rather more rapid decline from the average 1954–6 level to the average 1959–61 level.

3. THE BALANCE OF INVESTMENT AND SAVINGS

It is now possible to consider, in a very summary manner, the implications of the above projections, for the savings-investment balance and hence for the order of magnitude of the public authorities' current surplus that would be required to ensure full employment equilibrium without excessive demand. Total investment, including net overseas investment, can be extracted from the above tables and is presented in table 9.5.

Total savings may be classified as originating from three main sources:

(i) the savings, or undistributed income, of companies and public corporations,

(ii) private savings of households, and

(iii) the combined surplus of public authorities.

In the absence of any special study here of the determinants of savings, the following estimates are simply a rough back-of-the-envelope calculation of how savings would develop, given certain assumptions about how far past trends

Table 9.5. *Total investment, 1960 and 1975 : £ million at 1960 and 1975 relative prices*

	1960 (at 1960 prices)			1975			
	1961 Blue Book	1963 Blue Book	% GNP[a]	At 1960 prices	% GNP	At 1975 relative prices	% GNP
Change in stocks	591	591	2·5	600	1·5	547	1·4
Gross fixed domestic capital formation	4,103	4,105	17·2	7,980	19·9	7,066	17·6
Net exports of goods and services	−259[a]	−182	−1·1	150	0·4	637[b]	1·6
Current transfer to abroad net[c]	−85[c]	−90	−0·4	−200	−0·5	−200	−0·5
Total investment[c]	4,350	4,424	18·2	8,530	21·3	8,050	20·1

[a]The 1960 figure here is that shown in the *National Income and Expenditure, 1961* Blue Book in the interests of consistency with the 'SAM' estimates (table 7.1, p. 206, note (b)).
[b]See note to table 9.4.
[c]For purposes of estimating savings requirements it is preferable to define total investment including net exports on a balance of payments basis, that is including net transfers, for although this does not affect the measure of national product, it does both constitute a burden on the foreign balance and reduce the net investment overseas accordingly.

in these components of savings might persist in the future. They are no more than illustrative. Indeed it is hardly necessary to embark upon a detailed analysis of the investment-savings balance unless there is reason to believe, on the basis of preliminary rough estimates, that a really acute problem will arise in achieving the projected level of investment without an undue strain on internal financial stability. So long as the total investment effort does not seem unduly high, there is some justification for ignoring this aspect of the projections altogether; it can be assumed that the authorities will take such fiscal action as will be necessary to ensure that reasonably full employment equilibrium is combined with reasonable internal financial stability. And, in fact, as table 9.5 shows, total investment (including current transfers to abroad) is projected to rise from only 18·2 per cent of gross national product in 1960 to 20·1 per cent in 1975 (at 1975 relative prices). It is difficult to believe that this can possibly create any serious problems of financial stability when it is remembered that most Continental developed countries considerably exceed this figure. For example, taking the total of the Common Market countries, the corresponding share of total investment in gross national product at market prices in 1960 was 25·6 per cent; and in Germany the figure was 29·6 per cent[1].

Hence the only justification for further examination of the investment-savings balance is that, on an admittedly very conservative assumption as to house-

[1]These figures are on the basis of the national accounts definition of net investment overseas; but as can be seen from table 9.5, the corresponding British figure, on this basis, would still be only 20·6 per cent of GNP in 1975.

Table 9.6.   *Percentage shares in total savings, 1950–60*

	1950	Average 1954–6	Average 1959–61	1960
Persons	− 2·8	16·5	28·6	29·4
Companies	53·0	56·5	50·2	56·7
Public corporations	5·1	6·3	6·5	6·9
Central and local government	42·2	18·3	16·0	13·8
Residual error	2·5	2·5	− 1·3	− 6·8
Total	100·0	100·0	100·0	100·0

Source: National Income and Expenditure, 1961.

holds' savings, the required level of public authorities' savings might have to be fairly high in spite of the projected significant increase in the share of public consumption in gross national product.   In other words, the total current revenue of public authorities would have to rise faster than total incomes. But, as is suggested later, given the progressive nature of the tax system, the amount of extra revenue required would probably not involve any rise in tax rates and might even permit some decline.

Table 9.6 shows the per cent composition of total savings over the past decade. It will be seen that the share of corporate savings, together with the surpluses of public corporations, has remained very stable, and a rise in the share of personal savings has been matched by a fall in the share of the current surplus of the combined public authorities in the early part of the 1950s followed by a fall in the share of company savings during the latter part.

International comparisons suggest that the share of total savings provided by households (i.e. persons) in Britain (23·1 per cent in 1960) is now about the same as in some other developed countries such as the United States (23·7 per cent), Canada (22·4 per cent) and France (21·9 per cent) and lower than that in Belgium, Germany, the Netherlands and Sweden[1].   But because personal savings are usually estimated as a residual from other elements in the accounts and because in spite of the efforts at standardization made by international organizations, the comparability of the savings data between countries is probably far from satisfactory, not too much reliance can be placed on these comparisons for purposes of judging whether the British savings pattern is normal in any sense.

The rapid rise in the contribution of personal savings corresponds to a rapid rise in the proportion of personal disposable income that has been saved. In the immediate post-war years, backlogs of unsatisfied demand for consumer goods combined with large excess liquidity led to dissavings by households.

[1]Estimates derived from Account 5 of the national tables shown in OECD *Statistics of National Accounts, 1950–1961, loc. cit.*

Table 9.7. *Relationships between personal income, personal disposable income, GNP at factor cost, and personal savings, 1952–62 and 1975*

	Average 1952–4	1960	1961	1962	Average 1960–2	1975
Personal income as percentage of GNP	90·6	93·8	94·7	95·5	94·7	94
Personal disposable income as percentage of personal income	87·5	85·8	85·5	84·6	85·3	85
Personal disposable income as percentage of GNP	79·3	80·5	78·3	80·9	79·9	80
Personal savings as percentage of personal disposable income	3·8	7·8	9·8	8·4	8·7	8

Source: National Income and Expenditure, 1963 for past years.

This was soon converted into small net savings and the savings ratio has continued to rise without interruption until 1961. Table 9.7 shows that the share of personal disposable income in total gross national product (at factor cost) has remained remarkably steady, but the savings ratio has risen from about 3·8 per cent of personal disposable income in 1952 to about 9 per cent in recent years.

The share of personal income has remained basically very steady throughout the period. The sharp rise in 1961 and 1962 was partly the counterpart of a fall in corporate undistributed profits, but was mainly an increase in the stock appreciation element. This meant that it was offset by higher taxes, thereby keeping the share of personal disposable income in total income fairly steady[1].

Thus the main variable in the determination of personal savings has been not the share of personal disposable income in total national product but the average propensity to save of households. Because the exceptional circumstances of the early years of the decade are largely responsible for the upward trend in the propensity to save in the 1950s, it would be unwise to expect any continued increase; and, in fact, the behaviour of the personal savings ratio over the last few years suggests that the peak may have already been reached, or very nearly so.

The most relevant country for comparison is the United States, where per capita income in the late 1950s was of the same order of magnitude as is assumed here for 1975. The savings ratios of the two countries (allowing for incomplete comparability in definitions) are very similar already (see table 9.8); but if purchases of consumer durables (representing one form of personal 'investment') are added to savings the ratio in the United States is much higher. This combined ratio has however remained very stable in the United States over the last fifteen years. It seems reasonable to assume therefore that

[1] This is matched by a fall in the ratio of after-tax income from self-employment and rent, dividends and interest to the corresponding pre-tax income.

Table 9.8. *Comparison of personal savings and expenditure on consumer durables as percentage of personal disposable income, United Kingdom and United States*

	UK		USA	
	Savings	Savings plus expenditures on durables	Savings	Savings plus expenditures on durables
1952–3	3·9	9·5	7·8	20·3
1954–5	3·9	10·6	6·9	20·4
1956–7	6·2	12·4	7·7	20·5
1958–9	5·4	14·8	7·4	19·0
1960–1	8·8	16·1	6·9	18·7
1962	8·4	15·3	7·6	19·4

Source: National Income and Expenditure, 1963 and, for the United States, from the *Survey of Current Business,* July 1963.

roughly the same combined ratio will prevail in Britain in 1975—that is about 20 per cent of personal disposable income would be absorbed by savings and expenditure on consumer durables together. The projection of consumer durables in chapter 6 would imply a savings ratio in the region of 8 to 10 per cent. Such a figure would mean no further rise in the savings ratio as defined in table 9.7 above, and this appears to be a reasonable assumption. In fact, since a very large part of British personal savings comprises 'fixed' savings through life assurance and pension funds, the rise in net payments of pensions by 1975 (accompanying the increasing proportion of old people in the population, as shown in chapter 3) would tend to reduce the savings ratio. Hence we have adopted, for our projections, a personal savings ratio of 8 per cent of personal disposable income, and have also assumed that personal disposable income would be about 80 per cent of gross national product at factor cost, which is projected to be £37,600 million[1].

Whilst the future course of personal savings is, perhaps, the most interesting component of total savings, the savings of companies and public corporations are (see table 9.6) more important. They have also remained fairly stable, both as a share of total savings or as a percentage of total national product (at factor cost). During the last few years, the proportion of corporate income paid in taxes at home has fallen slightly, on account mainly of more generous investment allowance; but this has been offset by a rather higher proportion distributed in the form of dividends and interest, leaving the savings ratio of corporate income fairly steady at about 40 to 45 per cent, with corporate income remaining fairly steady at about 25 per cent of gross national product

[1]GDP at factor cost may be derived from table 7.10, being the sum of GDP at factor cost shown therein (£36,850 million) and the net income abroad shown therein of £750 million.

Table 9.9. *Relationship of corporate income to gross national product and corporate savings to corporate income, 1950–75*

					Percentages
	1950	Average 1954–6	Average 1959–61	1960	1975
Total corporate income as percentage of GNP at factor cost[a]	28·5	26·0	25·7	26·9	25
Corporate savings as percentage of total corporate income[b]	43·6	42·9	42·2	42·3	45

Source: National Income and Expenditure, 1963, tables 1 and 3; and National Institute of Economic and Social Research estimate for 1975.

[a]This includes the surpluses of public corporations as well as non-trading income earned in the United Kingdom and income earned abroad.

[b]This comprises undistributed income after taxation but before providing for depreciation and stock appreciation. The projection of corporate savings in 1975 assumes no stock appreciation since the investment-savings balance under discussion here is conducted in the context of overall stability of prices. If stock appreciation were excluded from the corporate savings for the past years, the corporate savings ratio would show a slight rise, in the above table, between 1954–6 and 1959–61, so that although the overall ratio would be slightly lower, there would be further justification for projecting that it would rise slightly to 45 per cent in 1975.

at factor cost[1]. Hence, other things being equal, there is little reason to expect any significant change in the share of corporate savings in total national product at factor cost. But some of the relevant 'other things' have been assumed to change, notably the rate of growth of gross national product and of capital formation. And a faster rate of capital formation is likely to be accompanied by a faster rise in depreciation allowances. Hence any change in the corporate savings ratio is likely to be in an upward direction. However, it is preferable, in an exercise of this kind, to err on the side of caution; so our assumption is that, with the share of corporate income remaining at about 25 per cent (and so equal to about £9,400 million), the savings ratio of corporations will not exceed 45 per cent, and so amount to about £4,230 million.

4. THE PUBLIC AUTHORITIES' SURPLUS

It is now possible to see what the above projections imply for the desired public authorities' surplus (table 9.10). Given the required total savings and the projections of personal and corporate savings discussed above, the public authorities' surplus is obtained residually.

The final item which needs to be examined, therefore, is the feasibility of a public authorities' surplus of the order of magnitude shown, that is of £1,330 million (at 1975 relative prices). Table 9.11 shows the evolution of total

[1]See also A. E. Jasay, 'Paying Ourselves More Money', *Westminster Bank Review*, May 1962.

Table 9.10. *Composition of savings, 1960 and 1975*

	1960		1975	
	£m.	% GNP (market prices) (at 1960 prices)	£m.	% GNP (market prices) (at 1975 relative prices)
Savings by persons	1,418	5·93	2,410	6·02
plus Persons' additions to tax reserves	95	0·4	(30)[a]	0·07
Savings by companies and public corporations	2,564	10·72	4,230	10·60
plus Additions to tax and dividend revenues	334	1·4	(50)[a]	0·08
Surplus of central and local government	449	1·88	1,330	3·33
Total	4,860	20·31	8,050	20·1
less stock appreciation	133		—	
less residual error	303		—	
equals: Total savings (balance of payments definition of net lending overseas)	4,424	18·5	8,050	20·1

Note: The 1960 figures shown here are from *National Income and Expenditure, 1963*, table 6, so that the total savings, £4,424, correspond to the estimate of total investment shown in the second column of table 9.5.

[a]Both of these rough estimates have been selected on the low side by comparison with the average of the past, in order to err on the side of caution as regards the ease with which total savings will be as projected without any unduly large public surplus being required.

public expenditure, receipts and surplus in the 1950s and it will be seen that while expenditure has been absorbing an increasing share of gross national product the surplus has fallen more than proportionately, so that the share of total receipts has declined.

Public current expenditure on goods and services has been projected to rise by 81 per cent, from £4,183 million in 1960 (at 1960 prices) to £7,590 million in 1975 (at 1975 relative prices); the sum of these expenditures and the surplus would need to rise by 92 per cent—about 50 per cent faster than gross national product. But goods and services form only just over half of total public expenditures, the remainder being composed of various subsidies, national insurance benefits, other current grants to persons and debt interest. Since about 1954, these transfer payments have been rising faster than the expenditure on goods and services. Table 9.11 shows that the total of consolidated expenditures of public authorities plus the surplus—that is, total public receipts—has represented a fairly stable proportion of national product in spite of the declining share absorbed by the surplus.

It may be instructive to estimate on certain fairly simple assumptions the required change in the proportion of national income that would have to be absorbed by receipts of public authorities. As is shown in table 9.11, if the ratio of public expenditures on goods and services to total public expenditures

Table 9.11.   *Share of public authorities' expenditure, receipts and surplus in GNP at factor cost, 1952–60 and 1975*

	Average 1952–3	Average 1956–7	Average 1959–60	1960	1975
			£ million		
1. Total public authorities' expenditure on goods and services	2,966	3,535	4,050	4,171	7,590
2. Total public authorities' current expenditure	5,046	6,018	7,198	7,456	14,310
3. Total surplus of public authorities	367	604	578	449	1,330
4. Total public authorities' receipts (equals 2 + 3)	5,413	6,622	7,776	7,905	15,640
5. Gross national product at market prices	15,357	20,185	23,287	23,931	40,000
6. Gross national product at factor cost	14,453	18,873	21,821	22,484	37,600
		Percentage			
7. Public authorities' current expenditure on goods and services as percentage of total (current) expenditure	58·8	58·7	56·3	55·7	53·0
8. Total public authorities' current expenditure as percentage of GNP at market prices	32·9	29·8	30·9	31·2	35·8
9. Total public authorities' current expenditure as percentage of GNP at factor cost	34·9	31·9	33·0	33·2	38·1
10. Total public authorities' receipts as percentage of GNP at factor cost	37·5	35·1	35·6	35·2	41·5
11. Total surplus of central and local government as percentage of total (current) expenditure	7·3	10·0	8·0	6·0	9·3
12. Total surplus of central and local government as percentage of GNP at factor cost	2·5	3·2	2·6	2·0	3·5

Source: National Income and Expenditure, 1963: rows 1 and 2, table 43; row 3, table 6; rows 5 and 6, table 11.

continues to fall slightly, reaching about 53 per cent in 1975, then total public expenditures would rise to about £14,310 million in 1975 (at 1975 relative prices); this would represent a rise of from 31·2 per cent of gross national product (at market prices) in 1960 to about 35·8 per cent in 1975. If the public surplus, as defined in table 9.10 above, is added to the total public expenditures, total public receipts would have to rise from £7,905 million in 1960 to £15,640 million in 1975.

It thus appears that the 'claim' of public authorities' receipts on total national product (at factor cost) will have to rise from about 35 per cent in recent years to about 42 per cent in 1975. So far as this results from rising transfer payments, it does not constitute a net 'burden' on the economy as a whole, though the 'burden' it creates for the taxpayers is not likely to be ignored. The increase in the total receipts from taxes and other sources by public authorities required to yield the necessary surplus is unlikely to allow any significant reduction in rates of tax generally. The progressive nature of the income tax system on persons (and of the minor item of death duties) will result in an automatic rise in the ratio of tax receipts to gross national product. The more prices and money incomes rise, the bigger will be the proportionate rise in total tax receipts. It is doubtful whether the yield of indirect taxes—which fall very heavily on drink and tobacco for which income elasticity is low—or of company taxes, will rise more than proportionately to gross national product. A precise calculation is hardly practicable, but the general implication is that any reductions in tax rates will need to be at least balanced by increases in other tax rates[1]. Also, even if it were found necessary for a public surplus to finance a slightly larger share of total investment than has been the case in the last few years, it should be borne in mind that the rise in the overall investment ratio is partly the result of the projected rise in certain items of social investment, such as those for education, health and roads. These are alternative forms of 'consumption' in a wide sense of the term, so that it is appropriate that they should be reflected in higher total tax receipts of one kind or another.

Finally, it hardly needs emphasizing that the estimates above are highly tentative. Small errors in many of the key projections, such as of the savings ratio of corporations and of households, would have a disproportionately large effect on the implied surplus required of the public authorities. Quite a small error in the projections of either kind of private savings could lead to an imbalance, including a deficiency of total demand in the absence of a sizeable public deficit[2].

The estimate above of the required public authorities' surplus is the last link that closes the circle of the projections of this study, so it is perhaps appropriate at this point to survey the effort, or lack of effort, which the closing of the circle appears to imply. In a sense, it might appear that, after all, very little effort *is* required. The investment burden does not seem excessive, chiefly because of the apparent inverse relationship between growth rates and incremental capital-output ratios. The foreign trade objective seems attainable, though by no means painlessly. And the savings-investment equilibrium seems not difficult to attain at full employment without any threat to financial stability and without an onerous level of taxation. But this kind of statistical reckoning would, of course, be highly misleading if it were to be interpreted as stating that faster growth can be achieved without major efforts and changes in attitudes and institutions. It will be recalled that the key assumption made at the outset is that the British economy will be more competitive in foreign trade, and that this depends among other things on solving the problem of implementing an incomes policy—at least, solving it as much as will be required,

[1] See J. C. R. Dow, *The Management of the British Economy, 1945–60, op. cit.*, p. 192.
[2] Mr Jasay's point that possibly only a faster growth rate, by raising investment requirements, will ensure full employment equilibrium in the absence of a large public deficit is by no means disproved by the above tentative projections.

given the degree of success or failure that our main trading rivals will achieve in the same sphere (and assuming that the foreign trade position does not deteriorate so much in the near future that some more drastic means of restoring our competitiveness is unavoidable).

It is then proposed, mainly in chapter 2, that such an increase in competitiveness is likely, by itself, to induce a faster rate of growth of investment and productivity in response to more favourable expectations concerning long-run demand prospects. When the more favourable productivity assumption is then, as it were, fed back into the mechanics of the arithmetical estimates and projections, it is hardly surprising that faster growth will appear to be relatively painless. But this should not obscure the fact that the initial achievement of a sufficiently successful incomes policy may be an extremely painful process, given the traditions and institutions that will have to be changed in the course of it. Furthermore, for the British economy to respond to the resulting improved demand prospects through a rise in efficiency and productivity, many and varied changes in attitudes and policies may also be required.

In short, the conclusion may well be that while faster growth will not encounter insuperable obstacles such as production bottlenecks, excessive imports or a difficulty in raising the level of investment without running into inflationary pressures, it is dependent on changes in attitudes that, by virtue of being more intangible, incalculable and hence relatively unidentifiable, create the most difficult problems of all to solve.

PART III

ENERGY, TRANSPORT, HOUSING AND SOCIAL SERVICES

CHAPTER X

ENERGY

BY G. F. RAY[1]

This chapter starts with an analysis of the past relationship between energy and national output and discusses the reasons for the changing shares of various types of fuel in energy demand. It then attempts to project these various relationships into the future and so reaches a conclusion about the demand for energy in 1975, its division between different types of fuel, and the consequent investment requirements of the energy industries.

1. THE DEMAND FOR ENERGY

(a) *The past demand*

Between 1951 and 1962 Britain's gross domestic product rose $29\frac{1}{2}$ per cent; in the same period total energy consumption—in terms of all primary fuel, converted into coal equivalent and corrected for temperature[2]—increased from 230 to 266 million tons, by $15\frac{1}{2}$ per cent. Just over 0·5 per cent of additional energy was needed for every one per cent increase in the national output (table 10.1).

Table 10.1. *Changes in national output and primary energy consumption*

	Per cent rise GDP (1)	Energy use[a] (2)	Energy coefficient (2) ÷ (1)
1951–5	11·4	7·7	0·68
1955–9	7·1	1·3	0·18
1959–62	8·6	5·8	0·67
1951–62	29·6	15·5	0·52

[a]In coal equivalent, corrected for temperature changes.

In both the first four and the last three years of the period shown, demand for primary energy rose at two thirds the rate of growth of national output; in 1955–9, however, there was hardly any rise in energy use, whereas national output rose 7 per cent. Putting the figures into million tons of coal equivalent, if over the whole period the use of energy had risen in line with national output, it would have gone up by about 6 million tons a year; in fact it rose by $3\frac{1}{4}$ million

[1]Assisted by R. E. Crum.
[2]Conversion factors and the method of temperature correction are described in Appendix 10.

U

tons.   Over the period 1955–9, the rise in line with national output would have
been some 4¼ million tons a year (in coal equivalent), and the actual rise was
under 1 million tons a year.

The following paragraphs attempt to identify the reasons for these discrepancies.   They may occur because the pattern of output changes: the output of
industries using little fuel may rise more than average, and the output of industries which are heavy fuel users may lag behind.   Then there is the effect of
the more efficient use of fuel—particularly in the electricity industry itself.
Thirdly, industries which are still mechanizing rapidly may become more fuel-
intensive.

The effect of changes in the pattern of output can be estimated by calculating
what fuel consumption would have been if the output of each industry had risen
in line with national output (appendix table 10.1).   There are, however, three
fuel-consuming sectors for which this calculation is not very sensible, since there
are no good measures of 'output': they are domestic (or household) consumption, road transport, and miscellaneous users (including offices, large shops, and
public administration).   For these three we have calculated, directly, what the
difference would have been if energy consumption itself had risen in line with
national output.   On this basis, household use showed an average annual
'saving' of ⅔ million tons over the period 1951–62.   However, in 1962 and 1963
there was an excess rather than a saving; domestic use of energy rose much faster
than national product.   This may have been due to concealed stock movements, or to imperfections in the method of temperature correction, or possibly
to a change in consumer tastes—a growing preference for cosy homes.

On the same basis of calculation, road transport's use of energy rose faster
than national output, and thereby added about ½ million tons a year to energy
use; and consumption by miscellaneous users 'saved' ¼ million tons a year.
Taking the three categories together, energy consumption rose more slowly than
national output in the early 1950s; it was at about the same rate in the later
1950s, and in 1959–62 it rose faster.

For other energy-using sectors the trend of output can be brought into the
calculation.   The comparatively slow rise in output in the mining and railway
industries produced a saving in energy consumption; these were largely offset
by increased demand in two industries whose output went up very rapidly—
oil refineries and air transport.

For manufacturing industries the pattern effect is divided into two: the change
in pattern between manufacturing industries and the rest of the economy, and
the change in pattern within manufacturing industries themselves.   The first
caused an addition to energy consumption, with manufacturing output rising
faster than average over the whole period.   Changes in pattern within manufacturing industry, on the other hand, reduced energy consumption over the
whole period—though most of this effect was in the years 1955 to 1959.   This
effect can fluctuate a good deal from year to year with the fortunes of the big

fuel-using industries such as steel and building materials.

Finally, there is the combined effect of fuel efficiency on the one hand and increased mechanization on the other—combined, because there is no way of disentangling them: all that can be done is to compare the actual increase in the use of fuel in each industry with the increase that would have occurred if fuel consumption had risen in line with that industry's output. The result shows a large saving on the fuel bill of the order of $1\frac{1}{8}$ million tons a year for the whole period, with no very large fluctuations in the annual average savings in the first or second half of the 1950s, or in the last three years 1959–62.

The figures for the various industries should not be used to praise or blame them. It is not only that both increased fuel efficiency and increased mechanization are at work (in opposite directions); it is also that the term 'fuel efficiency' is used in a rather wide sense. The electricity and gas used by industries have been valued according to the amount of coal needed to produce them; and there has been a big increase in efficiency at power stations, with a more modest one at gas-works. These savings have been transferred (in appendix table 10.1) to the final users in proportion to their use of electricity and gas. So industries which are heavy users of secondary energy will show big savings from this transferred efficiency[1].

Improved fuel efficiency, in this rather wide sense, in six industry groups (collieries, railways, iron and steel, chemicals, textiles, building materials) accounts for about 2 million tons of fuel saved each year in the period, and explains a good deal of the divergence between the movement of energy consumption and national output. It is of some interest to do the same analysis excluding from each industry's figures the savings resulting from improved efficiency at power stations and gas-works—that is, by using constant factors to convert gas and electricity to their coal equivalent (appendix table 10.2)[2]. On this basis, there were only three major industrial categories of fuel consumers using more fuel in relation to output in 1962 than in 1951: agriculture, refineries, and engineering. In these groups, it seems that the effects of mechanization and other technical factors have outweighed the savings due to higher fuel efficiency. In all other groups, there were considerable fuel savings. At the end of the period, collieries were using one third less fuel per unit of output than at the beginning; the saving was between one tenth and one quarter in the food, chemical, and building materials industries; and in manufacturing as a whole it was 11 per cent.

---

[1]Further, fuel efficiency, as defined here, may show a rise because, for example, when production increases in a factory, the amount of fuel used for heating does not rise proportionately; in this sense part of the energy used in industry is an overhead. Again, when a consumer changes to a different fuel (and in this period there was a very appreciable shift towards oil and electricity), he installs more modern equipment and saves fuel in that way.

[2]This method is described in more detail in Appendix 10.

To sum up (appendix table 10.1): over the whole period 1951–62, total energy consumption rose more slowly than national output, to the extent of $2\frac{3}{4}$ million tons a year. Two million tons of this is explained by greater fuel efficiency, either in industry or in the conversion of primary to secondary energy. Half a million tons is explained by the relatively slow rise in fuel consumption in domestic and commercial use, only partly offset by a relatively fast rise in road transport. The pattern of output was changing in such a way as to increase fuel consumption, on balance. These various factors together explain about $2\frac{1}{4}$ million tons of the $2\frac{3}{4}$ million tons annual saving, leaving some $\frac{1}{2}$ million tons unaccounted for. The exceptionally high figure of fuel saving in the period 1955–9 is explained partly by a larger saving from fuel efficiency than in the rest of the period—particularly in the iron and steel and brick industries— and partly by a change in the pattern of output, particularly within manufacturing, which was tending to reduce fuel consumption.

This tendency for fuel consumption to rise more slowly than output was not unique to Britain. In a number of countries with a comparable economic structure, less energy has been needed, per unit of output, in recent years than ten years earlier (table 10.2). In Western Germany, 'fuel saving' in this sense was slightly greater than in Britain.

Table 10.2.   *Fuel used per unit of national output in selected industrial countries,
1959–61 (1951–3 $= 100$)*

Canada	104·5
Denmark	105·0
France	90·7
Germany	81·9
Italy	128·7
Netherlands	97·2
Sweden	110·0
United Kingdom	**85·0**
United States	95·3

Source: United Nations, *Statistical Yearbook*; United Nations, *World Energy Supplies* (New York, annual).

Notes:

1. The above figures are derived by dividing gross national product, at constant prices, by energy used, and converting the resultant figures into index numbers.

2. The factors used by the United Nations for conversion into coal equivalent differ from those used in other parts of this chapter.

(b) *Sources of energy*

At the beginning of the 1950s, coal was the source of some nine tenths of Britain's primary energy supplies. By 1962, coal's share had declined to 70 per cent; in absolute terms the fall in demand was from about 213 million tons per annum in the mid-1950s to about 190 million in the years 1959-62. Apart from some hydro-electricity, generated mainly in the north of Scotland, and a small but gradually increasing amount of nuclear energy, the rest of our energy needs were supplied by oil.

Table 10.3. *The share of various types of energy in total consumption*

Per cent of total

Primary sources	1951	1962	Final consumption	1951	1962
Coal	89	70	Coal (direct use)	51	30
Oil	11	29	Oil (direct use)	11	25
Hydro-electricity	—	} 1	Electricity	16	27
Nuclear power	—		Gas	8	7
			Coke and other solid fuel	14	11

Source: Appendix tables 10.3 and 10.4.

The direct use of coal (that is, the quantity used outside power stations, gas-works and coke ovens) is now responsible for less than one third of total final consumption—as against more than 50 per cent in the early 1950s (appendix table 10.3).   The share of directly used oil more than doubled; and even if road and air transport are excluded, oil's share in final consumption still rose from 6½ per cent in 1951 to 15 per cent in 1962.   Electricity has also become almost twice as important as in 1951, and in 1962 it supplied over one quarter of the country's energy.   The share of gas was fairly stable over the period; that of coke declined appreciably.

The use of oil advanced rapidly in the iron and steel industry and in the building materials industry, where its share rose over the eleven years from 1951 to 1962 from 5 per cent to 32 per cent.   Oil was also making headway at power stations in the second half of the 1950s; in 1959 it supplied 13 per cent of all their fuel (appendix table 10.4) and its further spread had only been stopped by government action dissuading the electricity authorities from further major conversions of existing coal-fired thermal stations to oil.   Oil has also become a significant source of fuel for gas-making.   There was only one category where oil lost ground to electricity: this was in agriculture, because of the success of the rural and farm electrification programme.

The advance of electricity appears less dramatic, because already in 1951 it was the main source of energy for a number of major users, such as the engineering, food, chemicals and textile industries.   In all these industries electricity gained more ground; furthermore, by 1962 it supplied about 40 per cent of all energy used in agriculture and over one third of domestic consumption.

The shift to oil as a source of primary fuel can be explained by a number of major factors.   First, in the middle 1950s there was an acute shortage of coal, leading to large coal imports.   This induced industrial and other consumers to look for other sources of energy, and oil was a convenient answer.   Secondly, oil proved to be in many respects a more convenient fuel, which was easier to handle and to control than coal.   Thirdly, relative price movements favoured oil (appendix table 10.5).   Fourthly, in view of the coal shortage in 1954-5 government policy at that time welcomed the substitution of oil for coal. Later, when demand for coal began unexpectedly to fall, measures were introduced in order to protect its markets.   But for these measures (notably the tax on fuel oil and the stopping of the trend to oil fuel for power stations) the part played by coal would have declined even further.

(c) *Projection for 1975*

The movement of demand for total energy depends on the rate at which national output grows, on the industrial pattern of this growth, and on any changes in 'fuel efficiency' in the widest sense—the input of fuel required per unit of output. The division of energy demand between the various types of fuel will depend on price, availability, convenience and so on.

The projections which follow[1] suggest that energy demand will continue to rise more slowly than national output—but that the energy coefficient (at 0·7 per cent) will be appreciably higher than it was over the 1951-62 period (0·57 per cent) and a little higher than it was from 1959-62 (0·67 per cent).   The past trend to improved fuel efficiency is expected to continue, and for the same reasons as in the past: the introduction of more efficient appliances, economies from conversion to the use of secondary instead of primary fuels, and also economies in the conversion of primary energy into secondary forms.   However, there will also be the strong contrary tendency to greater mechanization, involving an increase in the input of energy per unit of output.   And, for domestic consumption, it is assumed that there will be a rather more marked trend than over the period 1951-62 towards better-heated homes.

The projections of the division of energy demand between the various types of energy require assumptions both about technical changes and new sources of energy, and about government policy.   For the first of them, the main unknown is the chance of finding natural gas under the North Sea.   This could alter the whole pattern of energy supply by 1975.   The present projections make no allowance for this: they do, however, assume that by 1975 about a fifth of gas requirements will be met by purchase of natural gas from abroad— either from the Netherlands or, in liquid form, from Algeria or elsewhere.

For government policy, the projections assume that coal will continue to enjoy some protection: that is, that the present tax on fuel oil will be retained; that the share of oil in electricity generation will not be allowed to rise further; and that the conversion from coal carbonization to oil gasification in the manufacture of gas will be gradual.   The projections also assume that nuclear

[1]The trends for different types of energy are discussed in detail in the sections which follow.   The energy projections match, of course, the general forecast of the industry pattern given in chapter 7, table 7.11.

power will be developed, as at present planned, up to 1975—though it is possible that there will be more ambitious plans for the years after 1975, which might have some effect on investment before that date; they also assume some further exploitation of hydro-electric potential.

The method of projection was as follows. For each of the major fuel consuming sectors, 1960 fuel consumption (corrected for temperature) was extrapolated in line with the expected increase in output. Then, for each sector, an allowance was made for improved efficiency—a further reduction in fuel input per unit of output. This allowance took into account the experience of recent years, and made appropriate adjustments where it was known that technological developments either had altered the relationships of fuel to output recently, or were likely to do so in the near future. The resulting 1975 demand was allocated between various types of energy, on the basis of assumptions derived in the following sections about the relative attractiveness of the different types of fuel. Finally, balance sheets for secondary energy were drawn up, so that an internally consistent picture was obtained both for primary and secondary fuels.

The main details of the projections are given in appendix tables 10.3 (for final use) and 10.4 (for secondary producers and for primary energy). They are summarized in table 10.4:

Table 10.4. *Projections for 1975*

	Unit	1960	1975	Percentage distribution[a] 1960	1975
All primary energy	Million tons coal equivalent	264	370–410	*100*	*100*
of which:					
Direct use of coal and oil	Million tons coal equivalent	146	160–190	*55*	*45*
Secondary energy production	Million tons coal equivalent	118	210–230	*45*	*55*
Primary sources					
Coal	Million tons	196	180–200	*74*	*48*
Oil	Million tons	39	95–105	*25*	*42*
Hydro-electricity	Thousand m. kWh	2·5	5–6	*1*	*1*
Nuclear power	Thousand m. kWh	2·1	55–65	*1*	*7*
Natural gas	Thousand m. therms	—	1·0	—	*2*
Final consumption					
Coal	Million tons	91	40–50	*35*	*10*
Coke	Million tons	30	25–26	*12*	*6*
Oil	Million tons	32	75–85	*21*	*31*
Electricity	Thousand m. kWh	105	300–360	*24*	*46*
Gas	Thousand m. therms	2·6	4·8–5·0	*7*	*7*

Source: Appendix tables 10.3 and 10.4.

[a]Percentage distribution calculated on basis of coal equivalent.

The main structure of the projection can also be set out as follows. If the demand for energy were to increase simply in line with total national output, the 1960 consumption of 265 million tons would become 440 million tons by 1975. If allowance is made for the changing pattern of output—by assuming that energy demand rises in each sector in line with the output of that sector, the 1975 figure is hardly altered: it becomes 442 million tons. The changing pattern of output is not likely to be very important.

The more efficient use of energy by final industrial consumers is expected to yield a 'saving' of about 24 million tons between 1960 and 1975. Moreover, an allowance has been made for a further saving (corresponding to the 'unexplained residual' in appendix table 10.1 on page 555) of the order of 1 million tons a year, reducing 1975 requirements by 15 million tons. Partly offsetting these two savings, we assume that the demand for energy by households, public administration, and miscellaneous users will, with the trend to higher standards of living, rise by 3·2 per cent a year—that is, faster than national product. (This is a considerable change from the experience of 1951–62, when demand in this sector was only rising 2·2 per cent a year.) This assumption will add some 21 million tons to the figure of 440 million tons—the figure derived by assuming simply that energy demand rises in line with output.

So far, this figure has been modified to 424 million tons; but no account has yet been taken of improving fuel efficiency at power stations and gas-works[1]. Greater efficiency here can be expected to result in a reduction of total primary energy requirements of about 36 million tons. The 1975 total thus becomes 388 million tons—or, to give a range, between 370 and 410 million tons, in coal equivalent.

The assumptions about fuel efficiency are cautious ones; a considerably larger saving could be achieved[2]. British consumption of energy per head was in 1961 the highest among European industrial countries (with the sole exception of Norway); the quantity of solid fuel consumed was also far above that in any other country (appendix table 10.6). Even allowing for differences in climate this suggests that the scope for further economies in Britain is considerable.

(d) *The division between fuels*

The projected division between the primary fuels implies that the share of coal will continue to decline—from about 70 per cent in 1962 to around 50 per cent

---

[1]The quantities of electricity and gas projected have been converted into coal equivalent at constant 1960 factors. (For explanation see Appendix 10.)

[2]'Statistical evidence, based on more than 2,000 heat and power surveys carried out by the National Industrial Fuel Efficiency Service engineers in the past 9 years, shows that, on average, the outcome is a 15 per cent saving in energy costs. In the smaller factories saving more often than not exceeds 20 per cent' (NIFES *Ninth Progress Survey with Report and Accounts, 1962–1963*, p. 17).

in 1975; this would leave the home demand for coal, in absolute terms, at roughly its present level.   Oil's share is expected to rise, from about 29 per cent in 1962 to around 40 per cent in 1975.   The main change from the 1951–62 trends is in the share of new sources of energy; nuclear energy and natural gas between them are likely to provide almost one tenth of total energy supplies by 1975.

There will be keen competition for the division of the market for secondary energy: for there should be no shortages (except possibly of coke and smokeless fuels).   In the 1950s, both technical and economic factors were working in favour of oil and electricity; in particular, the movement of relative prices gave them considerable advantages over gas and coal.   In the next decade, price movements are not likely to favour oil and electricity so much.   New methods of gas-making, together with increasing possibilities of supplies of natural gas, should keep down gas costs (table 10.11).   Productivity in coal mining has been rising sharply in recent years, as reorganization and mechanization begin to have their effects; and—though it is open to question whether productivity will be able to keep pace fully with the rise in wage costs—at least coal prices, relative to those of other forms of energy, are likely to rise more slowly than in the last decade.   If coal prices do rise, electricity prices are quite likely to rise too, since coal accounts for such a large part of electricity generation costs; and it may not be open to the electricity industry to increase the share of oil in its supply of primary fuel.

The pattern of movement of relative prices, therefore, seems likely to be rather different in the future from that of the past; and this has been allowed for in the projection of the division of demand between the various forms of secondary energy.   The fastest-growing sector will still be electricity, demand for which is likely to more than treble between 1960 and 1975.   However, following an initial period of even more rapid rise (part of which has already happened between 1960 and 1963) the growth rate is projected to slow down.   The direct use of oil in 1975 may be about $2\frac{1}{2}$ times that of 1960, but the rate of growth of demand for oil in direct use (excluding secondary energy producers) will, on our projections, be lower than in the past.   Demand for gas is projected to double between 1960 and 1975; this will be a substantial change after a long period of near-stagnation.

The contribution of coal to the final market seems likely to be about 40–50 million tons, or about one tenth of final demand, by 1975; the rise of demand for coal at power stations will balance most of the lost market in final use.   By 1975 less coke will be available, mainly because the quantity of coal carbonized in gas-making will be less than half the amount in 1960.   The unsatisfied consumers will probably use other fuels, mainly electricity and gas.

2. COAL

Coal was the basis of Britain's development as a leading industrial power and it is still the most important source of her energy supplies. It is the only industrial material available in abundance within the country; reserves of British coal are immense[1].

(a) *The demand for coal*

In the early post-war years coal supplied virtually all the market for primary fuel, apart from petroleum products for vehicles. In the second half of the last decade, however, oil began to replace coal to such an extent that, even although the total demand for energy was rising, the demand for coal began to fall. From an annual level of home demand of 213 million tons in 1954–6, coal consumption fell rapidly to around 190 million in 1959–62. The fall was the result of the steep decline in demand for directly used coal; rising consumption at the secondary producers (mainly at power stations) did not fully offset this.

Table 10.5. *Inland coal consumption*

	Total	Direct use	*Million tons, annual averages* Consumption for energy production
1946–7	185	113	72
1948–9	193	115	78
1950–3	204	116	88
1954–6	213	113	100
1957–8	203	102	101
1959–60	191	91	100
1961–2	190	83	107

Source: Ministry of Power, *Statistical Digest, 1962.*

Coal demand fell because, over a period when coal was scarce, industrialists began to turn to oil, and found it a more convenient and cheaper fuel. In 1950 the National Coal Board's *Plan for Coal*[2] expressed the view that the demand for solid fuel in the 1960s could not be met in full. This prediction appeared to be confirmed by the coal shortage around 1955, when large quantities of coal had to be imported—over 20 million tons in the four years 1954–7. Industrial and other consumers started to look to oil as an alternative. Oil proved to be a more convenient fuel, easy to handle and to control. Electricity had the same advantages.

Further, the movement of relative prices probably explains a good part of coal's decline. Between 1954 and 1958, coal prices rose more than twice as

[1]Estimates vary; coal in the ground in seams of 1 ft. thickness and over, and lying within 4,000 ft. from the surface, is probably of the order of 170,000 million tons. A large part of this is not economically workable, but even so the amount of reserves which are believed to be mineable within the present limits of economic operation may still be between 50,000 and 100,000 million tons). A. M. Wandless, 'The British Coal Resources', in *Economic Aspects of Fuel and Power in British Industry,* conference organized by the Manchester Joint Research Council, Manchester, 1960, pp. 45–6).

[2]*Loc. cit.*

fast as the scheduled price of fuel oil (appendix table 10.5).   For gas-making, from 1949 to 1957 the coal price almost doubled, that of gas oil rose by only one half; after 1957 the price of oil products fell sharply, and coal could not compete with this.   Whereas from 1950 to 1960 coal became 90 per cent more expensive, in the same period the price of electricity rose by one quarter for domestic and one third for industrial consumers, oil prices rose some 40 per cent, and even the rise of the gas price was considerably less than that of coal. Moreover, the oil prices used here are scheduled prices; if all discounts and allowances could be taken into account (there are no reliable indicators for them) the price of fuel oil and other products would probably turn out to have been fairly stable from the mid-1950s on.

In the period from 1950 to 1954, oil was only replacing about half a million tons of coal a year[1]; the figure rose to $1\frac{3}{4}$ million tons in 1955–6 and—after a pause in 1957 because of the closing of the Suez Canal—to the rate of over 6 million tons a year in 1958 and 1959.   Then in 1960 the conversion of power stations to oil was checked; substitution of oil for coal continued, but at a slower rate of about 2 million tons a year.

The introduction of smokeless zones, the recognition of the inefficiency of the traditional open fires, the gradual disappearance of the steam-engine and the replacement of rail by road transport have all served to accelerate the decline in coal's share of the energy market.   Technological developments in the iron and steel industry were also important; they led to an appreciable relative fall in the use of coke.   In other coke-consuming industries (such as in engineering, food, chemicals, other industries and public administration) coke had gradually been replaced by other fuels.

(b) *The reorganization of the coal industry*

The British coal industry has been substantially reorganized in recent years: the major changes have been summed up in table 10.6.   A large number of uneconomic pits have been closed down; production has been concentrated in the more promising areas, the more efficient pits and the more productive coalfaces.   In 1962 alone, the number of coalfaces in operation was reduced by 450.   In the five years to 1962 the manpower employed by the National Coal Board fell by more than 140 thousand.   Mechanization has been considerably increased and almost 60 per cent of total saleable output was produced by machinery in 1962—twice as much as in 1958, only five years earlier.   Productivity, measured by output in tonnage per man-shift, rose some 30 per cent for face-workers in the five years from 1958 to 1962, and only slightly less for all workers.   This reorganization (together with higher prices) led to much better

[1] G. F. Ray and F. T. Blackaby, 'Energy and expansion', *National Institute Economic Review*, September 1960, p. 33.

financial results: in 1962 the consolidated financial results of the Board showed a small profit, following an average deficit of £20 million a year in 1959–61.

Table 10.6.   *Coal: the last five years*

	1958	1960	1962
Output (million tons)			
Deep-mined, NCB	198·8	183·8	187·6
Opencast	14·3	7·6	7·3
Licensed mines	2·7	2·3	2·6
Total	215·8	193·6	197·4
Manpower (thousands) in NCB mines	693	602	551
Output per man-shift (cwt. NCB, saleable)			
Face-workers	70·7	79·5	91·0
All workers	25·6	28·0	31·2
Mechanized output (per cent of saleable coal)	27·8	37·5	58·8
Profit per ton of saleable deep-mined coal[a]	1s. 2d.	1s. 8d.	4s. 7d.
Consolidated financial results (£m.)[b]	−13·5	−21·3	+1·4

Source: National Coal Board, *Report and Accounts for 1962.*

[a]Excess of proceeds over costs, excluding interest charges.

[b]Deficiency or surplus of *all* activities (including opencast coal and ancillary operations) after charging interest.

By employing standardized techniques and making full use of mechanized equipment the National Coal Board can now produce coal at low cost in large quantities under very favourable geological conditions (as in the Midland coal-fields, which stretch over a large area with little geological faulting). Further mechanization will enable productivity to be raised continuously for some years to come. However, before the end of the 1960s full mechanization, within its technical limits[1], will probably be achieved and although by that time the National Coal Board will be pushing ahead with the automation programme devised for the mines, it remains to be seen whether its results will suffice to balance the rise in wages and thus keep prices stable.

The National Coal Board has said that around 200 million tons of coal a year must be sold in order to carry overheads and standing charges[2]; and has also claimed that any quantity, say another 10 or 20 million tons, additional to the 'basic' 200 million tons (which carry the overheads) could be produced at extremely low cost, with little sacrifice of resources, in the most remunerative Midland pits[3]. For the time being there appears to be no likelihood of selling any such additional quantity in the home market, which cannot even take up

[1]At the beginning of 1964 about 30 per cent of all deep-mined coal was still hand-mined; the technical limit for mechanized production and transport of all deep-mined coal can be put at about 95 per cent.

[2]National Coal Board, *Report and Accounts for 1962.* (London, H.M. Stationery Office, 1963.)

[3]For the possibility and cost of 'additional' production see E. F. Schumacher, 'Coal', *Aspect,* January 1964, and G. L. McVey, 'Policy for Fuel', *Political Quarterly,* January–March 1964.

the 200 million tons. In export markets, however, competitive pricing may produce additional sales, although demand for coal appears to be declining in most industrial countries. Export plans play an important part in the National Coal Board's endeavour to keep demand for British coal at a high level[1]. In 1963 the Board succeeded in raising coal exports to 8 million tons, almost twice the 1962 figure.

It is important on social and technical grounds, too, that coal production should not fall much more. There are still about half a million workers and other employees engaged in this industry, many of them living in mining villages where no other jobs exist; their redundancy would present grave social problems. Another important point is technical: once a pit has been closed down and abandoned, after a time the possibilities of reopening it are limited. Apart from strategic considerations and reasons connected with the balance of payments, these were the grounds on which the government introduced some measure of protection for coal. For the projections in this chapter, it has been assumed that existing protectionist measures (such as the tax on fuel oil, restrictions on coal imports, and no further conversion of existing coal-burning power stations to oil-firing) will be maintained, and also that the large-scale replacement of the coal carbonization process at gas-works by oil-gasification will be spread over a fairly long period—longer than would be justified on purely economic grounds.

Even with this degree of protection it will not be easy to keep demand for coal stable. It will depend on the Coal Board's success in keeping competitive, and in altering the image of coal as an old-fashioned fuel.

The direct use of coal will certainly continue to decline, probably to about 40–50 million tons in 1975 (table 10.7). This will be a result partly of technological changes (such as the gradual disappearance of steam traction on the railways and of the steamship, or the switch from generation to the purchase of electric power by collieries). Other consuming categories will substitute other fuels for coal; but, owing to coal's better competitive position, the rate of substitution is likely to be much below that in earlier years. Excluding railways, ships and collieries, the direct use of coal fell from 92 million tons in 1955 to 67 million tons in 1962, or by just under 4 million tons a year; the projected fall is another 25 million tons by 1975, or about 2 million tons a year, about half of which will be due to the changed structure of domestic energy use.

In the secondary energy industries, gas-works, one of the main traditional users of coal, will need, at maximum, half the present quantity of coal in 1975. The demand for coal will, on the other hand, grow very rapidly at power stations and these deliveries are likely to balance, in quantity, most of the expected falls elsewhere. But power stations use a lower-grade and cheaper coal than either gas-works or other categories (especially railways and domestic

[1]National Coal Board, *Report and Accounts for 1962, loc. cit.*, p. 5.

users) and consequently the structure of the coal market will change appreciably. This appears to fit reasonably well with the trend to mechanization since mechanized mining yields a much smaller proportion of large coal. Proceeds of all sales in the expected new structure will therefore be relatively lower than they used to be because of this shift from high to lower grade coal in both demand and supply. Thus, other things being equal, the National Coal Board will have to face a decline in the proceeds of coal sales. Under such circumstances it is rather doubtful whether in the long run coal prices can be kept stable—especially as the potential scope for further mechanization diminishes.

On balance, it seems reasonable to assume that the coal industry will succeed in maintaining a home market of around 190 million tons a year, and total output, including exports, of around 200 million tons a year.

Table 10.7. *Coal: the past and projected pattern of consumption*

Million tons

	1955	1960	1962	1975 projection
Direct use				
Collieries	8·7	4·9	4·1	1–1½
Iron and steel	6·1	3·8	2·6	1–2
Other industries	39·1	30·9	28·1	16–18
Railways	12·3	8·9	6·1	1–1½
Water transport	1·0	0·4	0·4	a
Agriculture	0·3	0·3	0·3	a
Domestic use	38·1	35·4	34·1	18–24
Public administration	4·8	4·0	3·8	2–3
Miscellaneous	3·4	2·5	1·8	1–2
Total	113·8	91·1	81·3	40–50
Secondary energy industries				
Electricity	42·9	51·1	60·4	105–115
Gas-works	27·9	22·3	22·1	10–12
Coke ovens	27·0	28·5	23·5	28–30
Manufactured fuel	1·7	1·4	1·6	2–3
Total[b]	213·5	195·5	190·9	180–200

[a]Less than a quarter of a million tons.
[b]Details for the past do not add up to the total because in some categories Northern Irish consumption is omitted.

(c) *Investment in coal mining*

The present investment activity of the National Coal Board more or less follows the plan outlined in *Revised Plan for Coal*[1] which revised downwards the original demand estimates published in 1950[2], and estimated total demand in 1965 as around 206 million tons—home demand of 196 million tons, and 10 million tons of exports. Capital investment, which had increased rapidly from

[1]*Revised Plan for Coal, loc. cit.*
[2]*Plan for Coal, loc. cit.*

fairly low levels in the early 1950s to an annual sum of about £100 million in
1958–9 has since come down to about £80 million a year. Investment will
probably stay at around this figure, or may rise slightly (at constant prices)
by 1975.

Table 10.8.   *Investment in coal mining*

	1958–9	1960–2	1975 projection[a]
		£million, annual averages	
Plant, machinery and vehicles	61	51	55–60
New building and civil engineering works	39	30	35–40
Total	100	81	90–100

Source: National Income and Expenditure, 1963.

[a]At 1960 prices; includes a small amount for investment in manufactured fuel plants.

3. OIL

(a) *The demand for oil*

In 1960 exactly one quarter of Britain's energy demand was covered by oil;
by 1962 its share had risen to 29 per cent. The rapidly increasing importance
of road transport is only one factor in this increase. In 1962 road, air, water
and rail transport made up only one third of the total oil demand of 46 million
tons. Oil has been gaining ground rapidly in industry, domestic space heating
and other uses, including gas-making and power generation.

The expansion of refinery capacity in this country has been even more rapid
by the end of 1960 it was five times as high as ten years earlier[1] and amounted
to about 50 million tons. In 1950 over half Britain's requirements for oil
products had to be imported; recently this proportion has fallen to about one
quarter, and these imports were balanced by exports and bunkering (appendix
table 10.9). The pattern of supplies has been changing rapidly. Motor
spirit has become very much less important; fuel oil much more important.
In 1962, fuel oil accounted for 45 per cent of all oil consumption, and for half
of all oil product imports. Feedstock for petrochemical plants, although the
quantity is still small, has also shown a very high growth rate in recent years[2].

According to our projection, demand for oil will rise from 38 million tons in
1960 (and 46 in 1962) to around 100 million tons in 1975.

[1]This is the capacity for crude oil distillation of all companies operating in the United
Kingdom. It does not include the overseas capacity of British oil companies.
[2]About 3 million tons of chemical feedstock had been used in 1962. In 1950, 9 per cent
of the total production of organic chemicals was made from petroleum feedstock; in 1962
it was 60 per cent and by 1975 it will be around 90 per cent. There has been a big increase
in the use of oil-based feedstock in the manufacture of inorganic chemicals as well, mainly
in the field of carbon black and ammonia. Before 1957, all the ammonia came from coal;
by 1962 half came from oil, and by the end of the 1960s probably almost all of it will be
produced from oil. ('A Look Ahead to 1975', *Esso Magazine*, Spring 1963, p. 4.)

Table 10.9. *Past and projected pattern of oil usage*

Million tons

	1955	1960	1962	1975 projection
Refineries	2·1	3·3	3·7	7½
Agriculture	1·0	0·9	1·1	1
Iron and steel	1·6	2·4	3·1	8
Other industries[a]	3·6	8·0	11·2	27
Railways	—	0·2	0·6	2
Road transport	7·4	9·9	11·3	23
Air transport	1·7	1·8	2·1	4
Water transport	0·7	1·1	1·2	2
Domestic	0·7	1·5	2·0	3
Public administration	0·5	1·6	1·7	3
Miscellaneous	0·3	1·4	1·1	2
Total direct users	19·5	32·1	38·9	75–85
Gas-works	0·5	0·8	1·1	7–8
Power stations	0·2	5·3	5·6	12
Total, all users	20·2	38·2	45·6	95–105

Source: Ministry of Power, *Statistical Digest, 1962.*

[a]The largest users in 1962 were the chemical, building material and engineering industries.

The pattern of growth which is projected is rather different from that of 1951–62. Transport will be responsible for the largest single addition to demand—for about 16 million tons of the 55 million tons projected rise between 1962 and 1975. The additional demand of industrial users (including petro-chemical plants) will probably add another 16 million tons. Gas-works will probably consume about 7–8 million tons in 1975, in place of the present 1 million tons. The oil consumption of the electricity industry will also more than double between 1960–2 and 1975, as there will be a limited number of large new power stations, based on oil-firing, such as the Fawley station already under construction.

The projections (shown in appendix table 10.3) imply that—except for the railways, water transport and the chemicals industry—the rate at which oil is substituted for coal will be appreciably slower than in the past. Despite this rather conservative projection, the contribution of oil to the country's energy supplies will rise to over 40 per cent (from 29 per cent in 1962).

The expansion of the world's oil reserves and the improvement in methods of exploration and production make a rise in oil prices unlikely in the foreseeable future; the projection is based on this assumption.

(b) *Investment in oil refineries*

By 1975 an additional 50–60 million tons of refined oil products will be needed for inland consumption. If the oil companies are to continue to hold a rough balance between imports and exports of refined products—which, probably partly at government instigation, seems to be the aim of their present policy—then about this quantity of new refinery capacity will be needed. Already, some 30 million of this has been announced[1].

This programme will probably require a rather larger annual capital investment than during the period 1950–62, when 42 million tons of new capacity was built. For during the 1950–62 period there was comparatively little need for replacement in addition to the construction of new capacity. In the coming period, on the other hand, replacement is likely to be a substantial item; by 1975, some 30 million tons of capacity would be over twenty years old, if it were not replaced in the interval.

The average level, therefore, of investment in the oil industry during 1962–75 will probably be well above the 1950–62 average of £35 million, at 1960 prices. Further, the trend of investment during 1962–75 will probably be rising, since demand for oil will be rising, in absolute terms, at an increasing rate. We have therefore put investment in 1975 itself at about £50–60 million a year[2].

4. GAS

In the period before 1963 gas consumption was fairly stable. Between 1955 and 1962 sales fluctuated between 2·5 and 2·7 billion therms, and the basic process of gas-making was the same as that at the end of the last century. The industry seemed doomed to be of gradually declining importance. However, technical developments of recent years—the oil-gasification process and the possibility of using natural gas—have altered the whole outlook for this industry

(a) *The composition of gas*

In 1950, the gas industry was based almost entirely on coal. Plant capacity at gas-works consisted of carbonization plant (70 per cent) and water gas plant (30 per cent), which is generally considered as a peak load carrier supplementing the base load supplied by carbonization. Already by 1963 carbonization plants

---

[1] In 1964 the new refinery of British Petroleum in Belfast (with a capacity of 1·3 million tons) started its operations and the Regent refinery in Milford Haven was due to come into production at the end of the year (capacity 5 million tons). In the first half of the same year the beginning of the building of seven further new refineries was announced:

Shell, Teesport	6 million tons capacity		
Gulf, Milford Haven	2 ,,	,,	,,
Total (French), Humber	3 ,,	,,	,,
ENI (Italian), Canvey Island	2 ,,	,,	,,
ICI-Philips (US), Tees-side	5 ,,	,,	,,
Continental (Jet), Humber	3 ,,	,,	,,
Petrofina, Humber	6 ,,	,,	,,

These should be gradually coming into operation in the years 1966–8.

[2] This projection of investment requirements relates to oil refineries only and excludes new tankers, investment in the marketing and distributive network, and the cost of exploration.

accounted for less than half of total capacity; and oil-gasification plant supplied one eighth[1]. Another important change was the increasing trend towards buying gas from other producers. Traditionally, the only source was coke oven gas, supplying 12 per cent of all gas consumed in 1950 (table 10.10). Already by 1963, outside producers supplied 26½ per cent, and nearly half of this came from new sources—liquid petroleum gas, refinery gas, and a small quantity of colliery methane.

The new sources of gas—either from oil-gasification or from purchases from outside—are, without exception, considerably cheaper than gas produced by conventional methods. Already in 1960 (table 10.11) refinery gas was only two thirds as expensive as gas produced by coal carbonization; since then, further technical advances make the margin in favour of oil even larger[2].

Table 10.10.   *The composition of total gas available and residuals made*

	1950		1960		1963		1975 projection	
	Million therms	Per cent	Million therms	Per cent	Million therms	Per cent	Million therms	Per cent
Gas made at gas-works								
Coal gas	1,887	72	1,732	59½	1,659	51	820	15
Water gas	374	14½	425	14½	503	15½	480	9
Oil gas	3	..	65	2	170	5	1,730	32
Other gas	31	1	21	1	60	2	50	1
Total gas made	2,295	87½	2,243	77	2,392	73½	3,080	57
Gas bought								
Coke oven gas	314	12	504	17	464	14	500	9
Liquid petroleum gas	—	—	—	—	124	4	200	4
Refinery gas	7	½	152	5½	259	8	600	11
Methane	—	—	13	½	21	½	20	—
Natural gas	—	—	—	—	—	—	1,000	19
Total gas bought	321	12½	669	23	868	26½	2,320	43
Total available	2,616	100	2,912	100	3,260	100	5,400	100
Residuals made at gas-works (million tons)								
Coke	11·8	..	9·9	..	9·8	..	5·0	..
Coke breeze	2·7	..	2·5	..	2·4	..	1·0	..
Tar (crude)	1·8	..	1·7	..	1·7	..	0·8	..

Source: Ministry of Power, *Statistical Digest, 1963.*

[1]Oil used for gasification is exempt from the fuel oil tax.

[2]The great cost advantage of oil-gasification put an end, at least temporarily, to the further application of the Lurgi process (that is, the complete gasification of coal). Even the cost advantage of imported natural gas may become questionable with further technical advances in oil-gasification.

Table 10.11. *The costs of gas[a]: pence per therm*

	Cost of production	Price paid by gas-works
Coal carbonization gas	12–15	..
Water gas	$9\frac{1}{2}$–15[b]	..
Oil gas	8–10[b]	..
Coke oven gas	..	$6\frac{1}{2}$[c]
Refinery gas	..	8–9
Methane from collieries	—	$5\frac{1}{2}$[c]

Source: Report from the Select Committee on Nationalised Industries: The Gas Industry (London, 1961, pp. 72 and 105).

Note: In countries with indigenous natural gas, distributors pay 1d. to 4d. per therm for that gas.

[a]The figures are intended to give a rough guide only. They assume favourable load factor, and refer to the period 1960–1.

[b]Depending on the raw material (gas, oil, light distillate, etc.) and covering both high and low load factors. For more details, see Appendix 39 in the Volume of Evidence to the Select Committee.

[c]The gas needs additional purifying, costs of which are not included.

In the early 1960s the gas industry introduced natural gas into this country. Two special ships were constructed to transport natural gas in liquified form from Algeria to Canvey Island, and a grid was built from Canvey Island terminus to Manchester and Leeds to distribute this imported natural gas to eight area boards. These projects were completed in 1964 and are capable of supplying about one tenth of the total present demand for gas. Another possibility is the purchase of Dutch natural gas. This could either be liquified and delivered by tanker or a pipe-line could be constructed; whether either system would be economical depends on the offer price.

On the basis of pure cost comparisons most, if not all, coal carbonization plants ought to be replaced in the near future by oil-gasification plants. In our projections we have assumed, however, that this process will be spread over a fairly long period. There are the technical difficulties of changing the whole fuel basis of the industry without disturbing supplies; there is also the fact that some of the carbonization plants are fairly new and therefore there will be strong resistance to scrapping them. Thirdly, if oil were suddenly substituted for coal, it would be very unsettling for the coal industry, which in the early 1960s supplied over 20 million tons of coal for gas-making. On this assumption of a fairly gradual programme of conversion, gas-works will still use about 10–11 million tons a year in 1975, or half of their present requirements. This quantity of coal will, however, only provide 15 per cent of total gas requirements, as against about a half in 1963.

(b) Projections of demand and supply

Between 1960 and 1975, we have projected a doubling of the demand for gas—after a long period in which it has hardly risen. This is partly because the new sources of supply should enable the industry to avoid price increases. Gas should continue to make headway in space-heating: the number of gas appliances sold for central heating rose sixfold between 1959–60 and 1963–4, and the number of gas fires trebled. There is reason for considerable further expansion: at the end of 1960, only about one fifth of gas consumers used gas for water-heating, and one third for space-heating.

Table 10.12. *Past and projected pattern of gas supply and usage*

	1955	1960	1962	1975 projection
Coke oven gas		*billion cubic feet*		
Output at ovens	294	317	261	320
Disposals to:				
Collieries	3	1	—	—
Steelworks	80	98	81	100
Other industries	7	7	3	8
Power stations	2	—	—	—
Gas-works	77	100	93	100
Total	169	205	177	208
Gas bled or wasted	6	4	2	2
Used at coke oven plants	119	108	81	110
Town gas		*billion therms*		
Gas made	2·50	2·24	2·33	3·1
Gas bought	0·40	0·67	0·75	2·3[a]
Gas available	2·90	2·91	3·08	5·4
Usage:				
Iron and steel	0·15	0·14	0·13	0·2
Other industries	0·60	0·72	0·71	1·0
Domestic	1·39	1·30	1·40	2·7
Public administration	0·09	0·07	0·06	0·2
Miscellaneous	0·39	0·41	0·44	0·8
Total use by final consumers	2·62	2·64	2·74	4·9

Source: Ministry of Power, *Statistical Digest, 1962.*

[a]Includes about 1,000 million therms of imported natural gas.

The idea that gas might be especially used to meet peak demands for energy is theoretically attractive, since gas can conveniently be stored, whereas electricity cannot be. However, this is a limited possibility, since a good deal of the evening peak demand is caused by the demand for light, and this gas can hardly meet.

The pattern of gas supply will continue to change rapidly. The supply of coke oven gas is not likely to alter much; so its importance in total gas supply by 1975 will probably be about half that of 1960. On the other hand, the supply of natural gas will increase sharply: just how sharply it is very hard to forecast. In the projection, a fairly arbitrary figure of one thousand million therms has been put in as the annual quantity of natural gas imports in the years around 1975; this equals about three to four times the volume of natural gas for which arrangements have been made at present, and would cover one fifth of all gas requirements. The rate of growth will depend on the success of Algerian imports, on the progress of purchase of gas from Holland, and on the success or failure of exploration in the North Sea.

There is also likely to be a big increase in the supply of refinery gas from 1960 to 1975; this would account for one tenth of gas supplies in 1975, compared with 5 per cent in 1960.

Thus, by 1975, nearly half of the total gas consumed is likely to be bought from outside sources. For the rest, the dominant method of manufacture will be oil-gasification, requiring some 7–8 million tons of various oil products a year, compared with 1 million tons in 1962. (This assumes the fairly gradual conversion from the carbonization process already described.)

(c) Investment in gas

Capital expenditure in the gas industry rose quite sharply in 1962–3 (table 10.13); and the technical changes required will probably necessitate a continued —though not a very rapid—rise. Although a substantial quantity of new plant will be needed, fortunately the capital requirements both of oil-gasification and of the reforming of gas bought from outside are considerably lower than those of the old type of carbonization plant[1]. (The capital cost of a new gas plant using oil works out considerably cheaper per therm produced than that of a generating station, even if an allowance is made for the difference in the use-

Table 10.13. *Capital expenditure in the gas industry: £ million*

	1960–1	1961–2	1962–3
Gas manufacture	15	16	21
Distribution	25	26	30
Natural gas import scheme (terminals, pipe-lines, etc.)[a]	—	—	4
Other (including research)	3	4	4
Total	43	46	59

Source: Gas Council, *Annual Report and Accounts, 1962–3*, Appendix II, Summary Schedule no. 15.

[a]Excluding ships.

[1]Capital costs are given in the *Report from the Select Committee on Nationalised Industries: The Gas Industry (loc. cit.)*, vol. II, *Minutes of Evidence, Appendices and Index*, p. 601, as follows:

	£ per therm per day
Coal carbonization	57–60
Coke ovens	50
Lurgi plant	45
Oil-gasification plant	20–30
Carburetted water gas	15
Gas reformer (for the processing of bought gas)	10

It is known that since the date of the above evidence (early in 1961) the capital costs of oil-gasification plant have been reduced considerably because of technical development.

fulness for final consumption of the energy produced[1].) So a slow rise in investment towards a level of £60–80 million (at 1960 prices) in 1975 should allow for the creation, between now and then, of about 2,000 million therms a year of oil-gasification capacity, equipment for the reception and processing of about 2,500 million therms a year of bought gas, and an improved distribution network[2].

5. COKE AND OTHER SOLID FUEL

Consumption of solid fuel other than coal—that is, coke, coke breeze, manufactured fuel (briquettes) and various types of 'smokeless' fuel—has been declining in recent years. The iron and steel industry is the major consumer of this group of fuels, using nearly half of total supplies; its coke consumption has come down appreciably since the mid-1950s, in spite of higher steel output[3]. Indeed the only sector where coke consumption has been rising is the domestic sector; this is the consequence of the introduction of smoke control zones. Domestic consumption rose from under 4 million tons in the late 1950s to $5\frac{1}{4}$ million tons in 1963.

The present pattern of supply (table 10.14) is roughly that coke ovens produce about two thirds of the total output of coke and breeze, and that three quarters of this coke oven output is used by the iron and steel industry. The remainder of coke oven output, together with some 10 million tons from gas-works, was available for other industries. This pattern will change radically between now and 1975; the supply of coke from gas-works will roughly halve, as the gas industry gradually changes over to oil-gasification[4]. If coke oven production, and the iron and steel industry's coke consumption[5], are about the same as now (table 10.14), then there will be a sharp reduction in the amount of coke available for other purposes.

This fall in the amount of coke for sale outside the iron and steel industry seems likely to cause something of a problem for the clean air policy in Britain[6]; if sufficient smokeless fuel were available, it is likely that its consumption would rise quite rapidly between now and 1975. It is quite possible, however, that the

[1]See 'Gas Forges Ahead', by Sir Henry Jones, *FBI Review*, October 1963.
[2]It also includes moderate amounts for investment in 'smokeless' fuel manufacture. This will be dealt with in the next section.
[3]In 1946, 22·6 cwts. of coke and coke breeze were needed to produce one ton of pig iron; in 1960 the average consumption was 18·3 cwts. only. By 1963 that quantity declined to 16·9 cwts. (Iron and Steel Board, *Development in the Iron and Steel Industry: Special Report, 1961, loc. cit.*, table 27.)
[4]The gas-works could produce coke from coal without making gas for sale; for the time being, however, the production cost of such coke appears prohibitive.
[5]See footnote 3 above. It has been assumed that coke consumption by iron and steel works will be stable at their 1962–4 level despite the rise in the output of ferrous metals.
[6]Ministry of Housing and Local Government, *Domestic Fuel Supplies and the Clean Air Policy*, Cmnd 2231 (London, 1963).

shortages of coke and briquettes will seem to drive up the price, and that the gas and electricity industries will stand to gain most from the faster spread of smoke control areas.

Investment in the coke industry in recent years amounted to about £20 million a year. For replacement of the ageing plants and a moderate expansion of the capacity of certain 'smokeless' varieties, further capital expenditure of the same order will be needed which by 1975 should be about £20–30 million[1].

Table 10.14. *Coke, breeze and briquettes: supply and distribution*

| | 1960 | | Projection for 1975 *Million tons* | |
	Supply	Distribution[a]	Supply	Distribution[a]
Coke				
Gas-works	9.9		5	
Coke ovens	18.8		19	
Iron and steel		15.6		15
Other industries		2.4		1½
Railways and agriculture		0.2		b
Domestic		4.1		3
Public administration		1.4		½
Miscellaneous		4.5		2½
Electricity		0.9		½
Gas-works		2.3		2
Exports		1.6		1½
Coke breeze				
Gas-works	2.5		1	
Coke ovens	1.3		1½	
Total, coke and breeze[c]	32.5	33.0	26½	26½
Briquettes[d]				
All producers	1.5		3.0	
Railways		0.6		¼
Other inland		0.8		2½
Exports		0.1		¼
Total	1.5	1.5	3.0	3.0

Source: Ministry of Power, *Statistical Digest, 1962.*

[a]The division between coke and breeze is not available; distribution figures include both.
[b]Negligible.
[c]The difference in 1960 between output and distribution was covered from stocks.
[d]All types (ovoids, rectangulars, etc.).

6. ELECTRICITY

The electricity supply industry has for a long time been the fastest-growing industry in Britain, and—with investment between 1951 and 1962 of £3,600

[1]A considerable part of 'smokeless' fuel is being made by gas-works, and briquettes by the National Coal Board. The requirements for capital expenditure projected in the coal and gas sections cover the relatively small amounts needed for the development of these plants.

million—it has also had the largest investment programme of any industry. In 1962, investment in the electricity industry accounted for 8½ per cent of all capital expenditure in the economy.

(a) *The demand for electricity*

The industry's problem is, of course, the peak load problem. The maximum load[1]—the daily peak within the seasonal winter peak—is usually more than twice the average hourly quantity of electricity sent out during the year. This problem has not in fact been getting more acute: if anything, the peak has been becoming slightly less sharp. Expressed as a percentage of the maximum load, the average hourly quantity of power sent out rose from between 30 and 35 per cent in the mid-1930s to over 40 per cent in the early 1950s and to 48–50 per cent in the early 1960s: in other words, base load demand has been rising rather faster than the peak demand[2]. Even so, the growth of capacity failed to keep pace fully with the growth of peak demand—in that there was still some load shedding (by voltage reductions or disconnections) at maximum loads in 1962 and 1963 (table 10.15). Of course, the economic importance of this failure to meet peak demand is small; supplies were interrupted in only a few areas, for a few hours.

Our projection suggests that demand for electricity will rise at about 8¼ per cent a year between 1960 and 1975[3]. This is a little slower than the rate between 1955 and 1960, appreciably slower than the rate between 1960 and 1962, and also somewhat slower than the rate (for England and Wales) recently adopted by the Electricity Council for the next few years. (We expect that peak demand will continue to rise rather less rapidly than the base load demand.) The very high increase in demand in the 1960–63 period was partly due to the abnormally cold winter in 1962–3. The effect of temperature cannot be calculated with any great accuracy; rough adjustments suggest that the adjusted demand increase between these two years was around 7½ per cent a year, as against the actual 9 per cent[4].

Table 10.16 gives the details of the projection for demand. First, domestic consumption is projected to rise at 9 per cent a year—below the recent rate of growth. There are two main reasons for this slower rate. First, household consumption is very vulnerable to cold spells; this explains why the 1960–2 increase was so high. Secondly, since about 1954 there has been an exceptionally fast rise in the ownership of all types of household durables—radios, television sets, and labour-saving appliances of all kinds. On balance, it

---

[1] The various technical expressions are explained in the notes to table 10.15.

[2] Between 1945 and 1963 total sales rose 8·3 per cent per annum and the peak load 7·5 per cent per annum.

[3] The projected range of 310 to 370 thousand million kWh is equal to an annual growth rate of between 7·8 and 8·8 per cent.

[4] See notes to table 10.16.

Table 10.15. *Electricity: capacity and loads*[a]

	Unit	1935	1945	1950	1955	1960	1963
Installed capacity[b]	Million kW[c]	8·1	12·3	15·0	22·5	31·9	39·3
Output capacity[d]	Million kW	..	..	13·5	20·6	29·6	36·5
Output capacity in per cent of installed capacity	Per cent	..	..	90	92	93	93
Simultaneous maximum load met during the year[e]	Million kW	5·7	9·0	11·9	18·4	26·9	33·1
Simultaneous maximum potential demand during the year[f]	Million kW	6·0	10·8	13·8	19·8	26·9	33·3
Apparent unsatisfied demand[g]	Million kW	0·3	1·8	1·9	1·4	0	0·2
Maximum demand in per cent of output capacity	Per cent	..	..	102	96	91	91
Maximum load met in per cent of output capacity	Per cent	..	..	88	89	91	91
Plant load factor[h]	Per cent	24·8	34·5	45·8	44·3	44·7	46·9
System load factor[i]	Per cent	31·8	37·6	42·8	43·5	48·4	50·4
Number of generating stations	No.	398	356	337	347	319	334
Average size of stations	Thousand kW (installed capacity)[b]	20	35	45	65	100	118

Source: Ministry of Power, *Statistical Digest, 1963.*

[a] Public supply stations in Great Britain.

[b] The maximum continuous rating of the generating sets in the stations, including auxiliary and stand-by sets capable of use, but excluding disconnected sets.

[c] At end of year.

[d] Capacity installed after allowing for station consumption and any limitation in the capacity of prime movers.

[e] This is the maximum load on the grid as a whole at any one time together with the load on any stations not connected to the grid. (The maximum load is defined here as twice the largest number of units sent out in any consecutive 30 minutes commencing or terminating at the hour.) This occurs near the end of the year or early in the following year.

[f] The maximum load met, plus an allowance for any load shed (by voltage reduction or disconnection) or any reduction in frequency. This is therefore the estimated total demand as opposed to the demand actually met. Owing to the severe winter the figure for 1962 was 35·2.

[g] As a result of load shedding, or reduction in frequency (2·6 in 1962).

[h] The average hourly quantity of electricity sent out during the year, expressed as a percentage of the average output capacity during the year.

[i] The average hourly quantity of electricity sent out during the year (including purchases from other sources) expressed as a percentage of the maximum potential demand nearest the end of the year or early in the following year.

seems likely that the yearly increase in ownership (which is not, of course, the same as the increase in sales, because of replacement demand) will be rather slower in future[1]. For certain appliances, such as vacuum cleaners and electric

[1] The index reflecting sales of the seven most important consumer durables, published regularly in the *National Institute Economic Review* (table 3 of the Statistical Appendix) indicates a marked peak in 1959–60, which has never been reached since. Indeed, sales in 1961–2 were about one quarter, and in 1963 still one sixth below the level of the 1959–60 boom.

Table 10.16.   *Electricity: the trend of sales*[a]

	1955	1960	1962	1975 approximate projection	*Thousand million kilowatt hours* Annual per cent change		
					1955–60	*1960–62*[b]	*1960–75*
All consumers	69·6	104·9	125·3	338 (310–370)	*8·5*	*9·3*	*8¼*
Main consuming categories:							
Collieries	3·3	4·6	4·8	8	*7*	*2*	*3*
Agriculture	1·2	2·1	2·5	5	*12*	*8½*	*7*
Iron and steel	4·2	6·0	6·2	19	*7½*	*4*	*8*
Other industries	27·6	39·9	43·2	127	*7½*	*4½*	*8*
Railways	1·4	1·8	2·1	5	*5*	*8*	*7*
Domestic	20·3	33·7	45·7	123	*10½*	*16½*	*9*
Public administration	3·6	4·7	5·7	15	*5½*	*9½*	*8*
Miscellaneous	6·9	10·6	14·0	35	*9*	*16*	*10*

Source: Ministry of Power, *Statistical Digest.*

Note: Sales to all consumers in this table differ from total sales as given in table 10.15 because they include Northern Ireland and industrial production of hydro-electricity.

[a]In the United Kingdom.

[b]The past figures have not been corrected for changes in the temperature: an allowance for the different temperature in the years 1955, 1960 and 1962 does not affect appreciably the period 1955–60 but it makes a considerable difference to the 1960–2 period. The growth rates of electricity consumption in the most affected industries may be estimated on a tentative basis and are likely to have been in 1960–2 3½ per cent for other industries, 12½ per cent for domestic consumption, 8 per cent for public administration, 11 per cent for miscellaneous uses, and between 7 and 7½ per cent for all consumers.

irons, saturation point in ownership has nearly been reached[1]: for others, such as washing-machines, the rate of increase in ownership is likely to be lower than it has been.   There seem only to be a few appliances—such as food mixers—for which ownership is likely to rise as fast as, or faster than, in the past.

There seems no reason to suppose that household demand for lighting will rise faster than before.   Although there are no details of the various purposes for which household power consumption is used, it is probable that the use of electric power for light increases more slowly than the overall use of electricity in households.   The remaining sector of household consumption is heating. Electric space heating certainly became popular in the post-war period because of its convenience, and in spite of its price.   It will increasingly meet the competition of forms of central heating.   It is difficult to assess, in the longer run, how successful block storage heaters will be in competition with oil, coal, and gas-fired central heating appliances; for it is uncertain how, and at what speed, the present block heaters will be developed[2].

[1]Early in 1964, 92 per cent of British households had an electric iron and 77 per cent a vacuum cleaner.   See appendix table 10.16.

[2]By the end of the 1963–4 heating season about 600,000 storage heaters were in use on domestic and commercial premises (Electricity Council, *Statistical Digest, 1963*).   More detailed information on central heating is given in Appendix, 10, pp. 573–5.

Industrial consumption of electricity is projected to rise rather faster than in the period since 1955. There are two forces here working in opposite directions. On the one hand, industrial production—in line with the general assumptions of this study—is assumed to rise much more rapidly in the future. On the other hand, in a number of industrial sectors the shift to electricity has been particularly fast in recent years; and—although it is assumed that a very large part of the energy use by the main categories is covered by electricity in 1975[1]— even so the shift to electricity from now on will, it seems, probably be slower than in recent years.

The agricultural use of electricity will rise at a slower rate because a large part of the rural (farm) electrification programme has already been fulfilled; similarly, the scope for further electrification of collieries (that is, the substitution of power purchased from the public system for self-generated electricity) appears rather limited. The railways, on the other hand, will need more power, in the light of their electrification plans, and the rate of growth of their need for electricity will be quite rapid. For public administration and the miscellaneous category the projected rate of growth is higher than that of the period 1955–62 when allowance is made for the past effects of temperature.

In sum, given the forecast for the total demand for energy, an annual growth rate for electricity demand lying between 7·8 and 8·8 per cent a year seems the most likely. If it is to be faster than this, then it implies either that the direct use of coal or other solid fuel will have to decline even more rapidly, or that the growth envisaged for oil or gas will be smaller. It does appear that the trend of prices—particularly as between electricity and gas—will be much less in electricity's favour than it has been in the past. The price of electricity depends on fuel costs—that is, by and large, on the cost of coal[2]; on balance, the price of coal seems more likely to go up than the price of oil or gas.

Competition from gas for the heating market, in particular, seems likely to be much stronger in future. There seems no reason at all to assume any government intervention to favour electricity as against other fuels.

(b) *The supply of electricity*

The electricity industry produces most of its power in the new, large stations where thermal efficiency is highest, and generation costs are lowest; and the older, less efficient stations are brought in to meet peak demands[3].

[1] Calculated in coal equivalent, it is assumed that 46 per cent of all final energy will be consumed in the form of electricity. The percentages for the various industries and sectors are 80 per cent in collieries, between 60 and 70 per cent in agriculture, chemicals, household and miscellaneous consumption, between 50 and 60 per cent in engineering, textiles, clothing and other industries, between 30 and 50 per cent in the food industries, paper and printing, building materials, railways and in public administration, and 24 per cent in iron and steel-making (appendix table 10.3).

[2] Fuel costs accounted for 87 per cent of generation costs in 1962 (appendix table 10.14).

[3] Analyses of the operations at power stations are given in the Appendix, by size of the stations (appendix table 10.12) and by specific fuel costs (appendix table 10.13).

In 1961–2, out of 353 public power stations (including 246 steam stations), the 58 largest produced about 70 per cent of all electricity sent out and were loaded at over 50 per cent of their capacity; in these stations, with a capacity of 200 megawatts and over, thermal efficiency exceeded 28 per cent, and generation costs were between 0·45 and 0·7 pence per kilowatt-hour. An analysis based on fuel costs gives the same picture. In 1961–2 there were 66 steam stations (out of a total of 246) where average works costs per unit were lower than the national average; these accounted for a quarter of all steam stations, for about half of installed capacity, and for two thirds of the electricity sent out. The difference in production costs are substantial. At 72 small stations operating at peak time the electricity generated cost over four times the national average; however, the load on these was very small and these stations—29 per cent of all plants in operation—produced in 1961–2 only 1 per cent of total output[1]. They acted as stand-by reserve producers.

(c) *Future needs*

Allowing for losses in transmission and power used on works, the projected $8\frac{1}{4}$ per cent rise in demand will require the generation of about 400 thousand million kilowatt-hours by 1975 (table 10.17). A considerable part of this, about 60,000 million kWh, will be supplied by nuclear power stations[2]. The rest will be generated by conventional steam stations, mostly with coal-firing, although a small number of new oil-using power stations will be built (in particular, near large oil refineries). The quantity of coal required will rise from 51 million tons in 1960 to about 110 million tons in 1975; this will be supplemented by about 12 million tons of oil. Hydro-electricity generation will show a moderate rise only, from 3,100 million kWh in 1960 to 5,000–6,000 million kWh in 1975[3].

This projection of fuel requirements assumes further improvement in the efficiency with which coal and oil are used. During the 1950s, thermal efficiency increased, on average, by over 2 per cent every year (table 10.18) and the rate of improvement was only slightly smaller ($1\frac{1}{2}$ per cent) in the early 1960s. This figure, of $1\frac{1}{2}$ per cent a year, was used for the projection. It may be on the

---

[1] The operating costs of hydro-electric stations were much lower: 0·04 d/kWh compared with 0·64 d/kWh at all steam stations. The unit cost of electricity produced by oil engines was about twice the cost of that produced at steam stations; this, however, is a process definitely reserved for peak periods and emergencies as an auxiliary source, and the electricity generated by oil engines was less than $\frac{1}{2}$ per cent of the total.

[2] This projection assumes that, apart from the stations built (with a capacity of about 5,000 MW and to be completed in 1969) under the first nuclear programme (Ministry of Power, *The Nuclear Power Programme*, Cmnd 1083, London, 1960) most of the stations to be built under the second nuclear power programme (*The Second Nuclear Power Programme*, Cmnd 2335, London, 1964) will be in normal operation in 1975.

[3] These figures are shown in detail in appendix table 10.4.

cautious side. In the United States, where the size of the stations has for a long time been larger than in Britain, higher annual improvement rates have been achieved (appendix table 10.15).

Table 10.17. *Electricity: the trend of supply*[a]

	1955	1960	1962	1975 projection
		Thousand million kilowatt hours		
Generation (including purchases from outside sources)	80·4	121·3	144·7	392
of which:				
Nuclear power stations	—	2·1	3·5	60
Used on works	4·8	7·0	8·7	23
Total electricity available	75·6	114·4	136·0	369
Losses, etc.[b]	8·2	12·0	13·6	37
Total sales	67·4	102·4	122·4	332
				(300–360)
		1955–60	*1960–62*	*1960–75*
Annual growth rates[c] (per cent)				
Generation	..	8·6	9·2	8¼
Total sales	..	8·7	9·3	8¼

Source: Ministry of Power, *Statistical Digest.*

[a]Public stations in Great Britain only.

[b]Losses in transmission mainly, but also including consumption in offices and showrooms of electricity authorities and boards, and delays in reading meters.

[c]Data in this table have not been adjusted for temperature. Deviations from the normal (long-term average) temperature in the years given were −0·3°F in 1955, +0·4°F in 1960 and −1·6°F in 1962. No temperature correctors have been worked out because of the insufficiency of the basic data—specifically referring to electricity usage; the application of tentative adjustments does not affect appreciably the growth rate of total sales in the period 1955–60 but reduces it to about 7 to 7½ per cent in the period 1960–2.

(d) *Investment in electricity*

It is the statutory duty of the industry to satisfy the demand of all consumers entitled to be supplied; the statutory obligation does not distinguish between demand occurring at peak and at other times. Electricity cannot be stored[1]. The Central Electricity Generating Board therefore considers that it should have a margin of plant capacity over demand in average cold spell weather of about 14 per cent; at the end of 1963 this margin was down to 7 per cent[2].

[1]A kind of storage, however, has been attempted in the pumped power station at Ffestiniog. This consists of two large water reservoirs at different levels. At off-peak times the water is electrically pumped up to the upper lake, whereas at peak times it is allowed to flow down generating hydro-electricity. This plant, together with the work of creating the reservoirs, cost about £16 million. According to some estimates, it replaces conventional plant of the size of 360 MW which would have cost £23 million (C. L. Boltz in *The Financial Times*, 24 July 1963). Another station on similar principles is now being planned for construction in North Devon.

[2]'Long-Term Planning for Electricity Supply', by C. T. Melling (London, Electricity Council, 1963).

Table 10.18.   *Fuel efficiency at public power stations*

(A) Average thermal efficiency of steam stations (the total calorific value of the electricity sent out as per cent of the total calorific value of fuel input)[a]

	Per cent	Average per cent improvement per annum over the period since previous year given
1920	8·7	..
1930	15·9	6·2
1940	21·0	2·8
1950	21·6	0·3
1960	26·7	2·1
1962	27·5	1·5

(B) Electricity generated per ton of fuel used[b]

	1950 = 100	
1950	100·0	..
1955	109·5	1·8
1960	115·4	1·1
1962	118·4	1·3

Source: Ministry of Power, *Statistical Digest.*

[a]Change in the calorific value of the coal used: 11,500 B.T.U. per lb. prior to 1940, 11,000 in 1945, 10,935 in 1950, 10,247 in 1960 and 10,083 in 1962.
[b]Based on tons, in coal equivalent, disregarding changes in the calorific value of the coal used.

The problem for investment is to decide how far the capacity which is needed for meeting peak load should consist of new 'high-merit' stations, with low operating costs, and how far of older 'low-merit' stations, with higher operating costs—allowing for the fact that some of the low-merit stations will only be operated for a small part of the year, in many cases for a few days only.

The investment programme suggested here begins with the assumption that only the stations with the best working results are likely still to be in operation as base load suppliers in 1975; these accounted in early 1963 for an aggregate capacity of about 14,000 megawatts[1].   New capacity of the order of 48,000 MW would then have to be built between early 1963 and 1975 to supply the rest of the base load, making in all about 62,000 MW of 'high-merit' stations for bulk production. Of this 62,000 MW, some 2,000 would be hydro-electric plants, perhaps about 9,000 would be nuclear stations (assuming that most nuclear stations in the second programme will be in operation by 1975)[2], and about

[1]Those stations have been taken into account here which in 1962–3 were loaded at around 60 per cent or over, with less than 0·6 d/kWh generation cost, and over 28 per cent thermal efficiency.   Altogether only 28 conventional steam stations fulfilled these requirements out of a total number of 247.   All nuclear and hydro-stations can be considered as still of 'high-merit' in 1975; in 1963 these accounted for about 2,000 MW capacity.
[2]The *Second Nuclear Power Programme, loc. cit.,* provides for 5,000 MW to be commissioned before 1975, raising total nuclear capacity (together with the plants in the first programme) to about 10,000 MW.

51,000 MW coal and oil-fired stations. In addition to these high-merit stations, there would be 1–2,000 MW of gas turbines and oil engines[1] and a large number of old low-merit steam stations as stand-by reserves. These would produce

Table 10.19. *Electricity: capital cost of power stations*

(A) Conventional stations	Commissioning dates	Number of sets	Size of sets 000 kW	Average cost £ per kW
	1958–64	36	120	53·6
	1959–64	12	200–300	45·4
	1962–66	12	275–376	36·6
	1963–68	14	500–550	34·4

(B) Nuclear stations	Works begun	Capacity 000 kW	Estimated cost £ per kW
Bradwell	1957[a]	300	176
Berkeley	1957[a]	275	186
Hinkley Point	1957[b]	500	150
Trawsfynydd	1959	500	137
Dungeness	1960	550	114
Sizewell	1961	580	107
Oldbury	1962	562	114
Wylfa	1963	1,180	100

Source: Report from the Select Committee on Nationalised Industries: The Electricity Supply Industry, loc. cit.; Ministry of Power, *The Second Nuclear Power Programme, loc. cit.*; 'Atomic Energy—A Reassessment', A. Cassuto, *Moorgate and Wall Street*, Spring 1961, p. 46, and information supplied by the Central Electricity Generating Board.
[a] January.
[b] September.

about the same quantity of power as they did in recent years (70,000–80,000 kWh a year): this would naturally be a much smaller part of all generation than it was in 1962–3. On this assumption about the way in which the demand for electricity will be met in 1975, one might expect commissioning of new plant in that year to be running at the rate of some 7,000–8,000 MW a year.

(e) *Cost of new capacity*

The average capital cost of new capacity has been declining steadily (table 10.19). For conventional plant, this is mainly due to the growth of plant size; for nuclear plant, technical advance is a better explanation. It is reasonable

[1] These are aircraft-type gas turbines with relatively low capital cost and high running costs which can be installed quickly. Their role is to act as emergency suppliers in case of breakdown and to provide reserve capacity at times of peak. The economies of these turbines lie in the saving of transmission loss and of the expenditure on the distribution network by providing ancillary safeguard generating capacity locally, in the place of supplying power through the national grid from other plants further away. It is estimated that about 1,000 MW of gas turbine plant could be economically included in the system of the industry by 1968 (Sir Ronald Edwards, 'The Expansion of Electricity Supply', *National Provincial Bank Review*, May 1963).

to assume that the downward trend will continue for both types of plant, though at a much less rapid rate than in the last decade[1]. We assume that in 1975, calculated at 1960 wage and material prices, the capital cost of a conventional station will be £30 per kW, and that of a nuclear station £75[2]. Further we assume that of the 7,000–8,000 MW commissioned in 1975, about 1,500 will be nuclear.

However, if there are rapid technical advances in the development of nuclear energy, and if the rate of interest were to fall considerably, the proportion of nuclear stations in the total might well be higher, and total capital expenditure in 1975 would consequently be significantly greater. Recent developments indicate that if the lifetime of nuclear stations is more than 20 years (admittedly assumed for lack of experience) the cost comparison becomes very much dependent on the expected return on capital, and if only 3 per cent interest is charged, the newest nuclear stations may compete favourably with large new coal stations on all counts (appendix table 10.17). Even more optimistic announcements have been made for the further prospects of a larger nuclear

Table 10.20. *Capital expenditure in the electricity industry*

			£ million, annual averages
	1957–9[a]	1960–2[a]	1975 projection[b]
Conventional stations	116	109	170–200[c]
Nuclear stations	46	73	110–120[d]
Hydro-electric stations	11	8	10–15
Main transmission	36	50	130–150
Distribution[e]	97	127	290–320
Other[f]	6	14	40–45
Total	312	381	750–850

Sources: Electricity Council, *Annual Report and Accounts;* annual reports of Central Electricity Generating Board, South of Scotland Electricity Board, North of Scotland Hydro-Electric Board.

[a]At current prices, financial years beginning in years stated for England and Wales and calendar years for Scotland; excluding Northern Ireland.

[b]At approximate 1960 wage and material prices but allowing for the reduction in specific capital costs due to technical development.

[c]5,500–6,500 MW conventional steam stations at £30 per kW.

[d]1,500 MW nuclear stations at £75 per kW.

[e]Area boards.

[f]Including the cost of initial charges of nuclear fuel.

[1]'In 1921, when the largest generating set was about 25 MW, an eminent British engineer offered the opinion that the tendency to increase the capacity of generating units was probably approaching its limits' (C. T. Melling, 'Long-Term Planning for Electricity Supply', *op. cit.*, p. 13).

[2]For stations commissioned in 1963 these costs were £34·4 for conventional, and £100 for nuclear stations, at current prices.

programme[1]. If, for example, nuclear energy were to provide half the commissioning in 1975, then even with further reduction of the capital cost of nuclear power stations to—say—£65 per kW, capital expenditure in 1975 would be about £80 million higher than the projection shown in table 10.20.

New generating capacity, however, has in recent years accounted for only about half the capital requirements of the electricity industry. Transmission of the power generated at the stations through the grid system to the area boards forms an equally important part of the supply system[2], as does the local final distribution by the area boards. The transmission and distribution of the trebled volume of power will necessarily require higher capital expenditure.

This approximate assessment ought to be interpreted with caution. Many factors influencing the capital requirements may change between now and 1975. There is not only the question of nuclear power; technical advances may greatly affect the capital requirements for transmission, or other items.

At present the plans of the Central Electricity Generating Board are based on the assumption that the demand for electricity grows at a faster rate than the $8\frac{1}{4}$ per cent a year rise assumed here. Their capital programme, at least in the early years, is consequently a good deal higher. According to their revised plan, 24,400 MW will be commissioned between 1963 and 1968; and between 1963 and the end of 1974 they probably envisage commissioning around 59,000 MW of new plant; and their total annual requirements of capital for the years 1963-4 to 1966-7 will be of the order of £640–£660 million a year—not much

---

[1]'Later programmes could well include reactors generating 1,000 MW. This size, and design improvements, could lead to a capital cost per kW which is 10–20 per cent below the £80 kW quoted a year ago. With overheads spread over a 6,000 MW plant at 75 per cent load factor, with a station life of 20 years and 6 per cent interest, the generating cost might fall in the later reactors below 0·40d. per unit, allowing for the improvements expected in fuel costs; 25 year life and 85 per cent load factor would bring it down to 0·35d.' (United Kingdom Atomic Energy Authority, *Ninth Annual Report, 1962–1963*, p. 12).

[2]The grid system consists of primary transmission (the Supergrid) and secondary transmission (the Grid). The Supergrid is planned to operate at high voltages (275 and 400 KV) for the purpose of linking power stations—mainly the large stations sited on cheap coalfields or near oil refineries, and also the (mainly coastal) nuclear stations—providing the main arteries through which supplies can be transferred in bulk from area to area in order to maintain the security and selective operation of the system and the economic pooling of the plant. The secondary system radiates from the Supergrid substations to carry bulk supplies at lower voltages (66 and 132 KV) to the points where the area boards receive them for further distribution.
The first grid, at 132 KV, was established in 1928; after the war it had to be changed to 275 KV and even this proved to be insufficient. The introduction of the 400 KV system has been gradually progressing (the first section on a distance of 53 miles came into operation in 1963). Research on a system consisting of 700 KV transmission has started.
According to present plans, at the end of 1967 there will be 1,900 route-miles and 41 substations working at 400 KV (there were none in March 1963); transformer capacity on the Supergrid (from 400/275 KV to 132 KV) will be more than trebled; and the secondary Grid will also be very considerably extended.

Y

less than the £750–£850 million we have projected for 1975[1].   However, as the industry is, for the time being, short of reserve capacity, there is no danger of wasted capital expenditure attached to these plans.   It is true that the larger power stations take five years to build; even so, the investment plans for the mid-1970s will not have to be settled finally for some time.   Energy forecasts are notoriously difficult to make for a long period ahead, and to foresee generation capacity requirements is especially delicate because of the high capital requirements on the one hand, and the risks involved in a chronic shortage on the other.   Frequent reassessments of any forecast or projection are therefore essential.   If, in the long run, the rise in demand for electricity should be nearer to our projection than to the higher growth rate which the electricity authorities are expecting for the coming five years, then the present estimates of the Electricity Council for capital requirements for the years until 1967 would have to increase only moderately until 1975.

7. SUMMARY OF INVESTMENT REQUIREMENTS

The projections for investment requirements, detailed in the various earlier sections, have been summed up in table 10.21.   According to this, capital expenditure of the order of £920–£1,120 million will be required in 1975 in the energy industries.   At comparable (1960) prices, the upper end of the range of the projected capital expenditure is about twice as high as actual investment was in 1962.

Table 10.21.   *Investment in the major energy industries*

						£ *million, annual averages*
						Projection
	1951–3	1954–6	1957–9	1960–2	1962	for 1975[a]
Coal mining	41	76	97	82	81	90–100
Oil refining	36	17	35	21	24	50–60
Gas	44	55	49	50	55	60–80
Electricity	163	237	301	370	406	750–850
Coke ovens	13	15	18	17	18	20–30
Total	297	400	500	540	584	970–1,120
At 1958 prices (1957–9 = 100)[b]	70	90	100	105	110	180–225

Source: National Income and Expenditure, 1963.

[a]At 1960 prices but allowing for lower capital cost of power generation due to technical advance (see page 320).
[b]Rounded to nearest 5.

[1]Electricity Council, *Finance for More Power* (London, 1963), p. 11. The capacity to be commissioned rises from 2,100 MW in 1963 and 3,800 MW in 1964 to 6,300 MW in 1967, and then declines to 5,000 MW in 1968.   This source gives estimates for England and Wales only—of £594 million a year from 1963–4 to 1966–7; the figure in the text of £640– £660 million allows for capital needed by the Scottish boards.

These projections have been based on the present technology of energy production. Only those developments have been taken into account which can already be foreseen, such as the expected advance in nuclear power production, or the radical change in the structure of the gas industry. If natural gas is found in substantial and accessible quantities under the North Sea, then the division of demand between the main forms of energy which we have postulated for 1975 could be altered a good deal. There are other advanced research projects which in time may well alter the picture—developments such as the fuel cell, or thermionic or magneto-hydrodynamic generation: but these are rather less likely to have developed sufficiently on a commercial scale to make a radical difference to the energy picture during the next decade.

CHAPTER XI

PROBLEMS AND POLICIES FOR INLAND TRANSPORT

By G. F. RAY AND C. T. SAUNDERS[1]

Inland transport of goods and passengers employs well over 2 million people—about one tenth of total employment in Britain, or about a quarter of the number employed in manufacturing industry[2]. This estimate of employment, as shown in table 11.1, takes into account—naturally by approximation only— the numbers employed in the current maintenance of road vehicles and of the roads, as well as in transport operations, so as to be reasonably comparable with total employment on the railways. In terms of employment, the 'road transport industry' is more than three times as large as the railways—allowing nothing for transport by private car. Even if we omit most of the employment on vehicle maintenance and about half that on road maintenance as attributable to private cars, then road transport other than private cars still occupies nearly three times as many workers as the railways: but road transport carries less than twice as much traffic, in passenger-miles or in ton-miles of freight, as the railways. Such a comparison must, however, be qualified by the shorter average distances and greater flexibility of road transport. Coastal shipping and inland waterways carry about one sixth of the total freight traffic.

Capital investment in inland transport is about 14 per cent of total investment, on the conventional definition (table 11.1) which excludes from investment personal purchases of motor vehicles. If such personal purchases were included in investment, the proportion would rise to 23 per cent[3]. Including all private motor vehicles, investment in roads and road transport is almost six times as great as in railways, while the total volume of traffic is greater by perhaps a rather smaller proportion[4].

[1]Assisted by R. E. Crum.

[2]If all sea and air transport, and not only inland transport, were included, the total employment would be about 2½ millions.

[3]Table 11.1 shows total investment in inland transport in 1960–2 as £656 million a year, against total fixed investment of £4,430 million. Net personal purchases of motor vehicles were £509 million.

[4]The difficulties of valuing assets—especially of valuing the infra-structure of rail and road—render comparison of capital stock of doubtful significance. However, the most recent estimates put the total volume of inland transport assets, at gross replacement values (1958 prices), at about £12 billions—about 13 per cent of total national capital. Of the assets in inland transport, railways account for £5½ billions, and road transport assets, including all private cars, for about £6 billions (G. A. Dean, 'The Stock of Fixed Capital in the United Kingdom in 1961', *Journal of the Royal Statistical Society*, Series A, vol. 127, part 3, 1964 ; £1·5 billion is added to Dean's estimates for motor vehicles in personal ownership).

Table 11.1. *Inland transport in Great Britain: employment, traffic and investment*

	Employment in operation and maintenance 1962 ('000s)	Traffic, 1962 Passengers billion passenger-miles	Freight billion ton-miles	Fixed investment average 1960–2 (£m)[i]
RAIL				
British Railways	450[a]	19·8	16·3[g]	140
London Transport	20	3·1	—	10
Total rail	470	22·9	16·3	150
ROAD				
Buses and coaches	270	42·4[f]	··	36
Road haulage	950[b]	—	33·6[h] }	316[j]
Private cars	··	103·7[f]		
Vehicle maintenance	250[c]	—	—	25[k]
Roads	100[d]	—	—	109[l]
Total road	1,570	146·1	33·6	486
AIR	15	0·7	—	10[m]
WATER (Coastal shipping and inland waterways)	75[e]	—	11·0[h]	10[n]
PIPELINES	—	—	0·4[h]	··
Total	2,130	169·7	61·3	656

Source: Annual Abstract of Statistics, 1963, except as noted below.

[a]This is a rough estimate, based on British Transport Commission *Annual Report and Accounts, 1962*, vol. II, pp. 140–1, and is intended to exclude staff engaged on new construction.

[b]196,000 in road haulage industry plus rough estimate of about 750,000 for employment as transport workers on 'C' and Contract A licensed vehicles (based on respective ton-mileages).

[c]Rough estimate related to 376,000 employed in 'motor repairers, distribution, garages and filling stations'.

[d]Rough estimate for employment on road maintenance, corresponding to about £170 million current expenditure on maintenance, etc., of roads and public lighting by public authorities (*National Income and Expenditure, 1963*, table 44).

[e]Rough estimate, related to 143,000 employed in 'port and inland water transport'.

[f]'Passenger Transport in Great Britain', *Economic Trends*, November 1963.

[g]Including rough estimate of 0·2 billion ton-miles for 3·4 million tons of freight by passenger train.

[h]Ministry of Transport, *Survey of Road Goods Transport, 1962: Final Results, Part 1* (1964), (table V). Of the total of 11·0 billion ton-miles, coastal shipping accounts for 10·8 billions.

[i]From *National Income and Expenditure, 1963*. Figures relate to United Kingdom.

[j]Goods vehicles plus net *business* purchases of private cars.

[k]Rough estimate based on capital expenditure per head in retail distribution.

[l]Capital expenditure on roads and public lighting.

[m]Related to £45 million total capital expenditure in air transport.

[n]Related to £23 million total capital expenditure on harbours, docks and canals.

326 THE BRITISH ECONOMY IN 1975

The pattern of transport, of which the main features are displayed in table 11.2, is changing under two major influences. There is the competition between railway and road and, perhaps more significant, the competition between public carriers (railways, road haulage operators, coastal shipping, and buses) and private transport (user-operated lorries and private cars). But in practice this competition is limited to only a part—though quite an important part— of the transport system. The changing structure of industry and the growth of incomes have also led to new kinds of demand for transport and travel which could not, in contemporary conditions, be satisfied by public carriers. The growth of road transport, and particularly of private cars, has, moreover, encouraged low density urban development, to which railways cannot economically be adapted and which creates difficulties even for public road transport.

Within the area of competition, neither direct cost considerations nor the rate of technical development is the only dominating force. Convenience and punctuality, and perhaps long-term and indirect cost factors, play as large a part. Low direct costs cannot explain why user-owned lorries have doubled their share of total goods transport in the past ten years, while the road haulage operator has done little more than maintain his share. Nor can it explain the doubling of the share of private cars in total passenger traffic, while the shares of the railways and to an even greater extent, of buses, have declined. The effects are bound to be cumulative. The manufacturer with his own fleet of lorries will

Table 11.2. *Trends in rail and road traffic*

| | Volume of traffic | | Percentage shares | |
	1952	1962	1952	1962
Passengers (billion passenger-miles)				
Railways	24·1	22·8	*21*	*13*
Roads				
Public transport	50·1	42·4	*45*	*25*
Private	37·9	103·7	*34*	*61*
Total road	88·0	146·1	*79*	*87*
Total	112·1	168·9	*100*	*100*
Freight (billion ton-miles)				
Railways	22·4	16·1	*54*	*32*
Roads				
Hauliers[a]	10·2	13·9	*25*	*28*
User-operated[b]	8·6	19·7	*21*	*40*
Total road	18·8	33·6	*46*	*68*
Total	41·2	49·7	*100*	*100*

Sources: Passengers: 'Passenger Transport in Great Britain', *Economic Trends*, November 1963.
Freight: Ministry of Transport, *Survey of Road Goods Transport, 1962: Final Results, Part I,*

[a]'A' and 'B' licensed vehicles.
[b]'C' and Contract A licensed vehicles.

certainly use them, just as the car owner will use his car, almost without regard to the cost of a particular journey. Indeed the costs of user-operated transport, whether lorries or private cars, are not always fully recognized. Thus private cars now account for 60 per cent of the estimated total of passenger traffic: ten years ago the proportion was one third. And user-owned lorries now account for 40 per cent of total goods traffic, against one fifth ten years ago.

1. OUTLINE OF A FUTURE TRANSPORT SYSTEM

In this chapter, we propose to deal first with the trend of demand for transport of freight and passengers, and then with the implications for investment in transport facilities. To estimate total demand or investment alone would be of little interest, because the facilities are specific. The interest lies in the pattern of demand, between road and rail and between public and private transport. The purpose is to set out some of the considerations which should govern the direction of public policy; about half of investment in transport is public investment, and there are many ways in which government can influence the pattern of transport usage—by taxation as well as by provision of facilities.

Investment in transport has certain special characteristics. First, many of the assets are particularly long-lived. If mistakes are made, society must endure them for a very long time. Secondly, the criteria for assessing costs and returns on investment in one form of transport against another are less calculable in advance than in most industries. This is partly because specific costs cannot be estimated accurately: on the railways, cost allocation is notoriously difficult; on the roads, there is the additional difficulty that track costs—although roughly calculable—are not paid directly by the user; for both rail and road, any commercial calculation is complicated by consideration of social costs and benefits some of which, even if calculable, are highly subjective. But the further problem is that the cost relationships must themselves be greatly influenced by what is in fact done.

Hence it is impossible to forecast demand for each kind of transport without some general presuppositions about the shape of policy. Extrapolation of recent trends *may* provide the most plausible forecast—but even that implies an extrapolation of recent policy (or of its absence). In what follows, we are taking the view that the next few years will see a certain reversal of recent trends. This does not necessarily mean that the increase in road traffic will be any slower than it has been—indeed, on the calculations made below it will on balance accelerate because of faster economic growth. But it does imply that railway traffic and public road passenger transport, which have been declining, will at some time begin to increase again.

Some impetus towards such a revival of the public transport systems may well spring from a change in the terms on which the different forms of transport at present compete. Such a change might take the form of a more discriminating method of taxing road vehicles than the existing vehicle licences and oil duties. The purpose of any such reorganization would be to base charges, so far as practicable, not just on ownership of a vehicle or use of motor fuel, but on the particular use of road space. Technical methods have now been devised, and appear feasible, for achieving this[1]. The main application of any such system would be in congested urban areas where the social costs of congestion caused by the use of private vehicles far exceed the costs to the individual vehicle user.

It must be recognized, of course, that owners of road vehicles already pay in licences and oil duties substantially more than the cost to public authorities of providing and maintaining roads. It also seems that each major category of road users—lorries, vans, cars, buses—pays more in taxes than the *total* road costs attributable to that category, so far as an attribution of costs can be estimated[2].

There are two possible justifications for a more discriminating method of charging for the use of road space—which certainly should not increase the total costs of road transport to users as a whole. The first is that the cost of road usage, in a particular place and at a particular time, should be related to the social costs—particularly the cost of congestion—caused by the vehicle in that particular use. If we allow for these additional costs, then it seems clear that some vehicle users, on some occasions (for example, commuters by private car), pay very much less than cost; others, in other circumstances, pay very much more than the costs caused.

The second justification, which is to be preferred, is simply that a system of discriminating pricing is the best way of adapting the demand for road space to the *existing* supply—by deflecting those users who are not prepared to pay either to alternative routes or to public transport. No such system can be ideal. 'Road pricing' cannot balance supply and demand, like the free market price of a commodity, simply because the supply of road space in the short run is inelastic. And in the longer run, the provision of road space must be based on a general policy for urban planning, in which the effective demand for the use of road space by private vehicles should play a part, but by no means the only part.

Any such change in the charging system would be designed to have the general effect of slowing down the expansion of private vehicle traffic within towns. This is the major problem of transport policy which has to be faced.

However, because prices and costs are far from the only determinants of choice of transport, the introduction of a different system of charging might not in itself go far enough to change the pattern. The major impetus to the revival of

---

[1]Ministry of Transport, *Road Pricing* (Smeed Report) (London, 1964).
[2]The calculation is worked out in the fullest detail in the Transport Holding Company, *Road Revenues and Costs: Memorandum submitted to the Committee on Carriers Licensing* (Geddes Committee) (London, 1964.)

public transport must come from an improvement in the quality of service offered by the public transport systems themselves. This is not, of course, just a matter of technical development. It depends much more on efficient organization—for passengers, on convenience, comfort and punctuality; for goods, on reliability and reduced delays (particularly for cutting down transhipment delays).

We take the view that the railway system will recover from the discouraging trading experience and lack of direction from which it has suffered during a long period when an increasing degree of freedom in rate fixing was used in somewhat unselective efforts to retain traffic; and that both arms of the general lines of policy now reinforced by Dr Beeching will have some success. It is true that the principles of the Beeching proposals[1] have been the declared basis of railway policy at least since the Modernization Report of 1955[2], and that for some years costs and the deficit were mounting and traffic had not increased. Nevertheless, we suggest that traffic will in future be attracted by the provision of fast and reliable services for passengers and goods between the major industrial centres; and that, at the same time, costs will be reduced by the closing of little-used lines and stations, by continued substitution of diesel (and to a smaller extent electric) traction for steam, by staff reductions and by concentration of freight depots. As we see it, the railways are capable of competing effectively on medium- and long-distance through-routes if they can succeed in concentrating their efforts on this kind of service by an appropriate rates policy and by offering appropriate facilities. This leaves two issues.

The first issue is the excess capacity of the transport system away from the main through-routes. A transport system, like any other national network—the postal service, electricity or water supply—is bound to suffer from a highly uneven distribution of use and of costs. The British Railways Board has proposed the closing down of perhaps one third of the total route mileage, routes which at present carry only about 1–2 per cent of total traffic[3]. It is often pointed out that the distribution of road traffic is roughly similar: the least used third of the total road mileage also carries about 2 per cent of total motor traffic[4]. Moreover, the geographical patterns of rail and road

[1]British Railways Board, *The Reshaping of British Railways*, known as the Beeching Report (London, 1963).

[2]British Transport Commission, *Modernisation and Re-equipment of British Railways* (London, 1955).

[3]The report proposes the closing of about 5,000 route miles to passenger traffic, out of 17,500 miles existing (in 1962). The extent of routes to be closed to freight is not stated but must be broadly similar. Since 1948, just over 2,000 miles have been closed (although services have been withdrawn from about 4,000 miles). If total route mileage were reduced to about 12,000 miles, it would be back to approximately the mileage open in 1867. The estimates of traffic carried on the lines proposed for closure were given by Dr Beeching and reported in *The Guardian*, 10 April 1963.

[4]J. C. Tanner, H. D. Johnson and J. R. Scott, *Sample Survey of the Roads and Traffic of Great Britain*, Road Research Technical Paper 62 (London, 1962): see figure 8 on page 45.

traffic are much the same.   There is, it may be said, as good, or as bad, a case for closing the least-used third of the road system as of the railway system— disguised only by the accident that commercial tests can be applied more easily to the railways than to the roads.   This is not, however, the issue.   The case for closure of a large proportion of railway route is: (a) there is indeed a social need for a comprehensive transport system with much 'excess capacity', one section subsidizing another—but not for two; (b) the real costs of providing and maintaining the less-used sections of the system are much less for roads than for railways.

This is not to justify every one of the closures proposed by the British Railways Board.   The facts so far produced in the Beeching Report, or in evidence at inquiries, are often so inadequate, and the allocation of costs or receipts to sections of route is so uncertain, that no outsider can be satisfied with the machinery for reaching decisions in particular marginal cases.   Nor is it by any means established that some at least of these lines could not usefully operate as light railways with rail-cars, unstaffed halts, and with signalling and track services below traditional standards[1].   They might still be more expensive than buses—but also much faster (which could be important on semi-commuter lines originally proposed for closure though now reprieved, such as Manchester-Buxton and Liverpool-Southport, where the alternative of a bus service would be slow because of the high proportion of built-up areas on the route).   But even if we discount heavily the new enthusiasm of the British Railways Board to cut free from as much doubtfully profitable traffic as possible, there is no escape from the general conclusion that the continuance of at least one third of the existing railway mileage is an extravagant waste of real resources and that much of it should have been cut out long ago[2].

The second issue is transport within cities—and particularly the commuter traffic which, because of its concentrated peak, is rapidly leading to an intolerable waste of time and resources in almost every industrial area.   We take the view—although it may never be proved beyond doubt—that the solution of reconstructing cities to accommodate smoothly the rising tide of private cars at peak periods is an impracticable one.   It may not be physically impossible but it is not worth its cost.   The solution must, then, lie in diverting as much as possible of the inevitable growth of urban traffic back to public transport.

It will be suggested that the expansion of suburban railways cannot for some years play a large part in the solution, although some expansion is desirable, especially in London.   Much more of the future increase in traffic must be carried by the buses.   But a main obstacle to the necessary improvement of the

---

[1]D. L. Munby, 'The Reshaping of British Railways' (*Journal of Industrial Economics*, July 1963).

[2]For further discussion, see G. F. Ray, assisted by R. E. Crum, 'Transport: Notes and Comments', *National Institute Economic Review*, May 1963.

frequency and reliability of the bus services is the congestion caused by the growth of car traffic.   To resolve this problem, a system of charging cars, and commercial vehicles, for the amount of congestion that they cause in movement or in parking is probably essential.   Methods of determent applied to the use of cars and lorries are likely to make a much larger contribution to the solution of urban traffic problems than to longer-distance traffic.   They can usefully be supported by traffic engineering measures such as reserved traffic lanes for buses or other preferences for public transport.

Finally, there is the question of subsidies.   It is inconceivable that every part of each system of transport should 'pay its way'—or disappear.   A large element of cross-subsidization is inevitable.   This can be conveniently arranged within the railway system as a whole even though it may imply some 'unfairness': it may not seem right that long-distance passengers or users of profitable freight services should in effect thereby subsidize commuters or expensive short hauls of goods.   But cross-subsidizing between various parts of the road system cannot be operated in the same way, because of the multiplicity of enterprises. From the point of view of society as a whole, there may be two reasons for subsidizing a particular transport service.   One reason—probably the most important—is that a subsidy (even if it causes a risk of extravagant operation) may be the cheapest way of meeting a particular demand for transport.   For example, if an urban public transport service is unable from its own resources to provide the facilities, at the right fares, to divert passengers from the growing use of cars, then it may well be cheaper to subsidize the public service than to engage in the physical reconstruction required to accommodate the cars. Secondly, there are many rural areas where bus services are not provided because they would not pay, yet where the provision of some form of public transport service is regarded as socially necessary—especially if a railway service has been withdrawn[1].

Within this framework of presuppositions, we may now review the prospects for each of the main categories of freight and passenger transport.   To illustrate what is implied by the projections of total transport demand and by the shifts between different forms of transport, projections are expressed in precise figures. It should be recognized that we are doing no more than illustrate general trends and that the projected numbers are meant only to indicate orders of magnitude.

It should also be recognized that nearly all the statistics of recent trends in road traffic are themselves no more than rough estimates, based partly on very infrequent sample surveys, partly on a limited number of traffic counts, partly on deductions from other statistics.   It is only recently that the long-standing concern with traffic and transport problems has led to a serious effort to begin to collect the information vitally needed for a solution.

[1]The report of the Committee on Rural Bus Services suggested a subsidy of £1 million a year, with the prospect of some annual increase (Ministry of Transport, *Rural Bus Services*, London, 1961).

The general method of analysis is not very different from that used in the Hall Report[1]—the first official published report to attempt a quantitative forward look at the problems of inland transport as a whole. But at several points the projections made here differ from those in the Hall Report, since the latter worked in broad ranges and without the same presuppositions about the future development of the transport system as those adopted here[2].

In this review, we have not entered in any detail into the possible future trend of freight by *coastal shipping*. Nearly half of the coastal traffic is coal; the tonnage carried by coastal shipping, and also its share of the total coal delivered, were falling during the 1950s but have been stabilized more recently.

Of the rest of coastal traffic, the bulk is presumably petroleum and has been rising. Consequently total coastal traffic has been increasing, only slowly in the 1950s but quite fast in 1960–2.

2. FREIGHT TRANSPORT

(a) *Coal*

Coal traffic (including coke) is still the mainstay of the railways, accounting for nearly a quarter of gross receipts and now the only class of traffic (apart from parcels and mails) which is reckoned to cover both direct and indirect costs—though only by the very small margin of £3 million in 1961 (table 11.3). But traffic has been falling off—from 10·5 billion ton-miles in 1952–4 to 7·6 billion in 1963 (table 11.4). One major reason for the decline is, of course, the general decline in coal usage. Other factors have contributed. Dispatches from the pits by road have been rising: by 1962 about 20 per cent of total coal disposals was moved by road from the pit. The average length of haul from the pits has been falling; this is partly because of the increasing proportion of coal used for electricity generation combined with the tendency to site new power stations near the source of fuel, and partly because the disappearance of coal shortages has made it possible to rationalize the distribution and minimize long hauls.

At the same time, the railways themselves are endeavouring to concentrate coal traffic on a smaller number of distribution depots, and into full train loads. The direct haulage cost for a single wagon consignment (over half the present coal traffic) can be twice as heavy (per wagon-mile) as for a through train load[3]: hence the contracts with the Central Electricity Generating Board for block train loads.

[1] *The Transport Needs of Great Britain in the Next Twenty Years* (London, 1963). This was the report of a group appointed by the Minister of Transport under the chairmanship of Sir Robert Hall, Economic Adviser to the Ministry of Transport.

[2] Some of the data for past years also differ, because the results of inquiries since the date of the Hall Report have led to revised estimates of road transport. Particularly important are (a) 'Motor Car Ownership and Use', *Economic Trends*, June 1963 (report of the first comprehensive official survey of private cars); (b) Ministry of Transport, *Survey of Road Goods Transport, 1962: Final Results, Part 1, loc. cit.* (report of the third sample survey of goods transport by road, incorporating revised estimates of previous trends).

[3] Beeching Report, *op. cit.*, p. 32.

Table 11.3. *Estimates of relative profitability of traffic on British Railways, 1961*

	Receipts	Direct costs	Surplus over direct costs	Allocated indirect costs	£ million Surplus over total costs
Passengers					
Fast and semi-fast	91·2	72·7	18·5	40·3	−21·8
Stopping	30·8	56·9	−26·1	29·8	−55·9
Suburban	39·8	40·3	−0·5	24·5	−25·0
Total	161·8	169·9	−8·1	94·6	−102·7
Freight					
Coal	108·3	83·5	24·8	22·0	2·8
Minerals	44·5	36·9	7·6	11·3	−3·7
General merchandise	102·8	148·1	−45·3	29·8	−75·1
Total	255·6	268·5	−12·9	63·1	−76·0
Freight by coaching trains	57·3	40·2	17·1	10·3	6·8
Total, all traffic	474·7	478·6	−3·9	168·0	−171·9

Source: British Railways Board, *The Reshaping of British Railways*, Beeching Report, *op. cit.*, table 1.

Note: The definitions of direct and indirect costs are not stated in the Report. Indirect costs are, however, stated to include interest and central charges (£49 million) and provision for depreciation calculated 'in terms of present money values'. (In 1961, the depreciation allocated to the railways at historic cost appears to have been about £50 million, to which about £20 million appears to have been added to allow provision at current price levels—see British Transport Commission, *Annual Report and Accounts, 1962, loc. cit.*)

The total usage of coal, however, is unlikely to increase (see chapter 10) and may well decline further; and the average distances for which coal is hauled by rail will almost certainly continue to fall. By 1975 electricity generation may well account for over half the total usage of coal and many power stations may take their coal direct from the pit by conveyor.

Coal may in future yield a higher net revenue to the railways, but the total coal traffic, in ton-miles, will fall; we suggest, in table 11.4, that it will fall from 7·6 billion ton-miles in 1963 to not much more than 5 billion in 1975. Road haulage of coal may increase with concentration of rail traffic on fewer depots. It must also be remembered that the railways are in competition with water transport and with the potential development of pipe-lines; and that total coal traffic may fall further still if the gas industry ceases to be a major user of coal.

(b) *Iron and steel*

A second distinguishable major class of heavy freight, of great importance for the railways, is iron and steel materials and products[1]. Together, they account

[1]In the regular statistics of railway traffic before 1963 these are not distinguished; iron and steel materials (in tonnage, chiefly iron ore) take up most of the 'minerals' category; iron and steel products are classed as general merchandise. The source of the separate figures for iron and steel is the Hall Report, *op. cit.*

Table 11.4. *Trends in inland freight transport*

	Average 1952-4	1960	1961	1962	1963	Average 1960-2	Projection 1975	Percentage change 1952-4 to 1960-2 Per year	1960-2 to 1975 Per year	Total
1. Traffic originating (million tons)										
Coal and coke										
Rail[a]	173·2	148·1	145·7	145·0	151·4	146·3	120	-2·1	-1·4	-18
Road[b]	26	38	39	38	..	38	50	4·9	2·0	32
Total	199	186	185	183	..	184	170	-1·0	-0·6	-8
Iron and steel materials and products										
Rail	48·6	50·9	42	33	..	42	64	-1·8	3·1	52
Road	7	13	13	12	..	13	21	8·0	3·5	62
Total	56	64	55	45	..	55	85	-0·2	3·2	55
General goods										
Rail	64	50	50	50	..	50	107	-3·0	5·6	114
Road	849	1,141	1,188	1,198	..	1,176	2,093	4·2	4·2	78
Total	913	1,191	1,238	1,248	..	1,226	2,200	3·8	4·3	79
All freight[c]										
Rail	286	249	238	228	235	238	291	-2·3	1·4	22
Road	882	1,192	1,240	1,248	1,300	1,227	2,164	4·2	4·1	76
Total	1,168	1,441	1,478	1,476	1,535	1465	2,455	2·9	3·8	68

2. Net ton-miles (billions)

Coal and coke									
Rail[a]	10·5	8·1	7·7	7·3	7·6	7·7	5·2	−3·8	−2·8	−32
Road[b]	0·5	1·0	1·0	1·0		1·0	1·3	9·1	1·9	30
Total	11·0	9·1	8·7	8·3	··	8·7	6·5	−2·9	−2·1	−25
Iron and steel materials and products										
Rail	3·5	3·6	3·1	2·7	··	3·1	4·4	−1·5	2·5	42
Road	0·4	0·9	1·0	1·0	··	1·0	1·6	12·1	3·4	60
Total	3·9	4·5	4·1	3·7	··	4·1	6·0	0·6	2·8	46
General goods										
Rail	8·4	7·0	6·8	6·1	··	6·7	15·8	−2·8	6·3	136
Road	19·0	28·2	30·3	31·6	··	30·0	50·2	5·9	3·7	67
Total	27·4	35·2	37·1	37·7	··	36·7	66·0	3·7	4·3	80
All freight[c]										
Rail	22·4	18·7	17·6	16·1	16·5	17·5	25·4	−3·0	2·7	45
Road	19·9	30·1	32·3	33·6	35·0	32·0	53·1	6·1	3·7	66
Total	42·3	48·8	49·9	49·7	51·5	49·5	78·5	2·0	3·3	59

Source: Total rail traffic and coal and coke traffic from *Annual Abstract of Statistics, 1963*. Total road traffic from Ministry of Transport, *Survey of Road Goods Transport, 1962: Final Results, Part 1, loc. cit.*, and *Highway Statistics, 1963*, Statistical Paper 3 (London, 1964). Iron and steel traffic estimated from data in Ministry of Power, *Statistical Digest* and Ministry of Transport, *The Transport Needs of Great Britain in the Next Twenty Years* (Hall Report, *op. cit.*).

[a]Revenue carryings: excludes railways' own coal.
[b]Dispatches direct from pits and open-cast sites.
[c]Excluding freight by passenger train.

for about 3 billion ton-miles of rail traffic—approximately half as much as coal, and yielding nearly half as much in revenue—and more than another billion ton-miles by road traffic.

The steel industry itself is expected to expand rather more slowly than total national output[1] and its transport requirements for materials, which are almost wholly carried by rail, may well increase less than its output.   The steel industry, like electrical supply, is tending to develop most on sites nearest to its sources of bulk supplies—the coast, or domestic ore fields; further geographical integration within the steel industry is also likely, to take full advantage of the development of continuous processes.   Moreover, one of the features of technical progress in the industry is savings in the tonnage of materials and fuel used in relation to output of finished steel.   For these reasons, iron and steel materials have not, over the past ten years, been an expanding traffic on the railways, in spite of the expansion of the steel industry itself.   But if steel output rises faster in future, its transport requirements for materials should in fact begin to increase.   As for coal, the advantages of block train operation for minerals are very substantial and could yield savings in transport costs[2].

For finished steel products, accounting for about 2 billion ton-miles of road and rail traffic, total transport requirements have been increasing—though not quite so fast as steel output—but road haulage has invaded the market effectively (table 11.4).   It is estimated that over half the products are now carried by road, and rail carryings have not increased over the past ten years.   This is a competitive market.   One of the reasons for the declining share of the railways is the risk of damage to the light products (such as sheets for car production) which are of growing importance; this risk should be reduced by improved methods of operation.   Reliable and quick delivery is also essential for firms (like the car producers) subject to violent fluctuations in demand.

So total transport requirements will increase, and rail traffic will rise significantly if road competition can be resisted more successfully than it has been so far.   It is suggested that total transport requirements might rise from 4 to 6 billion ton-miles, and rail traffic from just over 3 billion to nearly $4\frac{1}{2}$ billion ton-miles.

(c) *General goods traffic*

If coal, and iron and steel, are left aside, the remaining freight traffic[3] amounted in 1960–2 to about 37 billion ton-miles.   Of these 37 billion ton-miles, the railways held 6·7 billion—18 per cent—in 1960–2.   Ten years ago, the railways carried $8\frac{1}{4}$ billion ton-miles—nearly one third of the smaller total (27 billion) then available.   The decline in the railways' *share* of this traffic has been fairly

[1]Iron and Steel Board, *Development in the Iron and Steel Industry: Special Report, 1964* (London, 1964).   See also table 7.6.
[2]Beeching Report, *op. cit.*, p. 33.
[3]'General merchandise', in the classification of the usual railway statistics, *plus* minerals other than iron and steel materials and *less* iron and steel products.

continuous, but the absolute amount of ton-mileage by rail has not always been falling; it recovered temporarily in 1958–60—when economic activity generally was increasing fast—and has been rising again in the general economic upturn of 1963–4.

It is, naturally, on the longer hauls that the railways have the best hope of regaining traffic. And it is important to note that in the longer-distance traffic the public haulier, rather than the user-operated lorry, is the main competitor. The competition at this end of the market may therefore offer the railways a more hopeful opportunity for competition by price and service. This is brought out by table 11.5, which also shows what kinds of present road traffic the railways now hope to recapture.

Of the general goods traffic now carried by rail, about half was estimated to cover its *direct* costs in 1961[1]. The loss on the rest is greater, for this class of freight as a whole failed to cover its costs (table 11.3). The paying traffic is predominantly that moving from siding to siding, conveyed for 75 miles or more in sizeable wagon loads[2]; movements between sidings and docks, or between stations and sidings, more or less break even (they represent about a quarter of the total). It is road traffic suitable for movement in these terminal conditions and for these distances which the railways hope to recapture; such traffic is believed to make up more than half the total of 54 million tons of goods now carried by road which the railways regard as suitable for rail transport[3]. Most of this traffic, too, is concentrated in flows between the major industrial areas—'matching the better-used rail routes'. Goods collected from a private siding must be assumed to mean—for the most part—products of factories which are large enough to provide a number of full wagon-loads (or, better still for the railways, train loads). The present view of the railways appears to be that other kinds of goods traffic—goods collected from the factories by road, or at stations —will generally not yield a return in present conditions; only a proportion of it is regarded as worth chasing—that which can be carried by the proposed new liner trains in the dense inter-city flows. It is admitted that much of this traffic which the railways wish to reject is also traffic which 'road hauliers would reject or carry only at very high prices'[4]. A certain number of small factories and traders who now use the railways for small consignments may find their transport costs rising.

The implication of the Beeching Report for the future of general goods traffic is that a strong effort will be made to capture from the roads as much as possible of a tonnage amounting in total to some two thirds of that already carried by rail. But at the same time it seems evident that the railways will be content to lose up to a quarter of their present general goods traffic in the unremunerative categor-

[1]Beeching Report, *op. cit.*, table on p. 36.
[2]*Ibid.*, tables I to IV, pp. 82–86.
[3]*Ibid.*, p. 41.
[4]*Ibid.*, p. 36.

Table 11.5. *Freight transport (other than coal)*

	Now carried by rail	Now carried by road		*Million tons* Traffic regarded as potentially suitable for rail
		Public hauliers	Private	
0–24 miles	27	160	770	5
25–49 miles	16	45	130	15
50–99 miles	19	40	65	13
100 miles and over	22	32	26	21
	84	277	991	54

Source: From table 2 in Dr R. Beeching, 'The Rationalisation of Transport', *Institute of Transport Journal*, March 1964. The figures given by Dr Beeching for road traffic are only approximations. They are further adjusted, arbitrarily, to exclude the small amounts of coal. The date to which the analysis relates is not stated but it is presumably based on the traffic surveys made in 1961 for the Beeching Report. They do not exactly match the figures in table 11.4.

ies. The competition between road and rail in effect concerns only a very small proportion of total goods traffic—at most, the 15 per cent (table 11.5) of tonnage carried for distances of 50 miles or more. If the railways were completely successful in achieving these aims (and making no allowances at this stage for the growth in total traffic available), total general goods tonnage would increase by some 40 per cent (34 million tons). This would hardly affect the total volume of goods traffic on the roads, but—if it happened—it would make a serious dent in the amount of long-distance goods traffic and in particular would remove a large fraction of the business of road hauliers including that of British Road Services. The railways are unlikely to achieve so much. But it seems possible that they might capture an additional 20 million tons of remunerative traffic whilst giving up, say, about 10 millions of traffic which does not at present pay them.

More important, however, is the amount of potential new traffic which would be generated by the growth of industrial output. It is natural to expect that the total amount of goods transport will be directly related to the total volume of goods produced (or imported). Significant changes in this relationship could occur for the following reasons:

(i) divergent trends in output (or imports) between goods requiring substantially different amounts of transport per unit of product;
(ii) locational changes leading to longer or shorter average hauls of inputs or output;
(iii) technical changes affecting, in particular, the weight or origin of materials or fuel used.

The first of these reasons could affect the relationship between output and transport needs even from year to year, and might be important in the long run, too. The second and third reasons could operate only slowly and over long periods. In looking far ahead, it is important to see whether in fact there is

Table 11.6. *General goods traffic by rail and road in relation to goods requiring transport*

	Traffic in billion ton-miles			Total (1952 = 100)	Index of physical supplies (1952 = 100)	Per cent change from previous year	
	Rail	Road	Total			Total traffic	Total physical supplies
1952	8·5	16·9	25·4	100·0	100·0	..	..
1953	8·4	17·8	26·2	103·1	106·9	3·1	6·9
1954	8·1	19·0	27·1	106·7	112·4	3·5	5·1
1955	7·6	20·3	27·9	109·8	118·9	2·9	5·8
1956	7·4	20·6	28·0	110·2	118·8	0·4	−0·1
1957	7·3	20·4	27·7	109·1	121·8	−1·0	2·5
1958	6·5	22·5	29·0	114·2	121·6	4·7	−0·2
1959	6·6	25·1	31·7	125·2	129·3	9·6	6·3
1960	6·9	26·5	33·4	131·5	137·5	5·0	6·3
1961	6·8	28·6	35·4	139·4	138·0	6·0	0·4
1962	6·3	29·9	36·2	142·5	139·2	2·2	0·9
1963	6·0	31·0	37·0	145·0	144·8	2·2	3·4

Sources: Traffic: as for table 11.4, except that local distribution by road is deducted (on basis of estimates of van traffic in the Hall Report, *op. cit.*, table 1).
Index of supplies: indices of manufacturing output, excluding ferrous metals, agricultural output and volume of imports weighted roughly by transport requirements.

evidence of any long-term structural changes in demand for goods transport.

So far as the evidence goes (table 11.6), it suggests that over the past decade or so there has been no significant long-term change in the relation between output (plus imports) and transport needs, for general goods. The year to year changes are not very closely correlated, partly perhaps because cyclical changes in the economy have unevenly affected different industries, partly because of the repercussions of the Suez crisis in 1956–7, which temporarily held back the growth of road transport.

The figures as they stand in table 11.6 suggest some tendency in the early part of the period (before the Suez crisis) for total transport to increase less fast than supplies to be moved, and a tendency since 1958 for the amount of transport to increase faster than total supplies, indicating a greater 'input' of transport per unit of product. But the period is too short, and the margin of error in the statistics too great, to make it possible to attach much significance to the apparent trend.

In projecting the total demand for inland transport of general goods, therefore, we assume an increase from 1960 to 1975 of 80 per cent—which corresponds with the expected increase in total physical supplies of goods to be moved[1].

[1] From 1960 to 1975, total manufacturing output is assumed to increase by 85 per cent (4·2 per cent a year—see chapter, 7 table 7.6), and the total volume of 'general' goods to be moved by a slightly smaller proportion.

Table 11.7. *Basis for projection of general goods freight traffic*

	Ton-miles (billion)			Tons (million)			Average length of haul (miles)		
	Rail	Road	Total	Rail	Road	Total	Rail	Road	Total
Traffic in 1960–2	6·7	30·0	36·7	50	1,176	1,226	134	25·5	30·0
Projected changes to 1975									
1. Shift from road to rail of traffic remunerative to rail	+2·5	−2·5	—	+20	−20	—	125	125	125
2. Shift from rail to road of traffic unremunerative to rail	−0·4	+0·4	—	−10	+10	—	40	40	40
3. Distribution of 80 per cent additional traffic from growth of supplies	+7·0	+22·3	+29·3	+47	+927	+974	150	24	30
Traffic in 1975	15·8	50·2	66·0	107	2,093	2,200	148	24	30

Note: The method of projection is as follows: each change is calculated in tons, and converted into ton-miles taking what appears to be a reasonable average haul for each category. For item 3, it is assumed that the railways will gain more in the longer-distance traffic.

The division between road and rail will depend on the outcome of the competitive struggle of the railways to maintain and increase their share. We are prepared to assume that they will in fact succeed in recapturing some of the better-paying traffic and in capturing about a quarter—the proportion of *present* traffic in ton-miles which it is assumed they may get—of the increased traffic resulting from faster growth; at the same time, we assume that they will succeed —by closure of lines and stations, increases in rates, and general discouragement —in casting off much of the traffic which fails to pay. In total, on the very arbitrary proportions set out in table 11.4, the result is a rise of over 6 per cent a year in the ton-miles carried by rail, and of under 4 per cent in that carried by road. By 1975, on this basis, the railways would hold nearly a quarter of total traffic in general goods; this is a bigger share than that now held (under a fifth) but remains less than in 1952–4 (nearly a third).

3. PASSENGER TRANSPORT

Of total consumers' expenditure, about 9 per cent is now devoted to transport (of which about one third is for net purchases of vehicles). At the beginning of the century, and indeed up to the 1920s, the proportion was only about 5 per cent; by 1975, it may be expected to increase to about 14 per cent according to the general analysis of expenditure patterns described in chapter 6. The total volume of expenditure would be substantially more than double what it is now (increase of 140 per cent from 1960 to 1975) and additional expenditure on transport in all forms is expected to take up a fifth of the increase in total real consumption—as it has done fairly consistently over the past half-century (tables 6.2 and 6.15).

The whole of this increase, and more, in expenditure on transport represents, of course, the increase in private motoring. There is every reason to expect this pattern to continue, even though it may be moderated by improvements in public transport and the increasing inconvenience, or even discouragement, of private motoring.

Development of passenger traffic can best be considered in three groups: long-distance traffic between major centres, medium distance traffic between towns or in the country and traffic within cities (the largest part being 'commuter' traffic). The third group probably accounts for 40 per cent of the total expenditure. A very rough distribution of expenditure and passenger-mileage is set out in table 11.8.

(a) Long- and medium-distance traffic

Of these groups of traffic, about one third is carried by public transport, and one eighth by rail. At present, British Railways is losing money both on the long-distance and the medium-distance traffic (assuming that these can roughly be identified with the division in the railway statistics between 'fast and semi-fast' and 'stopping' trains); the average distance for the former category is something under 100 miles and for the latter about 10 miles. But the long-distance traffic at least covers its direct costs and makes a substantial contribution to the overhead costs of the system; the receipts from medium-distance traffic cover little more than half the direct costs (table 11.3).

No evidence is available about whether long-distance traffic has been increasing in the recent past. There should be a tendency for growth with rising incomes. But private cars compete extensively, and the cost difference—taking running costs only—is not very large for small or medium sized cars with more than one passenger; the airlines have made serious inroads on the London–Scotland routes, where they may now be carrying the same order of magnitude of passenger traffic as the railways; and the long-distance coaches offer marginal competition based on substantially lower fares. It can hardly be expected that the volume of long-distance rail traffic will increase much.

The principal change affecting the long-distance rail services is the proposal to eliminate six stretches of duplicated main lines, and some terminals and accompanying facilities (for instance, to cut out one of the three trunk routes to Scotland, one of the three to the West Riding, two of the five trans-Pennine routes)[1]. The financial improvement from these closures, 'together with better handling of bulk commodities', is expected to amount to about £50 million a

---

[1] This was not included in the Beeching Report, but a preliminary announcement appeared in *The Times*, 7 October 1963.

Table 11.8. *Trends in inland passenger transport*

Passenger-miles (thousand million)

	Average 1952–4	1960	1961	1962	1963	Average 1960–2	Projection 1975	Per cent change 1952–4 to 1960–2 Per year	Per cent change 1960–2 to 1975 Per year	Per cent change 1960–2 to 1975 Total	Total receipts or expenditure (£ million) 1960
RAIL											
British Railways											
Long-distance	⎰ 15–16	..	..	..	..	⎰ 11·8	13·5	..	1·0	14·4	86
Medium-distance	⎱	..	..	..	..	⎱ 3·8	2·0	..	−4·5	−47·4	28
Urban (excluding LTB)	(5)	..	..	..	..	5·2	6·0	..	1·0	15·4	37
Total British Railways	20·6	21·5	21·1	19·7	19·6	20·8	21·5	0·1	0·2	3·4	151
London Transport	3·5	3·2	3·1	3·1	3·1	3·1	3·5	−1·5	0·9	12·9	26
Total rail	24·1	24·7	24·2	22·8	22·7	23·9	25·0	−0·1	0·3	4·6	177
ROAD											
Public services											
Long-distance	⎰ 28·0	⎰ 25·6	25·1	24·8	..	⎰ 2·6	⎰ 3	⎰ −1·4	1·0	15·4	16
Medium-distance	⎱	⎱			..	⎱ 22·5	⎱ 24	⎱	0·5	6·7	150
Urban (excluding LTB)	14·0	12·4	12·3	11·9	..	12·2	15	−1·7	1·5	23·0	92
London Transport	8·3	5·9	5·7	5·7	5·6	5·8	8	−4·4	2·3	37·9	56
Total public road services	50·3	43·9	43·1	42·4	41·5	43·1	50	−1·9	1·1	16·0	314

Private motor vehicles											
Long-distance	..	..	..	..	..	15	60	..	10·4	300·0	200
Medium-distance	..	..	..	..	..	34	165	..	11·9	385·3	350
Urban	..	..	..	..	..	48	75	..	3·2	56·3	750
Total private motor vehicles	42·4	88·9	97·7	103·7	110·5	96·8	300	10·9	8·4	209·9	1,300
Total road	92·7	132·8	140·8	146·1	152·0	139·9	350	5·3	6·8	150·2	1,614
AIR											
Long-distance	0·2	0·5	0·6	0·7	..	0·6	2·5	14·7	10·7	316·7	10
TOTAL INLAND TRAVEL	117·0	158·0	165·6	169·6	..	164·4	378	4·3	6·1	129·9	1,801
of which:											
Long-distance	..	..	..	..	..	30	79	..	7·2	163·3	312
Medium-distance	..	..	..	..	..	60	192	..	8·7	220·0	528
Urban	..	..	..	..	..	74	108	..	2·7	45·9	961
Private motor vehicles	42·4	88·9	97·7	103·7	..	96·8	300	10·9	8·4	209·9	1,300
All other	74·6	69·1	67·9	65·9	..	67·6	78	-1·2	1·0	15·4	501

Sources and notes: See Appendix 11 (detailed notes to table 11.8) for a description of the methods of arriving at the detailed projections.

year.   If savings on this scale can be realized, the operation of the fast and semi-fast passenger service as a whole will become very profitable (present direct plus indirect costs being put at £113 million—and revenue at £91 million). The resulting concentration of long-distance traffic should also increase the attractions of further electrification.

Medium-distance traffic—stopping services on the railways—presents a different picture.   The great bulk of the traffic, largely in rural areas, is by private car; the railways hold less than 5 per cent of it; the rest is held by the bus companies (a large proportion of them in the groups controlled by the nationalized Transport Holding Company—now split off from the British Transport Commission).

It is this sector (together with small-scale freight movements) that will mainly be affected by the station and route closures proposed in the Beeching Report. The railways at present take about £30 million in passenger receipts from stopping services, against direct costs of £57 million and allocated overheads of another £30 million.   The Beeching proposals imply that about half of this traffic will be given up, and the total costs reduced by about £45 million[1].   The slimmed-down services in this category should then approximately cover their direct costs (since the bulk of the savings must be on direct costs), but can hardly be expected to contribute to general overheads.   The traffic transferred to the roads will not be important in total; from the estimates in table 11.8, it should not add as much as 5 per cent to the road passenger-mileage in this category (more, in terms of vehicles, to the extent that the displaced passengers go by car, less to the extent that they can use existing bus services which are not fully loaded).

Nevertheless, it is the endeavour to reduce railway losses on this class of railway traffic which has brought to a head the whole question of public policy towards the railway system.   The case for withdrawing *most* of the services proposed for closure is obviously very strong.   Over the whole category of stopping services, the taxpayer is now contributing nearly half of the direct costs as well as all the overheads; on the services to be closed, the taxpayers' proportion must be much higher.   Whatever criticisms may be directed at the accounting methods of the railways, whatever calculable social benefits may be regarded as offsetting the loss to the railways, whatever increases in fares might be proposed, and whatever simplification of the railway services might be feasible— there can be no doubt that the railway is the wrong method of public transport in the majority of cases and that more economical means of transport are possible.   But there may well be marginal services proposed for closure where broader considerations than the financial results to British Railways would justify the maintenance of the service with a specific subsidy.

So far, however, the criticism that may reasonably be directed at public

[1]Beeching Report, *op. cit.*, pp. 19 and 54.

policy is that very few of the proposed closures have been effected and that no clear guidance has yet been given by the government about assistance for providing alternative forms of transport.   There is no evidence yet, for example, that the more extensive use of luggage-carrying buses is being promoted.   The British Railways Board itself has, however, paid subsidies (nearly £100,000 in 1963) to support bus services provided to alleviate hardships to passengers deprived of railway services through closures[1].

(b) Urban transport

The central problem for urban transport is that of carrying people between home and work at peak periods.   The concentration on peak periods is largely responsible for the high costs of operation of public transport systems and their consequent financial difficulties, for the high social costs—in terms of wasted time—of traffic congestion, and for the high costs to the public of the road improvements needed to keep pace with the increasing flow of traffic.

There is no comprehensive information on the rate at which traffic within towns has been increasing.   The extensive use of urban traffic surveys has only just begun.   Two facts, however, stand out from the statistics available for London, and may become broadly true of traffic in all the great cities.   The growth in the number of commuting travellers has not been remarkably rapid. In the ten years 1952–62 the number of *people* entering central London in the morning peak by rail or road rose only by 1 per cent a year—and the number entering by road was reduced.   But the flow of *vehicles* on the roads in central London increased by 3 to 4 per cent a year[2].

Urban traffic congestion is chiefly the result of the switch from public transport to the private car.   To take London again: only about 10 per cent of the commuters enter London by private transport, but (at $1\frac{1}{2}$ persons per car[3]) they account for half of the road vehicle flow[4].   In other big cities, the pattern is very

---

[1] British Railways Board, *Annual Report and Statement of Accounts . . . 1963*, p. 2.

[2] The average number of vehicles per mile of road in the day-time (excluding parked vehicles) in central London rose from 135 in 1954 to 167 in 1962—a rise of nearly 3 per cent a year.   The number of vehicles passing census points in the central London area in the day-time rose between 1952 and 1962 by $3\frac{3}{4}$ per cent a year.   The increase in other areas was faster still.   See Ministry of Labour and Ministry of Transport, *Report of the Committee of Inquiry to Review the Pay and Conditions of Employment of the Drivers and Conductors of the London Transport Board's Road Services* (London, 1964).

[3] Average occupancy of private cars is given as 1·54 on the journey to work, 1·69 for all journeys on Monday to Friday, and 1·93 for all journeys in the week.   Data from sample surveys begun in 1961 by the Social Survey for Ministry of Transport ('Motor Car Ownership and Use', *Economic Trends*, June 1963, *loc. cit.*).

[4] Taking buses and private cars alone, at the peak in central London, and reckoning a bus as the traffic equivalent of 3 cars, the private cars are reckoned to account for less than a quarter of the number of travellers, but for 70 per cent of the traffic flow (R. J. Smeed and J. G. Wardrop, 'An Exploratory Comparison of the Advantages of Cars and Buses for Travel in Urban Areas', *Institute of Transport Journal*, March 1964, p. 309).

Table 11.9.   *Usage of private cars*

Passenger-miles

	Total cars licensed ('000s)	Total billion	Passenger-miles ('000s) per car
1952	2,508	37·9	15·1
1953	2,762	42·1	15·2
1954	3,100	47·2	15·2
1955	3,526	54·3	15·4
1956	3,888	59·5	15·3
1957	4,187	59·9	14·3
1958	4,549	72·9	16·0
1959	4,966	82·1	16·5
1960	5,526	88·9	16·1
1961	5,979	97·7	16·3
1962	6,556	103·7	15·8

Sources: Cars licensed: *Annual Abstract of Statistics, 1963* (Great Britain, September of each year).

Passenger-miles: estimates from 'Passenger Transport in Great Britain', *Economic Trends,* November 1963, page v; figures based on traffic counts.

similar.   The proportion of commuters entering by car is estimated to be about 10 per cent or less in Birmingham, Glasgow and Manchester.   But it rises to 15–25 per cent in moderate-sized cities (Cardiff, Coventry, Leeds, Leicester, Newcastle upon Tyne)[1], and is higher still in many small towns.

If recent trends were to continue, the flow of road passenger vehicles in urban areas would probably increase by at least 5 per cent a year.   Passenger-mileage by urban *public* transport has fallen by more than 1 per cent a year over the past decade (table 11.8, taking the figures for British Railways season tickets, London Transport and 'mainly urban' bus services).   If we assume that this 1 per cent of passengers has transferred to private cars, that alone would imply an annual increase in the number of *vehicles* on the road of more than 5 per cent[2].   In fact, the total number of passengers has also increased, so that the rate of growth of urban traffic must have been somewhat faster.

A shift away from private transport is already beginning to be seen in inner London, where the rate of increase in private car traffic is now slowing down. Congestion itself may be partly responsible[3], but there can be no doubt that parking restrictions and the extension of parking meters have greatly contributed to checking the use of cars.

[1]From a special inquiry conducted by the NIESR in 1963.   See G. F. Ray, 'Transport: Notes and Comments', *National Institute Economic Review*, May 1963, *op. cit.*, p. 26.

[2]Assuming that about two thirds of the traffic consists of private cars.

[3]Increasing congestion does not in itself seem to be a major factor; average traffic speed in central London, even at peak periods, has been increasing slightly since 1960, as a result of improved traffic regulation.

There are three ways of attack on the urban transport problem. First, road improvements and developments in traffic engineering on a substantial scale will be required to speed the flow of traffic even if the size of the flow increases only moderately. Second, the improvement of public transport facilities, both rail and road, is necessary to attract traffic. Whether this will be possible without subsidy is an open question. Because of the high costs of peak operations (and it seems unlikely that the staggering of working hours will go far to eliminate the peaks), the subsidizing of public transport may often be the only way of keeping fares low enough to attract traffic, and be very much cheaper than the massive expenditure on road improvements that will be insisted upon if private car traffic continues to grow fast. Third, as suggested above (page 328), methods are known by which road users can be charged specifically for the use of particular roads. As a result, the relative costs of private and public transport could be substantially changed; in these circumstances, the use of cars for commuting should be checked (except to the extent that the costs would often be spread by treatment as a business expense). It must be recognized, too, that although road charges may at first be confined to the most congested central areas, one of the effects will be to spread congestion to the suburbs; as time goes on, the areas to which road charges must apply will inevitably be extended.

On British Railways, commuting traffic has been fairly stable, and in total the suburban services just cover the direct costs, but contribute nothing to overheads (table 11.3). The London suburban services, however, do come 'near to covering their full cost' in spite of the intense concentration on peak periods[1]. As is recognized in the Beeching Report, this is only because of the saturation of the services and the consequent 'extreme discomfort' to which passengers are reduced. To extend the capacity of the London suburban railway services, which already carry nearly 40 per cent of the peak period commuters into central London, would be difficult and expensive south of the Thames because of the congestion near the terminals. To the north, there is still spare capacity. The London Transport underground services have been losing traffic slowly; financially they cover direct costs with a margin for overheads. Again, the limits on frequency of service must restrict the possibilities of increasing the amount of peak hour traffic. They now carry just over one third of the peak period commuters. The extension of the system—the Victoria Line—will allow some addition, but a very large proportion of its traffic is expected to be diversions from other public transport, for time-saving and comfort. For some years, the necessary increase in public transport of commuters in London must fall largely on the buses. The question is how much extra traffic the buses can take. At present they carry only about 17 per cent of the peak period commuters. If half of the natural growth of total passenger traffic (which must be

---

[1]Beeching Report, *op. cit.*, part 1, p. 20.

put at over 1 per cent a year[1]) were to be carried by the buses, this would mean an expansion of bus traffic of just over 4 per cent a year[2] (over the past ten years it has been falling by 4 per cent a year). This is probably more than can be expected.

In the longer term, more drastic and expensive solutions will be necessary to break the bottlenecks caused by the capacity limits for the suburban railways and the underground. Such solutions—which could take the form of further underground extensions running through the centre, new river bridges, the building of a new railway or a monorail system through built-up areas—must be seriously considered in formulating investment requirements for the next 10–15 years[3].

The alternative form of radical solution is to direct away from London the future expansion of industry, commerce, finance and administration (and not only away from inner London, because the traffic congestion problems of outer London threaten to become as serious as those of the centre).

Outside London, the possible solutions of the urban transport problem are somewhat different. The numbers of commuters—in relation to population—are much less than in London. But this advantage is offset by the relatively minor role played by the suburban railways in nearly all these cities. The suburban railways are significant in Birmingham, Cardiff, Glasgow, Leeds, Liverpool, Manchester and Newcastle upon Tyne; but in these, and all other towns outside London, the bulk of public transport falls on the bus services. Hence the road problem, although now less acute in most towns than in London, is different in degree rather than in kind; and the growth of private car traffic—generally accompanying, as in London, a declining use of buses—will in time lead to a road problem of the same intensity.

As in London, the main solution, at least in the short term, is likely to lie in the diversion of additional traffic from cars to buses. The existing suburban railways at present lose money heavily[4]. The Beeching Report, indeed, proposes the withdrawal of certain suburban services. The Report recognizes that in some cases 'it may be cheaper to subsidise the railways than to bear the other costs which will arise if they are closed'. It is, however, unlikely that an economic solution could be found in the extension of suburban railways, just

---

[1]Ministry of Housing and Local Government, *The South East Study* (London, 1964), p. 43, suggests an increase of not less than 20,000 a year (about 1½ per cent) in the number of daily commuters.

[2]This does not just mean carrying more passengers on existing bus routes. It may also mean new services to take some of the load of natural growth off suburban railways and the underground system.

[3]The present equivalence of underground and bus fares does not necessarily encourage the best distribution of passengers.

[4]As shown in table 11.3, all suburban railway services, including those in London, just cover their direct costs, making no contribution to overheads. Since the London railways come near to covering their total costs, and account for 85 per cent of the revenue, the accounting loss on other suburban railways must be relatively very large indeed.

because of the 'peakiness' of the demand. What is desirable, in many cities, is a more imaginative co-ordination between the railways and the municipal bus services[1].

For urban passenger transport we envisage, therefore, both for London and for other cities: (i) the introduction of policies which will check the rate of growth of private car traffic in towns by charges both for parking and for movement in the more congested areas; (ii) a reversal of the declining trend in urban bus traffic; and (iii) a limited growth in the suburban and underground railway traffic. If recent trends could be modified to the extent illustrated by our statistical projections, this would go far towards solving the biggest of our transport problems and one of the major problems for better urban planning.

(c) *Passenger transport as a whole*

The implications for expenditure on passenger transport as a whole are summarized in table 11.8. Precise figures are given for 1975 but it will of course be understood that the discussion from which the figures derive allows very wide margins of uncertainty. In particular, for passengers as for freight, the allocation of future traffic between the different forms of transport depends on the outcome of what is essentially a competitive process. We are suggesting that the terms on which competition operates will be modified by public policy, in the interests of minimizing the social costs of the inevitable expansion of the volume of transport. We are, further, suggesting that the drastic reorganization of the railway system now in progress will achieve at least some of the desired results. Both these suggestions are assumptions rather than forecasts. Both imply reversals of existing trends.

The major factor in the increase of expenditure on transport has been, and will continue to be, the growth of car ownership. Car ownership is not likely to be much affected by discouragement of the use of private cars in congested areas. Hence the estimate in chapter 6 (page 195) of the future trend of consumers' expenditure on purchase of vehicles may be regarded as consistent with some modification of the recent swing from public to private transport. The estimates used in chapter 6 imply an increase in the total number of cars in use from 5·5 million in September 1960 (7·4 million in 1963) to about 13–14 million in 1970, and perhaps around 17 million in 1975—tripling in 15 years[2]. The figure for 1975 would represent about one car per household.

[1]Beeching Report, *op. cit.*, part 1, p. 22
[2]An extrapolation of the estimates of cars in use from the study used in chapter 6 would in fact lead to around 22 million cars in 1975 (the figure relates to Great Britain). It seems reasonable, however, to suppose that the income and long-term trend determinants will not continue to operate indefinitely on the total number of cars in use; some of their effect may be transferred to more rapid replacement or higher quality, as the number of cars approaches 1 per household.

For considering traffic problems, it is of course the *usage* of cars which is relevant, not the total stock.   But in recent years, there seems to have been no significant tendency towards any change in average mileage per car (see table 11.9).

4. INVESTMENT IN THE RAILWAYS

For British Railways, the upshot of the projections (summarized in table 11.10) is:

> (a)   a rise, taken as about 3 per cent a year, in total freight traffic—roughly the same rate of increase as the rate of decline during the past decade; this would bring total freight traffic in 1975, at 25 billion ton-miles, to a somewhat higher volume than has been achieved before, on a smaller route mileage[1];

> (b)   approximate stability in passenger traffic at about 21–22 billion passenger-miles, but again on about two thirds of the existing system.

The concentration of a higher volume of traffic on two thirds of the present system would not in itself create a problem since the sections expected to be closed already carry so little traffic (although traffic might approach capacity at a few places).   Greater expansion seems possible for freight than for passenger traffic, because the only potential gains in passenger traffic are concentrated in two categories: first in long-distance traffic, where the railways already hold a large proportion of total traffic; second in suburban traffic, especially in London. It seems highly desirable that schemes for further development of suburban railway systems—including extensions of the London Transport railway system —should be elaborated.   This may still prove the cheapest way of coping with the further expansion of London.   But, just because of the unavoidable peaks of traffic, it is improbable that such extensions would offer a reasonable profit to British Railways (or London Transport).   Their justification, like that of the Victoria Line, may rather be found in the contribution that they might make to speeding up the flow of traffic generally and to avoiding the need for more radical physical reconstruction.

The modernization of the railway system—as set out in the modernization programme of 1955[2] and subsequent revisions[3]—was first conceived as involving massive capital expenditure.   The first proposals (of 1955) envisaged a total of £1,200 million (1954 prices) of which about half was regarded as normal

---

[1]In wartime, under heavy pressure, total ton-mileage rose to 24 million ton-miles.   In the inter-war peak years, about 18–19 million ton-miles were carried (in 1923–4, 1929 and 1937); in 1912, about 20 million ton-miles.

[2]British Transport Commission, *Modernisation and Re-equipment of British Railways*, *loc. cit.*

[3]British Transport Commission, *Proposals for the Railways*, Cmd 9880 (London, 1956), and *Re-appraisal of the Plan for the Modernisation and Re-equipment of British Railways*, Cmnd 813 (London, 1959).

Table 11.10. *Summary of railway traffic projections*

	1952–4	1960–2	1975	Percentage changes 1952–4 to 1960–2 Per year	1960–2 to 1975 Per year
Freight (billion ton-miles)	22·4	17·5	25·4	−3·0	+2·7
Passengers (billion passenger-miles)					
British Railways	20·6	20·8	21·5	+0·1	+0·2
London Transport	3·5	3·1	3·5	−1·5	+0·9
Total passengers	24·1	23·9	25·0	−0·1	+0·3

Source: Tables 11.4 and 11.8.
Note: The figures relate to Great Britain.

maintenance. Actual investment began to increase substantially in 1957—after many years in which it can have represented little more than maintenance of assets. The *Re-appraisal* of 1959 increased the estimate of new investment required to £1,500 million (1958 prices); and proposed a greater concentration of the programme within the years 1959–63. Investment was to increase from about £180 million in 1959 to £200 million or more in each of the years 1961 to 1963[1]. It was expected in 1959, on certain assumptions about the growth of the economy and the improvements which it was hoped to make in railway operations, that the working results (excluding interest payments) would turn from a deficit of £27 million a year to a surplus of £25 million or more by 'about the end of the year 1963', through cost reductions, increased traffic (passenger but not freight) and higher fares (again, from passengers only)[2].

The policy of rapid and heavy re-equipment was reversed not long after it had been reappraised and confirmed. Nothing like the projected amounts of capital expenditure were in fact spent. The years 1959–60 proved to be the peak and investment fell back rapidly to about £100 million (current prices) in 1963 and 1964. The Beeching Report (1963) put comparatively little emphasis upon expensive physical re-equipment and more emphasis on the reduction of working costs[3]. The financial expectations of 1959 were not realized, but the year 1963 at least saw a substantial reduction of the deficit on railway working, to £87 million (from £109 million in 1962)[4]. The improvement was the result

[1] These figures relate to total investment by British Railways and appear to cover a wider range than the statistics of investment in railways in *National Income and Expenditure* (although the latter also includes London Transport railways and Northern Ireland).
[2] British Transport Commission, *Re-appraisal, loc. cit.*, para. 111.
[3] There is no specific estimate of total capital investment in the Beeching Report. But (p. 55) it notes that continuing replacement of steam by diesel traction, the introduction of liner trains and reorganization of sundries traffic 'would involve capital expenditure of the order of £250 million' over an unstated period. It also notes, however, that existing modernization schemes, including electrification on the London Midland Region, would go ahead.
[4] These figures exclude interest charges, but include depreciation and amortization of £55 million in 1963. It is pointed out that if depreciation were reckoned at replacement cost, it—and the deficit—would be higher by £24 million (British Railways Board, *Annual Report and Statement of Accounts, 1963, loc. cit.*).

of falling expenses while receipts were constant. Excluding the effect of wage increases (and some minor price changes) which wiped out part of the gains, the reduction in working costs in 1963 is estimated at £34 million[1], or 6 per cent, on a 1962 total of £570 million.

One big reason given for the improvement is the saving resulting from replacement of steam by diesel traction, with its lower fuel and labour costs. This is the major item in the original modernization programmes on which progress has been rapid. By 1963, diesel traction, which was introduced on a substantial scale only about 1957–8, accounted for 46 per cent of total traction hours; electric traction for only 9 per cent. It was only in 1962 that steam traction fell below 50 per cent.

The biggest reason for the improvement in 1963, however, must have been the better use of labour and train capacity. While total traffic, in terms of passenger-miles and ton-miles, was constant, total train-miles were reduced by 3 per cent; and the total staff was reduced by 8 per cent. Line closures had hardly begun to affect costs in 1963.

This suggests that the goal of financial balance on working account may not be so far out of sight as the disappointments of 1959–62 might suggest. The potential annual cost reductions outlined in the Beeching Report, to be achieved over a period of years, were put at £95–£111 millions[2]. To this may be added the £50 million expected to be saved from cutting out duplicated main lines. These various savings are not wholly additive and will not all be realized. Yet savings increasing by £10–£15 million each year (2–2½ per cent of total working expenses) may well be feasible over a number of years.

These estimates are made at 1962–3 wages and prices. It may be assumed that rising fares and freight rates could compensate for increases in wages and other costs equal to those in the economy as a whole. But it must also be accepted that part of the effect on the deficit will be eroded by a rise in relative wages of railway workers. A rise in relative wages of 10 per cent would add £35 million to costs once for all. On the other hand, an increase in the more profitable classes of traffic, as suggested in our projections, will add about £6 million a year (at 1963 fares and freight rates) to gross receipts and should make some contribution to net earnings.

It is thus just possible to envisage an approximate balance of working receipts and expenses by about 1970. The chances of achieving a working surplus anything like sufficient to pay interest charges must be regarded as very small[3].

[1]British Railways Board, *Annual Report . . . 1963 loc. cit.*, p. 27 of the *Report*.
[2]Beeching Report, *op. cit.*, pp. 54–5. The figures quoted above relate to cost reductions only, and exclude potential increases in net earnings in the Report.
[3]In 1963, the deficit, before interest, of the British Railways Board (taking into account activities other than the railways—ships, letting of property, etc.) was £76 million. In addition, interest charges were put at £58 million; and will increase. Working expenses include provision for depreciation only at historic cost. If (following the principles laid down in the Treasury, *The Financial and Economic Obligations of the Nationalised Industries*,

It seems likely that effective concentration of the British Railways Board's own efforts on cost saving, reinforced by Treasury caution, will continue to accompany a much slower rate of physical re-equipment than was originally intended—at least until the financial position is restored. For some years, investment may remain at not much over £100 million a year. This probably implies, among other things, a rather slow progress of main line electrification.

It is not unreasonable to suppose that after a few years a new programme of re-equipment will be desirable, if the railways have succeeded in turning the tide. Besides re-equipment—and possibly further electrification if relative fuel costs justify it—provision must be made for new development of suburban services. A preliminary appreciation by British Railways of the possibilities of expanding London suburban services to provide for the expected additional peak hour movements arrives at a total capital cost of £100 millions; it is suggested that the cost to London Transport might be even heavier[1].

The London Transport Board (with total investment of about £11—£12 million a year) is already engaged in the Victoria Line scheme, which is scheduled for completion by about 1967; the total cost is estimated at over £50 million.

Comparatively little planning has so far been done for suburban railway expansion (apart from the Victoria Line), and similar developments may eventually be needed in some other cities than London. It seems quite probable that in the late 1960s there will be a very substantial increase in investment in railways—both main line and suburban—that will continue well into the 1970s. For the projections of the investment level around 1975 (table 11.15), a figure of £175 million has been adopted for the railway systems.

5. INVESTMENT IN ROADS AND ROAD TRANSPORT

Total road traffic is expected, according to the projections described above, and summarized in table 11.11, to rise by $6\frac{1}{2}$ per cent a year. By 1975 it would be nearly $2\frac{1}{2}$ times as great as in 1960–2. This projection is not very different from the 5–6 per cent annual increase which has occurred in the past ten years and which is now accepted as a basis for future road and traffic planning[2]. But we are suggesting that the pattern of the traffic increase may change somewhat—with a 9 per cent annual increase in inter-urban traffic (which on the arbitrary definition here includes rural traffic—indeed all traffic outside towns), and a

Cmnd 1337, London, 1961) depreciation at replacement cost were included, the working surplus at which the Railways Board should aim, for all its activities, would be over £80 million in 1963.
[1]Ministry of Housing and Local Government, *The South East Study*, loc. cit., p. 45. The estimates appear to be based on what are considered the maximum physical possibilities, allowing British Railways alone to cater for another 450,000 peak hour commuters for the London area as a whole. On the forecast in the *The South East Study*, this would cover requirements for much longer ahead than 1975.
[2]Hall Report, *op. cit.*, para. 63.

Table 11.11. *Summary of road traffic projections*

	Vehicle-miles 1960–2 (billions) (1)	Equivalent private car miles 1960–2 (billions) (2)	Percentage increase in traffic 1960–2 to 1975 Total (3)	Per year (4)	Equivalent private car miles, 1975 (billions) (5)
Inter-urban					
Private motor vehicles	28	28	*359*	*11·5*	128
Public service vehicles	0·9	2·7	*7·6*	*0·5*	2·9
Commercial vehicles (excluding vans)	5·1	15·3	*66*	*3·7*	25·4
Light vans	4·4	4·4	*66*	*3·7*	7·3
Total	38	50	*228*[a]	*8·9*[a]	164
Urban					
Private motor vehicles	27	27	*56*	*3·2*	42
Public service vehicles	1·5	4·5	*27·8*	*1·8*	5·7
Commercial vehicles (excluding vans)	4·7	14·1	*68*	*3·8*	23·8
Light vans	5·4	5·4	*50*	*2·9*	8·1
Total	39	51	*57*[a]	*3·3*[a]	80
Total all areas	77	101	*141*[a]	*6·5*[a]	244

Sources: Col. (1) estimated from table 19 of J. C. Tanner, H. D. Johnson and J. R. Scott, *Sample Survey of the Roads and Traffic of Great Britain, op. cit.* This paper, based on traffic counts in 1959–60, analyses traffic in each class of vehicle between 'rural' and 'urban' roads—the distinction is not exactly the same as that made in other tables between 'long-and medium-distance' and 'urban' traffic.

Col. (2) uses the usual equivalents: 1 private car = 0·33 heavy commercial vehicle or bus = light van.

Col. (3): the projections for each line are those made in table 11.8 for passenger traffic, in passenger-miles, and in table 11.4 for freight traffic, in ton-miles (all coal and iron and steel traffic is treated as 'inter-urban').

[a]Increase in total equivalent private car miles.

3 per cent annual increase within towns[1]. This difference in rates of expansion, as has been emphasized, depends on a successful policy of attracting urban passengers back to public transport. It may well be over-optimistic to expect this to happen.

The present programme of investment in roads is inevitably concentrated on going some way towards catching up with the past growth of traffic. Total

[1]In urban areas generally, traffic has been growing at about the same rate as in rural areas over the past few years. But traffic in central city areas may have been increasing more slowly (Ministry of Transport, *Roads in England and Wales ... 1962–63*, para. 31),

Table 11.12. *Investment in roads*

£ million

	1961–2	1962–3	1963–4 estimate	1964–5 programme	1967–8 estimate	Five-year programme 1964–5 to 1968–9 Total	Annual average	1975 projection
Motorways and trunk roads	53	66	84	100	..	over 500	over 100	250
Classified roads	38	47	57	63	..	under 500	under 100	325b
Total officially programmed	91	113	141	163	225	1,000	200	575
Unclassified roads, street lighting, etc.a	18	19	22	22	25	..	25	75
Total	109	132	163	185	250	..	225	650

Source: (except for last column) Treasury, *Public Investment in Great Britain, October 1963*, Cmnd 2177 (London, 1963); Ministry of Transport, *Roads in England and Wales . . . 1962–63*; *Public Expenditure in 1963–64 and 1967–68, loc. cit.*

Note: All figures relate to Great Britain. Figures for 1964–5 and later are at 1963 prices; others are current prices. All include cost of land purchase.
aIncludes local authority expenditure on car parks.
bIncludes at least £250 million for urban roads.

capital expenditure[1] began to increase significantly only in 1956–7, with the first serious long-term programme—envisaging expenditure of about £60 million a year in 1957 to 1960.   By 1961, expenditure for the first time exceeded £100 million.   In 1964–5, it is planned to reach £185 million.   Under the current five-year programme which exceeds £1,000 million (1964–5 to 1968–9), expenditure will mount to about £250 million a year (at 1963 prices—see table 11.12).

The five-year capital programme is divided about equally between expenditure on motorways and trunk roads on the one hand (these are wholly financed by central government) and, on the other, expenditure on classified roads, on which expenditure is shared between the central government and the local authority. (Capital expenditure on unclassified roads is relatively small and is mainly financed by local authorities; it is not included in the programme.)   The bulk of the programme for classified roads consists of expenditure on major improvements of main roads in the conurbations and large cities[2]; the main roads in cities and large towns are classified roads, not trunk roads.

Although the programmed expenditure is about equally divided, the weight of expenditure in the early years—as for some years past—falls on the development of the motorway and trunk road systems.   However, if the present programme is kept to, expenditure on these roads will already have nearly reached its peak in 1964–5, at £100 million—over half of it on the motorways.   Expenditure on classified roads (£63 million in 1964–5) has still a long way to climb.   By the later 1960s, to achieve the programme, it may well need to rise to around £110 million a year or more.

(a) The trunk road network

Expenditure on the motorways and trunk roads is still aimed at completing 1,000 miles of motorway—most of it new roads—by the early 1970s, of which about 750 is expected to be completed by 1969; together with modernizing by 1969 about 750 miles of existing trunk roads and improving others[3].   The whole trunk road system of the United Kingdom in 1964 is about 9,000 miles.

[1]Capital expenditure on roads, both for Parliamentary Vote purposes and for national accounts, is defined as new construction and major improvements.   It should be noted that in addition about £200 million a year is now spent on maintenance and 'minor improvements' ('essentially improvements within the limits of the existing highway which betters the structure or alignment of the road'—Roads in England and Wales 1962-63, loc. cit., Ministry of Transport, para. 83).   The figures of capital expenditure used in the text are generally those published by the Ministry of Transport and Scottish Development Department.   They relate to Great Britain.   They differ only slightly (see notes to table 11.12) from the figures in the National Income and Expenditure Blue books.

[2]Roads in England and Wales . . . 1962–63, loc. cit., p. 31.   Indeed of £12 million of classified road schemes costing over £100,000 each, completed during 1962–3, over £5 million is accounted for by the Park Lane–Hyde Park Corner scheme alone.

[3]Roads in England and Wales . . . 1962–63, p. 7, suggests that about 600 miles will have been modernized between 1958 and 1969.   Since then, the five-year programme has been accelerated; and an allowance must be made for expenditure in Scotland.

It is indeed doubtful whether the present programme is calculated to keep pace with the growth of traffic.   One of the methods of assessing the need for road improvements is to measure the extent to which existing roads are 'overloaded' by relating the volume of traffic, from traffic censuses, with the estimated design capacity of the roads.   One such estimate showed that in 1960 about 2,600 miles of trunk roads were overloaded (table 11.13)[1].   The authors went on to show that at the current rate of increase of traffic—about 6 per cent a year—the mileage of overloaded roads would rise by about 10 per cent a year; on this rather theoretical basis, about 250 extra miles a year of trunk roads would stand in need of major improvement—generally widening—or replacement by new roads.   This seems to be more than the annual mileage of new motorways and reconstructed existing trunk roads to be provided under the present programme[2].

It seems clear that by the middle 1970s there will still be a backlog to be made up before an efficient trunk road network can be said to exist.   Moreover, if we are right in projecting for inter-urban traffic an annual rate of expansion significantly greater than in the past few years, then the growth of traffic will require substantially greater annual expenditure than that now provided.   For these reasons, we suggest that the annual rate of expenditure on the trunk road network—£100 million now and, under the present programme, for the rest of this decade—will have to rise well before 1975 to about £250 million.   At present costs, this would allow the annual construction of perhaps 300–500 miles of new and modernized roads.   If expenditure could be more than doubled by the early 1970s, then by 1975 there could be well over 1,000 miles of new road (including the motorways) and about 3,000 miles of the 8,500 miles of existing trunk roads could have been completely modernized.   It seems likely that expenditure at something like this rate would be needed for some years after 1975, even if, as is possible, the rate of expansion of traffic begins to slow down with the declining rate of growth in car ownership.

(b) *Classified roads—inter-urban and rural*

Of 86,000 miles of classified roads almost 70,000 can be described as 'non-urban' (table 11.13).   Even if the bulk of inter-urban traffic could be carried by the main trunk network, many of the non-urban classified roads will continue to be needed as feeder roads and will be affected by the growth of traffic.   At present, it is estimated that about 2,700 miles of classified non-urban roads are overloaded—as large a mileage as that of overloaded trunk roads.

[1]J. C. Tanner, H. D. Johnson and J. R. Scott, *Sample Survey of the Roads and Traffic of Great Britain, op. cit.,* table 34.

[2]The Ministry of Transport's calculation is that early in 1963 about 1,170 miles of trunk road in England and Wales were' severely' overloaded.   The Ministry pointed out that improvement of 'a substantial mileage of overloaded trunk road must wait until the 1970s. During the present decade, therefore, conditions on many trunk roads must continue to get worse' (*Roads in England and Wales . . . 1962–63*, p. 7).

Table 11.13. *The road network of Great Britain*

| Type of road | Urban roads | | | Non-urban roads | | |
| | Total miles | 'Overloaded' | | Total miles | 'Overloaded' | |
		Miles	Per cent		Miles	Per cent
Trunk	1,723	1,100	*64*	6,543	2,600	*40*
Class I	6,296	3,000	*48*	13,376	2,000	*15*
Class II	3,927	800	*20*	13,721	600	*4*
Class III	5,456 ⎤	700	*2*	43,370 ⎤	100	*0·1*
Unclassified	38,927 ⎦			55,854 ⎦		
Total	56,329	5,600	*10*	132,864	5,300	*4*

Source: J. C. Tanner, H. D. Johnson and J. R. Scott, *Sample Survey of the Roads and Traffic of Great Britain, op. cit.,* tables 2 and 34.   The estimate of overloaded roads relates to 1960.   'Overloaded' roads are those which traffic counts showed to be carrying traffic in excess of design capacity.   The total mileage of roads relates to 1956; but there was very little change in total mileage in any of these categories between 1956 and 1960.

The present level of capital expenditure on such roads is not stated.   Part of the overloading will disappear as the trunk road system is improved, and the costs of improvement of the rest will be much less than for trunk roads.   Nevertheless, it seems not unreasonable that capital expenditure of up to £50 million will be needed to bring this part of the road system up to the standards required for the traffic of the 1970s.

(c) *Classified roads—urban*

Measured simply by the mileage of overloaded roads, the order of magnitude of the urban road problem is the same as for non-urban roads—there are about 5,000–6,000 miles of overloaded roads in each category (table 11.13).   The proportion of roads which are overloaded is, of course, much greater in the towns.   Under the present five-year programme, rather less is likely to be spent on urban than on non-urban roads—perhaps substantially less on actual construction since the programmed cost of urban roads includes a much larger proportion for purchase of land than for non-urban roads[1].   Moreover, the rate of total expenditure on urban roads is at present at a very much lower level, in relation to the five-year average under the 1964–9 programme, and will need to be more than doubled by 1969.   By that date (see page 356) total expenditure on classified roads will probably need to rise to about £150 million a year compared with about £60 million now.

A survey of the present road plans of a considerable number of British towns (other than London) was undertaken by the National Institute of Economic and Social Research in early 1963; and is summarized in table 11.14.   Of the 54 towns approached, nearly all had plans (of some kind) for major road develop-

---

[1]See table 11.12.   The bulk of expenditure on classified roads, which is rather less than half the total programme, is for urban roads (see p. 355).   On urban roads, over 20 per cent of the cost is for land purchase. against an average of under 5 per cent for non-urban roads.

Table 11.14. *Road development plans of some British towns*

	Population ('000)[a]	Estimated cost of road development plans (£m.)[b]		Estimated number of years the work would take[c]	Expenditure on construction	
		Con-struction	Land		Per head	£ per head per annum
Bristol	436	59·0	16·0	20	46	2·3
Cambridge	95	1·6	0·4	5	17	3·4
Darlington	84	1·5	1·0	20	18	0·9
Dundee	183	0·6	0·5	9	3	3·3
Glasgow	1,055	20·0	4·0	15	19	1·3
Huddersfield	130	4·0	2·8	20	31	1·6
Manchester[d]	661	65·1	18·3	20	98	4·9
Newcastle upon Tyne	269	26·0	9·0	20	93	4·7
Newport, Mon.	108	5·5	5·2	20	51	2·6
Northampton	105	1·6	1·1	10	15	1·5
Norwich	120	3·6	2·1	6	30	5·0
Preston	113	2·5	2·4	20	22	1·1
Southend on Sea	165	3·2	1·8	16	19	1·2
Sunderland	190	0·8	1·9	8	4	0·6
Swansea	167	5·5	1·5	25	33	1·3
Wolverhampton	150	7·0	3·0	15	47	3·1
Cardiff	256	6·0	2·0[f]	20	23	1·2
Doncaster	86	3·0	1·0[f]	14	35	2·5
Ipswich	117	16·5	5·5[f]	21	141	6·7
Leeds	511	20·0	5·0[f]	15	39	2·6
Luton	132	1·5	0·5[f]	10	11	1·1
Middlesbrough	157	2·7	0·8[f]	8	17	2·1
Walsall	118	2·0	0·6[f]	7	17	2·4
Total of above	5,408	259·2	76·4	15[e]	48	3·2

Source: NIESR survey carried out in January 1963. We are indebted to the town clerks, city architects and surveyors and other officials of the cities and towns co-operating with us in this survey.

Note: The *Birmingham* Inner (Bull Ring) Road scheme cost £23 million; of this approximately £10 million was represented by constructional costs of road works. The cost of one mile of dual carriageway within this scheme was £2¾ million per mile.

[a]Census of Population, 1961. The figures indicate the population of the city or town proper; they exclude those living in adjoining but administratively separate boroughs.

[b]Plans as reported in January 1963. As far as possible the figures refer to the estimated cost of roadbuilding and exclude the cost of acquisition of land and property as well as the cost of erection of buildings connected with the road development.

[c]These figures are necessarily vague as many of the plans have not yet passed the necessary stages of approval.

[d]In addition, a comprehensive development plan has been worked out for the whole SELNEC (South-East Lancashire and North-East Cheshire) area. This is, for the time being, the most elaborately phased programme of this kind. It totals £242 million and covers an area with a population of 2·3 million, thus giving a per head expenditure of £105 (some £80–£85 excluding land costs). Of this total, works valued at £93 million are being scheduled for the ten-year period 1963–72, equalling a per head quota of £4 per annum.

[e]Weighted average.

[f]The land cost data for these towns have been estimated: the basis of the estimate was the average of the data in the first group of cities and towns for which the division of total costs into construction and land acquisition costs had been given by the city authorities. It appears that, on the average, about one quarter of the total estimated costs of road development is accounted for by land and property acquisitions though this varies widely (e.g., 22 per cent in Manchester, 37 per cent in Norwich, 45 per cent in Dundee and Preston).

ments, ranging from a number of small projects to ambitious rebuildings of whole city centres. The local authorities of 23 towns, with a total population of over 5 million, were able to express their plans in expenditure figures and to say how long they might take. Much of the work in these programmes, of course, has not yet been officially approved, and the periods covered vary between 5 and 20 years, with an average of 15 years.

A general average of the figures received shows annual expenditure on construction alone, excluding land, of £3·2 per head. If these figures may be grossed up to cover all towns and conurbations with a population of 50,000 or more, including London (a total population of 30 million in Great Britain) the total expenditure would amount to £100 million a year, excluding land, or about £125 million a year including land. Allowing a rather smaller proportionate figure for smaller urban areas might bring the total up to about £125 million excluding land, or £150 million including land. This figure is not very different from that implied for the late 1960s by the present five-year programme.

Is it possible to estimate the 'adequacy' of capital expenditure on this scale?

Only the first steps have yet been taken towards assessing the total cost of urban road development. It is clear that road development cannot be considered in isolation from the much larger problems of urban reconstruction as a whole. It is bound up with the problems of raising the whole standard of housing and urban living. Moreover, the discussion above of the possible growth of traffic in towns shows that a policy for the development of public transport might substantially slow down the growth of traffic. The usual basis for urban road planning at present is a doubling of traffic in 10 years—an annual growth rate of 7 per cent a year. We have suggested that this rate of growth could possibly be halved. Even if this were accepted, however, it would not proportionately affect the need for road development, because so much is needed—and will continue to be needed well into the 1970s—to provide for the present volume of traffic.

The best known studies of radical schemes for reconstruction of urban road systems are those made by Professor Buchanan[1]. The emphasis in the Buchanan Report was not of course on costs, but rather on a demonstration of the practicability of a systematic analysis of the urban traffic problem not only now but for 50 years hence. For this purpose, case studies were conducted in a handful of urban areas leading to proposals for a complete transformation of the road patterns. This transformation was based on rapid expansion in the use of cars—though not perhaps for the full demand potential that might be implied by doubling the motor vehicle stock in ten years, or trebling it in twenty. The Buchanan Report gave the roughest estimates of capital cost for two towns— Leeds (population of 511,000) and Newbury (37,000)—with no suggestion that

---

[1]Ministry of Transport, *Traffic in Towns: a Study of the Long Term Problems of Traffic in Urban Areas* (Buchanan Report) (London, 1963).

these were to be regarded as typical for towns of their size.   So far as they go, the cost figures were: for Leeds £90 million, or £175 per head of population; for Newbury, £4½ million, or £120 per head[1].   In both cases, the costs include land acquisition, but are for the 'primary networks' of roads only.   They appear to cover what might be needed to provide for the traffic of the year 2010.   The precise period is not of major importance, since so much of the reconstruction would be needed for catching up present needs and providing for the faster rate of traffic expansion in the earlier years.

If any conclusion may be drawn from these estimates, it is that existing plans (the figures quoted above of around £4 a head, including land, for 15 years) fall far short of what would be needed to create a substantially smoother flow of road traffic within the next 10–20 years.

It would be absurd, taking into account our present very limited knowledge even of present traffic requirements, and of the wide scatter of potential benefits to be gained by different schemes of development, to propose any precise figures as an estimate of the total need for capital expenditure on urban needs. Nor is it possible to assess relative priorities.

However, we suggest that if expenditure on urban roads were to rise from its present level of under £60 million a year to a figure of around £275 million in the mid-1970s[2], then a quite substantial advance would have been made towards the solution of the urban traffic problem.   This figure is intended to allow for the change in traffic patterns, suggested above, towards the revival of public transport (and to this extent is based on much easier assumptions than that of the Buchanan Report).   It is a figure, too, which appears to us broadly in line with the scale of investment in other sections of the economy, in relation to the needs for development so far as they can at present be assessed.

(d) *Total investment in roads*

Table 11.15 below summarizes the projected levels of capital expenditure in 1975.   Is so great an increase over the present rate of investment expenditure on roads feasible?   Investment expenditure and current maintenance of roads should be considered together.   Maintenance expenditure is now nearly £200 million a year and should increase—but not proportionately to investment. In real terms, it has risen about 50–60 per cent in the past ten years.   If maintenance expenditure is put at £300 million in 1975, then total expenditure on road construction and maintenance (excluding land) would increase about two and a half times over about twelve years—an annual rate of increase of about 8 per cent a year.   Over the past ten years, the rate of expansion in real

---

[1]Buchanan Report *op cit*: for Leeds para. 218, for Newbury para. 173.
[2]This figure includes land purchase.   Excluding land, it can be put at about £225 million. In terms of annual expenditure per head of population in cities of 50,000 or over, this might represent about £7, including land.

Table 11.15. *Total investment in roads*

	1963–4	1964–5 planned	£ million 1975 projection (1963 prices)
As in official programmes for Great Britain, including land			
Motorways and trunk roads	84	100	250
Classified roads			
Non-urban	} 57	63	{ 50
Urban			275
Total programmed	141	163	575
Unclassified roads, and street lighting, etc. (including local authority parking places)	22	22	75
Total	163	185	650[a]

[a]In *National Income and Expenditure*, the figures for fixed capital in roads, etc., are generally somewhat higher than the 'programme' figures given here. The Central Statistical Office figures exclude land, but include Northern Ireland and other adjustments are made. However, the projected figure for 1975 includes a much larger element for land purchases than current figures (especially because of the increasing proportion of urban roads). Hence in the summaries of investment projections in table 11.15 and in chapter 8, table 8.14, which are based on *National Income and Expenditure* definitions, the £650 million for 1975 at 1963 prices is regarded as equivalent to £600 million at 1960 prices.

terms may have been about 9 or 10 per cent a year[1].

Road work is at present only a little over 10 per cent of the total output of the construction industry as a whole (it is of course recognized that only a part of the construction industry is able to undertake large-scale road work). And it has been shown that the total of the central projections for demand for construction work of all kinds (including these projections for road work), would not lead to an increase in total output of the construction industry of more than about 3 per cent a year from 1960 to 1975 (chapter 7, table 7.7.). Hence, it is not suggested that these projections for expenditure on roads represent the maximum that the construction industry could do. It may well be physically possible to accelerate the present five-year programme and to provide for a higher rate of road construction in the 1970s than we have projected. Nor would this imply—in view of the scale of ultimate requirements, especially in urban areas—any slowing down in the second half of the 1970s.

It may easily be represented that a much larger volume of investment in roads during the next 10–15 years would be not only possible but desirable. Certainly, investment on the scale proposed here will leave much still to be done after

[1]On the basis of the Central Statistical Office figures of public authorities' current plus capital expenditure (*National Income and Expenditure, 1962*, table 44) deflated by the index of building prices (other than for dwellings) in *National Institute Economic Review* Statistical Appendix. But this price index is not necessarily appropriate for road work, and the calculation of the real increase in the past is very dubious.

1975, to make good long-standing arrears as well as to keep pace with growth of traffic. The work of reshaping the urban road system will only have begun. We have done no more than make an impressionistic guess at the appropriate scale of expenditure in relation to other calls on an expanding economy. A more precise assessment is impossible until far more systematic analysis has been made of needs, of potential benefits, and of alternative methods of solution.

(e) Investment in road transport

To complete the picture of investment in road transport estimates must be added for investment in vehicles for *public passenger transport*. A significant increase in expenditure seems to be required to provide for expansion, in place of contraction, of bus transport. Investment has been running at about £36 million a year. An increase to £50 million in 1975 is suggested.

6.   TOTAL INVESTMENT IN INLAND TRANSPORT BY RAIL AND ROAD

The investment projections for rail and road transport are brought together in table 11.16. The total at 1960 prices rises from under £300 million in the last few years to a suggested total of £760 million in 1975 (at 1960 prices). Its share of total investment as shown in chapter 8 (table 8.14) rises from 7 to $9\frac{1}{2}$ per cent.

The projections provide not only for the growth of transport business, but also for catching up with past arrears in modernizing the rail and road network. It has been emphasized, too, that the size and form of network that will be appropriate to the 1970s depends in part on the determination of a clear policy, especially for coping with urban transport. We have also suggested that even if policy were determined, far more information and analysis is needed before the capital costs of an appropriate network can be estimated more than impressionistically. What is required first is a programme of what should be done over the course of 10–20 years. It might then be possible to consider how quickly it should be done. For all these reasons, any figures put down for a particular year, such as 1975, must be regarded as not much better than an order of magnitude. It cannot be claimed with any assurance that a system of expansion leading to £100 million more or less in 1975 would be inconsistent with the qualitative objectives which the projections given here are intended to accomplish.

It does, however, seem certain that the projected general scale of investment in road development in urban areas would fall very far short of meeting future needs if the use of private motor vehicles continued to grow at the same rate as in recent years. We have assumed, in particular, a substantial slowing down in the rate of expansion of car traffic in towns. As was made clear at the beginning of this chapter, this is most unlikely to happen unless public transport can be

Table 11.16.   *Total investment in transport*

	1960	1961	1962	1963	1975 at 1963 prices	£ million 1975 at 1960 prices
		(current prices)				
Railways	171	153	119	96	175	160
Roads and public lighting	88	109	132	149	650	600
Public road passenger transport	31	34	44	..	50	50
Total	290	296	286	279	825	810
Air transport (including airports)	54	47	35	40	..	125
Harbours, docks and canals	25	22	23	20	..	75
Shipping	162	132	107	84	..	250
Grand total	531[a]	497	451	423	..	1,260

[a]From *National Income and Expenditure, 1964*. The corresponding figure of 522 used in table 8.14 comes from the 1961 issue, which has been used for all the central calculations in this work.

improved and also unless policy is directed towards a system of charging motor vehicles according to their use of the roads. If these solutions are ruled out, then the projected scale of road investment in urban areas may do no more than stabilize the present degree of congestion.

7. INVESTMENT IN OTHER TRANSPORT

Problems of investment in air and sea transport have not been studied in the present work. But these branches at present absorb about £150–£200 million of investment and at least a rough projection for 1975 must be made as part of the estimate of overall investment requirements in chapter 8. Figures are given in table 11.16 but they are intended only as orders of magnitude.

For *air transport*, a substantial increase must be expected both in aircraft and in airport facilities. Most of the investment of £40–£50 million a year in recent years has been devoted to aircraft. But a continuing need for airports is bound to arise; by the mid-1970s, airports might be absorbing up to £50 million a year of capital expenditure.

The need for drastic improvements and reconstruction of British *ports* has become urgent. The Rochdale Committee's report[1] suggested total expenditure of £150 millions on certain major schemes of port development over the past ten to fifteen years—quite apart from the modernization of existing facilities. Mounting difficulties and delays in the shipping of exports have shown that the present facilities and methods of working in the ports are already overstrained. Without substantial improvements, the capacity of the ports may soon prove

[1]Ministry of Transport, *Report of the Committee of Inquiry into the Major Ports of Great Britain* (Rochdale Report), Cmnd 1824 (London, 1962).

to be a real bottleneck preventing the expansion of overseas trade which, as we have emphasized throughout this study, is a necessary condition for the faster growth of the economy.   We are therefore suggesting that by 1975 a tripling of recent rates of investment (which have been £20–£25 millions a year) may well be needed to provide an efficient port system.

The general expansion of international trade, and improving competitiveness of British shipbuilding and of the British merchant fleet implied by the general assumptions of this study, will call for greatly increasing investment in *shipping*. Investment in recent years has been rather more than £100 million a year (at 1960 prices), and completion in British yards of new vessels (excluding exports) about one million gross tons on average.   A round figure projection of £250 million investment in 1975 is suggested, although so high a figure may well be an overestimate of the long-term average.

CHAPTER XII

HOUSING

BY D. C. PAIGE

For the last hundred years or more nearly all the new houses built have been needed to add to the total stock of dwellings and replacement of old or sub-standard houses has been relatively small. This has been caused partly by a rapid growth in the number of households needing homes, and partly by the length of time required to make up for the cessation of new building during two world wars. In 1951 there were over 0·6 million more households than dwellings. Over the following ten years the number of dwellings increased by 2·4 million and the number of households by only 1·8 million (see table 12.2 below). By 1961 the overall shortage of dwellings was relatively small, although there were still local shortages particularly in the London area.

In future the rate of growth of the housing stock required will be determined almost entirely by the rate of growth in the number of households. This we expect to be slightly smaller than in the past. Substantial investment in dwellings will still be needed, but it will be needed mainly to raise housing standards through replacement—and improvement—of old houses. The level of investment required will be decided by the demand for improved standards of housing, and the rate of replacement that this involves.

The demand for housing, in this sense, can be considered either in terms of the market demand which depends upon incomes, prices and the elasticity of demand of householders for better houses, or in terms of some social assessment of housing needs. We have taken the view that a realistic appraisal of demand must involve a combination of both approaches. Because of the long period needed to correct imbalance in the housing stock it is a community responsibility to ensure that new building is adequate for long-term needs. It is also a recognized social responsibility to see that minimum housing standards are raised to an acceptable level. But at the same time we do not regard it as desirable or practicable to treat housing only as a social service like education or health. This is undesirable because expenditure on housing involves a wide field of choice which should be decided by individual consumer preferences. It is impracticable because of the enormous variety in the housing stock. We can aim to give every child a free education or every sick person free medical care according to some social assessment of need, but it would be impossible to allocate a highly heterogeneous stock of houses according to varying family needs.

Our aim is then to assess the rise in housing standards that consumers may demand as incomes rise, but without necessarily accepting this as the upper limit for which we should plan. If the demand for better housing at a full economic rent does not ensure the building of sufficient new houses of high enough quality both to raise minimum standards and to meet probable long-term needs we expect this to be supplemented by subsidy or other means.

In practice any assessment of the rise in consumer demand can only be extremely crude. After many years of rent control, housing shortage and slow income growth, past experience gives little guide to the rate at which house-holders may wish to improve their housing standards in free market conditions, with an adequate total supply of houses and more rapidly growing incomes. We have only attempted to assess how fast housing standards have improved in the past, and the rate of replacement that will be needed to ensure a continuation of this improvement.

In section 1 we consider housing requirements over the period 1960 to 1990 and alternative levels of investment for 1975 that this suggests. The analysis covers the rate of household formation and growth of the total stock of dwellings; the quality of the housing stock in terms of size and amenities; the age structure and replacement requirements; and, finally, total investment requirements both for new building and improvements. In section 2 we consider the implications of these proposals in terms of house tenure, rents, and the likely need for subsidies.

1. HOUSING REQUIREMENTS

(a) *The rate of household formation*

The rate of household formation depends mainly on demographic change, but it is also affected by changes in the extent to which people of different age groups and marital circumstances set up independent households. In 1951, the latest date for which we have complete information, 90 per cent of married men were heads of households; and among those over 40 years old the proportion was almost 97 per cent (appendix table 12.1). Among widowed and divorced people over 40, rates ranged from 64 per cent for men over 60 to 78 per cent for women between 40 and 59. The rates for single men and women over 40 ranged from 27 per cent to 47 per cent increasing with age. There were very few unmarried heads of households under 40.

Demographically then, the rate of household formation is determined mainly by the rate of growth of the total population over 40 and the number of married couples under 40. Between 1960 and 1975 we expect these groups to increase by 9 per cent, and from 1975 to 1990 by 7 per cent. With no change in the proportion of each group who are householders, the number of households would also increase by 9 per cent between 1960 and 1975 and by 8 per cent between 1975 and 1990.

In addition, however, we must make some allowance for the probable rise in headship rates. Between 1951 and 1961 the number of households increased

Table 12.1.   *Adult population^a by household status*

	Head of household	Spouses of heads	Other	Total adult population	Adult population per household
1931^b	37·9	28·2^c	33·9	100·0	2·95
1951	41·5	31·5	27·0	100·0	2·41
1960	46·2	35·3^d	18·5	100·0	2·21
1975^e	47·4	36·2	16·4	100·0	2·11
1990^e	47·7	36·6	15·7	100·0	2·09

Source: General Register Office and General Registry Office, Scotland, *Census 1951, Great Britain: One Per Cent Sample Tables* (London, 1952).

^{a}Defined as all married persons plus single persons of 20 and over.
^{b}England and Wales only (in 1951 the proportions for England and Wales were the same as those for Great Britain).
^{c}Average headship rates did not change from 1931 to 1951. It has been assumed, therefore, that average married headship rates were also the same.
^{d}Based on estimated married headship rates in appendix table 12.1.
^{e}Based on forecast headship rates in appendix table 12.1.

by 12 per cent, although on 1951 headship rates the increase would only have been about 7 per cent. Thus headship rates must have increased by about 5 per cent. We do not yet have information from the 1961 census to indicate where this increase occurred but as hardly any increase was possible in rates for married men over 40 it suggests a rise of some 10 per cent for younger married people, and the unmarried groups.

This rise was mainly due to the reduction in the housing shortage over the period. In 1951 many younger married couples and single people were sharing homes because of the shortage of accommodation. We expect some further rise over the next twenty years, but it cannot be very big. Headship rates have in the past only risen rather slowly, and in addition there is a limit set by the number of people choosing to live alone.

In 1931, 34 per cent of the adult population were non-householders in the sense that they were neither heads of households nor the wives of heads[1], and the number of adults per household was 2·6 (table 12.1). By 1961 there were only 2·2 adults per household and only 21 per cent of all adults were non-householders. As this 21 per cent includes the part of the adult population (3·7 per cent in 1951) living in institutions, and a fairly big proportion of young adults living with their parents prior to marriage, we do not think that it can fall very much further. Our assumptions on headship rates imply that by 1990 only 16 per cent of the adult population will be non-householders, and the number of adults per household may be little more than 2·1.

These estimates are probably a maximum. Income elasticity for separate houses seems to be fairly small. It is not possible to calculate headship rates by income group or social class, and not all members of households are of the same

[1]The adult population is defined as the population over 20, plus married persons under 20.

Table 12.2. *Dwellings and households in Great Britain, 1951–90*

	Number of dwellings	Number of households	Dwellings per 100 households
1951	13,831	14,482	95·5
1960	16,230	16,307	99·5
1975	18,990	18,421	103·1
1990	21,200	20,356	104·1

Source: Census 1951, Great Britain: One Per Cent sample Tables, loc. cit. and NIESR estimates.

social class. But estimates have been made of the distribution of adults in households of two persons or more according to the social class of the head (appendix table 12.2). In 1951 the number of persons over 15 per household fell by 2 or 3 per cent with each rise in social class, giving a total difference of 10 per cent between social class V and social classes I and II. The figures suggest, as we would expect, that a disproportionate number of the households that consisted of two primary families sharing a home were in the lower social classes. Many of these probably formed new households between 1951 and 1961. The rise in household formation that occurred from 1951 to 1961 was equivalent to raising the level of social class V to that of class III and the other classes proportionately. That envisaged over the next thirty years, would be roughly equivalent to raising each social class to the level of the one above.

In total our estimates indicate a rise of 2·11 million in the number of households between 1960 and 1975, and 1·94 million between 1975 and 1990 (table 12.2). Most of the increase is due to demographic change. If headship rates remained at their 1960 level there would still be increases of 1·52 million in the first period and 1·44 million in the second period (appendix table 12.1). Not every household requires a separate dwelling. Some people, particularly among those living in one-person households, will always prefer to share dwellings. But this factor will be more than offset by the need for some vacant houses, and, as incomes rise, a probable increase in the number of households with more than one dwelling. In total, therefore, we expect the stock of dwellings to need to rise by 2·76 million between 1960 and 1975, and by 2·21 million between 1975 and 1990.

(b) *The size of dwellings and households*

It is not possible to try to predict the sizes of dwellings required in twenty-five years' time without a detailed regional analysis which cannot be made here. The size and age distribution of houses varies considerably from one locality to another. A large-scale replacement programme such as we envisage should be able to meet the needs of population movement without adding to the total number of new houses. In general, the areas with an outward drift of population probably have the oldest housing stock and are likely to need a large amount of demolition. They should, therefore, get a reasonable share of new

Table 12.3.   *Distribution of households by size, Great Britain, 1951–90*

Percentages

	1951	1960[a]	1975[b]	1990[b]
All households				
1 person	9·9	11·3	16·3	16·6
2 persons	30·0	29·8	31·3	30·4
3 persons	24·9	24·6	20·5	20·5
4 or more persons	35·2	34·3	31·9	32·5
Total	100·0	100·0	100·0	100·0
Average size of households with 4 or more persons	4·8	4·3	4·7	4·8
Households with heads over 60				
Married heads				
2 persons	54·2	..	74·5	80·2
3 or more persons	48·8	..	25·5	19·8
Total	100·0	..	100·0	100·0
Unmarried heads				
1 person	42·2	..	77·9	79·1
2 or more persons	57·8	..	22·1	20·9
Total	100·0	..	100·0	100·0

Source: General Register Office, *Census 1951, England and Wales: Housing Report* (London, 1956) and P. G. Gray and R. Russell, *The Housing Situation in 1960: Inquiry Covering England and Wales*, Social Survey SS319 (London, 1962).

[a]England and Wales only.

[b]The forecasts are made on the assumption that the proportion of the population in institutions, hotels, etc., is the same as in 1951; that children and young people under 20 are distributed among households with heads under 60 in broadly the same proportions as in 1951; and that adults who are neither householders nor their wives are distributed among all households similarly to their distribution in 1951. As the number of children is expected to rise, and the number of non-householder adults to fall sharply this implies some increase in the size of households with younger heads, and a substantial fall in the size of households with heads over 60.

building even if some 'replacements' are built in other areas. But a balance of this kind is unlikely to be obtained for houses of particular sizes. There may well be a shortage of houses for larger families in the north currently with a surplus of large houses in the south.

We shall therefore only attempt a general view of trends in average size as they affect costs. Changes in the size of new homes required are likely to result from three factors: the effect of changes in family size and the size distribution of households; the demand for bigger houses as shortages disappear and incomes rise; and the size distribution of the dwellings demolished.

We do not expect the average size of households to change very much over the next thirty years. The small further fall that we expect in the number of adults per household will be offset by an increasing number of children. The total number of persons per household fell from 3·37 in 1951 to 3·13 in 1960 but is not expected to change between 1960 and 1990 (appendix table 12.1). There will, however, be a substantial change in the dispersion. We expect the proportion of one-person households to rise from 11 per cent to 16 per cent (table 12.3). This will be offset by some rise from 1960 onwards in the average size of households of four or more.

The increase in one-person households is due primarily to the rising proportion of elderly people in the population, but is increased further by their rising headship rates. In 1951 about a quarter of the single and widowed population over 60 lived alone, and 42 per cent of households with heads in this category were one-person units. By 1975 the proportion of the elderly unmarried population living alone may rise to nearly 50 per cent and about 78 per cent of households with unmarried heads over 60 may consist of people living alone. In addition we expect the proportion of older married couples living by themselves to rise from 54 per cent in 1951 to 75 per cent by 1975. This change will almost certainly entail an increase in the number of small easily managed dwellings for older people, many of which should be in small groups where help and some communal facilities can easily be given[1]. But it is not likely to result in a reduction in the average size of new building in general. Younger families with children will be increasing in size, and the indications are that as shortages disappear their demand for house space may rise significantly.

The rather crude indicator of rooms per person shows that there is quite a wide continuous spread between the space available per household according to social class (table 12.4). In 1960, 84 per cent of households in social classes I and II had more than one room per person compared with 65 per cent of those in social class V. Differences by tenure were even bigger; 87 per cent of owner-occupiers' houses had more than one room per person, compared with 64 per cent of local authority tenants. This can only be partly due to income differences, for in fact a large proportion of owner-occupiers have incomes below the average of council tenants (see table 12.13 below).

Council tenants are usually only offered a dwelling considered appropriate to the size of the family, so that their house-space is in fact rationed. This is a sensible way of dealing with a shortage of houses but not a system for which to plan. Another factor accounting for the low density of occupation of owner-occupiers is that families who own their houses tend to stay in them after the children are grown up. This is an institutional factor which might change if a larger supply of small homes for elderly people were available. But small new houses are always liable to cost more than larger older ones, and the problems of adapting furnishings and equipment remain.

Our conclusion is, therefore, that we should cater for an appreciable demand

[1]See chapter 13, 'Health and Welfare', p. 434.

Table 12.4.   *Density of occupation by fitness of dwellings, social class and tenure
of occupation in England and Wales*

	More persons than rooms	Persons equal to rooms	More rooms than persons	*Percentages* All sizes
All households				
1951	13·3	19·3	67·4	100
1960	9·8	15·2	74·9	100
1960				
By fitness of dwelling				
Short life	18·5	19·2	62·3	100
Medium life	10·6	15·2	74·2	100
Long life	8·1	14·4	77·5	100
By tenure				
Local authority	15·2	20·9	63·9	100
Other rented	13·4	18·8	67·8	100
Owner-occupied	3·8	8·8	87·2	100
By social class				
I and II	4	12	84	100
III	11	17	72	100
IV	12	20	68	100
V	17	18	65	100

Source: General Register Office, *Census 1951, England and Wales: Housing Report, loc.
cit.*, and P. G. Gray and R. Russell, *The Housing Situation in 1960, op. cit.*

for more space per head as incomes rise.   This would be partly because wealthier
families want bigger homes and partly because many people do not willingly
relinquish a house that is theoretically too big for present needs.   The results
of the Social Survey inquiry support this conclusion.   One of the most frequent
reasons given by people trying to move was that the present accommodation
was too small but few housewives who considered their accommodation too
large were trying to move.[1]

At the same time that the size distribution of households is expected to
become more widely dispersed, demolition will narrow the dispersion of dwelling
sizes because the older dwellings include a disproportionate share of the very
small and very large units (table 12.5).   The first two million houses to be
demolished will be well below average size.   Old houses tend to have small
rooms and the difference is in floor area rather than number of rooms.   The
short-life houses include more than a third of the dwellings with a floor area of
under 500 square feet and less than a tenth of those of over 750 square feet.
(For many dwellings the short life assessment may be partly due to the fact that
they are too small to modernize satisfactorily.)   The occupants of these substandard houses include a fairly high proportion of pensioners who will need

[1] P. G. Gray and R. Russell, *The Housing Situation in 1960, op. cit.*

Table 12.5. *Size of dwellings[a] and their length of life, England and Wales, 1960*

	All dwellings, per cent in each size class	Short life[b]	Medium life[c]	Long life[d]	Total
		Per cent of all dwellings of given size			
All dwellings (per cent)	100	13·3	19·4	67·3	100
Internal floor area (sq. ft.)					
Under 500	5	35	20	45	100
500–749	24	24	24	52	100
750–999	40	9	17	74	100
1,000–1,249	17	8	16	76	100
1,250 and over	14	7	23	70	100
Number of rooms[e]					
1–3	13	21	21	58	100
4	27	17	21	62	100
5	35	10	17	73	100
6	17	9	19	72	100
7 and over	8	11	22	67	100

Source: P. G. Gray and R. Russell, *The Housing Situation in 1960, op. cit.*

[a]Rateable units.
[b]Dwellings assessed by local authorities as unfit or likely to become so in less than 15 years.
[c]Dwellings assessed as having a life of 15 to 30 years.
[d]Dwellings assessed as having a life of over 30 years.
[e]'Habitable' rooms excluding bathrooms, structurally unusable rooms; kitchens are included if used for eating.

small houses, but they also include families at present overcrowded. (Nineteen per cent of households in short-life dwellings have less than one room per person, compared with 8 per cent of those in long-life dwellings (table 12.4)).

Replacement of medium-life houses is likely to start during the 1970s. This is a more heterogeneous group including many large old houses. The group contains a disproportionate number of converted flats and shared dwelling units, mainly in Greater London, so that actual sizes per household will be somewhat smaller than the figures based on rateable units imply. But the group also includes the main stock of big cheap houses for larger families.

Over the last 120 years the floor area of typical working-class houses has increased by about 0·5 per cent a year (table 12.6). In the period from 1840 to 1880 it rose rapidly by about 0·9 per cent a year, but over the last 80 years the rise has been slower, 0·3 per cent to 0·5 per cent a year. From 1880 to 1920 there was little measurable improvement in standards of new housing and since 1920 more than half of the improvement has been in quality (measured by cost per square foot at 1962 prices) and has taken place rather slowly. This has been caused partly by falling family size and partly by recent economies in public sector building standards.

In the future we expect the demand for space for a family of given size to grow more quickly than in the past, but this will be slightly offset by the increased

Table 12.6.   *Changes in size and quality of typical houses, 1840–1960*

New houses[a]	1840	1880	1920[b]	1962
Floor area, sq. ft.	435	625	705	825
Replacement cost (£1962)	700	1,200	1,375	2,025
Cost per sq. ft. (£1962)	1·61	1·92	1·95	2·45
Annual percentage increase				
Area		*0·9*	*0·3*	*0·4*
Cost per sq. ft.		*0·5*	—	*0·5*
Total cost		*1·4*	*0·3*	*0·9*

Total stocks[c]	1900	1920	1940	1960
Average replacement cost (£1962)	872	948	1,175	1,366
Annual percentage increase		*0·4*	*1·1*	*0·8*

Source: Appendix table 12.3 (estimates made for NIESR by D. Rigby Childs, ARIBA, AMTPI, in association with D. B. Connal, FRICS, and J. F. Green, FRICS).

[a]Based on the replacement cost in 1962 prices of typical working-class housing of each date, ranging from a 2-room cottage with privy in yard for 1840 to a Parker Morris type house with garage for 1962.

[b]The small increase in costs between 1880 and 1920 results from the introduction of cheaper materials, e.g. bricks of fletton type and tiles in lieu of slates.   These economies (which may largely depend on the price base used for valuation) offset the additional amenities in 1920 houses.

[c]Based on valuations in appendix table 12.3 with rough estimates for pre-1840 houses and those built from 1845 to 1875.   The average is calculated with weights based on the age structure of the total housing stock.

number of one- and two-person households, and the small size of many units being replaced.   The exact balance will vary from one locality to another and national policy must be flexible.   In an area with a good stock of family houses, it may be sensible to build subsidized old persons' dwellings fairly liberally in order to release houses for young families.   But in areas where the family houses are older and smaller and do not meet current needs, demand may be met most easily by encouraging the construction of family houses, and allowing the cost of small, older, five-room houses to fall.   In the latter circumstances few retired people would find such a house too big for them.

On balance we estimate that average dwelling size may increase by about 0·5 per cent a year, that is, at the same rate as from 1840 to 1880 and from 1920 to 1960.

(c) *The rising standard of the housing stock*

Rising housing standards do not consist solely of extra space.   They also include quality improvements in structure and amenities.   The improvement in these quality factors may be measured, extremely roughly, by the replacement cost per square foot (in constant prices) of typical houses (table 12.6).   Between 1840 and 1880 this increased by about 20 per cent, or about 0·5 per cent a year.

From 1880 to 1920 increasing use of cheaper materials offset improvements in structure and amenities and so costs barely changed, but from 1920 to 1962 they again increased by about 25 per cent or 0·5 per cent a year. For the future we have assumed that real cost per square foot will continue to rise at this rate. More rapidly rising incomes may eventually result in a demand for a faster rate of increase, particularly through higher demand for amenities and equipment; but for the next fifteen or twenty years we believe the main task will be to reduce the present extremely wide spread between the standard of old and new houses.

In the past most of the general improvement in the standard of housing, has come from the rapid growth in the total stock, continuously adding new houses that were of higher quality than those of earlier generations. Demolitions seem to have been relatively few, and probably more than three quarters of the stock of houses that existed in 1900 is still in use. But three fifths of the present stock consists of newer houses of higher quality and the average replacement values, at 1962 prices, of the stock of low to middle income houses probably rose from about £870 in 1900 to nearly £1,370 in 1960. This represents an increase, due both to size and other quality factors, of 57 per cent or about 0·8 per cent a year.

This increase in the real value of specimen working-class houses is probably a fair indication of the rise in the housing standard of the two thirds of households with lowest incomes[1]. Upper income standards declined between 1911 and 1951 in terms of space. In 1911, 29 per cent of households had six or more rooms, in 1951 only 15 per cent (table 12.7). Moreover at the earlier date the third of households with most rooms had an average of 7·1 rooms each and in 1951 only 5·8. The total quality of the stock of high income houses has certainly not fallen in proportion to this fall in their average size. The standard of equipment in new housing has risen and, whereas few of the older working-class houses have had bathrooms and other conveniences installed, almost all old housing that has remained in middle-class occupation has been extensively improved. Plumbing is expensive. Consequently the average replacement value of the total stock, as improved, may not have fallen, but it is unlikely that it has risen much.

It seems likely that between 1951 and 1960 the trend to smaller houses for upper income groups has been reversed. The number of houses with six or more rooms has started to increase. This was to be expected: the effects of the changes in income distribution, relative prices, and availability of domestic service, which led to the decline, are probably fully implemented by now. In future we expect all grades of housing to improve at broadly comparable rates.

If we assume no rise in upper income housing standards over the last sixty

[1]In 1911, 71 per cent of households occupied 5 rooms or less and at that date there were probably rather few high income households who occupied less than 6 rooms.

Table 12.7. *Distribution of households by numbers of rooms occupied, England and Wales, 1911–60*

	1911	1921	1931	1951	1960
Percentage of all households occupying:					
1–3 rooms	*25·4*	*29·6*	*28·4*	*25·5*	*18·6*
4–5 rooms	*45·7*	*45·2*	*48·4*	*59·1*	*61·6*
6 or more rooms	*28·9*	*25·2*	*23·2*	*15·4*	*19·8*
	100·0	*100·0*	*100·0*	*100·0*	*100·0*
Average number of rooms per household	4·78	4·54	4·48	4·34	4·56
of which:					
2/3 with fewest rooms	3·85	3·65	3·69	3·78	3·90
1/3 with most rooms	7·06	6·67	6·35	5·75	5·81

Source: Census 1951, Great Britain: One Per Cent Sample Tables, loc. cit., and P. G. Gray and R. Russell, *The Housing Situation in 1960, op. cit.*

years, and a rise of 0·9 per cent a year in that of the remaining stock, this would give an average rise of 0·6 per cent. The number of houses also increased by about 1·3 per cent a year. Thus the total increase in real income from housing seems to have been about 1·9 per cent a year, over a period when the national product was growing at 1·4 per cent a year.

Over the next thirty years we expect the national product to rise at about 4 per cent a year, but an increase of only about 0·8 per cent a year will be needed in the number of dwellings. Household income will therefore increase much faster than previously and a more rapid increase in housing standards is likely to be called for. With a slower rate of growth in the stock of houses, much less of this increase can come simply from adding better houses to the stock. Over the past hundred and fifty years the stock of houses has almost doubled every fifty years; in the future we expect it to double only every seventy-five years.

In the future, therefore, extensive replacement will be needed, not merely to clear slums and insanitary houses that offend the social conscience, but as the only way in which an adequate rise in general housing standards can be achieved.

(d) *Minimum standards and age structure*

There can be little doubt that the minimum standards of the present housing stock are far below those now considered socially acceptable. In 1960 about 4 per cent of the housing stock in England and Wales was considered already unfit for habitation, and a further 9 per cent likely to become so within fifteen years. Many houses were in need of extensive repair and improvement; 28 per cent still lacked bathrooms, 21 per cent their own w.c. and 40 per cent were without a proper hot water system (appendix table 12.8).

Some of these deficiencies are due to neglect, but the basic problem is that a substantial proportion of the housing stock is excessively old. Over the period 1880 to 1960 total demolitions of all houses except those severely damaged by bombing do not appear to have amounted to more than 2·0 or 2·2 million dwellings (see appendix table 12.4). Thus nearly four million of the six million houses recorded in the 1881 census must still be in use. About a quarter of the original six million were erected before 1800, and a very substantial part of the remainder were cheap workers' dwellings of small size and low quality built before minimum building standards were first established under the Public Health Act of 1875. Few of them are capable of adaptation to today's needs. The cost of erecting such houses today is estimated at £700 to £1,000 (see appendix table 12.3), to and owing deterioration their present value is far below their replacement cost. Thus the least fortunate fifth of households lives in houses whose real value is probably only a quarter or a third of that of a small modern council house costing £1,900 to £2,000.

The long-term problem of maintaining adequate housing standards is not merely one of replacing an existing stock of inadequate and obsolete dwellings. We have also to ensure a pattern of replacement that does not permit the bulk of low and middle income dwellings to get excessively old. In the past there has been no provision for this. Up to 1930 demolitions averaged only about 0·25 per cent of the housing stock a year; with the stock growing at 1·3 per cent a year, a continuation of this rate would mean that on the average houses would come up for demolition at an age of 140 years. Over the last thirty years demolitions have averaged about 0·3 per cent of the stock a year, and they may currently be about 1·5 per cent. But over the last eighty years as a whole the average demolition rate has only been 0·27 per cent. This gives a life expectation of about 135 years.

Had houses been demolished strictly according to age we should, in 1960, have just finished replacing the housing stock of 1825. The housing stock in 1820 was only about 2·8 million dwellings. Supposing, as a maximum, that half of these still survive and are houses of architectural and historic value that should be preserved, this would mean that only 1·4 million of the many poor quality houses of later date could have been replaced by 1960.

There is no way of determining precisely what the average life of a house ought to be. The Social Survey investigation suggests that at least a third of our present housing stock will require replacement by 1990. The number of houses thus estimated to require demolition by 1990 is almost equal to the present pre-1890 stock.

This suggests an average age at demolition of 100 years. This assessment is probably a minimum as it is unlikely to have made any allowance for rising standards due to higher incomes. With more rapidly rising living standards a life of 70 to 90 years appears more appropriate. Rather few of the houses built before 1880 are acceptable today, and even fewer of those built before 1920 are likely to meet the needs of households in 2000. However, if the typical life of houses fell much below 70 years this would materially increase the annual cost, by shortening the period of amortization[1].

In a state of equilibrium, with the housing stock increasing at 1 per cent a year, an average life of 70 to 90 years would require the replacement of 0·7 to 1·0 per cent of the housing stock each year. The present rate of about 0·5 per cent a year would be consistent with an average life of 110 years. But higher demolition rates are needed to overcome the present arrears of replacement within a reasonable period (see appendix table 12.7).

The next thirty years provide an exceptional opportunity to improve the age structure and conditions of the housing stock. We expect the demand for additional dwellings to be smaller than in the past. After 1990 it may rise again although it is unlikely to be as high as during the last fifty years. Also the structure of the housing stock makes it easier to shorten the replacement period now than it will be in twenty years time.

Largely as the result of the first world war the number of houses less than 35 years old is atypically large and the number between 35 and 50 years old extremely small. Building only averaged 80,000 a year from 1890 to 1924, compared with nearly 200,000 from 1925 to 1949, and nearly 300,000 since 1950. Replacement of the earlier stock is relatively easy now, but if there is still a big excess of old houses when the post-1925 houses begin to need replacement, the task of renewal will be herculean.

To reach an average life of 90 years before the products of the building booms of the 1930s and 1950s require renewal, we should need to replace the pre-1925 stock by the year 2015. This would require an average of a little over 160,000 demolitions a year over the next fifty years. To reach an average life of 70 years we should need to demolish the pre-1930 stock by the end of this century—an average rate of nearly 240,000 a year for just under forty years.

Although over the last fifty years as a whole new building has averaged only 1·5 per cent of the housing stock a year, in the three peacetime decades it has been much bigger than this. From 1930 to 1940 it was 2·4 per cent a year, and from 1950 to 1960, 1·9 per cent a year. Consequently the resources that have so far been devoted to making up arrears in the total number of houses can now be turned to making up arrears of replacement, and a much smaller expansion of building capacity will be needed than would normally be necessary.

(e) *Future housebuilding and investment levels*

Two estimates have been made of possible building levels over the next thirty years. It takes a long time to alter the stock of a commodity that may last a hundred years or more, and estimates of numbers of houses required from 1975

---

[1]Local authorities normally amortize their houses over 60 years, and as the actual life of houses is dispersed fairly widely about the average, the normal amortization period must be shorter than the average life, so that the majority of houses are amortized before their useful life is over.

Table 12.8. *Housebuilding in Great Britain, 1958–90*

Output ('000s)[a]

Actuals		
1958		266
1959		297
1960		304
1961		304
1962		315
1963		334

| | Lower | Upper |
Forecasts	estimate	estimate
1970	390	420
1975	415	495
1980	420	520
1985	420	440
1990	420	440

Source: Monthly Digest of Statistics and NIESR estimates.
[a]Average of starts and completions.

to 1990 are included in order that 1975 levels may be judged in terms of progress towards a more distant target. But whereas it is possible to make some estimate of the numbers of new houses likely to be needed in 1990, it would be extremely hazardous to try to predict their type and quality. This will depend largely on technological development, which over thirty years may be dramatic. Our investment estimates are, therefore, limited to 1975.

Our lower estimate assumes that housebuilding will rise from about 330,000 houses a year in 1963 to about 415,000 in 1975 and then level off at about 420,000 (table 12.8)[1]. This would allow for the building of 5·5 million new houses from 1960 to 1975, about half of which would be required as additions to the housing stock and half as replacements (table 12.9). Demolitions would increase from their 1960 level of perhaps 70,000 to 80,000 a year to about 250,000 by the early 1970s and level off at 270,000 to 280,000. In the second period from 1975 to 1990 total new building would amount to about 6·3 million dwellings. As requirements of additional houses are expected to be rather smaller after 1975, almost two thirds of this total would be for replacement. Total demolitions over the thirty-year period would total 6·8 million, which is about equal to the 1960 stock of pre-1900 houses, so that by 1990 the average

[1]The very rapid rise in housing starts between mid-1963 and end-1964 suggests that the level of building activity (measured by both starts and completions) forecast for 1975 may be reached by 1965 or 1966. It is not entirely valid to compare the present sharp upswing (which is certainly above any long-term trend) with trend estimates for 1975. The comparison does, however, emphasize the point that if necessary housing requirements can be met in the long term with very little expansion of present capacity. The choice between our lower and higher estimates will not be determined by capacity, but by financial provisions, and the priority given to *early* solution of present difficulties.

Table 12.9.   *Estimates of housing requirements in Great Britain, 1975–90*

Millions

	1960	1975 Upper estimate	1975 Lower estimate	1990 Upper estimate	1990 Lower estimate
Stock of dwellings	16·2	19·0		21·1	
Change over previous 15 years					
Building		5·9	5·5	7·2	6·7
Demolitions		−3·1	−2·7	−5·1	−4·6
Net increase		2·8	2·8	2·1	2·1
Annual rate as a percentage of the stock					
Building		*2·2*	*2·1*	*2·4*	*2·2*
Demolitions		*1·1*	*1·0*	*1·7*	*1·5*
Net increase		*1·1*		*0·7*	

Source: NIESR estimates.

age at replacement would be about 90 years. A continuation of this rate of demolition would reduce the normal life further to about 70 years by the end of the century and it would then level off when the products of the building boom of the 1930s came up for demolition.

The higher estimate assumes that housebuilding will rise more rapidly, approaching 500,000 houses a year by 1975 and 520,000 before 1980. This would permit a more rapid replacement of the stock of obsolete houses but to maintain this level of new building after 1980 would in time reduce the normal life of houses to 40 or 50 years. Consequently after 1980 new building would probably fall rapidly and level off at about 440,000 houses a year. Total new housebuilding would amount to 5·9 million between 1960 and 1975 and 7·2 million between 1975 and 1990. Demolitions would rise rapidly reaching almost 350,000 by 1975 and 370,000 by 1980; they would then fall to about 300,000. Over the whole thirty-year period total replacements would amount to just over 8 million houses and by 1990 the average age at replacement would be about 70 years. A continuation of this level of demolitions would reduce the normal life to about 65 years by the end of the century.

The increase envisaged in our higher estimate is not likely to be beyond the capacity of the building industry. Housebuilding has expanded very rapidly in the past. Between 1926 and 1936 output, in numbers of houses, rose by 64 per cent in ten years, from a level that was already unprecedented; from 1948 to 1954 it increased by 53 per cent in six years, and the rate of increase in the building booms of the 1860s and 1890s was even faster. Our estimate only requires an increase of about 50 per cent over the period 1963 to 1978 or 1979. But it might not, in conditions of full employment, be justified to devote to housing the share of resources that this higher programme implies considering that building rates of 450,000 to 520,000 a year would only be needed for ten or twelve years.

Table 12.10. *Age structure of the housing stock, 1911–90*

Percentages of total stock

Age in years	Under 10	10–40	40–70	Over 70	Of which over 100	Total
Estimates[a]						
1911	15	34	20[b]	31[b]	..	100
1921	3	35	25[b]	37[b]	..	100
1931	15	25	22	38	(20)[b]	100
1951	7	35	23	35	(18)[b]	100
1960	18	34	16	32	(17)	100
Forecasts[c]						
1975						
Lower estimate	20	36	20	24	(7)	100
Upper estimate	23	36	20	21	(4)	100
1990						
Lower estimate	20	49	25	6	(—)	100
Upper estimate	21	54	25	—	(—)	100

Source: NIESR estimates.

[a]Estimates are based on new building, and assume that demolitions of houses under 40 years old are negligible, and that demolitions of those between 40 and 100 years old are offset by increases in the number of dwellings of this age by subdivision of larger units.

[b]For houses built before 1800 the standard age structure (see appendix table 12.6) was assumed.

[c]The forecasts are hypothetical and assume that future demolitions would be in chronological order. To the extent that houses over 70 or 100 years old are in fact preserved the number of houses aged 40–70 or 70–100 years would be reduced.

As it takes some time to reach a higher level of output the effect of the higher estimate on the housing stock would be small until after 1975. By this date it would increase the stock of houses under 10 years old, and lower the proportion over 100 years old, by an extra 3 per cent. Over the past fifty years the age structure of the housing stock has not changed very much, apart from the short-term effects of the two world wars; 40 or 50 per cent of the housing stock has been less than 40 years old, and 30 to 40 per cent over 70 years old (table 12.10). For the last thirty years or more over a sixth of all dwellings have been over 100 years old. By 1975 we expect 55 to 60 per cent of the stock to be under 20 years old, and only 20 to 25 per cent to be more than 70 years old. By 1990, 70 to 75 per cent of all dwellings would be less than 40 years old and very few over 70 years old.

The effect of this change would be to raise minimum housing standards very sharply. In 1960 the replacement cost of the oldest 20 per cent of houses in the stock was probably only £700 to £750, or barely a third of average current construction costs. By 1975 replacement cost (in 1960 prices) of the oldest quintile may have increased by some 60 per cent to £1,100 or £1,200, and by 1990 to £1,450 to £1,600. Under the higher building programme in 1990 the typical

Table 12.11.   *Gross fixed capital formation in dwellings, United Kingdom 1960 and 1975*

	1960	1975 Lower estimate	1975 Upper estimate
New construction			
Number of dwellings ('000s)a	311	425	510
Average cost (£1960)	2,250	2,600	2,600
Total cost (£1960 million)	704	1,105	1,326
Improvements			
Number of dwellings ('000s)	130	10	5
Average cost (£1960)	385	385	385
Total cost (£1960 million)	50	4	2
Total investment (£1960 million) 1960 = 100			
Number of dwellings	100	137	164
Average cost	100	116	116
Total cost, new dwellings	100	157	188
Total investment including improvements	100	147	176

Source: Central Statistical Office, *National Income and Expenditure, 1963;* Ministry of Housing and Local Government, *Housing Return for England and Wales* (London, quarterly); and NIESR estimates.

aAverage of starts and completions.

home of the most poorly housed section of the population would be an estate house of the 1920s.

From 1960 to 1975 we have assumed that the average construction cost of new houses (at 1960 prices) will rise by about 1 per cent a year from about £2,250 in 1960 to £2,600 in 1975.   Because of the necessity of rehousing a large number of low income families living in the houses to be demolished, substantial changes in policy and some subsidies may be necessary to maintain even this rate of rise[1].   After 1975 when building rates level off, and the minimum standard of housing has been raised substantially, the average quality of new houses might rise much faster.

In addition to replacement of substandard houses, there is also an urgent need for large-scale improvement.   This is, however, essentially a short-term problem.   We expect the number of houses improved in respect of basic amenities to remain at the 1960 level of about 130,000 houses a year under the high programme for new building, and to rise to about 200,000 a year under the lower programme for new houses.   These rates would only be required until the early 1970s.   By 1975 the remaining houses that still lack bathrooms and basic facilities will have a very short life—less than 5 years in most cases.

[1]These policies are discussed in section 2 below.

Expenditure is thus expected to fall from about £50 million in 1960 to a nominal £2–£4 million by 1975[1].

We expect, therefore, that a fall in expenditure on improvements will offset part of the rise in new housebuilding. The number of houses built in 1975 is 37 per cent higher than in 1960 in the lower estimate, and 64 per cent higher in the upper estimate. Allowing for higher quality, the increase in the volume of new construction would then be 57 per cent or 88 per cent, and total investment, including improvements, would be 47 per cent above the 1960 level under the lower programme, and 76 per cent above under the higher programme. Our estimate of total housing investment in 1975 at 1960 prices is between £1,110 million and £1,330 million. For purposes of the projection of national investment as a whole in 1975 in this study a middle level of £1,200 million has been used.

2. RENT POLICY AND HOUSE OWNERSHIP

In this part we shall consider housing finance with particular reference to the level of rents and the subsidies that might be needed to ensure an adequate rate of new building and replacement. At the present time direct and indirect subsidies vary widely for different kinds of tenure, and this together with rent control and overall shortages has influenced the pattern of house ownership that has developed. First, therefore, we need to consider present tenure and the kinds of tenure that are likely to be possible in the future.

(a) *Housing tenure*

The main feature of house tenure over the last fifty years has been the rapid decline in the volume of privately rented houses. In 1914, 90 per cent of housing was privately rented[2]; by 1963 this share had fallen to less than one third. Since 78 per cent of privately rented houses were built before 1919, this trend can be expected to accelerate with more rapid redevelopment. Owner-occupied and publicly owned houses make up most of the modern stock and whereas the privately rented sector accounts for 52 per cent of all pre-1919 houses, it covers only 12·5 per cent of those built since 1919, and only 6 per cent of those built since 1945 (table 12.12). Not only has little new housing been built for renting, but more and more of the stock of pre-1919 houses has been transferred to owner occupation. There are now, in absolute terms, more than three times as many pre-1919 houses in owner occupation as there were in

---

[1]For technical reasons these figures only cover expenditure on specific basic improvements financed by government grants. A fuller discussion of the problem is given in Appendix 12.

[2]M. F. W. Hemming, 'The Price of Accommodation', *National Institute Economic Review*, August 1964.

Table 12.12. *Distribution of the housing stock by age and tenure,*
Great Britain, 1960

	All dwellings	Date of erection		
		Pre-1919	1919–45	1945–60
Number of dwellings ('000s)				
Owner-occupied	6,550	2,970	1,390	2,300
Rented: private	5,530	4,560	760	210
local authority	4,150	460	2,400	1,180
Total	16,230	7,990	4,550	3,690
Distribution by tenure, analysed by age (percentages)				
Owner-occupied	*100*	*45*	*37*	*18*
Rented: private	*100*	*82*	*14*	*4*
local authority	*100*	*11*	*33*	*56*
Total	*100*	*49*	*28*	*23*

Distribution by age, analysed by tenure (percentages)

Date of erection	All dwellings	Owner-occupied	Rented	
			Private	Local authority
Pre 1919	*100*	*38*	*56*	*6*
1919–45	*100*	*53*	*17*	*30*
1945–60	*100*	*32*	*6*	*62*
Total	*100*	*40*	*34*	*26*

Sources: P. G. Gray and R. Russell, *The Housing Situation in 1960, op. cit.* for England and Wales, with NIESR estimates for Scotland.

1919. Much of this represents owner occupation of substandard dwellings undertaken unwillingly because of the shortage of houses to rent.

If present trends continue, by 1980 the privately rented sector would be unlikely to account for more than 12 to 15 per cent of the total housing stock, and at least one third of this would probably be short-life substandard property awaiting demolition. We need first then to consider whether it is desirable or possible to reverse this trend and if not what form of tenure will replace it.

The decline in privately owned housing has been partly due to fifty years of rent control, and partly to its unfavourable position in relation to subsidies. Local authority housing has benefited from direct subsidy and even more from the reduction of capital costs on older houses as the result of inflation. Only owner-occupiers of long standing have gained through inflation, but all have been subsidized indirectly first through very low Schedule A assessments and subsequently by the abolition of this tax. Privately rented housing has not had corresponding tax or subsidy benefits, and capital gains due to inflation have been eaten away by rent controls. Without these disadvantages the decline over the last fifty years might have been smaller, but it seems unrealistic to believe that either removal of controls, or more equal tax and subsidy status would reverse the trend[1]. Firstly, confidence has already been lost and will not easily be regained. Secondly, it is highly unlikely that it will ever be possible, or indeed socially desirable, for the bulk of low and medium income housing to offer a return on capital equal to that obtainable from other forms of commercial investment.

It is to be expected that owner occupation would rise with rising real incomes. But there can be little doubt that the rapid rise in recent years has been largely due to a shortage of rented housing, and that there is at present a big unsatisfied demand for houses to rent. We should not expect, therefore, that as private rented dwellings disappear they could be replaced mainly or wholly by owner occupation. There will have to be a big expansion of publicly owned housing or of housing rented by non-profit making bodies such as housing associations and co-operatives. In the Netherlands, Sweden and West Germany housing associations and co-operatives own 25 to 30 per cent of the housing stock. In this country the movement is still tiny. So far housing associations account for less than 1 per cent of ownership in England and Wales and many legal, tax and subsidy handicaps will have to be remedied before much expansion is likely[2]. Expansion is desirable if only to provide greater freedom of choice and to avoid a virtual monopoly of rented housing by local authorities. But it seems unlikely that the maximum encouragement of both commercial and private non-profit renting will do much more than provide a small-scale alternative to publicly rented housing.

Consequently as replacement of obsolete housing and urban redevelopment proceeds it is inevitable that the proportion of publicly owned housing should expand at least fast enough to replace most of the privately owned houses demolished. Historically, the object of municipal housing was to provide adequate inexpensive dwellings for those unable to afford full economic rents. This function still underlies much of local authority rent and subsidy policy. But local authorities now own two thirds of all dwellings built since 1945, and more than three quarters of rented dwellings built since 1919. In the future we must expect local authorities to own an ever increasing share of rented housing and most of the best quality dwellings available for rent.

If the quality of the housing stock is to rise with rising incomes, it is essential that the function of local authorities as planning authorities and general landlords should be clearly differentiated from their original aim of providing for those in special need. If these functions are not differentiated the possibility of getting an adequate housing replacement programme will be greatly reduced

[1] The Rent Act 1957 was expected to produce more private houses for rent, but the transfer of houses to owner occupation has continued since decontrol.
[2] This is fully discussed in PEP (Political and Economic Planning), 'Housing Associations', *Planning*, no. 462, May 1962.

and artificial housing shortages may replace real ones. We should continue in an 'Alice in Wonderland' world where only those poor enough qualify for the best housing, where the standards of new housing are kept below long-term requirements because of the necessity of providing cheap housing for the needy, and where because of queues and waiting lists, provision cannot be made for many of those in greatest need.

(b) *Rents and rent policy*

(i) *The present dual market.* The incongruities and injustices of the present structure with its partial controls and complex network of direct and indirect subsidies are indefensible on social, ethical or economic grounds[1]. But before considering alternatives to the present system we must recognize that it is, in one respect, supremely successful. It enables a flourishing demand for unsubsidized private building to continue although for half the housing stock rents are probably only 50 or 60 per cent of the level necessary for unsubsidized new building.

This situation is possible because of the existence of two virtually independent markets: local authority and private rent-controlled housing on the one hand, and a free market sector of owner-occupied and uncontrolled rented dwellings on the other. We have estimated, extremely roughly, that uncontrolled rents and the rental value of owner-occupied dwellings may be 80 to 100 per cent above controlled rents and those of local authority houses. Demand for free market houses continues because their potential purchasers or tenants cannot become controlled tenants and are unlikely to be eligible for a council tenancy within a reasonable period.

Socially, this split of the housing market into two worlds is unacceptable because it bears little relationship to need. Controlled tenants are simply those who happened to live in a house below a certain rateable value before a certain date. There is no reason to believe that their need for low rent dwellings is greater than that of many other householders. Local authority tenants are, on the average, somewhat poorer than owner-occupiers, but by no means uniformly. In 1962, 33 per cent of owner-occupiers, including 10 per cent of those still paying for their houses, had household incomes of less than £15 per week, while 40 per cent of local authority tenants had incomes over £20 per week (table 12.13). Moreover, the high demand for low rent local authority dwellings makes it impossible for the authorities to provide housing for many of those most in need. Economically the system is objectionable because, in the low rent sector, houses are in effect rationed so that consumer demand gives no guide to the best use of resources between different kinds of houses

---

[1]A full description of anomalies in the present system is given in M. F. W. Hemming, 'The Price of Accommodation', *National Institute Economic Review, op, cit.*

Table 12.13. *The incomes and rents of different kinds of householders, 1962*

Income range (£ per year)[a]	Tenants			Owner-occupiers			All house-holders
	Council	Private	All	Still paying	Paid up	All	
Per cent of all households	28	31	59	21	20	41	100
Per cent of households in each income group							
Under 312	10	13	12	1	14	7	10
312–779	25	33	29	17	34	26	28
780–1,039	25	20	22	26	14	20	21
1,040–1,559	26	22	24	40	19	29	26
1,560 and above	14	12	13	17	19	18	15
Total	100	100	100	100	100	100	100
Average income of highest group	1,991	1,967	1,981	2,176	3,133	2,687	2,325
Total outgoings on rent, rates, 'owners' maintenance'[b] and mortgages[c] (£ per annum)							
Under 312	58	50	54	··	37		
312–779	75	64	69	115	43		
780–1,039	85	73	80	129	··		
1,040–1,559	85	82	83	176	50		
1,560 and above	97	92	95	273	104		
Average	82	71	77	169	55		
As per cent of income							
Under 312	25·2	23·2	24·1	··	15·9		
312–779	12·9	11·1	11·9	18·4	7·5		
780–1,039	9·3	8·1	8·6	14·2	··		
1,040–1,559	7·0	6·5	6·8	13·8	3·9		
1,560 and above	4·9	4·7	4·8	12·5	3·3		
Average	8·2	7·8	8·1	13·9	6·3		

Source: Ministry of Labour, *Family Expenditure Survey: Report for 1962* (London, 1963).

[a]The incomes shown are normal household income, including incomes of all members, but excluding special temporary income.

[b]To make the outgoings of owners more comparable with tenants' rents an amount equal to the expenditure of tenants in the same income group on maintenance has been deducted from total repair and maintenance expenditure.

[c]Actual outgoings on mortgage repayment (including capital repayment) rates.

and restriction of consumers' choice reduces the total satisfaction gained from a given stock of houses. Mobility of labour is greatly reduced because half of all households, living in the low rent sector, stand to lose heavily if they move.

In 1960 almost exactly half of the housing stock was in the low rent sector, and although the share is diminishing it is probably still over 40 per cent. If low rents resulted solely from direct subsidies, a doubling of subsidies, which would not be an intolerable burden, would permit the establishment of a unified market with little need for rent increases. Unfortunately this is not the case. Less than one third of the difference between an economic rent and the actual rents paid by local authority tenants in 1960 resulted from direct subsidy (see table 12.17 below). The low rents charged are possible because of past inflation. The capital cost of older local authority houses is substantially below their present annual value because they were financed at much lower price levels, and this enables authorities to fix rents well below current annual costs, less subsidy. This factor not only increases the gap between the low rent and high rent sectors, but results in gross anomalies between different authorities according to the age of their housing stock. The privately rented sector is not publicly subsidized, but controlled rents can be regarded as an enforced subsidy of tenants by their landlords. The extent of this subsidy can be seen in the price difference between houses sold with sitting tenants and those sold with vacant possession. This situation is also possible only as the result of past inflation. If landlords incurred capital charges in line with today's prices, controlled rents could not be enforced; there would be too many bankruptcies.

While the existence of a substantial gap between values in the low rent sector and the open market is apparent, the extent of the gap cannot be assessed with any accuracy. We have no reliable measure of the relative values of houses in each sector. Market prices at which owner-occupied houses change hands exist, but the statistics are inadequate. A small sample of prices paid by purchasers over the period 1957–60 suggests an average price over this period of £2,500[1]. But average prices of houses mortgaged to one major building society in 1960 were about £2,040[2]. The difference between these two estimates may not actually be very big because building societies lend chiefly on the less expensive houses. (The average price of houses costing less than £4,000 in the former survey was £2,090.) We have estimated an average price in 1960 of £2,125 for houses bought through borrowing[3]. In 1962 owner-occupiers purchasing their houses spent on the average 15·8 per cent of household income on mortgage repayments, rates and maintenance. The full annual cost of buying a £2,125 house with 100 per cent mortgage would amount to £242 or 20 per cent of 1962 owners' income. This appears reasonably consistent if we assume an average mortgage of twenty years covering 70 per cent of the price[4]. The equivalent rent of a house of this value would be £182 or 15 per cent of income[5].

---

[1]P. G. Gray and R. Russell, *The Housing Situation in 1960, op. cit.*

[2]This is a weighted average of new and second-hand houses mortgaged to the Co-operative Building Society.

[3]The lower figure of £1,950 given in table 12.19 below includes decontrolled rented houses.

[4]In 1960 building society mortgages appear to have averaged 79 per cent, and in 1961, 73 per cent of the purchase price. But the average period may be shorter than 20 years.

[5]The relationships between capital cost and annual cost to buy or to rent are taken from L. Needleman, 'A Long Term View of Housing', *National Institute Economic Review*, November 1961, pp. 19–36.

Compared with this, local authority tenants in 1962 were paying on average £90 or 9·0 per cent of their rather lower incomes in rent. The rateable value of their houses appears to be about 10 per cent higher than those of owner-occupiers. Age for age council houses are smaller, but two thirds of them have been built since the second world war compared with only one sixth of owner-occupied houses. However, part of the high cost of local authority dwellings may be the choice of the community rather than of individuals. A proportion are flats costing more than houses of equivalent size, but we have no reason to believe that they would rent for more in an open market. We have, therefore, assumed that the free market rent of the average council house would be about the same as that of the average owner-occupied house. Even on this basis economic rents of local authority houses appear to be about 100 per cent higher than actual rents and would amount to about 18 per cent of their tenants' incomes.

Tenants of privately owned houses, both controlled and uncontrolled, spent on the average £80 or 8·8 per cent of still smaller incomes on rent, rates and maintenance. But they lived in very much inferior houses. We have roughly estimated that the average value of their houses was only 55 to 65 per cent of those of owner-occupiers and council tenants[1]. Average market rents and maintenance costs might thus be between £100 and £120. This is 20 to 50 per cent above actual average rents, but covers a range including many controlled tenancies whose rents were, quality for quality, almost as low as those of local authority tenants[2], and tenants of uncontrolled property often—because of restricted choice—paying more than a normal market rent.

In 1960 the low rent sector amounted to 50 per cent of all accommodation units but by 1962 this may have fallen to 45 per cent. Controlled tenancies in England and Wales have been falling at a rate of over 300,000 a year, while local authority houses are increasing at a rate of only about 110,000. Rents for both groups were probably only about half of those in the free market and the biggest gap was not in the shrinking group of controlled tenancies but in the expanding group of council tenancies.

(ii) *Future prospects and policy.* The aim of long-term policy should be to work towards a unified housing market in which price differentials of different kinds of houses reflect consumer preferences. Houses are a singularly bad subject for rationing because of their heterogeneity. At no time shall we be able to give every one a new house, and if rents of new houses are too low in

[1] An attempt to assess values of privately rented houses by comparing their age structure and probable qualities suggested an average value of about two thirds of local authority and owner-occupied houses. An estimate made on the basis of rateable values (calculating those of the private rent sector as a residual) suggested an average value of 55 per cent.
[2] In 1960 local authority rents averaged about 1·9 times the rateable value and private controlled rents were 2·0 times the rateable value (see M. F. W. Hemming, 'The Price of Accommodation', *op. cit.*).

relation to those of older dwellings the removal of overall shortages will not stop queues, allocations and inevitable injustices. But if the price of older houses is too low in relation to current building costs there will be no effective demand for new building.

The burden of economic rents as a share of income will fall over the next twenty years. We expect the average quality of the housing stock to rise by about 1·4 per cent a year, or 32 per cent between 1960 and 1980. Household incomes are expected to increase by about 68 per cent or 2·7 per cent a year. Consequently by 1980 an average economic rent per dwelling would, in 1960 prices, represent only 13 or 14 per cent of an average income compared with 16 or 17 per cent in 1960. This shift will facilitate rent increases in the low rent sector, but it will not remove the need for them. If rents remained at their 1960 level, relative to other prices, by 1980 local authority tenants would only be paying 7 per cent of their incomes in rent.

As the overall housing shortage disappears there will probably be some fall in prices in the free sector, relative to the general price level. Indeed the possibility must be recognized that as shortages disappear market rents might fall below the level necessary to create an effective demand for new building. This would place a still larger burden on the public sector for the provision of new houses. The larger the proportion of recent construction in the public sector and the slower the rate of increase in building costs the smaller will be the amount by which local authorities will be able to subsidize rents from past capital gains. Consequently ever larger direct subsidies would be needed to maintain 1960 rent levels. Moreover no amount of public building for rent could meet the demand for rented houses as long as the present wide difference between local authority rents and owner-occupiers' housing costs remains. No sensible person buys a house if he is able to rent one at half the cost. An additional problem arises because the tenants of older privately rented houses are in general poorer than present local authority tenants; 46 per cent of all private tenants had incomes under £15 per week in 1962 compared with 35 per cent of council tenants. Without a unified housing market and some filtering up, attempts to rehouse the whole of the poorest section of the community in heavily subsidized public housing would lead inevitably to economy building standards and failure to provide houses of high enough quality to meet the long-term needs of a growing economy[1].

The establishment of a unified housing market, at least for the majority of dwellings, is essential if there are ever to be an adequate number of dwellings to rent, and a replacement programme based on long-term requirements. Theoretically it is possible to do this either by raising the level of local authority and controlled rents to those of the free market sector, or by subsidizing free

---

[1]The effect of this dilemma can already be seen in lower standards and reduced average size of recent local authority houses.

Table 12.14.   *Distribution of housing units^a by tenure and length of life, England and Wales, 1960*

A. Distribution by length of life analysed by tenure   *Percentages*

	All housing units	Owner-occupied	Rented Private Controlled	Decontrolled	Local authority[b]
Short life[c]	13	7	30	17	7
Medium life[d]	20	20	32	29	4
Long life	67	73	38	54	89
Total	100	100	100	100	100

B. Distribution by tenure analysed by length of life

	All housing units	Short[c]	Medium[d]	Long
Owner-occupied	42	23	42	45
Rented				
Private controlled	20	47	33	12
Private decontrolled	13	17	20	11
Local authority	25	13	5	32
Total	100	100	100	100

Source: P. G. Gray and R. Russell, *The Housing Situation in 1960, op. cit.*

[a]The figures are based on 'accommodation units' and not structurally separate dwellings. They exclude private vacant units.

[b]Including requisitioned, temporary, and empty dwellings.

[c]Unfit houses and those estimated as likely to become so within 15 years. Under our high building programme these would be demolished by about 1972 and under the low programme by 1974.

[d]Houses estimated as likely to remain fit for 15–30 years. Under the high building programme they would be demolished by 1980, and under the low programme by 1990.

market housing costs and reducing them to the level of the low rent sector. The latter policy would, however, entail very big subsidies. It would probably be necessary to subsidize over 60 per cent of the cost of three quarters to four fifths of all new housebuilding. In 1965 this would cost about £500 million and by 1975 probably £700 million (see appendix table 12.10).

(iii) *The low rent sector.* How far then is it possible to increase rents in the low rent sector to an economic level? This is mainly a question of public sector rents. Although controlled rents are very low, so is the quality of much of the housing. In the long run the problem of the private rent-controlled sector is self-liquidating; over the next fifteen to twenty years most of this group will disappear. The number of controlled tenancies is at present falling by rather more than 300,000 a year. Probably 15 to 20 per cent of this is due to demolition and the remainder to changes of tenancy. The share due to demolition will rise rapidly as replacement proceeds because 47 per cent of all unfit and short-life dwellings are rent-controlled (table 12.14).   It is likely that 50 or 60 per cent of them will have been demolished by 1975, and over 90 per cent by 1985.

Most of this substandard rented property will have to be replaced by publicly owned dwellings, supplemented by housing owned by non-profitmaking organizations.   The tenants of private rented controlled housing are poorer than present local authority tenants, and two problems arise.   The first is to maintain and improve these dwellings for the remainder of their lives.   This is not likely to appear an economic investment to private landlords even when they can afford it, which many cannot[1].   The second is to rehouse these tenants as demolition proceeds at rents which they can afford.

Both these problems can only be solved by the acquisition by public authorities of the bulk of rent-controlled dwellings.   By 1965 these are not likely to number much more than 2 million.   Adequately maintained houses which landlords desire to retain could be decontrolled, and the remainder, together with similar decontrolled dwellings, purchased at values based on the income they now produce[2].   Rents could then be increased as improvements proceed. Probably the biggest gain from such increases would be that occupiers would become accustomed to a rent level high enough to facilitate rehousing.   Both the tenants being rehoused and others in acquired property could be offered new houses at rents nearer to the economic level than could be imposed if no choice existed.   Most important of all, perhaps, an opportunity of better housing could be offered not merely to those who happened to live in condemned dwellings but to the majority of the tenants of old houses.   Such a policy would require the acquisition of a sizeable block of dwellings most of them with a life of ten years or more; we cannot expect tenants being rehoused to move into houses with a life of only two or three years.   But these very short life houses, as they become vacant, could be made available for homeless families, recent migrants and others for whom there is hardly any provision now.

To combine the low rent sector in one publicly managed group would facilitate rent increases to a more economic level, but it would not entirely solve the problem.   The 68 per cent of local authority tenants with incomes of over £740 a year had in 1962 an average income of £1,250, and paid less than 8 per cent of this in rent (table 12.15).   In the rent-controlled sector the corresponding group probably had an average income of about £1,150 and may have paid only about 6 per cent in rent.   For these tenants substantial rent increases might be unpopular but they would not be onerous.   But both local authority and private tenants with incomes of less than £6 a week already pay almost a

---

[1]A survey of Lancaster in 1960 showed that over 75 per cent of landlords owned only one or two houses, and 67 per cent had incomes of less than £10 per week (see J. B. Cullingworth, *Housing in Transition*, London, 1963).

[2]The most satisfactory form of purchase might be by compensating the owner with an annuity based on the expected life of the house (see M. F. W. Hemming, 'The Price of Accommodation', *op. cit.*).

quarter of their income in rent. Those with incomes between £6 and £15 per week pay 11 per cent to 13 per cent, which, as there is a wide dispersion of rents, must involve many paying well over 15 per cent of income in rent (table 12.13). Here rents could not be increased without hardship unless there was a sizeable expansion in incomes.

For this group both housing and income subsidies are needed. If whole groups such as old age pensioners, large families or unsupported mothers cannot afford the rent of any reasonable house they need bigger incomes, by means of increased pensions or family allowances. In particular the National Assistance policy of paying actual rents plus subsistence allowance will need to be reviewed. This policy is quite appropriate to cover temporary hard times when people should not be expected to move, and unavoidable so long as acute housing shortage prevents people from moving. But as shortages disappear long-term help should include a rent element with the right to retain this whatever actual rent is paid. We cannot, however, meet all low income needs by income subsidy, because the quality of housing available varies widely between areas. In some localities local authorities will have stocks of older houses whose economic rent is low, but in others, such as new towns or extensively redeveloped areas, the only dwellings available are likely to be beyond the means of low income households even after income increases. It would be unlikely that we could afford to pay all the present low income groups sufficient allowances for them all to be able to afford modern dwellings. We must, therefore, give subsidies where only modern houses are available, but the subsidies should leave room for a choice of home at differential rents that reflect preferences. Otherwise the decision which pensioner gets the new bungalow and which stays in the slum must be invidious and arbitrary.

The method of rent adjustment proposed to meet these requirements is that rents should be increased by amounts corresponding to 0·5 per cent to 1·0 per cent of incomes per year, subject to a maximum rent of say 15 per cent of income, for a modern post-war house[1]. Since many tenants will not get the opportunity of such a house, those tenants qualifying for a rent reduction would also pay correspondingly less for lower grade accommodation. The average level of rents on this basis would thus be unlikely to exceed 12·5 per cent of income.

Different authorities would need to adopt varying programmes according to their present rent structure and level and local housing availabilities. But it should be incumbent on all:

(a) to increase rents of those paying less than the economic 'replacement' rent of the house they occupy by, say, 1 per cent of income a year until they reach the economic level or a determined income ceiling;

[1]This would be based on 'normal' income and would not vary with casual earnings or windfalls.

Table 12.15. *Household incomes, 1962–80*[a]

	1962	1965	1970	1975	1980
All households (£)					
Average income	990	1,060	1,220	1,380	1,590
Local authority tenants	1,000	1,045 ⎫	1,100	1,225	1,390
Private controlled tenants	810	860 ⎭			
Private decontrolled tenants ⎫ Owner-occupiers ⎭	1,035	1,105	1,315	1,500	1,750
Low income households (£)[b]					
Maximum income	740	740	920	1,030	1,190
Average income	470	540	660	770	900
Percentage who are:					
Local authority tenants	*25*	*28* ⎫	*54*	*60*	*67*
Private controlled tenants	*(21)*	*(17)* ⎬			
Private decontrolled tenants	*(18)*	*(18)* ⎫			
Owner-occupiers			*20*	*14*	*7*
Still paying	*10*	*11* ⎭			
Paid up	*26*	*26*	*26*	*26*	*26*
Total	*100*	*100*	*100*	*100*	*100*
Upper income households (£)[c]					
Average income, all	1,270	1,340	1,520	1,710	1,960
Local authority tenants	1,250	1,310 ⎫	1,431	1,615	1,845
Private controlled tenants	(1,150)	(1,200) ⎭			
Private decontrolled tenants ⎫ Owner-occupiers ⎭	1,310	1,370	1,555	1,755	2,005

Sources: NIESR estimates based for 1962 on the Ministry of Labour, *Family Expenditure Survey: Report for 1962, loc. cit.*

[a]The definition of household income used is that given in the *Family Expenditure Survey.*
[b]Average: these households made up 35 per cent of all households in 1962 and this relationship is assumed to continue.
[c]Households with incomes over 75 per cent of the general average.

    (b) to provide dwellings at appropriate rents for low income households;
    (c) to ensure that rents paid for different qualities of accommodation by households of similar income reflect the differences in quality.

Rent increases directly related to income would remove present anomalies most rapidly. There is really no reason why those council tenants spending £97 a year on rent and rates from incomes of almost £2,000 should not have big rent increases quite quickly! But those authorities who do not now operate rebate schemes, and object to universal means tests, would obtain the same final result by standard increases with a right of appeal if the increase exceeds a certain proportion of income.

For the purpose of estimating rents and costs we have assumed that all households with incomes below 75 per cent of the overall household average will need special rent reductions. In 1962 this group accounted for 35 per cent of all households; their maximum income was £740, and average £470 (table 12.15). This low average is mainly due to the inclusion here of many pensioner

Table 12.16. *Public sector incomes and rents, 1960–80[a]*

	1962	1965	1970	1975	£1960[b] 1980
Average income					
Upper income households[c]	1,250	1,307	1,430	1,615	1,845
Low income households[c]	470	540	660	770	900
Per cent of low income group in total	32	34	43	46	48
Economic rent[d] including rates					
New dwellings[e]	204	209	218	227	237
All publicly built[f]	186	188	195	200	206
Acquired dwellings[g]	113	116	118	122	130
Average	181	184	171	181	193
Average net of rates	154	156	146	154	162
Actual rents including rates					
Upper income households	97[h]	111	157	200	206
Low income households	78[h]	78	83	96	113
Average	91[h]	100	125	152	161
Average net of rates	63	72	103	125	130
Rents as percentage of income					
Upper income households	7·7	8·5	11·0	12·4	11·2
Low income households	16·6	14·5	12·5	12·5	11·2
Average	9·1	9·6	11·4	12·4	11·6

Source: NIESR estimates.

[a]Including sponsored private non-profitmaking ownership.
[b]At 1960 general price level but allowing for rent increases.
[c]See table 12.15.
[d]Based on amortization of current value over 60 years at 6 per cent.
[e]Based on capital cost of £2,400 in 1962 rising to £2,840 in 1980.
[f]Based on capital value of £2,185 in 1962 rising to £2,410 in 1980.
[g]Based on capital value of £1,200 in 1962 rising to £1,430 in 1980.
[h]Estimated from national accounts series which give an average 10 per cent higher than the *Family Expenditure Survey* series in table 12.13. This is probably because the latter deducts rent received from subletting.

and National Assistance households with incomes under £6 per week. We have assumed, therefore, that as the result of more adequate pension policies the average income of the group will rise faster than household incomes generally, but that the proportion of such households will remain at 35 per cent, and the maximum income of the group at three quarters of the general average.

In 1962, 25 per cent of such households were local authority tenants, nearly 40 per cent were tenants of privately rented dwellings, and about 36 per cent were owner-occupiers, although only 10 per cent of the latter were still paying for their houses (table 12.13). There will always be some retired paid-up owner-occupiers of low income, but apart from these the public sector will need to provide for the great majority of these low income households. As the privately rented sector diminishes, and substandard owner-occupied houses are replaced, public authorities may have to cater for about two thirds of the poorest group compared with a quarter at present[1]. The total amount of public housing will also be increasing, but the proportion of the poorest households in this total may increase from 32 per cent to 48 per cent between 1962 and 1980. At present this group are only paying 40 per cent to 45 per cent of the full economic rent. As their incomes rise this will increase and may reach 70 per cent to 75 per cent by 1980 (table 12.16).

Average incomes of the better-off local authority tenants are expected to rise by about 50 per cent between 1962 and 1980. Rents are widely dispersed at present and all rents would not need to rise equally fast. We have assumed, therefore, that a maximum increase of 1·0 per cent of income a year for those now paying the lowest rents would result in an average increase on all rents of about 0·5 per cent a year. This would enable rents for the upper income households to reach an economic level at a little under 12·5 per cent of average income over ten years, say by 1975. In terms of the 1960 general price level the average rent would need to double between 1962 and 1975 and the increase would absorb about a quarter of the rise in real income over the period. Only about 10 per cent of this would be due to rising quality of houses; the present dwellings built by local authorities are relatively modern and rather homogeneous in quality and so quality improvement will be smaller than in private house-building. The tenant who remained in the same house over the period might experience a rent rise of nearly 90 per cent.

In view of the present low level of council rents compared wi·h housing costs of decontrolled tenants and owner-occupiers, increases of this order do not appear unreasonable, particularly over a period of rapidly rising real incomes. They may not, however, prove politically feasible. In this case an alternative would be to introduce some subsidy applicable to both free market and public housing, which would permit the establishment of a single housing market at rents below the full economic level. This alternative is discussed further below.

With the rent increases proposed, the financing of local authority housing, including rebates for low incomes, could be covered without direct subsidy from 1970 onwards. This is because for most authorities actual expenses incurred on management, maintenance and debt redemption are not as big as a full replacement rent. A large part of the public housing stock was built and financed at lower price levels and local authorities have benefited by a substantial capital appreciation of their housing stock. In 1962 rents and subsidies only covered 55 per cent of our estimate of the full economic rent, and 45 per cent of the economic rent was in fact financed out of capital appreciation. If

---

[1]For simplicity of presentation we refer throughout to a single group of public sector housing. In practice we hope that this group would be divided among various kinds of authorities, including local authorities, public corporations, and voluntary non-profitmaking housing associations.

Table 12.17. *The financing of public sector housing, 1960–80*

Costs £ million	1960	1965	1970	1975	1980
			£1960 million[a]		
Annual value publicly built[b]	527	630	810	993	1,223
Acquired[c]	19	28	188	159	128
Total	546	658	998	1,152	1,351
of which:					
Actual capital charges[d]	(257)	(345)	(643)	(742)	(886)
Appreciation[e]	(289)	(319)	(355)	(410)	(465)
Maintenance[f]	91	110	185	198	216
Total	637	768	1,183	1,350	1,567
Receipts £ million					
Rent	229	359	832	1,093	1,248
Capital appreciation	289	319	355	410	465
Subsidy (+) or surplus (−)	119	96	−4	−153	−146
Total	637	774	1,183	1,350	1,567
Receipts per house			*£1960*[a]		
Rents	55	72	103	125	130
Capital appreciation	69	71	44	36	48
Subsidy (+) or surplus (−)	29	22	−1	−17	−14
Total	153	155	146	154	164

Source: NIESR estimates.

[a]At 1960 general price level but allowing for rent increases.

[b]The full cost of amortization over 60 years at 6 per cent based on current replacement value of the housing stock.

[c]A rate of £74 per house in 1960 rising to £89 in 1980 is assumed; no capital appreciation is allowed for this short-life property.

[d]Obtained as a residual by deducting appreciation from the annual value.

[e]1960 estimated as the difference between full cost and receipts from rents and subsidies. For later years the amount has been increased by 1 per cent of the annual value of purpose-built houses, on the assumption that the general price level will rise at this rate.

[f]1960 average of £22 per unit used for publicly built houses, and £25 per unit for acquired property.

current house prices rise at about 1 per cent a year over the next twenty years the total capital appreciation fund will continue to grow, but more slowly than in the past, and it will have to be spread over a larger number of houses (table 12.17).   From 1970 onwards it would finance only 30 per cent of the full rent.   But it would continue to be more than sufficient to subsidize rent reductions for poorer householders, and would, after 1975, leave a surplus for general amenities or the improvement of older houses.

This position is, however, an average for all authorities.   It would entail elaborate equalization between them.   This is not impossible.   Capacity to pay would be measured by the gross value of the housing stock in relation to outstanding capital charges.   Needs would be primarily related to the total number of low income households in the locality, with some adjustment according to the quality of the housing stock. Another problem would be that some outstanding payments under former central government subsidies to local authorities would be superfluous, but it might be difficult to cancel them. This may be another reason—although a slightly odd one—why in practice it might be easier to subsidize the free sector rather than remove subsidy altogether from the public sector.

(iv) *The private free market sector.* In 1960, 40 per cent of all dwellings were owner-occupied and the proportion was rising, both because private new building was almost entirely for owner occupation and because of transfers of rented houses to owner-occupiers. We expect this trend to continue while there is an overall shortage of houses to rent, perhaps until 1970 or 1975, but it may then level off at least temporarily. Twenty per cent of owner-occupied houses have only a medium life expectation and are likely to be demolished between 1975 and 1985. When this occurs it is likely that many of their owners will opt for a rented house rather than the purchase of a more expensive house. Consequently although we expect owner-occupation of good quality housing to rise with rising incomes this may do no more than offset the fall in ownership of older houses by people of moderate income.

Nearly half of the decontrolled privately rented dwellings in 1960 were short- and medium-life dwellings of which few will be left by 1980, and this group has since been augmented by decontrol of dwellings whose life expectation is even shorter. In addition privately rented dwellings are transferring to owner occupation and many of the older ones may come into the category to be acquired by public authorities. Consequently by 1980 we expect the privately rented sector to fall from the 1960 level of about 14 per cent of the housing stock to a basic minimum of about 1·5 million or perhaps 7 per cent (table 12.18). This would cover little more than the rented dwellings built since 1919, a few dwellings rented temporarily by owner-occupiers and some new high income urban flats.

Consequently we expect the stock of privately owned houses, which has increased rapidly in the last six to eight years, to level out in about 1965. New private building may continue to rise slowly, but it is unlikely to retain its present high share of the total. Over the period 1965 to 1980 as a whole we have assumed that the public sector, including housing associations, will account for slightly over half of all new houses built[1]. This will be partly because the demand for private houses to buy is unlikely to go on rising at recent rates and partly because replacement will form an ever increasing proportion of new building and this is unlikely to be undertaken by private builders. If, however, the private demand for new houses proves bigger than we anticipate there is no

---

[1]The public share of investment will be slightly under half because the most expensive houses are private ones.

Table 12.18. *The housing stock by tenure, 1960–80*

	1960	1965	1970	1975	*Thousands* 1980
Low rent sector					
Publicly owned	4,150	4,990	8,080	8,740	9,540
of which: Purpose-built	(3,900)	(4,630)	(5,700)	(6,800)	(8,000)
Acquired	(250)	(360)	(2,380)	(1,940)	(1,440)
Private controlled	3,200	2,040	—	—	—
Total	7,350	7,030	—	—	—
High rent sector					
Uncontrolled rented	2,330	2,950	2,300	1,900	1,500
Owner-occupied	6,550	7,340	7,840	8,350	8,700
Total	8,880	10,290	10,140	10,250	10,200
All dwellings	16,230	17,320	18,220	18,990	19,740
Percentage distribution					
Low rent sector					
Publicly owned	*26*	*29*	*44*	*46*	*48*
Private controlled	*20*	*12*	—	—	—
Total	*46*	*41*	*44*	*46*	*48*
High rent sector					
Uncontrolled rented	*14*	*17*	*13*	*10*	*8*
Owner-occupied	*40*	*42*	*43*	*44*	*44*
Total	*54*	*59*	*56*	*54*	*52*
All dwellings	*100*	*100*	*100*	*100*	*100*

Source: NIESR estimates.

reason why houses built by public authorities for replacement should not be sold to owner-occupiers.

The amount of private building that we envisage, together with demolition and transfer to public ownership of older rented dwellings, will, however, raise the value of the average privately owned house by about 35 per cent between 1960 and 1980.   By 1980 over three quarters of privately owned houses will have been built after 1919, and 60 per cent of them since 1945.

There does not appear to be a great risk that the costs of owner occupation will prove excessive because we envisage that most low income households will rent public sector dwellings.   After 1970 we expect only about a quarter of private dwellings to be occupied by low income families and most of these will be retired owner-occupiers who have finished buying their houses.   We have therefore examined capacity to meet housing costs in terms of the incomes of upper income households.   In 1962 the average household in this group would have needed to spend 17 per cent of income on mortgage repayment, rates and

Table 12.19   *Private sector incomes and housing costs, 1960–70*

	1962	1965	1970	1975	1980
Average income (£)					
All households	1,035	1,104	1,314	1,499	1,750
Upper income households[a]	1,310	1,370	1,556	1,755	2,004
Per cent of upper income groups in total	67	68	73	74	77
Economic rent[b] including rates (£)					
New houses[c]	241	250	261	272	284
Post-1945 houses[d]	224	228	235	242	250
Average of all dwellings[e]	165	170	186	203	222
Annual cost of purchasing[f]					
New houses[c]	322	336	350	366	381
Post-1945 houses[d]	247	305	314	324	334
Average of all dwellings[e]	220	226	247	269	296
Percentage of upper household income required:					
To buy					
New house	*24·6*	*24·5*	*22·5*	*20·9*	*19·0*
Post-1945 house	*22·7*	*22·2*	*20·2*	*18·5*	*16·7*
Average house	*16·8*	*16·5*	*15·9*	*15·3*	*14·8*
To rent					
New house	*18·4*	*18·2*	*16·8*	*15·5*	*14·2*
Post-1945 house	*17·1*	*16·6*	*15·1*	*13·8*	*12·5*
Average house	*12·6*	*12·4*	*12·0*	*11·6*	*11·1*

Source: NIESR estimates.

[a]See table 12.15.
[b]Based on amortization of current value over 60 years at 6 per cent.
[c]Based on capital cost of £2,900 in 1962 rising to £3,500 in 1980.
[d]Based on capital cost of £2,650 in 1962 rising to £3,000 in 1980.
[e]Based on capital cost of £1,950 in 1962 rising to £2,630 in 1980.
[f] Includes mortgage repayments over 20 years at 6 per cent for full value, maintenance at £25 a year (intended to represent 'landlords' repairs' only) and rates.

maintenance if they bought an average house entirely out of income, or 13 per cent of income to rent one (table 12.19). For a new house the cost would have been 25 per cent of income to buy, or 18 per cent to rent. By 1970 the cost of purchase of the average house will have fallen to 16 per cent of income and by 1980 to 15 per cent. In 1980 it would take 17 per cent of average income to buy a post-war house. Purchasers have in fact to meet part of the cost out of savings and so actual payments would be less. In 1962 actual payments by these income groups amounted to about 13 per cent of income. By 1980 they could obtain a modern house for this outlay, and a new house for only slightly more.

(c) *House prices, productivity and subsidies*

The above analysis of future rents and housing costs depends upon two assumptions: that incomes will rise significantly faster than the real value of the housing stock and that house prices will move in line with the general level of prices.

The first assumption is a fairly safe one because of the slow growth expected in numbers of households and the long time required to alter the average quality of the whole housing stock. Our upper building estimate allows for a rise of 76 per cent in investment from 1960 to 1975, and our lower estimate for a rise of 47 per cent. But up to 1975 the effect of this difference on the total housing stock is small; with the higher building level the real value of the average house might increase by 25 per cent between 1960 and 1975, and with the lower level by 21 per cent. A rate of replacement fast enough to increase the average value of all houses much more than we have assumed is inconceivable unless there were dramatic increases in productivity which led to big changes in the requirements of labour and other inputs per house.

When we consider likely movements in house prices relative to prices in general, there is a much wider range of possible developments. Relative movements in prices of new houses will depend upon relative productivity of the house construction industry compared with that of other industries. Although in recent years output per man in housebuilding seems to have risen rather fast in the longer term[1], productivity in house construction has tended to increase more slowly than productivity in general and, including quality improvements, prices of typical houses have risen more rapidly than wages[2]. This is probably because housebuilding is a labour-intensive industry and includes a big proportion of small firms. On the other hand the present trend towards system building and prefabrication, could, during the next ten or fifteen years, lead to a major breakthrough, rapid rationalization of the industry, and a sharp rise in productivity. If this occurred relative prices of new houses might fall sharply. This has happened often enough with other commodities when factory methods and large-scale production were introduced. A big reduction in costs would probably result in more rapid replacement than we have envisaged, but would not lead to higher rents or a larger volume of resources going to the building industry.

If prices of new houses fell sharply, so would those of existing houses, and some kind of compensation might be necessary for lower income owner-occupiers[3]. Existing houses have no supply price and their values are determined solely from the demand side. In recent years, because of the shortage of houses, house prices have risen more rapidly than construction costs, particularly in city centres and the London area. This abnormal rise should slacken as the overall housing shortage disappears, but other policies to change the location of employment will be needed to reduce excess demand in particular areas where there is insufficient land to expand housebuilding much[4].

[1]See for example *National Institute Economic Review*, February 1964, p. 40.
[2]L. Needleman, 'A Long Term View of Housing', *National Institute Economic Review. op. cit.*
[3]See Appendix 12.
[4]M. F. W. Hemming, 'The Price of Accommodation', *op. cit.*

We do not know what the elasticity of demand for better houses may be once general shortages disappear. If demand continues to rise faster than the supply can be increased, it might be necessary, at least in some areas, to reduce excess demand first by reducing direct and indirect subsidies and other incentives to house purchase, and possibly even by some kinds of taxation or controls. But the income-elasticity of demand for housing seems to be rather low and it is equally possible that when scarcity disappears house prices may fall below current construction costs. Whether this happens depends partly on consumers' preferences between old and new houses. If there is a strong preference for modern houses, prices of new houses would still cover their building costs even if those of second-hand houses fell. But this would not happen if, as the range of choice increased, many householders who could afford new houses preferred houses of the 1930s or 1950s, either because of lower cost or because the higher quality of current construction did not outweigh the disadvantages of the higher density of development and smaller choice of site which appear inevitable for much of new building in the future. In this case subsidies might be needed to stimulate the demand for new building.

New housing subsidies might also be required if public authorities, with big reserves from capital appreciation, were unwilling to increase rents to current economic levels. In this case, unless all dwellings were subsidized, the dual market would be perpetuated and there would be an excess demand for council houses, together with insufficient demand for owner-occupied houses or those rented by newer authorities and housing associations who had insufficient reserves to charge low rents. Finally, subsidies might be necessary to ensure that new building was of high enough quality to meet long-term needs. We are aiming to overcome large arrears of replacement in a fairly short period. Much of this effort would be wasted if the new houses built are not adequate to meet requirements in forty years' time.

If for any of these reasons the demand for new houses at a full economic rent proves inadequate we should be prepared to subsidize new building. Such subsidy must be available to all types of houses and not one which will perpetuate the existing dual market. Once the overall shortage of houses has disappeared, a general subsidy on new houses would bring a corresponding fall in existing house prices and help to narrow the gap between market rents and those paid in the low rent sector. Too sudden a fall would cause hardship and loss of confidence, but a gradual fall in real values is desirable for a regular replacement policy. Houses can no longer be regarded as a perpetual asset. Depreciation over a period of about 70 years implies an average fall in the value of the building of about $1\frac{1}{2}$ per cent a year, or of perhaps rather over 1 per cent a year in the total value including the site. Houses are usually financed by fixed-value loans and so a fall of this order need not cause the annual cost to rise to cover depreciation so long as the general price level is rising by at least 1 per cent a year. In this case real values would fall but monetary values remain constant, and capital appreciation due to inflation would be shared by all householders, instead of—as at present—being concentrated on those owner-occupiers, local authorities, and landlords who bought before the price rise.

This effect will not, of course, occur as long as there is an overall shortage of houses; but the housing market is a relatively local one. In Scotland and the north of England a general subsidy to increase the volume of resources going to housebuilding would be appropriate already[1]. In London and the south-east it would probably merely be inflationary since the demand for new housing is already as high as can be met with the resources available.

The aim of a general housing subsidy would be to increase demand and to lower prices. Publicly owned, privately rented and owner-occupied housing should be eligible without discrimination or means test, but it need not fall evenly on all types of housing. Very expensive houses would not be eligible, but the proportion of the building cost eligible for subsidy should taper off gradually so that building is not arbitrarily concentrated at the particular values that attract most subsidy. In the north, where average house sizes are very small, it may be desirable to extend the upper limit to increase the proportion of higher quality houses[2].

The most satisfactory form of general subsidy of new building appears to be an annual grant payable over a period of ten to twenty years.[3] This could be graduated to apply in part to recently built houses as well as new ones and thus avoid sudden fluctuations in values. It could also be reduced gradually for more expensive houses, so as to avoid a concentration of building at the values attracting most subsidy. The amount of subsidy required would, of course, depend on the extent of the stimulus to demand that was needed. Present expenditure on direct housing subsidies, increased proportionately to the rise in total national product, would amount to over £200 million in 1960 prices by 1975. This would cover the cost of a subsidy of $17\frac{1}{2}$ per cent of the construction cost of new houses, or perhaps 14 per cent of the total rent or selling price (including land). But rates are an indirect tax on housing and with the present level of subsidies housing is, on a net basis, fairly heavily taxed. If it were necessary new building could be subsidized to the extent of 30 per cent or 40 per cent without the total subsidy being bigger than the total tax.

[1]Scotland, with almost 10 per cent of the population of Great Britain and 10 per cent of total housebuilding, had in the period 1954 to 1962 only 3·5 per cent of the private housebuilding. In the first quarter of 1964 it still only received 4 per cent of the private housebuilding orders.

[2]A shortage of houses suitable for executives is one factor limiting the movement of industry to some development areas.

[3]This is discussed fully in Appendix 12, section on subsidies.

CHAPTER XIII

HEALTH AND WELFARE

By D. C. Paige and K. Jones

In this chapter we make estimates of current and capital expenditure on the health and welfare services in 1975, consider the administrative needs of these services, and some alternative policies. The estimates vary in quality. In some instances the time and resources available have not permitted a complete investigation of needs. In others the information necessary for a full study is lacking. But much of the pattern of the health services in 1975 is being determined by decisions taken now. The new hospitals being planned will influence medical practice for many years to come and the careers of health service personnel now in training may last as long as the new buildings.

We have, therefore, paid most attention to requirements of buildings and skilled manpower. Most of the other current expenditures of the health services are dispersed over a wide range of goods and services, and are negligible in terms of the total distribution of resources. Moreover our results suggest that the level of expenditure in 1975 is more likely to be limited by shortages of trained staff and suitable buildings than by considerations of finance.

Our estimates are linked to the national accounts definition of public authorities' expenditure on health and welfare. This means that the financial series exclude expenditures on the school medical services and child care, and only cover those expenditures by voluntary and private organizations that are reimbursed by public authorities.

The factors chiefly affecting the total demand for health and welfare services are the rate of growth, age structure and marital status of the population; the rate of medical and sociological advance, or 'technical progress'; the effect of rising incomes and the distribution of income on the demand for social services; and the extent of present unsatisfied demand.

(a) *Population changes*

An increase of 12·7 per cent in the population is expected between 1960 and 1975. But the total effect of population change on health requirements will be substantially bigger because by far the greater part of the increase is expected in the non-productive age groups. The population over 65 is expected to increase by 26 per cent, that over 75 by 24 per cent, and the number of babies under 2 by 27 per cent. These are the groups whose needs for health and welfare services are the biggest.

(b) *Technical progress*

The rate of medical advance, or technical progress, is the most difficult factor to predict. It seems safe to assume that general trends towards shorter hospital stays and more effective but more expensive treatments will continue. We can also, with limitations, try to assess the long-term effects of new treatments such as the new drugs and rehabilitation programmes for the mentally sick. But we can barely hazard a guess in which direction will lie the major new developments, parallel to the big reductions during recent years in infectious diseases, and the length of hospital stay for tuberculosis cases.

The effect of medical progress on health expenditure is not all in one direction. Shorter hospital stays and virtual elimination of certain diseases may reduce expenditure, but immunization programmes and the control of chronic illness by drugs may increase them. Better diagnosis and treatment may either reduce or increase the demand for hospital care. Full antenatal care may avoid postnatal complications and long hospital stays, but twenty or more babies with possible rhesus blood complications may need to be born in hospital for the one who subsequently needs transfusion to receive maximum protection. Similarly while medical advance may prevent or cure some forms of chronic illness formerly needing lifelong care, parallel advances increase the survival rate of handicapped babies, and the life expectation of the severely disabled.

Thus, although 'technical progress' in the health field may greatly increase the 'productivity' of the resources devoted to health, it is not likely to lead to a reduction in the resources required. The concept that increased health expenditures would, by reducing the incidence of illness, eventually reduce the need for such expenditures, has already proved to be an illusion. But the precise deployment of the resources needed cannot be predicted. We need buildings that can be adapted to new needs and purposes, and we need to train staff who are able to adjust to new demands and new functions as conditions change.

(c) *Rising incomes*

The changing pattern but undiminished total of health needs described above is partly a reflection of rising demand as standards improve and incomes rise. As we get richer we can afford protection against more remote risks. A domiciliary confinement for a mother with possible postnatal complications, or an operation in a hospital without full modern equipment, will appear to be quite acceptable risks in a poor country with high mortality rates. But they are not acceptable in a prosperous country where the more immediate risks to life and health are catered for.

But the effect of rising incomes on health service requirements is wider than this. Health and welfare services are not solely concerned with acute emergencies. As standards of living rise people want better food, more congenial surroundings and more privacy in hospital as well as at home. Moreover, it is now accepted in principle—if not always in practice—that the standard of living of the aged and the handicapped should rise with that of the working population. So it is reasonable that expenditure on institutional house-keeping should rise with that of private consumers, and the quality of goods supplied for health needs to keep pace with those supplied for general consumption purposes.

Although higher standards of living may be expected to increase the demand for health services, the reduction of poverty should reduce it. A significant part of the need for care of old people is at present caused by inadequate pensions and poverty rather than by unavoidable physical needs[1]. This is a problem of the distribution of income rather than the average level, and is not automatically eliminated by a rise in total national product. The estimates made of the future demand for health services assume an adequate pension policy for the old and permanently disabled.

(d) Present unsatisfied demand

In addition to allowing for changes in the numbers of people needing services, and in the rising standard of service they may reasonably expect, we must take account of the serious deficiencies that still exist in the quantity or the quality of the services available. Deficiencies in quality can be seen in the excessive variation in present standards of medical and hospital care, in hospitals that spend less than three fifths of the national average on the patients' food[2], and in 41,000 old people still housed in nineteenth century Poor Law institutions. Deficiencies in quantity are seen in the number of general practitioners with excessively long lists, the present acute shortage of maternity beds, long waiting lists for old people's homes and beds for the mentally subnormal, and the wide variation in provision of services by different local authorities.

1. THE PRESENT HEALTH SERVICES

(a) The users of the health service

The biggest group of users of the health service are ordinary families suffering the normal ailments and disabilities of life, which call on the family doctor, and related dental, pharmaceutical and ophthalmic services[3]. These general medical services account for 26 per cent of total health service expenditures, before deduction of charges made to patients (table 13.1). Everyone is at risk of more serious illness or accident requiring specialist care and may need hospital

[1]Peter Townsend, *The Last Refuge* (London, 1962), and Dorothy Cole with J. E. G. Utting, *The Economic Circumstances of Old People* (Welwyn, 1962).
[2]In 1962 three hospital regions spent 18 shillings to 19 shillings per head per week on food in hospitals for the chronic sick or mentally subnormal. National average expenditure was 32 shillings.
[3]For brevity we refer to these throughout as the 'family practitioner services'.

Table 13.1.   *Distribution of health manpower and expenditure, 1960[a]*

	Expenditure	Staff
		Percentages
General hospitals[b]	47	57
of which facilities for acute illness	(38)	..
Other residential care[c]	17	25
Family practitioner services[d]	26	6
Community health and welfare services[e]	8	12
Other expenditures[f]	2	..
	100	100

Sources: See tables 13.2 and 13.22.

[a]Expenditures are gross, i.e. before deduction of payments by staff and patients.
[b]Hospitals catering mainly for acute and chronic illness, maternity and geriatric care. Outpatients expenditure included.
[c]Specialist psychiatric hospitals and welfare homes.
[d]General practitioners and the general dental, pharmaceutical and ophthalmic services. Staff figures include doctors and dentists only.
[e]National Health Service local authority services.
[f]Medical Research Council and public health.

facilities—for acute illness—either as an inpatient or an outpatient.   The general hospital is the most expensive of the health services, accounting for 47 per cent of gross expenditures[1].   Perhaps 38 per cent of total expenditure is related to the treatment of acute illness.   Thus the general medical services and hospital facilities for acute illness together account for nearly two thirds of all health service expenditure.

The remaining third of expenditure is devoted to the care of special groups whose needs are more intensive and more continuous than those of the general population.   These are mothers and babies, young children[2], old people, the mentally ill, mentally subnormal and physically handicapped.   Just over a quarter of total expenditure is devoted to their residential care—about 9 per cent to maternity and geriatric care within the general hospital group, and 17 per cent to the specialist psychiatric hospitals and welfare homes.   In addition these special categories probably use about 90 per cent of the domiciliary services provided by local authorities, which include clinics, day care, social work and home nursing.   These services—which we shall call the community health and welfare services—accounted in 1960 for only 8 per cent of total

[1]General hospitals, properly speaking, are hospital units providing a variety of care for acute illness, maternities, geriatric and chronic illness, and some psychiatric care.   Facilities for the latter categories are provided sometimes within the general hospital and sometimes in specialist units.   For descriptive purposes we use the term general hospitals to cover all hospitals except the specialist psychiatric hospitals, and distinguish the type of care by the type of bed: acute, geriatric, maternity, etc.
[2]The specialist needs of children of school age are provided for mainly by the school medical service and child care services, neither of which are included in health and welfare on national accounting definitions.

Table 13.2. *Staff of the health services, England and Wales, 1960*

Thousands

	Total	Health and welfare services Hospital and residential	Other	School health and child care
Doctors	40·9	17·4	23·5[b]	1·0
Dentists	10·5	0·2	10·3[b]	1·0
Nurses and midwives	197·2	184·2	13·0	c
Residential care[a]	10·0	10·0	—	5·0
Health visitors	4·8	—	4·8	3·0
Social workers	4·2	1·4	2·8	2·0
Other professions	25·8	18·8	(7·0)	2·2
Domestic	224·0	200·0	24·0	(5·0)
Other, mainly clerical, administrative and ambulance	56·0	36·0	(20·0)	(2·0)
Total	573·4	468·0	105·4	21·2
Medical and dental	51·4	17·6	33·8	2·0
Other professions	242·0	214·4	27·6	12·2
Other	280·0	236·0	44·0	7·0

Sources: Ministry of Health annual *Report*; Ministry of Education, *The Health of the School Child*; Ministry of Health, *Health and Welfare: The Development of Community Care*, Cmnd 1973 (1963); Institute of Municipal Treasurers and Accountants and Society of County Treasurers, *Children Services Statistics, 1961–62*.

Note: This table is intended to give only a broad general picture of the staffing of the health services in whole-time equivalents. Many of the figures are rough estimates and they may not, in all cases, be complete.

[a]Excluding domestic.
[b]On lists—not necessarily whole-time.
[c]School nurses are included with health visitors who usually do this duty.

expenditure. But they are increasing rapidly, and present provision varies widely between different areas, so that their share in the total may be expected to grow.

The specialist hospital and residential services for geriatric and psychiatric care and for the physically disabled are used by only a small proportion of the old and the handicapped, and the hospital maternity services only cover three fifths of all births. The total numbers of the special groups needing other services are much bigger, and their demands on the family practitioner and community health and welfare services are higher than those of other sections of the population. Consequently although they may include only 20 to 25 per cent of the population these groups probably account for 50 to 60 per cent of total health service expenditure[1]. Changes in the size of these groups therefore have a more than proportionate effect on the demand for health services as a whole.

[1]The population under 5 and over 65 accounts for almost 20 per cent, and the subnormal for about 0·6 per cent. There is no way to count the mentally ill and physically disabled, except in terms of those receiving help, and they are certainly not all the potential clients.

Table 13.3. *Hospital and residential care, England and Wales, 1960*

| | Beds or places | | Expenditure[a] |
	Thousands	Per cent	Per cent
Acute illness[b]	184·1	*32·9*	*60*
Maternity	20·5	*3·7*	*6*
Mental illness	151·9	*27·1*	*14*
Mental subnormality	59·8	*10·7*	*5*
Care of the aged and handicapped:			
in hospital[c]	59·1	*10·5*	*7*
in welfare home[d]	84·6	*15·1*	*8*
Total	560·0	*100·0*	*100*

Sources: Ministry of Health, *A Hospital Plan for England and Wales* (*1962*); Ministry of Health annual *Report*; NIESR estimates.

[a]Rough estimates based on running costs of different kinds of hospitals.
[b]Includes 4,600 beds in special units, mainly convalescent.
[c]Geriatric beds only.
[d]Residents at end of year. The figures include 73·9 thousand old people, 2·9 thousand younger mentally handicapped and 6·6 thousand younger physically disabled. 12·5 thousand places are in voluntary homes paid for by local authorities.

(b) *The staff of the health services*

In total the health and welfare services directly employ about 570,000 people (table 13.2), and the school health and child care services, which are outside our terms of reference, probably employ a further 21,000. Another 15,000 to 25,000 may be employed indirectly, as auxiliary staff employed by doctors and dentists, and in homes run by voluntary organizations for which the local authorities pay the fees.

Doctors and dentists account for less than 10 per cent of the total, and other professional health and welfare workers account for 41 per cent. Of these, nurses and midwives constitute 35 per cent and the remainder includes social workers, health visitors, physiotherapists, teachers of the handicapped and a wide range of other professional and technical staff. The remaining 50 per cent consists largely of domestic staff but includes also ambulance staff, and clerical and administrative staff at all levels. Our estimates for the latter groups may be incomplete.

Residential care takes the major part of the staff employed. The general hospitals alone account for 55 per cent and other kinds of residential care for 25 per cent. The community services in 1960 employed only 14 per cent of health service staff.

(c) *Hospital and residential care*

In addition to employing 80 per cent of the total health service staff, the provision of hospital and other residential facilities accounts for nearly two thirds of current expenditures on health and welfare and 90 per cent or more of capital expenditures. Hospital provision for acute illness is the most expensive item: it accounts for 60 per cent of expenditure on hospitals and homes but only a third of the number of beds (table 13.3). Facilities for the mentally ill and subnormal account for about a fifth of expenditures and two fifths of the beds, and those for the care of the old and handicapped for 15 per cent of expenditures and just over a quarter of the beds.

(d) *Other kinds of care*

The amount of residential care needed, particularly in the case of the old, handicapped and mentally ill, depends largely on the alternative facilities available. Adequate domiciliary help can enable old people and the disabled to continue living in their homes when it would not otherwise be possible. Grouped housing with some communal facilities can meet a similar need. Day hospitals and day centres, for the elderly and disabled and for psychiatric patients, can often meet needs both for active treatment and for welfare care without the necessity for residential care. Training centres for the subnormal also reduce the necessity for admission to institutions, both by providing social training and by relieving families of some of the burden of care.

Provision of many of these kinds of facilities is increasing rapidly but is still only able to meet a tiny part of total need. The number of infirm and handicapped people living in private households is many times the number in institutions. But the staff of the community services is barely half of that devoted to the residential care of these groups; and a substantial part of this staff is engaged in the longer established services for mothers and children. In 1963 there were 36,000 persons in sheltered housing units in England and Wales among an elderly population of over 5 million. There were 220 hospitals giving geriatric or psychiatric day treatment to about 18,000 people, and some 90 local authority workshops and social centres for the mentally ill. Provision of centres for the physically disabled is more liberal; there were over 1,300 in use or under construction in 1964. Training centres for the mentally subnormal have also been expanding rapidly. The number attending such centres increased from 8,300 to 32,000 between 1952 and 1964. But there is still a big shortage of places.

2. THE TRIPARTITE ADMINISTRATION OF THE HEALTH AND WELFARE SERVICES

The services provided under the National Health Service are divided among three separate administrations with largely different geographic coverage. The division of functions is haphazard, based partly on historic accident, and partly on compromises necessary to utilize fully the limited resources available and to secure the co-operation of the medical profession at the time when the health service was initiated in 1948.

The hospital services are organized under fifteen regional hospital boards responsible to the Minister of Health. Their members are appointed by him in consultation with the university of the region, the medical profession, the relevant local authority and other organizations involved. Under the regional hospital board each hospital or group of hospitals is administered by a hospital management committee, appointed by the board with similar consultations, and including both lay members and senior medical staff of the hospital. The teaching hospitals are not responsible to the regional hospital boards but are administered by boards of governors appointed by the Minister on nomination by the university, the regional hospital board, and medical and dental teaching staff of the hospital The ambulance services, of which the hospitals are a major user, are a local authority function[1].

The general practitioner, dental, ophthalmic and pharmaceutical services are organized under about 140 executive councils, responsible to the Minister. Approximately half of their membership is appointed by the professions, one third by the local authorities, and one fifth by the Minister.

The remaining services are provided by 146 local authorities, at county or county borough level, and are not under the direct control of the Minister of Health. In addition to the ambulance service the local authorities provide the domiciliary maternity services, mother and baby clinics, health visitors, home nurses, home helps and social workers. They are also responsible for the mental welfare services including hostels and training centres for the mentally ill and mentally subnormal, and welfare homes for the elderly and handicapped. The extent of provision varies widely from one authority to another, with a complementary variation in the burden falling on the hospitals and general practitioners.

The functioning of the health service under this divided administration depends heavily on the degree of co-operation and co-ordination achieved by the officers concerned assisted by joint representation on the hospital boards and executive committees. At its best this separation is not a real handicap simply because a unified service has been created for practical purposes by means of joint staff appointments and shared facilities. At its worst it is disastrous, providing ready opportunity for avoidance of responsibility, lack of co-ordination between the services and failure to make best use of the small numbers of highly trained staff available.

There is almost no limit to the examples that can be quoted. In areas where the centrally financed hospital services cannot, or do not, provide adequate outpatient and early admission facilities for the mentally ill, more comprehensive locally financed community health services are needed[2]. If, on the other

---

[1]The arrangements described above, and throughout the present section, relate to England and Wales. Slightly different arrangements apply in Scotland and Northern Ireland. In Scotland the teaching hospitals are not separately administered and the ambulance services are not a local authority responsibility.

[2]Ministry of Health, *On the State of the Public Health, 1962* (London, 1963), p. 135.

hand, the local authority services are inadequate, the only choice open to the mental hospitals is to retain patients who no longer need their full facilities, or to discharge them with a high probability of early readmission. The inhuman policy of shifting old people between welfare homes and hospitals as their condition changes continues—in spite of official exhortation—largely because both welfare and hospital authorities, faced with shortage of staff and long waiting lists, consider that the sick (or the well) are someone else's responsibility. Sometimes such transfers become the subject of a bargain between authorities, neither authority being in a position to judge the relative needs of the patients concerned.

Apart from the basic inhumanity of such arrangements they greatly increase the difficulty of assessing needs and creating an efficient service. Without integration, we do not believe that the services can be effectively expanded. Further, if there is expansion on paper, we do not believe that the more extensive services thus created could operate competently with the limited trained staff available, unless all the staff in an area are employed by, or contracted to, one authority. This is not simply a question of goodwill and co-operation. (In fact a large number of skilled man-hours are now spent 'co-operating'.) If there is a shortage both of family doctors and home nurses, only a common authority can make the policy decision how much nursing time should be devoted primarily to relieving doctors. If there are only three fully qualified psychiatric social workers in an area with a case load for six, only a unified team responsible for all cases can allocate them sensibly between highly trained and less skilled staff. Where needs are specialized and numbers small, as they are particularly in some mental welfare services, only a wider regional organization can supervise and guide small numbers of local professional staff.

For these and other reasons explained elsewhere[1] we endorse the recommendation of the Porritt Committee[2] that 'one administrative unit should become the focal point for all the medical services of an appropriate area'. Administrative units must be big enough to include expert skills in all specialities but the field services must meet the needs of reasonably compact local areas. Area health boards, analogous to the regional hospital boards but possibly of different size, and operating through local management committees, would appear to provide the best solution.

On one point we would go rather further than the Porritt Committee. They recommend giving 'care and after-care' to the area health boards but leaving welfare homes with the local authority. We believe that the border-line between residential care necessary for medical reasons and that needed only for social

[1]The arguments on many of the points made in this chapter will be set out more fully in a paper on health and welfare by D. C. Paige and K. Jones to be published shortly in the Occasional Papers series of the National Institute of Economic and Social Research.
[2]A report of the Medical Services Review Committee (Porritt Committee), A Review of the Medical Services in Great Britain (London, 1962).

reasons is often hard to distinguish, and that correct diagnosis and continuity of care at this point are vital to the patient.   This will only be achieved if area health boards cover both health and welfare functions.

3. TRENDS AND POLICIES

Estimates of future expenditure can only be made within a particular framework of social and medical policy.   At the present time much of the policy concerning health and welfare care is in a state of flux, and many of the issues are controversial.   We cannot here defend the choices we have made on controversial issues.   But an outline of the main changes contemplated is necessary to understand the estimates that follow.

(a) *The general hospital*

Current trends in hospital care for acute illness show shorter stays, more intensive treatment and more expensive equipment.   The full range of services of a modern hospital can no longer be provided in the small units of less than 200 beds, which now make up 72 per cent of our hospitals and 41 per cent of all the beds (table 13.4)[1].   The principle underlying the Hospital Plan is that of the integrated general hospital, ideally of perhaps 800 beds and covering all specialities, including chronic and geriatric care and some beds for mental illness[2].

The advantages of this structure are that it can provide the full range of facilities required both for inpatients and outpatients and for teaching purposes. The inclusion of chronic and geriatric wards and beds for mental illness will open to these specialities—which have tended to be the Cinderellas of the hospital service—the full facilities, research and specialization of the general hospital, and make it easier to provide adequate staffing for them.   It will also make possible an expansion of teaching facilities for the care of these groups, both in hospital and in community services.   It will help to provide hospital care for the mentally ill nearer to their homes and to remove the stigma attached to mental illness.

A number of disadvantages must be set against these gains.   The general hospital may tend to get too big in relation to population, so that patients, relatives and general practitioners may have to travel excessive distances.   The closure of small cottage hospitals may reduce local facilities for the care of minor illness, and the opportunities for general practitioners to use hospital facilities.   The inclusion of chronic and mental illness beds in a general hospital orientated to the short-stay care of acute illness may not provide the best environment for patients needing longer hospital treatment[3].

[1]Throughout this section specialist psychiatric hospitals are excluded.
[2]Ministry of Health, *A Hospital Plan for England and Wales*, Cmnd 1604 (London, 1962).
[3]K. Jones, 'The Role and Function of the Mental Hospital', in *Trends in the Mental Health Services*, edited by H. Freeman and J. Farndale (Oxford, 1963).

Table 13.4. *Size distribution of general hospitals, 1960 and 1975*

Size of hospitals (beds)	Hospitals		Beds ('000s)	
	1960	1975	1960	1975
Under 50	848	438	23·3	11·9
50–199	889	611	88·7	62·5
200–399	282	208	78·3	57·5
400–799	108	168	59·0	93·1
800 and over	23	54	23·0	53·1
Total	2,150	1,479	272·3	278·1
Percentage distribution				
Under 50	*39·4*	*29·7*	*8·6*	*4·3*
50–199	*41·4*	*41·3*	*32·5*	*22·4*
200–399	*13·1*	*13·9*	*28·8*	*20·6*
400–799	*5·0*	*11·4*	*21·7*	*33·6*
800 and over	*1·1*	*3·7*	*8·4*	*19·1*
Total	*100·0*	*100·0*	*100·0*	*100·0*

Source: NIESR estimates from *A Hospital Plan for England and Wales*, 1962, *loc. cit.*

How far these advantages and disadvantages outweigh one another will be learned when we have more experience of this new type of general hospital. We cannot, in a global study of this kind, assess how far the selection of small hospitals for closure has been wise.   But we do not believe that the amount of centralization given in the plan up to 1975 is excessive, looking at the country as a whole.   By that date, only one eighth of all the beds for mental illness will be in general hospitals; 71 per cent of the hospitals, and 26 per cent of the beds, will still be in units of less than 200 beds, and there will still be over 400 hospitals with less than fifty beds.   If these are properly distributed they should make adequate provision for local care.   There is greater cause for concern about the 450 hospitals, many of them small, which are planned to be closed after 1975. But before their closure is due there should be opportunity for review in the light of greater experience.

(b) *Community care*

The need for a big expansion in the domiciliary services is undisputed.   At the present time the provision is so patchy, and in many cases so inadequate, that it is impossible to calculate potential need.   We have, therefore, estimated particular needs of staff for the community services by calculating the numbers that would be needed to bring the standard of all local authorities up to that planned by the best authority in each of a number of different classes[1].   This

---

[1]As far as possible allowance was made for alternative types of provision but there appeared to be no general tendency for local authorities to treat residential care and the various community services as alternatives.

suggests a big expansion. For many types the numbers of staff are doubled. Such provision may still not meet all needs, but probably gives a reasonable estimate of potential achievement by 1975.

(c) *Residential care*

We do not believe that this expansion of the domiciliary services will result in any big reduction in the number of people needing a long period of residential care. There are still acute shortages to be made good, and there will always be a number of elderly and handicapped people who cannot live in normal families and for whom domiciliary services alone would be inadequate. They may not need large scale hospital care, but they need shelter. We do not distinguish between hospital and other residential facilities, because—under a unified administration—this does not seem to be the most meaningful distinction. The important distinctions are in the size of units, the type of facilities offered and their location in relation to population.

The main reason for providing care in small units is social and humanitarian. The trend against large-scale institutions, which is fully evident in the current policy on homes for normal children and for old people, is equally applicable to the care of the subnormal and many categories of the mentally ill. But for these groups it will take longer to get rid of the old, isolated, large asylums and hospitals.

There is also a strong economic case for building small units in the next decade or so because they provide greater flexibility for changes in methods of treatment. We seem to be on the edge of a revolution in the mental health services, and no one can now predict the final pattern of services that will develop over the next fifteen or twenty years. But the state of our mental hospitals is such that rebuilding and replacement cannot wait until the trend of development is clearer. Small units can be built piecemeal, more readily adapted to changing practices and more readily converted to different kinds of care if needs change. But the new 1,000-bed hospital may become a white elephant tying future generations to outdated treatment because it is too expensive to scrap[1].

The frequently quoted disadvantages of small units relate to dis-economies in staffing and administration. We believe these to be exaggerated. Somewhat higher staffing ratios are needed but the difference is not big[2] and staff are easier to obtain for units offering more amenities and more satisfying occupations[3]. Problems of relief staff, common user services, and technical administration

---

[1]Consider, for example, Greaves Hall, the new 900-bed hospital for the subnormal under construction in the Liverpool region at a cost of £3 or £4 million.

[2]We estimate that small units may require 20 per cent more staff but this will also provide a higher standard of care, and better conditions of service.

[3]Small purpose-built homes for old people appear to meet their needs of staff more easily than large homes (see P. Townsend, *The Last Refuge, op. cit.,* pp. 123–4).

Table 13.5. *Distribution of psychiatric beds by size of hospital, 1960 and 1975*

Size of hospitals (beds)	Mental illness 1960	1975	Mental subnormality 1960	1975
		'000s		
Under 200	2·9	1·0	9·4	7·2
200–499	4·3	7·5	11·8	11·5
500–799	10·8	21·1	7·6	14·3
800–1,199	34·5	17·4	5·0	8·6
1,200 and over	94·5	28·4	19·0	15·3
Unspecified[a]	—	4·3	5·4	6·2
Beds in general hospitals	4·9	12·3	1·6	0·5
Total	151·9[b]	92·0	59·8	63·6
		Percentage distribution		
Under 200	*1·8*	*1·2*	*15·6*	*11·3*
200–499	*2·9*	*8·2*	*19·8*	*18·1*
500–799	*7·1*	*22·9*	*12·8*	*22·5*
800–1,199	*22·7*	*18·9*	*8·4*	*13·5*
1,200 and over	*62·3*	*30·8*	*31·7*	*24·1*
Unspecified[a]	—	*4·6*	*9·1*	*9·7*
Beds in general hospitals	*3·2*	*13·4*	*2·6*	*0·8*
Total	*100·0*	*100·0*	*100·0*	*100·0*

Source: NIESR estimates from *A Hospital Plan for England and Wales*, 1962, *loc. cit.*
[a]Groups of hospitals for which individual size not given.
[b]Total excludes 200 beds allocated for mental subnormality.

can be met by local grouping of units covering different kinds of care. Policy guidance and professional supervision require a functional administration over a wider geographic area. We thus envisage a two-tier system of small units. A small home caring for particular categories of the mentally ill would share catering, domestic and secretarial facilities, and many categories of relief staff, with other local homes responsible perhaps for elderly or subnormal people. It would draw on the regional administration for specialist skill, supervision and guidance in respect of its professional responsibilities for mental illness.

How much of the total provision should be in small units is still uncertain. But for a considerable period virtually all modernization and replacement can be in such units without any risk of their share becoming too great. At the present time practically all the available institutional accommodation for the mentally sick and subnormal is in excessively large hospitals. In 1960 less than 2 per cent of mental hospital beds were in units of less than 200 beds; 62 per cent were in units of over 1,200 beds, including 36 per cent in hospitals of over 2,000 beds (table 13.5). According to the Hospital Plan two thirds of the group of small hospitals with less than 200 beds will be closed by 1975, but more than 30 per cent of all beds will still be in hospitals with more than 1,200 beds. The reduction expected in the number of mentally ill patients automatically results in some reduction in the average size of hospitals, but far too many excessively large hospitals are scheduled to remain.

There is more serious cause for concern over hospitals for the mentally subnormal because in this group a number of new hospitals and major extensions are planned. The implementation of these plans will reduce the number of beds in very large hospitals; the proportion of beds in hospitals with more than 1,200 beds will fall from 32 per cent to 24 per cent. But extensions to existing hospitals that are already above the optimum size will increase the number of beds in hospitals with between 500 and 1,200 beds from 21 per cent to 36 per cent. Nearly all the new hospitals planned are in the 400- to 500-bed category. The Ministry of Health recommends the care of the moderately subnormal in units not exceeding 200 beds[1], and a good case can be made for caring for many other categories in units of this size, or even substantially smaller. But in 1960 only 16 per cent of beds were in units of less than 200 beds and only 6 per cent in units of less than 100 beds; by 1975 these proportions will fall to 11 per cent and 3 per cent. In this sector we believe that present plans are devoting scarce building resources to a kind of provision that is already approaching obsolescence.

(d) *Facilities in the general medical services*

Our estimates suggest that there will still be a shortage of doctors in 1975; and it becomes increasingly important both to attract a sufficient number of the doctors available into general practice within the health service and to ensure that the best use is made of their services. This will certainly involve some reconsideration of the form and level of remuneration. In addition it is necessary to ensure that the general practitioner has good physical facilities for practice, adequate auxiliary staff, and both opportunity and encouragement for greater integration with the hospital service and with the domiciliary family services.

Increased integration, in a functional sense, will not be provided automatically by unified administration, but it will be facilitated. For example, a raising of minimum obstetrical standards among general practitioners within the service can be more readily achieved within a unified maternity service where senior obstetricians have a greater degree of responsibility for policy and standards[2]. General practitioners, on their side, can make a bigger contribution towards

---

[1] Ministry of Health, *A Hospital Plan for England and Wales* (1962) *loc. cit.*, p. 8.
[2] The urgent need of this has been demonstrated by the inquiry of the National Birthday Trust into perinatal mortality (N. R. Butler and D. G. Bonham, *Perinatal Mortality*, Edinburgh, 1963).

EE

obtaining improvements in hospital and domiciliary services available to them if these are provided by the authority with whom they are contracted.

Adequate auxiliary staff is allowed for in our estimates, partly by increased financial provision for the direct employment of nursing and secretarial assistance by general practitioners, and partly by increased domiciliary staff in the family services. This more liberal staffing of community services would make it possible to adopt generally the system of attaching home nurses, midwives and health visitors to practices. This is already done in some 300 practices to advantage of both doctors and patients[1].

Both the provision of auxiliary staff and better physical facilities can be provided more effectively under group practice or by means of health centres, if these are serving at least four or five doctors caring for 8,000 to 10,000 patients.[2] We have made some allowance for increased provision of this kind of facility in our capital expenditure estimates. But local authorities already plan for the provision of 26 new health centres and a considerable extension and rebuilding of clinics, and we believe that considerable provision can be made within the finance already allocated provided that premises are suitably used and planned. In areas of more scattered population the remaining cottage hospitals may be the most useful focal point for both general practitioner and family services. Concern should be more with the provision of adequate and efficient premises that permit easy co-operation between the services than with elaborate prestige building.

(e) *Pensions and National Assistance policy*

Our estimates assume an adequate pension policy and we do not provide for admission to institutions resulting from poverty, or the effects of poverty. But we believe also that the practical administration of the health and welfare services requires that the real cost of institutional care should be apparent to the officers responsible for matching needs to resources. Old age pensioners already contribute to their maintenance in old people's homes; this fails to cover the full cost of maintenance—other than staff costs—simply because pensions are inadequate. It does not cost more to feed, clothe and house a person in this kind of institution than in a private household. If pensions were adequate, and equally favourable provision made for the permanently disabled and handicapped, who are now mainly dependent on National Assistance, the health and welfare budgets would carry no long-stay housekeeping costs. National Insurance and National Assistance budgets would be responsible for the support of all elderly and handicapped people, most of whom will always be in private

---

[1]See Porritt Committee report, *A Review of the Medical Services in Great Britain, op. cit.,* and Ministry of Health, Standing Medical Advisory Committee, *The Field of Work of the Family Doctor: Report of the Sub-committee* (Gillie Committee) (London, 1963).

[2]Porritt Committee, *A Review of the Medical Services in Great Britain, op. cit.*

households. The health and welfare services would be responsible for meeting their other needs either by residential care or by family services.

(ƒ) *Alternative costs*

Our original intention was to provide estimates showing the difference in cost of alternative policies, such as extensive domiciliary help, day centres or residential care. The aim was to provide a framework within which economic choice could be made. This has not proved practicable because the quality of provision varies so widely that averages are not meaningful. The range of capital costs per place in different kinds of institutions is such that it is feasible to select any one of a considerable variation of types of accommodation at a given per capita cost, even when average costs might suggest that one form was cheaper than another[1]. This is in itself an important conclusion. For it means that the basic choice is far more social than economic.

Similar variation occurs in running costs. Day hospitals only require a single staff shift, provide fewer meals and no sleeping accommodation, and so it is evident that a given standard of care must cost less than in a residential institution. But the average cost of care in existing day hospitals appears to be about the same as the cost of corresponding inpatient treatment[2]. This is because day hospitals are relatively new, small-scale institutions and include none of the cheap substandard hospitals which keep down the average cost of maintaining long-stay patients in mental and geriatric hospitals.

Even as between residential and domiciliary care, the saving in staff from maintaining people in their own homes is much less than might appear at first sight. The average number of man-hours per week required to provide domiciliary help for one old or handicapped person is quite small. But this includes a lot of people whose needs are very small. The marginal case where the choice between domiciliary or residential care is a real one needs more than average help. On the other hand the staff ratio in old people's homes tends to be higher in homes with a large proportion of infirm residents than in those where most residents are active[3]. The average staff ratio, including domestic staff, is 1:3·5.

The residents for whom domiciliary or residential care are practicable alternatives are the more active. Their resettlement in private households would raise the average staff ratios required in residential care. We must not assume therefore that if those discharged could be looked after in their own

---

[1]The one important exception appears to be in group housing, which is more economical both in capital costs and in the deployment of staff than other forms of care (see page 434 below).

[2]J. Farndale, 'British Day Hospitals', in *Trends in the Mental Health Services*, edited by H. Freeman and J. Farndale, *op. cit.*

[3]See page 444 below.

homes with less than one home help/home nurse/social worker to every 3·5 old people it would result in a saving of staff. The choice here is again mainly a social rather than an economic one; and the motive for wanting to retain as many old people as possible in their own homes is the belief that this will give them happier lives.

4. REQUIREMENTS IN 1975 : PEOPLE AND PLACES

In this section we shall consider the numerical requirements for beds for acute illness in general hospitals and beds for the mentally ill, subnormal, elderly and disabled in general hospitals and in other residential units. Day care in training centres for the subnormal is also included, but it has not been possible to make similar assessments of day care and day hospital needs of the other groups. Present provision is so small that potential requirements cannot be estimated. Financial allowance for considerable expansion is, however, made in the provision for staffing and rebuilding of general and psychiatric hospitals and in the expansion of the family services. The assessments made in this section will form the basis of our capital expenditure estimates. They are also needed to calculate staff requirements of hospitals and other institutions and to estimate other current expenditures by institutions.

The analysis falls into two parts. The whole population is at risk of acute illness or mental illness and for these groups demographic factors play a rather small part. Expected changes in requirements are mainly due to changes in the incidence of illness, kinds of treatment and the length of hospital stay. For both groups a fall is expected in requirements per head of population; in beds for mental illness it will be substantial. Extensive building will be needed, but it will almost all be for replacement and modernization. Both for beds for acute illness and for provision for short-stay mental illness, our view is that the official estimates may be over-optimistic about future trends and may somewhat underestimate requirements. But the basis of these estimates is hazardous and in view of the extensive building programmes we do not consider the difference big enough to justify making an alternative estimate. If in fact requirements prove rather higher, it would be possible to reduce the rate of closures of obsolete hospitals to avoid a shortage of beds.

Our estimates of the needs of the elderly and the subnormal have a more demographic basis. We start from estimates of the special populations in need of care and try to assess the proportion that may need residential or other facilities. For both these groups big expansions in accommodation are needed, partly because of rising populations and partly because of current shortages. Replacement forms too small a part of the total estimate for any shortage in total provision to be met by postponing closures. On the other hand we shall still have a big proportion of undesirable accommodation in use in 1975[1].   So there is little risk of over-supply.   For both groups, our estimates are above official plans; for the subnormal they are substantially higher, but part of the difference may be accounted for by different objectives.   Our aim is to make the best guess possible of total needs in 1975—however inadequate the data.   The official plans are obtained by adding up assessments of local needs and in many cases are expected to be revised upwards as the level of needs becomes clearer.

(a) *General hospitals*

(i) *Beds for acute illness.*   The Hospital Plan allows for a fall in the number of beds for acute illness from 3·9 to 3·4 per thousand population.   The factors determining the demand for beds are the number of patients requiring treatment, their average stay in hospital and the average occupation of available beds[2]. We have tried to assess probable future trends of these three factors by comparison both with recent developments in England and Wales and with the present position in the few other developed countries for which moderately comparable figures are available[3].   For this purpose it is desirable to distinguish between beds for tuberculosis and infectious diseases, and other beds for acute illness.

The figures for these beds which cover all chest diseases as well as infectious diseases have fallen sharply from 40,400 in 1953 to 23,300 in 1962 (table 13.6). Even with this reduction, occupancy rates in these specialities are low and the downward trend seems likely to continue.   Thus only about 10,000 beds may be needed for these specialities by 1975.

Beds for other acute illnesses increased slightly between 1953 and 1963 but only enough to offset a small fall in the proportion occupied.   The number of beds per thousand population fell by about 2 per cent.   The number of cases treated per thousand population—measured by discharges—increased by 17 per cent.   The number of discharges per bed increased by about 20 per cent, as the result of a fall of 20 per cent in the average length of stay.

The fall in occupancy rates over this period appears to reflect an improvement in the service rather than a fall in efficiency.   Shorter length of stay makes it more difficult to achieve a high rate of occupancy.   It is perhaps for this reason that occupancy rates in this country are still slightly above those in other countries (table 13.7), but we do not envisage that they will fall further, because more efficient use of beds has already partly offset this factor and the greater flexibility of larger modern hospitals may permit further improvement.

The fall in the length of stay seems likely to go on.   The average stay in Eng-

---

[1]This will consist mainly of old people's homes in unsuitable converted buildings, and excessively large and obsolete hospitals for the subnormal.

[2]These factors are in turn affected by changes in the age/sex structure of the population, but the influence of this will be small between 1960 and 1975.

[3]International comparisons in this field can only give a very broad picture, because it is extremely difficult to get comparable figures.   The level of needs is also affected by institutional differences between countries.

Table 13.6. *Hospital beds for acute illness. England and Wales, 1953–63*

| | Staffed beds allocated '000s | | | Dis-charges '000s | Beds | Dis-charges | Dis-charges per bed | Per cent of beds occupied | Average stay (days) |
| | | | | | per 1,000 population | | | | |
	Total	TB and infectious diseases	Excluding beds for TB and infectious diseases[a]						
1953	193·1	40·4	152·7	2,674	3·45	60·6	17·5	80·4	16·74
1954	194·3	39·9	154·4	2,776	3·46	62·7	18·0	80·0	16·23
1955	192·9	38·7	154·2	2,765	3·46	62·2	17·9	79·6	16·21
1956	191·0	36·7	154·3	2,814	3·45	63·0	18·2	79·7	15·94
1957	188·5	34·0	154·5	2,819	3·44	62·8	18·2	78·1	15·61
1958	188·6	32·5	156·1	2,883	3·46	63·9	18·5	78·4	15·39
1959	186·5	30·1	156·4	2,970	3·45	65·4	19·0	77·4	14·88
1960	185·0	28·2	156·8	3,059	3·43	66·9	19·5	77·6	14·50
1961	184·7	26·7	158·0	3,132	3·41	67·8	19·8	76·3	14·04
1962	183·1	24·8	158·3	3,218	3·38	68·9	20·3	76·9	13·80
1963	181·7	23·3	158·4	3,336	3·37	70·9	21·1	77·9	13·50
Forecast									
1975	177·0	10·0	167·0	4,800[b]	3·21	90[bd]	28·8[b]	78·5[b]	10
				4,200[c]		82[c]	25·2[c]	76·0[c]	11

Sources: Ministry of Health annual *Report*; *A Hospital Plan for England and Wales*, 1962, *loc. cit.*

[a]The figures include a small number of beds (mainly convalescent and for special purposes) that are not classified as acute illness in table 13.24. The number of these (4 per cent in 1960) is not sufficient to affect the ratios. Staff wards and special care babies are excluded here. The earlier years are not strictly comparable.

[b]Assuming an average stay of 10 days and 78·5 per cent occupancy.

[c]Assuming an average stay of 11 days and 76 per cent occupancy.

[d]A continuation of the rate of growth of 1·6 per cent a year in discharges per 1,000 of the population experienced over the period 1953–63 would give a figure of 86 per 1,000 of the population or 4,500 in all.

land and Wales is about the same as in Norway and Sweden and substantially above that in Saskatchewan[1]. This is so in spite of the fact that these three places appear to have more acute beds per thousand population. The length of stay in this country for maternity cases has been deliberately shortened because of the current shortage of beds[2]. But there is no evidence that this has been so for acute illness. In fact it has been shown that for comparable diagnoses the hospitals that are most efficient in other respects have the earliest discharges.[3]

[1]They are more than twice as high as those in the United States. But we believe short stays in the United States are partly due to the high cost of medical care.

[2]D. C. Paige, 'Births and Maternity Beds in England and Wales in 1970', *National Institute Economic Review, op. cit.*

[3]R. W. Revans, 'The Morale and Effectiveness of General Hospitals', in *Problems and Progress in Medical Care*, edited by Gordon McLachlan (London, 1964).

Table 13.7.   *International comparisons of hospital beds for acute illness, 1960[a]*

	Beds	Discharges		Occupa-tion rate	Length of stay
	Per 1,000 population		Per bed	Per cent	(days)
England and Wales	3·59	68·4	19 1	76·2	14·5
United States[b]	3·55	128·0	36·0	74·7	7·6
United States[c]	3·09	105·9	33·9	74·7	8·0
Canada (Saskatchewan)[d]	6·20	170·3	27·5	78·3	10·4
Sweden[e]	4·93	96·3	19·5	76·7	14·3
Norway	5·58	102·7	18·4	75·0[f]	14·9[f]

Sources: World Health Organization; Ministry of Health annual *Report; Statistical Abstract of the United States; Statistical Yearbook of Norway; Statistical Abstract of Sweden; Annual Report of the Saskatchewan Hospital Services Plan, 1963.*

[a]Excluding TB, maternity, psychiatric, and chronic beds, but including those for infectious diseases.

[b]Figures include maternity beds.

[c]Adjusted to exclude maternity beds on the basis of number of hospital births and an assumed average stay of 5·5 days (including antenatal).

[d]Figures are for 1961 and relate to the Saskatchewan Hospital Service, which by 1961 covered almost all the bed-days in the province.   Maternity and mental cases have been excluded.   Occupancy rates are calculated from the total of bed-days, and rated bed capacity in the province.   The number of beds is derived from the other data, and includes in principle beds used by the service in other provinces.

[e]Discharges and length of stay are partly estimated to exclude maternities and a few psychiatric cases.   This has been done on the assumption of about 100,000 maternity cases staying 8–10 days.

[f]Derived figures based on the discharges and number of beds.   It has been assumed that both occupancy is a little lower and length of stay a little higher than in Sweden.   If the actual length of stay is shorter, occupancy rates would be still lower and vice versa.

If the number of discharges continues to rise at the same rate as in the past—1·6 per cent a year—there would be 86 per thousand population by 1975.   The Hospital Plan bed allocation could handle this without any increase in occupancy rates if length of stay fell to 10½ days.   This is about the same percentage fall over the next fifteen years as has occurred over the past nine years.   If occupancy rates rose to 78·5 and length of stay fell to 10·0 days, which seems likely to be the upper limit for these factors, it would permit the treatment of 90 cases per thousand population.   Present levels in Norway, Sweden and the United States range from 96 to 106.

It would appear, therefore, that the methods used in the Hospital Plan may not make sufficient allowance for a lowering of the threshold of admission, and consequent increase of cases for treatment, that may occur as more facilities become available.   The Plan seems, however, to allow for a more rapid increase in the number of cases than has been experienced in the past, and in view of the uncertainty of length of stay, and the hazardous nature of international comparisons in this field, we do not feel that the evidence is sufficient to justify an alternative set of estimates.   We have, however, made allowance for the higher population estimates used in this study.   This increases the number of beds for acute illness in 1975 from the Hospital Plan figure of 168,600 to 173,600 compared with a total of 179,500 in 1960.

(ii) *Other beds in general hospitals.* We have allowed for 33,000 *maternity beds* in England and Wales by 1975, compared with 20,500 in 1960, and the 1962 Hospital Plan provision of 27,500[1]. This estimate is linked to a birth forecast of 960,000 in 1975, and aims to provide for 80 per cent to 85 per cent of births to be in hospitals[2].

Our estimates also include the provision of 12,300 beds in general hospitals for *mental illness* and 65,900 *geriatric beds.* These estimates are taken from the Hospital Plan. In the following section we discuss the total residential needs of these groups. We have also included the Hospital Plan estimate of 4,600 convalescent and other special category beds, but have increased the provision for the *subnormal* from 500 to 1,000. The latter are all intended to be beds in paediatric departments for very severely handicapped children. These provisions bring the total number of beds in general hospitals in 1975 to 289,000 compared with 270,000 in 1960 (see table 13.24 below).

(iii) *Replacement and modernization.* A substantial proportion of existing hospitals is in need either of replacement or of extensive modernization and improvement. In 1953 it was found that in a group of hospitals covering 90 per cent of all hospital beds[3], 45 per cent of hospitals were originally erected before 1891 and 21 per cent before 1861[4]. Many of these have been added to or partly rebuilt since the original date of erection, but the hospital survey carried out at the end of the war revealed many hospitals in quite appalling condition, and a big proportion of the 2,800 hospitals taken over by the National Health Service in 1948 were in obsolete buildings[5]. Capital expenditure since 1948 has been too small to have changed the situation significantly. In the thirteen years from 1948 to 1961 it provided only 35,600 beds in new or converted buildings; this represents a replacement rate of only 0·6 per cent a year.

The Hospital Plan provides for the replacement of about one quarter of the

---

[1]The 1963 revision of the Plan states that the official figures have also been revised upwards following revised birth projections, but new totals are not stated. The revised birth figures are still, however, below those used in this study (see Ministry of Health, *A Hospital Plan for England and Wales (Revision to 1972–73)* (London, 1963).

[2]Details of the basis of these estimates are given in D. C. Paige, 'Births and Maternity Beds in England and Wales in 1970', *op. cit.* Since that article was prepared later studies suggest that larger provision will be needed for antenatal care and that rather lower occupancy rates are to be expected (see D. J. Newell, 'Statistical Aspects of the Demand for Maternity Beds', *Journal of the Royal Statistical Society,* Series A (1964), vol. 127, part I). We believe, however, that this extra provision will be offset by a reduction in normal postnatal stay so that further beds will not be needed.

[3]The figures given throughout this paragraph relate to both general and psychiatric hospitals.

[4]B. Abel-Smith and R. M. Titmuss, *The Cost of the National Health Service in England and Wales* (Cambridge, 1956).

[5]Ministry of Health, *A Hospital Plan for England and Wales,* 1962, *loc. cit.,* p. 1.

existing beds in general hospitals by 1975. Allowing also for additional beds to be made available by that date, 28 per cent of all beds will then be in buildings less than fifteen years old, and probably 35 to 40 per cent will be less than 27 years old. In view of the age structure of the present stock of hospitals this will still leave a substantial number of obsolete hospital buildings—some of them over eighty years old—for replacement in the following decade. But a continuation of the rate of rebuilding that will be reached by 1975 should provide for complete renewal of all general hospitals built before the second world war by about 1990 or 1995. Taking into account other health service and social service needs we do not consider that a more rapid rate of replacement would be justified.

(b) Mental illness

(i) *Number of beds.* The number of beds needed for mental illness is expected to fall dramatically over the next fifteen years. The Hospital Plan allows provisionally for 92,000 beds in England and Wales, or 1·9 beds per thousand population in 1975 compared with 152,000 beds or 3·3 per thousand population in 1960. The reduction expected is almost entirely in long-stay patients (those remaining in hospital over two years). This group is expected to fall from perhaps 2·1 per thousand in 1960 to 0·9 in 1975. The forecast is based on a study of the accrual of long-stay patients admitted in 1954 and 1956[1]. The evidence we have is open to several interpretations which could lead to different forecasts, but we believe that the most likely explanation of the available data is that the reduction in the number of patients becoming chronic occurred some time ago[2]. There does not appear to have been a big fall in the number of patients remaining in hospital for more than a year during the 1950s. If this view is correct, we may expect a fairly rapid running down of long-stay patients between now and 1975 as the large number of chronic patients admitted in the 1920s and 1930s die off, but have no grounds, on the evidence now available, for believing in much further reduction thereafter. On this analysis the fall expected in the immediate future does not justify an assumption that in the longer term there will be no need to provide suitable facilities for a fairly large number of chronic patients.

The prediction made by C. G. Tooth and E. M. Brooke of 0·88 beds per thousand population for short- and medium-stay patients appears over-optimistic. It is based on admissions in 1956 and does not allow for a continuation of the steady upward trend in admission that has continued over many years. Allowing for changes in coverage, total admissions probably increased

---

[1]C. G. Tooth and E. M. Brooke, 'Trends in the Mental Hospital Population and Their Effect on Future Planning', *The Lancet*, 1 April 1961, pp. 710–13.

[2]The grounds for this belief, which cannot be firmly established from the data available, are given in the forthcoming paper by D. C. Paige and K. Jones, *op. cit.*, footnote 1, page 412.

Table 13.8. *Mental illness: hospital population and admissions, England and Wales, 1951–61*

Thousands

	Admissions			Resident population, end-year
	First	Re-admissions	Total	
National Health Service mental hospitals				
Voluntary, temporary and certified patients				
1951	38·7	20·6	59·3	143·2
1952	39·2	23·1	62·3	144·6
1953	42·8	24·6	67·4	146·6
1954	43·2	28·5	71·7	148·1
1955	45·9	32·7	78·6	146·9
1956	47·4	36·6	84·0	145·6
1957	48·3	40·7	88·9	143·2
1958a	48·6	43·0	91·6	138·1
National Health Service mental hospitals				
Voluntary, temporary, certified and informal patients				
1958a	50·1	44·0	94·1	142·8
1959b	55·0	50·7	105·7	139·1
1960	58·6	56·0	114·6	136·2
All mentally ill patients in National Health Service or special hospitals				
1.11.60 to 30.4.61c	..	..	138·7	137·1d
1.5.61 to 31.12.61c	..	..	140·2	135·4
1.1.62 to 31.12.62	..	..	146·5	133·7
1.1.63 to 31.12.63	..	..	160·4	127·6

Sources: Ministry of Health annual *Report*; *Registrar General's Statistical Review of England and Wales for the year 1959*; *Supplement on Mental Health.*

aThe figures for 1958 including informal patients cover 4,000 more beds than those covering voluntary, temporary and certified patients only.
bThe figures for 1959 cover 2,000 more psychiatric beds than those for 1958.
cAnnual rate.
dEnd-April 1961.

by about 70 per cent between 1951 and 1959 (table 13.8). There may have been some levelling off recently but this is difficult to determine because of the statistical and administrative effects of the 1959 Mental Health Act. The increase in admissions has been partially but not wholly offset by a fall in the average length of stay of short- and medium-stay patients. Between 1952 and 1959 the average stay of patients in hospital for less than one year fell from 57 to 50 days, but this is not sufficient to offset the rise in short-stay admissions and the number of beds needed for these patients has continued to rise.

Present indications are that some allowance should be made for a further rise in the number of beds needed for short- and medium-stay patients, but this trend might be offset by the effects of better provision of mental health facilities for outpatients and in community services. Also the total provision in the Hospital Plan is slightly above the detailed forecast (1·9 beds per thousand compared with 1·77) and we have not therefore made any alternative estimate for additional provision.

(ii) *Modernization and replacement.* The majority of the existing mental hospitals are quite unsuited to modern needs and the substantial fall expected in the number of beds will not obviate the need for extensive replacement. The Hospital Plan aims to provide an additional 7,400 beds for mental illness in general hospitals but only about 2,000 new beds are specifically listed in the plan, or in schemes in progress[1]. Modernization schemes are referred to for hospitals covering about 30 per cent of the beds that will remain in 1975, but the extent of the improvement is difficult to assess from the information available. Well over half appears to be limited to special facilities such as engineering services, kitchens or staff accommodation. Such improvements may be highly necessary but they cannot alter the basic layout of unsuitable buildings and their cost is often very high.   In addition the local authority plans for the period up to 1972 include the provision of 4,000 hostel places for the mentally ill, but this total includes many areas with no planned provision at all.

We aim, therefore to increase the hostel places to 10,000, and to replace with small or medium size units a quarter of the 72,000 beds in specialist mental hospitals that will still be in use in 1975. On this basis 36 per cent of mental illness beds of all kinds would in 1975 be less than fifteen years old.   This is a slightly bigger proportion than for the general hospitals, which is necessary if any significant impact is to be made on the main group of specialist mental hospitals. Almost all the hostel places will be new as there is hardly any provision of this kind at present, and so will three fifths of the mental illness beds in general hospitals.

(c) *Mental subnormality*

(i) *Incidence.* Probably about one baby in every 200 is born with a mental handicap amounting to 'severe subnormality', which means he will always need some care and protection and be incapable of living an independent life. Severe subnormality is often associated with physical handicap, and for many categories life expectation is still short, but it has increased substantially over the last thirty years[2]. We estimate that there may be nearly 140,000 severely subnormal individuals in England and Wales, about 43,000 children under 16

[1]It is difficult to identify bed replacements in the Hospital Plan because the size of most hospitals is to be reduced.   The total amount of new ward accommodation planned may be substantially bigger than that we have been able to identify.

[2]The number of mongol children who survive to the age of 10 is estimated to be four times greater than in 1929 (see C. O. Carter, 'A Life Table for Mongols with Causes of Death', *Journal of Mental Deficiency Research*, vol. 2, part 2, 1958, p. 64).

Table 13.9.   *Estimated number of mentally subnormals needing health and welfare care, England and Wales, 1960 and 1975*[a]

Age group	1960			1975		
	Idiots and imbeciles	Others[b]	Total	Idiots and imbeciles	Others[b]	Total
Total number						
0–4	14,800	3,500	18,300	19,900	4,700	24,600
5–15	28,000	7,600	35,600	34,600	9,400	44,000
16–24	17,600	34,100	51,700	20,700	39,700	60,400
25–64	64,200	59,300	123,500	67,200	64,400	131,600
65+	13,000	10,900	23,900	16,500	13,900	30,400
Total	137,600	115,400	253,000	158,900	132,100	291,000
Number in a total population of 100,000[c]						
0–4	32	8	40	38	9	47
5–15	61	17	78	66	18	84
16–24	39	74	113	40	76	116
25–64	140	130	270	129	124	253
65+	28	24	52	32	27	59
Total	300	253	553	305	254	559

Source: Forthcoming paper by D. C. Paige and K. Jones, *op. cit.*, footnote 1, page 412.

[a]The estimates aim to include all the severely subnormal (roughly equated to imbeciles and idiots) and the proportion of moderately subnormal (feeble-minded) likely to be in need of special help.

[b]This is an arbitrary estimate of the proportion of the moderately subnormal who may need care. During childhood the incidence is taken as only 1·0 per 1,000 population because most moderately handicapped children are at school. The proportion needing help rises sharply at the school-leaving age, and falls again as the majority reach independence.

[c]Calculated from unrounded figures.

and possibly as many as 95,000 adolescents and adults (table 13.9)[1].

There is a large number of subnormal people whose incapacity is smaller, but who may need care and help at least during part of their lives. Most of the children are able to attend educationally subnormal schools but need guidance or further training for perhaps five or ten years after leaving school. About 10 or

[1]These estimates were extrapolated from assessments for children aged 10–14 given by J. Tizard in *The Needs of Mentally Handicapped Children*, a report of a working party set up by the Paediatric Society of the South East Metropolitan Regional Hospital Board (London, 1962). Since our estimates were prepared Dr Tizard has made a full study of the requirements of this group (see J. Tizard, *Community Services for the Mentally Handicapped*, Oxford, 1964). Direct comparison of the two assessments is complicated by differences in classification and coverage, and in assumptions concerning general population movements and availability of resources. Dr Tizard's much more complete and expert estimates suggest that we have probably been unduly conservative in our assessments considered as estimates of the full need for residential care, but perhaps not as estimates of reasonable achievement over the country as a whole by 1975. Our one serious error seems to have been in underestimating the number of children likely to require full nursing and hospital care.

Table 13.10. *Care of the subnormal: some tentative estimates, England and Wales, 1962 and 1975, by age group*

	0–4	5–15	16–24	25–64	65+	Total
1962						
Hospital	500	8,000	50,200[a]		2,500	61,200
Poor Law institution			1,900[a]		3,600	5,500
Other local authority homes			900[a]		3,000	3,900
Training centre		13,500	11,200[a]		..	24,700
Home training		300	1,000[a]		..	1,300
Subtotal	500	21,800	(22,700)	(42,500)	9,100	96,600
No residential or day care	17,800	13,800	29,000	81,000	14,800	156,400
Receiving local authority services		7,200	41,400[b]			48,600
Awaiting hospital		(1,000)	(4,800)[b]			5,800
Awaiting training		1,700	3,400[a]			5,100
Total of subnormal	18,300	35,600	51,700	123,500	23,900	253,000
Total places:						
residential	500	8,000	53,000		9,100	70,600[c]
training		13,800	12,200[a]			26,000
1975						
Children's hospital	400	600				1,000
Children's home	1,500	4,500				6,000
Home and training centre		6,000				6,000
Training centre only	3,000	25,000				28,000
Hospital			15,000	40,000	5,000	60,000
Hostel or small unit			4,000	16,000	1,000	21,000
Old people's home				2,000	15,000	17,000
Hostel and training centre			3,000	4,000	..	7,000
Training centre only			19,000	18,000	..	37,000
Subtotal	4,900	36,100	41,000	80,000	21,000	183,000
Domiciliary services only	19,700	7,900	19,400	51,600	9,400	108,000
Total of subnormal	24,600	44,000	60,400	131,600	30,400	291,000
Total places:						
residential	1,900	11,100	22,000	62,000	21,000	118,000[d]
training	3,000	31,000	22,000	22,000	..	78,000

Sources: Estimates of those in care in 1962 are based on Ministry of Health annual *Reports*. End-1961 or 1962 figures are related to 1960 estimates of the subnormal, because some services are expanding rapidly and this gives a more up-to-date picture. The allocation by age groups is partly estimated. Estimates for 1975 are tentative suggestions which aim only at giving the order of magnitude of services likely to be needed.

[a]Age groups 16–64.
[b]All age groups over 16.
[c]Including 8,500 places in general welfare homes.
[d]Including 17,000 places in general old people's homes.

20 per cent may remain permanently dependent. The number of moderately subnormal individuals of various ages who may need special health and welfare services is probably between 110,000 and 120,000.

We thus estimate that there may be about 250,000 subnormal children and adults in England and Wales. Of these in 1962 about 60,000 were in hospital, 10,000 in welfare homes, 25,000 in day training centres and another 60,000 receiving some local authority services or awaiting a hospital bed or place in a training centre (table 13.10). In all about 145,000 are known to the authorities; but the standard of ascertainment and service varies widely between different local authorities and this number might reach 200,000 if the standard of all authorities was as high as that of those with the most developed mental welfare services[1].

We do not expect much change in the incidence of mental subnormality over the next fifteen years. Medical research may eliminate some causes of severe subnormality and improved training permit more of the moderately handicapped to reach independence. But these factors are likely to be more than offset by increased life expectancy and increased survival at birth of severely handicapped babies. As our estimates of the incidence are very rough we have taken the same rates for 1975. On this basis there would be nearly 300,000 mentally subnormal people in England and Wales in 1975, of whom 70,000 would be children. For the United Kingdom the corresponding numbers would be 330,000 and 80,000.

(ii) *Provision required.* There are at present long waiting lists both for hospitals and for training centres for the subnormal and these have not been reduced by increases in facilities. We believe that, in addition, the demand may increase sharply as the quality of residential care is improved. The families of severely subnormal people often carry an excessive burden, which they may tolerate only because there is often no alternative except residential care in a large substandard hospital[2].

The Hospital Plan aims to increase the number of hospital beds for the subnormal from 60,000 in 1960 to 64,000 in 1975. In addition local authorities plan to provide 51,000 training centre places and 10,000 hostel places by 1972. Some of the hostel places would be for those attending training centres. On our estimates of the total population this would make some kind of provision for regular care or training for about 40 per cent of the subnormal population, or for perhaps half of those aged 5 to 64. The great majority of those in need of services are in one of three groups: children of school age needing the best training available to minimize their handicaps; young retarded adults whose development to independence largely depends on the guidance and training they

[1]Based on incidences quoted in Ministry of Health, *Health and Welfare: The Development of Community Care*, Cmnd 1973 (London, 1963).
[2]Working party on *The Needs of Mentally Handicapped Children, op. cit.*

are given; and severely handicapped adults with the mental age of young children. We do not believe that provision for regular residential or day care for only half the people in these groups will be adequate. Our estimates aim therefore to provide regular care for 60 per cent of all the subnormal population needing help (table 13.10). The ratios range from about 20 per cent for children under school age[1] to over 80 per cent for children of 5 to 15 and 65 per cent for young adults aged 16 to 24. For older adults of working age we tentatively assume regular care for about 55 per cent. This is well above present levels, but as we have excluded from the population the moderately subnormal expected to reach independence, and as many will be beyond the age when their immediate families can look after them, it may still be optimistic to assume that 45 per cent can manage with only occasional care and guidance. We assume that most of the elderly, apart from those who have grown old in hospital, can be fitted into normal welfare homes.

Our estimates of the number needing residential and day care respectively are highly tentative. In total we allow for 78,000 training centre places, and 111,000 residential places, of which 13,000 would be for those attending centres.

All new provision should be in small units, because most of the present 60,000 hospital beds, which are mainly in large hospitals, will have to remain in use; our plans therefore incorporate the modernization schemes for these included in the Hospital Plan. We regard it as of prime importance that the residential care for children should be in small homes offering them maximum opportunity of development[2], and that junior training centres should be integrated with the main educational system. This is necessary both to facilitate transfer of those children who make sufficient progress and to permit them to share the benefits of the main stream of educational research and training.

(d) Care of the aged and handicapped

(i) *Family circumstances.* The proportion of the population over 65 who are in institutions or receiving family services is small. About 5 per cent of those over 65 and nearly 7 per cent of those over 75 are in various kinds of residential homes, or general, chronic or mental hospitals. Perhaps another $3\frac{1}{2}$–4 per cent get some domiciliary help but it is often slight.

The need for help is greatly dependent on family circumstances, chiefly marital status and the availability of help from children. In nearly all categories a bigger proportion of men than women, go into institutions in their old age (table 13.11). Very few married people come into residential care; only about 0·25 per cent are in welfare homes, and less than 2 per cent in institutions of any

[1] Much of this would be in training centres of nursery school type for 3- and 4-year-olds.
[2] We have also estimated a token allowance of 1,000 beds in general hospitals for children with gross physical and mental handicaps. Tizard's estimates (see footnote 1, p. 428) suggest that a total of some 8,000 beds might be needed for children of this category, but in 1975 some would be likely still to be in the large specialist hospitals.

kind.   Rates for the widowed are higher, rising from 2 per cent for widows aged 65 to 74, to 8·5 per cent for widowers of 75 and over.   The proportion of single people in institutions is much higher.   Even at ages 65 to 74 over 12 per cent of elderly single men are in some residential care—nearly half of them in welfare homes.   For the age group 75 and over, 12 per cent are in homes, and over 20 per cent in some sort of institution.   Rates for single women are lower than those for men at all ages under 84, but among those over 85—where women substantially outnumber men—15 per cent are in old people's homes, and possibly over a quarter of the group are in some institution.

There will be a smaller proportion of single old people in 1975, and this factor, together with minor changes in age and sex composition, would slightly reduce the need for residential care.   But the difference is small.   Using residence rates applicable in 1956–9, the same scale of provision could be made in residential homes with 17·1 places per thousand old people in 1960, and 16·4 in 1975.   The total requirement including hospitals would fall on this account from 38·6 per thousand to 37·5.

But one of the main reasons underlying the differences in institutional requirements is the amount of help people receive in old age from their children. Because of the smaller families that resulted from marriages after the first world war fewer of the old people of 1975 will have surviving children.   The proportion with three or more may fall from 43 per cent to 30 per cent of those who married.   The number of married and widowed people with no surviving child will rise from perhaps 18.5 per cent in 1960 to 25 per cent in 1975, and the number with only one child from 18 per cent to 24·5 per cent.   In addition the old people of 1975 will have fewer siblings and substantially fewer unmarried children living at home.

It is not possible to take account of this factor very precisely.   It would seem that residence rates for widows and widowers without children are probably only 20 or 25 per cent lower than those for single people.   Rates for those with only one or two children may be 40 or 60 per cent higher than for those with three or more[1].   On this basis the effect of smaller families may just about offset the changes in marital status, and we expect little net change in total needs arising from changing family circumstances between 1960 and 1975 (table 13.11).
(ii) *The kind of facilities required.*   It is more difficult to assess how far present facilities fall short of needs.   On the one hand there is evidence of a big unsatisfied demand for residential places.   The number of beds in homes increased by 80 per cent between 1949 and 1960, but long waiting lists remain.   And those local authorities which provide about twice the national average number of places relative to population do not seem to have too many.   About one third

---

[1]These estimates are based on proportions of new residents in different categories given by Townsend, *The Last Refuge, op. cit.,* combined with our own estimates of the proportions of these groups in the general population.

Table 13.11. *The proportion of elderly people in homes and hospitals, England and Wales*

Age group	Marital status	Old people's homes[a]		General hospitals[b]		Hospitals for mental illness		Total	
		M	F	M	F	M	F	M	F
	Number in institutions per 1,000 population of group, 1956–9[c]								
65–74	Married	1	1	7	5	4	7	12	13
	Widowed[d]	2	5	15	9	5	6	22	20
	Single	59	19	27	14	38	24	124	57
75 and over	Married	7	6	10	10	5	14	22	30
	Widowed[d]	56	32	24	18	5	9	85	59
	Single	122	77	49	28	33	26	204	131
All over 65	Married	3	2	8	6	4	9	15	17
	Widowed[d]	37	14	20	13	5	7	62	34
	Single	82	42	35	19	36	25	153	86

Total number in institutions

	Old people's homes	General hospitals	Hospitals for mental illness	Total
1960				
Requirements on above ratios[e]: '000s	93·2	66·8	50·8	210·8
Per 1,000 over 65	17·1	12·2	9·3	38·6
1975				
Requirements on above ratios: '000s	114·0	83·2	62·8	260·0
Per 1,000 over 65	16·4	12·0	9·0	37·4
Adjusted for surviving children: '000s	119·1	85·1	62·8	267·0
Per 1,000 over 65	17·1	12·3	9·0	38·4
Expected needs: '000s	163·0	82·0	43·0	288·0
Per 1,000 over 65	23·5	11·8	6·1	41·4

Sources: Ministry of Health, *Report on Hospital In-patient Enquiry, 1956–1957*; Registrar General's Statistical Review . . . 1959: Supplement on Mental Health, loc. cit.; B. Abel-Smith and R. M. Titmuss, *The Cost of the National Health Service in England and Wales, op. cit.*; P. Townsend, *The Last Refuge, op. cit.*; and NIESR estimates.

[a]Including voluntary and private homes.
[b]All National Health Service hospitals other than psychiatric hospitals.
[c]The ratios for old people's homes relate to 1958–9, those for general hospitals to 1956 and for mental hospitals to 1959. Information for the latter two categories related only to age and sex, rates by marital status were extrapolated from 1951 assuming a proportionate change within each age/sex group.
[d]Including divorced.
[e]The actual number in old people's homes in 1960 was 96,700 or 17·7 per 1,000; we do not have information for hospitals in 1960.

of the beds available are still in substandard former public assistance institutions and demand might rise further if this deterrent were removed. On the other hand it is argued that much of the current need arises from poverty, poor housing, insufficient housing and lack of domiciliary facilities; and that we already have more old people's homes and geriatric wards than we should need if these other deficiencies were met[1].

[1]P. Townsend, *ibid.,* chapter 12.

We believe that the most urgent need is for adequate financial provision, more liberal and more flexible domiciliary services and sufficient housing suitable for the elderly and infirm, much of it in supervised group units. Only when these needs are met will the genuine demand for *residential* care become apparent.

We agree with Townsend that large-scale provision of sheltered housing is the greatest need. Not only does this provide a reasonable social compromise between the need for care and the need for independence but it is the most economical form of care. Our housing plans include large-scale rebuilding and improvements[1]; it does not cost more to arrange for many of the smaller units to be in small groups where some communal facilities can be given. The capital cost of these is only about £1,500 a unit compared with about £1,900 a place for residential homes. Grouped units provide a similar saving in staff costs, partly by saving travelling time for domiciliary staff, but mainly by enabling the provision of a little help at frequent intervals; and this may often avoid the need for admission to full residential care. There are already about 1·3 million people over 75 living quite alone, and perhaps 0·75 million married couples of this age group with no younger person in the house. By 1975 these numbers will be much bigger. It may well be therefore that 0·5 million or even 1·0 million of new homes or new conversions should be in grouped schemes.

(iii) *Residential care.* Since the present provision of residential places is far below the need, we do not believe that these alternative facilities are likely to bring an actual reduction in the provisions required. It is more likely that, with more liberal alternative care, a small increase in the residential care per thousand elderly people will, by 1975, meet needs that it would not satisfy now. This still implies a big increase in the number of places in welfare homes, partly because of the population increase and partly because there will be fewer old people in mental hospitals, and a slight fall in the proportion in geriatric beds (table 13.12). We expect that the number of residents in old people's homes of all kinds may need to rise from about 97,000, or 17·7 per thousand old people, in 1960, to about 165,000, or 22·8 per thousand in 1975.

Not all the present accommodation is in homes run by public authorities. In 1960 there were about 23,000 residents in private homes and homes run by voluntary bodies not supported by public funds. A further 9,000 residents in voluntary homes were paid for by local authorities. The standard of voluntary and private homes varies a lot. We believe that rising incomes and better pensions will increase the demand for private and voluntary care, but that more stringent regulations and competition with improved public provision will eliminate much inferior accommodation. On balance, therefore, we expect the beds in homes unsupported by public funds to increase but barely to keep pace with population growth. We expect the total public provision will need to increase from 74,000 places, or 13·5 per thousand, in 1960, to 138,000 or

[1] See chapter 12 above.

Table 13.12.   *The population of old people's homes and other institutions, England and Wales, 1960 and 1975*

	1960		1975	
	'000s	Per 1,000 population over 65	'000s	Per 1,000 population over 65
Elderly people in institutions				
Welfare homes: public authority	64·5	11·8	138	19·9
sponsored[a]	9·4	1·7		
Other voluntary and private homes[b]	22·8	4·2	(27)	(3·9)
Hospitals: geriatric departments[c]	55·9	10·2	62	8·9
mental illness	50·8	9·3	42	6·2
mental subnormality	3·1	0·6	6	0·9
Total	206·5	37·8	275	39·8
Beds in welfare homes[d]				
Public authority	77·0	14·1	..	..
Sponsored[a]	13·0	2·4	..	..
Total	90·0	16·5	154	22·2
All residents of welfare homes[d]				
A. Total				
Public authority	72·0	13·2	..	..
Sponsored[a]	12·5	2·3	..	..
Total	84·5	15·5	148	21·3
B. Residents under pensionable age[e]				
Mentally handicapped	6·6	..	7	..
Physically handicapped	2·9	..	2	..
Other	1·1	..	1	..
Total	10·6	..	10	..

Sources: Ministry of Health annual *Report*; *A Hospital Plan for England and Wales, 1962, loc. cit.*; and NIESR estimates.

[a]Accommodation provided for local authorities by voluntary organizations. The estimated number of beds assumes the same occupancy rate as in voluntary homes generally.
[b]Private homes, and residents in voluntary homes not supported from public funds.
[c]Assuming 94·5 per cent occupancy of geriatric beds.
[d]Excluding residents and beds not supported from public funds.
[e]Of these 3,000 of the mentally handicapped, 100 of the physically handicapped and 100 of the rest were in sponsored homes in 1960.

almost 20 per thousand in 1975.   Residents should have a choice, and a fair share of accommodation will still need to be in voluntary homes.   But with staff costs and higher physical standards voluntary organizations will need full public support, and we have not, therefore, distinguished between direct provision and voluntary provision sponsored by public authorities.

Welfare homes also provide for some younger residents, mainly among the physically and mentally handicapped.   In 1960, 10,600 out of 84,500 residents in publicly supported accommodation were under pensionable age. By 1975 there will be better provision for the younger mentally handicapped but some, entering residential care in middle age, may fit most happily into welfare homes. The younger physically handicapped mainly need help to live independently, but some residential care will always be needed, though it should not be in the same units as that for old people.

Allowing for these younger categories and for an adequate number of vacancies, we estimate that for England and Wales in 1975, 154,000 publicly supported beds will be needed. This is an addition of 64,000 to the number in 1960. A further 34,000 new places will be needed to replace the beds still in use in old workhouses. This will still leave many homes in unsuitable converted premises which it would be desirable to replace. But, unless actual requirements prove to be smaller than we expect, it seems unlikely that this will be possible before 1975.

5. REQUIREMENTS IN 1975 : STAFF

Supply of skilled staff is likely to be the limiting factor in the development of the health and welfare services over the next ten or fifteen years. The numbers of doctors and dentists cannot be expanded rapidly because of the length of training. Were it possible to double the intake of medical students immediately, this would have no effect until after 1970 and would then increase the number of active doctors by only about 3 per cent a year. The training period for nurses, social workers and other professional staff is shorter, and wastage—largely through marriage—is very high. Consequently a given expansion in training facilities would have a bigger effect on numbers, but, as with teachers, the main difficulty is to retain trained staff. These are predominantly women's occupations and the demographic trend to earlier marriage and larger families increases the demand for this kind of staff and at the same time reduces its supply.

In the following paragraph we shall consider separately the demand for and the supply of doctors and dentists; nurses and other attendant staff in hospitals and residential homes; and the staff of the family services. Finally we shall estimate total staff requirements in 1975.

(a) *Doctors and dentists*

(i) *Present shortages.* A shortage of doctors and dentists in 1975 is unavoidable. The maximum training and recruitment programmes that are possible can barely keep pace with population growth over this period and can do little to overcome present shortages. To consider how much training can be expanded we must therefore look further ahead than 1975. Short-term policy will be concerned mainly with making the best possible use of the staff available and avoiding undue wastage.

Table 13.13.   *International comparisons of doctors and dentists in relation to population*

	Total population per doctor		Total population per dentist	
	1950	1960	1950	1960
Great Britain	1,128[a]	874[b]	3,700[a]	3,700[b]
Canada[c]	960	900	2,730[a]	3,010
France	1,180	930	3,780[d]	3,000
West Germany	800	720	1,914	1,740
Netherlands	1,200[d]	900	5,620	4,500
Norway[e]	850	840	1,900	1,430
Sweden	1,400	1,100	2,000	1,470
United States	750	780	1,920[d]	1,920

Sources: J. F. Dewhurst and others, *Europe's Needs and Resources* (New York, 1961); World Health Organization and national statistics.

Note: The figures shown are not strictly comparable between countries.   The aim has been to include only active doctors and dentists, omitting the retired and those working overseas.   This has not always been possible and in addition definitions vary in respect of personnel in administrative or industrial work.

[a]1951.
[b]NIESR estimates.   The WHO estimate is 935 persons per doctor.
[c]All doctors and dentists (including non-active).
[d]1952.
[e]Including doctors and dentists practising overseas.

The shortage of dentists is of longer standing and is more conspicuous than that of doctors.   In this field Britain lags badly by comparison with other developed countries (table 13.13).   International comparisons of the numbers of doctors and dentists are difficult, and differences of classification and coverage might easily account for the relatively small differences that appear in the number of doctors in relation to population.   Seven of the eight countries for which we have figures had between 760 and 950 persons per doctor in 1958.   But no classification differences can explain away the fact that Britain has half—or less than half—as many dentists in relation to population as Norway, Sweden, Germany and the United States.   Moreover, there was no improvement in Britain from 1950 to 1958, whereas in France and the Netherlands, the only countries worse off than Britain in 1950, the number of dentists had expanded sharply by 1958.

The shortage of British dentists has been a subject of concern for over twenty years[1].   In fact it is true to say that there have never been sufficient qualified dentists.   Formal qualifications for all new practitioners were not successfully enforced until 1921 and at that time only one third of the dentists practising had approved qualifications,   From 1921 to the early 1950s, recruitment was barely

[1]Ministry of Health, *Interim Report of the Inter-departmental Committee on Dentistry* (Teviot Committee), Cmd 6565 (London, 1944).

sufficient to replace wastage and the age distribution of dentists became progressively more unfavourable. The problem was for many years one of recruitment, and it is only in the last few years that the dental schools have been able to fill the training spaces available[1].

By contrast the shortage of doctors is a failure of planning. There is no shortage of applicants for medical training, and as a much larger proportion of senior doctors than of dentists are centred on hospitals, expansion of medical schools should be easier than that of dental schools. But in 1955 the Willink Committee decided that there was a risk of over-supply of doctors and recommended a reduction of 10 per cent in recruitment[2]. This is generally recognized as having been a mistake[3]. As far as can be judged from the limited figures available, the committee did not go seriously wrong on the supply side. Both recruitment and total wastage from 1955 to 1965 will probably be much as they forecast. But the inquiry appears to have substantially underestimated the expansion in demand, partly because they reported at a time when over-expansion of the health services was feared, partly because they failed to recognize that rising medical standards and rising incomes would increase the demand for medical care, and partly because the population projections available in 1955 anticipated a fall in birth rates and a much smaller rise in total population. Over the last decade the number of doctors has grown faster than the population in most developed countries (table 13.13).

(ii) *Future requirements and recruitment of doctors.* The students already in medical schools will decide the number of new doctors at least until 1970. If we accept the estimate of death and retirements made by the Willink Committee, and assume that better conditions of service will reduce net emigration to about a hundred a year, we can expect a net increase of about 4,100, or 7 per cent, in the number of active doctors between 1960 and 1970 (table 13.14). This will barely keep pace with the growth in population and cannot ameliorate present shortages.

The present total number of university students is expected to increase by 40 per cent between 1960–1 and 1966–7. We have estimated that within this general rise in the student population it should be possible to increase the intake of medical students by about 60 per cent between 1965 and 1970. This would enable the output of medical graduates to rise from about 1,900 in 1972 to about 3,000 in 1977. The age structure of doctors is such that a substantial rise in

---

[1] Ministry of Health, *Report of the Committee on Recruitment to the Dental Profession* (McNair Committee), Cmd 9861 (London, 1956).

[2] Ministry of Health, *Report of the Committee to Consider the Future Numbers of Medical Practitioners and the Appropriate Intake of Medical Students* (Willink Committee) (London, 1957).

[3] See for example the reports of the Porritt Committee, *A Review of the Medical Services in Great Britain, op. cit.*, and the Gillie Committee, *The Field of Work of the Family Doctor, op. cit.*

Table 13.14. *Estimated supply of doctors, Great Britain, 1955–85*

Thousands

	1955–60	1960–5	1965–70	1970–5	1975–80	1980–5
Number of active doctors, beginning of period[a]	56·3	58·3	59·9	62·4	66·3	73·2
New graduates[b]	8·9	8·3	9·1	10·7	14·8	15·0
Wastage[c]	−5·8	−5·9	−6·1	−6·3	−7·4	−8·4
Net emigration	(−1·1)[d]	(−0·8)	−0·5	−0·5	−0·5	−0·5
Active doctors, end of period	58·3	59·9	62·4	66·3	73·2	79·3
Population per doctor, end of period (number)	877	888	887	869	818	787

Source: NIESR estimates.

[a] 1955 estimate from Willink Committee report including its figures for service doctors.
[b] Assuming an increase from 1,900 in 1972 to 3,000 in 1977, continuing at that annual rate.
[c] Based on Willink Committee estimates.
[d] Based on the forecast of immigration by the Willink Committee and the estimates of emigration in *British Doctors at Home and Abroad* by B. Abel-Smith and K. Gales (Welwyn, 1964).

retirements must be expected after 1975 and this would partially offset the rise in recruitment. If output continued at 3,000 a year it would increase the number of active doctors from about 60,600 in 1960 to 67,250 in 1975 and perhaps just over 80,000 by 1985. This would improve the doctor/population relationship from about one doctor to 875 persons in 1970 to one to every 775 in 1985. To judge whether this level of recruitment would be adequate, or whether it would be likely to lead to an eventual surplus, we need to look at probable requirements both for general practice and the hospital service which together account for 80 per cent of the employment of doctors.

One result of the general shortage of doctors during the last ten years has been the failure to attract an adequate number of doctors into general practice. Over the period 1953 to 1962 the number of hospital doctors increased by 22 per cent, but the number in general practice by only 6 per cent (table 13.15). This development was probably due to a number of causes. Part of the expansion in the hospital medical service was probably only possible because of the increasing number of young doctors from abroad coming to this country for postgraduate training. In addition the staffing structure of the hospital service resulted in a large number of young doctors at registrar level with no prospect of promotion to more senior posts, but whose training and experience did not incline them to general practice[1]. In addition, general practice under the health service does not seem to have been attractive enough financially, or in the kind of work it offered. Ways in which these disadvantages might be relieved are discussed more fully elsewhere[2].

[1] Ministry of Health, *Report of the Joint Working Party on the Medical Staffing Structure in the Hospital Service* (Platt Report) (London, 1961).
[2] D. C. Paige and K. Jones, *op. cit.*

Table 13.15. *Doctors in the hospital and general practitioner services, Great Britain, 1949–80*

	1949	1953	1959	1962	1980
Hospital doctors[a]					
Senior[b]	9,300	10,650	11,450	12,000	..
Junior	6,650	7,850	9,500	10,700	..
Total	15,950	18,500	20,950	22,700	32,400
Rate of increase					
Per cent per annum		*3·8*	*2·1*	*2·7*	*2·0*
General practitioners					
Principals:					
unrestricted list	..	20,501	22,330	22,964	..
restricted list[c]	..	912	785	740	..
Assistants	..	1,871	1,572	1,175	..
Trainees	..	393	339	304	..
Total	..	23,677	25,026	25,183	33,700
Patients per doctor[d]		2,054	2,005	2,047	1,775

Sources: Report of the Joint Working Party on the Medical Staffing Structure in the Hospital Service, loc. cit.; annual reports of the Ministry of Health and the Department of Health for Scotland; and NIESR estimates.

[a]Estimates for 1949–59 are taken from the Platt Committee. They exclude general practitioner hospital appointments.

1962 estimates are based on the change in numbers from 1959–62 adjusted to the same basis as the earlier series.

[b]Consultants, senior hospital medical officers and senior registrars.

[c]Doctors only acting for members of a particular institution, or only offering maternity services.

[d]Based on civilian population per doctor in general practice (including assistants and trainees).

Although there has been little increase in the number of general hospital beds during the last ten years, the number of hospital doctors has continued to grow at about 2·3 per cent a year. This shows little sign of flattening and there are still a number of junior posts which cannot be filled. We should, therefore, allow for a continued growth of at least 2 per cent a year and this would imply a total increase of almost 50 per cent by 1980. This is conservative. A more liberal interpretation of the recommendations of the Platt Committee would imply a growth of 3 or 4 per cent a year at least for the earlier years.

The total expansion in the number of doctors required depends very largely on the requirements of general practice. We need to allow for the increased demands that will be made on the medical service by a population containing more elderly people and more children, and with more of the handicapped and mentally ill living in the community. Doctors' lists are already considered to be too long. In 1962, 52 per cent of patients were on lists of over 2,500 and 26 per cent were on lists of over 3,000. To reduce maximum lists to 3,000, re-distributing the extra patients on lists between 1,500 and 3,000, might require an increase of about 8·5 per cent in the number of doctors in general practice. To reduce maximum lists to 2,500, which most people would regard as a reasonable maximum for a proper family doctor service, would probably need about 15 to 20 per cent more general practitioners, and might involve a reduction in the average number of patients per doctor (including assistants and trainees) from the 1962 level of about 2,050 to about 1,775[1]. If we aimed to achieve this latter target by 1980, we should need 33,700 general practitioners, or an increase of 35 per cent over the number in 1960.

Allowance must also be made for a continued rise in the number of doctors in other kinds of employment. These include the public health services, teaching, research, occupational health, doctors in the armed services and in private practice. In all requirements in 1980 might amount to over 82,000 active doctors, a rise of just over 40 per cent spread over the twenty years from 1960. Such a rise would secure an improvement of about 1 per cent a year in the ratio of doctors to population. This estimate may be compared with our estimate of potential supply in table 13.14, which would provide about 74,000 doctors by 1980 and 80,000 by 1985. It will therefore be a very long time before there is any serious risk of an over-supply of doctors.

(iii) *Future supply of dentists*. Ten years ago the age structure of dentists was highly unfavourable; in 1953, 43 per cent of the dentists practising in the general dental services in England and Wales were over 55 and 27 per cent were over 60. Consequently wastage over the last decade has been heavy and the increase in the number of practising dentists has been small. But during this period a more balanced age structure has been achieved and, since younger dentists have a higher output[2], the dental services available have probably expanded more than the change in numbers suggests; the number of courses of treatment per dentist has risen by 70 per cent.

Over the next ten to fifteen years wastage will be abnormally low. The dentists due to retire in this period will be those who trained in the inter-war period when the annual intake was unusually small. Consequently even if re-cruitment were to increase no further, and the present very high age of retirement were to fall somewhat, we should expect an increase in the number of dentists of about 4,500 over the fifteen years from 1960 compared with 440 over the nine previous years (table 13.16, estimate A). On this basis, even by 1980, we should still have more than 3,000 persons per dentist. If retirement ages were to re-main as at present, and dental school places could be increased from the present number of about 650 to say 1,100 by 1970[3] (and if this increased number of

---

[1] These estimates assume that with maximum lists of 3,000 per principal, the patients on lists over this size could be redistributed on lists averaging 2,250 and with a maximum of 2,500 on lists averaging 2,000. In 1962 the lists per principal for doctors with less than 3,000 patients averaged 2,000 and for doctors with less than 2,500 the average was 1,800.

[2] Royal Commission on Doctors' and Dentists' Remuneration, 1957–1960 (Pilkington Commission), *Report*, Cmnd 939 (London, 1960).

[3] This allows for 10 per cent student wastage, and assumes an output of graduates reaching 1,000 a year by 1975.

Table 13.16. *Dentists in relation to population, Great Britain, 1951–75*

	Total number of dentists	Population per dentist
1931	n.a.	3,480[a]
1951	13,400	3,650
1955	13,600	3,640
1960	13,840	3,690
Estimate A		
1965	15,100	3,520
1970	16,700	3,320
1975	18,300	3,140
1980	19,900	3,010
Estimate B		
1965	15,400	3,460
1970	17,500	3,160
1975	20,600	2,800
1980	23,900	2,510
Estimate C		
1965	15,400	3,460
1970	17,700	3,120
1975	22,500	2,540
1980	29,300	2,040

Source: Ministry of Health, *Report of the Committee on Recruitment to the Dental Profession, loc. cit.*, 1951 Census, and NIESR estimates.

Notes: Estimate A assumes that recruitment continues at the same rate as in 1955 to 1960, but that retirement rates are increased for age groups over 60.

Estimate B assumes that recruitment increases reaching an intake of 1,000 students a year by 1970, and that retirement rates remain at the level of 1960 to 1962.

Estimate C assumes that recruitment increases to 1,500 a year by 1970, retirement rates as in estimate B.

[a]England and Wales only.

places could be filled), the number of dentists would rise by 6,800, or about 50 per cent, by 1975. In the following five years, when the build-up was complete, the rise would be about 4,700 (table 13.16, estimate B). For forecasting purposes we have assumed an achievement somewhere between these two estimates.

There is little risk of over-supply of dentists. Even if preventive measures such as fluoridation of water supplies were to reduce the need for dental care, this would take many years to affect the demand of the total population, and present standards of care for many people are very low. If recruitment could be raised to an intake of 1,650 by 1970, we should be able to increase the total number of dentists to almost 30,000 by 1980 (table 13.16, estimate C). Such an achievement, which is not very likely, would still leave us with slightly more persons per dentist in 1980 than most developed countries had in 1958 (table 13.13).

(b) *Nurses and attendant staff*

(i) *General hospitals.* Between 1951 and 1960 the number of patients in general and chronic hospitals increased by only 1 per cent but the number of nurses increased by 20 per cent and the ratio of nurses to patients fell from 1:1·8 to 1:1·5 (table 13.17). Part of the increase in nursing staff was needed to offset a reduction in hours: in most hospitals during this period hours were reduced by $8\frac{1}{2}$ per cent, from 96 to 88 a fortnight.

The improvement in nurse/patient ratios over this period was associated with shorter hospital stays. Whereas the ratio of patients to nurses fell by almost 20 per cent, the number of cases treated per nurse rose slightly from 25·8 in 1951 to 27·1 in 1960. This is likely to reflect a need for more intensive nursing. When maternity cases are discharged early it is evident that the saving in beds will not be accompanied by an equal saving in nursing requirements, and this is probably also true of most surgical and some medical cases.

We expect both the reduction in nursing hours and the trend to shorter hospital stays to continue and have allowed for a continued improvement of 30 per cent in nurse/patient ratios between 1960 and 1975. This assumes a further reduction in hours of 10 per cent, from 88 to 80 hours per fortnight. Nursing staff are expected to increase by about 38 per cent, but the number of discharges from acute beds is expected to rise by 45 per cent (see page 423 above) and the number of maternity cases by about 65 per cent. This will be slightly offset by an increased number of geriatric and mental illness beds in general hospitals but our estimates imply some further increase in the cases treated per nurse.

(ii) *Mental illness and mental subnormality.* The most serious shortage of nurses at the start of the National Health Service was in mental hospitals and mental deficiency institutions. Between 1951 and 1960 staff/patient ratios in hospitals for mental illness were improved by nearly 25 per cent and those in hospitals for the subnormal by over 30 per cent. But there is still a severe shortage. Moreover the increase was almost entirely in untrained staff. Between 1949 and 1961 the total nursing staff of psychiatric hospitals increased by 35 per cent but the number of trained staff and students increased by only 12 per cent; their share fell from 73 per cent to 51 per cent of the total.

The reduced number of mental illness patients in hospital will not reduce the need for psychiatric nurses, because a much bigger proportion of the total will consist of short-stay patients receiving active treatment. In addition small units for the mentally ill and subnormal may involve an increase of 15 to 20 per cent in staff ratios, and improved treatment and training for the mentally subnormal, particularly for children, will require considerably more liberal provision of staff. We aim therefore to improve staff/patient ratios by 55 to 60 per cent, from 1:5·0 to 1:3·0 for mental illness, and from 1:5·6 to 1:3·6 for mental subnormality. Not all of the additional staff however will need to be

Table 13.17. *Nursing and attendant staff in hospitals and residential homes, England and Wales, 1951–75*

| | General hospitals[a] | Hospitals and homes for: | | Welfare homes[b] |
		Mental illness	Mental sub-normality	
1951				
Nurses/attendants ('000s)[c]	122·4	22·6	6·8	..
Patients/residents ('000s)	215·4	141·1	50·2	..
Ratio	1·8	6·2	7·4	..
1960				
Nurses/attendants ('000s)[c]	146·9	27·6	9·9	12·1
Patients/residents ('000s)	217·8	136·8	55·7	84·5
Ratio	1·5	5·0	5·6	7·0
1975				
Nurses/attendants ('000s)[c]	203·0	26·2	24·8	34·4
Patients/residents ('000s)	234·0	87·3	89·3	148·0
Ratio	1·15	3·3	3·6	4·3

Source: Ministry of Health annual *Report* and NIESR estimates.

[a]General and chronic hospitals.
[b]The figures include residents supported by public authorities in voluntary and private homes (see table 13.12) and estimates of the staff caring for them. The staff estimates in table 13.19 are reduced by 2,000 in 1960 and 3,700 in 1975 to exclude these.
[c]Whole-time equivalent.

psychiatric nurses. These will be needed in increased numbers for active treatment of the mentally ill, but the increase in proportion of care of subnormal and confused elderly patients in hostels and smaller units may call for staff with training and experience in mental health and residential care but without full nursing qualifications.

(iii) *Care of the elderly and handicapped.* The ratio of attendant staff to residents that is needed in old people's homes depends partly on the size of institution and partly on the degree of infirmity of the residents. Townsend found that the ratio of total staff (including domestic) to residents was 1:3·2 in post-war old people's homes with less than 35 beds, compared with 1:4·0 in those of over 35 beds. In former Poor Law institutions the proportion of housebound residents in homes with an attendant staff ratio of less than 1:5 was 83 per cent compared with 29 per cent in the homes with a staff ratio over 1:15[1].

In estimating staff requirements in 1975 we need to allow for substantial improvements in staff ratios to relieve present shortages, to allow for the replacement of old large institutions by small homes and to allow for the larger proportion of infirm residents that is likely when better alternative facilities

[1]P. Townsend, *The Last Refuge, op. cit.*

become available for moderately active old people[1]. Local authority plans indicate an improvement in ratios for attendant staff from about 1:7 in 1960 to perhaps 1:6 in 1972. Townsend advocates an immediate increase in attendants to 1:3, and an eventual further increase to 1:2. We have estimated a ratio between these two extremes, of 1:4·3. This would increase the attendant staff of a 30-bed home from about four at present to seven, and should permit a substantial improvement both in the standard of care and in staff conditions.

(iv) *The supply of staff.* Staff for psychiatric institutions and residential homes are acutely short now. Hospital nurses appear to have suffered from a chronic shortage for thirty years or more, but this seems to be due mainly to unrealistic recruitment standards and high wastage[2]. The shortage has been rather less acute during recent years in spite of the rapid decline in numbers of single women. However, the number of fully trained nurses in general hospitals in 1961 was 10 per cent less than the number of student nurses, partly because of excessive wastage during training, and partly because many trained nurses leave hospital very shortly after completing training.

In spite of these difficulties we have allowed for a substantial improvement in staffing; we believe that it will only be possible to obtain staff if hours and conditions of work are fundamentally improved. The total numbers involved are not big and in spite of unfavourable demographic trends they should be obtainable if this field of work is made more attractive. Both attitudes and hours will need to be adjusted to permit more employment of married women. There has been much improvement in nurses' pay in recent years but further increases may be necessary particularly to retain senior staff, and the pay of staff in residential homes needs substantial increase. In addition new building programmes must provide staff accommodation comparable with that which might be available for workers in similar non-residential occupations, and suitable for staff with dependants.

(c) *Professional staff in the family services*

In this section we consider requirements for social workers of all kinds, health visitors, home nurses and other nurses employed in clinics, health centres and group practices[3]. The main part of the work of this group is with the elderly, mothers and children, the mentally ill, subnormal and the physically handicapped, but the services may also provide help for all sections of the population when called for on account of illness or social problems. Much of the work is integrated with that of the family doctors.

[1]These estimates do not include wardens for sheltered housing as these would probably be part-time and recruited from outside the labour force.
[2]B. Abel-Smith, *A History of the Nursing Profession* (London, 1960).
[3]Midwives are not included. With a larger proportion of hospital births an effective separate domiciliary service is not possible and we have allowed for an increase in hospital staff to cater for home care of confinements and postnatal care in the home.

Many of these services are new and are expanding rapidly, so that a projection of trends would be misleading. But needs are so various that a comprehensive estimate on the basis of numbers needing help would be impossible. Both present provision and future plans vary widely between different local authorities: estimated requirements of social workers in 1972 range from 5 to 28 per 100,000 population in county boroughs and from 2 to 20 per 100,000 among the county authorities. The method adopted, therefore, was to estimate what future requirements would be if the provision in each of thirteen groups of local authorities was raised to that planned by the authority in each group aiming at the most liberal facilities. The aim was to calculate the requirements needed to raise the standards of all areas to those of the best 20 per cent, while taking account of varying needs due to different social characteristics in different localities[1].

Between 1962 and 1972, local authorities plan to increase the number of social workers they employ by 66 per cent, the number of health visitors by 44 per cent, and that of home nurses by 27 per cent (table 13.18). To raise the standard of all authorities to that of the best quintile in each group would require an increase of 145 per cent in social workers, 88 per cent in health visitors, and 70 per cent in home nurses. A continued, but slower, rate of growth was assumed from 1972 to 1975. Rather smaller increases were estimated for hospital and psychiatric social workers as these services have been established longer and their recent growth has been smaller.

The increases estimated in this way appear reasonably in line with other recommendations. In 1959 the Younghusband Report recommended a ten-year recruitment programme of social workers which starting from the 1956 level would produce a staff of 5,750 for England and Wales somewhere between 1966 and 1970[2]. This may be compared with local authority plans for 4,880 by 1972, and our estimate of 7,600 by 1975. It is more difficult to compare figures for health visitors because much of their work is in the school health services, which are not covered in our estimates of the local authority plans. But in 1956 the working party on health visitors recommended an increase of 3,500 over about ten years, mainly for work other than with schoolchildren[3]. Local authority plans for 1972 are only 3,000 above the 1955 level. Our plans for 1975 give an increase of 6,000 over the twenty years from 1955.

---

[1]County boroughs were divided into 10 groups, based on Moser's classification (C. A. Moser and W. Scott, *British Towns: a Statistical Study of Their Social and Economic Differences*, Edinburgh, 1961). Counties were divided into 3 groups according to population density. A separate estimate was made for the London County Council area which assumed an increase in LCC plans similar to that in plans of other large cities.

[2]Ministry of Health, *Report of the Working Party on Social Workers in the Local Authority Health and Welfare Services* (Younghusband Report) (London, 1959), adjusted to exclude Scotland.

[3]Ministry of Health, *An Inquiry into Health Visiting: Report of a Working Party on the Field of Work, Training and Recruitment of Health Visitors* (London, 1956).

Table 13.18. *Selected professional staff of the family services, England and Wales, 1962–75*

| | 1962 Actual | Numbers employed 1972 | | 1975 Estimates | Per 100,000 population | |
		Local authority plans	NIESR estimates		1962	1975
Social workers						
Almoners	1,020	—	—	1,300	*2·1*	*2·5*
Hospital PSWs	470	—	—	700	*1·0*	*1·3*
Other university trained	280a	790⎫		1,200b	*0·6*	*2·3*
General	430	1,570⎬	7,200	3,800	*0·9*	*7·3*
Other	2,230	2,520⎭		2,600	*4·8*	*5·0*
Subtotal	4,430			9,600	*9·5*	*18·4*
of which: in local authority plans	(2,940)	(4,880)	(7,200)	(7,600)	*(6·3)*	*(14·6)*
Welfare assistants	250	745	850	900	*0·5*	*1·7*
Health visitors	5,270	7,610	9,900	10,500	*11·3*	*20·2*
Home nurses	7,700	9,745	13,100	13,900	*16·5*	*26·7*
Other nurses	980	1,235	1,350	1,400	*1·9*	*2·7*
Total	18,540			36,300	*39·7*	*69·7*
of which: in local authority plans	(17,050)	(24,215)	(32,400)	(34,300)	*(36·5)*	*(65·9)*

Source: *Health and Welfare: The Development of Community Care*, Cmnd 1973, *loc. cit.* and NIESR estimates.

aIncluding almoners and psychiatric social workers employed by local authorities in 1962.
bIncluding almoners and psychiatric social workers additional to those shown above.

The implications of our estimates can be judged by considering the team available for a local area of 100,000 population. In 1962 such an area had just under fifty general practitioners, eighteen home and clinic nurses, eleven health visitors and ten social workers and welfare assistants. But, of the latter group, more than half were quite untrained and three of the five trained workers were employed in the separate hospital administration. In 1975 we envisage an integrated team, still containing only about fifty general practitioners, but they would be supported by thirty home and clinic nurses, twenty health visitors and twenty social workers. Among the social workers perhaps six would have advanced university training, seven general training, and seven would still have no formal training.

(d) *Total staff requirements in 1975*

Estimates of total staff requirements of the health services in England and Wales in 1975 are summarized in table 13.19. These include the estimates for the groups already discussed. Other staff needs were estimated as follows:
(i) *Other professional staff* includes a variety of professional and technical employees in hospitals, ranging from laboratory technicians and pharmacists.

to physiotherapists and teachers in hospital schools. Numbers increased by 52 per cent, or 4·8 per cent a year, from 1953 to 1962 but there are still shortages. Over the period 1960 to 1975 we have therefore assumed a rate of increase of 5·5 per cent a year. Other professional staff in the family services includes teachers in training centres, whose numbers will expand rapidly, and the staff of day nurseries and centres for the handicapped.

Table 13.19. *The staff of the health services, England and Wales, 1975*

	Total		Hospital and residential		Other	
	'000s	1960=100	'000s	1960=100	'000s	1960=100
Doctors	48·0	117	21·2	122	26·8[a]	114
Dentists	14·9	142	0·3	150	14·6[a]	141
Nurses and midwives	223·0	140	208·0[b]	137[b]	15·3	185
Residential care[c]	82·0	171	82·0[d]	171[d]	—	—
Health visitors	10·5	217	—	—	10·5	217
Social workers	10·5	225	—	—	10·5[e]	225[e]
Other professional	57·0	219	42·0	223	15·0	214
Domestic	300·0	134	244·0	122	56·0	234
Other[f]	79·0	141	49·0	136	30·0	150
Total	824·9	144	646·5	138	178·7	170
of which:						
Medical and dental	62·9	122	21·5	122	41·4	123
Other professional	383·0	158	332·0	155	51·3	186
Other	379·0	135	293·0	124	86·0	195

Source: NIESR estimates.

[a] Doctors and dentists on general medical lists: not whole-time equivalent.
[b] Excluding nurses in specialist psychiatric hospitals, but including, as part of the maternity services team, domiciliary midwives. The corresponding figure in 1960 was 152,000.
[c] Excluding domestic staff.
[d] Including nurses in psychiatric hospitals. The corresponding figure in 1960 was 48,000.
[e] Including almoners and psychiatric social workers attached to hospitals in 1960.
[f] Mainly clerical, administrative and ambulance staff.

(ii) *Domestic staff* in hospitals and residential homes are expected to increase more slowly than the professional staff. Over the period 1953 to 1962, numbers rose by 24 per cent but modernization and better equipment should raise productivity. We have allowed for an increase of 22 per cent from 1960 to 1975; during this period the number of occupied beds will increase by about 12 per cent and the total number of professional staff by nearly 50 per cent.

Requirements of home helps were estimated by calculating the number needed to raise the plans of all local authorities to the level of the best. This gives an increase of 134 per cent over the fifteen years 1960 to 1975, compared with an increase of 46 per cent planned by local authorities over the ten years 1962 to 1972.

(iii) *Other staff* includes mainly clerical and administrative workers at all levels and ambulance staff. Ambulance staff, who account for nearly two thirds of the non-residential group, were estimated in the same way as home helps.

This gives an increase of 57 per cent from 1960 to 1975, compared with a rise of 22 per cent planned by local authorities from 1962 to 1972. Numbers of clerical and administrative staff could only be roughly estimated.

We expect total employment in health and welfare services to increase by 42 per cent, that in hospitals to rise by 36 per cent and in the family services and general medical services by 68 per cent. Numbers of medical and dental staff will rise by only 22 per cent but an increase of 55 per cent is expected in nurses, social workers and other professional staff.

6. CURRENT EXPENDITURE ESTIMATES

(a) *The overall level*

In order to make realistic estimates of total future expenditures on health and welfare we need to consider the general trend of expenditures as well as the cost of the various services needed. It is too easy to build up a big shopping list of all the services that we would like to have, and to justify them individually. We can only judge whether such a list is reasonable, and how far the economy can afford to satisfy it, by an assessment of the share of the gross national product that it is reasonable to devote to health and welfare.

The volume of public expenditure on health and welfare has increased by about 30 per cent over the last eleven years (table 13.20). Private expenditures have probably added another 5 or 6 per cent to the total but from the little evidence that we have it would not appear that their share has changed very much[1]. The proportion of the total national product spent on health is almost the same as it was in 1950 (table 13.21). It fell between 1950 and 1954 but rose again from 1954 to 1962. This may be compared with movements in the United States where the share of total health expenditures—private and public— also fell between 1949 and 1951 but has been rising steadily ever since and in 1961 was 25 per cent above the 1951 level. Comparisons of the absolute level of expenditure in different countries are vulnerable because of classification and measurement problems. As far as we can see there is not much difference between the share of total national resources devoted to health in Britain and America but comparison in this form combines both price and quantity differences and the prices of health services—like those of services in general—are relatively high in the United States.

Over the period from 1960–75 our proposals add about 50 per cent to public expenditure at constant prices. This means that the share of health expenditure in gross national product at constant prices will remain at about its 1960 level.

---

[1]There has been a substantial increase recently in the number of group insurance schemes. This appears, however, to be partly a shift due to advantages in premiums and taxation. There is little evidence of a big rise in the total number of people paying for private health treatment in cash and through insurance policies together.

Table 13.20. *Current expenditures on health and welfare, United Kingdom, 1951–62*

£ *million*

		At current prices						At 1960 prices Public expenditure		
		Public[a]			Private[b]					
	Total expenditure	Total	Hospitals	Other	Total	NHS charges	Other	Total	Hospitals	Other
1951	580	487	276	211	93	8	85	665	418	247
1952	609	502	289	213	107	20	87	655	421	234
1953	632	520	299	221	112	24	88	669	426	243
1954	655	536	315	221	119	25	94	683	446	237
1955	703	577	343	234	126	27	99	704	456	248
1956	772	635	376	259	137	29	108	735	475	260
1957	834	684	404	280	150	33	117	762	480	282
1958	883	726	434	292	157	33	124	788	498	290
1959	950	784	468	316	166	35	131	823	510	313
1960	1,031	853	510	343[c]	178	37	141	853	510	343
1961	1,122	926	555	371[c]	196	48	148	863	517	346
1962	1,162	952	601	351	210	52	158	877	554	323

Sources: National Income and Expenditure, 1963; Annual Abstract Statistics; Ministry of Health Report, part I, 1961; NIESR estimates.

[a]*Public expenditure* includes total central and local government expenditure on the NHS, other health, and care of the aged and handicapped. Estimates at 1960 prices are based on a price index for the NHS derived from *National Income and Expenditure.*

[b]*Private expenditure* on items other than NHS charges are estimates based on the Family Expenditure Survey for 1957–9, and extrapolated from consumers' expenditure on 'chemists' goods', and 'other sources'. About 60 per cent of the item consists of purchases of non-NHS drugs, and the remainder of private medical and nursing fees.

[c]These figures include arrears of an increased remuneration award to general practitioners.

However, some increase in relative prices is likely to occur so that the share of health expenditure at current prices is likely to rise. Incomes of health service personnel must keep pace with those in the economy as a whole but in few instances will rising productivity mean that we can meet our needs with smaller numbers of doctors, nurses or social workers.

(b) *Private health expenditures*

We do not include private expenditures on health in our estimates for 1975[1]. But our estimates for public health services assume that they will continue at 5 or 6 per cent of the total. About a quarter of private expenditures consists of charges for dentists, spectacles and drugs supplied by the National Health Service. If policy were to be changed in respect of these charges it would alter the cost but not the overall volume of health expenditures[2]. Three fifths of

[1]They are included in consumers' expenditure.

[2]For simplicity we have ignored here any secondary effect, i.e. the argument that people might use more—or even in certain cases less—of these services if they were completely free.

Table 13.21. *Current expenditures on health and welfare in the United Kingdom and the United States, 1949–61*

| | United Kingdom | | | | United States | | | |
| | Public | Personal | Total | Total as per cent GNP | Public | Personal | Total | Total as per cent GNP |
		£m.				$m.		
1949	437	78	515	4·66	2,870	8,051	10,921	4·23
1950	480	83	563	4·80	2,907	8,741	11,648	4·09
1951	487	93	580	4·49	3,150	9,440	12,590	3·83
1952	502	107	609	4·35	3,151	10,172	13,323	3·84
1953	520	112	632	4·23	3,227	11,072	14,299	3·91
1954	536	119	655	4·13	3,441	11,925	15,366	4·23
1955	577	126	703	4·17	3,667	12,827	16,494	4·15
1956	635	137	772	4·20	3,848	14,126	17,974	4·29
1957	684	150	834	4·30	3,464	15,417	18,881	4·26
1958	726	157	883	4·35	3,893	16,645	20,538	4·62
1959	784	166	950	4·49	4,034	17,169	21,203	4·39
1960	853	178	1,031	4·59	4,412	18,504	22,916	4·55
1961	926	196	1,122	4·67	4,792	20,752	25,544	4·92
1962	952	210	1,162	4·67				

Source: United Kingdom, see table 13.20.

United States, public: *Statistical Abstract of the United States* (1952–62). The figures include expenditure on health, welfare and veteran expenditure, but exclude as far as possible expenditures on construction, defence research, school lunches and child welfare. Some earlier figures are partly estimated.

Personal: Office of Business Economics, *US Income and Output* (Washington, 1958), and *Survey of Current Business*, July 1962.

the remainder consists of privately purchased drugs, which are very largely items such as laxatives and aspirins for which no big change in the share of expenditure seems likely. Private expenditures that compete with the National Health Service are less than a third of the total. They might fall as the public services improve or they might rise as incomes rise, but they are unlikely to become very important.

(c) *Public expenditures in 1975*

In total we expect health expenditures to rise by 54 per cent between 1960 and 1975 (table 13.22). The distribution between the three major kinds of service will not change very much but there are important changes within each group. Expenditure on the general hospitals will rise by almost 50 per cent although we expect only a small increase in the number of beds. These beds will handle more cases per year and this means more drugs and equipment as well as more staff. The big increases we have discussed in residential care for the old and subnormal are partly offset by the fall in mental illness beds.

Table 13.22. *Public expenditures on health and welfare, 1960 and 1975*

£ (1960) million

	Total	General hospitals[a]	Other residential[b]	Family practitioner services[c]	All other[d]
1960					
Wages, salaries and fees	581	284	102	137	58
Other goods and services					
Drugs and medical supplies	152	(36)	(5)	108	(3)
Other	202	118	48	—	36
Subtotal	354	154	53	108	39
Gross expenditures	935	438	155	245	97
less: charges to patients	−50	−6	−11	−29	−4
charges to staff[e]	−43	−30	−13	—	—
Net expenditures[f]	842	402	131	216	93
1975					
Wages, salaries and fees	837	396	160	177	104
Other goods and services					
Drugs and medical supplies	250	60	7	178	5
Other	348	196	92	—	60
Subtotal	598	256	99	178	65
Gross expenditures	1,435	652	259	355	169
less: charges to patients	−82	−8	−22	−46	−6
charges to staff[e]	−59	−40	−19	—	—
Net expenditures[f]	1,294	604	218	309	163

Sources: 1960, total net expenditures and the wage and salary component are from *National Income and Expenditure, 1963.* Expenditure on fee-paid services and charges to patients are from the *Annual Abstract of Statistics, 1963.* The further breakdown is partly estimated using data on hospital and local authority expenditures and numbers employed. 1975, NIESR estimates.

[a]Hospitals dealing predominantly with acute and chronic illness, and a small number of convalescent and other specialist units (the breakdown is given in table 13.1).

[b]Psychiatric hospitals, and all welfare homes and hostels.

[c]Executive committee services for which payments to doctors and dentists are gross of their expenses.

[d]Community health and welfare services, together with public health and Medical Research Council expenditures.

[e]Includes a small amount of 'other income' sale of garden produce, etc.

[f]These figures differ from those in chapter 9 and appendix 9.1 because expenditure on care of the aged and handicapped is included here.

(i) *Staff.* In 1960 about 62 per cent of health and welfare expenditures consisted of wages, salaries and medical fees[1]. On the basis of the estimates made in the previous section we expect these to rise by about 44 per cent between 1960 and 1975. In addition to the increases in numbers shown in table 13.19 we have allowed for an increased payment of 5 per cent to general practitioners to enable them to employ more auxiliary staff.

[1]This figure is actually a little inflated because most doctors and dentists are paid by gross fees, out of which they must pay their own auxiliary staff and other expenses.

(ii) *Drugs and medical supplies.* This category accounted for 16 per cent of expenditures in 1960. We have not made any proper estimate of future levels. This is a field liable to technical change which is difficult to predict, and for the more expensive ethical drugs it is extremely difficult to determine movements in the volume of consumption[1]. But total expenditure on drugs has, in the past, remained a fairly constant share both of health expenditures and of the total national product. We have assumed that this will continue.

(iii) *Institutional housekeeping.* Most of the remaining 22 per cent of expenditures in 1960 consisted of the current running costs of homes and hospitals. They are dependent on four factors:

(a) The change in the number of patients.

(b) The rise in living standards required to keep pace with increases in the standard of living in the country as a whole.

(c) The need to increase standards in some institutions more than the general rise in the cost of living because they are now well below tolerable current standards.

(d) Changes in staff ratios. In 1951 staff meals accounted for a fifth of hospital catering expenditure[2]; with the improvement in ratios since then the proportion is bigger today[3].

Part of the increase required ought to be obtained from the increased efficiency in hospital kitchens, engineering services and other services that will result from the large-scale rebuilding and modernization programmes that are planned. We hope that for the general hospitals this will provide the general levelling up that is needed. The hospitals to be closed are mainly the smallest which are in fact the cheapest to run but this is because they provide a lower level of services.

For the general hospitals we expect a rise in institutional housekeeping expenditures of 66 per cent; of this 8 per cent results from an increase in the number of patients, 8 per cent from an increase in staff, and 50 per cent from the need to keep standards in line with the growth in per capita consumers' expenditure. For other residential care—including psychiatric hospitals—we expect a total rise in costs of 92 per cent. Of this total 15 per cent results from more patients, 8 per cent from more staff, 10 per cent from levelling up of substandard institutions and 58 per cent from the need to keep standards in line with the national standard of living. For the institutions in this group we do not reckon that modernization and rebuilding will provide a sufficient increase in

---

[1] This is because all drugs are expensive when first produced and fall in price as production expands. Consequently it is difficult to make a realistic estimate of price changes.

[2] B. Abel-Smith and R. M. Titmuss, *The Cost of the National Health Service in England and Wales, op. cit.*

[3] This is really an income in kind because staff pay for their emoluments but not the full cost. If by 1975 increased staff wages and salaries allow for them to pay the actual cost of residence and meals in institutions the rise in running costs due to higher staff ratios would—in current prices—be fully offset by an increased deduction for charges to staff.

efficiency to account for the levelling up process. The units being reduced or closed include the inhumanly large and incredibly cheap, as well as the un-economically small.

7. CAPITAL EXPENDITURE

In 1948 the National Health Service took over a stock of hospital buildings many of which were already obsolete. In the following ten years capital expenditure in the health and welfare services was very small. Throughout this period it was less than 1 per cent of total gross fixed capital formation, and averaged only about 3 per cent of total investment by the public sector (table 13.23). Between 1958 and 1963 the volume of investment in the health and welfare services more

Table 13.23. *Capital expenditure on health and welfare services, selected years, 1951–75[a]*

| | Current prices | 1960 prices | As percentages of: | |
	£ million		All fixed capital formation	Public authorities capital formation
1951–5 average	20	24	*0·8*	*2·7*
1956	23	25	*0·7*	*2·9*
1957	29	30	*0·9*	*3·6*
1958	32	32	*0·9*	*4·1*
1959	38	38	*1·0*	*4·6*
1960	43	43	*1·1*	*5·0*
1961	52	51	*1·2*	*5·8*
1962	63	59	*1·4*	*6·2*
1963 estimate	71	65	*1·5*	*6·4*
Forecasts				
1966		99		
1969		129		
1972		152		
1975		160	*2·0*	*9·3*

Source: National Income and Expenditure, 1963 and NIESR estimates.

[a]Estimates exclude expenditure by private health and welfare organizations and expenditure on doctors' cars.

than doubled, but substantial further increases are stilll required. Official plans envisage an average expenditure of at least £91 million a year for England and Wales over the period 1964 to 1973[1]. Our estimates expect an average expenditure for the United Kingdom of about £121 million over this period.

[1]The Hospital Plan revision to 1973–4, May 1964, suggests expenditure on hospitals of £750 million over the decade 1964–5 to 1973–4, and the local authorities' plans for the decade ending in 1971–2 total £223 million. In 1960 prices this might total £910 million, but the Ministry of Health commentary on the local authority plans indicates that upward revision of a number of items is to be expected (see Ministry of Health, *A Hospital Plan for England and Wales (Revision to 1973-74)* (London, 1964)).

Table 13.24. *Estimated cost of provision of recommended new beds or places, England and Wales, 1960–75*

	\begin	Beds or places					Expend-iture per new bed or place[a]
	1960	1975	Net addition	Replace-ment	Total require-ment	Total cost	
			Thousands			£m.	£
General hospital							
Acute	179·5	173·6	−5·9				
Maternity	20·5	33·0	12·5				
Geriatric	59·1	65·9	6·8				
Mental illness	4·9	12·3	7·4				
Mental subnormality	1·6	1·0	−0·6				
Other	4·6	3·4	−1·2				
Total	270	289	19	62	81	786	9,700
Psychiatric							
Mental illness							
Residential	148	90	−58	30	30	90	3,000
Mental subnormality							
Children's homes	··	12	12	··	12	30	2,500
Other residential	59	81	22	10	32	89	2,780
Training centres	20	78	58	10	68	48	700
Total						257	
Other residential homes							
Elderly	65	128	63	34	97	180	1,860
Younger physically handicapped	3·6	4·1	0·5	1·5	2·0	4	2,060
Total						184	
TOTAL						1,227	

Source: NIESR estimates.

[a]Including expenditure on additional facilities and improvements not providing new beds.

Of this perhaps £100 million would be for England and Wales. We expect a rapid rise during the decade, reaching a level of £150 million by 1972, and about £160 million by 1975.

Over 90 per cent of health and welfare capital expenditure in the past and nearly 95 per cent of expected future expenditure is accounted for by the four main items already discussed. These are the general hospitals; hospitals and other residential care for the mentally ill; residential care and training for the mentally subnormal; and residential homes for the elderly and physically handicapped. The results are summarized in table 13.24, which shows the total expenditure needed for England and Wales to implement 1975 requirements.

Costs are estimated as follows:

(i) *General hospitals.* Total expenditure, as given in the original Hospital Plan, has been increased to allow for the additional beds we have included, and to incorporate schemes started before 1961–2 (which were included in the beds available in 1975 but not in the financial provision of the Plan).   But estimated expenditure on special psychiatric hospitals is excluded from this item.   The estimate suggests an average expenditure per new bed of £9,700.   This includes the full cost of 41,000 beds in over seventy new hospitals and modernization schemes in existing hospitals which include the provision of at least 40,000 new beds[1].   For schemes completed and in progress the cost per bed in new hospitals does not differ much from the average cost per new bed in modernization schemes (including those schemes which do not involve changes in ward accommodation)[2].   It seems reasonable, therefore, to regard the number of new beds as a rough estimate of the amount of hospital accommodation renewed.

(ii) *Mental illness.*   On the basis of the local authority plans we have estimated the cost of hostel accommodation at £2,000 a place.   Mental hospital replacements, which would include outpatients, day centre, training, and other facilities, may cost £3,000 to £3,500 a bed.   Total capital expenditures per new bed is, however, raised by the inclusion of other modernization schemes which do not provide ward replacements.

(iii) *Mental subnormality.*   Nearly all the new residential accommodation we envisage would be in small units probably costing only £2,000 to £2,500 a place, but the inclusion of modernization schemes for existing hospitals raised total expenditure per new place to nearly £2,800.   Training centre costs have been estimated at £700 a place on the basis of the local authority plans.

(iv) *Care of the aged and physically handicapped.*   The average cost of £1,860 per place in welfare homes is estimated from the local authority plans.

Because of the length of time needed to complete large hospital schemes, the programme required to meet needs in 1975 does not give us a complete estimate of capital expenditure up to 1975.   Some of the schemes included were already in progress before 1960, and a substantial part of the work done after 1971 or 1972 will be on projects for completion after 1975.   Table 13.25 makes allowance for this factor, includes estimates of other capital expenditures and increases the estimates to include Scotland and Northern Ireland.   The total investment estimate for the fifteen-year period is £1,700 million.   This is about four times the annual rate of investment in the decade ending in 1960.

(v) *Other capital expenditure.*   The 10 per cent of capital expenditure not covered in the major groups discussed above consists of items that are less easy to quantify.   They include health centres, group practice facilities, clinics for mothers and children, day nurseries, ambulance stations, and centres and clubs

---

[1]This figure includes the additional maternity beds in our estimate.   The Hospital Plan allows for at least 33,000 new beds in existing hospitals, but the actual number may be bigger as it is not always possible to identify all replacements (see Ministry of Health, *A Hospital Plan for England and Wales*, 1962, loc. cit.).

[2]Ministry of Health, *Hospital Building, England and Wales: Progress Report*, nos. 1–5 (London, 1962–3).

Table 13.25. *Total capital expenditure on health and welfare services, United Kingdom, 1960–75*[a]

£(*1960*) *million*

	General hospitals[d]	Psychiatric care[e]	Care of elderly and physically handicapped[f]	Other[g]	Total
1951–60					
United Kingdom	178	49	36	22	285
1960–75					
England and Wales programme[b]	786	257	184	..	..
Change in schemes in progress[c]	144	25	6	..	..
Total	930	282	190	83	1,485
Scotland and Northern Ireland	130	50	25	12	217
United Kingdom	1,060	332	215	95	1,702
1960–75 as per cent of 1951–60 United Kingdom annual rate	*397*	*452*	*393*	*288*	*398*

Source: NIESR estimates.

[a]Figures exclude private expenditure (which includes doctors' cars).
[b]As table 13.24.
[c]The programmed expenditure includes the full cost of schemes completed after 1960, but excludes work on schemes to be started before 1975 but not due for completion by then. Large hospital projects may take 4 or 5 years to complete, and it is assumed that most projects started after 1971–2 will be unfinished. For smaller residential units the volume of work on hand is much smaller.
[d]Including geriatric beds and psychiatric beds in general hospitals.
[e]Figures include hospital and hostel accommodation but exclude psychiatric beds in general hospitals. Centres for the mentally ill are included in 'other'.
[f]Excluding centres for the physically handicapped (which are included in 'other').
[g]Includes health centres, maternity and child welfare clinics, day nurseries, centres for the physically handicapped and mentally sick, ambulances, ambulance stations, and miscellaneous expenditure.

for the mentally sick. Many of these are established services where the need is for replacement of old or unsuitable buildings, and expansion to meet population growth, and we expect their share in total capital expenditure to be lower in the future than in the past. Our estimate is based mainly on extrapolating local authority plans from 1972 to 1975.

(vi) *Long-term investment trends.* After 1975 a continued high rate of investment will still be needed but it is unlikely to increase further. We expect by that date to have replaced nearly 30 per cent of the general hospital beds, one third of the beds in special hospitals and hostels for mental illness and about half of those for the mentally subnormal. But there will still be a large number of obsolescent beds awaiting replacement in general and psychiatric hospitals. It will also still be necessary to replace many of the post-war old people's homes in unsuitable converted premises, and after 1975 there will be a big increase in the population over 75 who account for most of the elderly needing residential care.

CHAPTER XIV

EDUCATION

By J. Vaizey and R. Knight

Education, it is generally agreed, contributes in some way to economic growth. The richest countries give their citizens more education than the other countries do. What the connexion is it is hard to say in precise terms. In differing degrees, obviously, education adds to knowledge through research; it adds to the skills of the labour force; and it adds to the general efficiency and competence of the population at large. Efforts have been made to assess these contributions in precise terms. Some writers calculate the private and social returns on education, and make them high[1]. Other writers calculate the residual element in growth, after the contributions of labour and capital have been deducted, and assign to the residual a large education content[2]. Others argue from more particular cases—the folk high schools and Danish agriculture, or the Soviet experience, for instance. But the major connexions have yet to be authoritatively demonstrated[3]. However, it can be said with a fair degree of certainty that the growth of gross national product requires more skilled workers, and a more highly educated population, and that the faster the rate of growth, the bigger the requirements of skill.

It can be demonstrated with much greater certainty that education is income-elastic. As income rises, so does the proportion devoted to education[4]. The background to this rise in the demand for education is complex. The accumulation of education itself creates a demand for it; children's voluntary staying on at school is closely related to parental (especially the mother's) educational background[5]. And, as national income rises and brute poverty is eliminated, people grow more concerned with the quality of life. As Tawney says, 'What a wise parent would desire for his own children, that a nation, in so far as it is wise, must desire for all children'[6].

---

[1] See, for example, T. W. Schultz, 'Investment in Man: an Economist's View', *Social Service Review*, June 1959.

[2] See O. Aukrust, 'Investment and Economic Growth', *op. cit.*, and E. F. Denison, *The Sources of Economic Growth in the United States and the Alternatives Before Us, op. cit.*

[3] See John Vaizey, *The Economics of Education* (London, 1962), chapter 3, and OECD, Conference of the Study Group in the Economics of Education, *The Residual Factor and Economic Growth* (Paris, 1964).

[4] See, for example, John Vaizey, *The Costs of Education* (London, 1958) and F. Edding, *Internationale Tendenzen in der Entwicklung der Ausgaben für Schulen und Hochschulen* (International Trends in Educational Expenditure), Kiel, Institut für Weltwirtschaft, 1958, p. 36.

[5] B. Jackson and D. Marsden, *Education and the Working Class* (London, 1962) and J. W. B. Douglas, *The Home and the School* (London, 1964).

[6] R. H. Tawney, *Equality*, 4th ed. (London, 1952), p. 159.

Table 14.1. *Combined public authorities' current and capital expenditure on education and other outlays in the United Kingdom in 1962*

	£ million	Per cent
Education: current expenditure and grants	988	*11·3*
capital expenditure and grants	211	*2·4*
Total education	1,199	*13·8*
National Health Service	952	*10·9*
Military defence	1,849	*21·2*
Other public expenditure	4,712	*54·1*
Total public expenditure	8,712	*100·0*
of which:		
Local authorities' contribution	1,642	*18·8*

Source: National Income and Expenditure, 1963, table 44.

A long-term view of educational requirements is essential because teachers cannot be trained quickly, and because it takes time to build new schools and universities. In making our long-term plans we have to make forecasts of the birth rate; we have to take a view about changes in the types of skill that will be needed in the future; and we have to decide whether we can adopt the various reforms needed in the educational system such as raising the school-leaving age and reducing the size of classes. The priorities here are partly dictated by the nature of the logistic relations in education. We cannot have more teachers in the schools unless the teacher-training sector of higher education is expanded; but before that can be done it may be necessary to make increased provision in the secondary schools that supply the entrants to teacher-training colleges. In addition, in making our plans for the future we have to take account of the continuous widening in educational horizons. The Organisation for Economic Co-operation and Development made an effort to quantify international expectations of this rise in educational requirements[1]. Enrolments among the age group 15–19 in the northern European countries including Britain were 21 per cent in 1958, and are expected to reach between 30 and 35 per cent in 1970; in France and Benelux countries they were 31 per cent in 1958, and they are expected to reach 40 to 45 per cent in 1970. For the United States and Canada the enrolment percentage for this age group in 1958 was 64 per cent, and it is expected to reach between 68 and 73 per cent in 1970.

Finally, we have to be sure that our plans do not make impossible demands on the country's resources. This is particularly important because the cost of education falls largely on the public sector and competes with other public expenditure for public funds: in 1960 it took 37 per cent of total local expenditure and one eighth of all public expenditure capital and current.

[1]OECD, *Policy Conference on Economic Growth and Investment in Education, part II: Targets for Education in Europe in 1970* (Paris, 1962).

Table 14.2.   *Economically active population with scientific and technological qualifications in teaching service, Great Britain, 1961*

Total	249,800
of which: In teaching	50,180
As percentage of total	*20·1*

Source: Census 1961, Great Britain: Scientific and Technological Qualifications.

In addition, education makes two demands on real resources—manpower and building. Teachers represent a large proportion of trained manpower: in 1961 education absorbed a fifth of all those with scientific and engineering qualifications (table 14.2). Nor can we ignore the effect on the labour force of withdrawing able people to become students[1]. Finally, the demand for educational building represents a significant part of the total public demand on the building industry.

In some ways the expansion of the educational system will be eased by the growth of the economy itself. As national income grows, there is more to spare for expenditure on children. The greater the rise in the building industry's output the easier it is to build more schools without sacrificing other construction. The major constraint which is not likely to be eased by the process of growth itself is the shortage of teachers. If this constraint is to be removed, the teachers have to be trained in advance of the expected demands. This is one of the most important aspects of projecting future demand. In making our forecasts we have not tried to prescribe a new educational order. What we have done is to estimate the demand for education and the cost of meeting it, on reasonable standards of staffing and equipment. This exercise enables policy to be discussed in realistic quantitative terms, so that choice can be posed as precisely as possible when resources available fall below those required to meet all the foreseen demands.

1. THE PRESENT SYSTEM—AND ITS INADEQUACIES

An expected growth of population or in the numbers who will stay on at school will automatically suggest that a corresponding expansion of the educational system is required. Yet the present system is judged inadequate by widely accepted criteria. So in our targets for 1975 we have not only to allow for growth; we have also to close the existing gap between what is required now and what is provided. The present system may be judged inadequate in the following ways:

---

[1]Calculations are made in the report of the Committee on Higher Education, *Higher Education* (Robbins Report), *Appendix 4*, Cmnd 2154–IV (London, 1963), of the costs of withdrawing students from the labour force.

(a) *Lack of places*

At the level of higher education there are known to be too few places for qualified candidates. In 1962 very many qualified candidates were unable to find places at universities[1], and 2,000 qualified candidates were turned away from the training colleges[2]. The numbers of those who were qualified but did not apply, or of those who could have qualified but were discouraged from doing so is not known. During 1960–1, 24 per cent of school-leavers with one or more A level passes and 20 per cent of boys and girls with two or more A level passes did not proceed to any full-time further education in England and Wales[3]. Other examples of an actual shortage of places are at nursery school level, where there were long waiting lists of children who would have attended a nursery school had one been available; and at Special Schools, where there were 15,384 children awaiting admission in 1961.

(b) *Size of classes*

There is also evidence of inadequacy of provision judged by accepted standards. The maximum size of classes laid down (in Regulations) under the Education Act 1944, in primary schools is forty pupils. By this criterion (without implying that this is acceptable), 19 per cent of primary pupils were in oversized classes in 1963 and 75 per cent were in classes with over thirty children. The statutory maximum size of classes in secondary schools is thirty pupils. By this criterion 53 per cent of senior pupils were in oversized classes in 1963 (table 14.3).

(c) *International comparisons*

International comparisons suggest that Britain may lag behind some other industrial countries in the rate at which various age groups are enrolled in schools and colleges. As British children start school a year or in some cases two years earlier than other children, the proper comparison is with length of school life. But it is commonly agreed that school life after 15 is educationally highly significant, and the importance of enrolment in higher education is beyond question. The law provides that on a day to be appointed the school-leaving age shall be raised to 16. In 1963 only 45 per cent of the children aged 15 were at school. In England and Wales the enrolment ratio for 17-year-olds in 1962–3 was 13 per cent or 16 per cent including full-time further education; in the United States it was 74 per cent; in France it was 28 per cent in 1959. About 8 per cent of British young people entered full-time higher education in 1955–9, while in the United States the proportion was 30 per cent and in Sweden

[1]See Universities Central Council on Admissions, *First Report, 1961–3* and *Second Report, 1963–4* (London, 1964–5).
[2]Association of Teachers in Colleges and Departments of Education, Annual Registration Survey.
[3]Ministry of Education, *Statistics of Education, 1962*, part 1, p. 65.

Table 14.3. *Staffing standards and deficiencies at maintained primary and secondary schools (excluding nursery and special schools) in England and Wales*

	1952	1960	1963
Junior classes			
Pupils ('000s)	3,947·3	4,098·7	4,096·3
Teachers ('000s)[a]	126·8	140·4	142·1
Pupils per teacher	31·1	29·2	28·8
Percentage of pupils in classes of:			
Over 40	*39·9*	*21·4*	*19·2*
Over 30	*80·5*	*74·4*	*75·2*
Teacher deficiency on current policy ('000s)[b]	19·4	9·5	9·6
Senior classes			
Pupils ('000s)	2,022·7	2,825·6	2,829·1
Teachers ('000s)	96·7	135·8	146·7
Pupils per teacher	20·9	20·8	19·3
Percentage of pupils in classes of:			
Over 40	*8·3*	*5·6*	*2·6*
Over 30	*60·1*	*62·9*	*52·8*
Teacher deficiency on current policy ('000s)[c]	29·7	40·8	30·1

Source: Statistics of Education, 1963, part 1, table 8, p. 30.

[a]Full-time plus full-time equivalent of part-time.
[b]To eliminate classes of over 40 a pupil-teacher ratio of 1:27 is required.
[c]To eliminate classes of over 30 a pupil-teacher ratio of 1:16 is required.

it was 10 per cent[1].   Five per cent entered degree courses in Britain compared with 20 per cent in the United States and 7 per cent in Sweden.   These international standards are difficult to establish in any rigorous manner.   For example, though British enrolments are lower than those in other countries, the proportion of those enrolled who eventually graduate is higher.

(d) *Comparisons of occupational groups*

Another approach to existing deficiencies is to present evidence showing the number of talented people who do not stay on at school or who do not go on to universities and colleges.   A survey of army recruits, taken between 1956 and 1958 and published in the Crowther Report[2], showed that more than three quarters of the men in the top two of five ability groups did not proceed to higher education.   These were men who should have been capable of advanced academic work (table 14.4).

A 1961 survey of school-leavers from maintained grammar schools contains a comprehensive analysis of their attainments in relation to their ability grading on entering the school and in relation to their father's occupation[3].   Table 14.5 summarizes some of the findings on leaving ages.   It shows, for example, that in the top third of the grammar school ability distribution 56 per cent of sons of professional class parents left grammar schools at 18 and over, while only 26 per

[1]Robbins Report, Appendix 5, p. 9.
[2]Ministry of Education, *15 to 18*, vol. 2 (London, 1960).
[3]See Ministry of Education, *Statistics of Education, 1961: Supplement to part 2.*

Table 14.4. *Parents' occupation and educational level of recruits to the army, in ability groups 1 and 2 (out of 5 ability groups)*

Parents' occupation	Percentages of army recruits					Number in sample
	Gradu- ate	Inter- mediate	A-level	Other	Total	
Professional and managerial	*12·2*	*9·4*	*21·3*	*57·1*	*100*	564
Clerical and other non-manual	*8·5*	*4·8*	*10·5*	*76·1*	*100*	352
Skilled manual	*3·1*	*3·6*	*7·5*	*85·8*	*100*	1,164
Semi- and unskilled manual	*1·9*	*2·3*	*5·2*	*90·6*	*100*	427
Total number in sample	143	122	266	1,976		2,507

Source: Crowther Report, vol. 2, p. 122.

cent of the sons of the semi-skilled and unskilled workers did so. For girls the position was worse. A comparison with the Crowther sample survey of school-leavers in 1954 and 1955 from grammar and technical schools confirms these findings. Even though the increase in the numbers staying on to 17 and 18 between the two dates is striking in all social groups, far more 'top ability' children of fathers in semi-skilled and unskilled occupational groups tend to leave school than in other social classes: the proportion of boys from unskilled homes leaving at 16 or earlier was five times as high as that of boys from professional homes, and table 14.5 suggests that working-class boys and girls, ability level for ability level, are under-represented in sixth forms. While the distribution of measured intelligence may be class-biased, it is not biased to the extent that the over-representation of white-collar family children would suggest. Nor is there any evidence that girls are less bright than boys[1].

(e) *Geographical variations*

A similar disparity between opportunities available to different groups of the community manifests itself geographically. The proportion of children going on to higher education varies from area to area, and so does the proportion of children staying on at school after 15. While 23 per cent of local authorities had fewer than one tenth of their 16-year-old boys at school, 21 per cent of local authorities had a quarter or over of their boys of that age at school. Eight authorities had over 80 per cent of their 13-year-olds at selective or comprehensive schools, while five had fewer than 10 per cent at such schools. While eight authorities spent less than £44 per child on primary schools in 1960, ten

---

[1]See *Ability and Educational Opportunity*, ed. A. H. Halsey (Paris, OECD, 1961), pp. 23–9. In the Robbins Report (p. 51) it is pointed out that, of children born in 1940–1, it was over eleven times more likely that children of fathers in the 'higher professional' occupational groups would proceed to higher education than children of fathers in the 'skilled manual workers' category.

Table 14.5. *Leaving age at maintained grammar schools in 1960–1 related to father's occupation and 11+ grading*[a]

Percentages

Leaving age	All occupations[b]		Professional		Semi and unskilled manual	
	Boys	Girls	Boys	Girls	Boys	Girls
Top grading						
16 or less	28·7	41·5	13·4	20·1	66·4	68·6
17	22·3	19·6	30·3	26·2	7·5	11·8
18 and over	49·0	38·8	56·3	53·8	26·2	19·6
Total number (= 100 per cent)	10,760	11,100	2,840	2,790	1,070	1,020
All grades						
16 or less	45·3	54·3	22·1	34·4	63·8	73·2
17	19·5	19·0	26·8	24·5	15·4	13·8
18 and over	35·2	26·7	51·1	41·1	20·8	13·0
Total number (= 100 per cent)	52,710	54,510	10,770	12,520	7,130	7,990

Source: Ministry of Education, *Statistics of Education, 1961: Supplement to part 2.*

[a]'Grading' refers to the ability level defined at the tests at age 11 for transfer from primary to secondary schools.
[b]Including occupation unknown.

spent over £60 per child. At secondary level, some authorities were spending over £100 per child, while eight were spending less than £72[1].

In 1960 there were ten authorities where over 31 per cent of classes in primary schools had more than forty children in them, while fifty-one authorities had fewer than 10 per cent of such classes[2]. The disparity at secondary level is no less striking. While 13 per cent of the 15- to 18-year-olds were at school in London and the south-east, only 7 per cent of those in the north were[3]. An index of educational deficiency is the percentage of senior children in all-age schools, where children of primary and secondary age are taught in one school. In 1960, in London and the south-east, it was less than 1 per cent. In the north it was 8 per cent.

The proportion of grammar and other selective school places varies from area to area, and may reflect differences in local educational policy. Nevertheless, the differences are largely historical and social—those areas which were well endowed with secondary education in 1944 remain so, while those that were not are still, in general, relatively behind. Those areas with large middle-class

[1]See appendix table 14.1.
[2]See appendix table 14.2.
[3]One explanation of this is that some parts of England and Wales have more children per 1,000 people than others, because of the age structure of the population. London and the south-east have only 133·7 children of school age per 1,000 population, while the northern region has 167·8. Yet the yield of a 1*d.* rate is 176*d.* in London and the south-east while it is only 71·4*d.* in the north.

populations tend to be ahead; those with heavy industry to lag behind. The consequences are that in areas with a small proportion of their children at grammar schools, fewer children are able to progress to O and A level courses, which are the main roads to higher education[1].

The streaming in primary schools, early selection for secondary education, and the division of secondary education are held by many observers to be the reason for a great deal of wastage of natural talent. Where changes have already been made from one or all of these there has been a tendency for ability to manifest itself[2]. For instance, H. R. King stated that in his school a third of the pupils originally classed as grammar school type had changed places with a third of other ability groups (as graded by 11 plus)[3].

(f) *Age and condition of school buildings*[4]

The existing stock of building is seriously inadequate. In 1962 the National Union of Teachers undertook a survey which showed that over half of all primary schools were built before 1900[5], and that in 17 per cent of primary schools sanitary conditions were still unsatisfactory[6]. The Newsom Report revealed that secondary modern schools, especially, had a stock of old buildings urgently requiring to be replaced[7].

The existing state of the educational system is therefore widely held to be inadequate. Consequently, in making projections for 1975 we have to make allowances for an improvement in the present situation in order to achieve a desirable situation in the future. What are the major factors likely to affect expenditure on education in the next ten or twenty years? In the next section of this chapter we consider the administrative background and educational policies on which our projections are based. In the following sections we project future requirements and consider the implications for the demand for schoolteachers; finally we consider the cost of our proposals and ways of financing them.

[1]See Robbins Report, table 24, p. 54.

[2]R. Pedley, *The Comprehensive School* (Harmondsworth, 1963), pp. 95–105, and *Ability and Educational Opportunity*, ed. A. H. Halsey, *op. cit.*, especially pp. 130–33, where Professor Torsten Husén reported on the experience of Swedish comprehensive schools.

[3]H. Raymond King, 'The Comprehensive School in England', *Yearbook of Education*, 1962, pp. 191–203.

[4]The Ministry of Education survey of school buildings in 1962 was not published at the time of going to press.

[5]*The State of Our Schools* (London, 1963).

[6]See table 14.19 for our estimate of the percentage distribution of pupils in schools built at different dates derived from the NUT data.

[7]Ministry of Education, *Half our Future: Report of the Central Advisory Council for Education (England)* (London, 1963). Forty per cent of all secondary modern schools were shown (by sample) to be seriously inadequate, and 79 per cent of schools in slum districts are so (pp. 21–2).

2. TRENDS AND POLICIES

The interrelationships of various parts of the education system are such that a long-term policy is necessary if serious imbalances are not to occur. In recent years for example the success of the secondary schools in discovering and teaching talented pupils has created a serious pressure on universities and other higher educational institutions for places. Similarly, the expansion of primary and secondary education has entailed substantial demands for teachers which can only be met by a major expansion of higher education. Education is now so large a part of the public sector that it is necessary to co-ordinate it with other aspects of government and national economic policy in a way which was not the case when it was a much smaller enterprise. In addition, it is a source of skills at all levels and is a major contributor to the changing technology of the economy. Therefore, in a policy designed to promote economic growth, the educational system occupies a crucial position.

(a) *The administration of the educational system*

At present education falls under the Department of Education and Science in England and Wales, under the Secretary of State for Scotland in Scotland, and the Northern Ireland Ministry of Education. The universities in Great Britain are the responsibility of the Department of Education and Science, through the University Grants Committee. The educational system is administered in England and Wales by 164 local education authorities, counties and county boroughs, of varying sizes, ranging from the population of nearly three million administered by the Inner London Education Authority to a county borough like Oxford with 100,000 inhabitants.[1] The Ministry of Labour is responsible for apprenticeship schemes (under the Industrial Training Acts, with co-ordinating arrangements with the Department of Education and Science), and for the youth employment services. The links between these bodies have not in the past been as close as might have been wished. But changes have occurred in recent years. For example, there has been a substantial improvement in the quality of the data provided by the Department of Education and Science, enabling general policies to be laid down which are capable of co-ordination with other aspects of national policy.

The problem in all educational planning is that it takes a considerable amount of time to create new schools or to change existing ones and the implications of decisions taken now may take up to fifteen years to come to final fruition. For example, a radical change in primary education might have consequences in increasing the demand for higher education fifteen years later. Thus, the general period of educational planning is longer than that which is considered appropriate for many other services and, in particular, it tends to exceed the lifetime of any particular Minister or any particular Parliament.

---

[1] The counties often devolve many of their powers to Divisional Executives which, while not elected bodies, are broadly representative of local interests.

Thus political responsibility is frequently assumed by a Minister for decisions taken by his predecessor but one.

Until recently, the constitutional doctrine that the budgetary year was the optimum period for planning, and the lifetime of a Parliament the maximum period during which a long-term look could be taken, considerably inhibited any attempt to provide in time for any anticipated changes in the supply or demand conditions in education. This doctrine has now been dropped and long-term looks for the next five to ten years are the fashion. But, although the doctrine has been dropped, the practical problems still exist and raise issues going far beyond this chapter.

The capital programme is subject to much detailed control and, broadly speaking, although the initiative comes from local authorities, the decision about the size of the programme in each area is effectively the Minister's. Current expenditure is determined by local authorities in the light of their revenues from the rates and from the general grant. This grant is arranged in such a way that, broadly speaking, 60 per cent of the educational expenditure is borne by the central government, although, in particular instances, such as school meals and higher technical education, the expenditure attracts a higher rate of grant. In other instances, such as expenditure on scholarships and teacher training colleges, the pooled total is split and allocated to individual authorities according to a formula.

There has been much criticism of the general grant as an instrument of government, since it is held that a number of authorities have restricted their expenditure from time to time in order to diminish the rate of increase of the local rates, particularly during critical local election years. Others maintain, however, that this effect has not been important, for certainly the rate of growth of expenditure on the education system since the inauguration of the general grant has been higher than for over eighty years[1].

The local authorities, having lost many functions to central government or *ad hoc* authorities from 1945 onwards (hospital, electricity, and gas undertakings, for instance) have become to an increasing extent primarily education authorities. In a recent year, for example, one Home County with a total budget of £39 million was spending £33 million on education. This has tended, in the opinion of many people, to distort the former role of local authorities as local forums where issues of priority between the various public services were debated and to substitute for it a degree of confusion over the ultimate source of authority in education.

Many parents obviously feel no deep loyalty to the 'traditions' and practices of their own locality. In a country where frequent change of abode is common (and likely to become more so as economic growth takes place), the argument for local diversity becomes less forceful. Many parents protest bitterly to their

[1]John Vaizey, *The Control of Education* (London, 1963), pp. 151–4.

Member of Parliament when they move from one authority to another and find that the education system is different and, in their opinion, inferior.

In addition, in recent years the teaching profession has become more militant and preoccupied with questions of status. The role of H.M. Inspectors in the classroom has been resented by some teachers, and their advisory status to the individual school has been emphasized. Many authorities prefer, where possible, to appoint 'organizers' in particular subjects—physical education and art— rather than local inspectors because the connotations of that word imply that the teacher is liable to require professional advice and help in a way which is not true of—say—doctors or dentists.

In the past, the Inspectorate has been a great source of innovation in the educational system. To some extent this is still true, but to a diminishing extent. More and more new educational techniques depend upon research in teaching methods and in the curriculum, and upon technological advances in book preparation and production, in television and in other teaching aids. The criticism which the teaching of mathematics and foreign languages has encountered in the last few years has been succeeded by a forceful attack on these problems by research workers, acting in co-operation with the technologists, and the results are being brought to the attention of the teachers through the universities and the Department and the local authorities directly, rather than by the advice and exhortation of the inspectors[1].

This analysis suggests that the role of the central government is likely to increase and that larger authorities are likely to be more successful than smaller authorities in promoting educational change. At the same time, the fact that the rates are regarded as a regressive tax and an unsuitable source of revenue for a rapidly expanding service and that they are, to an increasing extent, for educational purposes rather than local purposes in general, makes it likely that an increasing amount of finance will be found by the central government. This probably means an increased assumption of power by the central government. The alternative to this is to give additional taxing powers to local authorities, but it would be difficult for 164 local education authorities to administer one major tax, whether an income tax or a turnover tax.

On the other hand, a regional authority covering several millions of people is conceivable as a local tax authority. Since there are substantial arguments in other services (for instance, in transport and in town and country planning) for regional authorities, it may well be the case that this is the future pattern of administration in education.

(b) *The type of educational system*

The type of education to be given is not so much a question of overall resources as of what to do with them when you have got them. The exceptions to this are

---

[1]Since much of the new technology requires television centres, language laboratories, etc., to embody it, the centralization process is bound to continue.

Table 14.6.   *Number of passes at advanced level of boys and girls in England and Wales*

| | Number of passes, '000s | | Science subjects as per cent of | |
	All subjects	Science subjects	All subjects	'Academic' subjects[a]
1952	77·4	36·8	48	49
1955	97·3	47·3	49	51
1960	146·4	74·9	51	55
1962	182·2	89·7	49	53

Source: Statistics of Education, 1962, part 2, table 8.

[a]After excluding general studies, technical drawing, art, music, craft and domestic subjects from the total. See Robbins Report, p. 164.

subjects—such as science and mathematics—which use more equipment than, say, history or English, and which require a scarce kind of specialist teacher.

Throughout the world there has been a swing towards science and mathematics teaching[1].   The majority of sixth-form boys, for example, are now on the science side[2], whereas in 1938 the majority were on the arts side, though for boys and girls taken together it is just under half.   The number of passes at advanced level in science subjects is now more than half of the academic subjects and the proportion of full-time graduate students at universities reading science and technology has grown from 33 per cent in 1953–4 to 45 per cent in 1962–3, although this has been mainly at the expense of medicine and dentistry rather than arts and social subjects (see tables 14.6 and 14.7).   It is thought likely by some people that the trend towards science will continue for three reasons:

(i) The need of the economy and the government service for more and more scientists and engineers (forecasts of this trend have underlain both the British and the French plans for expanding the science faculties of the universities).

(ii) The general cultural drift towards science.   Many of the brightest minds are now in science who fifty years ago would have been in the classics.   Increasingly this is a civilization whose mode of thought is characteristically mathematical and scientific.   Able and enquiring boys and girls will want to work at subjects which are clearly at the frontiers of knowledge.

(iii) It seems possible that the scarcity of scientists and technologists is likely to guarantee them higher incomes than could be expected by arts specialists, at least for a time.   Belief that there is an opportunity for higher earnings is a basis for many boys opting for science.   Nevertheless, it is important to realize that in the decade 1952–62 the swing

[1]See, for example, J. A. Lauwerys and J. Vaizey, *Supply, Recruitment and Training of Science and Mathematics Teachers* (Paris, OECD, 1962) and Oxford University Department of Education, *Arts and Science Sides in the Sixth Form* (Peterson Report, 1960).

[2]In 1962 the percentage was 60 per cent.   In 1952 it had been 56 per cent, and in 1960 it was 61 per cent.

Table 14.7. *Percentage distribution of full-time students by subject*

	Universities		Universities and CATs	All higher education
	1953–4	1960–1	1962–3	1962–3
Arts and social studies	41·5	42·1	40	39
Pure science	20·0	23·8	26	22
Technology	12·6	15·1	19	17
Medicine and dentistry	21·8	15·9	13	8
Other subjects[a]	4·1	3·1	2	14
Total	100·0	100·0	100	100

Source: University Grants Committee, *Returns from Universities and University Colleges in Receipt of Treasury Grant, 1960–1961*, p. 3; Robbins Report, p. 166.

[a]'Other subjects' includes agriculture, veterinary science, domestic science, physical education, music, art.

away from arts subjects to science was only moderate at sixth-form and at undergraduate level. This may have been the result of policy, or the accidental consequence of the inability of the educational system to expand more rapidly in one direction than in the other.

There has not been much study of the influences that make up the total curriculum; however, two main tendencies can be discerned. Firstly, because of the exaggerated specialization in English grammar and public schools, so often condemned, there is a growing concern to establish a broad curriculum giving both verbal and mathematical skills. Despite the importance of vocational skills, it is clear that their effective development depends upon a broad base of educational attainment, and that the argument for this broad base is strengthened by the reflection that the need to change skills frequently is likely to be the common experience of those living in the flexible economy of the last quarter of the twentieth century. This, taken with the growing complexity of knowledge (what the Americans have called the 'explosion' of knowledge) requires a higher level of general education by many people before specialization can take place. The old division between science and the arts, between academic and non-academic, is less valid than it was for this reason. It is probable, too, that specialization in schools is itself the result of intense competition for university places and, possibly, once the expansion of universities has caught up with the demand for places, the pressure for specialization may ease.

The second tendency runs in the same direction. The demand for education among the former 'working class' is now high and the demand for an adequate secondary education is the most immediate manifestation of this. In country after country, the division between the 'academic' school (grammar school, *lycée*, gymnasium) and the 'non-academic school' (secondary modern, elementary school)—a division which corresponds strikingly to a division by social class—is breaking down[1]. The increase in the number of comprehensive (or

[1]*Ability and Educational Opportunity*, ed. A. H. Halsey, *op. cit.*

comprehensive type) schools, and the development of academic streams in the secondary modern schools, are strong evidence that it is happening in this country. Whatever form of secondary organization is eventually adopted, there can be no doubt that it will be far more flexible than the tripartite system that was implemented in the years 1945–9 by the Ministry of Education, on the basis of the Hadow Report, and under the influence of the psychologists of the time[1].

This is partly because the selection tests for secondary schools have increasingly been called into question by sociologists and psychologists, as well as by a dissatisfied electorate[2]. Not only is there increasing doubt about their validity as predictors (as many as one third of the children chosen for grammar schools might not have been chosen on another day or if tested in another way) but the basis of the tests has itself been attacked[3]. The notion of 'pure' intelligence, shorn of environmental factors, is no longer generally accepted as a useful hypothesis[4]. Thus, if selection procedures are doubtful at eleven, the case for a wider range of opportunity, where second chances are possible, is strengthened. This is a case that becomes overwhelming when it is clear that vast 'reserves of ability' are untapped by the present system[5].

(c) *Regional policies*

The different economic and social character of the various regions of Britain suggests that there should be emphasis on different kinds of education in different areas. The most obvious differences are between largely rural areas, like East Anglia, and conurbations, like London, but the difference between those places requiring large numbers of workers for heavy engineering and other heavy industries and those areas requiring workers for light assembly plants are enough to imply a difference in the educational structure. This is undoubtedly one of the reasons for the importance of apprenticeship and part-time technical education in towns like Rugby and for the importance of full-time academic education in outer London suburban areas.

In making projections for future needs, it is important that the desire to equalize educational opportunity throughout the country should not be mistaken for an attempt to impose a uniformity of system upon the whole country, for to do this might merely be a method of introducing intellectual unemployment in some areas and shortages of skill in others.

The education system must also be looked at in the light of the need to cure regional unemployment and the need for urban renewal. The higher education programme has an important role to play here. The provision of institutions

[1]Board of Education, *Report of the Consultative Committee on the Education of the Adolescent* (London, 1926).
[2]Robbins Report, Appendix 1, pp. 82–4.
[3]R. Peers, *Fact and Possibility in English Education* (London, 1963), p. 54.
[4]Robbins Report, Appendix 1, p. 80.
[5]Robbins Report, Appendix 1, Parts III and IV.

of higher learning is itself a potent weapon of regional planning. For a university or regional college can be a source of new ideas, new skills and a cultural focus for an area. It has been proposed that the building of new universities should, in part at least, be connected with the renewal of urban twilight zones. Hitherto new universities have, on the whole, been placed on vacant sites, outside towns.

Substantial shifts of population to new towns or substantial increases in income per head in certain areas entail disproportionate increases in the demand for education. These shifts allow freedom for experiment in educational organization which may not exist in other places[1].

3. REQUIREMENTS IN 1975: NUMBER OF PLACES

(a) Pre-primary education

An important part of the demand for educational provision is that for younger children. It has been government policy in recent years not to increase the number of nursery schools. Nevertheless, mainly because of the increase of admission classes at infant schools, the number and enrolment ratios of children aged 2–4 at maintained schools have risen, though they are still substantially below what they were earlier in the century. The vast majority of the under fives at primary schools are aged 4 (and presumably approaching 5).

It is difficult to estimate the trend in the number of children at private nursery schools because registration was not complete before 1959. From the available data it looks as though numbers have recently decreased slightly, presumably with the enforcement of minimum educational standards. In addition to registered nursery schools and those recognized as efficient by education authorities, there are numerous nurseries only subject to inspection by local health departments without minimum educational requirements.

Half-day nursery care is desirable for many 3- and 4-year-olds, and provision of nursery schooling for 17 per cent of the 3- and 4-year-olds (in addition to 4-year-olds in admission classes) would not seem excessive in view of the widespread provision in other European countries[2]. Thus, we might seek to provide half-time places by 1975 for 616,000 children in the United Kingdom for those aged 3 and 4 (see table 14.8). At the same time, a number of people have urged half-time schooling for 5-year-olds for their first year at school. This would slightly reduce the teacher requirement for an age group of 1,060,000 children in 1975. In other words, half-time schooling for 5-year-olds might go

[1]For example, Shropshire County Council is providing comprehensive schools for the new town of Dawley (population 90,000) while in other towns the bipartite system has been maintained.

[2]For example, in France in 1955–6 the enrolment percentage of 3- to 5-year-olds was 60 per cent compared with 43 per cent in Britain. See Institut National de la Statistique et des Etudes Economiques, *Coût de développement de l'enseignement en France* (Paris, 1958).

Table 14.8. *Projections of pre-primary education*

| | 1960[a] | | 1975[e] | |
	'000s	Per cent of age group	'000s	Per cent of age group
ENGLAND AND WALES				
Population aged 3 and 4[b]	1,326		1,887	
Enrolment[c]:				
In nursery schools and classes	56·3	*5·0*	321	*17*
In admission classes	162·8	*11·5*	216	*11·5*
Total	219·1	*16·5*	537	*28·5*
Included above in independent schools	20·4	*1·5*	24	*1·3*
UNITED KINGDOM[d]				
Population aged 3 and 4[b]	1,559		2,166	
Enrolment:				
In nursery schools and classes	n.a.		368	
In admission classes	n.a.		248	
Total	235·3		616	
Included above in independent schools	21·9		26	

Source: Statistics of Education and NIESR estimates.

[a]Includes a small number of 2-year-olds.

[b]See appendix tables 14.3 and 14.4.

[c]For nursery classes and admission classes at primary schools, the total number of under 5s has been split up to distinguish those almost 5 from others aged 3 and 4 at primary schools.   The usual practise is to allow enrolment of 4-year-olds who will reach their 5th birthday during their first term.   However, some head teachers will admit younger children and others will only admit children once a year, for example in September.   Twenty-three per cent was the actual percentage of 4-year olds in 1960 after deducting the estimated number of 4-year-olds in nursery schools and classes and an estimated 2 per cent who prefer to stay at home until legally forced to start school.

[d]Scotland and Northern Ireland estimated as follows:

	1960
Grant-aided schools	'000s
Scotland	7·0
Northern Ireland	7·7
	14·7
Independent (estimate)	1·5
Total under 5s	16·2

[e]Projection assumes an annual increase of 1 per cent in enrolment ratios at nursery schools, a constant 2 per cent of the population aged 3 and 4 enrolled in nursery classes and a constant 23 per cent of 4-year-olds in admission classes at primary schools.

a small way to meeting the needs for half-time schooling of the 3- to 4-year-olds.

The fact that the system of part-time education for substantial numbers of children aged 3–6 is generally prevalent in Europe and North America[1] is a

---

[1]John Vaizey, 'Primary Schools on the Continent', *New Society,* 3 January 1963.

Table 14.9. *Population aged 3–24, 1960–75*

Age 1 January	England and Wales			United Kingdom		
	1960	1970	1975	1960	1970	1975
3–4	1,326	1,723	1,887	1,559	1,997	2,166
5–10	3,954	4,804	5,298	4,619	5,570	6,119
11–14	2,955	2,770	3,227	3,420	3,217	3,731
15–17	1,930	1,970	2,179	2,235	2,292	2,523
18–20	1,667	2,029	2,002	1,954	2,346	2,318
21–24	2,339	3,031	2,666	2,707	3,459	3,067
Indices (1960 = 100)						
3–4	100	130	142	100	128	129
5–10	100	121	134	100	121	132
11–14	100	94	109	100	94	109
15–17	100	102	113	100	103	113
18–20	100	122	120	100	120	119
21–24	100	130	114	100	128	113

Sources: 1960, *Annual Abstract of Statistics*; 1970 and 1975, appendix tables 14.3, 14.4, 14.5 and 14.6.

powerful prima facie case for considering that our age of five for full-time attendance may be too low, and our provision for under fives far too small. There are good educational reasons for the advantages of half-day schooling for very young children[1].

(b) *Number of children aged 5–15*

Because all children aged from 5 to 15 years are obliged to go to school, changes in the birth rate are a direct and relevant factor in determining the size of the school population. Between 1960 and 1975 it is expected that the primary school population will rise substantially[2]. In 1960 there were 4·6 million children aged 5 to 10 in the United Kingdom. By 1975 there may be 6·1 million. In 1960 there were 3·4 million children aged 11 to 14. By 1975 we expect 3·7 million.

Between 1960 and 1970 the primary school population will increase while the secondary school population below the age of 15 will fall. After 1970, the primary school population will continue to rise and the secondary school population will rise as well. Thus the major factor dominating the expansion up to 1975 will be the significant increase in the number of children of primary school age. This will require more teachers for children under the age of 11. Initially the fall in the numbers of children aged 11 to 15 attending secondary

[1]The argument for making 5 the compulsory starting age in 1870 was that since most children would leave for employment when they reached 10 or 11 it would be better to start essential instruction as early as possible. See W. O. Lester-Smith, *Compulsory Education in England* (Paris, UNESCO, 1951).
[2]See appendix tables 14.3, 14.4, 14.5 and 14.6.

schools will release some teachers if the ratio of teachers to pupils is left unchanged, or result in improved staffing ratios, but after 1973 a substantial increase in the secondary school population will take place.

The increase in the total number of children at school, because of the population changes, will not initially increase the total spent on education in direct
proportion because younger children are cheaper to educate than older children.
Nevertheless, as the increase in population sweeps into the secondary schools
there will eventually be a tendency for costs to rise in a fairly direct relation with
the total number of pupils.

(c) *Staying on after 15*

A major influence affecting future expenditure is the tendency for children to
stay on at school voluntarily after the age of 15.   The proportion staying on rose
gradually up to 1954 and has risen steeply since then.   There are a number of
factors which are probably responsible for this trend, some of which may act
with accelerated force in the future.   In the first place, people in higher income
groups expect their children to stay on at school longer than in lower income
groups.   The rise in per capita real income itself seems to increase the demand
for education.   But a second factor is a changing 'social' appetite for education.
A comparison of maintained grammar schools and non-maintained schools
(that is, independent and direct grant schools together) shows that the proportion
staying on in 1963 was higher at maintained grammar schools than at other
schools, for all ages over 15.   The proportion of 17-year-old boys at school
(as a percentage of 13-year-olds four years earlier) was 51 per cent at maintained
grammar schools in 1963 compared with 31 per cent in 1956[1].   The 1963
percentage was higher than that for boys at independent and direct grant schools,
whereas in the earlier year the percentage at maintained grammar schools was
below that for non-maintained schools[2].

This indicates changes in parental attitudes and ambitions, particularly
among the 'skilled manual' group, which are likely to persist.

The change towards less rigorous secondary selection will also accelerate the
tendency to stay on at school[3].   There is evidence that in comprehensive schools,
easy transfer between streams provides encouragement to children who would
normally have had no opportunity to enter courses for the General Certificate
of Education: there has been a rapid increase in the proportion of 15- and 16-
year-olds staying on, although the numbers are still very small.   Where extended

[1]The figure of 17-year-olds may overstate the percentage staying on at maintained grammar schools since it includes transfers after 13, but these are just as likely to occur at non-
maintained schools.
[2]Table 2, *Statistics of Education, 1963*, part 1, pp. 6–8.
[3]London County Council, *London Comprehensive Schools* (London, 1961) and Stewart C.
Mason, *The Leicestershire Experiment and Plan*, rev. ed. (London, 1963); see also H. R.
King, 'The Comprehensive School in England', *op. cit.*

courses are provided the tendency is for children to take advantage of them and the introduction of the Certificate of Secondary Education in 1965 will lead to a further expansion in the numbers staying on after 15.

Another factor which may accelerate the trend to 'staying on' voluntarily in the future is the rising educational level of parents. The demand for the education of children tends to be related to the education of the parents[1]. As the number of people in the population with an extended education increases there will be an increasing demand for education arising from the parental educational background. Although this is related to the socio-economic forces just discussed it was found to be a dominant variable in cross-sectional studies undertaken in the United States[2] and also in this country[3].

The trend projections of enrolment ratios in table 14.10 below imply that opportunities for sixth-form work will increase rapidly at all schools, both as a natural continuation of a five-year course and as a result of less selective types of education.

In addition, there will be a big increase in enrolment ratios when the school-leaving age is raised. The Crowther Committee recommended 1965–8 as the best years for the change because of the dip in numbers of the population of secondary school age. The most recent official pronouncement on the subject fixes the year as 1970. The year 1966 was the date chosen for the raising of the leaving age in our projections. This would be fully effective by 1968[4]. The date chosen would affect the *phasing* of the programme but not the final enrolment figure for 1975. An additional 'policy' assumption made in our projection was that December leaving would be abolished for 16-year-olds as it has already been for 15-year-olds. This was also one of the Crowther Committee recommendations[5].

The broad implications of these assumptions are shown in table 14.10. The 'trend' is the projection made by the Department of Education and Science and is based on the enrolment trends since 1955[6]. The effect of raising the leaving age in our calculations is to make an addition to the 'trend'. We have made a further addition to the trend for the effect of increased opportunities for all children to go on to sixth-form work; in 1962 about 10,000 students (excluding students from overseas) in England and Wales in 'further education' prepared for the General Certificate of Education A level examination by full-time study,

---

[1]B. Jackson and D. Marsden, *Education and the Working Class, op. cit.* See also *Ability and Educational Opportunity*, ed. A. H. Halsey, *op. cit.*

[2]See 'Social and Economic Determinants of the Demand for Education', by H. E. Brazer and M. David in *The Economics of Higher Education*, ed. S. Mushkin, US Department of Health, Education and Welfare (Washington, 1962).

[3]Robbins Report, Appendix 1, part II, pp. 66–7.

[4]This is because of the difficulty of ensuring accommodation for the extra final year.

[5]*15 to 18, loc. cit.*, p. 140.

[6]The trend is an extrapolation of recent experience, according to assumptions spelt out by the Ministry of Education in *Statistics of Education, 1962*, part 2, p. 7.

Table 14.10. *Enrolment ratios for boys and girls aged 15 and over at all schools in England and Wales*

Age			1960		1975	
			Boys	Girls	Boys	Girls
15	(a)	Trend projection	40·8	38·7	74·6	71·7
	(b)	Raising leaving age	—	—	24·9	27·8
16	(a)	Trend projection	22·6	20·4	36·9	31·4
	(b)	No December leaving	—	—	21·0	22·8
17	(a)	Trend projection	12·4	9·7	22·1	16·1
	(b)	More A level courses at schools	—	—	3·7	2·7
18	(a)	Trend projection	4·9	2·5	8·8	4·7
	(b)	More A level courses at schools	—	—	1·4	0·8
		SUB-TOTALS				
15–18	(a)	Trend projection	21·4	19·0	36·2	31·6
	(b)	Additional factors	—	—	13·0	13·8
		(a) + (b)	21·4	19·0	49·2	45·4
19		Trend projection	0·6	0·2	1·1	0·3
		TOTAL				
15–19			17·6	15·5	40·3	37·0

Source: Statistics of Education and NIESR estimates.

and a further 27,000 part-time[1]. Better provision of five- and seven-year courses for pupils at school would obviate the need of many of these to 'catch up' in later years. The conclusions we reach are that while in 1960 there were 0·5 million pupils aged 15 and over in England and Wales, by 1975 there will be 1·4 million, of which only 0·2 million will be accounted for by the raising

Table 14.11. *Enrolment projections for boys and girls aged 15 and over at all schools in England and Wales*

				'000s
	1960		1975	
	Boys	Girls	Boys	Girls
Trend projections aged 15 and over	271	230	537	441
Additional effect of:				
Raising the leaving age	—	—	94	100
No December leaving	—	—	79	81
Greater access to A level courses at non-selective schools	—	—	19	12
Total number aged 15 and over	271	230	729	634

Source: Statistics of Education, 1962, part 2, table 3; and table 14.10.

of the school-leaving age (table 14.11). To some extent these increases in the number of children staying on at school compulsorily or voluntarily in full-time education will be offset by diminution in the demand for full-time and part-time further education.

[1]The latter include an unknown number of overseas students. There is also a large but unknown number preparing for GCE A level by private study.

(d) *Non-advanced further education*[1]

Further education is a field of immense complexity where changes have occurred more rapidly in the last ten years than in any other part of education. A number of additional changes can be foreseen. In the first place, the number of boys and girls under the age of 18 in institutions of further education undertaking full-time courses will, after a point in time, diminish as the full-time enrolments in the secondary system increase. From the age of 16 up to 18 part-time enrolments will increase until the one day a week attendance envisaged by the 1944 Act becomes compulsory. Thus, that part of the age group 16 and 17 not enrolled in full-time education will be making substantial demands on teacher supply. These boys and girls will follow courses some of which will lead to further education, particularly in the technical colleges. Higher education will itself expand in order to cover some of the courses now taken in further education. In particular, a number of degrees and diplomas now obtained by part-time work will be provided for by full-time courses. In this respect, therefore, the expansion of higher education will tend to slow down the expansion of the further education sector, but three forces will be working in the opposite direction.

The first is that as the desire for qualifications expands throughout the community, it is likely to expand at all levels. Therefore, the provision in higher education for degrees and diplomas will be matched, and probably out-stripped, by growth in requirements for semi-professional and trade qualifications. Secondly, part-time courses for further vocational qualifications and for leisure pursuits will undoubtedly be in increasing demand, partly because the rapidity of technical change makes it certain that an increasing number of people will feel the urgency of acquiring new skills or developing those they already have by part-time study. In addition, the expansion of full-time education will in itself lead to an increased demand for part-time courses: teachers, for example, form a high proportion of the student body in many part-time education courses and the virtual doubling of the teaching force which we foresee will itself be an important factor in increasing the demand for part-time education. Thirdly, the whole question of the further education and training of married women whose families have ceased to be entirely dependent upon them will undoubtedly receive far greater attention in the next fifteen years than it has until recently. All these factors, and especially the Industrial Training Act, will tend to increase the demand for further education and adult education.

For these reasons, we expect a rise of about 30,000 to a level of 130,000 in the numbers of those in full-time further education in the United Kingdom, and substantial increases in the numbers of people attending part-time day enrol-

[1]Further education is defined as education for people beyond the compulsory school-leaving age who are neither at school nor in higher education as defined by the Robbins Committee (i.e., universities, colleges of advanced technology, 'advanced' further education and teacher training colleges).

Table 14.12. *Projections of non-advanced further education*

	England and Wales		United Kingdom	
	1959–60	1974–5	1959–60[a]	1974–5
				'000s
Full-time and sandwich students				
Age 15–17[b]	57·5	50	67·5	55
Age 18 and over[c]	26·9	65	31·8	75
Total	84·4	115	99·3	130
Part-time day students				
Age 15–17[d]	194·5	815	215·2	940
Age 18 and over[c]	218·9	440	236·0	505
Total	413·4	1,255	451·2	1,445
Full-time equivalent (1/5th)	82·7	250	90·2	290
Evening students, 18 and over[c]				
Major establishments	553·5	885		
Evening institutes	563·4	1,000		
Total	1,117·0	1,885	1,356·1	2,285
Full-time equivalent (1/10th)	111·7	190	135·6	230
TOTAL full-time equivalent students	278·8	555	325·1	650

Source: Statistics of Education, 1961, part 2 and NIESR estimates.

[a]Partly estimated.

[b]Projected as percentage of the non-school population.

[c]Trend projection after deducting advanced students.

[d]Part-time day or block release assumed to be compulsory by 1970 for ages 16 and 17, 15-year-olds will remain at school.

ments, equivalent to a total in 1975 of well over a quarter of a million full-time students.   Then by 1975 in the United Kingdom there may be 420,000 full-time equivalent students outside the Robbins categories of higher education, plus nearly 2·3 million evening students (see table 14.12).   In addition, substantial provision will be made for courses conducted by television and by correspondence[1] and a certain amount of provision of further education will be in residential schools for week-end and vocational courses.

(e) *Higher education*

The higher education targets in this section are based upon the number of qualified leavers from schools and further education, together with students from overseas.   The methods we have used are the same as those used in the Robbins Report, but for several reasons our figures are higher than theirs. The reasons for our higher estimates—which exceed those in the Robbins Report by nearly 20 per cent—are that the earlier raising of the school-leaving age which we envisage has the effect of accelerating the trend to stay on in full-

[1]It has been estimated that 500,000 people took courses by correspondence in 1960 (Ditchley Park Conference on Long-Distance Education, June 1964).

Table 14.13.   *Home and overseas students in full-time higher education in Great Britain, 1960 and 1975*

'000s

	1959–60	1974–5 Robbins	NIESR[a]
Universities and CATs	113	227	304
Advanced further education	19	53	62
Colleges of education[b]	38	132	132
Total	170	412	498

Source: Robbins Report, Appendix 1, tables 47 and 53, and NIESR estimates.

[a]NIESR estimates for Northern Ireland are 11,000 in universities and CATs; 3,000 in advanced further education and 3,000 in colleges of education.

[b]Training colleges.

time education until 18.   The pool from which candidates for higher education places will be drawn is therefore larger than assumed in the Robbins Report. In addition, the earlier acceleration in the provision of places for those training as teachers, which is implicit in the targets for the larger teaching force (larger both because of the higher birth rate and the intention to eliminate oversize classes by 1975), will build up the higher education system at a more rapid rate than was envisaged in the Robbins Report.   We foresee a switch in the balance of higher education towards teacher-training in the period up to the early 1970s, and then a rapid build-up of the university sector, to provide teachers for the 15 + age group.   Our difference from Robbins is partly a matter of *timing*—our totals represent a bringing forward of the Robbins totals by several years—and partly a matter of *phasing*.   In addition, we have assumed a greater acceleration in the proportion of those qualified for entrance to higher education who actually do enter.   This is mainly because we assume that the growth of full-time education to replace part-time education, will make the route to higher education more direct for many boys and girls.   It is from the early 1970s onwards that our assumptions lead to increases in the demand for higher education.   To some extent we have allowed for such considerations in our projections for non-advanced further education, since that is the sector where the 'open door' policy for admission is followed.

Our estimates for Great Britain are compared with those in the Robbins Report in table 14.13.   Our total of 498,000 places in higher education by 1974–5 is 86,000 higher: we anticipate an additional 77,000 places in universities and 9,000 more in technical education.   Our United Kingdom estimates add 17,000 places in Northern Ireland.

(f) *Total number of places*

Table 14.14 summarizes the demands on the educational system.   It shows the number of pupils at school and the numbers in further and higher education in 1960 and gives our targets for 1975.

Table 14.14. *Summary table: numbers in full-time education, 1960 and 1975*

'000s

| | England and Wales | | United Kingdom | |
	1960	1975	1960a	1975
Under 5s	219	537	235	616
Age 5	645	918	756	1,060
All other primary	3,550	4,653	4,241	5,375
Total primary, nursery, special schools	4,414	6,108	5,232	7,051
Secondary: under 15	2,705	2,947	n.a.	3,407
age 15 and over	501	1,362	n.a.	1,587
Total secondary	3,206	4,308	3,575	4,994
Total schools	7,620	10,416	8,807	12,045
of which: Private sector	497	520	517	540
Percentage of total	6·5	5·0	5·9	4·9
Further educationb	279	555	325	650
Higher education	144	426	176	515

Source: NIESR estimates from tables 14.8, 14.9, 14.11, 14.12 and 14.13.

aThe United Kingdom estimate involved some guesswork, particularly for the private sector in 1960 in Scotland and Northern Ireland: Scotland, 17,000 pupils; Northern Ireland, 3,000 pupils in independent schools and establishments.
bFull-time equivalent.

4. TEACHER REQUIREMENTS IN 1975

(a) *Number of teachers needed*

We have worked out the requirements for teachers on a number of separate assumptions, basing the calculation initially on an analysis for England and Wales and adjusting subsequently for the United Kingdom. Table 14.15 presents the results for schools. We begin from the situation in 1960, when there were 312,400 full-time teachers in the nursery, primary and secondary schools and, including part-time teachers, 323,600 full-time equivalents. Rather more than half these last were in secondary schools—166,600—and rather less than half in the primary and nursery schools—157,000. The calculations for 1975 rely on teacher-pupil ratios which are examined below.

(i) *Nursery classes.* We expect the number of children in nursery classes and equivalents for children under 5, in England and Wales, to rise from 219,000 in 1960 to 537,000 in 1975[1]. The 1960 pupil-teacher ratio for maintained nursery schools was 22·0 (plus a nursery assistant for each trained teacher). A pupil teacher ratio of 19·5 would require 16,000 teachers for half-time schooling for this age group or 27,000 nursery school teachers for full-time schooling.

Numbers in the age group of five will grow (on our assumption) from 645,000 to 918,000 in England and Wales. At a ratio of 19·5 pupils per teacher, which

[1]Table 14.8.

II

Table 14.15. *Increase in the number of schoolteachers needed to achieve objectives, 1960–75*

Primary and second-ary school age groups	England and Wales								United Kingdom
	Percentage change due to:					Numbers ('000s)			
	Increase in population	Enrolment changes		Reduction of class size to 30	Total percentage increase	1960[c]	Net increases required	1975	1975
		Voluntary[a]	Statutory[b]						
3 and 4	+42	+73	−40	+34	+97	8	+8	16	18
5	+42	—	−40	+45	+23	23	+5	28	32
6–10⅛	+31	—	—	+45	+90	126	+113	239	276
10⅔–14	+9	—	—	+24	+35	141	+49	190	220
15–18	+16	+75	+35	+24	+240	26	+62	88	102
3–19	+24	+8	+7	+27	+73	324	+237	561	648

Source: NIESR estimates.

[a]Provision for 28·5 per cent of the 3 and 4 age group; provision for the trend of voluntary staying on at school and additional acceleration factors such as more comprehensive schools and 5- and 7-year courses at modern schools.

[b]Measures to introduce half-day schooling for those aged 5 and under and to raise the school-leaving age to 16.

[c]The breakdown by pupils' age group is estimated.

is probably what is necessary to achieve a maximum class size of thirty, 47,000 teachers would be required, or 28,000 if the pupils attended half-time[1].

(ii) *Primary schools.* The primary school population aged 6–10⅓ in 1960 was 3,550,000 in England and Wales. By 1975 it is expected to be 4,653,000. Allowing for this increase and a reduction of the pupil-teacher ratio to provide a maximum size of class of thirty, 239,000 teachers would be required in England and Wales.

(iii) *Secondary schools.* The secondary school population in 1960 was 3·2 million in England and Wales. Of this 0·5 million were 15 and over. In 1975 the total secondary school population will be 4·3 million, of whom 1·4 million will be 15 and over. The number of teachers will rise from its 1960 figure of 166,600 (full-time teacher equivalent), at the pupil-teacher ratio necessary to achieve a maximum class size of thirty, to 278,000 teachers.

(iv) *All schools.* Thus, while the total school population in England and Wales is likely to rise from 7·6 million to 10·4 million, the number of teachers required will rise from the figure of 323,600 (full-time equivalent) in 1960, to 561,000 at desirable staffing standards. This figure will be even larger if present differences in staffing between maintained and private schools persist, since the private schools' share of teachers is so much greater in relation to the number of pupils and the above estimate assumes an overall average staffing ratio consistent with a maximum class of thirty. A continuation of present inequalities would call for an additional 4 per cent of teachers.

For the United Kingdom we have set the same targets as for England and Wales and the number of teachers needed will be 648,000 in 1975. This is a net increase of 76 per cent, compared with 73 per cent for England and Wales. The slightly higher proportional increase is the net effect of a population increase of 23 per cent (slightly less than that of England and Wales), an increase in enrolment which would have to be greater than in England and Wales since in 1960 the enrolment percentage of those over leaving age was lower in Scotland[2] and Northern Ireland[3] and a greater than proportional reduction in class size[4].

---

[1]Three fifths as many teachers are required to teach half-time schoolchildren as are required to teach children attending all day.

[2]See Scottish Education Department, *Education in Scotland in 1960* and *Supply of Teachers in Scotland*, Cmnd 1601 (Edinburgh, 1962), particularly p. 13 and p. 9.

[3]Northern Ireland, Ministry of Education, *Education in Northern Ireland, 1961–62.*

[4]Average staffing ratios in Scotland were higher for primary schools (30·8) and lower for secondary schools (17·3) than in England and Wales. In Northern Ireland also staffing ratios were less favourable in primary schools (30·6 compared with 29·2 in England and Wales), despite the relatively large number of small rural schools (19 per cent of classes contained over 40 children). As in Scotland the maximum permitted size for primary classes was 45 compared with 40 in England and Wales. For secondary classes in Scotland it was 30 for years IV–VI but 40 for years I–III. The enrolment percentage of those aged 15–18 in 1960 was 20·2 per cent in England and Wales compared with 15·7 per cent in Scotland (and approximately 17 per cent in Northern Ireland).

The net effect on the United Kingdom figures of these differences in starting points between England and Wales and Scotland and Northern Ireland, however, is slight: for example, an enrolment ratio of 19·6 for the United Kingdom, compared with 20·2, for those aged 5–18, and an overall staffing ratio of 26·3 for the United Kingdom compared with 26·1 in England and Wales.

(v) *Non-advanced further education*. In table 14.12 it was shown that on our assumptions the numbers in non-advanced further education would increase— on a full-time equivalent basis—from 279,000 in 1960 to 555,000 in 1975. In 1962 the staffing ratio at major establishments was 14·9 full-time equivalent students to full-time staff. However, there are many part-time teachers in further education, particularly those teaching evening students. There is no satisfactory overall estimate of part-time staff. In order to gauge future requirements it is the supply of full-time rather than part-time staff which is of crucial importance. In 1960 the number of day students (full-time and one fifth part-time) to full-time staff was 11·3. This included students on advanced courses who often make more demands on teaching time than less advanced students. Excluding advanced courses there was a staffing ratio of about 12·5. We have used a ratio of twelve students per full-time teacher as an approximate measure of future needs. This appears very favourable compared with that of schools and it may well be higher if colleges expand student numbers in the future.

Table 14.16. *Full-time teachers of full-time students in further education and higher education*

| | 1959–60 Great Britain | | 1974–5 United Kingdom |
	Staffing ratios (students per teacher)	Teachers '000s	Teachers '000s
Further education	12·0	16·7	35·0
Higher education:			
Universities	7·6	13·6	} 42·0
CATs	7·8	1·1	
Advanced further education	7·3	2·6	9·0
Teacher training	11·9	3·2	11·0
Total higher education	8·3	20·5	62·0

Source: Robbins Report, Appendix 3, and NIESR estimates.

Some of the additional teachers will be recruited from the technical colleges themselves and the technical teachers' training colleges (although the latter are still very small). But it is hoped that more recruits from industry and commerce will fill the posts needed for vocational courses. The greatest expansion will be due to compulsory day release. Altogether day release students will require a three-fold increase in the number of teachers. The number of full-time teachers required in non-advanced further education in England and Wales will have to be more than double that of 1960, and rise from approximately

15,000 in 1960 to 31,500 by 1975, a net increase of 16,500. In the United Kingdom the total number of teachers required in non-advanced further education may be 35,000 (table 14.16).

(vi) *Higher education.* The range of student-staff ratios in higher education in 1960 was from 7·6:1 for universities to 16:1 for Scottish colleges of education. On the assumption that in 1974–5 the average ratio is the same as in 1960, the total of teachers in higher education would be about 62,000 compared with about 21,000 in 1960.

(b) *The supply and recruitment of school teachers*

Teachers are the key input of the education system. Without them, nothing can be done. They form the greater part of the costs which education lays upon society. Educational building is not a high proportion of total building. Teachers, however, are a large part of the total stock of highly educated manpower. Consequently, any proposals for the expansion and improvement of education services must depend ultimately upon adequate measures to supply teachers and to train them. The following analysis is confined to schoolteachers as this is the sector where the problems are likely to be greatest. The number of full-time teachers employed in further and higher education was less than one tenth of the total in 1960 and although the proportional increase will be much greater than for teachers in schools, the former will still be only about one eighth of the total in 1975. Moreover, the problem of wastage is much greater among schoolteachers than among teachers in further and higher education.

The increases in the total number of schoolteachers needed will be substantial. We estimate that an average net increase of 19,000 teachers per year, or a recruitment of 53,000 at given wastage rates (table 14.17) will be needed in England and Wales alone. This will not, however, be a steady recruitment. The number of teachers at present in training in England and Wales, and for whom provision for training has already been made, determines the supply until 1967. In 1962–3, 17,000 students entered the training colleges, in 1963–4 there were 21,000 entrants, and in 1964–5 between 26,000 and 28,000 are expected to enter[1]. After that, on plans in early 1964, the number would be held constant at 28,000. It is in fact clear that the number should rise to 40,000 in England and Wales by 1971 because to achieve the targets set for the 1970s would require higher rates of entry to teacher-training in the late 1960s, to compensate for the relatively low rates of entry in the mid-1960s. Consequently, the substantial expansion of teacher training provision which has already been made must be continued if the targets are to be achieved.

The changes in the structure of the teaching force on which our teacher

[1]Recruits from universities must be added to these figures.

Table 14.17.   *Teacher requirements to achieve targets, ten-year period 1965–74 inclusive (England and Wales)*

'000s

	Net increase	Wastage	Total additional needs
Number of schoolteachers needed, total	189	339	528
By level:			
Primary and nursery	91	171	262
Secondary	98	168	266
By sex:			
Men	122	76	198
Women	67	263	330
By qualification:			
Graduates	115	88	203
Non-graduates	74	251	325

Source: NIESR estimates based on the targets set out in table 14.15.

requirements are based are shown in table 14.18 below.   They are designed to provide graduate teachers for the larger number of pupils who will stay beyond school-leaving age and some of whom will prepare for entry to higher education. But a higher proportion of graduates and specialist teachers are also needed for younger children in secondary schools if all pupils are to be given some opportunity to enter courses for the General Certificate of Education.   The sex balance has been altered for two reasons: firstly, because the high wastage rate of women inevitably increases the proportion of men in the force.   Secondly, we are proposing increased recruitment of men in order to reduce the overall wastage rates and to lessen the instability in schools caused by high turnover of staff.

Table 14.19 sets out the supply position.   Even the expanded training college programme and the university expansion recommended by the Robbins Committee will still leave us short of 120,000 teachers if we wish to achieve our target by 1975.   The officially recommended expansion is aimed at reducing the size of primary classes to thirty by 1980.   If this is to be achieved by 1975 the timing of the expansion will have to be reviewed and the date brought forward by at least three years.   A rapid increase in the number of graduate teachers is essential.   The percentage of arts graduates recruited was 42 per cent in 1961, but that of science graduates only 26 per cent and hardly any of the engineering students consider teaching as a career.   Already the swing away from science in the schools is causing concern to the newly expanded university science faculties and to industry.   Recruitment of science graduates should be increased at least to the same percentage as of arts graduates, at any rate temporarily until the present severe gap between supply and demand is bridged.   We therefore propose that the overall percentage of graduates who take up teaching as a career should eventually reach 45 per cent.   The present percentage in

Table 14.18. *The structure of the teaching force, 1960–1 and 1974–5*

| | Men | | | Percentages Women | |
| | | Non- | | | Non- |
1960–1	Graduates	graduates		Graduates	graduates
Primary schools:					
England and Wales	1·9	23·6		1·8	72·7
Scotland	12·0	3·7		20·0	64·3
Secondary schools:					
England and Wales	24·4	32·1		14·3	29·2
Scotland	38·6	18·5		25·4	17·5
All schools:					
Great Britain, 1960-1	14·1	25·9		9·5	50·4
Great Britain, 1974-5	17·4	28·6		15·0	39·0

Source: Statistics of Education, 1962, part 1 and Education in Scotland, 1960.

Scotland is 42 per cent and the proportion of graduate teachers in Scotland is higher now than that of our planned proportion in Great Britain in 1975 (see table 14.18).

The supply and recruitment of the teachers needed to achieve our targets raise a number of issues.

(i) *The short-term emergency.* The acute shortage in the mid-1960s, especially of primary teachers, will require special measures to be taken which could become permanent. If the age of school entry were to be raised, if 5-year-olds were to attend half-day in nursery and admission classes, and teachers were to be helped by nursery assistants, as we have suggested, the number of trained teachers needed in the primary schools would be correspondingly reduced. Further examination of desirable pupil-teacher ratios may well change the notions of what targets for class sizes should be. In addition, the proposed alterations in the status of teacher training colleges and their full entry into the higher education system, could conceivably lead to an increase in the number of teachers because of the improved status of education as a course of study. On the other hand they might lead to a loss if other courses were found to be more attractive.

(ii) *Teachers' pay.* It is in this connection that the wider question of teachers' pay and status is raised. It is commonly held that the problem of recruiting teachers of adequate capabilities is one of paying large differentials for those with the highest academic attainments. There is evidence that this is not necessarily the case[1]. The shortage of mathematics and science teachers, for

[1]However, the sudden increase in the demand by government and industry for mathematicians led to competitive bidding and drained the supply of mathematicians at the source, since maintained schools were unable to offer high enough differentials. Mathematics teaching suffered in consequence. Flexibility in salary scales in the past might have been of advantage here.

Table 14.19. *Recruitment of schoolteachers, cumulative totals for ten-year period 1965–6 to 1974–5 inclusive (England and Wales)*

'000s

	Official Min. of Education plans	Revised by Robbins Committee	To meet 1975 target
From training colleges	231	230	284
From universities	91	96	150
Re-entrants	included above	80	94
Total	322	406	528

Sources: Ministry of Education, *The Demand and Supply of Teachers, 1960–1980* (London, 1962); Robbins Report, Appendix 1: training colleges p. 141, assuming three-year course and 10 per cent wastage; universities, p. 301; re-entrants, p. 299; and NIESR estimates.

example, has been shown to be largely structural and not immediately susceptible to differential payments of the kind usually advocated[1].

It is also clear that, higher education apart, the major task in teacher recruitment is to meet the needs of the primary school and the secondary school catering for children of ordinary attainments. It is in these schools that the chronic shortages of large numbers of teachers have been most handicapping and where the projections of future requirements are largest. It is for this reason that the pay and status of the ordinary teacher assumes a crucial role in the analysis of teacher supply.

The academic quality of teachers has risen consistently over the years (with the exception of the periods immediately after the two wars when emergency-trained teachers were recruited). The proportion of new entrants to the training colleges with one or two A level passes has increased in recent years and the proportion of entrants with degrees to the teaching profession in all types of school has also increased. Our projections allow for a steady increase in the proportion of graduates in the teaching force[2]. The proportion of trained teachers has increased as the untrained element has been withdrawn. Provision has now been made for a date to be fixed at which all graduate entrants to the profession will have to have been trained.

However, although the formal attainments of teachers have improved, the general capabilities of new entrants to the profession are sometimes said to have declined (apart from their academic quality and the adequacy of the training they have received). This is an untestable statement since it requires the comparison of the immeasurable over time. It is clear that, with such large numbers, the dedicated teacher must always have been in the minority and it must be unsound to build a profession on the assumption that they are the general rule.

[1]See J. A. Lauwerys and J. Vaizey, *Supply, Recruitment and Training of Science and Mathematics Teachers, op. cit.* and J. Vaizey, *The Control of Education, op. cit.*, pp. 205–6.
[2]See table 14.18.

Fortunately, as the size of the classes is reduced and as the quality of the buildings is improved, it would be reasonable to assume that the quality of the teaching would also improve.   There is a great deal of experiment and research being carried out in the United States and, to a lesser extent, in this country, which should improve pedagogical techniques.   There are, for example, experiments in team teaching and in the teaching of modern languages and of mathematics, using modern technological aids.   Thus, there are reasons to assume that the productivity of the typical teacher is rising and may rise more rapidly in the future.   This should enable policies to be pursued that improve their professional status.   Their relative pay will, however, depend on other factors[1].

(iii) *Married women in the teaching force.*   One major policy issue in the supply of teachers is the different supply and demand conditions prevailing for men and for women teachers.   The greater part of the shortage of teachers in recent years is the withdrawal of married women from the teaching force.   Recent research appears to indicate that up to one half of the married women can be expected to return to teaching within ten years of their withdrawal[2].   Should this rate of return increase, the proportion of women teachers in the teaching force would not decline as rapidly as it has recently.   Nevertheless the recruitment of men is, at the moment, more valuable as a long-term policy than the recruitment of women.

The use of married women in the schools, however, depends not only on their willingness to re-enter the labour market, but upon flexibility of the school system in making use of them.   This requires provision for part-time teaching and for nursery schools for their children.   The wide variation in rates of recruitment of married women throughout the country suggests that if the best practices of the best local education authorities were to be applied, the rate of recruitment of part-time women teachers would be higher than it is.

There are rigidities in the education system which militate against the best use of teachers.   One such rigidity is found in single-sex schools where it is difficult to use teachers of the opposite sex even when these are temporarily in surplus. This has undoubtedly been a major problem in the teaching of mathematics in girls' schools.

(iv) *Pupil-teacher ratios.*   Finally, an issue which is central to the discussion is the use of the pupil-teacher ratio to calculate requirements for teachers.   To achieve a maximum class size of thirty in secondary schools, a ratio of 1:16 is needed.   This is because of small schools, classes which fall just below thirty, and the growing use of teachers for educational purposes outside the classroom proper.   The size of classes is crudely estimated by numbers on the register—

[1]See Hugh Clegg, 'After Burnham—What?', *Education*, 7 and 14 June 1963.
[2]Ministry of Education, *Women and Teaching*, by R. K. Kelsall (London, 1963).

an increasingly irrelevant concept. Teacher requirements could be reduced by a far more effective use of teachers than in the past. This could make a substantial difference to our totals for 1975. Assuming a 10 per cent improvement in staff utilization, the number of teachers required by 1975 would fall from 648,000 to 585,000. Even so, this still represents substantial increases in the numbers to be trained.

5. BUILDING REQUIREMENTS

There are four major influences on the demand for new building. The first arises from the expansion of the child population. For each additional child there should, in principle, be a new place. In practice, of course, many places are created just by overcrowding. The second influence is much less easy to quantify. Since the war the major reason for additional school building has been movement of population as, for example, when people leave London for a new town or move from a town centre to an outer suburb. The degree of mobility of population could be substantially enhanced by a policy of regional dispersion and urban renewal; though such movements during and since the war have been substantial. This movement, by itself, raises enormously the demand for new school places even with a static or falling total school population.

In the third place the demand for new school building arises from the need to renew out-of-date buildings. In part, this is achieved by the movement of population, since the older buildings in the centres of town are left relatively empty, while there is pressure for new building in the newly built areas on the outskirts of towns. Fourthly the expansion of education services into new sectors often entails building additional accommodation. At present something like 2 million children are in new schools built since the war and over a million in places provided by extensions and alterations and minor projects. A distribution of the age of school buildings based on the National Union of Teachers' report, *The State of Our Schools* (see table 14.20) suggests that approximately 54 per cent of primary schools and 20 per cent of secondary modern schools were built before 1900[1]. Allowing for the average size of these older schools this would still leave 40 per cent of pupils at primary schools built before this century. Since compulsory primary education started fully between 1876 and 1880 one would assume that one third of these places will reach their centenary in 1970, half in 1976 and one sixth in 1980 or not long after. A modest estimate for replacement needs would be that schools built before 1900 should be replaced by 1975. Schools with a total of 2,542,000 places would need to be replaced in thirteen years, or 196,000 places annually.

---

[1]The Ministry of Education survey of school buildings was not published at the time of going to press.

Table 14.20. *Estimated age distribution of school buildings*[a]

Period of construction of oldest part	All primary schools[b]		Secondary modern	Primary and Sec. mod.	NIESR estimate[c]
	Per cent of schools	Per cent of pupils	Per cent of schools	Per cent of schools	Per cent of places
Post-war	17	25	35	20	46
1920–44	}29	35	45	31	14
1900–19					9
Pre-1899	54	40	20	49	31
Total	100	100	100	100	100
No. of schools in sample	2,355		696	3,051	

Source: National Union of Teachers, *The State of our Schools*, NUT, *loc. cit.*, pp. 36, 42, 48, 11 and NIESR estimates.

[a]The percentage distribution of pupils was derived by applying the average number of pupils per school in each construction period to the number of schools. The NUT survey gives the percentage age distribution of secondary modern schools in the sample but not the average size of school in each construction period which would enable us to derive the distribution of pupils. Grammar and comprehensive schools are excluded.

[b]Excluding all-age schools.

[c]Based on Vaizey's estimate made in 1956 of school places built before 1899 (see *The Costs of Education, op. cit.*, p. 90). This is a residual figure after deducting an estimate of places built since 1900 from the total number of school places. He stresses that places are not synonymous with pupils.

In addition 700,000 places built between 1900 and 1918 would need to be replaced or modernized. This would amount to approximately 250,000 places annually on the most conservative replacement assumption. To this must be added provision for the increase in the number of children of school age and for the reduction in the size of classes.

The prospective rise in the number of children at school is of the order of 3·0 million in the thirteen years between 1963 and 1975. This suggests an annual rate of building of over 236,000 places without making provision for the movement of population. In addition, places have to be provided to allow the reduction in the size of classes, which requires a total of 948,000 places in thirteen years, or 73,000 annually. The total requirement is likely to be 559,000 places annually, not allowing for population movement. This compares with 249,000 places completed in 1960.

As the rate of provision up to 1964 has been far below this, in the later years of our period up to 700,000 places a year would be required to meet our targets.

To provide an increase in higher education on the scale that seems desirable will require a substantial amount of accommodation. The target in the Robbins Report was to increase the number of places from 216,000 in 1962–3 to 412,000 in 1974–5—an increase of 196,000 in twelve years[1]. Our targets would raise this to an increase of 299,000 places between 1962–3 and 1974–5.

[1]Robbins Report, Appendix 4, p. 155.

Table 14.21. *Building requirements for schools, 1963–75; number of places*

'000s

	England and Wales			United Kingdom		
	Primary	Second-ary	Total	Primary	Second-ary	Total
To allow for increase in school population, 1962–75	1,732	1,021	2,753	1,863	1,207	3,070
To eliminate classes over 30	587	222	809	707	241	948
To replace or modernize schools built before 1900[a]	1,640	517	2,157	1,964	578	2,542
To replace or modernize schools built between 1900 and 1918[b]	300	300	600	352	352	704
Total number of places	4,259	2,060	6,319	4,886	2,378	7,264
Annual average	327	159	486	376	183	559

Source: NIESR estimates.

[a]40 per cent of primary and 17 per cent of secondary places in 1962.
[b]9 per cent of all places in 1962.

School building costs have been controlled since the late 1940s by a system of cost control now being widely adopted for other purposes. This has kept the cost of school buildings down. The procedures have only recently been adopted for universities. Higher education building has been exceptionally expensive since the war. There is no reason to suppose that there will be a substantial change in school building costs, but in higher education it would not be unreasonable to assume that costs per place will fall as methods of financial control are made more efficient.

The Robbins Report estimates these costs at £3,850 per place in technology, £2,640 in science and medical subjects and £1,320 in arts subjects. The cost of residence is estimated at £1,650–£1,705 per place[1]. These are clearly on the high side, and new techniques might reduce costs.

In general, school building has followed the movement of population. This has meant that the proportion of new school buildings is highest in the sub-urban areas of the great towns and lowest in those areas where social conditions are worst. A reversal of this policy would have significant effects on the standard of education in working-class areas but it would entail heavy costs in land acquisition. The cost of altering schools is higher per place than the cost of building anew.

6. CURRENT EXPENDITURE ESTIMATES

In this section we attempt to estimate total current expenditure on goods and services by all educational institutions, whether financed by public authorities or from other sources (fees, property income, etc.). These estimates are set out in table 14.22.

[1]Robbins Report, Appendix 4, p. 113.

Some costs vary with the number of pupils (and their age and kind of education)—scholarships and school meals, for example; others move with the number of teachers—teachers' salaries, superannuation, classrooms at primary schools, teaching equipment; still other costs—school maintenance—are a function of the composition of the stock of educational building. In general, because modern buildings are bigger and better than old buildings, they cost more per pupil to heat and clean.

We expect that the volume of current expenditure on schools and further education will increase proportionately to the number of teachers, that is by 78 per cent. For higher education, the projection of costs is based on the projected increase in the number of students. On this basis, the volume of expenditure on schools and further education (other than rents and maintenance grants) will rise from £626 million in 1960 to £1,113 million in 1975. Higher education will increase from £95 million in 1960 to £287 million in 1975. Total expenditure, including miscellaneous expenditure, rents and grants, will rise from £882 million in 1960 to £1,727 million in 1975, at 1960 prices and salary rates. Most of the increase will be in public expenditure. To conform with our projections, the private sector in schools will not expand. In further and higher education, fees and endowment income together will rise at about the same rate as total expenditure. Direct current expenditure by public authorities will increase from £685 million in 1960 to £1,265 million in 1975 at 1960 prices[1]. Public grants to universities, other institutions and persons will increase from £114 million to £328 million[2].

These calculations are based on the assumption that the relative salaries of teachers will not rise. In the projection of public authorities' expenditure in chapter 9 it has been assumed that incomes of teachers will have to rise *pari passu* with gross national product per head of the labour force (that is, 3·1 per cent per annum)[3]. Since salaries of teachers represent about two thirds of total current expenditure in schools and about half in higher education, this means that total current expenditure would rise by 2 per cent a year for schools, and about 1½ per cent a year for higher and further education above the estimates at 1960 prices.

By 1975 the average level of qualifications of teachers will have risen, but the profession's age distribution will have altered. In view of the large number of new recruits we expect, however, average salary increases due to higher quali-

[1] The 1960 figure used here differs from that used in chapter 9 and appendix table 9.1, partly because child care is excluded here and partly because current education expenditure was revised downwards from £702 million in *National Income and Expenditure, 1961* (used for chapter 9) to £685 million in *National Income and Expenditure, 1963* (used for this chapter).
[2] In chapter 9, as in the national accounts, expenditure by universities and other institutions financed by grants, is treated as consumers' expenditure.
[3] A similar assumption was made by the Robbins Committee in estimating the future cost of higher education.

Table 14.22. *Current expenditure on education in the United Kingdom*[a]
(*£ million, 1960 prices*)

	1960			1975		
	Combined public authorities	Private[b]	Total	Combined public authorities	Private[b]	Total
Maintained schools	489			900		
Non-maintained schools	20	56		20	57	
All schools	509	56	565	920	57	977
Non-advanced further education	55	6	61	121	15	136
Universities and CATs	63	10		177	28	
Advanced further education	13	1		45	2	
Teacher training	8	—		34	1	
All higher education	84	11	95	256	31	287
Miscellaneous expenditure[c]	56		56	90		90
Imputed rents[d]	66		66	114		114
Maintenance grants[e]	29	10	39	92	31	123
Total current expenditure and grants	799	83	882	1,593	134	1,727
of which:						
Direct public expenditure	685			1,265		
Grants to universities and other institutions	85			236		
Grants to persons	29			92		

Sources: National Income and Expenditure, 1963; Statistics of Education, 1962; Robbins Report; NIESR estimates.

[a]Including current grants.

[b]Expenditure from private sources includes expenditure of individuals as well as from donations and endowment income. Boarding expenditure is excluded. Most of the estimates of private expenditure in 1960 are arbitrary, since little is known about actual expenditure.

[c]Includes school health, recreation and youth service, administration and inspection, and other miscellaneous grants and expenditure. These items were projected by an increase in school enrolment with an allowance for improved services for health and dentistry, recreation and youth service.

[d]Imputed rents are assumed to be equal to loan charges in accordance with *National Income and Expenditure.*

[e]Maintenance in 1960 can be divided as follows: Schools   £1 million
                                         Further education   £4 million
                                         Universities   £14 million
                                         Teachers' training £10 million

fications may be offset to some extent by the generally lower average age of teachers. This may be too cautious an assumption and the average level of salaries could rise further as a result of the improvement of qualifications.

The forecasts of current expenditure in table 14.22 imply that the proportion of the total national product spent on education will be higher in 1975 than it is at present (and allowing for changes in relative prices it will be higher still). Moreover, on our assumptions the share of the public authorities will rise from 90·5 per cent in 1960 to 92·5 per cent in 1975. Within the public sector the share of the central government has been rising over the last forty years or so, and our forecast would suggest that in the absence of any radical change in the system of financing, this tendency will continue. This raises the issue of whether or not the share found by local finance should be reduced still further, by a reorganization of the system of central government grants to local authorities. In the discussion in section 2 above of the role of the central government in educational finance, we concluded that for various reasons an increasing amount of finance is likely to be found by the central government and that the proportion of educational finance met from the rates is likely to diminish.

There is another possible source of finance. In a general sense, education is income-elastic and there is some evidence that parents earning more than a given amount of income—and, the assumption is, also those possessing a certain amount of capital—are prepared to buy education for their children. Arguments have been advanced which would suggest that, as personal incomes rise, so the share of private education in the total would also tend to rise. In the more prosperous towns in the south, the proportion of privately educated children is higher than in the towns in the north. In recent years, however, the rise in the public sector has been relatively greater than that of the private sector.

Another possibility is that education authorities may look for additional private sources of revenue to assist the maintained schools. Fees could be charged for part of the cost of educating a child at a school, or for a particular part of the service—books, games, hobbies and so on. The case for greater private finance of maintained schools is, in part at least, a case for extending the market economy to education. We do not intend to argue the pros and cons of this case here. We do not believe, however, that these devices could make a substantial contribution towards reducing the financial cost of the education service. Any system of fee-charging has to be set alongside a complex system of subsidies and grants to poorer parents and to parents who are unwilling to do what most people would regard as the best for their children. In the history of education and other social services, complicated schemes of this kind have always ended in the assimilation of the fee-paying sector into the wholly free sector.

Different arguments apply to loans for students: these transfer payments could be met through a loan system which, although it would be administratively expensive to operate, would tend to diminish government expenditure on student aid. It would, however, have a dissuasive effect on student enrolment since it would discriminate against students from low income homes.

Another possible way of reducing public authorities' expenditure would be to reduce the unit costs of the more expensive parts of education[1]. As student

---

[1] The cost of educating British students is probably the highest in the world, even when compared with the United States. This is partly due to residence, partly to low staff ratios and the small average size of departments.

grants approximate more and more to the earnings of the people of that age in industrial or commercial employment and as higher education is also residential in large degree, the unit cost is high and rising. If student labour were regarded as a possible means, both of reducing the current costs of higher education and of helping to finance students, then the unit cost might be considerably reduced. Similarly, the adoption of new techniques might help to reduce the cost of education.

7. CAPITAL EXPENDITURE

It will be clear that total capital expenditure over the period 1960–75 will be very large. Additional school places for over 3 million children, plus nearly a million places to allow for smaller classes, together with replacement of about $2\frac{1}{2}$ million places in existing buildings, suggest that requirements will need to be of the order of about 560,000 places annually. Since building in the early 1960s has not provided more than about 250,000 places a year, a figure of 700,000 places a year should be aimed at by 1975, allowing for a build-up in the later 1960s. In 1960 the net cost per place in primary schools was £156, and for secondary schools was £277. This excludes land, playing fields and site works. Our total estimate for capital expenditure on schools was obtained by adjusting net costs per place in 1960 in the light of actual capital expenditure in 1960.

Table 14.23. *Capital expenditure, £ million*

	1960	1975 (1960 prices)
Schools and further education	113	190
Higher education	34	99[a]
	147	289

Sources: National Income and Expenditure, 1963, table 58; Robbins Report, Appendix 4, p. 106.

[a]The Robbins Report figure included £15 million per annum to replace existing buildings. Our figure for 1975 is arrived at by using Robbins average cost per place adjusted to 1960 prices and making a similar provision for replacement.

Capital expenditure on higher education will depend on the build-up of investment in the 1960s. The Robbins estimate for Great Britain was £87·3 million in 1974–5 at 1962–3 prices. At 1960 prices this would imply about £82 million for the United Kingdom. Our projected student body is 25 per cent larger, and it would not be unreasonable to suppose that proportionately greater capital expenditure will be required. This would raise the capital figure to £99 million by 1975, for higher education as a whole.

Total capital expenditure in 1975 would thus be of the order of £280–£300 million a year (table 14.23).

APPENDICES

Appendix table 1.1.   *Total employed labour force in various countries, 1950–62*[a]

'000s

	Austria	Belgium	Canada	Denmark[b]	France	Germany	Ireland	Italy	Netherlands	Norway	Sweden	UK	USA
1950	3,246	3,371	5,029	1,982	19,150	20,365	1,241	17,167	3,835	1,455	2,980	23,229	61,398
1951	3,270	3,488	5,174	2,109	19,240	20,895	1,220	17,232	3,858	1,460	3,020	23,588	63,884
1952	3,253	3,444	5,266	2,021	19,250	21,300	1,200	17,297	3,850	1,455	2,990	23,519	64,628
1953	3,241	3,428	5,340	2,042	19,140	21,810	1,182	17,363	3,929	1,453	2,942	23,636	65,492
1954	3,297	3,451	5,357	2,106	19,206	22,395	1,185	17,427	4,042	1,458	2,960	23,987	64,240
1955	3,406	3,489	5,481	2,025	19,218	23,230	1,181	18,255	4,125	1,473	3,008	24,280	65,992
1956	3,475	3,520	5,702	2,020	19,271	23,830	1,163	17,951	4,204	1,471	3,016	24,458	67,565
1957	3,513	3,544	5,843	2,030	19,329	24,360	1,141	18,762	4,248	1,473	3,003	24,491	67,811
1958	3,539	3,507	5,815	2,045	19,316	24,585	1,121	19,370	4,216	1,460	2,963	24,221	66,603
1959	3,584	3,478	5,976	2,100	19,259	24,865	1,112	19,530	4,270	1,465	3,001	24,296	68,133
1960	3,605	3,496	6,074	2,150	19,288	25,330	1,067	19,886	4,347	1,478	3,071	24,691	69,195
1961	3,617	3,537	6,170	2,185	19,387	25,735	1,062	20,063	4,420	1,494	3,111	24,938	69,368
1962	3,618	3,607	6,343	2,220	19,630	26,045	1,058	20,133	4,491	1,503	3,120	25,080	70,673
Trend growth rates of employed labour force, 1950–62													
	1·1	0·3	1·9	0·6	0·2	2·1	−1·3	1·6	1·4	0·2	0·6	0·6	1·0

Sources: OECD, *Manpower Statistics, 1950–1960* (Paris, 1961) and *1950–1962* (Paris, 1963); Economic Commission for Europe, *Economic Survey of Europe in 1962, Part 1: The European Economy in 1962* (Geneva, 1963); unpublished data from OECD.

[a]Figures include employers, persons working on their own account and certain categories of unpaid family labour. The total includes armed forces which cover personnel from the metropolitan territory drawn from the total available labour force, irrespective of whether stationed at home or abroad.

[b]Figures for Denmark exclude armed forces apart from draftees performing their military service.

Appendix table 1.2.   *Share of wages in national income in various countries, average 1950–60*

Percentages

Austria	68·3
Belgium	63·9
Canada	75·8
Denmark	67·2
France	68·4
Germany	69·6
Ireland	62·9
Italy	61·8
Netherlands	63·6
Norway	69·3
Sweden	74·7
UK	**82·7**
USA	78·4

Sources: OECD, *General Statistics*, November 1962; UN *Yearbook of National Accounts Statistics, 1957* and *1962*, and *Statistics of National Income and Expenditure*, Statistical Papers, series H, no. 10 (1957); OECD, unpublished data.

Note: 'Wages' includes salaries, payments in kind, employers' social security contributions and pay and allowances of the armed forces.

Appendix table 1.3.   *Indices of real capital stock for various countries, 1950–60[a]*

	Belgium	Canada	France	Ger-many[b]	Nether-lands	Norway	Sweden	UK	USA
1950	100·0	100·0	100·0	100·0	100·0	100·0	100·0	100·0	100·0
1951	103·8	105·1	102·5	103·9	103·5	106·2	102·1	103·6	105·3
1952	106·5	112·8	105·6	108·2	107·0	110·8	103·7	103·6	110·3
1953	109·1	120·5	108·1	112·8	110·5	116·9	105·9	107·1	115·0
1954	112·0	128·2	110·6	118·7	115·8	124·6	108·0	110·7	119·7
1955	115·6	133·3	113·7	126·5	121·1	130·8	110·2	114·3	124·5
1956	118·9	141·0	117·6	136·2	128·1	138·5	112·3	121·4	129·8
1957	122·9	151·3	122·3	146·7	136·8	144·6	114·4	125·0	135·3
1958	127·0	161·5	127·4	156·8	145·6	152·3	117·1	128·6	140·5
1959	130·2	171·8	133·0	167·3	152·6	160·0	119·8	135·7	144·7
1960	134·2	179·5	138·0	179·4	161·4	166·2	122·5	139·3	149·2

Source: OECD unpublished data.

Note: 'Real capital stock' includes all man-made durable goods in private and public enterprises excluding military installations, forests, land, livestock, inventories, and other consumer goods in the hands of the consumers. Real capital stock at 1954 prices for bench-mark years is the real capital stock at current prices shown in 'Statistics of National Wealth for Eighteen Countries', by Th. van Der Weide, in *Income and Wealth*, series VIII (London, 1959), p. 8, divided by the implicit price deflator of gross domestic fixed asset formation obtained from the OECD 1954 price series. For other years net asset formation at 1954 prices was added to or subtracted from real capital stock at 1954 prices in bench-mark years. Annual net asset formation at 1954 prices equals gross fixed domestic asset formation at 1954 prices minus depreciation at 1954 prices. Depreciation at 1954 prices is the depreciation obtained from countries' submissions to the OECD deflated by the implicit price deflator mentioned above.

[a] At 1954 prices.
[b] Excluding the Saar and West Berlin.

Appendix table 2.1. *Indicators of the pressure of home demand and export performance*

(a)

		Pressure of demand for labour in United Kingdom	United Kingdom share in world trade in manufactures
		(Half-yearly percentage relation to trend, seasonally adjusted)	
1955	2	100·35	102·4
1956	1	100·31	101·3
	2	100·10	99·6
1957	1	99·87	97·3
	2	99·95	99·8
1958	1	99·62	99·9
	2	99·32	102·7
1959	1	99·34	103·4
	2	99·72	101·3
1960	1	100·08	99·6
	2	100·32	96·4
1961	1	100·44	101·1
	2	100·38	100·4

(b)

		Home purchases of plant and machinery	United Kingdom share in world trade in plant and machinery
		(Half-yearly percentage relation to trend, seasonally adjusted)	
1955	2	103·5	104·3
1956	1	100·2	101·5
	2	100·8	94·8
1957	1	102·3	98·1
	2	103·1	95·3
1958	1	100·4	99·2
	2	98·0	98·0
1959	1	95·6	105·8
	2	96·3	102·3
1960	1	95·0	105·8
	2	98·8	97·1
1961	1	104·4	103·7
	2	104·0	95·2

(c)

		Home purchases of plant and machinery	Share of exports in total domestic production of plant and machinery
		(Quarterly percentage relation to trend, seasonally adjusted)	
1955	1	95·8	107·9
	2	100·3	96·8
	3	101·8	100·0
	4	105·1	100·3
1956	1	100·8	103·7
	2	99·6	105·9
	3	98·1	98·4
	4	103·4	92·8
1957	1	101·4	101·5
	2	103·2	102·0
	3	101·3	96·3
	4	104·8	97·5
1958	1	101·0	98·9
	2	99·8	96·3
	3	97·9	94·6
	4	98·0	95·6
1959	1	92·9	99·7
	2	98·3	101·6
	3	94·7	96·9
	4	97·8	100·4
1960	1	97·3	104·2
	2	92·6	106·5
	3	98·8	94·1
	4	98·7	100·7
1961	1	102·6	106·3
	2	106·2	101·9
	3	106·6	95·8
	4	101·4	102·3

Sources: The basic data on the UK share in world trade in plant and machinery were kindly supplied by the OECD Statistics Division. The other data are NIESR estimates based on NIESR series of the 'excess demand' for labour, and official series of purchases of, production of and trade in plant and machinery.

Appendix table 3.1.   United Kingdom total male population by 5-year age groups, 1960–75

Mid-year ('000s)

	1960	1961	1962	1963	1964	1965	1966	1967	1968	1969	1970	1971	1972	1973	1974	1975
0–	2,133	2,197	2,262	2,334	2,397	2,452	2,500	2,541	2,580	2,622	2,669	2,714	2,752	2,782	2,799	2,806
5–	1,947	1,950	1,988	2,022	2,067	2,128	2,194	2,256	2,323	2,388	2,442	2,490	2,531	2,573	2,616	2,663
10–	2,175	2,172	2,054	1,999	1,968	1,950	1,959	1,990	2,023	2,063	2,127	2,192	2,252	2,322	2,388	2,438
15–	1,815	1,893	2,062	2,140	2,169	2,182	2,164	2,060	2,003	1,971	1,956	1,962	1,992	2,026	2,066	2,128
20–	1,723	1,721	1,746	1,773	1,821	1,857	1,921	2,081	2,156	2,186	2,196	2,175	2,067	2,006	1,974	1,956
25–	1,665	1,674	1,703	1,719	1,745	1,756	1,753	1,777	1,798	1,839	1,874	1,938	2,092	2,167	2,197	2,207
30–	1,709	1,712	1,726	1,712	1,698	1,692	1,705	1,737	1,749	1,771	1,778	1,771	1,792	1,811	1,852	1,887
35–	1,867	1,818	1,785	1,756	1,734	1,715	1,722	1,741	1,724	1,707	1,699	1,710	1,740	1,752	1,774	1,781
40–	1,643	1,721	1,796	1,870	1,944	1,879	1,823	1,785	1,754	1,731	1,710	1,714	1,734	1,717	1,700	1,692
45–	1,830	1,804	1,762	1,686	1,596	1,646	1,711	1,775	1,846	1,918	1,853	1,801	1,762	1,736	1,713	1,692
50–	1,769	1,776	1,776	1,771	1,771	1,775	1,753	1,706	1,631	1,546	1,596	1,662	1,723	1,792	1,862	1,799
55–	1,568	1,596	1,616	1,633	1,646	1,658	1,674	1,668	1,662	1,665	1,672	1,654	1,608	1,541	1,461	1,508
60–	1,202	1,246	1,284	1,326	1,367	1,404	1,435	1,452	1,468	1,482	1,494	1,511	1,505	1,501	1,504	1,511
65–	918	936	957	973	997	1,018	1,047	1,080	1,122	1,157	1,193	1,214	1,230	1,244	1,257	1,268
70–	676	677	683	689	696	707	720	734	744	760	780	806	836	870	897	925
75–	447	448	449	449	450	451	451	454	461	469	476	484	492	505	519	535
80–	230	228	229	230	232	234	236	237	238	239	241	242	243	247	251	255
85+	106	106	105	106	106	107	108	108	109	110	111	112	112	113	114	115
Total	25,423	25,675	25,983	26,188	26,406	26,611	26,876	27,182	27,391	27,624	27,867	28,152	28,463	28,705	28,944	29,166
of which:																
0–14	6,255	6,319	6,304	6,355	6,432	6,530	6,653	6,787	6,926	7,073	7,238	7,396	7,535	7,677	7,803	7,907
15–64	16,791	16,961	17,256	17,386	17,493	17,564	17,661	17,782	17,791	17,816	17,828	17,898	18,015	18,049	18,103	18,161
65+	2,377	2,395	2,423	2,447	2,481	2,517	2,562	2,613	2,674	2,735	2,801	2,858	2,913	2,979	3,038	3,098

Appendix table 3.2.   United Kingdom total female population by 5-year age groups, 1960–75

Mid-year ('000s)

	1960	1961	1962	1963	1964	1965	1966	1967	1968	1969	1970	1971	1972	1973	1974	1975
0—	2,024	2,084	2,147	2,212	2,273	2,326	2,371	2,412	2,446	2,486	2,530	2,572	2,610	2,634	2,651	2,658
5—	1,855	1,856	1,886	1,922	1,964	2,019	2,084	2,142	2,205	2,267	2,320	2,365	2,406	2,439	2,479	2,523
10—	2,080	2,073	1,959	1,905	1,876	1,861	1,865	1,885	1,920	1,962	2,016	2,075	2,138	2,202	2,264	2,317
15—	1,753	1,824	1,976	2,046	2,072	2,083	2,061	1,961	1,905	1,876	1,861	1,863	1,885	1,920	1,962	2,013
20—	1,680	1,663	1,681	1,705	1,746	1,778	1,849	1,991	2,059	2,083	2,094	2,071	1,967	1,911	1,882	1,867
25—	1,632	1,612	1,622	1,635	1,661	1,683	1,676	1,687	1,711	1,751	1,787	1,848	1,988	2,056	2,080	2,092
30—	1,717	1,695	1,687	1,676	1,652	1,637	1,624	1,625	1,639	1,664	1,682	1,676	1,684	1,708	1,748	1,785
35—	1,908	1,844	1,796	1,759	1,732	1,709	1,698	1,683	1,672	1,648	1,632	1,617	1,618	1,632	1,657	1,675
40—	1,704	1,766	1,822	1,892	1,964	1,893	1,835	1,781	1,744	1,716	1,694	1,685	1,669	1,658	1,634	1,618
45—	1,894	1,863	1,820	1,742	1,643	1,684	1,741	1,793	1,864	1,935	1,866	1,809	1,756	1,719	1,691	1,669
50—	1,854	1,858	1,855	1,847	1,847	1,853	1,822	1,781	1,703	1,608	1,649	1,706	1,759	1,830	1,901	1,832
55—	1,729	1,750	1,765	1,775	1,783	1,790	1,799	1,794	1,785	1,786	1,793	1,766	1,726	1,649	1,554	1,596
60—	1,522	1,546	1,567	1,590	1,615	1,640	1,666	1,675	1,686	1,694	1,701	1,715	1,707	1,699	1,701	1,709
65—	1,296	1,314	1,337	1,359	1,382	1,399	1,415	1,435	1,455	1,479	1,505	1,523	1,539	1,551	1,560	1,567
70—	1,047	1,056	1,068	1,087	1,107	1,121	1,135	1,152	1,170	1,190	1,213	1,228	1,242	1,261	1,284	1,309
75—	757	772	781	789	798	806	814	822	836	850	865	879	893	908	925	945
80—	440	446	453	462	472	481	490	499	505	512	518	524	530	538	546	555
85+	224	228	236	242	248	254	259	265	271	277	284	290	296	299	305	310
Total	27,116	27,250	27,458	27,645	27,835	28,017	28,204	28,383	28,576	28,784	29,010	29,212	29,413	29,614	29,824	30,040
of which:																
0–14	5,959	6,013	5,992	6,039	6,113	6,206	6,320	6,439	6,571	6,715	6,866	7,012	7,154	7,275	7,394	7,498
15–64	17,393	17,421	17,591	17,667	17,715	17,750	17,771	17,771	17,768	17,761	17,759	17,756	17,759	17,782	17,810	17,856
65+	3,764	3,816	3,875	3,939	4,007	4,061	4,113	4,173	4,237	4,308	4,385	4,444	4,500	4,557	4,620	4,686

Appendix table 3.3.   *United Kingdom total population and population of working age, 1960–75*

Mid-year ('000s)

	1960	1961	1962	1963	1964	1965	1966	1967	1968	1969	1970	1971	1972	1973	1974	1975
Total males and females	52,539	52,925	53,441	53,833	54,241	54,628	55,080	55,565	55,967	56,408	56,877	57,364	57,876	58,319	58,768	59,206
Males 15–64	16,791	16,961	17,256	17,386	17,493	17,564	17,661	17,782	17,791	17,816	17,828	17,898	18,015	18,049	18,103	18,161
Females 15–59	15,871	15,875	16,024	16,077	16,100	16,110	16,105	16,096	16,082	16,067	16,058	16,041	16,052	16,083	16,109	16,147
Total population of working age	32,662	32,836	33,280	33,463	33,593	33,674	33,766	33,878	33,873	33,883	33,886	33,939	34,067	34,132	34,212	34,308

Appendix table 3.4. *Great Britain total male population by 5-year age groups, 1960-75*

Mid-year ('000s)

	1960	1961	1962	1963	1964	1965	1966	1967	1968	1969	1970	1971	1972	1973	1974	1975
0—	2,058	2,122	2,186	2,255	2,317	2,371	2,418	2,458	2,496	2,537	2,583	2,627	2,665	2,695	2,711	2,718
5—	1,879	1,882	1,918	1,951	1,995	2,056	2,121	2,181	2,246	2,310	2,363	2,410	2,450	2,491	2,533	2,578
10—	2,107	2,104	1,988	1,934	1,903	1,885	1,893	1,922	1,954	1,995	2,057	2,121	2,179	2,247	2,312	2,360
15—	1,753	1,832	1,999	2,075	2,104	2,116	2,098	1,996	1,939	1,907	1,892	1,897	1,926	1,958	1,999	2,059
20—	1,667	1,674	1,698	1,725	1,770	1,804	1,865	2,024	2,096	2,126	2,135	2,114	2,009	1,947	1,915	1,897
25—	1,623	1,633	1,660	1,677	1,704	1,715	1,714	1,736	1,754	1,793	1,826	1,887	2,042	2,112	2,142	2,151
30—	1,669	1,671	1,684	1,671	1,657	1,652	1,666	1,697	1,710	1,733	1,740	1,734	1,754	1,769	1,808	1,841
35—	1,824	1,774	1,743	1,713	1,692	1,674	1,682	1,700	1,685	1,669	1,661	1,673	1,702	1,715	1,738	1,745
40—	1,604	1,679	1,753	1,825	1,899	1,835	1,780	1,745	1,713	1,691	1,671	1,675	1,695	1,680	1,664	1,656
45—	1,787	1,762	1,722	1,646	1,557	1,606	1,669	1,733	1,802	1,874	1,810	1,760	1,723	1,696	1,674	1,654
50—	1,730	1,736	1,736	1,730	1,730	1,734	1,712	1,668	1,593	1,508	1,558	1,622	1,683	1,750	1,820	1,758
55—	1,533	1,561	1,581	1,597	1,612	1,622	1,637	1,631	1,624	1,627	1,634	1,616	1,572	1,505	1,425	1,472
60—	1,174	1,216	1,254	1,296	1,336	1,373	1,404	1,420	1,436	1,450	1,461	1,477	1,471	1,467	1,470	1,477
65—	896	913	934	949	973	994	1,022	1,056	1,096	1,131	1,166	1,186	1,203	1,216	1,229	1,239
70—	660	660	665	672	678	689	702	716	726	741	761	787	817	850	877	904
75—	436	437	437	438	439	440	439	442	449	457	464	472	480	493	506	522
80—	223	221	222	223	225	227	229	230	231	232	234	235	236	240	244	248
85+	104	103	102	103	103	104	105	105	106	107	108	109	109	110	111	112
Total	24,727	24,980	25,282	25,480	25,694	25,897	26,156	26,460	26,656	26,888	27,124	27,402	27,716	27,941	28,178	28,391
of which:																
0-14	6,044	6,108	6,092	6,140	6,215	6,312	6,432	6,561	6,696	6,842	7,003	7,158	7,294	7,433	7,556	7,656
15-64	16,364	16,538	16,830	16,955	17,061	17,131	17,227	17,350	17,352	17,378	17,388	17,455	17,577	17,599	17,655	17,710
65+	2,319	2,334	2,360	2,385	2,418	2,454	2,497	2,549	2,608	2,668	2,733	2,789	2,845	2,909	2,967	3,025

Appendix table 3.5. Great Britain total female population by 5-year age groups, 1960–75

Mid-year ('000s)

	1960	1961	1962	1963	1964	1965	1966	1967	1968	1969	1970	1971	1972	1973	1974	1975
0–	1,954	2,013	2,074	2,138	2,197	2,249	2,293	2,333	2,366	2,405	2,448	2,489	2,527	2,551	2,567	2,574
5–	1,791	1,791	1,821	1,856	1,897	1,951	2,014	2,070	2,132	2,192	2,244	2,288	2,328	2,360	2,399	2,442
10–	2,015	2,008	1,896	1,842	1,813	1,799	1,803	1,821	1,856	1,897	1,950	2,007	2,068	2,131	2,192	2,243
15–	1,695	1,763	1,913	1,983	2,009	2,020	1,998	1,900	1,844	1,815	1,800	1,802	1,823	1,858	1,899	1,949
20–	1,630	1,616	1,634	1,655	1,694	1,723	1,792	1,932	1,999	2,023	2,034	2,012	1,909	1,854	1,825	1,810
25–	1,586	1,568	1,579	1,592	1,618	1,640	1,634	1,644	1,665	1,702	1,736	1,795	1,933	2,000	2,024	2,036
30–	1,672	1,650	1,643	1,633	1,610	1,596	1,584	1,585	1,599	1,624	1,642	1,637	1,645	1,665	1,702	1,737
35–	1,861	1,797	1,750	1,714	1,688	1,666	1,655	1,641	1,631	1,608	1,593	1,579	1,580	1,594	1,619	1,637
40–	1,662	1,722	1,777	1,846	1,918	1,847	1,790	1,737	1,701	1,674	1,653	1,644	1,629	1,619	1,596	1,581
45–	1,848	1,819	1,776	1,700	1,602	1,643	1,699	1,749	1,820	1,890	1,821	1,766	1,713	1,678	1,651	1,630
50–	1,812	1,815	1,812	1,803	1,803	1,809	1,779	1,739	1,663	1,569	1,610	1,666	1,717	1,787	1,857	1,788
55–	1,690	1,712	1,726	1,736	1,743	1,750	1,758	1,753	1,743	1,744	1,751	1,725	1,686	1,611	1,517	1,559
60–	1,489	1,510	1,531	1,554	1,579	1,604	1,630	1,638	1,649	1,657	1,664	1,676	1,668	1,659	1,661	1,669
65–	1,268	1,285	1,306	1,329	1,351	1,368	1,383	1,403	1,423	1,446	1,473	1,490	1,506	1,517	1,526	1,532
70–	1,025	1,033	1,045	1,063	1,083	1,096	1,109	1,126	1,144	1,164	1,187	1,202	1,215	1,234	1,257	1,282
75–	741	756	765	773	782	790	798	805	818	832	846	860	873	889	905	925
80–	430	437	444	453	462	471	480	489	495	502	507	513	519	526	534	542
85+	220	223	230	236	242	248	253	260	265	271	278	283	291	292	298	303
Total	26,389	26,518	26,722	26,906	27,091	27,270	27,452	27,625	27,813	28,015	28,237	28,434	28,630	28,825	29,029	29,239
of which:																
0–14	5,760	5,812	5,791	5,836	5,907	5,999	6,110	6,224	6,354	6,494	6,642	6,784	6,923	7,042	7,158	7,259
15–64	16,945	16,972	17,141	17,216	17,264	17,298	17,319	17,318	17,314	17,306	17,304	17,302	17,303	17,325	17,351	17,396
65+	3,684	3,734	3,790	3,854	3,920	3,973	4,023	4,083	4,145	4,215	4,291	4,348	4,404	4,458	4,520	4,584

Appendix table 3.6. *Great Britain total population and population of working age, 1960–75*

Mid-year ('000s)

	1960	1961	1962	1963	1964	1965	1966	1967	1968	1969	1970	1971	1972	1973	1974	1975
Total males and females	51,116	51,498	52,004	52,386	52,785	53,167	53,608	54,085	54,469	54,903	55,361	55,836	56,346	56,766	57,207	57,630
Males 15–64	16,364	16,538	16,830	16,955	17,061	17,131	17,227	17,350	17,352	17,378	17,388	17,455	17,577	17,599	17,655	17,710
Females 15–59	15,456	15,462	15,610	15,662	15,685	15,694	15,689	15,680	15,665	15,649	15,640	15,626	15,635	15,666	15,690	15,727
Total population of working age	31,820	32,000	32,440	32,617	32,746	32,825	32,916	33,030	33,017	33,027	33,028	33,081	33,212	33,265	33,345	33,437

Appendix table 3.7. England and Wales total male population by 5-year age groups, 1960–75

Mid-year ('000s)

	1960	1961	1962	1963	1964	1965	1966	1967	1968	1969	1970	1971	1972	1973	1974	1975
0–	1,820	1,882	1,942	2,004	2,061	2,111	2,154	2,190	2,226	2,264	2,307	2,350	2,386	2,415	2,430	2,437
5–	1,664	1,668	1,701	1,733	1,773	1,827	1,887	1,944	2,000	2,059	2,108	2,151	2,188	2,226	2,264	2,306
10–	1,879	1,876	1,772	1,721	1,693	1,677	1,684	1,710	1,741	1,779	[1,833	1,892	1,947	2,006	2,063	2,111
15–	1,560	1,640	1,793	1,860	1,885	1,894	1,875	1,785	1,731	1,702	1,688	1,692	1,718	1,749	1,788	1,840
20–	1,482	1,494	1,518	1,546	1,590	1,623	1,682	1,826	1,891	1,916	1,923	1,900	1,804	1,746	1,716	1,699
25–	1,446	1,460	1,490	1,507	1,534	1,546	1,547	1,569	1,587	1,626	1,659	1,717	1,855	1,920	1,945	1,952
30–	1,494	1,499	1,516	1,506	1,495	1,491	1,506	1,537	1,550	1,572	1,580	1,577	1,596	1,612	1,651	1,684
35–	1,646	1,603	1,576	1,549	1,531	1,515	1,523	1,540	1,528	1,514	1,509	1,521	1,549	1,562	1,584	1,592
40–	1,451	1,522	1,590	1,656	1,725	1,667	1,618	1,585	1,558	1,537	1,519	1,521	1,541	1,529	1,515	1,510
45–	1,615	1,596	1,564	1,496	1,416	1,463	1,516	1,577	1,640	1,707	1,649	1,605	1,569	1,546	1,525	1,507
50–	1,565	1,572	1,570	1,567	1,567	1,575	1,557	1,518	1,452	1,376	1,422	1,479	1,534	1,595	1,660	1,604
55–	1,387	1,415	1,434	1,448	1,462	1,471	1,485	1,478	1,475	1,479	1,487	1,471	1,433	1,373	1,302	1,346
60–	1,064	1,101	1,134	1,175	1,212	1,247	1,276	1,291	1,307	1,319	1,327	1,342	1,336	1,325	[1,329	1,336
65–	813	830	851	865	886	905	931	958	997	1,030	1,063	1,081	1,096	1,111	1,121	1,129
70–	600	601	606	612	618	628	641	654	654	667	685	709	743	776	802	828
75–	395	397	398	399	400	402	401	404	411	419	425	432	440	452	463	478
80–	201	200	201	202	204	207	209	210	211	212	214	215	216	220	224	227
85+	94	93	92	93	93	94	95	95	96	97	99	100	100	101	102	103
Total	22,176	22,449	22,748	22,939	23,145	23,343	23,587	23,871	24,055	24,275	24,497	24,755	25,051	25,263	25,484	25,689
of which:																
0–14	5,363	5,426	5,415	5,458	5,527	5,615	5,725	5,844	5,967	6,102	6,248	6,393	6,521	6,647	6,757	6,854
15–64	14,710	14,902	15,185	15,310	15,417	15,492	15,585	15,706	15,719	15,748	15,763	15,825	15,935	15,957	16,015	16,070
65+	2,103	2,121	2,148	2,171	2,201	2,236	2,277	2,321	2,369	2,425	2,486	2,537	2,595	2,659	2,712	2,765

Appendix table 3.8. *England and Wales total female population by 5-year age groups, 1960–75*

Mid-year ('000s)

	1960	1961	1962	1963	1964	1965	1966	1967	1968	1969	1970	1971	1972	1973	1974	1975
0–	1,726	1,783	1,841	1,899	1,954	2,002	2,042	2,079	2,110	2,146	2,186	2,226	2,262	2,284	2,300	2,307
5–	1,586	1,586	1,613	1,645	1,681	1,732	1,790	1,843	1,899	1,954	2,002	2,042	2,079	2,110	2,146	2,186
10–	1,797	1,791	1,690	1,637	1,609	1,596	1,600	1,618	1,650	1,686	1,735	1,790	1,845	1,901	1,957	2,004
15–	1,509	1,576	1,714	1,773	1,793	1,804	1,783	1,698	1,644	1,615	1,602	1,604	1,623	1,655	1,691	1,740
20–	1,451	1,439	1,457	1,480	1,518	1,548	1,612	1,741	1,799	1,820	1,828	1,807	1,714	1,660	1,631	1,618
25–	1,414	1,400	1,411	1,424	1,450	1,472	1,468	1,479	1,502	1,537	1,570	1,625	1,751	1,810	1,831	1,841
30–	1,497	1,478	1,472	1,464	1,444	1,433	1,424	1,426	1,441	1,464	1,483	1,480	1,487	1,510	1,545	1,579
35–	1,680	1,622	1,578	1,545	1,520	1,501	1,489	1,477	1,469	1,449	1,437	1,426	1,427	1,442	1,465	1,484
40–	1,499	1,554	1,605	1,666	1,731	1,670	1,618	1,571	1,537	1,512	1,493	1,485	1,470	1,462	1,444	1,430
45–	1,665	1,641	1,605	1,536	1,449	1,486	1,537	1,584	1,647	1,710	1,649	1,599	1,552	1,519	1,494	1,475
50–	1,636	1,639	1,635	1,628	1,629	1,634	1,608	1,574	1,505	1,421	1,459	1,510	1,557	1,620	1,683	1,622
55–	1,525	1,547	1,562	1,571	1,577	1,583	1,590	1,585	1,576	1,578	1,585	1,563	1,529	1,461	1,376	1,415
60–	1,346	1,364	1,383	1,404	1,427	1,451	1,476	1,485	1,494	1,501	1,507	1,518	1,511	1,503	1,506	1,514
65–	1,149	1,166	1,185	1,206	1,225	1,239	1,252	1,271	1,289	1,312	1,337	1,353	1,369	1,380	1,388	1,394
70–	933	939	951	967	986	996	1,008	1,025	1,040	1,057	1,078	1,091	1,104	1,121	1,142	1,166
75–	676	690	699	706	715	723	730	736	748	760	773	785	798	811	825	843
80–	394	401	407	415	424	432	441	449	456	462	467	472	477	484	491	498
85+	203	205	212	218	224	230	235	241	247	253	260	265	271	273	278	283
Total	23,686	23,821	24,020	24,184	24,358	24,532	24,703	24,882	25,053	25,237	25,451	25,641	25,826	26,006	26,193	26,399
of which:																
0–14	5,109	5,160	5,144	5,181	5,244	5,330	5,432	5,540	5,659	5,786	5,923	6,058	6,186	6,295	6,403	6,497
15–64	15,222	15,260	15,422	15,491	15,540	15,582	15,605	15,620	15,614	15,607	15,613	15,617	15,621	15,642	15,666	15,718
65+	3,355	3,401	3,454	3,512	3,574	3,620	3,666	3,722	3,780	3,844	3,915	3,966	4,019	4,069	4,124	4,184

Appendix table 3.9. England and Wales total population and population of working age, 1960–75

Mid-year ('000s)

	1960	1961	1962	1963	1964	1965	1966	1967	1968	1969	1970	1971	1972	1973	1974	1975
Total males and females	45,862	46,270	46,768	47,123	47,503	47,875	48,290	48,753	49,108	49,512	49,948	50,396	50,877	51,269	51,677	52,088
Males 15–64	14,710	14,902	15,185	15,310	15,417	15,492	15,585	15,706	15,719	15,748	15,763	15,825	15,935	15,957	16,015	16,070
Females 15–59	13,876	13,896	14,039	14,087	14,113	14,131	14,129	14,135	14,120	14,106	14,106	14,099	14,110	14,139	14,160	14,204
Total population of working age	28,586	28,798	29,224	29,397	29,530	29,623	29,714	29,841	29,839	29,854	29,869	29,924	30,045	30,096	30,175	30,274

Appendix table 3.10   United Kingdom female population: age and marital status, 1960–75

Mid-year ('000s)

	1960	1961	1962	1963	1964	1965	1966	1967	1968	1969	1970	1971	1972	1973	1974	1975
Married																
15–	106	113	128	137	145	150	155	151	152	154	156	155	155	156	159	161
20–	946	948	970	996	1,032	1,063	1,119	1,218	1,275	1,302	1,321	1,311	1,249	1,217	1,203	1,196
25–	1,360	1,351	1,366	1,383	1,410	1,433	1,431	1,444	1,468	1,506	1,539	1,597	1,722	1,787	1,812	1,826
30–	1,521	1,503	1,498	1,490	1,470	1,459	1,450	1,454	1,470	1,496	1,515	1,513	1,524	1,549	1,587	1,623
35–	1,654	1,610	1,579	1,557	1,543	1,526	1,523	1,510	1,501	1,480	1,465	1,454	1,455	1,469	1,491	1,509
40–	1,469	1,529	1,583	1,650	1,719	1,661	1,617	1,574	1,547	1,527	1,512	1,506	1,494	1,484	1,464	1,450
45–	1,552	1,539	1,514	1,460	1,387	1,432	1,489	1,540	1,609	1,678	1,624	1,581	1,540	1,513	1,493	1,478
50–	1,429	1,440	1,447	1,450	1,459	1,473	1,459	1,437	1,385	1,311	1,361	1,416	1,467	1,534	1,601	1,550
55–	1,203	1,223	1,239	1,253	1,266	1,278	1,293	1,299	1,301	1,311	1,328	1,317	1,298	1,250	1,189	1,233
60–	924	943	961	979	1,000	1,020	1,043	1,055	1,069	1,082	1,095	1,113	1,118	1,123	1,135	1,150
65–	621	635	651	667	684	700	715	732	749	769	795	803	814	824	831	838
70–	375	378	382	389	397	404	411	419	429	440	452	461	468	478	489	501
75+	264	270	275	279	284	292	294	300	308	316	325	328	332	335	339	344
Total	13,424	13,482	13,593	13,690	13,796	13,891	13,999	14,133	14,263	14,378	14,488	14,555	14,636	14,719	14,793	14,859
of which 65+	1,260	1,283	1,308	1,335	1,365	1,396	1,420	1,451	1,486	1,525	1,572	1,592	1,614	1,637	1,659	1,683
Single																
15–	1,647	1,711	1,848	1,909	1,927	1,933	1,906	1,810	1,753	1,722	1,705	1,708	1,730	1,764	1,803	1,852
20–	734	715	711	709	714	715	730	773	784	781	773	760	718	694	679	671
25–	272	261	256	252	251	250	245	243	243	245	248	251	266	269	268	266
30–	196	192	189	186	182	178	174	171	169	168	167	163	160	159	161	162
35–	254	234	217	202	189	183	175	173	171	168	167	163	163	163	166	166
40–	235	237	239	242	245	232	218	207	197	189	182	179	175	174	170	168
45–	342	324	306	282	256	252	252	253	255	257	242	228	216	206	198	191
50–	425	418	408	397	388	380	363	344	318	291	288	290	292	296	300	282
55–	526	527	526	522	517	512	506	495	484	475	465	449	428	399	365	363
60–	598	603	606	611	615	620	623	620	617	612	606	602	589	576	566	559
65–	675	679	686	692	698	699	700	703	706	710	710	720	725	727	729	729
70–	672	678	686	698	710	717	724	733	741	750	761	767	774	783	795	808
75+	1,157	1,176	1,195	1,214	1,234	1,249	1,269	1,286	1,304	1,323	1,342	1,365	1,387	1,410	1,437	1,466
Total	7,733	7,755	7,873	7,916	7,926	7,920	7,885	7,811	7,742	7,691	7,656	7,645	7,623	7,620	7,637	7,683
of which 65+	2,504	2,533	2,567	2,604	2,642	2,665	2,695	2,722	2,751	2,783	2,813	2,852	2,886	2,920	2,961	3,003

Appendix table 3.11.   *Great Britain female population: age and marital status, 1960–75*

Mid-year ('000s)

	1960	1961	1962	1963	1964	1965	1966	1967	1968	1969	1970	1971	1972	1973	1974	1975
Married																
15–	104	111	126	135	143	148	153	149	150	152	154	153	153	154	157	159
20–	931	933	954	979	1,015	1,045	1,100	1,198	1,255	1,282	1,301	1,292	1,230	1,198	1,183	1,176
25–	1,334	1,325	1,340	1,357	1,384	1,407	1,405	1,418	1,440	1,476	1,508	1,565	1,688	1,752	1,776	1,790
30–	1,490	1,471	1,467	1,459	1,440	1,430	1,422	1,426	1,442	1,468	1,487	1,485	1,496	1,519	1,554	1,589
35–	1,619	1,575	1,545	1,524	1,511	1,494	1,491	1,479	1,471	1,451	1,436	1,426	1,427	1,441	1,463	1,481
40–	1,437	1,496	1,549	1,615	1,684	1,626	1,583	1,541	1,515	1,495	1,481	1,475	1,464	1,455	1,435	1,422
45–	1,519	1,507	1,482	1,430	1,357	1,402	1,458	1,507	1,576	1,645	1,591	1,549	1,508	1,483	1,463	1,449
50–	1,400	1,411	1,418	1,420	1,429	1,443	1,429	1,407	1,357	1,290	1,334	1,388	1,438	1,504	1,569	1,518
55–	1,178	1,200	1,215	1,229	1,241	1,253	1,268	1,274	1,275	1,285	1,302	1,291	1,273	1,226	1,166	1,210
60–	907	925	943	961	981	1,001	1,024	1,035	1,049	1,062	1,075	1,092	1,097	1,101	1,113	1,128
65+	1,237	1,259	1,283	1,309	1,339	1,370	1,393	1,424	1,458	1,497	1,543	1,563	1,585	1,606	1,626	1,648
Total	13,156	13,213	13,322	13,418	13,524	13,619	13,726	13,858	13,988	14,103	14,212	14,279	14,359	14,439	14,505	14,570
Single																
15–	1,591	1,652	1,787	1,848	1,866	1,872	1,845	1,751	1,694	1,663	1,646	1,649	1,670	1,704	1,742	1,790
20–	699	683	680	676	679	678	692	734	744	741	733	720	679	656	642	634
25–	252	243	239	235	234	233	229	226	225	226	228	230	245	248	248	246
30–	182	179	176	174	170	166	162	159	157	156	155	152	149	146	148	148
35–	242	222	205	190	177	172	164	162	160	157	157	153	153	153	156	156
40–	225	226	228	231	234	221	207	196	186	179	172	169	165	164	161	159
45–	329	312	294	270	245	241	241	242	244	245	230	217	205	195	188	181
50–	412	404	394	383	374	366	350	332	306	279	276	278	279	283	288	270
55–	512	512	511	507	502	497	490	479	468	459	449	434	413	385	351	349
60–	582	585	588	593	598	603	606	603	600	595	589	584	571	558	548	541
65+	2,447	2,475	2,507	2,545	2,581	2,603	2,630	2,659	2,687	2,718	2,748	2,785	2,819	2,852	2,894	2,936
Total	7,473	7,493	7,609	7,652	7,660	7,652	7,616	7,543	7,471	7,418	7,383	7,371	7,348	7,344	7,366	7,410

Appendix table 3.12. *Great Britain trend participation rates of married women, adjusted for level of unemployment, 1952–62 (numbers 'active' as per cent of total population of group)*

Age group	20–4	25–9	30–4	35–9	40–4	45–9	50–4	55–9
1952	43·05	30·99	27·77	29·58	31·23	31·20	27·41	21·04
1953	43·18	31·11	27·79	30·82	32·71	32·40	28·57	22·03
1954	43·13	31·23	27·92	31·94	34·10	33·64	29·78	23·08
1955	42·92	31·34	28·16	32·98	35·36	34·90	31·02	24·15
1956	42·59	31·49	28·51	33·92	36·53	36·17	32·31	25·25
1957	42·08	31·60	28·96	34·78	37·55	37·49	33·60	26·38
1958	41·41	31·72	29·51	35·52	38·48	38·85	34·92	27·56
1959	40·61	31·83	30·18	36·17	39·28	40·27	36·29	28·76
1960	39·69	31·98	30·94	36·73	39·99	41·69	37·69	30·00
1961	38·60	32·10	31·82	37·17	40·54	43·14	39·11	31·26
1962	37·34	32·21	32·80	37·53	41·00	44·62	40·57	32·56

Sources: Economic Trends, September 1962; *Ministry of Labour Gazette*, various issues; and NIESR adjustments indicated below.

Note: Unemployment was correlated with participation rates using the equation

Index of $P = a + b_{12}U + b_{14}U_{-1}$ $(R^2 = 0.973)$

where P = participation rates

U = total female unemployment

U_{-1} = total female unemployment lagged one year

b_{12} = -1.721

b_{14} = -1.413

a = 5.529

Appendix table 3.13. United Kingdom total male labour force by 5-year age groups, 1960–75

Mid-year ('000s)

	1960	1961	1962	1963	1964	1965	1966	1967	1968	1969	1970	1971	1972	1973	1974	1975
15–	1,373	1,454	1,564	1,630	1,665	1,693	1,684	1,486	1,233	1,188	1,166	1,154	1,198	1,191	1,188	1,198
20–	1,691	1,638	1,662	1,684	1,727	1,767	1,818	1,963	2,034	2,054	2,056	2,048	1,922	1,850	1,806	1,774
25–	1,661	1,661	1,692	1,708	1,733	1,744	1,741	1,765	1,785	1,826	1,861	1,925	2,078	2,152	2,182	2,192
30–	1,703	1,698	1,716	1,702	1,688	1,682	1,695	1,727	1,738	1,760	1,767	1,760	1,781	1,800	1,841	1,876
35–	1,863	1,806	1,774	1,745	1,723	1,705	1,712	1,730	1,713	1,697	1,689	1,700	1,729	1,741	1,763	1,770
40–	1,635	1,711	1,785	1,859	1,933	1,868	1,812	1,774	1,743	1,721	1,700	1,706	1,723	1,707	1,690	1,682
45–	1,779	1,773	1,734	1,659	1,571	1,620	1,684	1,747	1,817	1,888	1,824	1,773	1,734	1,708	1,686	1,665
50–	1,707	1,687	1,696	1,691	1,691	1,695	1,674	1,629	1,557	1,476	1,524	1,587	1,646	1,711	1,778	1,718
55–	1,489	1,506	1,527	1,543	1,557	1,567	1,582	1,576	1,571	1,574	1,580	1,563	1,520	1,456	1,381	1,425
60–	1,068	1,120	1,153	1,192	1,228	1,261	1,289	1,305	1,319	1,332	1,342	1,358	1,352	1,349	1,352	1,358
65–	411	408	417	420	426	431	439	449	463	473	483	486	487	479	469	458
70+	251	244	244	243	242	241	241	241	241	241	243	245	247	243	239	232
Total	16,631	16,706	16,964	17,076	17,184	17,274	17,371	17,392	17,214	17,230	17,235	17,305	17,417	17,387	17,375	17,348

Note: In this and related tables it had been assumed that the school-leaving age would be raised in 1967 (see chapter 3, page 94).

LL2

Appendix table 3.14.   *United Kingdom total female labour force by 5-year age groups, 1960–75*

Mid-year ('000s)

	1960	1961	1962	1963	1964	1965	1966	1967	1968	1969	1970	1971	1972	1973	1974	1975
Married																
15–	48	54	64	69	73	75	78	76	76	77	78	78	78	78	80	81
20–	377	378	391	401	415	427	450	489	512	523	530	527	502	489	483	480
25–	436	433	438	436	438	445	438	434	442	454	456	473	510	529	537	541
30–	469	478	491	481	475	465	462	456	454	455	461	453	448	455	465	477
35–	599	591	587	594	604	612	626	636	632	624	624	620	621	627	636	636
40–	584	615	644	671	708	684	674	656	653	659	661	673	675	671	662	648
45–	638	656	667	659	639	667	708	747	789	832	805	791	778	779	776	783
50–	533	558	582	604	630	657	672	683	672	652	687	729	770	813	855	835
55–	358	383	400	423	439	462	481	502	521	545	571	586	597	587	571	598
60–	146	154	157	164	178	186	201	208	221	229	243	252	264	276	290	300
65+	75	77	91	99	101	111	112	122	132	143	148	157	167	178	188	191
Total	4,263	4,377	4,512	4,601	4,700	4,791	4,902	5,009	5,104	5,193	5,264	5,339	5,410	5,482	5,543	5,570
Single																
15–	1,264	1,304	1,398	1,463	1,477	1,481	1,470	1,296	1,071	1,034	1,006	1,000	996	1,007	1,021	1,030
20–	720	690	677	671	674	675	690	731	738	735	724	711	658	633	616	606
25–	255	252	248	244	243	242	238	235	234	236	238	241	256	259	258	256
30–	185	183	178	177	173	170	167	164	162	161	160	157	155	153	155	155
35–	226	210	197	185	174	171	165	165	163	161	161	157	157	157	160	160
40–	198	200	204	209	214	205	194	186	179	174	170	169	167	166	163	161
45–	268	256	244	226	208	206	208	210	215	218	208	199	191	183	178	173
50–	304	300	295	289	286	282	273	260	242	224	223	227	230	236	242	230
55–	305	308	312	312	314	314	314	310	305	302	300	292	281	263	242	244
60–	178	184	197	199	200	205	206	205	210	211	215	219	217	212	211	209
65+	149	151	152	155	157	171	173	175	177	179	181	183	185	187	205	208
Total	4,052	4,038	4,102	4,130	4,120	4,122	4,098	3,937	3,696	3,635	3,586	3,555	3,493	3,456	3,451	3,432
Grand total	8,315	8,415	8,614	8,731	8,820	8,913	9,000	8,946	8,800	8,828	8,850	8,894	8,903	8,938	8,994	9,002

Appendix table 3.15. *Great Britain total male labour force by 5-year age groups, 1960–75*

Mid-year ('000s)

	1960	1961	1962	1963	1964	1965	1966	1967	1968	1969	1970	1971	1972	1973	1974	1975
15–	1,332	1,383	1,522	1,588	1,623	1,650	1,641	1,449	1,202	1,159	1,137	1,125	1,168	1,161	1,158	1,168
20–	1,650	1,609	1,621	1,641	1,681	1,709	1,768	1,910	1,978	2,000	2,001	1,993	1,868	1,795	1,751	1,720
25–	1,615	1,623	1,653	1,669	1,695	1,706	1,705	1,727	1,745	1,784	1,817	1,878	2,028	2,103	2,133	2,142
30–	1,661	1,660	1,677	1,663	1,649	1,644	1,658	1,690	1,701	1,724	1,731	1,725	1,744	1,763	1,804	1,834
35–	1,815	1,765	1,732	1,704	1,683	1,666	1,674	1,692	1,676	1,661	1,653	1,665	1,694	1,706	1,728	1,738
40–	1,596	1,671	1,743	1,816	1,890	1,826	1,771	1,734	1,704	1,683	1,663	1,669	1,687	1,671	1,654	1,648
45–	1,742	1,735	1,695	1,621	1,534	1,582	1,644	1,706	1,775	1,846	1,783	1,734	1,695	1,669	1,647	1,626
50–	1,652	1,650	1,658	1,652	1,652	1,656	1,635	1,592	1,521	1,440	1,488	1,549	1,607	1,672	1,739	1,679
55–	1,456	1,475	1,494	1,509	1,523	1,533	1,547	1,540	1,535	1,538	1,544	1,527	1,485	1,421	1,346	1,390
60–	1,039	1,094	1,127	1,166	1,202	1,235	1,263	1,278	1,292	1,305	1,314	1,329	1,323	1,320	1,323	1,329
65–	403	402	411	414	420	425	433	443	456	466	476	479	480	472	462	451
70+	249	242	242	241	240	239	239	239	239	239	241	243	245	241	237	230
Total	16,210	16,309	16,575	16,684	16,792	16,871	16,978	17,000	16,824	16,845	16,848	16,916	17,024	16,994	16,982	16,955

Appendix table 3.16. *Great Britain total female labour force by 5-year age groups, 1960–75*

Mid-year ('000s)

	1960	1961	1962	1963	1964	1965	1966	1967	1968	1969	1970	1971	1972	1973	1974	1975
Married																
15–	47	53	63	68	72	74	77	75	75	76	77	77	77	77	79	80
20–	368	369	382	392	406	418	440	479	502	513	520	517	492	479	473	470
25–	427	424	429	427	429	436	429	425	432	443	445	462	498	517	524	528
30–	462	471	484	474	468	458	455	449	447	448	454	446	441	448	458	469
35–	591	583	579	587	597	605	619	629	625	617	617	613	614	620	629	629
40–	575	606	635	662	699	675	665	647	644	650	652	664	666	662	653	640
45–	630	648	659	651	631	659	700	738	780	823	796	782	769	771	768	775
50–	525	550	574	596	622	649	664	675	665	645	680	722	762	805	847	827
55–	353	378	395	418	434	457	476	497	516	540	566	581	592	582	566	593
60–	145	153	156	163	177	185	200	207	220	228	242	251	263	275	289	299
65+	74	76	90	98	100	110	111	121	131	142	147	156	166	177	187	190
Total	4,197	4,311	4,446	4,536	4,635	4,726	4,836	4,942	5,037	5,125	5,196	5,271	5,340	5,413	5,473	5,500
Single																
15–	1,225	1,264	1,358	1,423	1,437	1,441	1,430	1,261	1,042	1,006	979	973	969	980	993	1,002
20–	696	666	653	646	648	647	661	701	707	704	693	680	628	604	587	577
25–	244	241	237	233	232	231	227	224	223	224	226	228	243	246	246	244
30–	177	175	171	170	166	163	160	157	155	154	153	150	148	145	147	147
35–	219	203	190	178	167	165	159	159	157	155	155	151	151	151	154	147
40–	192	194	198	203	208	199	188	180	173	168	164	163	161	160	158	154
45–	262	250	238	220	200	200	202	204	209	212	202	193	185	177	173	156
50–	297	293	288	282	279	275	266	254	236	218	217	221	223	229	236	224
55–	297	300	304	304	306	306	306	302	297	294	292	284	273	256	235	237
60–	175	181	194	196	197	202	203	202	207	208	212	216	214	209	208	206
65+	147	149	150	153	155	169	171	173	175	177	179	181	183	185	203	206
Total	3,931	3,916	3,981	4,008	3,997	3,998	3,973	3,817	3,581	3,520	3,472	3,440	3,378	3,342	3,340	3,321
Grand total	8,128	8,227	8,427	8,544	8,632	8,724	8,809	8,759	8,618	8,645	8,668	8,711	8,718	8,755	8,813	8,821

Appendix table 3.17. *Total labour force, United Kingdom and Great Britain, 1960–75*

Mid-year ('000s)

	1960	1961	1962	1963	1964	1965	1966	1967	1968	1969	1970	1971	1972	1973	1974	1975
United Kingdom																
1. Males	16,631	16,706	16,964	17,076	17,184	17,274	17,371	17,392	17,214	17,230	17,235	17,305	17,417	17,387	17,375	17,348
Females (2+3)	8,315	8,415	8,614	8,731	8,820	8,913	9,000	8,946	8,800	8,828	8,850	8,894	8,903	8,938	8,994	9,002
2. Married females	4,263	4,377	4,512	4,601	4,700	4,791	4,902	5,009	5,104	5,193	5,264	5,339	5,410	5,482	5,543	5,570
3. Single females	4,052	4,038	4,102	4,130	4,120	4,122	4,098	3,937	3,696	3,635	3,586	3,555	3,493	3,456	3,451	3,432
Total (1+2+3)	24,946	25,121	25,578	25,807	26,004	26,187	26,371	26,338	26,014	26,058	26,085	26,199	26,320	26,325	26,369	26,350
Great Britain																
4. Males	16,210	16,309	16,575	16,684	16,792	16,871	16,978	17,000	16,824	16,845	16,848	16,916	17,024	16,994	16,982	16,955
Females (5+6)	8,128	8,227	8,427	8,544	8,632	8,724	8,809	8,759	8,618	8,645	8,668	8,711	8,718	8,755	8,813	8,821
5. Married females	4,197	4,311	4,446	4,536	4,635	4,726	4,836	4,942	5,037	5,125	5,196	5,271	5,340	5,413	5,473	5,500
6. Single females	3,931	3,916	3,981	4,008	3,997	3,998	3,973	3,817	3,581	3,520	3,472	3,440	3,378	3,342	3,340	3,321
Total (4+5+6)	24,338	24,536	25,002	25,228	25,424	25,595	25,787	25,759	25,442	25,490	25,516	25,627	25,742	25,749	25,793	25,776

Appendix table 3.18.   United Kingdom total population by 5-year age groups, 1960–75

Mid-year ('000s)

	1960	1961	1962	1963	1964	1965	1966	1967	1968	1969	1970	1971	1972	1973	1974	1975
0–	4,157	4,281	4,409	4,546	4,670	4,778	4,871	4,953	5,026	5,108	5,199	5,286	5,362	5,416	5,450	5,464
5–	3,802	3,806	3,874	3,944	4,031	4,147	4,278	4,398	4,528	4,655	4,762	4,855	4,937	5,012	5,095	5,186
10–	4,255	4,245	4,013	3,904	3,844	3,811	3,824	3,875	3,943	4,025	4,143	4,267	4,390	4,524	4,652	4,755
15–	3,568	3,717	4,038	4,186	4,241	4,265	4,225	4,021	3,908	3,847	3,817	3,825	3,877	3,946	4,028	4,141
20–	3,403	3,384	3,427	3,478	3,567	3,635	3,770	4,072	4,215	4,269	4,290	4,246	4,034	3,917	3,856	3,823
25–	3,297	3,286	3,325	3,354	3,406	3,439	3,429	3,464	3,509	3,590	3,661	3,786	4,080	4,223	4,277	4,299
30–	3,426	3,407	3,413	3,388	3,350	3,329	3,329	3,362	3,388	3,435	3,460	3,447	3,476	3,519	3,600	3,672
35–	3,775	3,662	3,581	3,515	3,466	3,424	3,420	3,424	3,396	3,355	3,331	3,327	3,358	3,384	3,431	3,456
40–	3,347	3,487	3,618	3,762	3,908	3,772	3,658	3,566	3,498	3,447	3,404	3,399	3,403	3,375	3,334	3,310
45–	3,724	3,667	3,582	3,428	3,239	3,330	3,452	3,568	3,710	3,853	3,719	3,610	3,518	3,455	3,404	3,361
50–	3,623	3,634	3,631	3,618	3,618	3,628	3,575	3,487	3,334	3,154	3,245	3,368	3,482	3,622	3,763	3,631
55–	3,297	3,346	3,381	3,408	3,431	3,448	3,473	3,462	3,447	3,451	3,465	3,420	3,334	3,190	3,015	3,104
60–	2,724	2,792	2,851	2,916	2,982	3,044	3,101	3,127	3,154	3,176	3,195	3,226	3,212	3,200	3,205	3,220
65–	2,214	2,250	2,294	2,332	2,379	2,417	2,462	2,515	2,577	2,636	2,698	2,737	2,769	2,795	2,817	2,835
70–	1,723	1,733	1,751	1,776	1,803	1,828	1,855	1,886	1,914	1,950	1,993	2,034	2,078	2,131	2,181	2,234
75–	1,204	1,220	1,230	1,238	1,248	1,257	1,265	1,276	1,297	1,319	1,341	1,363	1,385	1,413	1,444	1,480
80–	670	674	682	692	704	715	726	736	743	751	759	766	773	785	797	810
85+	330	334	341	348	354	361	367	373	380	387	395	402	408	412	419	425
Total	52,539	52,925	53,441	53,833	54,241	54,628	55,080	55,565	55,967	56,408	56,877	57,364	57,876	58,319	58,768	59,206
of which:																
0–14	12,214	12,332	12,296	12,394	12,545	12,736	12,973	13,226	13,497	13,788	14,104	14,408	14,689	14,952	15,197	15,405
15–64	34,184	34,382	34,847	35,053	35,208	35,314	35,432	35,553	35,559	35,577	35,587	35,654	35,774	35,831	35,913	36,017
65+	6,141	6,211	6,298	6,386	6,488	6,578	6,675	6,786	6,911	7,043	7,186	7,302	7,413	7,536	7,658	7,784

Appendix table 3.19. *Projection of labour input, United Kingdom, total man-hours per year*

	Weights	1960	1961	1962	1963	1964	1965	1966	1967	1968	1969	1970	1971	1972	1973	1974	1975
Hours worked per week (million man-hours)																	
Males		765·5	768·5	780·3	785·5	790·5	794·6	799·1	800·0	791·8	792·6	792·8	796·0	801·2	799·8	799·3	798·0
Females (married)																	
Full-time	(80%)	139·8	143·6	148·0	150·9	154·2	159·1	160·8	164·3	167·4	170·3	172·7	175·1	177·4	179·8	181·8	182·7
Part-time	(20%)	18·8	19·3	19·9	20·2	20·7	21·1	21·6	22·0	22·5	22·8	23·2	23·5	23·8	24·1	24·4	24·5
Females (single)																	
Full-time	(95%)	157·8	157·3	159·8	160·9	160·5	160·6	159·6	153·3	144·0	141·6	139·7	138·5	136·1	134·6	134·4	133·7
Part-time	(5%)	4·3	4·2	4·3	4·3	4·3	4·3	4·3	4·1	3·9	3·8	3·8	3·7	3·7	3·6	3·6	3·6
Total hours worked per week		1,086·2	1,092·9	1,112·3	1,121·8	1,130·2	1,137·7	1,145·4	1,143·7	1,129·6	1,131·1	1,132·2	1,136·8	1,142·2	1,141·9	1,143·5	1,142·5
Index of yearly hours worked (unadjusted for holidays; adjusted for male/female mix)		100·0	100·6	102·4	103·3	104·0	104·7	105·5	105·3	104·0	104·1	104·2	104·7	105·2	105·1	105·3	105·2
Index of total labour force (unadjusted for male/female mix)		100·0	100·7	102·5	103·5	104·2	105·0	105·7	105·6	104·3	104·5	104·6	105·0	105·5	105·5	105·7	105·6
Index of yearly hours worked (adjusted for holidays and/or shorter working week, and male/female mix)		100·0	100·4	102·0	102·7	103·2	103·4	103·5	102·8	101·0	100·6	100·1	99·9	99·6	99·4	99·1	98·9

Appendix table 4.1. *National incomes and travel expenditure and receipts, 1954–63 (annual percentage rates of increase at current prices)*

	National incomes (National currencies)	(US dollars)	Travel expenditure (US dollars)	Travel receipts (US dollars)
Austria	8·5	8·5	23·8	20·0
Belgium/Luxembourg	4·7	4·7	17·7	15·9
Denmark	7·5	7·5	12·2	14·4
France	10·4	6·2	19·4	16·5
West Germany	10·1	10·7	26·5	14·1
Italy	9·3	9·3	29·4	22·0
Netherlands	7·8	8·4	17·4	16·3
Norway	6·2	6·2	6·1	11·1
Sweden	6·9	6·9	10·8	12·0
Switzerland	7·3	7·3	7·5	8·2
United Kingdom	**5·9**	**5·9**	**10·3**	**8·6**
Canada	6·8	5·4	4·1	7·0
USA	5·3	5·3	8·9	6·3

Sources: International Monetary Fund, *International Financial Statistics* and Organisation for Economic Co-operation and Development, *Tourism in OECD Member Countries* (annual).

Appendix table 5.1. *Competitive imports and exports by industry* (*national income basis*) (£ *million, 1960 prices*)

	1960 Competitive imports	Exports	1975 Competitive imports	Exports
Agriculture, forestry, fishing	297	66	375	100
Coal mining	1	35	—	75
Mining and quarrying n.e.s.	14	16	20	25
Food processing	419	109	510	100
Drink and tobacco	13	116	20	225
Coke ovens, etc.	—	11	—	10
Mineral oil refining	144	110	330	250
Chemicals n.e.s.	195	334	620	675
Iron and steel (excluding tinplate and tubes)	77	120	135	160
Iron and steel (tinplate and tubes)	4	96	10	125
Non-ferrous metals	72	102	90	175
Engineering and electrical goods	248	879	665	1,730
Shipbuilding and marine engineering	6	62	35	50
Motors and cycles	48	612	135	1,255
Aircraft	60	140	125	260
Railway locomotives and rolling stock	1	16	—	15
Metals goods n.e.s.	54	159	125	240
Textiles	168	368	330	435
Leather, clothing, footwear	59	62	175	135
Building materials	13	28	25	30
Pottery and glass	14	45	30	55
Timber, furniture, etc.	54	10	100	15
Paper, printing, publishing	110	86	205	160
Other manufacturing	47	101	110	130
Construction	—	10	—	10
Gas	—	8	—	10
Electricity	—	6	5	10
Water	—	8	—	10
Transport and communications	21	598	35	675
Distributive trades	—	16	—	25
Services n.e.s.	326	422	515	755
TOTAL	2,465	4,751	4,725	7,925

Appendix table 5.1 shows the debit and credit components of the net export figures given in table 7.2. The figures for merchandise trade in appendix table 5.2 have been adjusted to the basis of the national income accounts (from Central Statistical Office, *National Income and Expenditure, 1961,* in the case of 1960). In particular the adjustments to competitive imports allow for the inclusion of shipping services in the trade account valuation used in appendix table 5.2. Similarly the figures for exports include services (other than expenditure by foreign tourists, etc.) as well as merchandise trade[1]. The projections of services are discussed in chapter 4.

[1]See Cambridge University Department of Applied Economics, *A Programme for Growth, 2: A Social Accounting Matrix for 1960, op. cit.,* pp. 28 and 65.

Appendix table 5.2. *Balance of trade by industry[a] : £ million at 1960 prices*

		1954	1955	1959	1960	1961	1962	1975
1.	Agriculture, forestry and fishing	− 251	− 314	− 272	− 284	− 259	− 254	− 350
2.	Coal mining	+ 34	− 35	+ 12	+ 19	+ 20	+ 18	+ 45
3.	Mining and quarrying	− 12	− 10	+ 1	− 13	− 11	− 11	− 15
4.	Food processing	− 227	− 229	− 285	− 303	− 282	− 301	− 395
5.	Drink and tobacco	+ 52	+ 59	+ 64	+ 66	+ 76	+ 86	+ 135
6.	Coke ovens, etc.	+ 10	+ 10	+ 9	+ 9	+ 9	+ 9	− 10
7.	Mineral oil refining	− 4	− 34	− 52	− 47	− 46	− 56	− 105
8.	Chemicals n.e.s.	+ 73	+ 89	+ 103	+ 111	+ 143	+ 136	+ 25
9/10.	Iron and steel	+ 121	+ 66	+ 164	+ 128	+ 177	+ 157	+ 135
11.	Non-ferrous metals	− 39	− 36	− 73	− 25	− 31	− 48	− 75
12.	Engineering and electrical goods	+ 617	+ 656	+ 584	+ 567	+ 616	+ 624	+ 935
13.	Shipbuilding and marine engineering	+ 64	+ 66	+ 39	+ 45	+ 74	+ 5	—
14.	Motors and cycles	+ 376	+ 413	+ 499	+ 547	+ 509	+ 576	+ 1,090
15.	Aircraft	+ 40	+ 53	+ 117	+ 77	+ 105	+ 72	+ 125
16.	Railway locomotives and rolling stock	+ 53	+ 46	+ 30	+ 16	+ 12	+ 15	+ 15
17.	Metal goods n.e.s.	+ 129	+ 152	+ 125	+ 114	+ 123	+ 125	+ 140
18.	Textiles	+ 311	+ 293	+ 208	+ 182	+ 174	+ 177	− 80
19.	Leather, clothing and footwear	+ 21	+ 21	+ 5	+ 15	+ 38	+ 42	− 85
20.	Building materials	+ 22	+ 24	+ 17	+ 14	+ 10	+ 10	+ 10
21.	Pottery and glass	+ 29	+ 36	+ 29	+ 27	+ 29	+ 29	+ 20
22.	Timber, furniture, etc.	− 39	− 44	− 51	− 63	− 61	− 59	− 120
23.	Paper, printing, publishing	− 5	− 25	− 19	− 28	− 30	− 35	− 55
24.	Other manufacturing	+ 73	+ 78	+ 70	+ 69	+ 66	+ 63	+ 55
25.	Construction	+ 3	+ 3	+ 4	+ 4	+ 4	+ 4	+ 5
26./27.	Gas and electricity	+ 4	+ 9	+ 5	+ 5	+ 5	+ 5	—
30.	Distributive trades	+ 14	+ 25	+ 10	+ 19	+ 2	+ 15	+ 3
31.	Services n.e.s.	+ 4	+ 4	—	+ 2	+ 3	+ 3	+ 3
	All industries	+ 3	+ 9	+ 19	+ 2	+ 10	+ 27	+ 5
	of which: Manufacturing	+ 1,523	+ 1,398	+ 1,489	+ 1,260	+ 1,457	+ 1,419	+ 1,725
	Agriculture, food, drink and tobacco	+ 1,924	+ 1,960	+ 1,993	+ 1,816	+ 1,940	+ 1,907	+ 2,395
	Mining and fuel	− 426	− 484	− 493	− 521	− 465	− 469	− 610
	Miscellaneous	+ 28	+ 69	+ 30	+ 33	+ 28	+ 40	+ 65

Source: NIESR estimates, based mainly on *Annual Statement of the Trade of the United Kingdom* and *Accounts relating to Trade and Navigation of the United Kingdom.*

[a] Exports (f.o.b.) less retained imports (c.i.f.) of competing products at 1960 prices.

Appendix table 5.3. *Competitive trade and gross output by industry: £ million, current prices*

	Value of trade in 1960		Percentage share in gross output[a]					
			Exports			Exports less competing imports		
	Competing imports[b]	Exports	1954	1960	1975	1954	1960	1975
1. Agriculture, forestry and fishing	322	38	1·9	2·4	2·4	−18·2	−18·2	−16·9
2. Coal mining	—	19	8·4	2·3	5·3	6·0	2·3	5·3
3. Mining and quarrying	29	15	9·3	10·0	10·9	−16·0	−9·3	−6·5
4. Food processing	384	80	4·3	3·4	2·4	−11·8	−13·0	−12·7
5. Drink and tobacco	31	97	14·6	13·9	18·6	10·8	9·5	13·6
6. Coke ovens, etc.	1	10	7·3	4·3	3·9	7·0	3·8	3·9
7. Mineral oil refining	144	97	25·9	18·9	19·1	−1·6	−9·0	−8·9
8. Chemicals n.e.s.	211	322	17·3	16·1	11·3	8·2	5·6	0·4
9. Iron and steel (excluding tinplate and tubes)	77	120	7·6	6·8	6·2	5·5	2·4	1·0
10. Iron and steel (tinplate and tubes)	4	89	30·1	27·5	21·5	29·4	26·2	19·7
11. Non-ferrous metals	75	99	10·3	13·7	14·9	6·3	3·5	6·6
12. Engineering and electrical goods	259	826	23·5	22·0	21·4	19·8	14·6	12·3
13. Shipbuilding and marine engineering	14	60	13·8	13·2	7·4	13·3	9·9	—
14. Motors and cycles	46	592	35·5	35·2	33·2	34·5	32·5	29·8
15. Aircraft	59	136	13·0	22·2	23·0	8·1	12·6	11·5
16. Railway locomotives and rolling stock	1	17	22·8	8·4	9·9	21·9	7·9	9·9
17. Metal goods n.e.s.	39	153	13·3	10·8	9·4	12·2	8·0	5·7
18. Textiles	169	351	19·1	16·7	14·1	14·8	8·7	2·8
19. Leather, clothing and footwear	73	57	5·3	5·4	6·2	2·0	1·4	4·2
20. Building materials	12	26	7·6	6·0	5·0	6·4	3·2	1·7
21. Pottery and glass	14	40	21·4	18·1	14·3	17·5	12·2	5·7
22. Timber, furniture, etc.	69	6	0·9	1·1	1·1	−9·1	−11·3	−12·8
23. Paper, printing, publishing	109	81	5·8	5·6	5·0	0·1	1·9	1·8
24. Other manufacturing	28	98	17·6	15·0	8·6	14·9	10·6	3·0
Other	11	10						
Total for above industries	2,170	3,430	13·9	13·3	13·3	7·2	5·7	3·8
of which:								
Manufacturing	1,259	3,075	16·4	15·7	14·7	12·5	9·3	6·5
Agriculture, food, drink and tobacco	737	216	4·8	4·7	5·0	−11·2	−11·3	−9·9
Mining and fuel	173	141	12·5	8·3	11·9	2·8	1·9	−2·5

Source: NIESR estimates.

[a] A minus sign denotes net imports as a percentage of output. The estimates of output from which the percentages have been calculated contain a margin of error. For 1975 both trade and output are valued at 1960 prices.

[b] Retained imports (c.i.f.).

THE PROJECTION OF PERSONAL EXPENDITURE

For convenience of reference a brief mathematical statement of the linear expenditure system and some of its properties is given here. Fuller details will be found in the original article by Stone and the other sources quoted in chapter 6. The special method adopted for dealing with the subgroups of food, clothing, and drink and tobacco, is treated in the second section. Finally, some results obtained under alternative price assumptions are given.

The linear expenditure system

The basic form of the demand equations in the linear expenditure system may be written

$$q_i = \left\{ b_i m + \sum_j (\delta_{ij} - b_i)c_j p_j \right\} / p_i, \tag{1}$$

where, $i, j = 1, \ldots, n$, refer to the n commodities. The q's and p's are quantities and prices; m is total expenditure. The b's and c's are the parameters of the system and $\delta_{ij} = 1$ if $i = j$, otherwise zero.

Alternatively, the equations may be written in the form

$$p_i q_i = c_i p_i + b_i (m - \Sigma c_j p_j), \tag{2}$$

which lends itself to the interpretation of c_i as committed consumption, the term in brackets representing supernumerary expenditure.

With the restriction that $\Sigma b_i = 1$, the equality $\Sigma p_i q_i = m$ is always maintained, whatever the level of total expenditure or prices. The equations (1) are also homogeneous of zero degree. Furthermore, it is evident that

$$\partial q_i / \partial m = b_i / p_i \tag{3}$$

and

$$\partial q_i / \partial p_j = -\{b_i c_j + \delta_{ij}(q_j - c_j)\} / p_i. \tag{4}$$

The substitution terms are, therefore,

$$s_{ij} = q_j(\partial q_i / \partial m) + (\partial q_i / \partial p_j)$$
$$= (b_i - \delta_{ij})(q_j - c_j)/p_i \tag{5}$$

or, by using (2),

$$s_{ij} = (b_i - \delta_{ij})b_j(m - \Sigma cp)/p_i p_j, \tag{6}$$

which is clearly unaffected by an interchange of i and j.

Expressions for the elasticities are readily obtained from equations (3) and (4). Thus the expenditure elasticity is

$$e_i = \frac{m}{q_i} \cdot \frac{\partial q_i}{\partial m}$$
$$= b_i m / p_i q_i, \tag{7}$$

and the price elasticity is

$$E_{ij} = \frac{p_j}{q_i} \cdot \frac{\partial q_i}{\partial p_j}$$
$$= (\delta_{ij} - b_i)c_j p_j / p_i q_i - \delta_{ij}. \tag{8}$$

The estimated elasticities shown in table 6.4 (p. 187) were obtained by applying these formulae, using the calculated not the actual expenditures on each commodity group.

In the version of the system adopted for the applications reported in chapter 6 the parameters were regarded as subject to regular displacements through time. That is, they were assumed to take the form

$$b_i = b_i^* + b_i^{**}t \text{ and } c_i = c_i^* + c_i^{**}t \tag{9}$$

where t is a simple trend variable.

There are many other extensions to which the basic system is open, but they need not be pursued here. Likewise the computing procedures are best left for the interested enquirer to get from the primary sources.

A method for subgroups

It may be shown without much difficulty, though it is not attempted here, that the equations of the linear expenditure system for any subset of commodities may be rewritten in a form where expenditure on each commodity is dependent only on the expenditure and prices of the group. Expenditure on the group is, of course, determined in its turn by total expenditure and all prices, so that no contradiction is involved. Thus, for item i of group k we may write

$$p_{ik}q_{ik} = c_{ik}p_{ik} + a_{ik}(m_k - \sum_j c_{jk}p_{jk}), \tag{10}$$

where m_k is expenditure on the group, and

$$a_{ik} = b_{ik} / \sum_j b_{jk} \tag{11}$$
$$= e_{ik} \cdot p_{ik}q_{ik}/e_k \cdot m_k,$$

the last expression being obtained by using (7). Similarly, for the projected expenditures

$$\hat{p}_{ik}\hat{q}_{ik} = \hat{c}_{ik}\hat{p}_{ik} + \hat{a}_{ik}(\hat{m}_k - \sum_j \hat{c}_{jk}\hat{p}_{jk}), \tag{12}$$

where the circumflex accents are added to indicate that the values relate to the date of the projection.

The extra assumptions we shall make are simply that

$$a_{ik} = \hat{a}_{ik} \tag{13}$$

and

$$c_{ik}p_{ik} / \sum_j c_{jk}p_{jk} = \hat{c}_{ik}\hat{p}_{ik} / \sum_j \hat{c}_{jk}\hat{p}_{jk}. \tag{14}$$

Then from (10) and (12), making use of (13) and (14),

$$\hat{p}_{ik}\hat{q}_{ik} = a_{ik}\hat{m}_k + (p_{ik}q_{ik} - a_{ik}m_k)\underset{j}{\Sigma}\hat{c}_{jk}\hat{p}_{jk}\Big/\underset{j}{\Sigma}c_{jk}p_{jk} \qquad (15)$$

or, substituting for a_{ik} from (11),

$$\frac{\hat{p}_{ik}\hat{q}_{ik}}{p_{ik}q_{ik}} = \frac{e_{ik}}{e_k}\cdot\frac{\hat{m}_k}{m_k} + \left(1 - \frac{e_{ik}}{e_k}\right)\frac{\underset{j}{\Sigma}\hat{c}_{jk}\hat{p}_{jk}}{\underset{j}{\Sigma}c_{jk}p_{jk}}\cdot \qquad (16)$$

This last equation provides us with a feasible method of making projections for subgroups. Estimates of total expenditure and total committed expenditure for the group are available from the first stage of the projection. The elasticities can be obtained from cross-section data.

Alternative price assumptions

In making the projections for the eight main expenditure groups in section 3 of chapter 6 it was assumed that the average prices for the groups were the same in 1975 as in 1960. It is known, of course, that prices do not remain constant, but in the absence of an explicit model of price determination it seemed the most expedient assumption to make.

An indication of the degree of variation in the prices of the main expenditure groups in the past is given in appendix table 6.1. In this table the prices are shown as index numbers with $1938 = 1\cdot000$; they were obtained simply as the ratios of the expenditures at current and constant prices in tables 6.1 and 6.2. The very large movements in absolute prices reflect the changes in the value of money over this period, particularly the inflationary effects of war conditions. In the determination of the pattern of consumption the significant movements are the changes in relative prices shown in the lower half of the table. Here the variations are very much more moderate and the direction of the movement is more often reversed in the course of time. Indeed, very little regularity is apparent in these figures. This suggests that, at least, no very obvious bias in the projections is likely to be incurred by the assumption of fixed relative prices. It also implies that an extrapolation of recent price movements would not necessarily prove any more realistic.

Without a completely articulated model, taking account of the interaction of supply and demand, the problem of price projection is likely to remain intractable. Nevertheless certain implications regarding relative shifts in the prices of industrial outputs do emerge from the present study (see chapter 9), and it is of interest to convert these figures to consumer prices and examine their effect on the demand projections. In a complete model this would not be the end of the story. The revised demand figures would imply different industrial outputs and probably lead to new estimates of prices. Several rounds might be needed to reach an equilibrium position. In the present context, however, we are

Appendix table 6.1. *Consumer prices, 1900–60*

Index numbers, 1938 = 1·000

	1900	1910	1920	1930	1938	1950	1960
Absolute prices							
Food	0·604	0·660	1·857	1·076	1·000	1·801	2·760
Clothing	0·447	0·504	2·076	1·042	1·000	2·219	2·702
Household expenses	0·516	0·541	1·215	0·969	1·000	1·589	2·353
Communications	0·500	0·615	1·214	1·048	1·000	1·378	2·262
Transport	0·872	0·910	1·467	1·127	1·000	1·543	2·256
Drink and tobacco	0·311	0·355	1·061	1·011	1·000	3·211	3·562
Entertainment	0·788	0·735	1·195	1·007	1·000	1·596	2·300
Other	0·516	0·585	1·414	0·998	1·000	1·917	2·520
Total	0·504	0·562	1·498	1·028	1·000	1·911	2·625
Relative prices							
Food	1·198	1·174	1·240	1·047	1·000	0·942	1·051
Clothing	0·887	0·897	1·386	1·014	1·000	1·161	1·029
Household expenses	1·024	0·963	0·811	0·943	1·000	0·832	0·896
Communications	0·992	1·094	0·810	1·019	1·000	0·721	0·862
Transport	1·730	1·619	0·979	1·096	1·000	0·807	0·859
Drink and tobacco	0·617	0·632	0·708	0·983	1·000	1·680	1·357
Entertainment	1·563	1·308	0·798	0·980	1·000	0·835	0·876
Other	1·024	1·041	0·944	0·971	1·000	1·003	0·960
Total	1·000	1·000	1·000	1·000	1·000	1·000	1·000

concerned with a more loosely interrelated system and a completely rigorous treatment is not required.

The breakdown of consumers' expenditures by industrial origin in 1960 has been used to derive the implied consumer prices[1]. Relative price increases in the food, drink and tobacco, and distribution industries are balanced by falls for most manufacturing sectors and the same divergence is apparent in the pattern of consumer prices. In the case of the household expenses group, however, lower prices for fuel and equipment are more than offset by the relative increase in rent.

The two sets of prices and the resulting estimates of consumption are shown in appendix table 6.2. The figures used in chapter 6 (A) are compared with the alternative estimates derived from using the assumptions regarding output prices (B). It can be seen that none of the implied price changes is large; the proportionate changes all fall within a range of 10 per cent. The estimates of consumption, as a result of the generally low values of the price elasticities, show an even smaller dispersion. That the price and quantity changes do not offset each other in the case of communications and entertainment is a consequence of the negative marginal propensities obtained for these two groups. The changes are all small, however, and must be well within the margins of error attaching to the estimates.

[1] That is, using $T^{1.8}$, $T^{1.10}$ and $T^{1.11}$ of SAM.

Appendix table 6.2. *Alternative projections of consumption for 1975*

	Price: 1938 = 1·000			Expenditure at 1960 prices: £ per head		
	A	B	Ratio B/A	A	B	Ratio B/A
Food	2·760	2·904	1·052	110·0	109·8	0·998
Clothing	2·702	2·677	0·991	53·8	53·9	1·002
Houshold expenses	2·353	2·420	1·029	100·3	99·0	0·988
Communications	2·262	2·164	0·956	2·9	2·9	0·993
Transport	2·256	2·171	0·962	62·8	64·1	1·020
Drink and tobacco	3·562	3·664	1·028	49·1	48·7	0·994
Entertainment	2·300	2·212	0·962	10·4	10·3	0·988
Other	2·520	2·466	0·979	61·5	62·1	1·009

MM

NOTE ON RELATIONSHIPS BETWEEN OUTPUT PER MAN, OUTPUT
AND EMPLOYMENT

It has been shown in chapter 1 that, as among the different countries covered, there is no correlation between rates of growth of productivity on the one hand and rates of growth of employment on the other[1]. At the same time we have, for purposes of projecting employment, made extensive use of our results (in chapter 7) concerning the strong correlation, within any country, between rates of change in productivity and total output in different industries. It might appear that these two results are inconsistent, for the following reasons:

Let P = productivity (output per man)
Y = output
L = employed labour force
(with all variables defined as rates of change per unit of time)

then from our equations (for which there are high correlation coefficients) of the form

$$P = a + bY \tag{1}$$

and given that

$$Y = P + L \tag{2}$$

we can derive the equation

$$P = \left(\frac{b}{1-b}\right)E + \frac{a}{1-b} \tag{3}$$

which suggests that the rate of change of productivity is a function of the rate of change of employment, so that it is inconsistent to maintain that the contrary holds good as between countries, or even for one country. There are two reasons why there is no such inconsistency.

First, the existence of a strong correlation for the equation type (1) above, implies nothing at all about the strength of the correlation that would be obtained from applying equation (3). Given the three variables, P, Y, and L, three sets of correlation coefficients have been obtained (see table on page 531).

Secondly, even had the correlations for the equations of type (3) been good, it would still not follow that there would be any inter-country correlation of productivity on employment. For each country would have different parameters in its type (3) equation, and the cross-country comparison would be between points, one for each country, lying on different lines of the type shown in equation (3) above. Such a collection of points does not necessarily provide any correlation.

[1] Page 22.

MM2

Correlation coefficients of output, productivity and employment

Data	No. of observations	r_{12}^2	r_{13}^2	r_{23}^2
United Kingdom				
1952–5 ⎫ Fast growth periods	29	0·704	—	0·265
1958–60 ⎭	29	0·736	0·021	0·609
1950–2 ⎫ Slow growth periods	28	0·968	0·018	0·693
1955–8 ⎭	29	0·489	—	0·508
1955–60 Peak to peak	29	0·699	0·016	0·586
1952–8 Trough to trough	29	0·673	0·002	0·420
1950–60 (trend values of variables)	20	0·836	0·267	0·671
Germany				
1950–5 ⎫ Fast growth periods	24	0·710	0·138	0·913
1958–60 ⎭	24	0·440	0·004	0·662
1955–8 Slow growth period	24	0·293	0·096	0·335

Note: The variables used in the correlations, and indicated in the subscripts of the r^2s are as follows:

1 = productivity; 2 = output; 3 = employment.

The observations used for the correlation were, as indicated in section 2 of chapter 2, the rates of change in the variables indicated in various industries (the number of industries is shown in the above table) during the periods indicated.

Appendix table 7.1. *Gross output, final and intermediate sales*

SAM industry group	Total gross output 1960	Total gross output 1975	£ million (1960 prices) Total final sales 1960	Total final sales 1975	Total intermediate sales 1960	Total intermediate sales 1975	Index 1975 (1960 = 100) Total output	Final sales	Intermediate sales
1 Agriculture, forestry and fishing	1,562	2,071	1,339	1,897	223	174	133	142	78
2 Coal mining	808	845	259	439	549	406	105	169	74
3 Mining and quarrying (excluding coal)	150	230	19	34	131	196	153	179	150
4 Food processing	2,338	3,100	1,705	2,157	633	943	133	127	149
5 Drink and tobacco	697	995	683	990	14	5	143	145	36
6 Coke ovens	234	256	59	87	175	169	109	147	97
7 Mineral oil refining	513	1,178	176	357	337	821	230	203	244
8 Chemicals n.e.s.	1,993	5,734	548	687	1,445	5,047	288	125	349
9 Iron and steel (excluding tin plate and tubes)	1,757	2,583	83	35	1,674	2,548	147	42	152
10 Iron and steel (tinplate and tubes)	324	559	100	122	224	437	173	122	195
11 Non-ferrous metals	723	1,143	25	43	698	1,100	158	172	158
12 Engineering and electrical goods	3,887	7,630	2,464	4,974	1,423	2,656	196	202	187
13 Shipbuilding and marine engineering	453	675	326	547	127	128	149	168	101
14 Motors and cycles	1,682	3,655	1,301	2,922	381	733	217	225	192
15 Aircraft	612	1,086	337	666	275	420	177	198	153
16 Railway rolling stock	203	152	106	81	97	71	75	76	73
17 Metal goods n.e.s.	1,419	2,448	301	508	1,118	1,940	173	169	174
18 Textiles	2,098	2,908	442	623	1,656	2,285	139	141	138
19 Leather, clothing and footwear	1,051	2,007	967	1,845	84	162	191	191	193
20 Building materials	436	604	40	45	396	559	139	113	141
21 Pottery and glass	221	349	95	168	126	181	158	177	144
22 Timber, furniture, etc.	560	938	148	328	412	610	168	222	148
23 Paper, printing and publishing	1,454	3,023	259	338	1,195	2,685	208	131	225
24 Other manufacturing	653	1,457	236	377	417	1,080	223	160	259
25 Construction	3,043	4,671	2,307	3,716	736	955	153	161	130
26 Gas	373	466	170	237	203	229	125	139	113
27 Electricity	776	2,394	347	551	429	1,843	309	159	430
28 Water	98	130	86	114	12	16	133	133	133
29 Transport and communications	3,032	4,654	1,645	2,598	1,387	2,056	153	158	148
30 Distributive trades	3,589	6,353	3,015	5,340	574	1,013	177	177	176
31 Services n.e.s.	4,048	6,493	1,870	3,436	2,178	3,057	160	184	140
1–31 TOTAL	40,787	70,787	21,458	36,262	19,329	34,525	174	169	179

Note: For reconciliation with total GNP see table 7.2, page 207.

PROJECTION OF SELECTED COMPONENTS OF CAPITAL FORMATION

Distribution and other services

This has been divided into the following four components:

	Gross capital formation in 1960 (£ million)
Wholesale trade	94
Retail trade	172
Insurance, banking and finance	89
Other transport and services	245
	600

Source: National Income and Expenditure, 1963, table 58. It should be noted that the total of £600 million shown here is less than that shown in table 8.13 by £15 million. This is because the table 8.13 figure is from *National Income and Expenditure, 1961*.

As it is the retail trade component of the above which seems to be rising most rapidly special attention has been paid to this item and the other three items have been projected in line with fairly simple indicators. Wholesale trade proper has been assumed to rise more or less in line with gross national product in future, and the remaining two small components of total wholesale trade, namely dealing in coal, building materials, and agricultural supplies, and dealing in industrial materials and manufactures, have been assumed to rise respectively slightly faster and slightly slower than gross national product. Investment in *insurance, banking and finance* has risen very rapidly in the last few years, but it is not thought that this is likely to continue and it has been rather arbitrarily assumed to rise by not much more than another 100 per cent between 1960 and 1975. Capital formation in *other transport and services* is not expected to rise rapidly since the fast-rising components (such as catering, sport and betting, and motor repairs) seem to be more or less offset by slow-rising, or falling, components (such as cinemas, dry-cleaning and professional services).

The rise in *retail distribution* has been not only very rapid but, given the enormous scope clearly still left for changes in the organization of retail distribution, could probably continue to rise for some time to come. It seemed desirable to split the amount of capital formation in retail distribution into (i) that part resulting simply from the rise in total consumers' purchases of distributed goods and (ii) that part resulting from the change in the organization of retail trade. In principle it would have been desirable also to estimate separately that part of distribution capital formation that resulted from urban renewal and shifts in the geographical pattern of population. On account of lack of time, however, it has been assumed that this would be caught up to some extent in item (ii) above.

The rise in total consumers' purchases of distributed goods has been calculated from the *National Income and Expenditure* series of consumers' expenditure at constant prices on food, alcoholic beverages, tobacco, clothing, household durables and other household hardware, books, etc., chemists' products. These show that from 1952 to 1957, when the sharp upsurge in distribution began (presumably indicating the beginning of capital formation of type (ii)), there was about £0·28 of capital formation in retail distribution for every £1 extra retail sale.   Between 1974 and 1975 the projectures of private consumption imply an increase of £431 million in retail sales.   This figure, therefore, implies about £121 million of capital formation in retailing to cope with the normal expansion of retail sales.

As for type (ii), namely that resulting from the change in the structure of retail distribution, the method has been to estimate the rate at which supermarkets (and similar stores) will increase their share in total retail trade and the average cost, per unit turnover, of supermarkets.   The latter has been estimated from (a) the difference between capital formation in distribution after 1957 and that which would have resulted had the previous trend persisted (about £118 million) and (b) the number of supermarkets built during this period (about 1,000 according to W. G. McClelland[1] and Board of Trade data).   This gives an average cost of a supermarket as about £120,000 which is apparently reasonable according to informed opinion, though the degree of variation is stated to be very large indeed.

Assuming that the transformation of distribution does not apply to clothing, books and household durables among the above list of items, and adopting McClelland's very tentative estimate that the percentage of turnover would be rising by about 3 per cent per annum in 1975, we obtain the amount of turnover absorbed by new supermarkets in 1975 at about £290 million.

As their average turnover appears to be about £120,000 per annum[2], this gives the number of such outlets to be built (about 2,420), and given their average price as calculated above, gives a total investment of this type of about £290 million.

Thus total capital formation in retail distribution in 1975 would be about £(121 + 290) million (i.e. about £411 million).   Various modifications to this figure were, however, made in the final stages of the projection in the light of other considerations.

The total projection of distribution capital formation, before these final adjustments, is as follows:

GCF in distribution (£ million at 1960 prices)

	1960	1975
Wholesale trade	94	154
Retail trade	172	411
Insurance and banking	89	200
Other transport and services	245	365
Total	600	1,130

[1] W. G. McClelland, *Studies in Retailing* (Oxford, 1963) and unpublished estimates.
[2] Based on turnover for different size of establishments as given in *Board of Trade Journal*, 20 December 1963.

Agriculture and construction. These two components of total gross capital formation are important, but no satisfactory method has been found for projecting them, and given the nature of the processes involved this is hardly surprising. In particular, much of the capital equipment used in the construction industry appears to have a relatively short life, so that no check on apparently very erratic ICORs can be made by constructing a reasonably reliable capital stock series[1]. In the event, therefore, very rough extrapolations have been adopted on the basis mainly of *pro rata* adjustments to the growth of capital formation in these sectors projected by the National Economic Development Council for the 5-year period 1961–6, with some rounding off and adjustment for differences in the projected growth rates of output[2].

Appendix table 8.1. *Gross capital stock, end-1955 (£ million at 1960 prices)*

SAM industry group		Plant machinery	Industrial buildings	Vehicles	Total
4	Food processing	611·7	510·8	63·8	1,186·3
5	Drink and tobacco	252·4	356·8	24·9	634·1
6	Coke ovens	145·6	20·9	—	166·5
7	Mineral oil refining	101·5	72·0	—	173·5
8	Chemicals n.e.s.	983·6	395·8	33·9	1,413·3
9	Iron and steel (excluding tinplate and tubes)	} 1,005·7	351·5	14·0	1,371·2
10	Iron and steel (tinplate and tubes)				
11	Non-ferrous metals	190·0	156·3	6·6	352·9
12	Engineering and electrical goods	1,562·5	953·9	66·9	2,583·3
13	Shipbuilding and marine engineering	157·5	141·7	—	299·2
14	Motors and cycles	413·7	234·4	8·9	657·0
15	Aircraft	282·7	160·2	8·9	451·8
16	Railway rolling stock	48·4	54·8	—	103·2
17	Metal goods n.e.s.	325·5	226·8	26·5	578·8
18	Textiles	1,487·7	1,347·3	26·8	2,861·8
19	Leather, clothing and footwear	178·8	271·3	21·8	471·9
20	Building materials	189·4	182·3	21·4	393·1
21	Pottery and glass	72·9	74·4	7·4	154·7
22	Timber, furniture, etc.	99·8	154·5	25·3	279·6
23	Paper, printing and publishing	704·3	461·2	20·6	1,186·1
24	Other manufacturing	235·2	154·4	11·3	400·9
4—24	TOTAL	9,048·9	6,281·3	389·0	15,719·2

Based on (a) Feinstein total manufacturing and distribution in 1955—for total plant and machinery, and total industrial building separately; (b) estimated split between manufacturing and distribution; (c) Barna's breakdown on manufacturing by individual industry—adjusted to fit SAM.

[1] According to *The Builder*, big contractors very often 'write off' plant and equipment after the end of the first contract for which they have been purchased; and much of such investment is counted as work in progress in their accounts. This is no doubt one of the reasons why the margin of error in the estimates of capital formation is indicated, by the Central Statistical Office (in *National Income Statistics: Sources and Methods*, op. cit.) as being greater than ±10 per cent.

[2] The NEDC projections of agricultural capital formation also assume that agricultural investment in buildings has been abnormally high during the past few years and must fall back to more normal rates (*Growth of the United Kingdom Economy, 1961–1966*, London, 1963).

Appendix table 8.2.　Gross capital formation by SAM industry, 1950–60 (£ million at 1960 prices)

SAM industry group	1950	1951	1952	1953	1954	1955	1956	1957	1958	1959	1960a
4 Food processing	58·1	57·8	51·5	49·3	53·3	61·9	67·5	70·4	71·0	68·1	82
5 Drink and tobacco	19·7	19·5	17·3	16·7	17·9	20·8	22·8	23·7	24·0	23·0	28
6 Coke ovens	47·8	47·3	50·0	40·2	19·5	15·1	24·2	44·2	40·7	23·4	15
7 Mineral oil refining	8·9	10·7	10·3	11·4	12·2	12·4	16·1	17·1	17·7	17·2	15
8 Chemicals n.e.s.	76·4	91·7	89·8	99·5	104·0	106·2	136·6	143·1	149·6	144·4	133
9 Iron and steel (excluding tinplate and tubes) } 10 Iron and steel (tinplate and tubes)	73·3	74·4	68·6	63·3	83·9	80·1	90·8	112·5	128·3	111·9	163
11 Non-ferrous metals	13·5	12·5	12·3	12·0	13·2	16·0	20·8	22·9	14·1	17·2	21
12 Engineering and electrical goods	83·9	96·0	107·9	105·7	116·5	138·4	152·9	148·8	142·2	133·9	159
13 Shipbuilding and marine engineering	7·8	8·2	8·8	9·6	10·9	10·3	10·9	16·7	18·1	18·3	13
14 Motors and cycles	29·4	35·9	37·3	31·8	31·5	54·0	62·1	59·6	49·5	43·7	62
15 Aircraft	17·1	34·6	46·5	46·1	26·6	20·6	25·1	22·8	19·2	23·3	19
16 Railway rolling stock	2·3	4·1	3·8	3·7	3·7	3·5	3·3	4·2	4·1	5·1	3
17 Metal goods n.e.s.	26·5	22·9	22·9	23·6	26·4	33·1	37·9	34·4	31·2	36·5	42
18 Textiles	79·1	73·9	56·9	52·0	66·6	73·7	63·2	65·0	50·6	52·8	63
19 Leather, clothing and footwear	16·0	11·7	9·5	11·8	11·7	12·4	12·8	11·4	9·9	11·1	14
20 Building materials	20·9	17·9	15·3	18·8	20·3	20·2	23·0	22·9	21·4	20·4	29
21 Pottery and glass	8·3	7·6	6·2	7·6	8·3	8·2	9·4	9·3	8·8	8·1	12
22 Timber, furniture, etc.	15·8	13·0	9·4	9·3	11·7	13·3	10·6	10·2	10·9	15·1	19
23 Paper, printing and publishing	36·0	41·0	35·8	32·4	43·4	53·9	69·5	76·2	62·6	57·9	65
24 Other manufacturing	17·8	17·7	161	13·3	18·0	24·1	27·3	27·2	28·2	30·4	38
4–24 TOTAL	658·6	698·4	676·2	658·1	699·6	778·2	886·8	942·6	902·1	861·8	995

aThe 1960 estimates here do not correspond to those shown in chapter 8 where revisions have been made to maintain consistency with the 1961 *National Income and Expenditure* Blue book. As the above figures have been used to obtain the capital stock series, however, they have been retained here in the interests of consistency.

Appendix table 8.3. *Capital formation (net of retirements) (£ million at 1960 prices)*

SAM industry group	1950	1951	1952	1953	1954	1955	1956	1957	1958	1959	1960
4 Food processing	50·7	52·2	40·6	33·2	46·8	54·0	51·7	50·5	50·9	50·7	65·0
5 Drink and tobacco	16·5	17·0	12·8	9·0	15·1	18·0	17·8	15·2	14·6	14·6	17·5
6 Coke ovens	8·6	10·5	9·9	10·6	12·0	12·1	15·6	16·6	17·3	16·3	14·2
7 Mineral oil refining	47·7	47·2	49·9	39·9	19·4	14·9	24·2	44·2	40·4	23·0	14·7
8 Chemicals n.e.s.	70·7	87·5	81·8	85·3	99·8	99·6	128·3	131·6	134·7	121·8	113·1
9 Iron and steel (excluding tinplate and tubes) } 10 Iron and steel (tinplate and tubes)	65·0	68·4	57·3	48·4	77·7	68·2	68·1	94·1	111·0	91·3	144·0
11 Non-ferrous metals	12·8	12·0	11·4	10·7	12·8	15·0	19·0	19·8	12·3	13·7	18·8
12 Engineering and electrical goods	75·4	89·6	95·5	92·7	109·3	126·3	124·3	122·5	118·3	106·3	135·4
13 Shipbuilding and marine engineering	7·1	7·7	7·9	8·0	10·4	9·4	9·2	14·5	16·2	16·2	11·1
14 Motors and cycles	26·9	34·2	33·7	26·4	29·2	51·9	59·7	54·2	45·1	38·3	59·1
15 Aircraft	16·7	34·3	45·8	45·3	26·3	20·3	24·4	21·5	18·1	21·9	18·0
16 Railway rolling stock	1·6	3·6	2·9	2·1	3·2	2·6	1·6	2·0	2·2	3·0	1·1
17 Metal goods n.e.s.	24·5	21·3	19·9	19·7	24·8	30·4	30·8	25·8	23·8	27·9	34·0
18 Textiles	66·9	64·9	40·1	20·9	57·8	59·4	34·7	27·7	2·2	9·2	20·7
19 Leather, clothing and footwear	11·2	8·1	2·8	3·4	7·8	6·0	1·1	0·4	0·4	−1·0	−0·1
20 Building materials	18·8	16·6	12·3	13·8	18·5	18·3	17·3	19·2	15·6	15·5	20·4
21 Pottery and glass	7·1	6·5	4·7	4·7	7·4	7·2	7·0	7·7	3·7	4·2	5·1
22 Timber, furniture, etc.	14·8	12·1	7·9	7·9	10·7	12·0	7·5	6·1	6·7	10·9	15·2
23 Paper, printing and publishing	29·0	36·1	25·8	20·4	36·4	46·9	49·2	59·6	39·2	36·0	50·6
24 Other manufacturing	16·6	16·8	14·3	11·5	16·4	23·4	23·9	23·7	22·4	22·8	28·5
4–24 TOTAL	588·6	646·6	577·3	513·9	641·8	695·9	715·4	756·9	695·1	642·6	786·4

Appendix table 8.4. *Gross capital stock—all assets (£ million at 1960 prices)*

SAM industry group	1950	1951	1952	1953	1954	1955	1956	1957	1958	1959	1960
4 Food processing	959·5	1,011·7	1,052·3	1,085·5	1,132·3	1,186·3	1,238·0	1,288·5	1,339·4	1,390·1	1,455·1
5 Drink and tobacco	562·2	579·2	592·0	601·0	616·1	634·1	651·9	667·1	681·7	696·3	713·8
6 Coke ovens	111·4	121·9	131·8	142·4	154·4	166·5	182·1	198·7	216·0	232·3	246·5
7 Mineral oil refining	61·0	108·2	158·1	198·0	217·4	232·3	256·5	300·7	341·1	364·1	378·8
8 Chemicals n.e.s.	959·3	1,046·8	1,128·6	1,213·9	1,313·7	1,413·3	1,541·6	1,673·2	1,807·9	1,929·7	2,042·8
9 Iron and steel (excluding tinplate and tubes) } 10 Iron and steel (tin plate and tubes)	1,051·2	1,119·6	1,176·9	1,225·3	1,303·0	1,371·2	1,439·3	1,533·4	1,644·4	1,735·7	1,879·7
11 Non-ferrous metals	291·0	303·0	314·4	325·1	337·9	352·9	371·9	391·7	404·0	417·7	436·5
12 Engineering and electrical goods	2,069·9	2,159·5	2,255·0	2,347·7	2,457·0	2,583·3	2,707·6	2,830·1	2,948·4	3,055·0	3,190·4
13 Shipbuilding and marine engineering	255·8	263·5	271·4	279·4	289·8	299·2	308·4	322·9	339·1	355·3	365·4
14] Motors and cycles	481·6	515·8	549·5	575·9	605·1	657·0	716·7	770·9	816·0	854·3	913·4
15 Aircraft	279·8	314·1	359·9	405·2	431·5	451·8	476·2	497·7	515·8	537·7	555·7
16] Railway rolling stock	88·8	92·4	95·3	97·4	100·6	103·2	104·8	106·9	109·0	111·0	112·1
17 Metal goods n.e.s.	462·7	484·0	503·9	523·6	548·4	578·8	609·6	635·4	659·2	687·1	721·1
18 Textiles	2,618·7	2,683·6	2,723·7	2,744·6	2,802·4	2,861·8	2,896·5	2,924·2	2,926·4	2,935·6	2,956·3
19 Leather, clothing and footwear	443·8	451·9	454·7	458·1	465·9	471·9	473·0	473·4	473·8	472·8	472·7
20 Building materials	313·6	330·2	342·5	356·3	374·8	393·1	410·4	429·6	445·2	460·7	481·1
21 Pottery and glass	124·2	130·7	135·4	140·1	147·5	154·7	161·7	169·4	173·1	177·3	182·4
22 Timber, furniture, etc.	229·0	241·1	249·0	256·9	267·6	279·6	287·1	293·2	299·9	310·8	326·0
23 Paper, printing and publishing	1,020·5	1,056·6	1,082·4	1,102·8	1,139·2	1,186·1	1,235·3	1,294·9	1,334·1	1,370·1	1,420·7
24 Other manufacturing	318·5	335·3	349·6	361·1	377·5	400·9	424·8	448·5	470·9	493·7	522·2
4–24 TOTAL	12,702·5	13,349·1	13,926·4	14,440·3	15,082·1	15,778·0	16,493·4	17,250·3	17,945·4	18,587·3	19,372·7

Appendix table 8.5. Indices of capital stock (at constant prices)

SAM industry group	1950	1951	1952	1953	1954	1955	1956	1957	1958	1959	1960
4 Food processing	100·0	105·4	109·7	113·1	118·0	123·6	129·0	134·3	139·6	144·9	151·7
5 Drink and tobacco	100·0	103·0	105·3	106·9	109·6	112·8	116·0	118·7	121·3	123·9	127·0
6 Coke ovens	100·0	109·4	118·3	127·8	138·6	149·5	163·5	178·4	193·9	208·5	221·3
7 Mineral oil refining	100·0	177·4	259·2	324·6	356·4	380·8	420·5	493·0	559·2	596·9	621·0
8 Chemicals n.e.s.	100·0	109·1	117·6	126·5	136·9	147·3	160·7	174·4	188·5	201·2	212·9
9 Iron and steel (excluding tinplate and tubes) ⎫											
10 Iron and steel (tinplate and tubes) ⎬	100·0	106·5	112·0	116·6	124·0	130·4	136·9	145·9	156·4	165·1	178·8
11 Non-ferrous metals	100·0	104·1	108·0	111·7	116·1	121·3	127·8	134·6	138·8	143·5	150·0
12 Engineering and electrical goods	100·0	104·3	108·9	113·4	118·7	124·8	130·8	136·7	142·4	147·6	154·1
13 Shipbuilding and marine engineering	100·0	103·0	106·1	109·2	113·3	117·0	120·6	126·2	132·6	138·9	142·8
14 Motors and cycles	100·0	107·1	114·1	119·6	125·6	136·4	148·8	160·1	169·4	177·4	189·7
15 Aircraft ⎫											
16 Railway rolling stock ⎬	100·0	110·3	123·5	136·4	144·4	150·6	157·6	164·0	169·5	176·0	181·2
17 Metal goods n.e.s	100·0	104·6	108·9	113·2	118·5	125·1	131·7	137·3	142·5	148·5	155·8
18 Textiles	100·0	102·5	104·0	104·8	107·0	109·3	110·6	111·7	111·8	112·1	112·9
19 Leather, clothing and footwear	100·0	101·8	102·5	103·2	105·0	106·3	106·6	106·7	106·8	106·5	106·5
20 Building materials	100·0	105·3	109·2	113·6	119·5	125·4	130·9	137·0	142·0	146·9	153·4
21 Pottery and glass	100·0	105·2	109·0	112·8	118·8	124·6	130·2	136·4	139·4	142·8	146·9
22 Timber, furniture, etc.	100·0	105·3	108·7	112·2	116·9	122·1	125·4	128·0	131·0	135·7	142·4
23 Paper, printing and publishing	100·0	103·5	106·1	108·1	111·6	116·2	121·0	126·9	130·7	134·3	139·2
24 Other manufacturing	100·0	105·3	109·8	113·4	118·5	125·9	133·4	140·8	147·8	155·0	164·0
4–24 TOTAL	100·0	105·1	109·6	113·7	118·7	124·2	129·8	135·8	141·3	146·3	152·5

Appendix table 8.6. *Indices of employment*

SAM industry group	1950	1951	1952	1953	1954	1955	1956	1957	1958	1959	1960
4 Food processing	100·0	104·4	105·6	108·7	113·1	117·4	117·8	116·8	118·1	118·5	119·9
5 Drink and tobacco	100·0	99·5	100·0	98·5	98·0	95·5	97·5	101·0	101·5	102·5	104·0
6 Coke ovens	100·0	100·0	100·0	113·3	106·7	126·7	120·0	126·7	126·7	126·7	126·7
7 Mineral oil refining	100·0	100·0	113·3	113·3	116·7	113·3	123·3	123·3	130·0	136·7	133·3
8 Chemicals n.e.s.	100·0	103·0	102·7	102·7	105·4	109·1	110·6	111·6	111·8	113·1	116·0
9 Iron and steel (excluding tinplate and tubes) } 10 Iron and steel (tinplate and tubes)	100·0	100·0	100·4	99·3	98·9	101·5	103·3	104·0	99·3	96·0	104·9
11 Non-ferrous metals	100·0	104·4	109·7	101·8	109·7	115·9	119·5	116·8	114·2	115·0	125·7
12 Engineering and electrical goods	100·0	103·8	107·8	102·1	110·4	117·2	119·3	121·0	121·9	120·5	128·2
13 Shipbuilding and marine engineering	100·0	97·7	100·3	101·0	101·7	101·7	104·3	103·0	99·3	95·0	92·1
14 Motors and cycles	100·0	101·2	101·7	99·4	104·6	111·0	106·6	103·2	106·1	110·1	125·4
15 Aircraft 16 Railway rolling stock	100·0	102·5	112·4	118·0	125·0	127·8	132·9	132·9	130·1	124·4	122·2
17 Metal goods n.e.s.	100·0	102·4	100·8	98·0	100·0	104·3	104·3	103·9	102·4	103·9	111·0
18 Textiles	100·0	101·3	90·8	95·9	97·7	94·2	92·2	91·5	84·8	83·4	83·6
19 Leather, clothing and footwear	100·0	100·1	94·3	98·6	98·3	96·7	96·6	95·4	91·0	90·8	93·4
20 Building materials	100·0	102·8	105·5	107·7	108·8	108·3	108·3	106·6	101·1	103·9	108·8
21 Pottery and glass	100·0	102·7	99·3	96·0	97·3	101·3	100·7	96·6	96·0	94·6	96·0
22 Timber, furniture, etc.	100·0	100·7	96·2	98·0	100·3	101·7	98·0	96·9	95·2	97·6	100·0
23 Paper, printing and publishing	100·0	102·4	100·2	100·0	104·3	108·3	110·7	112·8	113·2	114·8	120·0
24 Other manufacturing	100·0	107·0	100·4	102·9	109·8	113·9	113·1	114·3	113·1	116·0	123·8
4–24 TOTAL	100·0	102·2	101·2	102·3	105·0	107·5	108·1	108·1	106·4	106·0	110·4

Appendix table 8.7. *Indices of net output*

SAM industry group	1950	1951	1952	1953	1954	1955	1956	1957	1958	1959	1960
4 Food processing	100·0	104·7	107·8	114·7	117·2	118·4	122·1	122·3	126·0	128·2	130·9
5 Drink and tobacco	100·0	101·9	100·4	100·8	101·1	105·4	107·7	110·7	111·5	119·5	124·5
6 Coke ovens	100·0	103·7	111·1	111·1	114·8	118·5	125·9	133·3	122·2	111·1	122·2
7 Mineral oil refining	100·0	166·7	233·3	266·7	300·0	300·0	311·1	288·9	344·4	400·0	455·6
8 Chemicals n.e.s.	100·0	103·7	96·3	108·4	122·3	130·4	135·9	141·8	141·3	162·9	180·2
9 Iron and steel (excluding tinplate and tubes) ⎫ 10 Iron and steel (tinplate and tubes) ⎬	100·0	104·2	108·8	109·3	113·9	122·3	126·5	128·3	114·2	118·6	138·5
11 Non-ferrous metals	100·0	113·5	111·5	97·1	114·4	126·9	123·1	122·1	121·2	129·8	148·1
12 Engineering and electrical goods	100·0	107·1	109·3	110·7	118·3	127·1	126·6	131·3	131·9	139·8	150·4
13 Shipbuilding and marine engineering	100·0	102·9	106·3	112·6	107·4	116·0	125·7	115·4	116·6	108·6	98·3
14 Motors and cycles	100·0	104·4	96·0	106·9	122·6	140·9	121·5	132·5	144·5	174·1	198·5
15 Aircraft ⎫ 16 Railway rolling stock ⎬	100·0	104·9	115·3	134·0	142·4	162·6	166·0	174·4	169·5	168·0	161·1
17 Metal goods n.e.s.	100·0	106·5	102·5	96·6	105·4	117·5	113·8	114·4	111·6	120·3	132·8
18 Textiles	100·0	99·8	81·8	97·4	100·0	97·4	96·3	96·5	87·1	92·0	95·4
19 Leather, clothing and footwear	100·0	94·7	89·8	98·1	97·5	100·6	101·5	100·9	97·2	106·2	113·0
20 Building materials	100·0	104·9	109·9	116·9	120·4	121·8	121·8	116·9	112·7	114·8	131·7
21 Pottery and glass	100·0	106·3	95·8	97·9	101·0	[110·4	106·3	104·2	107·3	124·0	122·9
22 Timber, furniture, etc.	100·0	107·7	95·2	106·0	119·0	119·0	111·9	114·3	111·3	120·2	122·6
23 Paper, printing and publishing	100·0	105·5	88·7	99·2	115·6	124·6	122·9	126·1	128·6	135·2	153·5
24 Other manufacturing	100·0	105·1	94·2	101·3	114·7	127·6	121·2	128·8	129·5	139·7	154·5
4-24 TOTAL	100·0	104·4	100·6	106·7	113·9	121·1	120·6	123·2	121·5	129·7	139·8

Appendix table 8.8.　*Indices of capital stock per head (1950 = 100)*

SAM industry group	1950	1951	1952	1953	1954	1955	1956	1957	1958	1959	1960
4 Food processing	100·0	101·0	103·9	104·0	104·3	105·3	109·5	115·0	118·2	122·3	126·5
5 Drink and tobacco	100·0	103·5	105·3	108·5	111·8	118·1	119·0	117·5	119·5	120·9	122·1
6 Coke ovens	100·0	109·4	118·3	112·8	129·9	118·0	136·3	140·8	153·0	164·6	174·7
7 Mineral oil refining	100·0	177·4	228·8	286·5	305·4	336·1	341·0	399·8	430·2	436·6	465·9
8 Chemicals	100·0	105·9	114·5	123·2	129·9	135·0	145·3	156·3	168·6	177·9	183·5
9 Iron and steel (excluding tinplate and tubes) } 10 Iron and steel (tinplate and tubes)	100·0	106·5	111·6	117·4	125·4	128·5	132·5	140·3	157·5	172·0	170·4
11 Non-ferrous metals	100·0	99·7	98·5	109·7	105·8	104·7	106·9	115·2	121·5	124·8	119·3
12 Engineering and electrical goods	100·0	100·5	101·0	105·9	107·5	106·5	109·6	113·0	116·8	122·5	120·2
13 Shipbuilding and marine engineering	100·0	105·4	105·8	108·1	111·4	115·0	115·6	122·5	133·5	146·2	155·0
14 Motors and cycles	100·0	105·8	112·2	120·3	120·1	122·9	139·6	155·1	159·7	161·1	151·3
15 Aircraft } 16 Railway rolling stock	100·0	107·6	109·9	115·6	115·5	117·8	118·6	123·4	130·3	141·5	148·3
17 Metal goods n.e.s.	100·0	102·1	108·0	115·5	118·5	119·9	126·3	132·1	139·2	142·9	140·4
18 Textiles	100·0	101·2	114·5	109·3	109·5	116·0	120·0	122·1	131·8	134·4	136·0
19 Leather, clothing and footwear	100·0	101·7	108·7	104·7	106·8	109·9	110·4	111·8	117·4	117·3	114·0
20 Building materials	100·0	102·4	103·5	105·5	109·8	115·8	120·9	128·5	140·5	141·4	141·0
21 Pottery and glass	100·0	102·4	109·8	117·5	122·1	123·0	129·3	141·2	145·2	151·0	153·0
22 Timber, furniture, etc.	100·0	104·6	113·0	114·5	116·6	120·1	128·0	132·1	137·6	139·0	142·4
23 Paper, printing and publishing	100·0	101·1	105·9	108·1	107·0	107·3	109·3	112·5	115·5	117·0	116·0
24 Other manufacturing	100·0	98·4	109·4	110·2	107·9	110·5	117·9	123·2	130·7	133·6	132·5
4–24 TOTAL	100·0	102·8	108·3	111·1	113·0	115·5	120·1	125·6	132·8	138·0	138·1

Appendix table 8.8a. Average capital-output ratios at 1960 prices (£ million at 1960 prices)

SAM industry group	1950	1951	1952	1953	1954	1955	1956	1957	1958	1959	1960
4 Food processing	2·31	2·33	2·35	2·29	2·33	2·42	2·45	2·54	2·57	2·62	2·68
5 Drink and tobacco	2·31	2·33	2·43	2·45	2·50	2·48	2·49	2·48	2·52	2·39	2·36
6 Coke ovens	3·96	4·21	4·26	4·58	4·81	5·06	5·20	5·38	6·35	7·48	7·26
7 Mineral oil refining	5·08	5·40	5·64	6·00	5·86	6·27	6·76	8·60	8·12	7·43	6·77
8 Chemicals n.e.s.	2·41	2·54	2·95	2·82	2·70	2·72	2·78	2·97	3·22	2·98	2·85
9 Iron and steel (excluding tinplate and tubes) } 10 Iron and steel (tinplate and tubes)	2·33	2·38	2·39	2·48	2·53	2·48	2·52	2·64	3·19	3·24	3·00
11 Non-ferrous metals	2·43	2·23	2·34	2·80	2·47	2·32	2·53	2·68	2·79	2·68	2·47
12 Engineering and electrical goods	1·72	1·67	1·71	1·76	1·72	1·68	1·77	1·79	1·85	1·81	1·76
13 Shipbuilding and marine engineering	1·40	1·40	1·39	1·35	1·47	1·41	1·34	1·53	1·59	1·78	2·03
14 Motors and cycles	1·98	2·02	2·34	2·21	2·02	1·91	2·41	2·38	2·31	2·01	1·88
15 Aircraft } 16 Railway rolling stock	1·72	1·81	1·84	1·75	1·74	1·59	1·64	1·62	1·72	1·81	1·94
17 Metal goods n.e.s.	1·25	1·23	1·33	1·47	1·41	1·33	1·45	1·50	1·60	1·54	1·47
18 Textiles	4·02	4·12	5·10	4·32	4·30	4·51	4·61	4·65	5·15	4·89	4·75
19 Leather, clothing and footwear	1·33	1·43	1·52	1·40	1·43	1·40	1·40	1·40	1·46	1·34	1·25
20 Building materials	2·18	2·19	2·17	2·12	2·17	2·25	2·34	2·56	2·75	2·79	2·54
21 Pottery and glass	1·27	1·26	1·45	1·46	1·49	1·44	1·56	1·66	1·65	1·46	1·52
22 Timber, furniture, etc.	1·35	1·32	1·54	1·43	1·33	1·39	1·51	1·51	1·59	1·52	1·57
23 Paper, printing and publishing	2·61	2·57	3·12	2·84	2·52	2·44	2·57	2·63	2·65	2·59	2·37
24 Other manufacturing	2·01	1·99	2·33	2·24	2·07	1·98	2·20	2·19	2·29	2·22	2·12
4-24 TOTAL	2·18	2·19	2·37	2·32	2·27	2·24	2·34	2·40	2·53	2·46	2·38

Appendix table 8.9.   *Indices of capital-output ratios (1950 = 100)*

SAM industry group	1950	1951	1952	1953	1954	1955	1956	1957	1958	1959	1960
4 Food processing	100·0	100·9	101·7	99·1	100·9	104·8	106·1	110·0	111·3	113·4	116·0
5 Drink and tobacco	100·0	100·9	105·2	106·1	108·2	107·4	107·8	107·4	109·1	103·5	102·2
6 Coke ovens	100·0	106·3	107·6	115·7	121·5	127·8	131·3	135·9	160·4	188·9	183·3
7 Mineral oil refining	100·0	106·3	111·0	118·1	115·4	123·4	133·1	169·3	159·8	146·3	133·3
8 Chemicals n.e.s.	100·0	105·4	122·4	117·0	112·0	112·9	115·4	123·2	133·6	123·6	118·3
9 Iron and steel (excluding tinplate and tubes) / 10 Iron and steel (tinplate and tubes)	100·0	102·1	102·6	106·4	108·6	106·4	108·2	113·3	136·9	139·0	128·8
11 Non-ferrous metals	100·0	91·8	96·3	115·2	101·6	95·5	104·1	110·3	114·8	110·3	101·6
12 Engineering and electrical goods	100·0	97·1	99·4	102·3	100·0	97·7	102·9	104·1	107·6	105·2	102·3
13 Shipbuilding and marine engineering	100·0	100·0	99·3	96·4	105·0	100·7	95·7	109·3	113·6	127·1	145·0
14 Motors and cycles	100·0	102·0	118·2	111·6	102·0	96·5	121·7	120·2	116·7	101·5	94·9
15 Aircraft / 16 Railway rolling stock	100·0	105·2	107·0	101·7	101·2	92·4	95·3	94·2	100·0	105·2	112·8
17 Metal goods n.e.s.	100·0	98·4	106·4	117·6	112·8	106·4	116·0	120·0	128·0	123·2	117·6
18 Textiles	100·0	102·5	126·9	107·5	107·0	112·2	114·7	115·7	128·1	121·6	118·2
19 Leather, clothing and footwear	100·0	107·5	114·3	105·3	107·5	105·3	105·3	105·3	109·8	100·8	94·0
20 Building materials	100·0	100·5	99·5	97·2	99·5	103·2	107·3	117·4	126·1	128·0	116·5
21 Pottery and glass	100·0	99·2	114·2	115·0	117·3	113·4	122·8	130·7	129·9	115·0	119·7
22 Timber, furniture, etc.	100·0	97·8	114·1	105·9	98·5	103·0	111·9	111·9	117·8	112·6	116·3
23 Paper, printing and publishing	100·0	98·5	119·5	108·8	96·6	93·5	98·5	100·8	101·5	99·2	90·8
24 Other manufacturing	100·0	99·0	115·9	111·4	103·0	98·5	109·5	109·0	113·9	110·4	105·5
4-24 TOTAL	100·0	100·5	108·7	106·4	104·1	102·8	107·3	110·1	116·1	112·8	109·2

Appendix table 8.10. Indices of output per head (1950 = 100)

SAM industry group	1950	1951	1952	1953	1954	1955	1956	1957	1958	1959	1960
4 Food processing	100·0	100·3	102·1	105·5	103·6	100·9	103·7	104·7	106·7	108·2	109·2
5 Drink and tobacco	100·0	102·4	100·4	102·3	103·2	110·4	110·5	109·6	109·9	116·6	119·7
6 Coke ovens	100·0	103·7	111·1	98·1	107·6	93·5	104·9	105·2	96·4	87·7	96·4
7 Mineral oil refining	100·0	166·7	205·9	235·4	257·1	264·8	252·3	234·3	264·9	292·6	341·8
8 Chemicals n.e.s.	100·0	100·7	93·8	105·6	116·0	119·5	122·9	127·1	126·4	144·0	155·3
9 Iron and steel (excluding tinplate and tubes) ⎫ 10 Iron and steel (tinplate and tubes) ⎭	100·0	104·2	108·4	110·1	115·2	120·5	122·5	123·4	115·0	123·5	132·0
11 Non-ferrous metals	100·0	108·7	101·6	95·4	104·3	109·5	103·0	104·5	106·1	112·9	117·8
12 Engineering and electrical goods	100·0	103·2	101·4	103·4	107·2	108·4	106·1	108·5	108·2	116·0	117·3
13 Shipbuilding and marine engineering	100·0	105·3	106·0	111·5	105·6	114·1	120·5	112·0	117·4	114·3	106·7
14 Motors and cycles	100·0	103·2	94·4	107·5	117·2	126·9	114·0	128·4	136·2	158·1	158·3
15 Aircraft ⎫ 16 Railway rolling stock ⎭	100·0	102·3	102·6	113·6	113·9	127·2	124·9	131·2	130·3	135·6	131·8
17 Metal goods n.e.s.	100·0	104·0	101·7	98·6	105·4	112·7	109·1	110·1	109·0	115·8	119·6
18 Textiles	100·0	98·5	90·1	101·6	102·4	103·4	104·4	105·5	102·7	110·3	114·9
19 Leather, clothing and footwear	100·0	94·6	95·2	99·5	99·2	104·0	105·1	105·8	106·8	117·0	121·0
20 Building materials	100·0	102·0	104·2	108·5	110·7	112·5	112·5	109·7	111·5	110·5	121·0
21 Pottery and glass	100·0	103·5	96·5	102·0	103·8	109·0	105·6	107·9	111·8	131·1	128·0
22 Timber, furniture, etc.	100·0	107·0	99·0	108·2	118·6	117·0	114·2	118·0	116·9	123·2	122·6
23 Paper, printing and publishing	100·0	103·0	88·5	99·2	110·8	115·1	111·0	111·8	113·6	117·8	127·9
24 Other manufacturing	100·0	98·2	93·8	98·4	104·5	112·0	107·2	112·7	114·5	120·4	124·8
4–24 TOTAL	100·0	102·2	99·4	104·3	108·5	112·7	111·6	114·0	114·2	122·4	126·6

Appendix table 8.11. *Net output, 1950–60 (£ million at 1960 prices)*

SAM industry group	1950	1951	1952	1953	1954	1955	1956	1957	1958	1959	1960
4 Food processing	415	434	447	475	486	491	506	507	522	531	543
5 Drink and tobacco	243	248	244	245	246	256	262	269	271	291	303
6 Coke ovens	28	29	31	31	32	33	35	37	34	31	34
7 Mineral oil refining	12	20	28	33	37	37	38	35	42	49	56
8 Chemicals n.e.s.	398	412	383	431	486	519	540	564	562	647	716
9 Iron and steel (excluding tinplate and tubes) } 10 Iron and steel (tinplate and tubes)	452	471	492	494	515	553	572	580	516	536	626
11 Non-ferrous metals	120	136	134	116	137	152	147	146	145	156	177
12 Engineering and electrical goods	1,206	1,292	1,318	1,336	1,427	1,533	1,527	1,584	1,591	1,687	1,814
13 Shipbuilding and marine engineering	183	188	195	206	197	212	230	211	213	199	180
14 Motors and cycles	244	255	235	261	300	344	297	324	353	425	485
15 Aircraft } 16 Railway rolling stock	214	225	247	287	305	348	355	373	363	359	345
17 Metal goods n.e.s.	370	394	379	357	389	434	421	423	412	445	491
18 Textiles	652	651	534	635	652	635	628	629	568	600	622
19 Leather, clothing and footwear	334	316	300	327	325	336	339	337	324	354	377
20 Building materials	144	151	158	168	173	175	175	168	162	165	189
21 Pottery and glass	98	104	93	96	99	108	104	102	105	121	120
22 Timber, furniture, etc.	170	183	162	180	202	202	190	194	189	204	208
23 Paper, printing and publishing	391	412	347	388	452	487	480	493	503	528	600
24 Other manufacturing	159	168	150	161	183	203	193	205	206	223	246
4–24 TOTAL	5,833	6,089	5,877	6,227	6,643	7,058	7,039	7,181	7,081	7,551	8,132

Note: The figures shown above for 1960 do not correspond exactly to those shown in table 7.10 as the latter have been adjusted in the light of more recent estimates.

Appendix table 8.12. *Employment and net output, 1950 and 1960*

SAM industry group	Employment					Output				
	Actual employment '000s	Index of trend level of employment (actual 1950=100)		Trend levels of employment '000s		Actual output £m. 1960 prices	Index of trend level of output (actual 1950=100)		Trend levels of output £m. 1960 prices	
	1950	1950	1960	1950	1960	1950	1950	1960	1950	1960
4 Food processing	518	103·0	122·5	534	635	415	102·8	132·2	426	548
5 Drink and tobacco	199	98·0	101·7	195	202	243	96·1	119·1	234	290
6 Coke ovens	15	99·4	132·2	15	20	28	105·4	126·2	29	35
7 Mineral oil refining	30	100·8	136·2	30	41	12	147·0	428·8	18	52
8 Chemicals n.e.s.	406	100·1	115·6	406	469	398	90·6	168·2	360	669
9 Iron and steel (excluding tinplate and tubes) } 10 Iron and steel (tinplate and tubes) }	452	99·8	101·5	451	459	452	102·4	131·2	463	593
11 Non-ferrous metals	113	101·9	122·2	115	138	120	101·0	136·8	121	164
12 Engineering and electrical goods	1,598	101·3	127·3	1,618	2,035	1,206	100·2	145·7	1,209	1,758
13 Shipbuilding and marine engineering	303	101·8	97·5	308	295	183	106·8	113·1	196	207
14 Motors and cycles	347	97·9	114·7	340	398	244	87·1	175·0	213	428
15 Aircraft } 16 Railway rolling stock }	356	107·6	133·9	383	477	214	107·8	182·8	231	391
17 Metal goods n.e.s.	493	99·1	106·5	489	525	370	97·8	124·2	362	459
18 Textiles	1,088	100·8	83·7	1,097	910	652	96·9	92·9	632	606
19 Leather, clothing and footwear	699	99·9	91·9	699	643	334	93·5	106·4	312	355
20 Building materials	181	104·1	107·1	188	194	144	106·2	125·1	152	180
21 Pottery and glass	149	100·8	95·6	150	142	98	96·1	117·7	94	115
22 Timber, furniture, etc.	293	99·5	97·7	292	286	170	101·5	121·6	172	207
23 Paper, printing and publishing	506	97·8	117·9	495	597	391	92·4	144·0	361	563
24 Other manufacturing	244	100·4	120·4	245	294	159	93·4	146·0	149	233
4–24 TOTAL	7,990	100·8	109·6	8,052	8,759	5,833	98·3	134·6	5,734	7,853

Appendix table 8.13.   *Capital stock per employee in manufacturing industries in 1960 from accounting data*

SAM industry group	(1) Capital stock from company data	(2) Estimated employment in enterprises covered by col. (1)	(3) Capital stock per employee from columns (1) and (2)
	£'000		£
Food processing	572,784	243,946	2,348
Drink and tobacco	936,600	131,330	6,962
Mineral oil refining	205,988	19,175	10,742
Chemicals n.e.s.	1,522,849	261,051	5,834
Iron and steel	1,093,663	320,947	3,408
Non-ferrous metals	242,791	88,910	2,731
Metal goods n.e.s.	432,164	180,669	2,392
Shipbuilding and marine engineering	154,148	172,168	895
Motors and cycles	466,635	340,072	1,372
Aircraft ⎫ Railway rolling stock ⎭	235,260	247,842	949
Leather and clothing	141,589	129,831	1,091
Building materials	303,871	80,781	3,762
Pottery and glass	66,292	69,791	950
Timber, furniture, etc.	49,996	47,798	1,046
Paper, printing and publishing	743,644	242,509	3,066
Engineering and electrical goods	1,529,973	1,090,341	1,403
Other manufacturing	296,689	129,235	2,296
Textiles	760,229	352,968	2,154

Note: These estimates, which are referred to on page 242n., have been derived from (i) Board of Trade published data on fixed assets and accumulated depreciation and (ii) Census of Production data on employment by firms grouped according to size and appropriate selection and interpolation of top size groups to obtain the number of companies in each industry corresponding to the Board of Trade data.   As companies' output may be spread over various industries this procedure is obviously subject to a large margin of error.

THE PROJECTION OF TOTAL CIVIL CONSUMPTION

Total civil public consumption (expenditure on goods and services) includes a very wide range of items but, as can be seen in the following table, expenditures on health and education are by far the two largest items, accounting, between them, for well over half of the total.

Appendix table 9.1. *Composition of public civil consumption in 1960 (at 1960 prices)*

	£ million	Per cent of total
Finance and tax collection	114	*4·4*
Police and justice	164	*6·3*
Overseas services	59	*2·3*
Housing	1	—
Education and child care	725	*28·2*
Health	823[a]	*31·9*
National insurance, pensions and assistance	100	*3·9*
Agriculture and food	36	*1·4*
Promotion and regulation of industry and trade	126	*4·9*
Provision of basic services	271	*10·5*
Other	159	*6·2*
Total	2,578	*100·0*

Source: National Income and Expenditure, 1961, table 42.

[a]This differs from the figure shown in chapter 13 (table 22) by virtue of the exclusion above of expenditure on care of the aged.

No attempt has been made to project separately all the individual items shown above. Projections of the two major items, health and education, have been obtained from chapters 13 and 14 respectively, and the remainder, amounting to £1,000 million in 1960, has been projected as one category, entitled 'miscellaneous public civil consumption'. Over the very long run this item has risen at about the same rate as gross national product (both at current prices). At current prices it amounted to 3·65 per cent of GNP in 1920, rising to 4·02 per cent in 1950, and falling back to 3·57 per cent in 1955[1]. However, with the faster rate of growth of GNP projected in this study, the share of this item should decline slightly, since many of the component items are in the nature more or less of overheads, or are related to the growth of the population rather than to the rise in income per head. Nevertheless, growing prosperity does lead to a demand for rising standards in many services. Also, some components, such as current expenditures connected with roads and public lighting,

[1]A. T. Peacock and J. Wiseman, *The Growth of Public Expenditure in the United Kingdom* (Princeton, 1961), pp. 80 and 133.

are linked to expanded capital investment programmes that have been projected in the related sectors.

Hence we have assumed that miscellaneous public civil consumption will rise at a rate about the average of the rates of growth of GNP in the 1950s and that projected for 1960–75 (3·5 per cent per annum). After making certain minor statistical adjustments, the final projection for this item is of an increase from £1,000 million in 1960 to £1,638 million in 1975 (at 1960 prices)—that is, an annual growth rate of 3·1 per cent per annum. Total public civil consumption is thus projected to rise as follows:

Appendix table 9.2. *Projection of total public civil consumption (£ million at 1960 prices)*

	1960	1975
Education (including child care)	725	1,300
Health	823	1,250[a]
Other	1,031	1,638
Total	2,578	4,188

[a]This differs from the figure shown in chapter 13 (table 22) by virtue of the exclusion here of care of the aged. As the division between this expenditure and the rest of the health expenditures shown above is somewhat arbitrary, depending on administrative arrangements, the chapter 13 projections have not followed this split. Hence, no significance should be attached to the apparent implied figure for the care of the aged, which, in fact, would probably rise much faster than appears to be implied.

NOTE ON THE MEASUREMENT OF TOTAL ENERGY USE

Most of the analyses and projections throughout chapter 10 have been done in the natural units (tons, kilowatts, therms) of the various types of energy. However, for certain purposes, such as measuring total energy or assessing the share of the different types of fuel, it was necessary to express all forms of energy, both primary and secondary, on a uniform basis.

The awkwardness of any form of conversion is fully recognized; but unfortunately it cannot be entirely avoided in this type of exercise. The 'coal equivalent' measure has been used for many years in official statistics and hence has become a familiar unit. Therefore, for the purposes mentioned above, the various types of energy have been expressed in terms of coal equivalent, on the basis of the conversion factors given below.

The major shortcomings of this procedure are: (a) that it neglects the changing average calorific value of coal, and (b) that it generalizes: for example, the relative usefulness of oil as related to coal fluctuates considerably in different uses around the generally applied factor of 1·7 tons of coal equivalent for 1 ton of oil.

The following conversion factors have been used:

(i) One ton of oil (including all petroleum gases and liquid fuels from coal) = 1·7 tons of coal.
(ii) 300 therms of colliery methane = 1 ton of coal.
(iii) 40,000 cu. ft. of coke oven gas = 1 ton of coal.
(iv) One ton of coke breeze = 0·9 tons of coal.
(v) The coal equivalent of gas coke and of hard coke is assumed to be one ton of coal to one ton of coke except that the coal equivalent of hard coke used by blast furnaces includes losses in conversion at coke ovens, i.e. it is calculated at the weight of coal used at coke ovens, less coke and breeze supplied to other consumers or exported or put to stock and sales of coke oven gas and liquid fuels derived from coal. Semi-coke is included with coke and breeze.
(vi) Other solid fuels which include briquettes, ovoids and Phurnacite are expressed in terms of coal used in their production.
(vii) The coal equivalent of town gas is taken to be the coal used at gasworks plus the coal equivalent of oil, colliery methane, coke oven gas purchased and all petroleum gases used, less sales of gas coke, coke-breeze and liquid fuels derived from coal.
(viii) The coal equivalent of electricity is taken to be the coal used at public supply and transport generating stations, plus the coal equivalent of coke breeze, oil, hydro and nuclear electricity and electricity purchased from collieries. The coal equivalent of hydro, nuclear and colliery electricity is taken as the amount of coal currently needed to produce the same quantity of electricity at steam stations.

In order to separate the effect of improved fuel efficiency at secondary producers of energy (mainly at the public power stations and gas-works) from the results achieved in this respect at final users, the electricity and gas consumed has been converted at a *constant* factor as well; 1951 constant factors were applied in the calculation of the data for fuel used per unit of output in appendix table 10.2 whereas 1960 constant factors were the basis of the projection of final demand in appendix table 10.3.

Apart from the coal equivalent, there are other ways of converting the quantities of various fuels into a commonly applicable unit, such as calories, therms, etc. For the first time, the Ministry of Power *Statistical Digest* for 1963 contained estimates of the thermal content of a fuel consumed in therms. Although this newer concept has not been used in this chapter a comparison of the two measurements—coal equivalent and therms—is given below.

Fuel used per unit of output[a]

Fuel	Index (1956=100)		Average annual per cent change				Energy coefficient[b]	
	1959	1962	1959–62		1956–62		1959–62	1956–62
			Fuel	Output	Fuel	Output		
In terms of coal equivalent	96	94	1·9	2·5	1·1	2·2	0·8	0·5
In terms of therms[c]	94	90	1·0	2·5	0·4	2·2	0·4	0·2

Source: Ministry of Power, *Statistical Digest*; *National Institute Economic Review.*

[a]Fuel consumption adjusted for changes in temperature.
[b]Per cent addition to total energy usage for 1 per cent rise in output.
[c]Includes losses in conversion and transmission.

There are several reasons for the difference between the two ways of measurement. The coal equivalent does not reflect the decline in the average calorific value of coal. The measurement in therms, on the other hand, appears for various reasons to reduce the part played by electricity, the fastest growing type of energy; this method measures the energy *input* (in therms) at the final stage of consumption without regard to the varying degree of efficiency with which various fuels are being used there. The coal equivalent, with all its shortcomings, attempts to make some allowance for that factor. The therm would be a very useful way of uniform measurement if it could be corrected for 'efficiency'; unfortunately, because of lack of information, this further step cannot generally be taken.

The table below illustrates the problem. Here the shares of various fuels in domestic (household) consumption in 1962 have been shown in three ways: first, based on coal equivalent, secondly, on therms, and thirdly, based on natural units but corrected by factors which take into account the relative efficiencies with which the fuel can be used in households. (The only available published information in this respect refers to household consumption and this illustration is therefore limited to that sector.)

Energy consumption by domestic users in 1962, approximate percentage distribution

	Coal	Coke	Gas	Electricity	Oil
Coal equivalent	43	7	11	35	4
Therms consumed	63	10	10	11	6
Efficient use[a]	42	7	14	29	8

[a]The raw data in units have been converted by the factors given in Ministry of Power, *Domestic Fuel Supplies and the Clean Air Policy*, Cmnd 2231 (London, 1963), Table 2, note (a), which are supposed to take into account the relative efficiencies with which the fuels can be used.

This allowance for efficiency actually is another form of the factor used for conversion into coal equivalent tailored to the special requirements of the consuming sector. Thus, if the relative efficiencies of the various fuels for the purposes of the different users were known and such individual factors substituted for the average ones given above the conversion into coal equivalent could be much improved. The introduction of such a procedure, however, requires more knowledge and detailed information on fuel usage than is at present available.

Appendix table 10.1.   *Changes in total primary fuel consumption, 1951–62 (million tons coal equivalent)*

+ indicates a factor *increasing* fuel consumption
− indicates a factor *reducing* fuel consumption

	Consumption in 1960a	Average annual changes				Annual changes		
		1951–5	1955–9	1959–62	1951–62	1960	1961	1962
Part 1. Changes in total fuel consumption:								
(1) Total fuel consumption if it had risen in the same proportion as GDP		+6·85	+4·25	+7·07	+5·96	+12·4	+9·6	−0·8
(2) Actual rise in fuel consumption, corrected for temperature changes	265·3	+4·43	+0·80	+4·90	+3·24	+14·2	+1·6	−1·1
(3) Difference to be explained: (2)−(1)		−2·42	−3·45	−2·17	−2·72	+1·8	−8·0	−0·3
Part 2. Difference between actual rise in consumptiona and rise in proportion to GDP:								
(1) Domestic consumption	72·4	−1·55	−0·38	+0·20	−0·65	−0·5	−1·2	+2·3
(2) Road transport	17·6	+0·10	+0·55	+0·50	+0·37	+0·5	+0·7	+0·3
(3) Miscellaneous usesb	32·2	−0·25	−0·18	−0·30	−0·24	+0·5	−2·5	+1·1
Total	122·2	−1·70	−0·01	+0·40	−0·52	+0·5	−3·0	+3·7
Part 3. The effect of changes in the pattern of outputc:								
(1) Decline in collieries	7·8	−0·35	−0·32	−0·28	−0·32	−0·7	−0·4	+0·3
(2) Decline in railways	11·1	−0·57	−0·17	−0·63	−0·44	−0·6	−0·7	−0·5
(3) Increase in refineries	6·1	+0·29	+0·41	+0·49	+0·39	+0·6	+0·5	+0·5
(4) Increase in agriculture	3·3	−0·04	+0·02	+0·02	—	—	−0·1	+0·1
(5) Increase in air transport	3·0	+0·23	+0·16	+0·20	+0·20	+0·3	+0·3	−0·1
(6) Increase in manufacturing	111·8	+1·23	+0·24	+0·88	+0·76	+3·6	−2·2	+1·2
(7) Changes within manufacturing		+0·01	−0·61	+0·07	−0·21	+3·7	−2·3	−1·4
Total	143·1	+0·78	−0·27	+0·75	+0·38	+6·9	−4·9	+0·1

Part 4. Changes in fuel efficiency:

	Consumption in 1960[a]	Average annual changes				Annual changes		
		1951–5	1955–9	1959–62	1951–62	1960	1961	1962
(1) Collieries	7·8	−0·28	−0·44	−0·46	−0·39	−0·4	−0·2	−0·7
(2) Railways	11·1	−0·21	−0·46	−0·58	−0·40	−0·6	−0·1	−0·1
(3) Refineries	6·1	+0·24	+0·05	−0·14	+0·07	−0·1	−0·2	—
(4) Agriculture	3·3	+0·04	—	+0·03	+0·02	−0·1	+0·2	−0·1
(5) Air transport	3·0	+0·18	−0·23	+0·03	−0·01	−0·2	+0·3	—
(6) Iron and steel	35·0	−0·39	−0·44	−0·22	−0·32	−0·2	+0·4	−0·9
(7) Engineering	18·7	−0·07	−0·08	+0·08	−0·03	+0·1	+0·2	−0·1
(8) Food, drink and tobacco	6·8	−0·07	−0·11	+0·05	−0·05	+0·1	+0·1	—
(9) Chemicals	16·0	−0·24	−0·42	−0·67	−0·42	−0·4	−0·1	−1·5
(10) Textiles, leather and clothing	7·7	−0·12	−0·22	−0·20	−0·18	−0·6	—	—
(11) Paper and printing	5·9	−0·04	−0·06	−0·10	−0·06	−0·3	+0·1	—
(12) Bricks	12·2	−0·09	−0·33	−0·22	−0·21	−0·8	−0·1	+0·3
(13) Other industries	9·4	−0·05	−0·05	+0·05	−0·02	−0·1	−0·1	+0·4
Total manufacturing (6) to (13)	111·8	−1·07	−1·71	−1·23	−1·29	−2·2	+0·5	+1·8
Total (1) to (13)	143·1	−1·10	−2·79	−2·35	−2·00	−3·6	+0·5	−3·6
Difference to be explained (Part 1 (3))		−2·42	−3·45	−2·17	−2·72	+1·8	−8·0	−0·3
Total, parts 2 to 4		−2·02	−3·07	−1·20	−2·14	+3·8	−7·4	+0·2
Unexplained residual		−0·40	−0·38	−0·97	−0·58	−2·0	−0·6	−0·5

Note: GDP is gross domestic product at factor cost constant (1958) prices.   The figures of fuel consumption within manufacturing do not add due to rounding and the temperature adjustment.

[a]Adjusted for changes in temperature.
[b]Public administration, water transport and miscellaneous uses.
[c]Lines (1) to (6) are changes relative to GDP, line (7) is the total of individual industry changes relative to the overall expansion in manufacturing.

Methods used in appendix table 10.1

(i) *Classification.* The main source of statistics of fuel consumption in the United Kingdom, analysed by class of consumer and type of fuel, is the Ministry of Power *Statistical Digest.* The Ministry of Power category 'other industries', i.e. all industries except iron and steel, which accounted for 30 per cent of total fuel consumption in 1962, has been further subdivided into seven industry groups with the aid of additional information obtained from the Electricity Council and the Gas Council. The industry groups are as follows:

Engineering:	Engineering and electrical goods, shipbuilding and marine engineering, vehicles, metal goods n.e.s., and non-ferrous metal manufacture
Food, etc.:	Food, drink and tobacco
Chemicals:	General chemicals and allied products
Textiles, etc.:	Textiles, leather and clothing
Paper, etc.:	Paper, printing and publishing
Bricks, etc.:	Bricks, pottery, glass, cement, etc.
Other industries:	Mining (other than coal), quarrying, timber and furniture, etc., other manufacturing industries, construction and water

Domestic consumption equals household use.

(ii) *Correction for changes in temperature.* The raw data of fuel consumption do not provide an adequate basis on which to discuss the efficiency of fuel usage or trends in fuel consumption over time since variations in temperature may affect fuel consumption to a significant degree. The following method was used to estimate coefficients with which to adjust fuel consumption for variations in annual average temperatures. First, a series of output indicators was obtained for as many of the classes of consumption as possible. These were:

The seven industrial groups:	The relevant indices of industrial production
Collieries:	Deep-mined coal production
Refineries:	Refinery throughout
Agriculture:	The index of output in the national accounts
Railways:	An index of net ton-miles plus passenger-miles weighted by engine-miles in 1958
Total fuel consumption:	Gross domestic product at factor cost

There were no reliable 'output' series for the other six classes of consumption and the following were used:

Air transport:	Domestic aircraft-miles flown
Road transport:	Motor-vehicle miles
Public administration: Miscellaneous:	Gross domestic product at factor cost
Domestic consumption:	Population

Consumption of fuel by water transport was assumed to be unaffected by variations in temperature.

The series for fuel consumption were then divided by 'output' to derive a series of fuel consumption per unit of output (per head for domestic consumption). Year to year percentage changes in this series were correlated with year to year percentage changes in annual average temperatures.

There are two possible sources of inaccuracy in this method. First, the units of the estimates of fuel consumption (0·1 million tons of coal equivalent) are in some classes large in relation to the overall consumption by that class, so that a change of 0·1 in units may be a relatively large percentage change. Secondly, the choice of a different 'output' series (e.g. traction-hours in traffic for railways) may lead to slightly different results.

The correlation of percentage changes in fuel used per unit of output (per cent F/O) with percentage changes in annual average temperatures (per cent T) leads to a regression equation of the form (per cent F/O) $= a + b$ (per cent T) where a may be interpreted as a constant change in fuel efficiency and b as the required temperature coefficient. This coefficient may be roughly converted into the more usual method of stating temperature dependence—the percentage change in fuel used for each °F deviation of the annual temperature from a long-term average annual temperature—by simply multiplying b by 2[1].

The results of this operation varied from the remarkably good (for total fuel consumption and the total of all industries except iron and steel) to the very bad. In some of the latter cases an improvement was obtained when scatter diagrams of (per cent F/O) and (per cent T) were drawn. It then became obvious that in some cases the omission of particular years would result in improved results[2].

The final temperature adjustments used are shown below:

Percentage change in fuel used per °F deviation from the average annual temperature, 1921–50

$+ \frac{3}{4}\%$: Iron and steel

$+1\ \%$: Collieries; food, etc.; chemicals

$+1\frac{1}{4}\%$: Textiles, etc.; paper, etc.; bricks, etc.; other industries; railways

$+1\frac{1}{2}\%$: Road transport; total fuel consumption

$+2\ \%$: Agriculture

$+2\frac{1}{4}\%$: Domestic; public administration; miscellaneous

$-\ \frac{3}{4}\%$: Refineries

A plus sign means that more fuel is used when the temperature falls.

[1] b in the equation multiplies a percentage change in temperatures that are near to 50°F. A percentage change at about 50°F is approximately twice a deviation at about 50°F so that: $b\ (\%\ T) \simeq b$ (twice deviation T) $\simeq 2b$ (deviation T).

[2] For example, the omission of 1962 resulted in the regression coefficient for collieries increasing from $R^2 = 0.04$ to $R^2 = 0.52$.

In some cases these coefficients are too refined in relation to the available data: the fact that a coefficient of $1\frac{1}{4}$ per cent is quoted for paper conceals the fact that any value between 1 and $1\frac{1}{2}$ per cent would achieve the same result. This was one of the reasons why such a relatively simple method has been used for estimating temperature coefficients. In order to approach the problem on a more precise basis separate monthly temperature deviations by major geographical regions ought to be taken into account, which in turn would necessitate a much more precise knowledge of fuel consumption than is at present available.

Since the corrections have been computed on the basis of data for the period 1951–62, strictly speaking they are averages applicable only to years in that period. For example, the coefficient for domestic consumption appears to have changed from about $1\frac{1}{2}$ per cent in the early 1950s to nearly $2\frac{3}{4}$ per cent in the early 1960s, indicating changes in heating habits and the altered pattern of household consumption. Therefore, using the coefficients given above for future periods may be misleading.

(iii) *Pattern effects.* Part 1 of appendix table 10.1 assesses the extent of the difference between the actual increase in fuel consumption and the increase that might have been expected if fuel consumption had risen in line with GDP. Part 2 then collects together the classes of consumption for which no suitable output data exists, using the same method as in part 1. In part 3 the effect of changes in the pattern of output relative to GDP was calculated by measuring the deviation of the year to year change in the production of each sector from the year to year changes in GDP on the basis of the following model:

$$P_n = (S_n - G_n) F_{n-1}$$

where P_n = effect of pattern change in year n

S_n = percentage change in the production of the sector since year $n-1$

G_n = percentage change in GDP since year $n-1$

F_{n-1} = total temperature-corrected fuel consumption in the sector in year $n-1$

Part 3 (7) was calculated similarly, comparing year to year changes in production by each industry sector with the year to year changes in industrial production.

(iv) *'Efficiency' change.* The efficiency changes in part 4 were calculated by comparing the actual change in total fuel consumption (corrected for changes in temperature) with the change that would have occurred if the previous year's fuel-output ratio had not changed:

$$E_n = F_{n-1} S_n - (F_n - F_{n-1})$$

An increase in fuel efficiency is indicated by a negative sign in the table.

Appendix table 10.2. Fuel used per unit of output[a]

Consuming sector	Indicator of output	Index (1951 = 100)			Average annual per cent change 1959–62		Average annual per cent change 1951–62		Energy coefficient[b]	
		1955	1959	1962	Fuel	Output	Fuel	Output	1959–62	1951–62
Collieries	Deep-mined coal	93	81	68	−6·7	−0·9	−4·4	−1·0	..	..
Refineries	Throughput of crude oil	138	147	138	7·7	10·2	14·4	11·1	0·8	1·3
Agriculture	Index of agricultural output	109	113	118	4·7	3·1	3·8	2·2	1·5	1·7
Iron and steel	Index of production of ferrous metals	96	93	93	0·8	0·8	0·7	1·4	1·0	0·5
Manufacturing (details below)	Index of production	96	93	93	2·3	3·3	1·9	3·0	0·7	0·6
Railways	Passenger-miles and ton-miles weighted by 1958 engine-miles	98	91	89	−6·8	−3·6	−4·6	−1·6	..	..
Road transport	Motor-vehicle miles[c]	..	82	69	5·3	6·7	5·6	7·8	0·8	0·7
Air transport	Domestic aircraft-miles[d]	144	107	109	8·7	8·2	10·5	9·7	1·1	1·1
Public administration	GDP	100	99	94	0·9	2·4	1·8	2·3	0·3	0·8
Miscellaneous[e]	GDP	100	102	104	3·4	2·5	2·7	2·3	1·4	1·2
TOTAL, all final consumers	GDP	98	96	95	2·4	2·5	1·8	2·3	0·9	0·8
Manufacturing industries:										
Engineering	Index of production	103	106	107	3·2	3·0	3·9	3·3	1·6	1·2
Food, drink and tobacco	Index of production	97	92	98	5·1	2·7	2·4	2·5	1·9	0·9
Chemicals	Index of production	94	87	77	1·3	5·4	2·7	5·2	0·2	0·5
Textiles, leather and clothing	Index of production	97	89	84	−1·7	0·3	−1·6	0	..	..
Paper and printing	Index of production	102	99	93	2·2	3·4	3·0	3·7	0·6	0·8
Bricks, etc.	Index of production	99	91	86	3·7	5·7	1·1	2·5	0·7	0·5
TOTAL, all final consumers (conversion at current factors)	GDP	96	91	90	1·9	2·5	1·3	2·3	0·8	0·6

Source: Ministry of Power, Statistical Digest; Annual Abstract of Statistics; National Institute Economic Review.

[a] Fuel measured in tons of coal equivalent; conversion at constant factors (for explanation, see Appendix, page 552) except for last line, consumption adjusted for changes in temperature (see Appendix, page 556).
[b] Per cent addition to total energy usage for 1 per cent rise in output.
[c] 1956 = 100.
[d] There is no possibility of measuring the performance of aircraft fuelled at British airports.
[e] Includes waterworks.

Appendix table 10.3. *Energy usage in the main sectors of final consumption by type of energy*

		Total energy consumption[a]	Coal	Coke[b]	Gas[b]	Electricity	Oil
			Approximate per cent distribution				
Collieries	1951	12·3	86		1	13	
	1955	11·0	79		1	20	
	1960	7·8	63		1	36	
	1962	7·0	59		—	41	
	1975	6·0	20		—	80	
Refineries	1951	1·6	—		—	6	94
	1955	3·7	—		—	5	95
	1960	6·1	—		—	7	93
	1962	6·8	—		—	7	93
	1975	13–14	—		—	8	92
Agriculture	1951	2·6	15	4	—	15	66
	1955	2·9	10	3	—	28	59
	1960	3·3	9	3	—	39	48
	1962	3·7	8	3	—	40	49
	1975	5·6	2	—	—	66	33
Iron and steel	1951	29·2	26	51	8	8	7
	1955	32·8	19	54	9	9	10
	1960	34·9	11	54	9	11	15
	1962	31·0	8	50	9	13	20
	1975	45–50	3	38	6	24	29
Engineering[c]	1951	13·8	30	9	16	35	10
	1955	16·6	27	8	15	37	13
	1960	18·6	18	4	16	42	20
	1962	19·6	16	4	13	42	25
	1975	36–44	4	2	7	54	33
Food, drink and tobacco	1951	6·0	55	10	8	17	10
	1955	6·3	54	6	8	19	13
	1960	6·8	43	3	7	24	24
	1962	7·3	37	2	7	25	29
	1975	9–11	9	1	6	43	41
Chemicals[d]	1951	12·3	56	11	1	27	5
	1955	13·8	55	10	1	28	6
	1960	15·9	44	8	1	36	11
	1962	15·6	42	7	1	36	14
	1975	31–35	15	2	1	60	22
Textiles, leather and clothing	1951	9·4	73	1	2	17	7
	1955	8·9	69	1	2	21	7
	1960	7·7	53	—	3	29	16
	1962	7·6	45	—	3	30	22
	1975	10–11	14	—	2	56	28
Paper and printing	1951	4·5	87	—	2	4	7
	1955	5·3	81	—	2	11	6
	1960	5·9	63	—	2	19	17
	1962	6·2	56	—	2	19	23
	1975	10–12	28	—	1	37	35
Bricks, etc.	1951	12·1	79	2	4	10	5
	1955	13·0	76	2	5	12	6
	1960	12·1	59	—	6	15	21
	1962	13·4	47	1	5	15	32
	1975	16–18	20	—	4	33	43

		Total energy consumption[a]	Coal	Coke[b]	Gas[b]	Electricity	Oil
					Approximate per cent distribution		
Other industries	1951	7·3	47	7	1	31	14
	1955	8·3	41	5	2	36	16
	1960	9·4	30	1	2	44	23
	1962	10·6	24	1	2	45	28
	1975	14–17	7	1	2	58	32
Railways	1951	15·5	92	3	—	6	—
	1955	14·0	88	6	—	6	—
	1960	11·0	81	5	—	10	4
	1962	9·1	67	7	—	14	12
	1975	7–8	16	4	—	43	37
Road transport	1951	11·7	—	—	—	6	94
	1955	13·5	—	—	—	4	96
	1960	17·5	—	—	—	2	98
	1962	19·5	—	—	—	1	99
	1975	35–40	—	—	—	—	100
Water transport	1951	2·2	59	—	—	—	41
	1955	2·2	45	—	—	—	55
	1960	2·2	18	—	—	—	82
	1962	2·4	17	—	—	—	83
	1975	3	5	—	—	—	95
Air transport	1951	1·2	—	—	—	—	100
	1955	2·9	—	—	—	—	100
	1960	3·0	—	—	—	—	100
	1962	3·6	—	—	—	—	100
	1975	6–8	—	—	—	—	100
Domestic	1951	65·4	58	7	16	18	1
	1955	66·7	57	7	14	20	2
	1960	71·8	50	7	11	29	4
	1962	79·2	43	7	11	35	4
	1975	110–125	16	5	13	62	4
Public administration	1951	10·0	46	23	8	18	5
	1955	10·9	44	20	6	22	8
	1960	11·7	34	12	3	27	23
	1962	11·8	32	11	3	29	25
	1975	15–18	15	3	5	47	30
Miscellaneous	1951	14·9	25	34	16	22	3
	1955	16·2	21	31	17	28	4
	1960	18·0	13	25	15	36	11
	1962	18·9	10	22	14	44	10
	1975	30–35	4	9	14	62	11
Total, all final consumers	1951	232·0	51	14	8	16	11
	1955	249·0	46	14	8	18	14
	1960	263·7	35	12	7	24	21
	1962	273·3	30	11	7	27	25
	1975						
(1) at 1960 conversion factors[e]		410–450					
(2) at current conversion factors		380–420	10	6	7	46	31

Source: Ministry of Power, *Statistical Digest;* NIESR estimates.

[a]In million tons coal equivalent.

[b]Coke includes other manufactured solid fuel; oil includes other liquid fuel and creosote-pitch mixture; gas is coke oven and town gas and in the case of collieries includes colliery methane.

[c]Including vehicles, shipbuilding, metal manufactures and non-ferrous metals.

[d]General chemicals.

[e]For electricity and gas (for explanation, see page 552).

Appendix table 10.4 *Primary sources of energy*

	Total primary energy consumption^a	Coal^b (m. tons)	%	Oil (m. tons)	%	Hydro-electricity^c ('000m. kWh)	%	Nuclear electricity ('000m. kWh)	%	Natural gas ('000m. therms)	%
I. All final users (direct use)											
1951	142·1	118·3	83	14·0	17	0·6	—	—	—	—	—
1955	147·0	113·8	77	19·5	23	0·6	—	—	—	—	—
1960	145·5	91·1	63	32·1	37	0·6	—	—	—	—	—
1962	147·5	81·3	55	38·9	45	0·6	—	—	—	—	—
1975	160–190	40–50	25	75–85	75	0–1	—	—	—	—	—
II. Secondary energy producers											
Electricity^d											
1951	36·0	34·9	97	0·1	—	1·1	3	—	—	—	—
1955	44·2	42·8	97	0·2	1	1·1	2	—	—	—	—
1960	63·1	51·3	81	5·3	14	2·5	3	2·1	2	—	—
1962	73·7	60·6	82	5·6	13	3·3	2	3·5	3	—	—
1975	155–170	105–115	68	10–14	12	5–6	2	55–65	18	—	—
Gas-works											
1951	31·4	30·5	97	0·5	3	—	—	—	—	—	—
1955	31·7	30·8	97	0·5	3	—	—	—	—	—	—
1960	26·0	24·6	95	0·8	5	—	—	—	—	—	—
1962	26·2	24·4	93	1·1	7	—	—	—	—	—	—
1975	28–32	12–14	40	7–8	38	—	—	—	—	1	22

Coke ovens	1951	23·5	23·5	100	—	—	—	—	—	—	—	—
	1955	27·1	27·1	100	—	—	—	—	—	—	—	—
	1960	28·7	28·7	100	—	—	—	—	—	—	—	—
	1962	23·6	23·6	100	—	—	—	—	—	—	—	—
	1975	28–30	28–30	100	—	—	—	—	—	—	—	—
Total	1951	90·9	88·9	98	0·6	1	1·1	1	—	—	—	—
	1955	103·0	100·7	98	0·7	1	1·1	1	—	—	—	—
	1960	117·8	104·6	89	6·1	9	2·5	1	2·1	1	—	—
	1962	123·5	108·6	88	6·7	9	3·3	1	3·5	2	—	—
	1975	210–230	140–160	67	18–22	14	5–6	1	55–65	13	1	3
III. Total, all users[e]	1951	232·0	206·2	89	14·6	11	1·7	1	—	—	—	—
	1955	249·0	213·5	86	20·3	14	1·7	1	—	—	—	—
	1960	263·7	195·5	74	38·5	25	3·1	1	2·1	1	—	—
	1962	273·3	190·9	70	46·2	29	3·9	1	3·5	1	—	—
	1975	370–410	180–200	48	95–105	42	6–7	1	55–65	7	1	2

Source: Ministry of Power, Statistical Digest.

[a]Million tons coal equivalent.
[b]Includes coke and coke breeze consumed at secondary producers.
[c]Includes electricity imported from France (102 million kWh in 1962).
[d]Public power stations.
[e]This is not the sum of the details above, partly because of minor duplication in the data and partly because of fuels of limited importance such as colliery methane, etc.

Appendix table 10.5. *Fuel prices*

(A) Wholesale prices, 1954 = 100

	Fuel used in manufacturing	Coal	Hard coke	Fuel oil[a]
1950	76	74	69	—
1952	91	90	85	—
1954	100	100	100	100
1956	117	124	130	111
1958	129	138	148	115
1960	128	137	152	119
1964[b]	139	151	164	139

(B) Coal prices (at pithead) for different consumers, 1949 = 100

	For gas-making	For electricity generation	For all consumers
May 1949	100	100	100
December 1951	122	199	119
May 1954	140	129	134
July 1951	193	171	178
September 1960	208	173	189

(C) Price of gas-making materials (delivered prices), 1957 = 100

	Coal	Gas oil	Heavy oil feedstock	Light distillate
1949	55	67	—	—
1954	77	87	77	—
1957	100	100	100	100
1959	101	91	79	89

(D) Price of non-solid fuel, 1950 = 100

	Domestic consumers			Industrial consumers		
	Gas	Electricity[c]	Kerosene	Gas	Electricity	Oil
1950	100	100	100	100	100	100
1955	135	112(123)	131	136	124	118
1960	173	123(166)	141	161	133	140

Sources: (A) *Annual Abstract of Statistics* and *Board of Trade Journal*; (B), (C) and (D) the *Report from the Select Committee on Nationalised Industries: The Gas Industry, loc. cit.*, vol. I, pp. 52, 55 and 79.

[a]Medium fuel oil, 950 secs.
[b]May.
[c]The indices in brackets show the price adjusted for sales increase, i.e. after allowance for the reducing effect of the two-part tariff in case of increasing use.

Appendix table 10.6. *Per capita consumption of energy and of solid fuels in European industrial countries (tons of coal equivalent)*[a]

	1955		1961	
	Total energy	Solid fuel	Total energy	Solid fuel
(A) Major coal producers				
Belgium	3·8	3·2	3·8	2·6
France	2·4	1·6	2·7	1·5
West Germany[b]	3·3	3·0	3·7	2·7
Netherlands	2·2	1·6	2·6	1·3
United Kingdom	4·9	4·3	4·8	3·7
(B) Others				
Austria	2·0	1·2	2·5	1·1
Denmark	2·5	1·6	2·9	1·2
Italy	0·9	0·2	1·4	0·2
Norway	4·1	0·4	5·4	0·3
Sweden	3·5	0·8	4·7	0·5
Switzerland	2·2	0·6	2·9	0·4

Source: United Nations Economic Commission for Europe, *The Coal Situation in Europe in 1961–62* (Geneva, 1963).

[a]United Nations conversion factors have been used.
[b]Including West Berlin.   For 1955, excluding the Saar.

Appendix table 10.7. *Some quality indicators of British deep-mined coal*

	1938[a]	1946	1955
Free dirt (per cent by weight)	4·5	6·7	7·0
Ash (per cent of air-dried coal)	4·8	5·3	6·1
Sulphur (per cent of air-dried coal)	1·3	1·4	1·6

Source: A. M. Wandless, 'The British Coal Resources', *op. cit.*, p. 57.
[a]England and Wales only.

Appendix table 10.8. *Petroleum: supplies and disposals (million tons and percentages)*[a]

	1938	1950	1956	1960	1962
Total supply of crude oil[b]	2·3	9·2	28·6	44·9	52·7
Total supply of refined products	11·9	18·8	35·9	54·4	63·0
of which, percentage:					
Output of UK refineries	*18*	*46*	*73*	*74*	*76*
Imports	*79*	*52*	*26*	*25*	*23*
Coal derivatives	*3*	*2*	*1*	*1*	*1*
Total disposals of refined products	10·7	18·9	35·9	53·8	61·9
of which, percentage:					
Inland deliveries	*82*	*77*	*64*	*73*	*76*
Shipments	*6*	*7*	*21*	*17*	*16*
Bunkers	*12*	*16*	*15*	*10*	*8*
Total imports	9·4	9·8	9·4	13·7	14·6
of which, percentage:					
Aviation spirit	—	*2*	*4*	*3*	*2*
Motor spirit	*50*[c]	*39*	*17*	*15*	*16*
Other spirit	*1*	*1*	*2*	*2*	*5*
Kerosene	*8*	*14*	*15*	*5*	*6*
Gas oil	*6*	*14*	*20*	*16*	*15*
Diesel oil	—	*2*	*2*	*1*	*1*
Fuel oil	*30*	*22*	*35*	*54*	*51*
Lubricating oil	*4*	*5*	*4*	*4*	*3*
Other sorts	*1*	*1*	*1*	*1*	*1*
Total deliveries for inland consumption (100)[d]	8·8	14·6	23·1	39·4	47·2
of which, percentage:					
Gases (200)	—	—	*1*	*1*	*1*
Feedstock (not comparable)	—	*1*	*3*	*5*	*6*
Aviation spirit (150)	*1*	*2*	*5*	*3*	*2*
Motor spirit (80)	*54*	*36*	*27*	*19*	*18*
Industrial and white spirit (50)	*1*	*1*	*1*	*1*	*1*
Kerosene (80)	*8*	*10*	*9*	*6*	*5*
Gas/diesel oil (130)	*14*	*18*	*18*	*15*	*16*
Fuel oil (100)	*7*	*21*	*28*	*44*	*45*
Lubricating oils (90)	*7*	*5*	*4*	*3*	*2*
Bitumen (100)	*7*	*4*	*4*	*3*	*3*
Paraffin wax (70)	*1*	*1*	—	—	—
Other (not comparable)	—	*1*	—	—	*1*

Source: Ministry of Power, *Statistical Digest, 1962.*

[a]Rounded.

[b]Includes crude and process oils and a small amount of indigenous production of crude petroleum and shale oil (between 0·1 and 0·2 million tons per annum).

[c]Including aviation spirit.

[d]Figures in brackets indicate the rounded percentage of home refinery output to inland deliveries in 1962.

Appendix table 10.9. *Plant capacity in gas-works*

	1950		1960		1963	
	Million cubic feet	Per cent	Million cubic feet	Per cent	Million cubic feet	Per cent
Carbonization plant	1,418	69	1,386	54½	1,223	46½
Water gas and similar plant	642	31	989	39	1,072	41
Oil-gasification plant[a]	3	—	165	6½	322	12½
Total	2,063	100	2,540	100	2,617	100

Source: Ministry of Power, *Statistical Digest, 1963.*
[a]This includes plant for reforming refinery gas and other gas purchased.

Appendix table 10.10 *Space-heating with gas*

			Annual sales: thousands
	1959–60	1962–3	1963–4
Central heating gas boilers	10	35	} 90
Gas warm-air units	3	21	
Gas fires	326[a]	533	750

Source: Sir Henry Jones, 'Gas forges ahead', *FBI Review*, October 1963; 'The Gas Industry', *Financial Times*, Supplement, 19 November 1963; Gas Council.
[a]1961–2.

Appendix table 10.11. *Domestic gas appliances, 1960*

	Percentage of domestic consumers operating the appliances listed
Cookers	90
Washing-machines and wash-boilers	45
Space-heaters	30
Water-heaters	20

Source: Report from the Select Committee on Nationalised Industries: The Gas Industry loc. cit., pp. 72 and 105.

Appendix table 10.12. *Analysis of public power stations by size, 1961–2*

Output capacity[a]	No. of stations[a]	Aggregate output capacity[a]	Electricity sent out	Plant load factor	Works cost of generation	Average thermal efficiency
(MW)	(No.)	(m. KW)	('000m. kWh)	(Per cent)	(Pence per kWh)	(Per cent)
All stations[b]	353	31·8	124·5	46·2	0·62	—

Steam stations	*Per cent of all stations*			*Average of all steam stations = 100*		
Under 25	14	2	—	10	417	49
25–100	24	15	8	52	142	82
100–200	15	23	20	82	118	89
200–300	9	25	27	108	98	103
300–400	5	19	26	132	90	105
400–500	1	6	8	155	73	119
Over 500	1	6	8	143	72	121
Total	69	96	97	100	100	100
Oil engine stations	10	—	—	33	190	122
Hydro electric stations	20	3	3	73	7	—
All stations[b]	100	100	100	99	98	—

Source: Ministry of Power, *Statistical Digest, 1962.*

[a]At end of year.
[b]Includes other stations not shown separately (waste heat, pumped storage, etc.).

Appendix table 10.13 *Electricity: works cost, 1961–2*[a]

Fuel cost per kWh sent out (pence)	No. of stations at end of year	Average capacity during year (*Percentage of total*)	Electricity sent out	Average works cost per kWh sent out (pence)			
				Fuel	Repairs and maintenance	Other operating costs	Total
Steam stations							
Less than 0·4	8	6	9	0·38	0·01	0·02	0·41
0·4–0·6	58	42	59	0·50	0·03	0·02	0·55
0·6–0·8	64	29	23	0·67	0·06	0·06	0·79
0·8–1·0	33	9	4	0·87	0·14	0·13	1·14
1·0–1·2	11	3	1	1·07	0·26	0·27	1·60
1·2 and over	72	7	1	1·58	0·53	0·69	2·80
All steam stations	246	96	97	0·55	0·04	0·04	0·64
Oil engines	34	—	—	0·74	0·23	0·24	1·21
Hydro-electric[b]	72	4	3	None	0·02	0·02	0·04
All stations	352	100	100	0·54	0·04	0·04	0·62

Source: Ministry of Power, *Statistical Digest, 1962.*

[a]Calendar year for the Scottish Boards.
[b]Excluding pumped storage station.

Appendix table 10.14. *Electricity: analysis of generation costs*[a]

	1931	1936	1941	1946	1951	1956	1962
Average cost: pence per 1,000 kWh sent out	247	186	289	429	512	632	623
Percentage of total costs							
Fuel	63	72	83	84	85	87	87
Repairs and maintenance	18	14	9	9	8	6	7
Other operating costs	19	14	8	7	7	7	6

Source: Ministry of Power, *Statistical Digest, 1963.*

[a] Works costs of generation based on kilowatt hours sent out from all stations, excluding capital charges. (Prior to 1948 the figures relate to financial years.)
[b] Including all costs of fuel handling.

Appendix table 10.15. *Electricity in the United States: the growth of efficiency*

	Coal (pounds)	Nat. gas (cu. ft.)	Oil (gall.)	Coal	Nat. gas	Oil	Total generation: annual growth rate in decade ending
		Fuel used per kWh generated			Annual improvement in decade ending		
1920	3·04	36·8	0·254	—	—	—	—
1930	1·60	19·0	0·132	6·2	6·4	6·4	8·7
1940	1·34	16·5	0·110	1·8	1·4	1·8	4·5
1950	1·19	14·1	0·094	1·2	1·6	1·6	8·8
1959	0·89	11·1	0·079	3·2	2·6	1·9	8·6

Source: Stanford Research Institute, *Industrial Economics Handbook* (Menlo Park (California), 1961).

Appendix table 10.16. *Estimates of the ownership of electrical household appliances (percentage of all households)*

	United Kingdom[a]	United States[b]	West Germany[c]	France[c]	Netherlands[c]	Sweden[c]
Blankets	37	30[d]	—	—	—	—
Coffee percolators	4	66[e]	—	5	3	—
Cookers	32	39	—	—	—	70
Floor polishers	2	—	5	—	4	—
Immersion heaters	35	20	—	—	—	—
Irons: all types	92	98	87	84	96	—
steam	27	71	—	—	—	—
Kettles	38	—	—	—	—	—
Mixers (food and drink)	5	68	23	24	22	—
Refrigerators	34	98[f]	52[g]	41[g]	23	75[h]
Spin-dryers	7	—	—	—	—	—
Dry-shavers[i]	41	80	—	—	—	—
Toasters	14	80	15	4	18	—
Vacuum cleaners	77	80	66	37	95	90
Washing-machines	49	78	36	32	69	35

Source: British Electrical and Allied Manufacturers' Association, *Statistical Review of Domestic Electrical Appliances*, vol. 4, no. 4, 1964.

Note: The estimates should be taken as broad guides rather than accurate data.

a End-1963 or early 1964.
b Early 1964.
c Early 1963.
d Bed coverings.
e Coffee makers.
f Plus deep freezers 22 per cent.
g Including gas refrigerators.
h Plus deep freezers 15 per cent.
i Per cent of adult males.

Appendix table 10.17. *Electricity: comparison of costs*

A. The position early in 1963[a]

	Capital cost (£ per unit)[b]	Fuel cost (pence per unit)[b]
1. Conventional thermal stations:		
Large station based on *coal*		
Near coalfield	35	0·35
Remote from coalfield	35	0·48
Based wholly on oil	32	0·37
2. Gas turbine	25	1·10

Source: *Report from the Select Committee on Nationalised Industries: The Electricity Supply Industry, loc. cit.*, p. 154.
[a]Costs of the stations in 1962–3; approximate averages.
[b]kWh sent out.

B. The position early in 1964

	Fawley (oil-fired[a])	Aberthaw B (coal-fired)	Pence per unit Wylfa (nuclear)
Running costs	0·42	0·46	0·23
Capital charges assuming 7½ per cent net return on capital[b]	0·12	0·13	0·44
Total	0·54	0·59	0·67
Assuming 3 per cent interest on capital[b]			
Total	0·49	0·54	0·52

Source: House of Commons, *Parliamentary Debates* (*Hansard*), written answers to questions, vol. 694, no. 100, 30 April 1964, col. *95*.
[a]Running costs include oil tax.
[b]Assumed useful life 20 years for nuclear and 30 years for other stations.

C. The development of generation costs at nuclear power stations

	Year of commissioning[a]	Station output	Cost of generation (pence per kWh sent out)		
		(*MW*)	Capital charges[b]	Running costs[c]	Total costs
Berkeley	1962	275	0·83	0·38	1·21
Bradwell	1962	300	0·77	0·30	1·07
Hinkley Point 'A'	1964	500	0·69	0·35	1·04
Trawfynydd	1964	500	0·63	0·33	0·96
Dungeness	1964	550	0·50	0·24	0·74
Sizewell	1965	580	0·47	0·26	0·73
Oldbury	1966	560	0·49	0·23	0·72
Wylfa	1968	1,180	0·44	0·23	0·67

Source: Information supplied by the Central Electricity Generating Board.
[a]Dates refer to the commissioning of the first reactor (all stations comprise two reactors of equal output).
[b]Capital charges are based on annuity over the assumed useful life of 20 years at an interest rate of 7½ per cent per annum. For initial capital costs of the stations, see table 10.19.
[c]Assumed load factor: 75 per cent. Fuel costs have been estimated on the basis of 3,000 MWD per tonne of uranium. The running costs of Berkeley and Bradwell are based on operating experience in the period between commissioning date and 31 December 1963 and relate to costs prevailing during that period.

CENTRAL HEATING

No reliable estimates are available regarding the number of central heating installations existing or newly installed. The Social Survey inquiry in April 1960 (referring to England and Wales only) gave the following information:

Appendix table 10.18. *Estimated percentage of households with central heating in April 1960*

	Greater London		Rest of England and Wales
		Per cent of all households	
Households with:			
Own central heating system		4·8	3·8
Solid fuel	3·8	3·1	
Oil	0·2	0·6	
Gas	0·4	0·1	
Electricity	0·4	—	
Central heating laid on		2·8	1·4
Solid fuel	1·5	1·3	
Oil	1·0	—	
Gas	0·1	0·1	
Electricity	0·2	—	
All households with central heating	7·6	5·2	
Without central heating	92·4	94·8	

Source: Social Survey, *The Housing Situation in 1960*, by P. G. Gray and R. Russell, op. cit., table 46.

Notes: (1) The number of all households in England and Wales was 12½ million in April 1960.

(2) In view of the small size of the sample *the above estimates should be treated with caution.*

During the last years of the 1950s and especially following the severe winter of 1962–3, interest in this type of heating installation had been becoming much livelier. The available information briefly detailed below still does not give a very trustworthy picture of new central heating installations in recent years.

(a) It has been estimated by N. S. Billington[1] that in 1962–3 central heating had been installed in about 100,000 homes.

(b) Estimates for 1963–4 are much higher. Thus, *The Economist*[2] put the number of central heating installations at around 240,000; of this total there were about 70,000 coal- or gas-fired systems, whereas there were about 50,000 using electricity or oil. These figures refer to full central heating systems, though the dividing line between full and partial heating cannot be drawn with great accuracy.

(c) The National Coal Board, on the basis of a large country-wide sample, estimated the number of all central heating systems installed in 1963 at over

[1] 'The Heating and Air-Conditioning Industry', *National Provincial Bank Review*, November 1963.
[2] 11 April 1964, pp. 175–6.

400,000. This admittedly included partial heating systems (such as back-boilers, kitchen boilers, or various electrical systems heating two or more rooms from one central source); according to the sample survey of the National Coal Board half of these systems used solid fuel, a quarter electricity, about one fifth gas, and the share of oil-fired central heating systems was not more than about 6 per cent. (The estimates for oil contradict all other estimates.)

(d) The Gas Council announced that in 1963–4, 90,000 gas-fired central heating installations (including warm-air units) had been installed.

(e) The Electricity Council had started their 'unit plan' domestic heating campaign in 1962 and by the end of the 1963–4 season some 600,000 free-standing storage heaters were in use in households and commercial premises. (These can, of course, be very partial solutions only; one of the attractions of the storage heaters is the possibility of installing piecemeal a heating system resembling a central heating unit.)

(f) The pattern of fuel usage in central heating is probably very different by region. The Heating Centre—an independent organization in London—analysed in July 1962 and 1963 'the recent 1,000 inquiries' and produced figures showing how inquirers decided to instal systems operating with various fuels. The samples were probably heavily biased geographically in favour of London. The result was this: the share of solid fuel was in both years just over one fifth; that of oil declined from 40 per cent in 1962 to one third in 1963; gas improved its position from 26 to 36 per cent from 1962 to 1963; and the share of electricity fell from 12 to 7 per cent.

From these pieces of evidence it is possible to put together the following very tentative data. These should be treated with caution because of the contradictions in the above sources.

Appendix table 10.19. *Central heating installations in 1963–4*[a]

			'000s
	Full	Partial	Total
Coal and other solid fuel	70–80	110–130	180–210
Gas	70–80	10–20	80–100
Electricity	50–60	40–50	90–110
Oil	30–40	10–20	40–60
Total	220–260	170–220	390–440

Source: The Economist, National Coal Board, Gas Council, Electricity Council.
[a]In households and other premises.

The following points are relevant to the problem:

(i) There are still certainly more than twelve million, or about 90 per cent of all households without central heating.

(ii) Only a relatively small number (probably under one fifth, according to very rough estimates) of new dwellings has in the last two years been equipped with central heating. If half of the present housing target of about 400,000 new dwellings per year were equipped with central heating, the required investment would be £80–£90 million in heating alone; as compared to the present situation this would be equal to an addition of about £40–£50 million to the investment requirements.

(iii) The heating and air-conditioning industry will more than double its output between 1964 and 1975. In 1963 the industry's turnover must have been about £300 million (about one third of the turnover was accounted for by boilers, radiators, etc., about one fourth by controls, pumps and pipework, and the rest by installation costs)[1].

Apart from the central heating of individual dwellings and premises, district heating (producing heat centrally and distributing it through a network of pipes) will probably play a more important part in the future.

[1]Billington, 'The Heating and Air-Conditioning Industry', *op. cit.*

THE PROJECTION OF INLAND PASSENGER TRANSPORT
(NOTE ON TABLE 11.8)

Sources of data for past years

(i) *Passenger mileage*

Rail. Tables for British Railways and London Transport Board from *Annual Abstract of Statistics*. Division by distance based on expenditure estimates (see below).

Road. Totals for public service vehicles from 'Passenger Transport in Great Britain', *Economic Trends*, November 1963, table 1, page v. Long- and medium-distance are estimates for non-municipal services (see Ministry of Transport, *The Transport Needs of Great Britain in the Next Twenty Years*, Hall Report, *op. cit.*, table 6); about 10 per cent are assumed to be 'long distance'; urban (excluding London Transport Board) figures from same source less estimates for LTB from British Transport Commission *Annual Report and Accounts* and London Transport, *London Transport* (annual report).

Private motor vehicles. Totals from *Economic Trends*, November 1963, *loc. cit.*, include taxis and hire cars. Division between journey distances for 1960–2 based on sample survey data of journeys by length in 1961 reported in 'Motor Car Ownership and Use', *Economic Trends*, June 1963, *loc. cit.* 'Urban' journeys are taken as those up to about 10 miles (36 per cent), medium-distance as 11–50 miles (45 per cent), for comparability with the division of rail traffic categories. These figures apply to 'household' cars, omitting cars owned by companies, hire cars, taxis and motor-cycles. The proportion of urban journeys is then increased (to 50 per cent) and the other categories correspondingly reduced to allow for the fact that a very large proportion of medium- and long-distance journeys must pass through urban areas. Some such adjustment is necessary because the estimate is required to give an indication of the trend of urban traffic. A very similar division is obtained by using the results of traffic counts (in terms of vehicle-miles) divided between 'urban' and 'rural' roads. (See table 19 of J. C. Tanner, H. D. Johnson and J. R. Scott, *Sample Survey of the Roads and Traffic of Great Britain, op. cit.*).

Air. *Annual Abstract of Statistics*. Figures include Northern Ireland and Channel Islands services as well as domestic routes and refer to scheduled services by aircraft corporations and private companies.

(ii) *Total receipts or expenditure*

Rail and public road services. Totals are receipts from *Annual Abstract of Statistics*. Division of rail by distance from analysis of 1961 receipts in the British Railways Board, *The Reshaping of British Railways* (Beeching Report, *op. cit.*), part 1, table 1, p. 8; 'fast and semi-fast' traffic taken very arbitrarily as long-distance, 'stopping' as medium-distance and 'suburban' as urban. (Note

that 85 per cent of suburban traffic consists of British Railways London suburban services).   The division of 1960 receipts is assumed to be the same as in
1961.

Private road vehicles (*including taxis*).   The estimates are those made by
R. F. F. Dawson in 'Estimated Expenditure on Road Transport in Great Britain,
1960' (*Journal of the Royal Statistical Society*, series A, vol. 125, part 3, 1962).
The figures include estimates of running costs, depreciation, interest on hire
purchase debt, maintenance, licences, garaging and parking, etc.   By comparing
the estimates for relevant items with those in *National Income and Expenditure*
it appears that consumers' expenditure accounts for rather over half the total
expenditure.

The allocation of car travel and expenditure by distance is based on the sample
surveys of motor car usage reported in *Economic Trends*, June 1963, *loc. cit.*
The estimate of expenditure allows for greater expenditure per passenger-mile
in urban journeys.   Somewhat similar proportions (in terms of expenditure)
are given in table 3 of 'The Rationalisation of Transport' by Dr R. Beeching,
Institute of Transport Journal, March 1964, *op. cit.*

Air.   Total passenger-miles, as above, multiplied by average receipts per
passenger-mile on domestic routes as given in British European Airways
Corporation, *Annual Report and Accounts*.

Projections

The figures are not intended to give more than orders of magnitude for the broad
tendencies described in the text.   We consider first *urban* traffic, and assume that
total passenger-miles in urban traffic rise by 3 per cent a year or 50 per cent from
1960–2 to 1975 (this is consistent with 'commuter' or peak hour traffic rising
somewhat less).   We then assume, in accordance with the text, that the passenger-miles carried by public transport, which have on balance been falling, will
increase, though only slowly (by about a quarter) and that this proportionate
increase, for reasons given in the text, will be bigger for road than for rail
services.   This leaves an increase of about 56 per cent in passenger-miles carried
by private vehicles in urban areas.   Since the total number of cars in use is
expected to treble in the period—in urban areas and elsewhere—this means a
considerable decline in *urban* passenger-mileage per car.   It should be noted
that the increase in commuter or peak hour traffic would be less, and the extent
of diversion (as compared with previous trends) from private to public transport
of commuter traffic much greater than the overall figures indicate.

For *medium-* and *long-distance* travel, we assume small increases in public
services except medium-distance rail travel; this is expected to decline substantially with the rationalization of the railway system, the greater part being
transferred to private cars (although some benefit to bus services is allowed for).

The projection of total *consumer expenditure* on travel in 1975 has been
determined by the method described in chapter 6; we assume further that the

PP

proportion of consumer expenditure to total expenditure in each category of travel remains approximately stable. Allowing for the relatively small (3 per cent a year) rise in urban usage of cars—although expenditure may rise more if the relative cost of urban motoring is increased by some form of road pricing—medium- and long-distance travel of private vehicles will increase very fast (by almost 10 per cent a year).

The result, for private motor vehicles, would be a tripling of expenditure which is about proportionate to the rise in the number of cars in use.

The weakest point in these projections is, perhaps, the assumption that business usage of private cars will increase as fast as consumer usage. Business travel, as suggested above, probably approaches half the total at present, and is not necessarily so sensitive as consumer usage to rising incomes. If this is so, the projections for private car traffic, especially outside urban areas, may well be overstated. On the other hand, a slower increase in business usage would imply a fall in average mileage per car, of which there has so far been no evidence.

NOTE ON HOUSING IMPROVEMENTS AND SUBSIDIES

Improvements

The need for improvement of existing dwellings has been estimated in terms of the number of dwellings lacking the four most important of the five basic amenities eligible for standard improvement grants. These are a w.c. indoors or attached to the dwelling, a bath, a fitted wash basin and a three-point hot water system connected to bath, basin and sink. This limited concept of improvement is used for statistical reasons[1]. It does not measure the full cost of improvement but as lack of basic amenities is closely associated with age and general condition it probably gives a fair measure of the number of houses involved.

In England and Wales in 1960, 41 per cent of households lacked at least one of the four basic amenities (appendix table 12.8). Nearly all of these were without proper hot water systems and 28 per cent of them lacked sole use of bathroom. Thus in Great Britain there may have been some 6·7 million households without sole use of at least one of the basic amenities. This figure includes, however, upwards of a million households sharing facilities[2]. These households are mainly in subdivided rateable units, a big proportion of them in London. They include both acceptable arrangements for single people in flatlet houses and some households still sharing dwellings. The latter group will diminish as the housing shortage is overcome. There will also be some seasonal dwellings and rural cottages for which it may not be sensible to plan the full range of facilities. We have, therefore, estimated that improvement or demolition is probably desirable for some 5·5 million dwellings. In many cases replacement will be the only practical solution because of size or structural defects.

There is a strong correlation between fitness and amenities: 72 per cent of short-life dwellings lacked bathrooms and 82 per cent lacked hot water systems. Among the fit houses the corresponding proportions are 21 per cent and 33 per cent. And 85 per cent of the short-life houses lacked at least one amenity. We have assumed that this proportion of the houses demolished will lack amenities. This means that by 1975, 2·3 million to 2·6 million of the substandard houses will have been demolished (appendix table 12.9), and by 1965 their life expectancy will probably be too short to make improvement worth while. There are, therefore, likely to be some 2·9 million to 3·2 million houses which in 1965 still have a long enough life expectancy to be worth improving. A few of the shorter-life houses may have been improved between 1960 and 1965 but as

[1] The greater part of improvement work cannot be separated from current repair and maintenance, and for the private sector only improvements subsidized by grant are included in residential capital formation in the national accounts. These subsidized improvements are highly concentrated on the four basic amenities. Improvements to public sector dwellings are included in investment charged to capital account but here also many items may be treated as current maintenance.

[2] In England and Wales 800,000 households share baths and 900,000 share a w.c.

choice tends to fall first on the most worthwhile houses the number is not likely to be very big.

The demand for improvement is more difficult to estimate. In 1960, 46 per cent of tenants in eligible dwellings lacking one of the four amenities were willing to pay extra rent if the house was improved. Among owner-occupiers who were aware of the grants scheme only 23 per cent of those in eligible houses proposed to apply[1]. Many of those unwilling to apply may, of course, have occupied houses that were too small or structurally too difficult to modernize. Many owner-occupiers of old property are fully extended to meet their mortgage commitments and the demand is likely to rise as incomes rise, and more rented property is available for poorer householders. But the biggest factor, as with the ownership of consumer durables, is likely to be the changing climate of opinion as the proportion of new and improved homes rises. Bathrooms and hot water systems get a higher priority when all the neighbours have them. Hitherto, most grants to private owners have been made to owner-occupiers. This is not surprising because the scheme offers little to the private landlord of substandard rent-controlled property. Policies are needed to ensure adequate standards of improvement for rented property[2]. There is less justification for bringing pressure to bear on owner-occupiers but higher rates of subsidy may be called for. In total we have assumed that 70 per cent to 75 per cent of houses which in 1960 had a life expectancy of more than twenty years may be improved, but much lower proportions of shorter-life dwellings.

On this basis we should need to improve 1·4–1·9 million houses before 1975. Under the lower building estimate the number of houses improved annually would probably need to rise from 130,000 in 1960 to about 200,000 in the late 1960s. After 1970 the number would fall sharply owing to the short life expectancy of the remaining unimproved dwellings. Under the higher building estimate with more rapid demolitions, improvement requirements could be met by maintenance of the present annual rate for ten to twelve years.

By 1975 there will still be 1·4 million to 1·6 million houses without basic amenities but only 400,000 to 500,000 of these will have a life expectation of more than five years and expenditure is likely to be very small. As housing standards rise other amenities such as central heating will become more general; but a shorter normal life for a house means a smaller gap between minimum standards and the standards of new housing, so that the problems are not likely to be as big. Expenditure may fall from perhaps £50 million in 1960 to £2–£4 million in 1975[3].

[1] Tables 51 and 52 in P. G. Gray and R. Russell, *The Housing Situation in 1960, op. cit.*
[2] See chapter 12, 'Housing', section 3, p. 392.
[3] Improvement grants to private householders totalled £14 million for 88,000 houses in 1960–1. This gives an average subsidy of £160 per house. The grant cannot exceed half of actual expenditure and it may be less. Moreover local authority improvements in the investment figures include other items besides the basic amenities. We have, therefore, assumed an expenditure of £385 per dwelling.

Subsidies

(a) *The form and cost of a general subsidy.* A general subsidy aimed at reducing the cost of new houses and lowering prices generally could take the form of an annual grant, a capital grant, or a subsidy of interest payments, but as the need for subsidy is likely to diminish with time, the period of payment should not be unduly prolonged. Capital grants for new building would have the advantage that the liability would be paid off immediately and they would not commit future policy. But they would be liable to cause sharp fluctuations in capital values. The introduction of a capital grant on new building or an increase in the amount would reduce the value of recently built houses, and its removal or reduction would give a windfall gain to past recipients.

Subsidized interest rates could be graduated more smoothly as they need not be available only on brand-new houses. High interest rates are the main cause of high rents[1]. A guaranteed low interest rate would, therefore, have the advantage that the cost of subsidy would fall automatically if a fall in interest rates reduced the need. The disadvantage of subsidizing interest rates is, however, that houses are often amortized over very long periods. Those owned by housing associations or local authorities are normally amortized over sixty years and it is certainly undesirable to commit future housing policy for as long a period as that. Subsidized interest rates for a restricted period would give most benefit to owners buying on a mortgage and would not reduce the cost of rented houses proportionately. Nor does there appear to be any reason to exclude from subsidy those who are not financing their house purchase by borrowing. A big proportion of those who can afford, or nearly afford, new houses are paid-up owners of older houses. To exclude these from subsidy benefit would restrict the effect of the subsidy[2].

The most appropriate form of general subsidy appears, therefore, to be an annual grant payable over a period of perhaps ten to twenty years. Provision could, if necessary, be made for downward revision if long-term interest rates fell significantly. It would be payable on the construction cost of all houses below a certain value, and should fall gradually for more expensive houses. If for example the average construction cost of new houses were £2,250, subsidy might be payable on the whole cost of houses costing less than £2,000, and on the first £2,000 of a house costing £2,000 to £2,500. For dearer houses the amount eligible for subsidy could fall by £200 for each increase of £100 in price. A house costing £3,500 would then receive subsidy on £500 and the subsidy would disappear completely at £4,000[3].

---

[1] If a local authority amortizes new building for 60 years at 6 per cent, over the whole period interest accounts for almost three quarters of the annual cost. In a 20-year building society mortgage, interest accounts for over 40 per cent of total repayments.

[2] In particular it would be undesirable to discourage retired people from moving into smaller new houses, perhaps in less congested areas.

The selling prices of eligible houses would be rather higher as these values do not include

New houses would be eligible for subsidy for the full period, and recently built houses for such period as remained before they reached the upper limit. A 15-year subsidy would, for example, be available for ten years on houses already five year old, and for three years on houses already twelve years old. The period of subsidy appropriate would depend on the level of subsidy and the amount by which it was considered that existing values could fall without undue hardship. Thus a subsidy of 1·9 per cent a year of the construction cost, payable for twenty years, would permanently reduce the annual cost of new houses by 16 per cent (appendix table 12.10). This would be likely to lower the price of comparable existing houses by a similar amount. But a house five years old would get a 15-year subsidy of 1·9 per cent which would reduce its annual cost by 11 per cent, so that the sale price would only be likely to fall by 5 per cent. Houses ten and fifteen years old would get shorter-period subsidies that would reduce their costs by 6 per cent and 3 per cent, and their prices might fall by 10 per cent and 13 per cent. If over the previous 15 years prices had been rising at about 1 per cent a year such falls would only offset capital appreciation. If, however, an equivalent subsidy were given in ten annual payments of 3 per cent of building costs, five-year-old houses would only get a subsidy equivalent to 8 per cent, and their prices might fall another 8 per cent. Houses ten and fifteen years old would get no subsidy and their prices might fall the full 16 per cent. This would be acceptable if prices of these houses had been rising at about 2 per cent a year since they were built but not in a period of fairly stable values.

The eventual cost of a 20-year subsidy is, of course, bigger than that of an equivalent ten-year one. On a house costing £2,000 to build the total subsidy payment needed to reduce the construction cost element of its annual value by 15 per cent would be about £560 if paid over twenty years, and £460 if paid over ten years. In addition many more older houses would receive part subsidies if payments were spread over the longer period.

This higher cost consists, however, of a longer future commitment at any time. The length of the period of the subsidy does not affect the immediate annual cost very much. Until after 1970 the annual cost of twenty-year subsidies would be slightly cheaper than those over shorter periods, because owing to the rapid rise in the money value of construction the value of the older construction included is relatively small. After 1970 when building rates level off this position changes, and the shorter period subsidy would be the most economical.

A reduction in total housing costs of 20 per cent would reduce the rents paid by upper income public sector tenants from 12·4 per cent to 10 per cent of their incomes in 1975. The cost of buying an average house entirely out of income would fall from nearly 15 per cent to just under 12 per cent. A reduction of this order would require a subsidy big enough to offset some 25 per cent of construc-

land. The site would not qualify for subsidy as this would only accelerate the increase in the cost of building land.

tion costs.   This would cost £340 million in 1970 rising to £430 million in 1980
if applied to 80 per cent of new building over the whole country.   If it were
restricted to areas of low housing demand the cost might be only half of this.

A subsidy of this order would be rather over twice the present level of subsidies, allowing for the general rise expected in national product.   But in
considering the total amount that it is reasonable to spend on housing subsidies
it must be remembered that at present housing receives no net subsidy but is in
fact fairly heavily taxed.   In 1960 housing subsidies on national accounting
definitions amounted to £119 million and rates levied on housing to £385 million,
giving a net tax of £266 million[1].   In 1962 this net tax had risen to £311 million.
These figures should be adjusted to take account of the subsidy that owner-
occupiers received through low Schedule A assessments, and the subsequent
abolition of this tax, but even including this item there was probably still a net
tax of some £180 million to £200 million in 1964[2].

If local authority responsibilities and methods of financing remain unchanged
rates are likely to increase roughly proportionately to national product.   Rates
may thus rise from £385 million in 1960 to £550 million in 1970 and over £750
million in 1980.   We should not exceed the present subsidy position if we were
to spend two thirds of this housing tax on housing subsidies.   A total subsidy
bill of £370 million in 1970 rising to £500 million in 1980 would not on this
basis appear excessive.

A small part of this might be needed to compensate owners of property whose
values had fallen (see section (b) below), but after about 1970 no special direct
subsidy should be necessary for public sector housing.   It is true that the amount
of capital appreciation in the public housing account would be reduced if capital
values fell as the result of a general subsidy.   But values are not likely to fall
below their 1960 level and so the public sector as a whole would still benefit
from the present appreciation of nearly £300 million on local authority pre-1960
houses.   Special subsidy of higher income tenants will cease soon after 1970—
perhaps sooner if the general level of costs is reduced.   From this time, therefore, over the country as a whole, housing authorities would, because of their
low historical costs, make a sufficient surplus on normal rents to meet the need
of subsidizing their low income tenants.

Nor should there by any justification by 1970 for continuing exemption from
Schedule A taxation.   This would by then be equivalent to a subsidy of about
£200 million in 1970 and over £260 million by 1980[3].   But this is a bad form of
subsidy because by giving most benefit to those who pay the highest tax rates it

[1]Central Statistical Office, *National Income and Expenditure, 1963, loc. cit.*
[2]This assumes that rates and subsidies rose at the same rate between 1962 and 1964 as
between 1960 and 1962, and that the full value of Schedule A exemption is £190 million
(see M. F. W. Hemming, 'The Price of Accommodation', *National Institute Economic
Review, op. cit.*).
[3]This estimate assumes the continuation of present tax rates, but allows for the rise in the
number of owner-occupiers and in the value of their housing.

increases rather than offsets the regressive nature of rates. In a situation where rents in the low rent sector are rising to an economic level, the abolition of Schedule A becomes increasingly unwarranted. It amounts in fact to a discrimination in favour of wealthy owner-occupiers, and against poor owners and tenants. Whatever alternative is adopted there is no justification for this kind of subsidy[1].

(b) *Compensation for falling values.* As shortages disappear and better rented housing becomes more generally available a fall may occur in the value of much pre-1919 property which is approaching the end of its useful life. Such a fall would be accelerated by a reduction in the cost to owners of new houses whether due to a rapid increase in productivity in housebuilding or to a general subsidy policy aimed at reducing the current values of existing houses. In general such a development is thoroughly desirable; it would reduce rents for the lowest income groups, narrow the gap between controlled rents and market rents, and reduce the cost of purchase for redevelopment. But among the owners of such property are many owner-occupiers of low income forced into house purchase because of the shortage of houses to rent. The householder who purchases through a mortgage in these conditions is in fact gambling on the margin; a fall of 20 per cent in capital values may mean the loss of 100 per cent of his savings. It would add insult to injury for the general gain to the economy to be made at the expense of low income owner-occupiers forced into house purchase by lack of houses to rent.

The cost of compensating for such losses would, however, be trifling compared with the total saving effected by falling values of older houses. The owner-occupier only suffers from a decline in capital values when he wishes to move, and even then his hardship is not severe if most of his original loan has been paid off. We need only to ensure that, if prices fall sharply, a low income owner-occupier receives some compensation if the general level of prices is substantially lower when he sells than when he purchased. In many cases this could be effected by taking price movements since purchase into account in fixing compensation for houses bought for redevelopment[2]. In addition purchasing authorities should be willing to buy, at this level of compensation, houses scheduled for demolition within ten years or so. It would not be easy to grant direct compensation in the case of sales between private parties, but special loan terms for another purchase could be made available to sellers who, as a result of falling prices, would otherwise lose their savings—and potential deposit on a new house.

---

[1]If conditions do not make some form of building subsidy necessary, the proceeds of Schedule A tax could be devoted to granting rates relief (refunded by the central government) to poorer householders. This would at least make rates less regressive instead of, as the present Schedule A exemption, increasing the regressiveness of housing taxes.

[2]We cannot compensate every purchaser for a bad buy, but those who suffer a loss (taking account both of purchase price and subsequent maintenance and improvements) should be compensated in terms of the general price level at which they bought.

Appendix table 12.1.   *Numbers of households, Great Britain, 1960, 1975, 1990*

Types of head	Population (Millions)			Headship rates[a] (Percentages)				Households on 1960 rates (Millions)			Households forecasts (Millions)	
	1960	1975 forecasts	1990 forecasts	1951[b]	1960[c]	1975 forecasts	1990 forecasts	1960	1975	1990	1975	1990
Married men:												
under 40	4·64	5·32	6·04	79	91	96	98	4·22	4·84	5·49	5·11	5·91
40–59	5·82	5·79	6·41	96	97	98	98	5·64	5·62	6·22	5·67	6·29
60 and over	2·60	3·36	3·46	97	98	98	98	2·55	3·29	3·39	3·29	3·39
All	13·06	14·47	15·91					12·41	13·75	15·10	14·07	15·59
Widowed and divorced[d]												
40–59 males	0·22	0·23	0·26	68	70	72	75	0·15	0·16	0·18	0·17	0·20
females	0·64	0·50	0·47	78	79	80	81	0·51	0·39	0·37	0·40	0·38
60 and over males	0·63	0·80	0·88	64	66	68	70	0·41	0·53	0·58	0·54	0·61
females	2·23	2·67	2·87	68	70	72	75	1·56	1·87	2·01	1·92	2·15
All	3·72	4·20	4·48					2·63	2·95	3·14	3·03	3·34
Single[e]												
20–4 both sexes	1·85	1·94	2·64	—[f]	3	6	12	0·06	0·06	0·08	0·12	0·31
25–39 both sexes	1·68	1·58	1·73	12	13	16	20	0·22	0·21	0·22	0·25	0·28
40–59 males	0·62	0·52	0·50	27	30	33	35	0·19	0·16	0·15	0·17	0·18
females	0·83	0·46	0·44	29	32	35	37	0·27	0·14	0·14	0·16	0·16
60 and over males	0·27	0·35	0·26	39	44	49	50	0·12	0·15	0·11	0·17	0·13
females	0·80	0·81	0·64	47	51	56	58	0·41	0·41	0·32	0·45	0·37
All	6·05	5·66	6·21					1·28	1·13	1·02	1·32	1·43
All households								16·31	17·83	19·26	18·42	20·36
Population, total and per households:												
Adults[h]	35·98	38·89	42·64					2·21	2·18	2·21	2·11	2·09
All	51·12	57·63	64·65					3·13	3·23	3·36	3·13	3·18

For sources and footnotes see overleaf

Appendix table 12.1

Sources: General Register Office, *Census 1951, England and Wales: Housing Report,* *loc. cit.*, and NIESR estimates.

aPercentage of total population in each group who are heads of households.

bBased on rates for England and Wales.   (Rates for Great Britain for major groups were almost the same.)

cEstimated from increase in total number of households.

dExcluding persons under 40.

eIncluding widowed and divorced persons under 40.

fIt is assumed that all heads of households were over 25 (see L. Needleman, 'A Long Term View of Housing', *National Institute Economic Review, op. cit.*).

gIncluding population not in private households.

hAll married persons, plus single persons of 20 and over.

Appendix table 12.2. *Number of adults^a in households by social class of head,
Great Britain, 1951*

| | All house-holds | Social class | | | | Un-classi-fied |
		I and II	III	IV	V	
Number of households ('000s)	14,482	2,674	6,111	2,028	1,523	2,144
of which:						
1 adult^b	1,776	217	414	186	141	819
Distribution of households with 2 or more adults (percentages)						
2 adults	*58·3*	*59·6*	*61·4*	*55·6*	*52·0*	*52·2*
3 adults	*22·3*	*23·4*	*20·7*	*21·4*	*21·4*	*28·8*
4 or more adults	*14·9*	*14·0*	*13·4*	*16·6*	*19·8*	*16·1*
Other large households^c	*4·5*	*3·0*	*4·5*	*6·4*	*6·8*	*2·9*
Total	*100·0*	*100·0*	*100·0*	*10·00*	*100·0*	*100·0*
Estimated number of adults per household						
All households	2·42	2·38^d	2·45	2·51	2·59	2·04
Households with 2 or more adults	2·61	2·50^d	2·56	2·66	2·75	2·69

Source: Census 1951, England and Wales: Housing Report, loc. cit., adjusted by NIESR
to exclude children in each size of household.

aAged 16 and over.
bNearly half of the households with only 1 adult could not be classified by social class,
and the analysis is, therefore, restricted to households of 2 or more adults.
cHouseholds of 6–7 persons including 3–4 children, and households of 8 or more including
5 or more children.
dExcluding domestic servants (on the assumption that all domestic servants are in households with heads of social classes I and II).

Appendix table 12.3. *The replacement costs of typical houses, 1840–1962*

Year of construction	Description of house	Floor area (sq. ft.)[a]	Replacement cost £ 1962 Total	per sq. ft.
1840	Two-room cottage, with privy in yard	435	700	1·61
1880	Four-room cottage, with w.c. in yard	625	1,200	
1890	Four-room cottage, with w.c. in yard and gas services	625	1,225	1·96
1905	Totterdown Fields Estate Type A 2nd class dwelling	672	1,250	1·86
1920	Garden city type dwelling	705	1,375	1·95
1925	Garden city type dwelling with electric light	755	1,500	1·99
1937	As Housing Act	760	1,600	2·11
1947	As Dudley Report[b] with 2 w.c.'s	800	1,875	2·34
1950	New town minimum standard with reduced floor area and 1 w.c.	800	1,775	2·22
1962	Parker Morris type with garage	825	2,025	2·45

Note: The above estimates were prepared for NIESR by D. Rigby Childs, in collaboration with D. B. Connal and J. F. Green. They show the cost of construction in 1962 of typical houses of the last 120 years, similar in status to local authority and new town houses of the 1930s and post-war period. They are used in this study to illustrate the way in which housing standards have risen over the last century, and the effect on average and minimum standards of replacing the nineteenth century houses by dwellings of modern type.

[a]To outside of external walls, excluding area of outbuildings (1947) or garage (1962). Garage is also excluded from costs but allowed for in planning.
[b]Ministry of Health, *Design of Dwellings* (London, 1944).

Appendix table 12.4. *New building, demolitions and the housing stock, Great Britain, 1881–1961*

'000s

	(1) Stock of dwellings recorded at census	(2) Net increase in dwellings	(3) New building	(4) Net disappearance of dwellings: (3) minus (2)[a]	(5) Estimated demolitions[a]
		Change since previous census			
1881	6,017				
1891	6,693	676	791	115	
1901	7,696	1,003	1,121	118	
1911[b]	8,652	956	1,252	296	
	8,814				
1921	9,400	586	301	−285	
1931	10,597	1,197	1,631	434	
1951	13,831	3,234	3,876[c]	642	
1961	16,230	2,399	2,868	469	
Total 1881–1961		10,051	11,840	1,789	2,200–2,400
of which: 1881–1931		4,418	5,096	678	900–1,000
1931–1961		5,633	6,744	1,111	1,300–1,500

Source: B. R. Mitchell and P. Deane, *Abstract of British Historical Statistics, op. cit.*

a*Estimated demolitions.* Demolitions can be obtained as the net disappearance of dwellings (column 4 above) ± changes in census definitions of dwellings + additional units obtained by conversion of large dwellings into smaller units — units lost by transfer to business or institutional use or by war damage.

Additional units obtained by conversion. In England and Wales in 1960 there were 480,000 separately rated flats in perhaps 190,000 converted houses, giving a net gain from conversion of 300,000 units (see P. G. Gray and R. Russell, *The Housing Situation in 1960, op. cit.*). In addition there were 900,000 'accommodation units' in excess of the number of rateable units, and the overall figures indicate that probably 700,000 of these were counted as separate dwellings in the 1961 census. We have estimated that including Scotland and allowing for some conversions prior to 1880 the total housing stock may have been increased by 950,000 through subdivision of dwellings from 1881 to 1961. From changes in room size it would appear that 300,000 to 400,000 units were converted before 1931 and 550,000 to 650,000 between 1931 and 1961.

Losses through war damage and transfer to other uses. 220,000 dwellings were totally destroyed by bombing, and a further 280,000 very severely damaged. Only about 50,000 of the latter appear to have been rebuilt by 1954, but some may have been demolished in normal clearance programmes. We have little information on the number of dwellings converted to business or institutional use but it probably totals several hundred thousand. We have, therefore, estimated total losses other than by deliberate demolition at 600,000 to 700,000 units, of which about 80 per cent will have occurred after 1931.

Total demolitions. These figures suggest that total demolitions (other than of houses severely damaged by bombing), were between 2·0 and 2·2 million units over the whole period 1881 to 1961. Between 1881 and 1931 they were probably about 0·9 to 1·0 million, and from 1931 to 1961 about 1·1 to 1·3 million. Public demolitions under the slum clearance and development programmes totalled over 800,000, so that private demolitions may have added about 50 per cent to this total.

b*Changes in definition.* Prior to 1911 figures relate to 'buildings used as habitations', and include residential institutions but count buildings containing several flats as only one unit. From 1921 onwards they relate to 'structurally separate dwellings' excluding institutions but counting each flat in a block separately. Both series are available for 1911 and show a net difference of only 2 per cent. From 1911 to 1921 the figures show a net gain by conversion of over 280,000 units. This might be partly due to inadequate adjustment for the change in definition, but there was certainly a substantial number of conversions. During this wartime decade of housing shortage and low building rates the number of households with only 1–3 rooms increased by nearly 600,000 and those with 6 or more rooms fell by about 120,000.

c Including 158,000 temporary dwellings.

Appendix table 12.5. *The growth of the housing stock since 1841*[a]

	Growth rate of stock	Building rate[c]	Houses per 1,000 persons	
			Total population	Population over 20
	Per cent per year			
1841	*1·8*		196	373
1851	*1·0*		191	350
1861	*1·3*		196	357
1871	*1·4*		199	367
1881	*1·5*		201	374
1891	*1·1*	*1·2*	203	371
1901	*1·4*	*1·6*	208	362
1911[b]	*1·2*	*1·5*	212	354
			—	—
			214	360
1921	*0·3*	*0·3*	212	338
1931	*1·5*	*1·6*	237	352
1941 ⎫	*1·3*	*2·4*	..	..
1951 ⎭		*0·7*	283	397
1961[d]	*1·7*	*1·9*	317	455

Sources: Census 1951, Great Britain: One Per Cent Sample Tables, loc. cit.; B. R. Mitchell and P. Deane, *Abstract of British Historical Statistics, op. cit.*

ᵃUp to 1881 figures relate to England and Wales, from 1891 onwards to Great Britain.
ᵇPrior to 1911 figures relate to 'buildings and habitations', i.e. they include residential institutions but count blocks of flats as one unit. From 1921 they relate to 'structurally separate private dwellings', excluding institutions but counting each flat in a block as one unit. Both figures are available for 1911 when the difference was only 2 per cent.
ᶜNew houses built as a percentage of the average stock over the period.
ᵈEstimated.

Appendix table 12.6. *Age structure of the housing stock in 1960*

Date built	Age in years	Standard age structure	1960 estimate	Deviation from standard
1811–20	Over 140	0·4		
1821–30	130–9	2·7		
1831–40	120–9	3·0		
1841–50	110–19	3·5		
1851–60	100–09	3·9		
	All over 100	(13·5)	(16·0)	(+2·5)
1861–70	90–9	4·5	3·9	−0·6
1871–80	80–9	5·1	6·2	+1·1
1881–90	70–9	5·8	4·9	−0·9
1891–1900	60–9	6·6	6·9	+0·3
1901–10	50–9	7·6	7·7	+0·1
	All 50–99	(29·6)	(29·6)	(0·0)
1911–20	40–9	8·6	1·9	−6·7
1921–30	30–9	9·8	10·1	+0·3
1931–40	20–9	11·2	17·4	+6·2
1941–50	10–19	12·8	7·3	−5·5
1951–60	0–9	14·5	17·7	+3·2
	All under 50	(56·9)	(54·4)	(−2·5)
	Total	100·0	100·0	0·0

Source: B. R. Mitchell and P. Deane, *Abstract of British Historical Statistics, op. cit.*; *Census 1951, Great Britain: One Per Cent Sample Tables, loc. cit.*; and NIESR estimates.

Notes: The above table compares the estimated actual age structure of the 1960 housing stock with a 'standard age structure' based on the assumption that the stock of houses has grown steadily at 1·3 per cent per year, new building amounting to 1·55 per cent and demolitions to 0·25 per cent of the stock. Demolitions are assumed to be in chronological order.

The estimated age structure is based on the stock of dwellings recorded in the censuses, and annual estimates of numbers built since 1861. It assumes that the number of post-1860 houses demolished is equal to the number of additional dwellings obtained by subdivision into flats.

The estimated actual age structure is very similar to the standard one for houses built before 1911. The age structure of more recent houses reflects two wartime decades when hardly any were built and three peacetime decades spent catching up on arrears. The slightly larger number of houses over 100 years old in the estimate of the actual age structure is due to the fact that the standard assumes demolition in strict chronological order and the estimates of actual ages allow for some demolition of newer houses.

Appendix table 12.7.   *Implications of alternative rates of replacement*

Percentage of current stock replaced annually		0·5	0·7	0·9	1·0	1·2	1·4
Annual demolitions ('000s)	1970	90	125	165	180	220	155
	1980	100	140	180	200	240	280
Eventual normal life (years)		110	89	75	70	61	54
Date by which life reduced to 100 years			2007	1988	1984	1978	1975

Note: The object of this table is to illustrate the implications of various rates of replacement if carried out consistently from 1960.

The eventual normal life and the date by which the life would be reduced to 100 years assume that the stock of houses is increasing at 1·0 per cent a year, and that the rate of increase in the past has been regular (i.e. it is based on the standard age structure in appendix table 12.6).

Appendix table 12.8.   *Households without standard amenities, England and Wales, 1960*

	Unfit and short-life dwellings[a]	Fit dwellings	All dwellings
Percentage of housing stock in each category	13	87	100
Percentage of dwellings in stated category lacking:			
Sole use of w.c.	52	16	21
bath	72	21	28
fitted wash basin	79	29	35
3-point hot water system	82	33	40
ventilated food store	..	..	33
At least one of the first four amenities listed above[b]	85	34	41

Source: P. G. Gray and R. Russell, *The Housing Situation in 1960, op. cit.*

[a]Dwellings already unfit or likely to become so within 15 years.
[b]The five basic amenities listed above are those eligible for standard grants. In considering the houses lacking at least one amenity the food store has been omitted, as with increased ownership of refrigerators this is not always in demand.

Appendix table 12.9.   *Improvement programme, 1960–75*

Thousand dwelling units

	Demolition period	Programme co-ordinated to new building programme	
		Lower estimate	Upper estimate
Estimated life expectancy of houses needing improvement in 1960[a]			
0–10 years	1961–70	1,240	1,370
10–15 years	1971–5	1,070	1,320
15–20 years	1976–80	1,150	1,550
20+ years	1981 onwards	2,040	1,360
Total		5,500	5,500
Demolished 1961–75			
Before improvement		2,260	2,620
After improvement		50	70
Improved 1961–75		1,870	1,410
Balance in 1975		1,370	1,570
of which life expectancy[b]:			
0–5 years	1976–80	860	1,160
5+ years	1981 onwards	510	410

Source: NIESR estimates.

[a]Assumes that 85 per cent of houses to be demolished are drawn from the 5·5 million awaiting replacement or improvement.

[b]Assumes that improvements in the period 1961–75 will cover the following proportions of the 1960 stock: dwellings due for demolition before 1975, 5 per cent; those due for demolition 1976–80, 25 per cent; those expected to continue after 1980, 75 per cent in the lower estimate and 70 per cent in the upper estimate.

Appendix table 12.10. *The cost and effect of alternative rates of general subsidy*

	Period of annual payments	Effective subsidy on new houses as per cent of construction cost[a]		
		15	20	25
Annual payments as per cent of construction cost[a]	20	*1·41*	*1·88*	*2·35*
	15	*1·71*	*2·28*	*2·85*
	10	*2·31*	*3·08*	*3·85*
Reduction in total annual cost (percentages)[b]				
New houses	20			
	15	*12*	*16*	*20*
	10			
Existing houses				
5 years old	20	*8·2*	*11·0*	*13·8*
	15	*7·5*	*10·0*	*12·5*
	10	*5·8*	*7·8*	*9·0*
10 years old	20	*4·6*	*6·2*	*7·8*
	15	*3·2*	*4·2*	*5·4*
	10	—	—	—
15 years old	20	*2·0*	*2·6*	*3·4*
	15	—	—	—
	10	—	—	—
Total annual cost (£1960 million)[c]				
1965	20	113	151	189
	15	123	163	204
	10	120	160	200
1970	20	146	194	243
	15	145	193	241
	10	149	198	248
1975	20	171	228	285
	15	174	232	291
	10	172	229	286
1980	20	200	266	333
	15	197	263	329
	10	192	256	321

Source: NIESR estimates.

[a]The annual payments necessary to reduce the original cost by a given amount are calculated as an annuity with interest at 6 per cent, of given total value at the time of construction, e.g. £200 would buy an annuity of £18·8 for 20 years or £30·8 for 10 years. The latter payments would be necessary, therefore, to give an effective subsidy of 20 per cent on a house costing £1,000 to build.

[b]Assuming that site costs are 20 per cent of total value, the reduction in annual costs shown are those obtained if interest and amortization (net of subsidy) are spread evenly over the whole period of repayment. The reductions are applicable, therefore, to the whole repayment period, not merely to the period of subsidy payments.

[c]At the 1960 general price level but assuming (for the calculation of payments on existing houses) a price rise of 1 per cent a year. It is also assumed that 85 per cent of new residential building over the period 1945–55 and 80 per cent of later construction is eligible for subsidy.

Appendix table 14.1. *Differences in expenditure per pupil among local education authorities in England and Wales, 1960–1*

Primary schools			Secondary schools		
Expenditure per pupil £	Number of authorities	Percentage distribution	Expenditure per pupil £	Number of authorities	Percentage distribution
40–	8	5·6	68–	8	5·6
44–	31	21·5	72–	9	6·2
48–	51	35·4	76–	23	16·0
52–	31	21·5	80–	25	17·4
56–	13	9·0	84–	25	17·4
60–	3	2·1	88–	27	18·7
64 and over	7	4·9	92 and over	27	18·7
Total	144	100·0	Total	144	100·0

Source: Institute of Municipal Treasurers and Accountants, and Society of County Treasurers, *Education Statistics 1960–61* (London, 1962).

Appendix table 14.2. *The incidence of oversize classes among different local education authorities in England and Wales, 1960[a]*

Junior classes of over 40			Senior classes of over 30		
Percentage of oversize classes	Number of authorities	Percentage distribution	Percentage of oversize classes	Number of authorities	Percentage distribution
1–	51	35·7	31–	14	9·6
11–	53	37·0	41–	41	28·3
21–	29	20·3	51–	70	48·3
31–	8	5·6	61–	16	11·0
41 and over	2	1·4	71 and over	4	2·8
Total	143	100·0	Total	145	100·0

Source: Ministry of Education, *List 71: Selected Statistics Relating to Local Education Authorities in England and Wales, 1960.*

[a]The percentages of oversize classes for England and Wales as a whole were 16·0 per cent for juniors and 53·5 per cent for seniors in 1960 and had improved to 13·9 and 47·3 per cent respectively in 1962.

Appendix table 14.3. United Kingdom population aged 0–14, 1960–75[a]

January ('000s)

	1960	1961	1962	1963	1964	1965	1966	1967	1968	1969	1970	1971	1972	1973	1974	1975
0	862	902	922	959	980	990	997	1,014	1,035	1,055	1,075	1,090	1,097	1,100	1,102	1,100
1	851	858	899	919	956	976	986	993	1,011	1,031	1,052	1,071	1,086	1,093	1,098	1,099
2	826	848	856	896	918	954	975	983	991	1,009	1,028	1,051	1,069	1,083	1,090	1,096
3	798	825	845	857	895	916	952	973	981	989	1,008	1,027	1,048	1,068	1,081	1,088
4	761	795	822	846	856	894	916	952	973	982	989	1,006	1,027	1,048	1,067	1,078
5	763	759	794	823	846	856	893	916	952	973	982	988	1,006	1,027	1,048	1,068
6	768	762	757	794	823	846	857	893	915	952	972	981	987	1,005	1,027	1,048
7	754	770	762	758	794	822	848	857	893	915	952	975	979	988	1,005	1,027
8	755	754	767	763	758	796	824	847	857	893	915	953	974	980	988	1,006
9	773	756	754	769	764	758	795	823	846	857	893	914	953	973	981	990
10	806	772	753	755	769	765	759	794	822	846	856	891	914	952	972	980
11	851	805	770	756	756	770	764	759	794	820	846	856	891	915	952	972
12	955	850	806	772	757	755	769	765	758	794	821	846	857	891	915	952
13	883	954	848	808	774	757	756	770	764	756	794	821	845	857	892	915
14	731	882	953	851	809	775	758	757	770	764	756	794	820	845	857	892
Total	12,137	12,292	12,308	12,326	12,455	12,630	12,849	13,096	13,362	13,636	13,939	14,264	14,553	14,825	15,075	15,311
0–4	4,098	4,228	4,344	4,477	4,605	4,730	4,826	4,915	4,991	5,066	5,152	5,245	5,327	5,392	5,438	5,461
5–10	4,619	4,573	4,587	4,662	4,754	4,843	4,976	5,130	5,285	5,436	5,570	5,702	5,813	5,925	6,021	6,119
11–14	3,420	3,491	3,377	3,187	3,096	3,057	3,047	3,051	3,086	3,134	3,217	3,317	3,413	3,508	3,616	3,731

[a]The figures in this table and the three following tables differ from those in the population tables in Appendix 3 because these are January figures, whereas those in Appendix 3 are mid-year.

Appendix table 14.4. *England and Wales population aged 0–14, 1960–75*

January ('000s)

	1960	1961	1962	1963	1964	1965	1966	1967	1968	1969	1970	1971	1972	1973	1974	1975
0	736	772	792	824	843	850	857	874	892	911	929	944	951	954	954	950
1	726	734	770	790	822	841	848	855	872	890	909	927	942	949	952	952
2	705	724	733	769	789	821	840	847	854	871	889	908	926	941	948	951
3	680	705	723	734	769	789	821	839	846	853	870	888	907	925	940	947
4	646	679	704	725	734	769	789	821	839	846	853	870	888	907	925	940
5	650	646	679	706	725	734	770	789	821	839	846	853	870	888	907	925
6	657	650	645	681	706	725	735	770	789	821	839	846	853	870	888	907
7	645	659	650	647	681	706	727	736	770	789	822	841	846	854	870	889
8	647	646	658	652	647	682	708	727	736	770	790	823	841	847	855	872
9	663	647	645	660	652	648	683	708	727	736	771	790	823	841	848	857
10	692	663	647	647	660	653	649	683	708	727	736	771	790	823	841	848
11	733	692	663	650	648	661	654	649	683	708	727	736	771	791	823	841
12	829	733	693	666	651	648	662	655	650	684	709	728	737	771	791	823
13	766	829	733	695	667	652	649	663	655	650	684	709	728	737	772	791
14	628	767	829	736	696	668	653	650	663	655	650	684	709	728	737	772
Total	10,403	10,546	10,564	10,582	10,690	10,847	11,045	11,266	11,505	11,750	12,024	12,318	12,582	12,826	13,051	13,265
0–4	3,493	3,614	3,722	3,842	3,957	4,070	4,155	4,236	4,303	4,371	4,450	4,537	4,614	4,676	4,719	4,740
5–10	3,954	3,911	3,924	3,993	4,071	4,148	4,272	4,413	4,551	4,682	4,804	4,924	5,023	5,123	5,209	5,298
11–14	2,956	3,021	2,918	2,747	2,662	2,629	2,618	2,617	2,651	2,697	2,770	2,857	2,945	3,027	3,123	3,227

Appendix table 14.5.   *United Kingdom population aged 15–24, 1960–75*

January ('000s)

	1960	1961	1962	1963	1964	1965	1966	1967	1968	1969	1970	1971	1972	1973	1974	1975
Males																
15	407	373	449	489	438	415	397	387	387	396	392	387	407	421	434	439
16	375	407	374	451	490	437	416	397	387	387	397	393	388	408	422	435
17	358	376	409	376	452	489	438	415	396	387	387	397	392	388	407	422
18	322	360	378	411	376	453	489	438	415	397	388	387	397	393	388	408
19	327	325	362	381	412	376	453	489	438	415	397	389	388	398	392	388
20	337	329	328	365	382	413	377	453	489	438	416	397	388	389	398	393
21	345	343	335	332	367	382	414	378	455	491	439	417	397	388	388	397
22	344	349	351	340	335	368	383	415	380	457	492	441	416	397	388	388
23	342	349	359	356	346	335	369	383	416	381	457	493	441	416	397	388
24	340	348	361	366	363	348	336	371	385	417	382	458	493	440	417	397
15–18	1,462	1,516	1,610	1,727	1,756	1,794	1,740	1,637	1,585	1,567	1,564	1,564	1,584	1,610	1,651	1,704
19–24	2,037	2,043	2,096	2,140	2,205	2,222	2,332	2,489	2,563	2,599	2,582	2,595	2,523	2,428	2,380	2,351
15–24	3,499	3,559	3,706	3,867	3,961	4,016	4,072	4,126	4,148	4,166	4,146	4,159	4,107	4,038	4,031	4,055
Females																
15	389	358	432	467	416	395	379	370	369	374	372	368	387	399	411	416
16	361	391	358	433	467	417	394	378	369	369	374	371	368	388	400	412
17	345	362	393	359	433	468	416	393	378	369	369	375	372	368	388	399
18	313	349	364	394	360	434	467	416	394	379	370	369	375	371	368	387
19	321	318	352	365	395	361	433	466	417	394	380	371	370	376	372	369
20	334	324	321	354	367	396	361	433	467	417	397	379	371	370	375	373
21	337	335	327	323	355	367	395	361	435	468	419	396	379	371	369	374
22	335	340	339	330	324	355	368	396	362	436	470	419	397	379	371	370
23	333	338	343	341	330	325	355	370	397	364	436	470	420	398	380	372
24	331	335	342	345	342	329	325	356	371	398	364	436	470	420	398	381
15–18	1,408	1,460	1,549	1,653	1,676	1,714	1,656	1,557	1,510	1,491	1,485	1,483	1,502	1,526	1,567	1,614
19–24	1,991	1,990	2,024	2,058	2,113	2,133	2,237	2,382	2,447	2,477	2,464	2,471	2,407	2,314	2,265	2,239
15–24	3,399	3,450	3,573	3,711	3,789	3,847	3,893	3,939	3,959	3,968	3,949	3,954	3,909	3,840	3,832	3,853

Appendix table 14.6. *England and Wales population aged 15–24, 1960–75*

January ('000s)

		1960	1961	1962	1963	1964	1965	1966	1967	1968	1969	1970	1971	1972	1973	1974	1975
Males	15	355	321	392	426	378	357	343	335	333	341	336	334	351	365	374	379
	16	323	355	322	394	427	378	358	343	335	333	342	337	335	352	366	375
	17	308	325	357	324	395	427	379	358	343	335	334	342	337	335	352	366
	18	273	310	327	360	325	396	428	379	359	344	336	334	342	338	336	353
	19	278	276	313	330	361	326	397	429	380	359	344	337	335	843	338	336
	20	290	280	280	317	332	363	328	398	429	381	360	345	337	336	344	339
	21	297	294	288	285	320	333	364	329	400	431	383	362	346	337	336	344
	22	297	303	305	295	290	322	335	365	331	402	433	385	362	347	337	337
	23	296	304	315	312	302	291	324	336	367	333	403	435	386	363	348	338
	24	295	304	318	323	320	304	292	325	338	370	335	405	435	386	364	348
	15–18	1,259	1,311	1,398	1,504	1,525	1,558	1,508	1,415	1,370	1,353	1,348	1,347	1,365	1,390	1,428	1,473
	19–24	1,753	1,761	1,819	1,862	1,925	1,939	2,040	2,182	2,245	2,276	2,258	2,269	2,201	2,112	2,067	2,042
	15–24	3,012	3,072	3,217	3,366	3,450	3,497	3,548	3,597	3,615	3,629	3,606	3,616	3,566	3,502	3,495	3,515
Females	15	338	307	375	406	359	340	326	318	317	322	319	316	333	344	354	359
	16	310	340	309	376	406	360	340	326	318	317	322	319	316	334	345	355
	17	296	312	342	309	376	407	360	340	326	318	317	323	320	317	334	345
	18	266	301	315	343	310	377	408	361	341	327	319	318	323	320	317	334
	19	274	272	305	317	344	311	378	408	362	341	328	320	319	324	321	318
	20	286	278	276	307	319	346	313	379	409	362	342	328	320	319	324	322
	21	290	289	282	278	308	319	346	314	381	410	364	344	328	320	319	324
	22	289	294	294	285	280	308	320	347	315	382	412	365	345	329	321	320
	23	288	293	298	297	286	281	309	322	348	317	383	413	366	346	330	323
	24	287	291	298	301	298	286	282	310	323	349	318	385	414	366	347	332
	15–18	1,210	1,260	1,341	1,434	1,451	1,484	1,434	1,345	1,302	1,284	1,277	1,276	1,292	1,315	1,350	1,393
	19–24	1,714	1,717	1,753	1,785	1,835	1,851	1,948	2,080	2,138	2,161	2,147	2,155	2,092	2,004	1,962	1,939
	15–24	2,924	2,977	3,094	3,219	3,286	3,335	3,382	3,425	3,440	3,445	3,424	3,431	3,384	3,319	3,312	3,332

LIST OF WORKS CITED

I. BOOKS, ARTICLES AND SERIAL PUBLICATIONS

ABEL-SMITH, B. *A History of the Nursing Profession* (London, Heinemann, 1960).

ABEL-SMITH, B. and GALES, K. *British Doctors at Home and Abroad* (Welwyn, Herts, Codicote Press, 1964).

ABEL-SMITH, B. and TITMUSS, R. M. *The Cost of the National Health Service in England and Wales*, National Institute of Economic and Social Research, Occasional Papers 18 (Cambridge, University Press, 1956).

ARROW, K. J. and HOFFENBERG, M. *A Time Series Analysis of Interindustry Demands* (Amsterdam, North-Holland Publishing Co., 1959).

ASHTON, A. S. 'Oil, Finance and the Future', *Esso Magazine*, Summer 1962, p. 2.

ASSOCIATION OF TEACHERS IN COLLEGES AND DEPARTMENTS OF EDUCATION. Annual Registration Survey (London).

AUKRUST, O. 'Investment and Economic Growth', *Productivity Measurement Review*, no. 16, February 1959, p. 35.

BALASSA, B. 'Trade Projections and Economic Model-Building', in *The United States Balance of Payments*, Joint Economic Committee, 88th Congress, 1st Session, 1963, p. 577.

BALOGH, T. *Unequal Partners* (Oxford, Blackwell, 1963).

BANNOCK, G. 'Productivity in Manufacturing, Pre-war to 1960', *Productivity Measurement Review*, no. 31, November 1962, p. 5.

BARNA, T. 'Du Capital Envisagé comme une Variable Economique', in Centre National de la Recherche Scientifique, *Cahiers du Séminaire d'Econométrie, no. 5: Production, Investissements et Productivité* (Paris, 1959).

BARNA, T. 'Export Growth Retarded by Technical Backwardness: Britain compared with US and Germany', *The Times*, 3 April 1963, p. 19.

BARNA, T. *Investment and Growth Policies in British Industrial Firms*, National Institute of Economic and Social Research, Occasional Papers 20 (Cambridge, University Press, 1962).

BARNA, T. 'The Replacement Cost of Fixed Assets in British Manufacturing Industry in 1955', *Journal of the Royal Statistical Society*, Series A, vol. 120, part 1, 1957, p. 1.

BARNA, T. 'Some Contrasts in Export Performance: the Key Role of Management', *The Times*, 1 February 1961, p. 16.

BECKERMAN, W. 'Projecting Europe's Growth', *Economic Journal*, vol. 72, no. 288, December 1962, p. 912.

BECKERMAN, W. and SUTHERLAND, J. 'Married Women at Work in 1972', *National Institute Economic Review*, no. 23, February 1963, p. 56.

BEECHING, R. 'The Rationalisation of Transport', *Institute of Transport Journal*, vol. 30, no. 9, March 1964, p. 316.

BILLINGTON, N. S. 'The Heating and Air-Conditioning Industry', *National Provincial Bank Review*, no. 64, November 1963, p. 10.

BOLTZ, C. L. 'How to Keep a Stock of Electricity', *The Financial Times*, 24 July 1963, p. 13.

BRAZER, H. E. and DAVID, M. 'Social and Economic Determinants of the Demand for Education', in *The Economics of Higher Education*, ed. S. Mushkin, US Department of Health, Education and Welfare (Washington, Government Printing Office, 1962).

BRECH, R. *Britain 1984: Unilever's Forecast* (London, Darton, Longman and Todd, 1963).

BRITISH ELECTRICAL AND ALLIED MANUFACTURERS' ASSOCIATION. *Statistical Review of Domestic Electrical Appliances* (London, quarterly).

BRITISH PETROLEUM COMPANY. *Statistical Review of the World Oil Industry* (London, annual).

BRONFENBRENNER, M. and DOUGLAS, P. H. 'Cross-Section Studies in the Cobb-Douglas Function', *Journal of Political Economy*, vol. 47, no. 6, December 1939, p. 761.

BROWN, E. H. PHELPS. 'The Meaning of the Fitted Cobb-Douglas Function', *Quarterly Journal of Economics*, vol. 71, no. 4, November 1957, p. 546.

BROWNE, G. W. G. 'The Production Function for South African Manufacturing Industry', *South African Journal of Economics*, vol. 11, no. 4, December 1943, p. 258.

BROWNLIE, A. D. 'Some Aspects of the Measurement of Aggregate Productivity with Special Reference to New Zealand Manufacturing', *Productivity Measurement Review*, no. 32, February 1963, p. 5.

BUTLER, N. R. and BONHAM, D. G. *Perinatal Mortality* (Edinburgh, Livingstone, 1963).

CAIRNCROSS, A. K. *Factors in Economic Development* (London, Allen and Unwin, 1962).

CAMBRIDGE UNIVERSITY. DEPARTMENT OF APPLIED ECONOMICS. *A Programme for Growth, 1: A Computable Model of Economic Growth* (London, Chapman and Hall, 1962); *2: A Social Accounting Matrix for 1960* (1962); *3: Input-Output Relationships, 1954–1966* (1963); *4: Capital, Output and Employment, 1948–1960* (1964).

CAMERON, B. *The Determination of Production: an Introduction to the Study of Economizing Activity* (Cambridge, University Press, 1954).

CARR-SAUNDERS, A. M., JONES, D. CARADOG and MOSER, C. A. *A Survey of Social Conditions in England and Wales as Illustrated by Statistics* (Oxford, Clarendon Press, 1958).

CARTER, C. O. 'A Life Table for Mongols with Causes of Death', *Journal of Mental Deficiency Research*, vol. 2, part 2, December 1958, p. 64.

CASSUTO, A. 'Atomic Energy—A Reassessment', *Moorgate and Wall Street*, Spring 1961, p. 44.

CHASE MANHATTAN BANK. *Future Growth of the World Petroleum Industry* (New York, 1961).

CLARK, F. LE GROS. *Women, Work and Age* (London, Nuffield Foundation, 1962).

CLEGG, H. 'After Burnham—What?', *Education*, vol. 121, nos. 3150 and 3151, 7 and 14 June 1963, p. 1128 and p. 1200.

COLE, D. and UTTING, J. E. G. *The Economic Circumstances of Old People* (Welwyn, Herts, Codicote Press, 1962).

COLLVER, A. and LANGLOIS, E. 'The Female Labor Force in Metropolitan Areas: an International Comparison', *Economic Development and Cultural Change*, vol. 10, no. 4, July 1962, p. 367.

CULLINGWORTH, J. B. *Housing in Transition: a Case Study in the City of Lancaster* (London, Heinemann, 1963).

DANIEL, G. H. 'Britain's Energy Prospects', 1955 Viscount Nuffield Paper, *Institution of Production Engineers Journal*, vol. 35, no. 2, February 1956, p. 76.

DAVISON, R. B. *West Indian Migrants: Social and Economic Facts of Migration from the West Indies* (Oxford, University Press, for the Institute of Race Relations, 1962).

DAWSON, R. F. F. 'Estimated Expenditure on Road Transport in Great Britain, 1960', *Journal of the Royal Statistical Society*, Series A, vol. 125, part 3, 1962, p. 462.

DEAN, G. A. 'Fixed Investment in Britain and Norway: an Experiment in International Comparison', *Journal of the Royal Statistical Society*, Series A, vol. 127, part 1, 1964, p. 89.

DEAN, G. A. 'The Stock of Fixed Capital in the United Kingdom in 1961', *Journal of the Royal Statistical Society*, Series A, vol. 127, part 3, 1964, p. 327.

DEANE, P. and COLE, W. A. *British Economic Growth, 1688–1959* (Cambridge, University Press, 1962).

DENISON, E. F. 'Measurement of Labor Input: Some Questions of Definition and the Adequacy of Data', in National Bureau of Economic Research, *Output, Input and Productivity Measurement*, Studies in Income and Wealth 25 (Princeton, N.J., University Press, 1961).

DENISON, E. F. *The Sources of Economic Growth in the United States and the Alternatives Before Us* (Washington, Committee for Economic Development, 1962).

WORKS CITED 603

WORKS CITED 603

DEUTSCHES INSTITUT FÜR WIRTSCHAFTSFORSCHUNG. *Produktionsvolumen und Produktionsfaktoren der Industrie im Gebiet der Bundesrepublik Deutschland: Statistische Kennziffern 1950 bis 1958*, and . . . *1959 bis 1960/61* (Berlin, 1960 and 1962).

DEWHURST, J. F. and others. *Europe's Needs and Resources: Trends and Prospects in Eighteen Countries*, by J. Frederic Dewhurst, John O. Coppock, P. Lamartine Yates and associates (New York, Twentieth Century Fund, 1961).

DICKS-MIREAUX, L. A. and others. 'Prospects for the British Car Industry', by L. A. Dicks-Mireaux, C. St. J. O'Herlihy, R. L. Major, F. T. Blackaby and C. Freeman, *National Institute Economic Review*, no. 17, September 1961, p. 15.

DOMAR, E. D. 'Depreciation, Replacement and Growth', *Economic Journal*, vol. 63, no. 249, March 1953, p. 1.

DOUGLAS, J. W. B. *The Home and the School: a Study of Ability and Attainment in the Primary School* (London, McGibbon and Kee, 1964).

DOUGLAS, J. W. B. and BLOMFIELD, J. M. *Children under Five* (London, Allen and Unwin, 1958).

DOW, J. C. R. *The Management of the British Economy, 1945–60*, National Institute of Economic and Social Research, Economic and Social Studies 22 (Cambridge, University Press, 1964).

DOW, J. C. R. and DICKS-MIREAUX, L. A. 'Price Stability and the Policy of Deflation', *National Institute Economic Review*, no. 3, May 1959, p. 16.

ECONOMIST INTELLIGENCE UNIT. *Studies on Immigration from the Commonwealth, 2: The Immigrant Communities* (London, 1962).

EDDING, F. *Internationale Tendenzen in der Entwicklung der Ausgaben für Schulen und Hochschulen*, Kieler Studien 47 (Kiel, Institut für Weltwirtschaft an der Universität, 1958).

EDWARDS, SIR RONALD. 'The Expansion of Electricity Supply', *National Provincial Bank Review*, no. 62, May 1963, p. 1.

EISNER, R. 'A Distributed Lag Investment Function', *Econometrica*, vol. 28, no. 1, January 1960, p. 1.

ESSO PETROLEUM COMPANY. 'A Look Ahead to 1975', *Esso Magazine*, Spring 1963, p. 2.

FARNDALE, J. 'British Day Hospitals', in *Trends in the Mental Health Services: a Symposium of Original and Reprinted Papers*, ed. H. Freeman and J. Farndale (Oxford, Pergamon Press, 1963).

FELLNER, W. and others. *The Problem of Rising Prices*, by W. Fellner, M. Gilbert, B. Hansen, R. Kahn, F. Lutz and P. de Wolff (Paris, Organisation for European Economic Co-operation, 1959).

FLORENCE, P. SARGANT. *Economics of Fatigue and Unrest and the Efficiency of Labour in English and American Industry* (London, Allen and Unwin, 1924).

FRANKEL, M. *British and American Manufacturing Productivity: a Comparison and Interpretation*, University of Illinois, Bureau of Economic and Business Research, Bulletin 81 (Urbana, Ill., 1957).

FRANKEL, M. 'The Production Function in Allocation and Growth: a Synthesis', *American Economic Review*, vol. 52, no. 5, December 1962, p. 995.

FRANKEL, P. H. and NEWTON, W. L. 'The State of the Oil Industry', *National Institute Economic Review*, no. 11, September 1960, p. 16.

GEARY, R. C., editor. *Europe's Future in Figures*, Association Scientifique Européenne pour la Prévision Economique à Moyen et à Long Terme, vol. 1 (Amsterdam, North-Holland Publishing Co., 1962).

GILBERT, M. 'Quality Changes and Index Numbers', *Economic Development and Cultural Change*, vol. 9, no. 3, April 1961, p. 287.

GILBERT, M. and associates. *Comparative National Products and Price Levels: a Study of Western Europe and the United States* (Paris, Organisation for European Economic Co-operation, 1958).

GILBERT, R. S. 'The Fall in Britain's Invisible Earnings', *National Institute Economic Review*, no. 12, November 1960, p. 45.

GILBERT, R. S. and MAJOR, R. L. 'Britain's Falling Share of Sterling Area Imports', *National Institute Economic Review*, no. 14, March 1961, p. 18.

GLANVILLE, W. H. and SMEED, R. J. 'The Basic Requirements for the Roads of Great Britain', in *Proceedings of the Conference on the Highway Needs of Great Britain, 1957* (London, Institution of Civil Engineers, 1958).

GLASS, R. *Newcomers: the West Indians in London* (London, Allen and Unwin, 1960).

GODLEY, W. A. H. and SHEPHERD, J. R. 'Long-Term Growth and Short-Term Policy', *National Institute Economic Review*, no. 29, August 1964, p. 26.

GOLDSMITH, R. W. 'The Growth of Reproducible Wealth of the United States of America from 1805 to 1950', in International Association for Research in Income and Wealth, *Income and Wealth of the United States: Trends and Structure*, Income and Wealth Series 2 (Cambridge, Bowes and Bowes, 1952).

GRAY, P. G. and RUSSELL, R. *The Housing Situation in 1960: an Inquiry Covering England and Wales*, SS 319 (London, Social Survey, 1962).

GRIFFITH, J. A. G. and others. *Coloured Immigrants in Britain*, by J. A. G. Griffith, Judith Henderson, Margaret Usborne, Donald Wood (Oxford, University Press, for the Institute of Race Relations, 1960).

HABAKKUK, H. J. *American and British Technology in the Nineteenth Century: the Search for Labour-Saving Inventions* (Cambridge, University Press, 1962).

HABAKKUK, H. J. and DEANE, P. 'The Take-off in Britain', in *The Economics of Take-off into Sustained Growth: Proceedings of a Conference held by the International Economic Association*, ed. W. W. Rostow (London, Macmillan, 1963).

HALSEY, A. H., editor. *Ability and Educational Opportunity* (Paris, Organisation for Economic Co-operation and Development, 1961).

HEMMING, M. F. W. 'The Price of Accommodation', *National Institute Economic Review*, no. 29, August 1964, p. 39.

HEMMING, M. F. W. and RAY, G. F. 'Imports and Expansion', *National Institute Economic Review*, no. 2, March 1959, p. 26.

HILHORST, J. G. M. 'Measurement of Production Functions in Manufacturing Industry', Netherlands Central Bureau of Statistics, *Statistical Studies*, no. 13, October 1962, p. 7.

HILL, T. P. 'Growth and Investment According to International Comparisons', *Economic Journal*, vol. 74, no. 294, June 1964, p. 287.

INDUSTRIAL BANK OF JAPAN. *Japanese Industries, 1964* (Tokyo, 1964).

INSTITUTE OF MUNICIPAL TREASURERS AND ACCOUNTANTS and SOCIETY OF COUNTY TREASURERS. *Children Services Statistics, 1961–62* (London, 1962).

INSTITUTE OF MUNICIPAL TREASURERS AND ACCOUNTANTS and SOCIETY OF COUNTY TREASURERS. *Education Statistics, 1960–61* (London, 1962).

ISAAC, J. *British Post-War Migration*, National Institute of Economic and Social Research, Occasional Papers 17 (Cambridge, University Press, 1954).

JACKSON, B. and MARSDEN, D. *Education and the Working Class: Some General Themes Raised by a Study of 88 Working-Class Children in a Northern Industrial City* (London, Routledge and Kegan Paul, 1962).

JASAY, A. E. 'Paying Ourselves More Money', *Westminster Bank Review*, May 1962, p. 2.

JONES, SIR HENRY. 'Gas Forges Ahead', *FBI Review*, no. 161, October 1963, p. 39.

JONES, K. 'The Role and Function of the Mental Hospital', in *Trends in the Mental Health Services: a Symposium of Original and Reprinted Papers*, ed. H. Freeman and J. Farndale (Oxford, Pergamon Press, 1963).

JONES, K., MAIZELS, A. and WHITTAKER, J. 'The Demand for Food in the Industrial Countries, 1948–1960', *National Institute Economic Review*, no. 20, May 1962, p. 40.

KALDOR, N. 'Capital Accumulation and Economic Growth', in *The Theory of Capital: Proceedings of a Conference of the International Economic Association*, ed. F. A. Lutz and D. C. Hague (London, Macmillan, 1961).

KALDOR, N. 'Increasing Returns and Technical Progress—A Comment on Professor Hicks's Article', *Oxford Economic Papers*, N.S. vol. 13, no. 1, February 1961, p. 1.

KELSALL, R. K. and MITCHELL, S. 'Married Women and Employment in England and Wales', *Population Studies*, vol. 13, no. 1, July 1959, p. 19.

KENDRICK, J. W. *Productivity Trends in the United States*, National Bureau of Economic Research, General Series 71 (Princeton, N.J., University Press, 1961).

KENEN, P. B. *British Monetary Policy and the Balance of Payments, 1951–1957* (Cambridge, Mass., Harvard University Press, 1960).

KINDLEBERGER, C. P. 'Foreign Trade and Economic Growth: Lessons from Britain and France, 1850 to 1913', *Economic History Review*, second series, vol. 14, no. 2, December 1961, p. 289.

KING, H. R. 'The Comprehensive School in England: Broadening the Field of Opportunity and Stimulating Response', *Yearbook of Education, 1962*, p. 192.

KLEIN, V. *Employing Married Women* (London, Institute of Personnel Management, 1961).

KLEIN, V. *Working Wives: a Survey of Facts and Opinions Concerning the Gainful Employment of Married Women in Britain* (London, Institute of Personnel Management, 1959).

KNAPP, J. and LOMAX, K. 'Britain's Growth Performance: the Enigma of the 1950s', *Lloyds Bank Review*, no. 74, October 1964, p. 1.

LAMFALUSSY A. 'Contribution à une Théorie de la Croissance en Economie Ouverte', *Recherches Economiques de Louvain*, vol. 29, no. 8, December 1963, p. 715.

LAMFALUSSY, A. *The United Kingdom and the Six: an Essay on Economic Growth in Western Europe* (London, Macmillan, 1963).

LAUWERYS, J. A. and VAIZEY, J. *Supply, Recruitment and Training of Science and Mathematics Teachers* (Paris, Organisation for Economic Co-operation and Development, 1962).

LESER, C. E. V. 'Commodity Group Expenditure Functions for the United Kingdom, 1948–1957', *Econometrica*, vol. 29, no. 1, January 1961, p. 24.

LESER, C. E. V. 'The Supply of Women for Gainful Work in Britain', *Population Studies*, vol. 9, no. 2, November 1955, p. 142.

LESER, C. E. V. 'Trends in Women's Work Particpation', *Population Studies*, vol. 12, no. 2, November 1958, p. 100.

LESTER-SMITH, W. O. *Compulsory Education in England* (Paris, UNESCO, 1951).

LEWIS, W. A. 'International Competition in Manufactures', *American Economic Review*, vol. 47, no. 2, May 1957, p. 578.

LLOYD'S REGISTER OF SHIPPING. *Statistical Tables* (London, annual).

LONDON AND CAMBRIDGE ECONOMIC SERVICE. *Key Statistics of the British Economy, 1900–1962* (London, Times Publishing Co., 1963).

LONDON COUNTY COUNCIL. *London Comprehensive Schools: a Survey of Sixteen Schools* (London, 1961).

LONDON TRANSPORT. *London Transport* (London, annual).

LONG, C. D. *The Labor Force under Changing Income and Employment*, National Bureau of Economic Research, General Series 65 (Princeton, N.J., University Press, 1958).

McCLELLAND, W. G. *Studies in Retailing* (Oxford, Blackwell, 1963).

McGIBBON, J. 'The Statistical Comparability of Rates of Growth of Gross National Product', *Productivity Measurement Review*, no. 36, February 1964, p. 5.

McVEY, G. L. 'Policy for Fuel', *Political Quarterly*, vol. 35, no. 1, January-March 1964, p. 46.

MADDISON, A. *Economic Growth in the West: Comparative Experience in Europe and North America* (New York, Twentieth Century Fund, 1964: London, Allen and Unwin).

MADDISON, A. 'Economic Growth in Western Europe, 1870–1957', *Banca Nazionale del Lavoro Quarterly Review*, no. 48, March 1959, p. 58.

MAIZELS, A. *Industrial Growth and World Trade: an Empirical Study of Trends in Production, Consumption and Trade in Manufactures from 1899–1959, with a Discussion of Probable Future Trends*, National Institute of Economic and Social Research, Economic and Social Studies 21 (Cambridge, University Press, 1963).

MAIZELS, A. 'Trade and Development Problems of the Under-developed Countries: the Background to the United Nations' Conference', *National Institute Economic Review*, no. 28, May 1964, p. 24.

MAJOR, R. L. 'World Trade in Manufactures', *National Institute Economic Review*, no. 10, July 1960, p. 18.

MASON, S. C. *The Leicestershire Experiment and Plan*, rev. ed. (London, Councils and Education Press, 1963).

MEDICAL SERVICES REVIEW COMMITTEE (Porritt Committee). *A Review of the Medical Services in Great Britain* (London, Social Assay, 1962).

MELLING, C. T. *Long-Term Planning for Electricity Supply* (London, Electricity Council, 1963).

MENDERSHAUSEN, H. 'On the Significance of Douglas' Production Function', *Econometrica*, vol. 6, no. 2, April 1938, p. 143.

MEYER, J. R. and KUH, E. *The Investment Decision: an Empirical Study* (Cambridge, Mass., Harvard University Press, 1957).

MITCHELL, B. R. and DEANE, P. *Abstract of British Historical Statistics* (Cambridge, University Press, 1962).

MORGENSTERN, O. *On the Accuracy of Economic Observations*, 2nd ed. (Princeton, N.J., University Press, 1963).

MORGENSTERN, O. 'Qui numerare incipit errare incipit', *Fortune*, vol. 68, no. 4, October 1963, p. 142.

MOSER, C. A. and SCOTT, W. *British Towns: a Statistical Study of Their Social and Economic Differences* (Edinburgh, Oliver and Boyd, 1961).

MUNBY, D. L. 'The Reshaping of British Railways', *Journal of Industrial Economics*, vol. 11, no. 3, July 1963, p. 161.

NATIONAL INDUSTRIAL FUEL EFFICIENCY SERVICE. *Progress Survey with Report and Accounts* (London, annual).

NATIONAL INSTITUTE OF ECONOMIC AND SOCIAL RESEARCH. 'Fast and Slow-Growing Products in World Trade', *National Institute Economic Review*, no. 25, August 1963, p. 22.

NATIONAL INSTITUTE OF ECONOMIC AND SOCIAL RESEARCH. 'Policies for Faster Growth', *National Institute Economic Review*, no. 19, February 1962, p. 55.

NATIONAL MANPOWER COUNCIL. *Womanpower* (New York, Columbia University Press, 1957).

NATIONAL UNION OF TEACHERS. *The State of Our Schools: a Report of the Findings of the National Survey of Schools, 1962* (London, 1963).

NEEDLEMAN, L. 'The Demand for Domestic Appliances', *National Institute Economic Review*, no. 12, November 1960, p. 24.

NEEDLEMAN, L. 'A Long Term View of Housing', *National Institute Economic Review*, no. 18, November 1961, p. 191.

NEILD, R. R. *Pricing and Employment in the Trade Cycle: a Study of British Manufacturing Industry, 1950–61*, National Institute of Economic and Social Research, Occasional Papers 21 (Cambridge, University Press, 1963).

NEWELL, D. J. 'Statistical Aspects of the Demand for Maternity Beds', *Journal of the Royal Statistical Society*, Series A, vol. 127, part 1, 1964, p. 1.

NEWTON, W. L. 'The Long Term Development of the Tanker Freight Market, *Journal of the Institute of Petroleum*, vol. 50, no. 489, September 1964, p. 209.

OXFORD UNIVERSITY. DEPARTMENT OF EDUCATION. *Arts and Science Sides in the Sixth Form: a Report to the Gulbenkian Foundation* (Peterson Report) (Oxford, 1960).

OXFORD UNIVERSITY. INSTITUTE FOR RESEARCH IN AGRICULTURAL ECONOMICS. *United Kingdom: Projected Level of Demand, Supply and Imports of Farm Products in 1965 and 1975*, ERS-Foreign-19 (Washington, US Department of Agriculture, 1962).

PAIGE, D. C. 'Births and Maternity Beds in England Wales in 1970', *National Institute Economic Review*, no. 22, November 1962, p. 22.

PAIGE, D. C., BLACKABY, F. T. and FREUND, S. 'Economic Growth: the Last Hundred Years', *National Institute Economic Review*, no. 16, July 1961, p. 24.

PAIGE, D. C. and JONES, K. Occasional paper of the National Institute of Economic and Social Research (in preparation).

PAISH, F. W. *Studies in an Inflationary Economy: the United Kingdom, 1948–1961* (London, Macmillan, 1962).

PEACOCK, A. T. and WISEMAN, J. *The Growth of Public Expenditure in the United Kingdom*, National Bureau of Economic Research, General Series 72 (Princeton, N.J., University Press, 1961).

PEDLEY, R. *The Comprehensive School* (Harmondsworth, Penguin, 1963).

PEERS, R. *Fact and Possibility in English Education* (London, Routledge and Kegan Paul, 1963).

PEP (Political and Economic Planning). 'Housing Associations', *Planning*, vol. 28, no. 462, May 1962.

PETROLEUM PRESS SERVICE. 'Energy Patterns in a Changing World', *Petroleum Press Service*, vol. 29, no. 11, November 1962, p. 404.

PETROLEUM PRESS SERVICE. 'Forty Years On', *Petroleum Press Service*, vol. 30, no. 12, December 1963, p. 447.

PETROLEUM PRESS SERVICE. 'Peering into the Seventies', *Petroleum Press Service*, vol. 29, no. 7, July 1962, p. 243.

PRAIS, S. J. and HOUTHAKKER, H. S. *The Analysis of Family Budgets, with an Application to Two British Surveys Conducted in 1937–9 and Their Detailed Results* (Cambridge, University Press, 1955).

PREST, A. R. and ADAMS, A. A. *Consumers' Expenditure in the United Kingdom, 1900–1919* (Cambridge, University Press, 1954).

RAY G. F. 'Transport: Notes and Comments', *National Institute Economic Review*, no. 24, May 1963, p. 23.

RAY, G. F. and BLACKABY, F. T. 'Energy and Expansion', *National Institute Economic Review*, no. 11, September 1960, p. 26.

REDDAWAY, W. B. and SMITH, A. D. 'Progress in British Manufacturing Industries in the Period 1948–54', *Economic Journal*, vol. 70, no. 277, March 1960, p. 17.

REDFERN, P. 'Net Investment in Fixed Assets in the United Kingdom, 1938–1953', *Journal of the Royal Statistical Society*, Series A, vol. 118, part 2, 1955, p. 141.

REVANS, R. W. 'The Morale and Effectiveness of General Hospitals', in *Problems and Progress in Medical Care*, ed. G. McLachlan (London, Oxford University Press, for the Nuffield Provincial Hospitals Trust, 1964).

REVIEW OF ECONOMIC STUDIES. 'Symposium on Production Functions and Economic Growth', *Review of Economic Studies*, vol. 29(3), no. 80, June 1962, p. 155 (whole issue).

ROBERTS, G. W. and MILLS, D. O. *Study of External Migration Affecting Jamaica, 1953–55*, supplement to *Social and Economic Studies*, vol. 7, no. 2 (Jamaica, Institute of Social and Economic Research, 1958).

ROSETT, R. N. 'Working Wives: an Econometric Study', in *Studies in Household Economic Behavior*, by T. F. Dernburg, R. N. Rosett and H. W. Watts (New Haven, Conn., Yale University Press, 1958).

ROWLATT, J. A. and BLACKABY, F. T. 'The Demand for Industrial Materials, 1950–57', *National Institute Economic Review*, no. 5, September 1959, p. 22.

SALANT, W. S. and others. *The United States Balance of Payments in 1968* (Washington, Brookings Institution, 1963).

SALTER, W. E. G. *Productivity and Technical Change* (Cambridge, University Press, 1960).

SCHULTZ, T. W. 'Investment in Man: an Economist's View', *Social Service Review*, vol. 33, no. 2, June 1959, p. 109.

SCHUMACHER, E. F. 'Coal', *Aspect*, no. 12, January 1964, p. 37.

SCOTT, M. FG. *A Study of United Imports*, National Institute of Economic and Social Research, Economic and Social Studies 20 (Cambridge, University Press, 1963).

SHELL TRANSPORT AND TRADING COMPANY. 'The Way Ahead', insert in *Shell Review*, 1961.

SMEED, R. J. and WARDROP, J. G. 'An Exploratory Comparison of the Advantages of Cars and Buses for Travel in Urban Areas', *Institute of Transport Journal*, vol. 30, no. 9, March 1964, p. 301.

SMITH, J. GRIEVE and MILES, T. P. 'Total Productivity of the British Iron and Steel Industry, 1950–60', in *Productivity in the Iron and Steel Industry*, Iron and Steel Institute Special Report 75 (London, 1962).

SOLOW, R. M. 'Comment', in National Bureau of Economic Research, *Output, Input and Productivity Measurement*, Studies in Income and Wealth 25 (Princeton, N.J., University Press, 1961).

SOLOW, R. M. 'Technical Change and the Aggregate Production Function', *Review of Economics and Statistics*, vol. 39, no. 3, August 1957, p. 312.

SOMERMEIJER, W. H., HILHORST, J. G. M. and WIT, J. W. W. A. 'A Method for Estimating Price and Income Elasticities from Time Series and its Application to Consumers' Expenditures in the Netherlands, 1949–1959', Netherlands Central Bureau of Statistics, *Statistical Studies*, no. 13, October 1962, p. 30.

SOUTH EAST METROPOLITAN REGIONAL HOSPITAL BOARD, NATIONAL SPASTICS SOCIETY and NATIONAL SOCIETY FOR MENTALLY HANDICAPPED CHILDREN. *The Needs of Mentally Handicapped Children* (London, 1962).

STANFORD RESEARCH INSTITUTE. *Industrial Economics Handbook* (Menlo Park, Calif., 1961).

STIGLER, G. J. *Capital and Rates of Return in Manufacturing Industries*, National Bureau of Economic Research, General Series 78 (Princeton, N.J., University Press, 1963).

STIGLER, G. J. 'Economic Problems in Measuring Changes in Productivity', in National Bureau of Economic Research, *Output, Input and Productivity Measurement*, Studies in Income and Wealth 25 (Princeton, N.J., University Press, 1961).

STONE, R. *Input-Output and National Accounts* (Paris, Organisation for European Economic Co-operation, 1961).

STONE, R. 'Linear Expenditure Systems and Demand Analysis: an Application to the Pattern of British Demand', *Economic Journal*, vol. 64, no. 255, September 1954, p. 511.

STONE, R., BROWN, A. and ROWE, D. A. 'Demand Analysis and Projections for Britain, 1900–1970: a Study in Method', in *Europe's Future Consumption*, Association Scientifique Européenne pour la Prévision Economique à Moyen et à Long Terme, vol. 2, ed. J. Sandee (Amsterdam, North-Holland Publishing Co., 1964).

STONE, R. and ROWE, D. A. 'Dynamic Demand Functions: Some Econometric Results', *Economic Journal*, vol. 68, no. 270, June 1958, p. 256.

STONE, R. and others. *The Measurement of Consumers' Expenditure and Behaviour in the United Kingdom, 1920–1938* (Cambridge, University Press, 1954).

STURMEY, S. G. *British Shipping and World Competition* (London, Athlone Press, 1962).

TAWNEY, R. H. *Equality*, 4th ed. (London, Allen and Unwin, 1952).

THOMAS, BRINLEY. *Migration and Economic Growth: a Study of Great Britain and the Atlantic Economy*, National Institute of Economic and Social Research, Economic and Social Studies 12 (Cambridge, University Press, 1954).

THOMPSON, B. and FINLAYSON, A. 'Married Women who Work in Early Motherhood', *British Journal of Sociology*, vol. 14, no. 2, June 1963, p. 150.

THOMSON, E. J. 'Productivity Change in Australian Manufacturing Industry, 1948–49 to 1954–55', *Productivity Measurement Review*, no. 28, February 1962, p. 25.

TIZARD, J. *Community Services for the Mentally Handicapped* (Oxford, University Press, 1964).

TOOTH, C. G. and BROOKE, E. M. 'Trends in the Mental Hospital Population and Their Effect on Future Planning', *The Lancet*, vol. 1, no. 7179, 1 April 1961, p. 710.

TOWNSEND, P. *The Last Refuge: a Survey of Residential Institutions and Homes for the Aged in England and Wales* (London, Routledge and Kegan Paul, 1962).

TRANSPORT HOLDING COMPANY. *Road Revenues and Costs: Memorandum to the Committee on Carriers Licensing* (Geddes Committee) (London, 1964).

UNIVERSITIES CENTRAL COUNCIL ON ADMISSIONS. *First Report, 1961–3* and *Second Report, 1963–4* (London, 1964–5).

VAIZEY, J. *The Control of Education* (London, Faber and Faber, 1963).

VAIZEY, J. *The Costs of Education* (London, Allen and Unwin, 1958).

VAIZEY, J. *The Economics of Education* (London, Faber and Faber, 1962).

VAIZEY, J. 'Primary Schools on the Continent', *New Society*, no. 14, 3 January 1963, p. 14.

VERNON, H. M. *The Shorter Working Week, with Special Reference to the Two-Shift System* (London, Routledge, 1934).

VIMONT, C. *La Population Active: Evolution Passée et Prévisions* (Paris, Presses Universitaires de France, 1960).

WANDLESS, A. M. 'The British Coal Resources', in *Economic Aspects of Fuel and Power in British Industry: Papers Presented at a Conference organized by the Manchester Joint Research Council, 5–7 November 1958* (Manchester, University Press, 1960).

WEIDE, TH. VAN DER. 'Statistics of National Wealth for Eighteen Countries', in International Association for Research in Income and Wealth', *The Measurement of National Wealth*, ed. R. Goldsmith and C. Saunders, Income and Wealth Series 8 (London, Bowes and Bowes, 1959).

WILLIAMS, J. 'Professor Douglas' Production Function', *Economic Record*, vol. 21, no. 40, June 1945, p. 55.

WINCOTT, H. 'Do the British Really Want to Grow?', *The Financial Times*, 7 January 1964, p. 10.

WORSWICK, G. D. N. and ADY, P. H., editors. *The British Economy in the nineteen-fifties* (Oxford, Clarendon Press, 1962).

II. OFFICIAL PUBLICATIONS

(1) UNITED KINGDOM

Board of Education. *Report of the Consultative Committee on the Education of the Adolescent* (Hadow Report) (London, HM Stationery Office, 1926).

Board of Trade. *Accounts Relating to Trade and Navigation of the United Kingdom* (later *Overseas Trade Accounts*) (London, HM Stationery Office, monthly).

Board of Trade. *Company Assets, Income and Finance in 1960* (London, HM Stationery Office, 1962).

Board of Trade *and* Central Statistical Office. *Input-Output Tables for the United Kingdom, 1954*, Studies in Official Statistics 8 (London, HM Stationery Office, 1961).

Board of Trade Journal (London, HM Stationery Office, weekly).

British Electricity Authority. *Report and Statement of Accounts* (London, HM Stationery Office, annual 1949–55).

British European Airways Corporation. *Annual Report and Accounts* (London, HM Stationery Office).

British Railways Board. *Annual Report and Statement of Accounts* (London, HM Stationery Office).

British Railways Board. *The Reshaping of British Railways* (Beeching Report) (London, HM Stationery Office, 1963).

British Transport Commission. *Annual Report and Accounts* (London, HM Stationery Office).

British Transport Commission. *Proposals for the Railways*, Cmd 9880 (London, HM Stationery Office, 1956).

British Transport Commission. *Modernisation and Re-equipment of British Railways* (London, 1955).

British Transport Commission. *Re-appraisal of the Plan for the Modernisation and Re-equipment of British Railways*, Cmnd 813 (London, HM Stationery Office, 1959).

Cabinet Office. Committee on Higher Education. *Higher Education* (Robbins Report), Cmnd 2154 and *Appendices 1–5*, Cmnd 2154–I to Cmnd 2154–V (London, HM Stationery Office, 1963–4).

Central Statistical Office. *Annual Abstract of Statistics* (London, HM Stationery Office).

Central Statistical Office. *Economic Trends* (London, HM Stationery Office, monthly).

RR

Central Statistical Office. *Monthly Digest of Statistics* (London, HM Stationery Office).

Central Statistical Office. *National Income and Expenditure* (London, HM Stationery Office, annual).

Central Statistical Office. *National Income Statistics: Sources and Methods* (London, HM Stationery Office, 1956).

Central Statistical Office. *United Kingdom Balance of Payments* (London, HM Stationery Office, annual).

HM Customs and Excise. *Annual Statement of the Trade of the United Kingdom with Commonwealth Countries and Foreign Countries* (London, HM Stationery Office).

Department of Education and Science (*formerly* Ministry of Education). *The Health of the School Child: Report of the Chief Medical Officer* (London, HM Stationery Office, biennial).

Department of Education and Science. *Statistics of Education* (London, HM Stationery Office, annual).

Department of Scientific and Industrial Research. *Woman, Wife and Worker*, Problems of Progress in Industry 10 (London, HM Stationery Office, 1960).

Electricity Council. *Annual Report and Accounts* (London, HM Stationery Office).

Electricity Council. *Finance for More Power* (London, 1963).

Electricity Council. *Statistical Digest* (London, annual).

Foreign Office. *Cereals: Exchange of Letters and Notes . . . Regarding the Changes which the Government of the United Kingdom Propose to Introduce in Their Production and Trade Policies Relating to Cereals*, Miscellaneous no. 10, Treaty Series no. 28 and Miscellaneous no. 16, Cmnd 2339, 2383 and 2404 (London, HM Stationery Office, 1964).

Gas Council. *Annual Report and Accounts* (London, HM Stationery Office).

General Register Office. *Census 1951, England and Wales: Housing Report* (London, HM Stationery Office, 1956).

General Register Office. *The Registrar General's Statistical Review of England and Wales* (London, HM Stationery Office, annual).

General Register Office. *The Registrar General's Statistical Review of England and Wales for the year 1959: Supplement on Mental Health* (London, HM Stationery Office, 1962).

General Register Office *and* General Registry Office, Scotland. *Census 1951, Great Britain: One Per Cent Sample Tables* (London, HM Stationery Office, 1952).

General Register Office *and* General Registry Office, Scotland. *Census 1961, Great Britain: Scientific and Technological Qualifications* (London, HM Stationery Office, 1962).

House of Commons. *Tenth Report from the Estimates Committee . . . Session 1962–63: Military Expenditure Overseas* and *Ninth Report from the Estimates Committee . . . Session 1963–64: Military Expenditure Overseas* (London, HM Stationery Office, 1963–4).

House of Commons. *Report from the Select Committee on Nationalised Industries: the Electricity Supply Industry, vol. I, Report and Proceedings* (London, HM Stationery Office, 1963).

House of Commons. *Report from the Select Committee on Nationalised Industries: the Gas Industry* (London, HM Stationery Office, 1961).

Iron and Steel Board. *Development in the Iron and Steel Industry: Special Report, 1957* (London, HM Stationery Office, 1957).

Iron and Steel Board. *Development in the Iron and Steel Industry: Special Report, 1961* (London, HM Stationery Office, 1961).

Iron and Steel Board. *Development in the Iron and Steel Industry: Special Report, 1964* (London, HM Stationery Office, 1964).

Iron and Steel Board. *Development of the Iron and Steel Industry, 1953 to 1958* (London, HM Stationery Office, 1955).

Ministry of Agriculture, Fisheries and Food. *Domestic Food Consumption and Expenditure* (London, HM Stationery Office, annual).

Ministry of Defence. *Statement on Defence, 1962: the Next Five Years*, Cmnd 1639 (London, HM Stationery Office, 1962).

Ministry of Education. *The Demand and Supply of Teachers, 1960–1980: Seventh Report of the National Advisory Council on the Training and Supply of Teachers* (London, HM Stationery Office, 1962).

Ministry of Education. *15 to 18: a Report of the Central Advisory Council for Education (England)* (Crowther Report) (London, HM Stationery Office, 1959–60).

Ministry of Education. *Half Our Future: a Report of the Central Advisory Council for Education (England)* (Newsom Report) (London, HM Stationery Office, 1963).

Ministry of Education. *List 71: Selected Statistics Relating to Local Education Authorities in England and Wales, 1960* (London, HM Stationery Office, 1962).

Ministry of Education. *Women and Teaching: Report on an Independent Nuffield Survey following-up a large National Sample of Women who Entered Teaching in England and Wales at Various Dates Pre-War and Post-War*, by R. K. Kelsall (London, HM Stationery Office, 1963).

Ministry of Health. *Health and Welfare: the Development of Community Care*, Cmnd 1973 (London, HM Stationery Office, 1963).

Ministry of Health. *Hospital Building, England and Wales: Progress Report* (London, HM Stationery Office, irreg.).

Ministry of Health. *A Hospital Plan for England and Wales*, Cmnd 1604 (London, HM Stationery Office, 1962); . . . *Revision to 1972–73* (1963); . . . *Revision to 1973–74* (1964).

Ministry of Health. *On the State of the Public Health: the Annual Report of the Chief Medical Officer of Health* (London, HM Stationery Office).

Ministry of Health. *Report* (London, HM Stationery Office, annual).

Ministry of Health *and* Department of Health for Scotland. *Interim Report of the Interdepartmental Committee on Dentists* (Teviot Committee), Cmd 6565 (London, HM Stationery Office, 1944).

Ministry of Health *and* Department of Health for Scotland. *Report of the Committee on Recruitment to the Dental Profession* (McNair Committee), Cmd 9861 (London, HM Stationery Office, 1956).

Ministry of Health *and* Department of Health for Scotland. *Report of the Committee to Consider the Future Numbers of Medical Practitioners and the Appropriate Intake of Medical Students* (Willink Committee) (London, HM Stationery Office, 1957).

Ministry of Health *and* Department of Health for Scotland. *Report of the Joint Working Party on the Medical Staffing Structure in the Hospital Service* (Platt Report) (London, HM Stationery Office, 1961).

Ministry of Health *and* Department of Health for Scotland. *Report of the Working Party on Social Workers in the Local Authority Health and Welfare Services* (Younghusband Report) (London, HM Stationery Office, 1959).

Ministry of Health, Department of Health for Scotland *and* Ministry of Education. *An Inquiry into Health Visiting: Report of a Working Party on the Field of Work, Training and Recruitment of Health Visitors* (London, HM Stationery Office, 1956).

Ministry of Health *and* General Register Office. *Report on Hospital In-patient Enquiry . . . 1956–1957* (London, HM Stationery Office, 1961).

Ministry of Health *and* Ministry of Town and Country Planning. *Design of Dwellings* (Dudley Report) (London, HM Stationery Office, 1944).

Ministry of Health. Central Health Services Council. Standing Medical Advisory Committee. *The Field of Work of the Family Doctor: Report of the Sub-committee* (Gillie Committee) (London, HM Stationery Office, 1963).

Ministry of Housing and Local Government. *Housing Return for England and Wales* (London, HM Stationery Office, quarterly).

Ministry of Housing and Local Government. *The South East Study, 1961–1981* (London, HM Stationery Office, 1964).

Ministry of Labour. *Family Expenditure Survey: Report for 1960 and 1961* (London, HM Stationery Office, 1962; . . . Report for 1962* (1963).

Ministry of Labour. *Statistics on Incomes, Prices, Employment and Production* (London, HM Stationery Office, quarterly).

Ministry of Labour. *Time Rates of Wages and Hours of Work* (London, HM Stationery Office, annual).

Ministry of Labour *and* Ministry of Transport. *Report of the Committee of Inquiry to Review the Pay and Conditions of Employment of the Drivers and Conductors of the London Transport Board's Road Services* (London, HM Stationery Office, 1964).

Ministry of Labour Gazette (London, HM Stationery Office, monthly).

Ministry of Power. *Domestic Fuel Supplies and the Clean Air Policy*, Cmnd 2231 (London, HM Stationery Office, 1963).

Ministry of Power. *The Nuclear Power Programme*, Cmnd 1083 (London, HM Stationery Office, 1960).

Ministry of Power. *The Second Nuclear Power Programme*, Cmnd 2335 (London, HM Stationery Office, 1964).

Ministry of Power. *Statistical Digest* (London, HM Stationery Office, annual).

Ministry of Transport. *Highway Statistics, 1963*, Statistical Paper 3 (London, HM Stationery Office, 1964).

Ministry of Transport. 'Motor Car Ownership and Use', *Economic Trends*, no. 1 June 1963, p. xiv.

Ministry of Transport. 'Passenger Transport in Great Britain', *Economic Trends*, no. 121, November 1963, p. ii.

Ministry of Transport. *Report of the Committee of Inquiry into the Major Ports of Great Britain* (Rochdale Report), Cmnd 1824 (London, HM Stationery Office, 1962).

Ministry of Transport. *Road Pricing: the Economic and Technical Possibilities* (Smeed Report) (London, HM Stationery Office, 1964).

Ministry of Transport. *Roads in England and Wales* (London, HM Stationery Office, annual).

Ministry of Transport. *Rural Bus Services* (London, HM Stationery Office, 1961).

Ministry of Transport. *Survey of Road Goods Transport, 1962: Final Results, Part 1,* Statistical Paper 2 (London, HM Stationery Office, 1964).

Ministry of Transport. *Traffic in Towns: a Study of the Long Term Problems of Traffic in Urban Areas* (Buchanan Report) (London, HM Stationery Office, 1963).

Ministry of Transport. *The Transport Needs of Great Britain in the Next Twenty Years: Report of a Group under the Chairmanship of Sir Robert Hall* (Hall Report) (London, HM Stationery Office, 1963).

National Coal Board. *Investing in Coal: Progress and Prospects under the Plan for Coal* (London, 1956).

National Coal Board. *Plan for Coal: the National Coal Board's Proposals* (London, 1950).

National Coal Board. *Report and Accounts* (London, HM Stationery Office, annual).

National Coal Board. *Revised Plan for Coal: Progress of Reconstruction and Revised Estimates of Demand and Output* (London, 1959).

National Economic Development Council. *Export Trends* (London, HM Stationery Office, 1963).

National Economic Development Council. *Growth of the United Kingdom Economy, 1961–1966* (London, HM Stationery Office, 1963).

Northern Ireland. Ministry of Education. *Education in Northern Ireland, 1961–62* Cmd 450 (Belfast, HM Stationery Office, 1963).

Oversea Migration Board. *Sixth Report*, Cmnd 1243 (London, HM Stationery Office, 1960); *Seventh Report*, Cmnd 1586 (1961).

Post Office. *The Inland Telephone Service in an Expanding Economy*, Cmnd 2211 (London, HM Stationery Office, 1963).

Road Research Laboratory. *Sample Survey of the Roads and Traffic of Great Britain,* by J. C. Tanner, H. D. Johnson and J. R. Scott, Road Research Technical Paper 62 (London, HM Stationery Office, 1962).

Royal Commission on Doctors' and Dentists' Remuneration, 1957–1960 (Pilkington Commission). *Report*, Cmnd 939 (London, HM Stationery Office, 1960).

Royal Commission on Population. *Report*, Cmd 7695 (London, HM Stationery Office, 1949).

Scotland. Home and Health Department. *Health and Welfare Services in Scotland* (formerly *Report of the Department of Health for Scotland*) (Edinburgh, HM Stationery Office, annual).

Scottish Education Department. *Education in Scotland* (Edinburgh, HM Stationery Office, annual).

Scottish Education Department. *Supply of Teachers in Scotland*, Cmnd 1601 (Edinburgh, HM Stationery Office, 1962).

Treasury. *Aid to Developing Countries*, Cmnd 2147 (London, HM Stationery Office, 1963).

Treasury. *Economic Survey* (London, HM Stationery Office, annual 1947–62).

Treasury. *The Financial and Economic Obligations of the Nationalised Industries*, Cmnd 1337 (London, HM Stationery Office, 1961).

Treasury. *Public Expenditure in 1963–64 and 1967–68*, Cmnd 2235 (London, HM Stationery Office, 1963).

Treasury. *Public Investment in Great Britain, October 1963*, Cmnd 2177 (London, HM Stationery Office, 1963).

Treasury. *United Kingdom Balance of Payments, 1959 to 1961*, Cmnd 1671 (London, HM Stationery Office, 1962).

Treasury. Committee on the Working of the Monetary System (Radcliffe Committee). *Minutes of Evidence* (London, HM Stationery Office, 1960).

Treasury. Committee on the Working of the Monetary System (Radcliffe Committee). *Principal Memoranda of Evidence* (London, HM Stationery Office, 1960).

United Kingdom Atomic Energy Authority. *Annual Report* (London, HM Stationery Office).

University Grants Committee. *Returns from Universities and University Colleges in Receipt of Treasury Grant* (London, HM Stationery Office, annual).

(2) OTHER NATIONAL

FRANCE. Institut National de la Statistique et des Etudes Economiques. *Coût de Développement de l'Enseignement en France*, Etudes Economiques 3 (Paris, 1958).

GERMANY. Statistisches Bundesamt. *Wirtschaft und Statistik* (Mainz, Kohlhammer, monthly).

NORWAY. Central Bureau of Statistics. *Statistical Yearbook of Norway* (Oslo).

SASKATCHEWAN. Department of Public Health. *Annual Report of the Saskatchewan Hospital Services Plan, 1963* (Regina, 1964).

SWEDEN. Central Bureau of Statistics. *Statistical Abstract of Sweden* (Stockholm, annual).

UNITED STATES. Bureau of the Census. *Statistical Abstract of the United States* (Washington, Government Printing Office, annual).

UNITED STATES. Bureau of Labor Statistics. *Tables of Working Life for Women*, Bulletin 1204 (Washington, Government Printing Office, 1957).

UNITED STATES. Office of Business Economics. *Balance of Payments: Statistical Supplement to the Survey of Current Business*, rev. ed. (Washington, Government Printing Office, 1963).

UNITED STATES. Office of Business Economics. *Survey of Current Business* (Washington, Government Printing Office, monthly).

UNITED STATES. Office of Business Economics. *US Income and Output: a Supplement to the Survey of Current Business* (Washington, Government Printing Office, 1958).

(3) INTERNATIONAL

EUROPEAN ECONOMIC COMMUNITY. *Treaty Establishing the European Economic Community, Rome, 25th March 1957* (English translation) (London, HM Stationery Office, 1962).

EUROPEAN ECONOMIC COMMUNITY COMMISSION. Groupe de Travail pour les Problèmes de Structure et de Développement à Long Terme (Uri Group). *Rapport sur les Perspectives de Développement Economique dans la CEE de 1960 à 1970* (Brussels, 1962).

ORGANISATION FOR ECONOMIC CO-OPERATION AND DEVELOPMENT. *The Flow of Financial Resources to Less-Developed Countries, 1956–1963* (Paris, 1964).

ORGANISATION FOR ECONOMIC CO-OPERATION AND DEVELOPMENT. *General Statistics* (Paris, 6 times yearly, 1951–65).

ORGANISATION FOR ECONOMIC CO-OPERATION AND DEVELOPMENT. *Manpower Statistics* (Paris, biennial).

ORGANISATION FOR ECONOMIC CO-OPERATION AND DEVELOPMENT. *National Accounts, 1955–1962: Supplement to the General Statistics Bulletin* (Paris, 1964).

ORGANISATION FOR ECONOMIC CO-OPERATION AND DEVELOPMENT. *Policies for Economic Growth* (Paris, 1962).

ORGANISATION FOR ECONOMIC CO-OPERATION AND DEVELOPMENT. *Policy Conference on Economic Growth and Investment in Education, Washington, 16–20 October 1961, Part II: Targets for Education in Europe in 1970*, by I. Svennilson, in association with F. Edding and L. Elvin (Paris, 1962).

ORGANISATION FOR ECONOMIC CO-OPERATION AND DEVELOPMENT. *The Residual Factor and Economic Growth* (Paris, 1964).

ORGANISATION FOR ECONOMIC CO-OPERATION AND DEVELOPMENT. *Statistics of National Accounts, 1950–1961* (Paris, 1964).

ORGANISATION FOR ECONOMIC CO-OPERATION AND DEVELOPMENT. *Tourism in OECD Member Countries* (Paris, annual).

ORGANISATION FOR EUROPEAN ECONOMIC CO-OPERATION. *Towards a New Energy Pattern in Europe* (Paris, 1960).

UNITED NATIONS. *Towards a New Trade Policy for Development: Report by the Secretary-General of the United Nations Conference on Trade and Development* (R. Prebisch) (New York, 1964).

UNITED NATIONS. Department of Economic and Social Affairs. *Demographic Aspects of Manpower, Report I: Sex and Age Patterns of Participation in Economic Activities*, Population Studies 33 (New York, 1962).

UNITED NATIONS. Economic Commission for Europe. *The Coal Situation in Europe in 1961/62 and Future Prospects* (Geneva, 1963).

UNITED NATIONS. Economic Commission for Europe. *Economic Survey of Europe in 1961, Part 2: Some Factors in Economic Growth in Europe during the 1950s* (Geneva, 1964).

UNITED NATIONS. Economic Commission for Europe. *Economic Survey of Europe in 1962, Part 1: The European Economy in 1962* (Geneva, 1963).

UNITED NATIONS. International Monetary Fund. *Balance of Payments Yearbook* (Washington).

UNITED NATIONS. International Monetary Fund. *International Financial Statistics* (Washington, monthly).

UNITED NATIONS. Statistical Office. *Demographic Yearbook* (New York).

UNITED NATIONS. Statistical Office. *Monthly Bulletin of Statistics* (New York).

UNITED NATIONS. Statistical Office. *Statistical Yearbook* (New York).

UNITED NATIONS. Statistical Office. *Statistics of National Income and Expenditure*, Statistical Papers, Series H, no. 10 (New York, 1957).

UNITED NATIONS. Statistical Office. *World Energy Supplies*, Statistical Papers, Series J (New York, annual).

UNITED NATIONS. Statistical Office. *Yearbook of National Accounts Statistics* (New York).

INDEX

Names of persons in capitals.
Abbreviations : n., footnote; t., table.

ss2

PUBLICATIONS OF THE
NATIONAL INSTITUTE OF ECONOMIC
AND SOCIAL RESEARCH

published by

THE CAMBRIDGE UNIVERSITY PRESS

Books published for the Institute by the Cambridge University Press are available through the ordinary booksellers. They appear in the three series below.

ECONOMIC & SOCIAL STUDIES

*I   *Studies in the National Income, 1924–1938*
　　Edited by A. L. BOWLEY. Reprinted with corrections, 1944. pp. 256. 15s. net.

*II *The Burden of British Taxation*
　　By G. FINDLAY SHIRRAS and L. ROSTAS. 1942. pp. 140. 17s. 6d. net.

*III *Trade Regulations and Commercial Policy of the United Kingdom*
　　By the RESEARCH STAFF OF THE NATIONAL INSTITUTE OF ECONOMIC AND SOCIAL RESEARCH. 1943. pp. 275. 17s. 6d. net.

*IV *National Health Insurance: A Critical Study*
　　By HERMANN LEVY. 1944. pp. 356. 21s. net.

*V   *The Development of the Soviet Economic System: An Essay on the Experience of Planning in the U.S.S.R.*
　　By ALEXANDER BAYKOV. 1946. pp. 530. 45s. net.

*VI *Studies in Financial Organization*
　　By T. BALOGH. 1948. pp. 328. 40s. net.

VII *Investment, Location, and Size of Plant: A Realistic Inquiry into the Structure of British and American Industries*
　　By P. SARGANT FLORENCE, assisted by W. BALDAMUS. 1948. pp. 230. 21s. net.

VIII *A Statistical Analysis of Advertising Expenditure and of the Revenue of the Press*
　　By NICHOLAS KALDOR and RODNEY SILVERMAN. 1948. pp. 200. 25s. net.

*IX *The Distribution of Consumer Goods*
　　By JAMES B. JEFFERYS, assisted by MARGARET MACCOLL and G. L. LEVETT. 1950. pp. 430. 50s. net.

*X   *Lessons of the British War Economy*
　　Edited by D. N. CHESTER. 1951. pp. 260. 30s. net.

*XI *Colonial Social Accounting*
　　By PHYLLIS DEANE. 1953. pp. 360. 60s. net.

*XII *Migration and Economic Growth*
　　By BRINLEY THOMAS. 1954. pp. 384. 50s. net.

*XIII *Retail Trading in Britain, 1850–1950*
　　By JAMES B. JEFFERYS. 1954. pp. 490. 60s. net.

XIV *British Economic Statistics*
　　By CHARLES CARTER and A. D. ROY. 1954. pp. 192. 30s. net.

XV   *The Structure of British Industry: A Symposium*
　　Edited by DUNCAN BURN. 1958. Vol. I. pp. 403. 55s. net. Vol. II. pp. 499. 55s. net.

XVI *Concentration in British Industry*
　　By RICHARD EVELY and I. M. D. LITTLE. 1960. pp. 357. 63s. net.

XVII *Studies in Company Finance*
　　Edited by BRIAN TEW and R. F. HENDERSON. 1959. pp. 301. 35s. net.

*At present out of print.

*At present out of print.

STUDIES IN THE NATIONAL INCOME AND EXPENDITURE OF THE UNITED KINGDOM

Published under the joint auspices of the National Institute and the Department of Applied Economics, Cambridge.

1 *The Measurement of Consumers' Expenditure and Behaviour in the United Kingdom, 1920–1938*, vol. I
   By RICHARD STONE, assisted by D. A. ROWE and by W. J. CORLETT, RENEE HURSTFIELD, MURIEL POTTER. 1954. pp. 448. £7 10s. net.

3 *Consumers' Expenditure in the United Kingdom, 1900–1919*
   By A. R. PREST, assisted by A. A. ADAMS. 1954. pp. 196. 55s. net.

5 *Wages and Salaries in the United Kingdom, 1920–1938*
   By AGATHA CHAPMAN, assisted by ROSE KNIGHT. 1953. pp. 254. 75s. net.

6 *Domestic Capital Formation in the United Kingdom, 1920–1938*
   By C. H. FEINSTEIN. 1965. pp. 284. About 90s.

THE NATIONAL INSTITUTE OF ECONOMIC AND SOCIAL RESEARCH

publishes regularly

THE NATIONAL INSTITUTE ECONOMIC REVIEW

A quarterly Review of the economic situation and prospects.

Annual subscription £2; single issues 12s. 6d. each.

The Review is available directly from N.I.E.S.R.

2, Dean Trench St., Smith Square, London, S.W.1

The Institute has also published
FACTORY LOCATION AND INDUSTRIAL MOVEMENT: *a Study of Recent Experience in Britain, VOLUMES I and II*
By W. F. Luttrell
N.I.E.S.R. 1962. pp. 1080. £5 5s. net the set.
This is also available directly from the Institute.